MY LIFE IN CRIME AND OTHER ACADEMIC ADVENTURES

My Life in Crime
and Other Academic
Adventures

160201

MARTIN L. FRIEDLAND

Published for The Osgoode Society for Canadian Legal History by
University of Toronto Press
Toronto Buffalo London

Printed in Canada
ISBN 978-0-8020-9790-3

∞

Printed on acid-free paper

Library and Archives Canada Cataloguing in Publication

Friedland, M.L. (Martin Lawrence), 1932–
My life in crime and other academic adventures / Martin L.
Friedland.

Includes index.
ISBN 978-0-8020-9790-3

1. Friedland, M.L. (Martin Lawrence), 1932–   2. Criminal justice,
Administration of – Canada.   3. Criminal law – Canada.   4. Law reform –
Canada.   5. Legal research – Canada.   6. Law teachers – Canada –
Biography.   7. University of Toronto – Faculty – Biography.
I. Osgoode Society for Canadian Legal History.   II. Title.

KE416.F74A3 2007   340.92   C2007-904282-1
KF345.Z9F74 2007

University of Toronto Press acknowledges the financial assistance to its
publishing program of the Canada Council for the Arts and the
Ontario Arts Council.

University of Toronto Press acknowledges the financial support for its
publishing activities of the Government of Canada through the
Book Publishing Industry Development Program (BPIDP).

Contents

Foreword

The Osgoode Society
for Canadian Legal History

Professor Martin Friedland has been involved in many areas of legal research and law reform in his career, and the Osgoode Society is very pleased to be able to publish his account of that involvement, especially as his public service includes many years as a director of the Society. This book examines his contributions and sets them in the broader context of public policy making across a range of issues. These include various aspects of criminal justice reform, securities regulation, judicial independence and accountability, anti-terrorism policy, and much more.

The purpose of The Osgoode Society for Canadian Legal History is to encourage research and writing in the history of Canadian law. The Society, which was incorporated in 1979 and is registered as a charity, was founded at the initiative of the Honourable R. Roy McMurtry, formerly attorney general for Ontario and chief justice of the province, and officials of the Law Society of Upper Canada. The Society seeks to stimulate the study of legal history in Canada by supporting researchers, collecting oral histories, and publishing volumes that contribute to legal-historical scholarship in Canada. It has published seventy books on the courts, the judiciary, and the legal profession, as well as on the history of crime and punishment, women and law, law and economy, the legal treatment of ethnic minorities, and famous cases and significant trials in all areas of the law.

Current directors of The Osgoode Society for Canadian Legal History are Robert Armstrong, Kenneth Binks, Patrick Brode, Michael Bryant, Brian Bucknall, David Chernos, Kirby Chown, J. Douglas Ewart, Martin Friedland, John Honsberger, Horace Krever, Gavin MacKenzie, Virginia MacLean, Roy McMurtry, Brendan O'Brien, Jim Phillips, Paul Reinhardt, Joel Richler, William Ross, Robert Sharpe, James Spence, Mary Stokes, Richard Tinsley, and Michael Tulloch.

The annual report and information about membership may be obtained by writing The Osgoode Society for Canadian Legal History, Osgoode Hall, 130 Queen Street West, Toronto, Ontario. M5H 2N6. Telephone: 416-947-3321. Email: mmacfarl@lsuc.on.ca. Website: Osgoodesociety.ca

R. Roy McMurtry
President

Jim Phillips
Editor-in-Chief

Preface

In the fall of 2003, I delivered the John Edwards Memorial Lecture at the University of Toronto. The topic that I chose was 'Criminal Justice in Canada Revisited,' which consisted of a personal look at criminal justice over the previous forty years. The talk was a return to my principal field of scholarly work after the publication of my history of the University of Toronto in 2002. A more formal version of my presentation was subsequently published in the *Criminal Law Quarterly*. The present book is a major expansion of that paper.

The book sheds light on the development of a number of criminal-law topics that I have worked on: double jeopardy, gambling, bail, legal aid, gun control, national security, and criminal-law reform – to mention some of the topics from the 1960s and 1970s. Each area discussed is brought up to date and recommendations are made about possible future developments in the law. The chapters, therefore, provide a historical and current analysis of a number of areas of law, much of which cannot be found elsewhere in the legal literature. Most of the subjects are controversial and many are currently before Parliament, so I am taking aim at a moving target. As this is being written, we do not know when a federal election will be called and what the result will be when it is called. Whatever the outcome, the issues that I have dealt with will not disappear. The manuscript is current as of 1 June 2007.

I have also included details about my own life in the law. Thus the book tries to integrate two genres – a personal memoir as well as a historical and analytical investigation of a number of areas of law. Both streams illustrate the accidental nature of one's life and of the development of the law and other institutions.

A study of the development of the law and of legal and other institutions, like one's own life, shows that what we have now was not preordained. There are always lots of twists and turns along the way. This is the main theme of the book, which is reflected in most of the chapters. In the conclusion to a detailed historical article on codification of the law in the nineteenth century, published in 1980, I ask what conclusions can be drawn from the story. My answer: 'Perhaps it is simply the obvious one that law reform is affected by a great number of factors apart from the merits of the proposals. Then, as now, a combination of politics, personalities and pressure groups affected the outcome. The crucial events seem, in retrospect, largely unplotted and accidental.'

I drew the same conclusion from my subsequent historical crime books. In *The Trials of Israel Lipski*, published in 1984, I examined the many factors that might affect a criminal trial, and stated:

> This story will place one trial in the context of the social, political and economic conditions of the time. A trial may in theory be an objective pursuit of truth, but in practice there are many subjective factors which influence the course of events. Justice may in theory be blind, but in practice she has altogether too human a perspective. The Lipski story is, no doubt, more dramatic, and the wealth of material richer, than in most cases; yet, by looking at this extreme example one can better understand some of the factors that may influence any criminal trial: the personality of the judge; the adequacy of counsel; the reaction of the press; the cry of popular opinion; the vulnerability of the Government; and many more.

A prologue to the present book sets the stage for the first chapter, on legal education. I believe that my early years shed some light on my later career, showing that I was fairly adventurous, filled with curiosity, entrepreneurial, and perhaps somewhat irresponsible. This may help explain why I tended in later life to break away from the more traditional forms of scholarship.

The book is primarily about criminal justice – my main subject of research and teaching, but other legal topics are included, such as securities regulation, pension reform, and judicial independence. I also discuss my involvement in the University of Toronto as dean of law and in other capacities. Hence the title: *My Life in Crime and Other Academic Adventures*.

Over the course of my career I have had well over one hundred excellent research assistants who assisted me with the many projects with which I have been involved. I also had first-class research assistance for this manuscript – from Lianne Cihlar, Andrew Elias, Matthew Gourlay, Colin Grey, Athar Malik, Melanie Ouanounou, and Bill Thompson. This book is dedicated to all of my many research assistants, past, present, and – with luck – future.

I am also grateful to the faculty of law for providing me with an intellectual home for almost my entire teaching career and for the years since my official retirement. The manuscript was more or less complete at the end of 2006. In January 2007 I taught an intensive course (fourteen hours over a two-week period) to about twenty upper-year law students, using the manuscript as the course material. This helped shape the final manuscript. For the previous three years, while I was writing this manuscript, I had taught a similar course as a fourth-year undergraduate seminar at Woodsworth College to a group of bright criminology students, who helped me probe many of the topics in the book. To my colleagues and former students I offer my sincere thanks.

A number of persons – including Harry Arthurs, John Beattie, Earl Berger, Alan Cairns, Michael Code, Stanley Cohen, Tony Doob, Horace Krever, Kent Roach, Peter Russell, Paul Schabas, Robert Sharpe, and Stephen Waddams – read earlier versions of the manuscript and made many helpful suggestions. I had the privilege of working with the University of Toronto Press and editor Len Husband, as well as with Jim Phillips, the editor-in-chief of the Osgoode Society. I am also grateful to John St James for his expert copy-editing. Further, Harold Averill and the University of Toronto Archives, as in the past, were of assistance in finding needed material. Funding for the research was provided by a generous research grant from the Donner Canadian Foundation.

My greatest debt is to my wife, Judy, who has offered love, support, and advice for the past fifty years, which I believe I have done in return. She encouraged me to become an academic, kept me on a relatively straight path, typed my thesis – I have been paying for the thesis typing ever since – and read and commented on a number of my manuscripts, including this one. In recent years I have been her unpaid research assistant in foreign lands while she has been researching the history of occupational therapy. Our three children and their partners have been lively and interested participants in my career. The publication of this manuscript will likely fall close to the date of our fiftieth wedding anniversary, as well as my seventy-fifth birthday, and about fifty years after my graduation from law school.

Martin L. Friedland
University Professor and Professor of Law Emeritus
University of Toronto
1 June 2007

MY LIFE IN CRIME AND OTHER ACADEMIC ADVENTURES

Prologue

In the spring of 1955, I went to see Caesar Wright, the dean of the University of Toronto Law School. His office was on the second floor of Cumberland House (then called Baldwin House), on the east side of St George Street. I was completing my fourth year of commerce and finance at the University and had just been selected to go on a World University Service study tour of West Africa. I would not be able to work over the summer to pay my tuition. Could the U of T law school assist me – I boldly asked – in waiving my tuition, then about $350 a year? I had no savings and my parents would have had difficulty assisting me further than they had already promised to do to enable me to go on the trip.

Like most students from Toronto I could continue to live rent-free at home in my parents' two-bedroom apartment in Forest Hill Village at the corner of Vesta Drive and Bathurst Street. We had moved from a fine home on Rosemary Road in the Village a year earlier because my father had suffered some losses in an unsuccessful venture manufacturing women's suits. He then turned to selling commercial real estate and was slowly getting back on his feet. Again, like most students, I was usually able to earn enough over the summer to pay my tuition and other expenses when the summer work was supplemented by various part-time jobs during the school year.

For the past two summers I had been the so-called athletic director at a Jewish summer resort, Muskoka Lodge. I arranged various games, including calisthenics each morning and the very non-athletic game of bingo one evening a week. The salary from the position did not go very far, but tips from serving wine at dinner – we offered only sweet Canadian wines – and acting as an extra bellhop on busy weekends enabled me to take home about a thousand dollars each summer. The previous summer, 1952, I had made a similar amount at the Gateway Hotel in Gravenhurst, where the athletic director and I profited handsomely from arranging moonlight cruises on the Muskoka Lakes for guests of the hotel. It was that summer that by chance I met my future wife, Judy Pless, then thirteen years old, who was spending a week or so at the resort with her aunt and uncle. I would not meet her again until the summer of 1957, five years later.

Employment at the resorts was normally supplemented by teaching swimming for the Toronto Board of Education in June and by work at the Canadian National Exhibition at summer's end. Part-time and summer jobs were reasonably plentiful in the early 1950s. Women had left the workforce after the war to produce the present baby boomers and the economy was doing well.

I was also entrepreneurial – a trait which the reader will probably conclude carried over to my academic career. Along with various partners I would sell peanuts and other items at the annual Santa Claus parade. One winter, our garage was filled with sacks of unsold peanuts, which delighted the upscale Forest Hill squirrels. I also sold Christmas trees at various locations on Eglinton Avenue West. Neither my colleagues nor I knew much about Christmas trees, but we believed it when we told the customers that the flattened trees would 'come down in the heat.' I continued to sell trees during my law-school days with a number of later distinguished Jewish lawyers, who probably do not wish to be publicly named.

I would seize other opportunities to bring in some cash. When the future Queen and Prince Philip visited Toronto in October 1951, I was on the cavalcade's route with a large crew that my partners and I had organized, selling flags. This was tricky, because few people are interested in buying a flag after the royal procession has passed. To overcome this problem, as soon as the royal couple passed us we would jump into a waiting car on a nearby street and drive a mile or so ahead of the cavalcade. This would be repeated throughout the cavalcade. I think I saw the future queen about six or seven times that day. Many years later my wife and I had a chance to talk briefly with the Queen and Prince Philip. We were on sabbatical in Cambridge in 1980 and

Mark MacGuigan, who had been my colleague as a law professor, had just become the minister of external affairs. He invited us to the centenary celebration at Canada House of the establishment of the office of Canadian High Commissioner. When Mark and the royal couple entered the room he brought them over to meet us. The Queen and the Prince may not have recognized the young lad they had seen half a dozen times on a fall day in Toronto thirty years earlier, and I did not raise the point in our brief conversation.

I cannot remember Caesar's exact reply, but I came away with a promise of a complete waiver of tuition – and then some – for the year 1955–6 – a total bursary of $400. He did not say: 'Perhaps' or 'I'll get back to you' or 'Why don't you take out a loan?' If anything, Caesar was decisive. He was not called Caesar for nothing. His real name was Cecil Augustus, and it was the combination of his imperial manner coupled with his middle name Augustus that brought about the nickname Caesar. President Sidney Smith had allocated to the law school that year about $3000 for bursaries and loans to – in Smith's words – 'attract able students to the institution, and thus maintain and indeed improve the caliber of our student body.'

Sidney Smith and Caesar Wright shared the dream of creating a major law school at the University. Smith had written shortly after his appointment as president in 1945 about the creation at the University of Toronto of 'a Law School that would rank first in Canada, and be among the leading schools of the North American continent.' In 1949 Wright, then the dean of Osgoode Hall Law School, had abruptly resigned from Osgoode and moved to the University law school along with his colleagues Bora Laskin, later the chief justice of Canada, and John Willis, a creative scholar and respected teacher.

I have a picture on my office wall that I am looking at as I write this of the three academics, said to have been taken on the day that they resigned from Osgoode. (There is a fourth person in the picture, but he went directly into practice.) All are in dark three-piece suits and all three are wearing glasses – Caesar's are rimless and he has a cigarette in his right hand. Over the years that I knew him, Caesar had the voice and cough of a heavy smoker. He also has a trim moustache in the picture, and had one over all the years that I knew him. He was forty-five at the time, but always looked much older than his years. He was only sixty-two when he died in 1967, shortly after announcing his retirement as dean.

Caesar wanted more students. The University law school was having trouble attracting them because it took an extra year to become a lawyer if one did not attend Osgoode Hall Law School, then located at Osgoode Hall on Queen Street West and University Avenue. Most of my undergraduate classmates at U of T who wanted to become lawyers – Mickey Cohen, Allen Linden, John McKellar, and Ian Scott, to name a few – were planning on going to Osgoode. The Benchers of the Law Society of Upper Canada, who governed the profession in Ontario and also ran Osgoode Hall Law School, gave U of T law graduates credit for only two years, thereby forcing them to attend Osgoode for a final and repetitive third year. Complaints by students and the University fell on deaf ears.

The graduation class pictures now lining the walls outside the classrooms in Flavelle House tell the story. The graduation class of 1950–1 had eight faculty members and ten students. The class of 1953–4 had nine faculty members but still only ten students. A frustrated John Willis left for practice in Nova Scotia, explaining to Wright that 'just two years after it started up as a professional school, the School of Law is to all intents and purposes dead.'

In those days anyone could study law. There was no law-school admission test and marks were unimportant as long as one had successfully graduated with an undergraduate degree – or had completed two undergraduate years towards a degree. There was no great incentive to get good marks, unless one was heading into medicine or to graduate school. Employers were eager to hire any graduates, particularly male commerce graduates. My marks were reasonably decent, although I had a first-class standing in only the first of my four years. With those marks I would certainly not be accepted into U of T law school today. I like to think, however, that in such a case I would have spent more time improving my grades. But then, I would not have been able to spend as much time on extra-curricular activities or attending non-credit lectures that had nothing to do with commerce and finance, such as Edward Carpenter's anthropology classes in the Royal Ontario Museum or Godfrey Ridout's music survey course at the Royal Conservatory of Music.

I am not sure when I decided to become a lawyer. As far as I can remember, I had only been in Osgoode Hall on one occasion, when my Sunday School teacher, Anne Brown, who was the librarian for the Ontario Court of Appeal, took me there when I was about ten or twelve. No member of my family was or had been a lawyer. It was simply the best of the various alternatives and would keep many doors open. My older brother Sheldon – my only sibling – was becoming an accountant, but accountancy did not interest me. I had mistakenly followed Sheldon into commerce – he was two years ahead of me – but I found the accounting lectures in the commerce course particularly uninspiring. The subjects that interested me were somewhat removed from the regular commerce courses. In the final chapter of my history of the U of T, I take a nostalgic personal tour of the campus on the last day of the old millennium and state: 'I look up at McMaster Hall, beside Philosopher's Walk, once the home of McMaster University and later of Toronto's department of political economy. I think of my favourite undergraduate classes there – the memorable lectures on economic history by Karl Helleiner, one of the relatively few refugee academics taken into the University before the Second World War, and the international relations seminar by Jim Eayrs.' I probably should have switched to political science and economics after first year, as some of my classmates did.

The law course in the commerce program, taught by Frederick Auld, a veteran of the First World War who started teaching in the law department in 1930, certainly did not inspire me to enter the law program. It was a nuts-and-bolts course on commercial law, given by a professor whose main interest was Roman law. He had a drinking problem that was apparent to his students. To our shame, the class gave him a present in his last class of the year in the large auditorium of the McMaster building. He opened it in front of us. It was a cheap bottle of liquor. I had had nothing to do with the gift, but still shudder when I think of the obvious humiliation he must have suffered.

There was never any thought of leaving Toronto to study law. Nor had there been any thought of leaving Toronto for my undergraduate program. Very few of my high school classmates did so. I cannot recall anyone from my class at Forest Hill Collegiate going to Queen's or McGill, although it is likely that some did. Some students went to Western, but often because they were a subject or two short in their grade 13 subjects and Western was more liberal in its admission standards than Toronto. Very few students from Forest Hill Collegiate that I knew went to American schools for their undergraduate degrees if they could get into the University of Toronto. No doubt, the same was true of other public high schools in Toronto.

I wanted to go to Caesar's law school in spite of and, indeed, because of the small number of students. The U of T law school had been developing a strong reputation for its academic program. Besides, I liked being at the University. I had been very active on the campus and Caesar must have viewed my attendance at his institution as a possible inducement for other potential students to attend the school. I had been the president of University College's male undergraduate student society, the University College Literary and Athletic Society, normally simply called 'the Lit.'

My credentials for being elected president of the Lit had not been particularly strong. Commerce students were for the most part cut off from their colleges. Almost all our classes were at the McMaster Building on Bloor Street, and a large number of the students spent most of their time there. Many spent their lunch hours playing bridge or cribbage – or was it hearts? – in the building, pastimes in which I did not participate. I had been the third-year president of the Lit and so spent some time in the Junior Common Room at UC. I had also been active in Hart House as a member of the music committee and spent a considerable amount of time in the House, particularly the record room, where I normally did most of my studying. Members of the music committee selected the musicians for the many concerts that were put on in the House, including Wednesday noon-hour recitals in the Music Room and the packed Sunday Evening Concerts. Members of the committee introduced the Wednesday noon recitalists. I had done very little public speaking before then and recall how nervous I was when I first had to introduce a performer. Members of the committee also had the privilege of putting our stamp of approval on the new Hart House Orchestra under the direction of the dean of music, Boyd Neel.

Membership on the music committee did not, however, consist wholly of such high-level work. We were also responsible for moving and rearranging the heavy oak tables and chairs in the Great Hall for each Sunday concert. On one occasion I was asked if I would turn the pages at one of these concerts for the pianist Leo Barkin, who was accompanying violinist Albert Pratz. I said yes. This was a mistake. Although I had completed grade 8 in piano at the Conservatory, I was not a good sight-reader and, moreover, the music had many repeats, which were difficult for me to follow. The pianist took over the page turning and I sat there, embarrassed, before perhaps five hundred persons in the audience. Although that occurred over fifty years ago, I think of it whenever I see someone turning pages for a pianist. I recently thought of it again as I watched someone turn the pages for a harpsichordist at a Tafelmusik concert, grateful that it was not me doing it.

I probably won the election as president of the Lit for two principal reasons. The first was the electoral speech that I made. Candidates for office for the Lit or the UC women's student society, the Women's Undergraduate Association (WUA) – they have since merged into one body – had to make an election speech if they hoped for a successful outcome. I do not know whether it is still the tradition, but in the early 1950s the speeches consisted entirely of off-colour jokes.

A couple of hundred persons – men and women – would gather at noon hour in UC's Junior Common Room, the JCR, to hear the election speeches by the candidates for the Lit and the WUA. One aspect of the room stood out above all – the faded gold lettering around the panelled walls of the names of officers of the WUA and of the Lit, going back to the Lit's founding in 1853. My joke, using language that is still not used in mixed company and was even less used in those days, brought down the house. Judy strongly suggests that I not tell it in this book.

My election was also helped by the future hockey promoter, Alan Eagleson. He was a jock, playing a number of sports, including lacrosse. Everyone knew Eagleson. Although I was not much of an athlete, I had managed to play on two intercollegiate teams – squash and water polo. Indeed, I was part of the water polo team that won the intercollegiate championship in 1953–4, helped by the fact that a number of talented players who had played for the Yugoslavian national team and had defected to Canada played for U of T. In the end, I played back-up goalie and rarely got wet during major games. I remember playing in one exhibition game against a Hamilton club in a pool with a shallow end. The goalie stood in waist-deep water. Of course the teams switched ends at half-time. I often think of that game when people talk about requiring 'a level playing field.' There are other ways to create fairness.

I did not enjoy the two-hour practices in the Hart House pool. I recall one routine that we had to master in order to stay as high as possible above the water: it required treading water furiously for about five seconds with one's finger tips touching the underside of the diving board. Unlike my teammates, I was not very powerful. Look at the picture of the team in the 1954 *Torontonensis*. I am the only player whose shoulders form an inverted 'V.' I also did not like leaving Hart House in the dark after a practice in the middle of winter, with my hair starting to freeze. I obviously wanted to make the team very badly. Since then I

have rarely entered a chlorinated indoor pool because of the unpleasant memories it brings back.

I was more successful as a squash player. I had played tennis in high
school, but, unlike those who had been at private schools, I had not
played squash before coming to the University. I would practise by
myself on one of the three undersized Hart House courts several times
a week, just hitting the ball back and forth. As it turned out, I managed
to make the intercollegiate team through sheer determination and
without an abundance of talent. It was not a bad lesson for my future
career as a scholar – concentrated hard work can pay off. I recently had
arthroscopic surgery on my right knee – the first time I have had an
operation since my tonsils were removed in a doctor's office when I
was about six or seven. Whether I will get back to a squash court
remains to be seen.

Having an 'athlete' heading the Lit – Eagleson must have thought –
would help the athletic side of the 'literary and athletic association.' In
those years, the department of Physical and Health Education (PHE)
was part of University College and its students were entitled to vote in
the elections. Eagleson arranged for all his friends in the program – and
Eagleson had a lot of friends – to come over to the JCR and vote for me.
It was a close vote and there is little question in my mind that the PHE
vote was the principal reason I was elected. My opponent was a good
friend of mine, Earl Berger, who had been UC's Student Administrative
Council representative and probably had a stronger claim to the office
than I had. He is still one of my closest friends.

The Lit and the WUA were active during my term in office, which
happened to coincide with the one hundredth anniversary of the establishment of University College. The Lit executive was composed of a
number of talented individuals, including the future publisher Peter
Martin and the future federal cabinet minister John Roberts, who was
the literary director. The first edition of the UC newspaper, the *Gargoyle*, was produced that academic year, edited by lawyer-to-be Aubrey
Golden. Like the stone gargoyles on the exterior of UC, the *Gargoyle* has
survived. We also supported a joint production between UC and St
Michael's College of the musical *Brigadoon*, directed by Leon Major.
Such productions continued for a few years and then ceased. We also
laid plans for the renovation of the JCR.

The year 1954–5 was also the year of the engineering frosh initiation
which, unfortunately, got out of hand. In the fall of 1954, hundreds of
engineering students were sent on a 'tour' of the campus. They entered

UC, looking for material that could form part of a later auction. In the course of the raid, the UC registrar was injured. 'Any question of retaliation,' I was quoted in the *Varsity* as stating, self-righteously, would be 'as juvenile as the entire incident itself.' The engineering society was suspended for several months and was fined $4000. Future engineering initiations involved cleaning up debris in parks and beaches.

I did not attend my undergraduate graduation, having already left on the World University Service study tour of West Africa. That trip was an eye-opening experience. I had never been abroad, although I had done a lot of travelling throughout North America. At least once a year during my undergraduate years I travelled for a couple of weeks to some place, driving a dealer's car from Detroit and usually hitch-hiking back to Toronto. The description of these trips may be more than the reader wants, but I believe that they illustrate an adventurous spirit which may have helped me expand the bounds of traditional scholarship in my later career. I leave that to the reader to judge.

The dealer would pay for the gas and give an allowance that, with careful spending, was often enough to cover almost all travel costs. I usually stayed in fraternity houses or flophouses, preferring the former. I was a member of Sigma Alpha Mu, a Jewish fraternity usually called Sammy – no Jewish student that I knew was a member of a non-Jewish fraternity at the U of T – and tried to arrange the route to allow me to stay in as many Sammy houses as I could along the way. This was not always possible, particularly when I was thumbing my way home. I recall staying in a flophouse in a city called The Dalles, Oregon, for $1 a night, while thumbing home from a trip to San Francisco. It was dormitory style and the man in the bed next to me had a seizure during the night and died – the first time I had seen someone die.

The destinations were determined by where the dealer wanted the car to go and usually were decided after I had arrived in Detroit. On most of these trips I went by myself. I continued to do this during my three years at law school. Over the years, I managed to cover forty-six of the then forty-eight states, in some cases by going out of my way to cut through the corner of a state. As of today, I still have not been in South Dakota or Wyoming, but my wife has tentatively agreed to a trip that will take in those states. Having already been to Alaska and Hawaii, I will then have hit all fifty states.

One result of travelling extensively throughout the United States in the 1950s before the establishment of the extensive interstate superhighway system and the many uniform fast-food outlets is that one could observe the cultural and social diversity of the various regions of the country. Route 66, which I followed on one trip to Los Angeles was not – and is not – a superhighway. It actually goes through Joplin, Missouri, and Oklahoma City, where I stopped to visit my mother's brother, is, as the song states, 'mighty pretty.' The United States, then and now, is not one monolithic entity.

I recall driving a new pink Cadillac convertible from Detroit to New Orleans and a new Buick Century to San Francisco. I would pick up hitchhikers in the Cadillac and pretend it was my own. On one occasion while I was standing beside the gas pump a driver pulled up and said to me: 'Fill 'er up.' I said nothing, but simply got into my pink Cadillac and drove away. The Buick trip must have been in the spring of 1954, because I listened to the Army-McCarthy hearings while driving through the western desert. The fate of Joseph McCarthy was being closely followed in Canada. Some of the trips were after Christmas and before classes started. In my second undergraduate year, a couple of upper-year medical students, Diz Disenhouse and Abe Chapman, needed a third driver for a trip in a 'drive-away' car to Los Angeles – this would be my first such trip – where they were headed to check out various hospitals for possible internships. I eagerly joined them and went to the hospitals with them, pretending to be a fellow medical student. There were at the time very few hospital internships in Toronto for Jewish medical students. My history of the University of Toronto confirms this and also shows that at that time there were even restrictions on the admission of Jewish students to the medical school. Both of my fellow drivers interned in the United States where there were more opportunities for employment for Jewish interns, became psychiatrists, and remained in the States. The following year I went with Diz, again courtesy of a Detroit drive-away, to Florida. For $10 we got a return plane ticket from Miami to Havana, obviously subsidized by the gambling syndicates in the pre-Castro days. The gambling syndicates did not get their money's worth from us.

These trips continued after I entered law school. There were two trips to Mexico, after I had dropped off the cars in one of the southern states. My fellow adventurer for one of those trips was my friend and law-school classmate Harry Arthurs, later the president of York University. We were then entering third year. The trip probably lasted about two weeks and I believe we missed a few classes in September. Harry had been hearing about my trips for years and wanted to see for himself what they were like. The only vehicle we could get was a pick-up truck with a standard gear shift. Harry had never driven a standard shift before, but he learned quickly, stripping the gears at the expense of the eventual owner of the truck. Thumbing back from Mexico we had a similar experience. We were just outside Cairo, Illinois, when the driver of a large tractor trailer pulled over and asked if either of us could drive one of those rigs. I said yes, having previously driven only a small truck that required double clutching when shifting gears, but I had never driven one with a dozen or more gears. The driver had a load of perishable produce that had to be in the Chicago market by dawn. It was then early evening and Chicago was over three hundred miles away. He had driven from the Deep South without stopping and was falling asleep at the wheel. Like Harry and the pick-up, I learned how to drive the rig. We arrived safely in Chicago early the next morning.

On the way down we had stopped at the University of Louisville's Brandeis School of Law, which houses the papers of Louis Brandeis, the first Jew on the United States Supreme Court. This was the first time that I had ever looked through archival papers and I still remember the exhilaration of the experience of touching papers belonging to a great public figure. I still find it thrilling.

One trip tends to blur into another. Harry's recollection of the events is probably sharper than mine. Unfortunately, I never made notes on any of the trips, although I would send postcards to my folks, who dutifully kept them. A few other incidents stand out from the trip with Harry. After dropping off the pick-up, we thumbed to the border town of Laredo, Texas. We either took a bus to Monterrey, Mexico, and hitchhiked back or hitch-hiked to Monterrey and took a bus back. (Harry thinks we took the bus back to Texas.) In retrospect, hitch-hiking on deserted mountainous Mexican roads was a rather stupid thing to do. Two other hitchhikers we met on the way showed us the knives they carried in case of trouble.

The hitch-hiking trip back to Toronto brought us through Little Rock, Arkansas, just at the time that the National Guard had been called out to ensure that black students could enter Little Rock High School. We heard about it while travelling north and went out of our way to see for ourselves what was going on. We circulated among the troops and the tanks. A United Press reporter interviewed us about our reaction to what was occurring, which I later heard made the national news in Canada. He then sent us out with a cameraman to a small college not far from Little Rock, where Governor Orville Faubus's son was a student. Faubus, it will be recalled, was resisting integration in spite of a court order made under the 1954 United States Supreme Court case of *Brown v. Board of Education*. Faubus's son agreed to a filmed interview, but it was never used because the authorities had been notified and the Arkansas police arrived to confiscate the film. Harry and I hid a roll of Kodak film we had taken in the hubcap of the cameraman's car – one of the pictures was of Faubus's son in his dormitory room with a poster saying 'Yankee Go Home.' Unfortunately, the quality of the prints made them unusable.

It was in New Orleans on the way south that I phoned Judy's father to formally ask for her hand in marriage. She had been my assistant on the waterfront over that summer at Camp White Pine in Haliburton, where I had been the head of the waterfront. The summer romance – it would be considered improper today because I was her boss – has now lasted close to fifty years. Joe Kronick, who ran the camp, claims – and I agree – that it has been the camp's most long-lasting and successful match. I had given Judy my fraternity pin just before Harry and I left for the trip. The actual 'pinning' had taken place on one of the many now torn-down and forgotten piers on the busy Toronto waterfront – the recently opened Seaway was bringing a large number of ocean-going ships to Toronto.

I phoned Judy's father, Mike Pless – collect – from Antoine's Restaurant in New Orleans. He said yes. The Pless and Friedland families knew each other. Like my father, Mike had a business life centred on Spadina Avenue. He travelled as a ladies' coat salesman throughout southern Ontario. My father, Jack, had successfully manufactured ladies' hats – at the Supreme Hat Company on Adelaide Street – and then, after the war, when many women stopped wearing hats, travelled as a dress salesman, covering roughly the same geographical area as Judy's father. I sometimes went with my father on those trips. He later became a ladies' wear jobber, with an office and showroom a few steps below street level at 129 Spadina Avenue. He was a well-known and much-loved figure on the Avenue, which he always pronounced 'Spadeena,' the proper pronunciation of the name. I picture him, bald, with a small mustache and somewhat overweight, standing on the sidewalk in the sunshine in front of his office, exchanging greetings with those passing by and smoking a large Topper cigar.

No one ever said a harsh word about my father, or my mother. Both were well-respected members of the Jewish community – my father was active in the service organization B'nai Brith and my mother in the women's Zionist organization Hadassah. I have nothing but admiration for their approach to life, and I cannot recall ever being physically disciplined by either of them. I was reasonably close with both of them, particularly my mother, who was kind, gentle, and devoted to her two children. Everyone who knew her loved her. She died in a nursing home in her late nineties, with the same wonderful disposition and respect for others that she had shown all of her life.

Spadina Avenue was an important part of my early life, even though we lived in the north end of the city. I had my haircuts at my father's barbershop on Spadina, Tetefs, where he would have a shave and a shoeshine on most days. My dentist, Reuben Brown, was above a bank at the south-west corner of Queen and Spadina, opposite the since-demolished Mary Pickford cinema. As stated above, after my father's unsuccessful foray into manufacturing women's suits, he switched to selling commercial real estate, which he did until his death in 1967 from a heart attack at age sixty-nine. My father-in-law, Mike Pless, continued on the road until he was almost ninety, using a driver in his later years. I had the experience of driving his van for him on one of his sales trips to Peterborough in the early 1990s. He could handle heavy garment bags in his eighties better than I could in my fifties. I never knew Judy's mother, who tragically died of leukemia in 1949, at the age of thirty-eight.

I am embarrassed to say that although I have carefully researched the history of a number of famous judges and alleged murderers, I have done very little research on my own family. I know – or so his passport says – that my father, Jacob Friedland, was born on 14 April 1898 in Minsk in the present republic of Belarus, then part of the Russian empire. He was two years old when he came in 1900 with his mother, Esther, and his older and younger brothers, Dave and Al, to Toronto, via the port of Montreal, to join his father, Asher Friedland. Asher, who seems to have been a Talmudic scholar in those years, had come to Toronto about a year earlier and was living with his wife's brother, Gershon Solway (grandfather of Herb Solway of the Goodmans law firm), in a large house on Brunswick Avenue, just north of College Street.

The Friedland family moved to New York within a year or two – Asher becoming a U.S. citizen in 1903 – and like many immigrants lived on the Lower East Side of Manhattan. My father graduated from the East Side Evening High School for Men in May 1917, and shortly thereafter came back to Toronto to live with and work as a bookkeeper for Gershon Solway, who had a thriving scrap-metal business. Gershon must have been in Canada for many years and was well established, because he was one of the original members of the board of directors of Goel Tzedec Synagogue when it opened in the early 1900s on the east side of University Avenue, just south of Dundas Street.

My father later moved to Brantford, Ontario, about 100 kilometres west of Toronto, to work as a bookkeeper. Coincidently, Judy's father – also from Minsk – lived in Brantford as well, and they knew each other in that city's small Jewish community. Mike Pless, several years younger than my father, remembered him as an excellent basketball player. My father and mother married in 1925, and my father became a Canadian citizen in 1932. I always heard him referred to as 'Jack,' but in Might's City Directory during the 1930s he called himself 'John.'

I rarely saw my New York grandparents. My earliest clear recollection of any event in my life that I can link with a specific date was travelling in our 1939 black Packard – we obviously were reasonably well off in those days – to New York City in August 1939 to visit my grandparents and to attend the New York World's Fair. I still clearly remember the Trylon and Perisphere and the General Motors exhibit that showed what highway travel would be like in the future. As it turned out, the predictions were not far off. It is not surprising that I would remember the World's Fair. It would be fixed in the memory of any child about to turn seven. I also remember from that trip the Queen Elizabeth highway, which had just opened. Of course, I have memories of the house we lived in at the time at 400 Castlefield Avenue, off Avenue Road, north of Eglinton Avenue, but those memories may be from a later period. So I do not know whether my memory of such events as deliberately breaking milk bottles which a friend (who also became a lawyer) and I took from neighbours' milk boxes, or adding butterflies to my large collection, or being told by the mother of a friend down the street not to tell her son that there was no Santa Claus, or being sent to my room without supper because I swore at my brother, or seriously gashing my leg on a nail protruding from a slide in the backyard of the house next door, occurred before or after the trip to New York. I know we had lived in a small house on Banff Road near Eglinton and Bayview until I was about four, but I have no recollection of it. Nor, of course, do I remember the rented duplex apartment on Oriole Parkway where I lived for two years after I was born or the Toronto Island cottage which I was told we rented for several summers when I was very young.

It was only when my father died in 1967 that his older brother Dave revealed to our family that his own father, my grandfather, Asher Friedland, had returned to Russia some time before the First World War and did not return to the United States to rejoin his family for at least ten years. An official document from 1922 that a New York cousin, Stuart Friedland, found required my grandfather to explain to a U.S. consular official in the Soviet Union his 'protracted residence in his native land' before they would allow him to return to the States. I do not know why he went to Russia or what he did there or how my grandmother with three children was able to survive in his absence. My New York cousin believes that he returned to Russia because of sympathy for the political changes going on there.

Perhaps tracing my roots will be a future project for me. It will not, however, be easy to find my paternal grandfather's origins in Eastern Europe. As far as I know, our family did not maintain contact with any relatives who remained there, although it may be that my grandfather or my grandmother, whose maiden name was Solway, had siblings who stayed behind. I recently examined the new Yad Vashem website that lists the names of persons who died in the Holocaust. There were well over fifty persons from Minsk alone with a name similar to Friedland. So the task of finding descendents might prove impossible.

I know somewhat more about my maternal grandparents, Samuel and Bertha Rogul. They came to Canada from Odessa in the Ukraine shortly after the turn of the last century, my grandfather preceding the family by a year or two. Although my mother always led her children and others to believe that she was born in Canada – a passport issued in 1941 said 'born in Canada' – in fact she was about two when she came to Canada. As a result, she was not automatically a Canadian citizen and did not become one until she was sworn in as a citizen in 1980, which was a requirement of getting her old-age pension. It is not clear where she was born – a later passport said that she was born in Leningrad, yet in a brief biographical sketch she did for me several decades ago she said she was born in Polsia in the Ukraine.

My mother's father, Samuel Rogul, was a committed Zionist all his life. No doubt it was his influence that caused my parents to give my brother the middle name of Benzion – Son of Zion – a name that Sheldon has never used. I had long talks with my grandfather, when he would stress the importance of trying to further the public good. I recall a walk through the woods on a farm, perhaps an hour's drive north of Toronto, where he and Bertha often spent part of the summer, during which he urged me not to spend my time chasing a little white ball around a golf course. He wrote in my bar mitzvah autograph book (I have corrected the spelling): 'We hope and trust you will be a successful man to yourself and a credit to your family and an honour to the Jewish race.' My mother's entry in the book was 'This is just the beginning – Aim High!'

It was only recently that I learned – through the memoirs of my mother's first cousin, Norman Rogul, a well-known Toronto furrier who was born in St Petersburg in 1918 – that my maternal grandfather's sister and their mother were both murdered in a pogrom in the Ukraine in about 1920. There was widespread anti-Jewish rioting throughout the former Russian empire after the 1917 Revolution, with hundreds of thousands of deaths. Norman's memoir also states that his great grandfather – my great-great grandfather – was one of the leading rabbis in Russia – another avenue that I might explore in the future.

My brother and I often stayed with the Roguls in their apartment above their ladies' wear store on Queen Street West in Parkdale. They had a set of the Book of Knowledge and the Book of History, which I often read when I was there. We had relatively few such books at home, although I would make frequent trips to the public library at Yonge and St Clements. I tended to borrow non-fiction, particularly biographies, travel adventures, and science stories. I cannot, however, say that I was an avid reader, and to this day do not know many of the children's classics that many of my contemporaries seem to have read.

As far as I am aware, none of my grandparents' siblings remained in Europe as the Second World War approached. As opposed to many other families, such as Judy's, I was not aware of any relatives who either perished in or survived the Holocaust. Perhaps for this reason, the destruction of the Jews in Europe was more abstract and less immediate for me than it otherwise would have been. I was twelve when the war ended. Like many young persons living comfortably in Forest Hill, I was not at the time very understanding of those who survived. Subsequently, Judy and I visited various Holocaust museums – in Jerusalem, Washington, Berlin, and other places – and the death camps of Auschwitz-Birkenau in Poland and Theresenstadt in the Czech Republic. It may be that researching and writing *The Trials of Israel Lipski* in the 1980s – a case which involved emigration from Eastern Europe and anti-Semitism – was a way of personally understanding the struggles of those seeking a better life in a new country and the fate of those who remained.

My childhood was a relatively easy one. I had been born in the Toronto General Hospital on 21 September 1932. My brother was twenty-one months older than me. Sheldon had the distinction of winning the Hadassah Bazaar prize as the most beautiful baby. Apparently I was never entered in any such contest. In fact, I gather that I was not a particularly beautiful baby, and weighed eleven and a half pounds at birth. A friend of my parents, Frank Goldberg, used to call me Young Firpo, after a serious contender for the light heavyweight boxing championship in the 1930s. We lived in a comfortable house at 400 Castlefield Avenue, close to Allenby Public School, before moving to 213 Rosemary Road in Forest Hill in 1944, when I was eleven. I cannot recall any serious anti-Semitic incidents and was only in one fight in my life. I do not remember the reason for the fight, but it was in the Allenby School playground and it lasted about ten seconds – I gave up after I received one punch in the temple.

I took piano and Hebrew lessons, had a respectable stamp collection, developed and printed my own photographs, had a small chemistry set, and built crystal radio sets. I also had an extensive butterfly collection – perhaps twenty or thirty varieties – all collected from the open fields at the end of Castlefield Avenue, just east of Bathurst Street. I obviously had broad interests and a sense of curiosity, which might be reflected in my later career, but I do not think that my activities were that different from those of other middle-class children growing up in Toronto in those years.

When we moved to Forest Hill in 1944, the comfortable life continued, although my mother regretted that they could not afford membership in the Oakdale golf club, to which most of my parents' friends belonged. We never had a record player and did not acquire a television set until long after most of my friends had one. I had only one record, Charlie Barnet's 'Pompton Turnpike,' which was given to me by radio personality Joe Chrysdale when I was selected from the audience attending his live radio broadcast, 'Club 580.' I was probably supposed to be at the synagogue across the street at the time. I did have my own radio – a brown plastic Admiral – and like most of Canada listened to the hockey games on Saturday nights, Jack Benny and Fred Allen on Sunday nights, and 'Lux Presents Hollywood' on Monday nights, but I also listened to Eric Severeid's analysis of the news at 11 o'clock each evening on a Buffalo station and CBC's 'Music of Mozart.'

Both my brother and I had traditional bar mitzvahs when we reached the age of thirteen. In each case there was a ceremony at Goel Tzedec

Synagogue on University Avenue, just north of the present courthouse, with a reception that evening at our house on Rosemary Road. There was drama connected with both our bar mitzvahs. My brother's was in January 1943. Like many other commodities, liquor was rationed during the war. My parents had carefully saved their liquor rations, getting ready for the bar mitzvah. On New Year's Eve, when Sheldon and I were alone at home – I was eleven years old – two men broke into our house and took all the liquor. I do not think they took anything else. I recall being asked by one of the robbers whether we had a safe and replying that we did not, but that 'my Auntie Anne had one.' The Forest Hill Village police came early the next morning. Sergeant Firstbrook showed me various mug shots, but although I had had a good view of one of the men, I could not identify either of them. I recall being asked if the robber I saw was sober. I said that he was not, thinking that the word sober meant drunk. The robbers were never caught, but friends donated some of their own supplies of liquor and the bar mitzvah celebration went on as planned.

My own bar mitzvah came after the war ended, and liquor was not the problem. The problem was that I had spent almost a year studying the wrong Torah and Haftorah portion. Once a week my Hebrew teacher, Mr Litchen, would bicycle to our house to give me a lesson. A few days before the date of my bar mitzvah it was discovered during a rehearsal at the synagogue that the portion I had learned was for the following week. It was too late to learn a completely new one and too late to switch the date of the event – the invitations had gone out weeks earlier. The bar mitzvah went on, with me reading the passages that I had learned. All the old-timers were asked to refrain from raising a fuss. Cantor Bornstein read the right portions after I had finished chanting the wrong ones. Although I now rarely get nervous speaking in public, whenever I am asked to participate in an event at the synagogue of a religious nature – I never volunteer – I fear impending doom. Even a simple act like opening the Ark causes unnatural stress.

My parents kept a kosher house – two sets of dishes and cutlery and no pork products. But we would eat Chinese food outside the house. I particularly remember the steamy upstairs restaurant at 12½ Elizabeth Street, where we would often go on a Sunday evening. Like my parents, Judy and I continue to maintain the same uneasy compromise.

My brother and I went to a summer camp, Balfour Manor Camp, in Muskoka, not far from Gravenhurst. The camp was owned and run by the Granovskys – Ted, a dentist, and his wife, Irene. She was a friend of my mother's – they were both in the Scopus chapter of Hadassah. Apparently, I had started going to the camp at the age of four, and continued for at least part of each summer for the next dozen years. I never felt abandoned, however, perhaps because in the early years the Granovskys also made room for my mother to stay at the camp for periods of time. The camp had always taken a strong interest in the arts, and my interest in music probably developed when the opera singer and actor Jan Rubes, who had just come over from Czechoslovakia, was my counsellor at camp. Rubes was also a championship tennis player and my interest in racquet sports developed over that summer. I recently talked with music professor and author Ezra Schabas, who is writing Rubes's biography, and I told him that I thought that Rubes probably had a significant effect on my life as a role model through his quest for excellence in everything he did.

Only one summer was spent in the city. I could not get a job as a camp counsellor in 1950 after grade 12, and so joined the air force for the summer. The 400 Fighter Squadron was recruiting students – there were about fifty of us – hoping that we would continue in the air force – some did – or at least become part of the reserve. Most of the summer was spent at the air-force station on Avenue Road north of Eglinton Avenue that had once been a hunt club. I was being trained as a communications technician and learned the intricacies of radio transmission. As stated above, I had built crystal radio sets when I was younger. My official designation was as an aircraftsman second class – M.L. Friedland AC2-90239. We also spent a surprisingly large amount of time drilling – understandable for the army, but surprising to me for the air force. I never did get the hang of marching. The drill leader would loudly single me out as 'loose as goose grease.'

We also spent about three weeks at the beginning of the summer stationed at the air base in Chatham, New Brunswick, flying there and back from Downsview air base in a large noisy turboprop North Star cargo plane with bucket seats around the interior. On weekends I thumbed around the province – I recall going to a lobster festival in Shediac and swimming in the ocean in Bathurst. We spent most evenings in New Brunswick playing a form of blackjack called 'stuke.' On one of those evenings in late June someone came into the tent where we were gambling to announce that war had been declared against North Korea and that Canada was sending over the 400 Fighter Squadron. I had just wanted a summer job and was not thrilled at the prospect of fighting in Korea. As it turned out, we did not go, but when the summer was over I lost no time in leaving the military. I still have my honourable discharge document.

Whether this experience in the air force influenced in any way my work in the 1990s for the Somalia inquiry on controlling misconduct in the military is hard to say. It probably did influence my later work on gun control, because it was in New Brunswick that I first did skeet shooting. Our superior officers often asked for volunteers. I liked volunteering, even though one risked unpleasant assignments. On one such occasion my task was to go skeet shooting with the commanding officer. I operated the contraption that shot the clay pigeons in the air, but for part of the time he graciously operated the machine and allowed me to do the shooting. Even though I ended up with a bruised shoulder because he failed to tell me to keep the gun tight to my shoulder to avoid damage from kickbacks, I learned that skeet shooting can be an enjoyable sport.

I was a fairly good student in high school, always in the class for the brighter kids that had the supposedly inconspicuous initial J at the end of it – 10J, 11J, etc. A large group from 13J went into medicine – one member of the class recently told me that over a dozen members of the 13J class became doctors –the toughest program to enter at U of T. In the end, I received five firsts out of the required nine subjects. One of the firsts was in English composition, with the remaining firsts in maths and sciences. The reader may find it interesting that I did not take history in my final year.

During high school I was not as involved in extra-curricular activities as I later would be in university, although my entry in the yearbook in my final year says that I was a member of the science club, took part in the production of *H.M.S. Pinafore*, won the intermediate tennis title, and was the vice-president of my class. I spent a large amount of time serving what were called 'detentions' – normally for misbehaviour – and at John's pool hall on Eglinton Avenue just east of Oakwood. My parents were not aware of the amount of time I spent shooting pool, but they must have been suspicious when John, the proprietor, called my home and told my mother that my wallet had been found in the pool hall. Needless to say, I was never invited to be a prefect, a coveted honour at Forest Hill Collegiate.

I was also involved in a Jewish high school fraternity, Beta Alpha Kappa, which a number of us had started when I was in grade 10. I was its first president. I recall one of the first meetings in our living room on Rosemary Road, a room normally reserved for very important events, such as my mother's hosting of a meeting of the Scopus chapter of Hadassah. Sociologist John Seeley's study of Forest Hill Village, which he titled *Crestwood Heights*, remarked on the sacredness of living rooms in Forest Hill. Our furniture was not covered in sheets, as in some homes, but we rarely used it. The fiftieth anniversary of the now-defunct fraternity occurred in 1996. The program set out the addresses of the members that could be located. The distinguished anthropologist Richard Lee, a fellow fraternity brother, observed the unusual feature that a significant percentage of the fraternity's members continued to live about a mile from the corner of Bathurst and Eglinton. He considered writing an academic paper on the subject, but never did so.

The trip to West Africa started in early June 1955 with a trans-Atlantic crossing by ship from Montreal to Southampton and briefings with West African experts in London. World University Service study tours were designed to increase contact between students throughout the world and to foster an interest in international affairs. The leader of the tour was Alan Cairns, later a noted political scientist but at the time a U of T graduate student doing a master's degree under Alexander Brady. He would go on to complete a doctorate at Oxford on the politics of Rhodesia. We continue to be close friends. There were four other members of the study group from other universities across Canada. We travelled by train across France and in Marseilles boarded a French passenger ship, whose ultimate destination was Vietnam. The French defeat at Dien Bien Phu had taken place the previous spring, but French troops were still in the non-communist south. The ship stopped to pick up and discharge passengers and cargo at ports of various French and English colonies along the way, including Casablanca, Dakar, Conakry, Abidjan, and Takoradi, allowing us to visit each of those cities. Most of those picked up in the French ports were black soldiers heading to Vietnam.

We spent about three weeks in Ghana, at the time called the Gold Coast, and about a month in Nigeria. The trip was also designed to lay the groundwork for a large World University Service summer program in the future, which took place two years later with Pierre Trudeau as one of its leaders. Very few persons, other than government officials, religious personnel, and businessmen, visited those colonies in those years. I cannot recall meeting any tourists or other travelling students while we were there. Forty years later, our eldest child, Tom, would – like other students – spend time travelling throughout Africa. But at the time our visit was a novelty and we had access to all the political and tribal leaders in both colonies. In the Gold Coast, we met with Prime Minister Kwame Nkrumah and with the leader of the opposition, Kofi Busia. We had meetings with colonial officials and had a formal audience in Kumasi with the Asantahene of Ashanti and his entourage, with their gold staffs and ancient ceremonial stools. There was great hope for the colony, which would gain its independence two years later. It had good economic resources: sources of power, bauxite for aluminum, cocoa and coffee and other crops. There was a solid infrastructure built up by the colonial administrators and a relatively new university, University College of the Gold Coast, near the capital, Accra, that was at the time affiliated with the University of London. As Alan Cairns recently wrote: 'There were great hopes that liberation and prosperity were just around the corner ... We all imbibed that atmosphere of hope.'

There was somewhat less promise of success for the much larger and more populous colony of Nigeria. Again, we met many of the key players: Nnamdi Azikiwe, known as 'Zik,' from the east, later the first president of the Republic of Nigeria; Yoruba Chief Obafemi Awolowa, the leader of the opposition from the west; the emir of Kano; and the Sardona of Sokoto from the Muslim north. We travelled by car and plane to all the regions, from Lagos on the coast in the western region and Onitsha across the Niger River in the east to the cities of Kaduna and the walled city of Kano, with its indigo dye vats outside the main gates, in the north. Like the Gold Coast, the country had important resources, including vast oil reserves, which unfortunately helped lead to the attempted secession of the oil-rich eastern region in 1967 and the devastating Biafran civil war. The promise that we had perhaps naively felt has still not yet been fulfilled.

One thing I brought back from West Africa was a small but good collection of authentic masks and other cultural items, such as Yoruba twin figures, an Ashanti fertility doll, and a small Benin bronze bell. I recall entering a small hut in Benin and offering a handful of coins and receiving the Benin bell in exchange. These objects were exhibited the following year in the Hart House Art Gallery. My wife and I have subsequently added to the collection on our travels.

In September 1955 I returned to Toronto from Southampton – on the

Greek Line's *Columbia*, the same ship on which we had travelled to England – to start law school. There is absolutely no doubt that the trip to West Africa further whetted my appetite for adventure – intellectually and otherwise. I was ready to be challenged in law school.

1

Legal Education

Classes started in Cumberland House in early September 1955. I returned home from Europe too late for the orientation program and so did not hear Caesar Wright's or Sidney Smith's opening addresses. Had I been there, I am sure I would not have forgotten the event. I cannot recall whether I missed any classes. In any event, I have no recollection of my first class. All our classes were in the large north front room overlooking St George Street. The small legal library was across the hall.

The class of about forty-five students was composed of talented and interesting individuals. Persons who attended the University of Toronto law school knew that it would cost them an extra year compared to those who attended Osgoode Hall Law School, and thus they tended to be highly motivated. The size of the class kept shrinking during the year, particularly after the Christmas test results were returned. Thirty-one persons graduated, which included some who had started out in the class a year ahead of us.

As it turned out, we did not have to spend an extra year before getting our call to the bar. On 14 February 1957, in our second year, we received a welcome Valentine's Day present. The Law Society of Upper Canada had decided that Osgoode Hall Law School would henceforth offer a three- rather than a four-year law degree and that other law schools in Canada would be recognized as qualified to offer degrees. The Law Society could not cope with the expected increase in the number of baby boomers who would soon be applying to study law. Osgoode was willing to and did, in fact, build a new wing on Osgoode Hall for 900 students, but could not handle the anticipated 1500 students a year who would soon want to enter law school in Ontario. Moreover, Queen's University had been pushing to be permitted to establish a law school. The final negotiations were worked out by Alex Corry of Queen's and two benchers, Park Jamieson and John Arnup. Caesar Wright had not been involved in the discussions. Principal Alex Mackintosh of Queen's wrote to Sidney Smith, stating: 'To be quite frank, I do not think Caesar Wright would help at this stage.' Caesar might have been a red flag to a bull and upset the apple cart, to mix a couple of metaphors.

During the summer between my first and second year, the law school moved north from Cumberland House to the Glendon Estate off Bayview Avenue, now Glendon College of York University. Cumberland House had not been able to accommodate the growing number of students. Some faculty members were unhappy about the move to Glendon, feeling cut off from the campus. One advantage for the students, however, was that faculty members were captive and would often eat lunch with us in the only available lunch room within half a kilometre of Glendon. We would take walks through the Glendon woods and down into the Don Valley ravine. I have it fixed in my mind that Bora Laskin sometimes joined us on these walks, but perhaps I am just imagining it.

The law school remained at Glendon until Caesar was able to persuade the University to allow the school to take over from the history department the magnificent Flavelle House, which has remained law's home ever since. Financier and businessman Sir Joseph Flavelle had built his residence on Queen's Park Crescent in 1903 and bequeathed it to the University in 1939. The history department, the members of which have never forgiven the law school, was moved to the new Sidney Smith Hall on St George Street. In 1962 the law school, with its complement of four hundred students, moved into Flavelle House.

Former dean Ron Daniels publicly announced in early 2005 that the University had given the law school permission to build an entirely new complex on Bloor Street and Devonshire Place. The present site, it was thought, could not be expanded to meet the growing needs of the law school. It now seems unlikely that the law school will have to move, because the unsuccessful attempt by the Royal Ontario Museum to build a tall condominium on the site of the planetarium beside the law school appears to have opened up the possibility of some modest growth on the law school's present site. In 2006 I was a member of a planning committee set up by Dean Mayo Moran to decide on a future site for the law school. We unanimously voted to stay where we are, assuming that some expansion is permitted.

I had known a number of the members of the first-year class from my University College days: Harry Arthurs, who would become a distinguished academic and the president of York University; Harvey Bliss, who became a successful civil litigator; and Joe Pomerant, who became an extraordinary criminal lawyer, but was later disbarred for taking money from one of his clients, a convicted drug dealer. I knew Ron Price, a Victoria College student, who had made a name for himself in honour history and went on to teach law at Queen's. We had all heard of John Sopinka, who had played for the Varsity Blues and the Toronto Argos, and during law school would play for the Montreal Alouettes. John became one of Canada's top counsel and later a strong member of the Supreme Court of Canada.

Jerry Grafstein, now a senator, came from the University of Western Ontario, where we had met when I was taking part in an intercollegiate squash tournament and Jerry was working part-time at the athletic centre. There was also Burt Kellock from McMaster, the son of a Supreme Court of Canada judge; Joe Cermak, a Czech poet with a civil law degree; Ross Husband, who had been a pilot in the air force; Bill Filipiuk, who had completed an MA in East European studies; and Bruce Hawkins, who became a superior court judge – to name only a few. There was only one woman, Diane Hillier, who did not practise law, but became a law librarian. There were relatively few women at the law school until the 1970s. When Jack Batten, who had been in the class a year ahead of me and then turned from the practice of law to a successful literary career, wanted to write a book about a specific class, he chose the one that graduated in 1975, because that was the first with a sizable number of women. Today, there are usually more women than men. There was only one visible-minority student, Julius Isaac, originally from Grenada, who later worked for the federal department of justice and ended up as the chief justice of the Federal Court of Canada. I had an exceptional group of classmates.

The faculty was also exceptional. It was – and probably still is – the best faculty ever assembled at one time in Canada. Caesar Wright, who taught us torts, was brilliant. He had graduated with gold medals from the University of Western Ontario, had stood first in all three years at Osgoode, and after only one year at Harvard Law School was given a doctorate at the age of twenty-two. He was not a follower of the Socratic method, widely used at Harvard. Although he occasionally asked questions, they were really rhetorical questions which he answered himself. He had his own strong ideas on what the law was and what it should be and was not very tolerant of other opinions. I always found him intimidating. Stan Schiff, who was two years ahead of me, accurately described Wright in a recent interview as 'a big man with a powerful booming voice and a personality that hit you in the face like a fist.' When I entered Wright's office, whether as a student or a professor, I was never invited to sit down. One stood in front of his desk waiting to be dismissed. He had two small magnets – one a black and the other a white terrier – at the front of his desk, and on several occasions I found myself nervously playing with them while he carried on his monologue.

Bora Laskin, who had done his master's at Harvard Law School, was more open to questions, but always had a tremendous amount of material to cover and so lectured most of the time. We had him for real property in first year, constitutional law in second year, and labour law in third. Today, most professors concentrate on one area of law, perhaps two. Laskin specialized in all three areas. Moreover, he was always busy with outside assignments, giving opinions, conducting labour arbitrations, involved in faculty association matters, participating in civil-liberties issues, and doing government reports. He also wrote headnotes for the *Dominion Law Reports*, the case-law series edited by Caesar. Law teachers were not well paid in those days. I expect that his appointment to the Ontario Court of Appeal in 1965 allowed him to slow down a bit. Laskin's first-year property course was the most technical course we had in law school. We learned in great detail such arcane subjects as future interests and shifting and springing uses.

Like Caesar, Laskin produced casebooks, and wrote a large number of articles and notes, particularly for the *Canadian Bar Review*, but, as with Caesar, he never produced a major text in any of his fields of expertise. Moreover, he had the misfortune of being on the Supreme Court of Canada just before the development of Charter jurisprudence, and so his judgments are perhaps not as frequently cited today as are those of Brian Dickson, his successor as chief justice. Nevertheless, as I will state in a later chapter on the Charter, I believe that he played an important role in its enactment. This was not because he was active behind the scenes, but because he looked and acted like a wise, fatherly, Solomon-type figure, whom the public could trust to deliver sound judgments under a new Charter of Rights and Freedoms.

Although Laskin's door was always open and he would deal with whatever you wanted to discuss with him, there was never time for much chit-chat at the law school. He was a no-nonsense professor. When he happened to mention critically to our first-year class something about the Queen's Counsel list that had been published that morning in the *Globe* and a voice in the back row – I'm quite certain it was Bruce Hawkins – shouted 'sour grapes,' Laskin walked out, although he returned to finish the class. Nor was Laskin amused in his second-year labour-law class when someone had secretly brought in a record player and opened the class with Pete Seeger's 'There once was a union maid.' He mellowed over the years, however, particularly after he became a judge.

My wife and I happened to be having dinner with the Laskins at an Italian restaurant in London, England, in early July 1965 when Laskin was called to the telephone. He did not say anything about the call when he returned to the table, although it was clear to us that it had been an important conversation. We later found out that the call had been from the solicitor general, Larry Pennell, telling Laskin that the cabinet had appointed him to the Ontario Court of Appeal. Jerry Grafstein, who had close ties with the Liberal Party and had played an important role in the appointment, had tracked Laskin down at the restaurant. The announcement would not be made until the Laskins returned to Canada from their holiday towards the end of August, and Laskin was asked to keep the appointment private. Laskin was not the first Jew to be appointed to the superior court in Ontario; that distinction belongs to Abe Leiff, who had been appointed to the trial division of the Supreme Court of Ontario several years earlier. Nor was Laskin the first Jew to be appointed to an appellate court. That honour belonged to Sam Freedman of Manitoba. Laskin's departure was a great loss to the University because he was the clear choice to succeed Wright as dean.

In contrast to Caesar and Bora, Jim Milner and Al Abel used the Socratic method – perhaps even more rigorously than had Socrates himself. Milner, a Dalhousie gold medallist who had also completed graduate work at Harvard, taught us contracts in first year and land-use planning in third year. He would ask questions and wait for the answers to come. Some of us – I was one of them – liked that approach, but others wanted more direction from the instructor. It taught one to think, but some of the long silences were painful. Al Abel, who did his doctorate at Harvard and taught at West Virginia University before coming to Toronto, followed the same approach, although he tended to keep his eyes closed during the silences. We had him for legal writing in first year and administrative law in second year. In administrative law he would either take two cases and spend the class comparing and contrasting them or just take one case to analyse. Milner allowed students to volunteer answers. Abel called on you after shuffling a deck of file cards. I recall one class where I had not read the material, which was obvious to most of my classmates and, I am quite sure, to Abel, but I was able to keep up the discussion for perhaps twenty minutes before he moved on to someone else. The first-year legal-writing class required an enormous effort on Abel's part. He would go over drafts of ours on such assignments as a *Harvard Law Review*–style case comment. To the extent that U of T law school has over the years contributed to the blossoming of legal scholarship in Canada, Al Abel has to take a fair amount of the credit as the person who showed the importance of clear written analysis to a generation of lawyers and judges.

Moreover, both Milner and Abel not only had open doors, but also encouraged students to discuss legal and other issues with them outside of class. Milner died at the very early age of fifty-one in 1969 after suffering a heart attack on a plane returning to Toronto from Ottawa. Abel died in 1977 at the age of seventy-one, still teaching a course at the law school. I was the dean and arranged the memorial service for him in the Hart House debates room. The room and the gallery were packed. Abel loved music and we asked the Orford String Quartet to play movements from Beethoven, Mozart, and Schubert quartets between speeches. Chief Justice Laskin came down from Ottawa. He had been Al's closest friend – they had done graduate work together at Harvard – and Laskin was responsible for Al's coming to Toronto. Although an American – Al did not become a Canadian citizen until shortly before he died – he learned French and included judgments written in French in his teaching materials. I had received a call from Al's cleaning lady one morning to come over to his house as soon as possible. He was sitting in a chair in his living room, having been asphyxiated by gas fumes. He died reading Balzac – in French.

The focus of the law school was shifting towards the United States. We studied English and Canadian cases, but also many American cases. Almost every faculty member had done graduate work in the

United States, and most of them did it at Harvard. This was part of the overall intellectual shift in the universities and in society after the Second World War away from the United Kingdom and towards American ideas and culture. One professor, Bob McKay, taught us criminal law from an excellent American casebook on criminal law, Michael and Wechsler's *Criminal Law and Its Administration*. I still have the text and my notes on the course – the only set that I kept. We covered the material in a straightforward manner. Some liked this approach, but I liked the classes where there were strong clashes of opinion. I cannot say that the course played a role in my later decision to specialize in criminal law, which owed more to Charles Dubin and Glanville Williams, whose influence will be described in later chapters. The course, however, did shape the approach I later took to teaching criminal law. When I started my own criminal-law casebook in 1967, I included material on criminal procedure and the administration of criminal justice. McKay, who had earlier moved to the new law school at the University of Western Ontario, used my casebook.

It is difficult to overestimate how tied we were to the English legal system when I was a student. Although appeals to the United Kingdom's Privy Council from the Supreme Court of Canada had been abolished in 1949, Canadian courts, including the Supreme Court of Canada, still felt bound by decisions of the British House of Lords and Privy Council. Indeed, there were Canadian cases saying that the Canadian courts were bound by English court of appeal decisions. The first Supreme Court of Canada case to refuse to follow a House of Lords decision was *The Queen v. Jennings* in 1966. Almost all of us knew most of the judges of the House of Lords. Today, few Canadian law students can name more than one or two judges in the House of Lords. Nineteenth-century judges such as Lord Lindley and Sir George Jessel, the first Jewish judge in England, both judges of the English Court of Appeal, were two of my heroes at law school.

The only person trained outside the common-law teaching at the law school was Wolfgang Friedmann, an international and comparative lawyer, who had studied in Germany and had come to the U of T via the University of London and the University of Melbourne. He never taught our class because he left Toronto at the end of our first year for Columbia University, where he established a stellar reputation in international law. When I became dean in 1972, I followed up on an invitation that Dean Ronnie Macdonald had extended to him to give a series of lectures at the U of T. Friedmann and I had worked out a date for the visit for early December 1972 and I had discussed the possible publication of the lectures with the U of T Press. In September, however, he was fatally stabbed in the Morningside Heights area near Columbia University while resisting some robbers who had demanded his wallet and his watch.

When Friedmann left for Columbia, the school hired Ted McWhinney, an international lawyer from Australia, who had done his doctorate at Yale. McWhinney taught us private international law, in which he was only one step ahead of us. His real love was public international law, but that slot was filled by Eugene LaBrie. McWhinney was a prolific and effective scholar. He was also a name dropper, but I did not mind because he actually knew most of the persons whose names he dropped. In the late 1960s he left for McGill University, unappreciated by many of his colleagues at the U of T, but not by this one. In later years he became a Liberal member of parliament, and one would often see his well-groomed countenance during question period behind Prime Minister Jean Chrétien.

Eugene LaBrie was our only professor who had been part of Dean W.P.M. Kennedy's law school. LaBrie taught us company law, tax law, and international law. Like Laskin, Milner, and others, he was the master of three subjects. He had come from Alberta to do his doctorate at the U of T. He kept – or perhaps invented – his slow western drawl and his gentle sense of humour. He would deliberately play with students' names, referring to Burt Kellock, for example, as Mr Cartwright or Mr Fauteux or another member of the Supreme Court. It does not seem as humorous now as it did to us then. Throughout his career, he resented the fact that Caesar Wright's professional law school, established in 1949, tended to forget that there had been a law school before Wright came – Kennedy's law school.

W.P.M. Kennedy was an eccentric Irishman who had never studied law, but produced some of the country's finest work on constitutional law. He had come to the U of T in the early 1920s as a professor of English, switched to history, then to political economy, and finally to law. The honour law program that the faculty offered was a four-year undergraduate course. It had many distinguished graduates, such as court of appeal members Charles Dubin, William Howland, G. Arthur Martin, and Sydney Robins, but its graduates did not receive any credit for the law courses they took when they went to Osgoode. I do not recall meeting Kennedy, and by all accounts one would not forget such a meeting. He was seventy-six when I arrived at the faculty as a student in 1955 and he died in 1964, the year before I joined the faculty as an academic. Not only was he an impressive scholar, but he was also a sparkling teacher. J.J. Robinette, one of Canada's greatest lawyers, who was taught by Kennedy in the 1920s, recalled that 'Kennedy was one of those brilliant Irishmen who could dazzle you ... a performer as much as a teacher.'

Despite not being taught by Kennedy, I feel I know him well because in 1983 Judy and I purchased a lakefront property that the Kennedy family had owned since 1940. The large 150-acre property on Beaver Lake and the Magnetawan River in the Town of Kearney, north of Huntsville and just west of Algonquin Park, was sold to us by his son, Reverend Frere Kennedy, who had inherited it from his father. A notice had been placed in each mail box at the law school saying that nothing would please the family more than to have the property remain in the hands of a member of the academic community. We visited the property in the early spring and loved it. We knew the area because we had once stayed at Rob Prichard's cottage on a connecting lake. The Kennedy property had been up for sale for many months without any takers, and so we purchased it for what turned out in retrospect to have been a very modest sum.

The purchase created a link with my fellow ex-dean, W.P.M. Kennedy, who is buried with his wife in a graveyard in the Town of Emsdale, close to the cottage. He had named the property 'Narrow Waters,' after a castle in Ireland, and we continue to use that name. Kennedy had kept a large collection of books and documents at the cottage. As other academics did in those years, he went north in May and did not return until late August. Records left at the cottage show that a number of faculty members visited the cottage and were made to saw logs and engage in other physical activities. Some of the old-timers in Kearney with whom I spoke over the years remember the eccentric but likeable dean. Unfortunately, Kennedy destroyed all his papers in Toronto before he died, making a full biography difficult to write. Several years ago, my colleague Dick Risk published an extensive article on Kennedy and his contribution to the law in the *U of T Law Journal*, which is probably as close to a biography as we are likely to get.

The property has another intriguing connection to the history of the University of Toronto Law School. It was there, during the summer of 1945, that a crucial part of the plan to create a strong university law school was executed. U of T president Sidney Smith and Caesar Wright, then the dean at Osgoode Hall Law School, had worked out a rather devious plan: Bora Laskin, then at the U of T Law School, would move to Osgoode Hall Law School and at a later and propitious time Wright, Laskin, and perhaps others would dramatically move to the University of Toronto. Indeed, this is what happened four years later. It was important to make sure that Kennedy, who thought very highly of Laskin and of his contribution to the law school, agreed to the plan. After conferring with Smith, Wright drove to Kennedy's cottage with Laskin in tow. While walking along the lakeshore trail, with Laskin walking slightly behind, Caesar somehow convinced Kennedy that he should allow Laskin to move to Osgoode. Why Kennedy went along with the plan is unclear. I often think about that story when I walk along that particular lakeside trail – which I keep very well groomed. A plaque could rightly say: 'On this trail a key part of the plan for creating the modern University of Toronto Law School was consummated.'

The only English-trained professor we had was Abe Weston, an Australian who had completed his law studies at Oxford and then taught at the University of Alberta. He also taught three different subjects, agency, real estate transactions, and jurisprudence. The jurisprudence course was one of my favourites at the law school. The class was broken down into small groups of about four or five students for discussions conducted each week in Weston's office – like the Oxford tutorials that he had experienced. I wrote an amateurish paper on free will and determinism and another paper on the nature of corporate liability. Weston stayed only a few years, later becoming the founding dean of law at University College in Tanganyika (Tanzania) and ending up as the dean of law at the University of Papua and New Guinea.

There were few choices of subject – none in first year and only a couple of electives in second and third years. In second year I chose insurance from a practitioner and international law from LaBrie, and in third year I took planning from Milner and jurisprudence from Weston. The widespread use of options was not adopted in North American law schools until the late 1960s.

We had very few lectures by practitioners. In addition to the practitioner who gave us insurance law, Edson Haines and Ben Grossberg, both of whom later became judges, gave us lectures on Saturday mornings on the practice of civil procedure. Other lectures by practitioners were introduced from time to time. A series of special lectures on mechanics' liens by a downtown lawyer were organized in our third year. We were not pleased to have these additional non-credit lectures imposed on us during the year. I recall that in one such lecture I was making a carbon copy of the notes I was taking for a classmate who could not be there – the photocopier was not available until many years later. The practitioner, future Ontario cabinet minister Robert Macaulay, asked me why I was making a carbon copy. To the best of my recollection, my answer was: 'I do it so that I can rip one up after the lecture.'

I guess my irreverent comment got a laugh from the class, although such smart-ass remarks and conduct often got me into trouble. In my younger days, I had the humiliating experience of spending at least a day in the kindergarten class at Allenby Public School when I was actually in grade 5. I cannot recall what caused me to be sent there. The exact same thing happened after we moved to Forest Hill, when I was in grade 7 at the South Prep. Moreover, I received 'the strap' at least twice at Allenby, once for standing on an outside water faucet. Why I was standing on the faucet remains a mystery to me. In my final year of high school I was kicked out of Pete Colgrove's geometry class for the remainder of the school year for making what I considered then a very clever remark. For some reason, we were discussing Dickens's *A Tale of Two Cities* in a geometry class and I said: 'That's one way of getting ahead.' The actual incident was no doubt only one of many disruptions. In later years I toned down this side of my nature. In any event, there was perhaps an increasingly greater acceptance or tolerance by society of these types of remarks.

Many of us got to know the professors at law school surprisingly well. It did not seem out of the ordinary for David Kilgour, whom we had for civil procedure in first year, to ask me to show my African slides at a faculty gathering one evening at his house. Jim Milner invited the class over to his house each year, and we often had dinner with Al Abel. When my wife and I got married in June 1958, at the end of my third year, we invited five or six professors and their spouses to our wedding. We are still using the vase that the Westons gave us.

Many of us formed small study groups in first year. Harry Arthurs, Harvey Bliss, Jerry Grafstein, and I got together every Sunday morning throughout the school year at each others' homes. At the end of the session, lunch would be served by the mother whose house we were in. Jerry's mother was in London, Ontario and I cannot recall who prepared lunch when we met occasionally at his home. It became clear, however, that Mrs Bliss was the best cook, and we tried to arrange to meet at Harvey's place as frequently as possible. Usually, one member of the group was assigned the task of taking us through the material in a particular course that had been dealt with in class but had not yet been covered by our small study group. We did this through all three years and there is no doubt that it helped us understand the material better than by going over it on our own. Study groups got a bad name because of the movie *Paper Chase*, but I always recommended them to my first-year class.

I loved law school. It was a welcome contrast from my experience studying commerce and finance. One's opinion mattered at law school. The material was always challenging. Unlike commerce, where I measured the amount of time I studied, at law school I measured the amount of time when I was *not* studying. I worked hard in first year, limiting my extra-curricular activities. I did, however, participate in one still-remembered Hart House debate on the future of NATO, with Lester Pearson as the guest speaker. Tim Armstrong, who later became a diplomat, and I supported Pearson's position in our speeches and by wearing bow ties. The debates room, including the balcony, was packed. My recollection is that when the house divided, the Pearson supporters won.

I read material that had not been specifically assigned by a professor. The new law journals were prominently displayed in the library and I made a habit of looking through them systematically – something that I continued to do until very recently. I recall accidentally coming across a hard-hitting review by Albert Abel in the *Iowa Law Review* of a book on administrative law, which quickly made the rounds of the Glendon community. The opening sentence was: 'This is a bad book. It is bad in gross and bad in detail.' Many of us read the law reports. Caesar was the editor-in-chief of the *Dominion Law Reports* and the publisher, the Canada Law Book Company, offered subscriptions to students at a very low rate, and so I subscribed, as did many of my colleagues. I am not sure that many of today's students keep up with current cases, unless they are discussed in class. Here is a bit of advice for law students: fact situations for exam questions are often drawn from recent cases that have not yet been included in the teaching materials, but are working their way up through the courts.

None of us knew how well – or how poorly – we would do in the exams. In December 1955 we wrote practice tests in all our subjects. They were handed back to us in class when we returned after the Christmas break. Caesar Wright, who taught torts, said he wanted to read a model paper to the class – mine. I could not believe it. I thought I had done all right, but had not expected that the paper was as good as Caesar obviously thought it was. Almost all the exams were of the same type, dealing with a detailed factual situation which contained a lot of issues to spot and to analyse. Law-school exams are still much the same today – at least mine were. My other test papers were also good, and I topped the class on the Christmas exams.

I learned that a straightforward analysis of the issues, without too many fancy tangents, would get good marks – if you knew the material and, I should add, if you had reasonably good handwriting. No one that I knew was permitted to type their examinations in those days. In later years, as a teacher, I found that poor handwriting might tend to hinder a student from getting an A, but it also helped prevent the student from getting a very low mark because most markers are willing to give the student the benefit of the doubt rather than take the time to decipher the writing. My handwriting was reasonably legible and I wrote relatively short answers. I cannot recall ever using more than one standard single-spaced exam booklet for an exam.

I was also at the top of my class at the end of first year. One learned one's standing by reading it in the *Globe and Mail*, which published all the results with actual names, in descending order from the top of the class to the bottom, including persons who failed. I had been alerted by Al Abel that I would be pleased with my marks. In third year Al Eagleson, who had been a year ahead and seemed to know everybody and everything, told me that I had topped the class and would receive the MacMurchy Gold Medal and the Butterworth Prize, the latter consisting of a complete set of about thirty volumes of the pale-green covered *Halsbury's Laws of England*. They looked good on my shelf, but became increasing less useful as they got more and more out-of-date and as Canadian lawyers relied less and less on English law. After moving the set of books to about five different offices I finally donated them to the law library.

Harry Arthurs stood second in our final year and also won the Dean's Key. Later, as dean, I would hand out the Dean's Key to the student or students who best combined academic and extra-curricular activities. Each time I presented it at the annual banquet I had to confess that I was not a winner of the coveted award. There is no question that there was academic rivalry between Harry and me throughout our careers. The rivalry probably helped both of us accomplish more than we might otherwise have done. We remain good friends.

Nobody said anything to me before my second-year standing was published in the *Globe*. I went downtown to pick up the early edition of the paper at the Globe building at the corner of York and King Streets – as students did in those days. When I opened the paper I discovered that there were no A standings in the second-year class, only a few Bs, and, for the rest of the class, including me, a C standing. I stood twelfth out of thirty-three students. Today, students who receive a C in a single subject at law school are usually very upset. When I would tell disappointed students about my C standing in second year – with a D in constitutional law from the future chief justice of Canada – they usually felt a bit better. It is probably a good thing that the law-school standing of judges who graduated in those years is not dug up by reporters. Law school marks started to creep up in the 1960s.

I had probably taken on too much extra-curricular activity in second year. I was a vice-president of the Student Law Society and national vice-chairman of World University Service of Canada, wrote a paper on the importance of foreign aid to underdeveloped countries for the university's Historical Club, which I joined in second year, and wrote a short non-credit article on the criminal-law power in the *British North America Act* for the *Faculty of Law Review*.

Marks were generally low in second year because of the enormous quantity of material covered in such heavily statute-based second-year courses as business organizations, taxation, real estate transactions, and administrative law. As mentioned above, in the 1960s the curriculum was changed to allow students more choice in the upper years in course selection and also in what year subjects could be taken. Moreover, all examinations in my time as a law student were closed-book exams, and in most cases the student could not even take statutory material into the exam. Almost no examinations today are closed-book – I think one or two professors still maintain that tradition. Some exams today are take-home exams, where the student has access to all available material.

Because of the quantity of material in second year, students would usually omit careful study of selected sections, hoping that the examiner would not cover that material in the examination. Most exams, however, did not give the student a choice in what questions to answer. I recall not carefully studying the material on securities regulation that had been covered on the last day of the business organization course. Naturally, one of the four questions required an intimate knowledge of the *Ontario Securities Act*. So, another piece of advice I would offer is that students should never miss studying the material covered in the last class in any subject.

Without question, one has to know the course material thoroughly in order to do well in exams. There is more, however. One has to know the material in each subject well enough that you can talk your way through it from page to page and also relate the material in one subject to that learned in others. One study technique that I applied in law school, which I still use, is to do my work where there is a certain amount of background noise, such as in a restaurant. I did my best work at a Hungarian restaurant, Hostos – on Eglinton Avenue, near Avenue Road – that is no longer in existence. (It was one of the first Central European restaurants in the city. La Chaumière was the only French restaurant I knew, but it would have been inappropriate to study in such a 'special' locale.) Blocking out the noise – at least for me – helps me to concentrate on the material I am working on. Whenever I am at a point where I have to do an outline of a project or synthesize a large amount of material, I go to a restaurant or coffee shop, or occasionally ride to the end of the subway line and back. One has to be careful, however, not to be too close to others and get caught up listening to their conversations. I always listen to music while I am working at home. As stated earlier, I did a lot of my studying as an undergraduate in the record room of Hart House. Judy says that I am actually not listening to the music. She may be right in thinking that I am blocking it out in order to concentrate on what I am working on. As this is being written, I am blocking out *Das Rheingold*, from Wagner's Ring Cycle.

There were relatively few extra-curricular activities of an academic nature at the law school apart from the *Faculty of Law Review*, which is still going strong, but now has to compete with several other student-run reviews, and with competitive mooting and many other activities. Harry and I co-edited the law review in our third year. To the best of my recollection, the issue we worked on was made available to the student body before the last exam was written. The *Review*, now published twice a year, is still entirely written and edited by students. I was the faculty adviser for a number of years and still attend many of the launches of issues of the *Review* to hand out the 'M.L. Friedland Prize,' which the student body established when I retired as dean and which I have topped up over the years. When I hand out the prize, I usually reminisce about the law review we published almost fifty years ago and tell students that the papers they will be editing are being written by future judges and chief justices. Some of the papers in our volume were written by future justices John Sopinka, Julius Isaac, and Bruce Hawkins from our class and justices John Morden and Stephen Borins from the year behind us.

I also refer to the advertisements by Toronto law firms at the end of each issue, which dramatically demonstrate the tremendous growth of the legal profession over the past fifty years. In my student days Torys listed a grand total of four lawyers, as did Goodmans. Blakes, then the largest law firm in Toronto, had a dozen lawyers and McCarthys had eight. Today, the numbers of lawyers in these four firms are about 300, 200, 500, and 800 respectively, with the last two firms having offices across the country and the first, Torys, having a large New York office.

2

Articling and the Bar Ads

In our third year of law school we applied for articling positions. I did not apply to any non-Jewish firms. It was assumed that Jewish students would not be hired by the large firms, although this was not an absolute bar. Charles Dubin, for example, had articled during the war with Mason Foulds (now WeirFoulds), and Jack Geller, later a vice-chair of the Ontario Securities Commission, who was called to the bar several years ahead of me, articled and practised with Arnoldi Parry and Campbell (now part of Fasken Martineau DuMoulin). Stan Schiff, who was two years ahead of me at the U of T law school and had stood first in all three years, had articled with what is now Borden Ladner Gervais and had been invited to return as a junior. All the members of our study group, however, articled with Jewish firms, after discussing the possibilities with Bora Laskin. Harry Arthurs went with Sydney Robins's firm, Harvey Bliss with Levinter Grossberg, and Jerry Grafstein started with a small Jewish firm and finished his articling with Senator David Croll's firm, Croll, Borins, and Shiff.

Jews were not integrated into all levels of the profession, as they are today. There were no Jewish superior court judges in Ontario at the time, although there had been a number of Jewish provincial court judges, then called magistrates. As stated earlier, the first Jewish superior court judge in the province was Abraham Lieff, an Ottawa lawyer and magistrate, who was selected by Prime Minister Lester Pearson in 1963. The Toronto legal community was a divided community. Indeed,

it was not really a community. Gentile lawyers belonged to the Lawyers Club of Toronto, Jewish lawyers to the Reading Law Club, named
after Lord Reading, the Jewish chief justice of England in the early
years of the twentieth century, who later became the Viceroy of India.
A number of the private clubs, such as the Granite Club and the York
Club, did not accept Jews. In my history of the University of Toronto I
tell of Ernest Sirluck, the first Jew to be appointed to a senior position at
the University of Toronto, who was not accepted for membership in the
York Club in the early 1960s because of his religion.

Like Grafstein, I also split my articling, starting with the general
practice firm of Pivnick and Chusid at the corner of York and Richmond, and then part-way through the articling period moved to
Charles Dubin's firm, Kimber and Dubin. Nathan Pivnick, a couple of
years behind Laskin at Kennedy's law school, was an extremely bright
lawyer, who lived a few doors up the street from my family when we
lived on Rosemary Road. Several years earlier I had helped organize
canvassers when he unsuccessfully ran to be a member of the Forest
Hill Council. Murray Chusid was starting to develop a strong reputation as a municipal lawyer. I learned a great amount from the firm and
was given a considerable amount of responsibility in connection with
real estate transactions, incorporations, simple wills, and small claims
cases. It became clear to me, however, that this was not the type of law
that I wanted to practise – if indeed I did want to practise – and so I
moved to Kimber and Dubin, which had just lost its articling student to
another firm. A number of years later, Pivnick died in unclear circumstances in a collision with a transport truck on a rainy evening, and it
was later discovered that he had been dipping into the firm's trust
account, had been leading a secret life with women outside his marriage, and was being investigated by the tax authorities. Large claims
were subsequently made by his clients against the Law Society's compensation fund. Chusid, who had nothing to do with these matters, is
now practising municipal and planning law with Blaney McMurtry.

Kimber and Dubin was a four-person firm. Jack Kimber, who was no
longer with the firm, was serving as a master of the Supreme Court of
Ontario, and would later become the chair of the Ontario Securities
Commission and, still later, the president of the Toronto Stock
Exchange. We would become friends when I worked as the research
associate for the Kimber Committee, which reported to the attorney
general in 1965 on the future of securities regulation in Ontario. Kimber's name remained part of the firm's name until the firm was

absorbed into Torys in 1973. When I started with Kimber and Dubin, they shared space with Goodman and Goodman in the Federal Building at 85 Richmond Street West – Dubin and Eddie Goodman were friends and fellow advisers to the Conservative Party – but midway through my articles the firm moved to other offices at 111 Richmond Street. Dubin was appointed to the Ontario Court of Appeal in 1973 and became the chief justice of Ontario in 1990. He is best known to the public for his work chairing two important federal royal commissions, one on the Ben Johnson doping scandal and another on aviation safety in Canada.

Other members of the firm included Dubin's wife, Anne, who had received her call in 1951 and who mainly handled solicitor's work. The two other members, both of whom became judges, were Horace Krever and Ed Eberle. Ed went to the trial division of the Superior Court in 1977. Horace, who became well known to the public as the head of the federal blood inquiry, was appointed to the Superior Court in 1975 and was elevated to the Ontario Court of Appeal in 1986. Both were excellent litigators and shared their expertise with their articling student.

Charles Dubin was one of the most brilliant, if not *the* most brilliant, lawyers who has ever practiced law in Ontario. He is still practising, having returned to Torys after his compulsory retirement from the bench at age seventy-five in 1996. Dubin grew up in Hamilton, Ontario, graduated from Kennedy's honour law program at the University of Toronto, and received the gold medal on his graduation from Osgoode Hall Law School. Like several other legendary lawyers in those years, such as J.J. Robinette and Joseph Sedgwick, he had great versatility in his practice, and was equally comfortable before a judge or jury, in both civil and criminal matters, in trials and appeals, and before courts and administrative tribunals.

Dubin would always prepare his cases carefully, writing out in detail his line of examination or cross-examination in handwriting so small that no bystander could read what he had written without considerable effort. His office had an air of mystery about it. The blinds were usually drawn and the one lamp on his desk cast very little light. One entered his office as if entering a shrine seeking guidance from an all-knowing sage – at least that is how it felt to this law student. His short stature, long, silken golden hair, and round face added to his sage-like appearance.

Over the years I would send him a copy of each of my books, appropriately inscribed. I tend to sign my books on the title page and not on the blank page next to the cover and so it is easy to miss the inscription. In the early nineties I went to see my old friend Ian Scott, who had suffered a serious stroke. Scott showed me with great amusement a gift that he had just been given by Dubin – a copy of my book *The Case of Valentine Shortis*, appropriately inscribed by me to Charles Dubin on the title page. Dubin obviously had not known that the book was so dedicated, but the leading lights of the legal community no doubt subsequently learned about it after they visited Scott.

I accompanied Dubin on a number of civil and criminal cases and several royal commissions, one in front of Judge Joe Sweet involving a scandal in the municipal government of York Township, and another before Judge Ian Macdonell involving alleged wrongdoing relating to the Niagara Parks Commission. I think Dubin liked having me along. For one thing, I always offered to carry his briefcase. He, in turn, then offered to carry my much lighter file-folder case. I was particularly valuable to him because I was then a smoker – a pack a day of Export A's – and Dubin had officially quit smoking – that is, he no longer bought cigarettes. Asking his articling student for a cigarette was only a slight lapse from his attempts to stop smoking. I should add that Judy and I stopped smoking cigarettes when Tom, our first child, was born in 1964.

The firm did a great amount of agency work for other lawyers throughout Ontario, such as appeals and pretrial motions before the master. At that time, the Supreme Court of Ontario was entirely centred in Toronto, where virtually all Supreme Court procedural motions were heard. I was often sent to argue motions before the master, such as motions for better particulars in the other party's statement of claim, or to strike out what was referred to as a special endorsement in the writ. It was excellent experience, without a lot at stake. I loved it.

The life of a litigator appealed to me as one of many possible careers. Even when I started teaching, I thought it likely that my teaching would be only for a short period and that I would eventually rejoin Kimber and Dubin. But after a few years in the academic world I became more excited talking about policy issues with academics than discussing procedural motions with my former classmates. I remained in the academic world.

Articling students in those days were used as messengers to serve documents on other lawyers. I had a rule, which I tried to stick to, that I would not do anything in connection with a file, including serving documents, without first looking through the file. In part, this came about because on one occasion I was asked by Dubin to look up something in the Great Library of Osgoode Hall – I think I was to find an earlier amendment to a statute – without knowing exactly why that amendment was relevant to the case. I brought back the wrong amendment and made the point to Dubin that I would have found the right one if I had known why I was doing the research. After that, I insisted upon at least glancing through the relevant parts of the file. One could learn a tremendous amount by doing that. I cannot recall anyone complaining about my rule. It was a reasonable quid pro quo. So I was happy to serve documents. I have sometimes suggested to articling students that they take the same approach, but the suggestion is usually met with a puzzled look.

I recall vividly one experience as an articling student that I was occasionally reminded of in later years by senior members of McCarthys. There had been a civil action by our client to obtain a crucial part of a 'Tastee Freeze' soft-ice-cream machine, which the other party had removed from our client's machine, probably because of unpaid bills. In any event, Ed Eberle had won the right to reclaim – or, as it was technically called, to 'replevy' – the part, which was at the time in the custody of McCarthy and McCarthy, then on one of the upper floors of the Canada Life building on University Avenue. Accompanied by two sheriff's officers, I went to McCarthys with the official replevin order and told the receptionist that I had come for the Tastee Freeze part. The receptionist said that she had been told to tell me that I had to find it myself. So the two sheriffs and I entered the McCarthy offices. The sheriffs were not happy doing so, but I assured them that we had the legal right to search the premises.

I poked my head into the various offices along the corridor, asking the occupant if he (I doubt if there were any women practising law in the firm at the time) had the Tastee Freeze part. No luck in George Finlayson's office, or Douglas Laidlaw's, or J.J. Robinette's. I was told to go to Senator Salter Hayden's office at the end of the hall. When I got there, a crowd of McCarthy lawyers had gathered to watch the show. Future cabinet minister Donald Macdonald later told me that he was part of that group. Hayden announced that the part I was looking for was in the locked cupboard behind his desk. I told him that under the law I had the right to break down the door. He said, 'Go ahead.' This went back and forth for a few minutes. Finally, I gave in, to the relief of the sheriff's officers. I was just a lowly articling student and was not 100 per cent sure of my grounds. I returned to the office at 111 Richmond

Street to report my failure. As it turned out, the Tastee Freeze part had been delivered to Dubin's office before I got back. I guess the moral is that nobody can tell McCarthys what they have to do.

During my articling at both Pivnick and Chusid and at Kimber and Dubin, and while I was in the bar admission course, I volunteered for a number of legal-aid criminal cases. You simply told the legal-aid official at city hall that you were prepared to take on a case. There was no paid legal-aid plan at the time. Even those defending murder cases did not get paid, as we will see in a later chapter. I took on perhaps half a dozen criminal cases during the articling year and while attending the bar admission course. Magistrates were usually prepared to hear articling students, although in a robbery case I had been assigned, Magistrate Tupper Bigelow said that an articling student could not appear for the accused in an indictable case. I threatened to appeal on constitutional grounds, but he was not intimidated. A lawyer sitting next to me, Alex Thompson, who was also a member of Toronto's board of education, offered to take the case for me. After a short adjournment to brief him, the trial proceeded. I cannot remember what the outcome was, but I think I would remember if there had been an acquittal.

I did better in another case, heard by Magistrate Joe Addison, where the charge was assault occasioning bodily harm. The accused was charged with assaulting a patron in Norm's Restaurant on Dundas Street near Jarvis Street – a tough part of town. I could not put my client in the witness box because he had a record three pages long, which included many assault charges, which could be put to him if he testified. He had told me he had acted in self-defence and I tried to draw the foundation for this defence out of the complainant and other witnesses. I won the case, but not on the basis of self-defence. Magistrate Addison entered an acquittal because the accused had not been identified in the Crown's case. I had not even argued the issue of identity. This was obviously a case of Addison feeling sorry for a struggling articling student.

In another case I almost won, and then lost. My client had been charged with indecent exposure. It was alleged that he had been seen by an elderly lady masturbating on the subway. (The Yonge Street portion of the subway was the only subway we had in those years.) She complained to a TTC attendant, and my client was arrested and charged. Again, I could not put him in the witness box because of his record, which included convictions for other sexual offences. I decided to telephone the complainant to check her story. I subsequently learned that it is considered unwise to speak to a complainant without a witness being present, lest the complainant later allege that you improperly tried to get the complainant to change his or her testimony. In the course of the conversation I asked if she had seen this type of conduct before. Yes, she said, in the little parkette at the corner of Avenue Road and St Clair, behind the statue of Peter Pan. I now had my defence strategy to shake her evidence. When she testified, she was made to appear unbalanced. 'Have you seen this type of conduct before?' I casually asked. 'Yes,' she replied. 'Where?' I asked: 'Was it in the little park at Avenue Road and St Clair, behind the statue of Peter Pan?' 'Why yes,' she said.

It appeared to everyone in the courtroom that I was about to get an acquittal. At that point, Assistant Crown Attorney Peter Rickaby, who would later become the city's crown attorney and prosecute the Yonge Street shoeshine-boy murder, jumped up and said that he would like to introduce evidence of the defendant's previous convictions for other sexual offences. The introduction of such evidence was entirely improper unless it came within what lawyers call the similar-fact rule or unless my client entered the witness box, which he was not going to do. Magistrate Norman Gianelli declared a mistrial, and the case was later heard by Magistrate John Prentice, who had no trouble convicting the accused. The element of surprise was gone. I thought about that case when I was later working on my doctoral thesis on double jeopardy. The Crown should not be permitted to deliberately blow a trial in order to have a second chance at a conviction.

That case made it into the weekly sensational tabloid publications, such as *Justice Weekly*, *Flash*, and *Hush*, magazines which often reported court cases that had a sexual angle. They could do so with reasonable safety from an obscenity prosecution by arguing that they were simply reporting court proceedings and had a right to do so. In one of my other cases that also made the sensational press, a beer bottle had been found in a women's abdomen. It was alleged that my client, the woman's husband, had put it there through her anus. She had been hospitalized for two months. He was charged with assault occasioning bodily harm, a serious charge. If the victim had died – and she easily could have – he would have faced a murder charge. The event took place in a rooming house on Granby Street, just off Yonge Street. My client told me that he was drunk and could not remember anything about the evening. The complainant did not remember the events either. I spoke over the phone to the doctor at the hospital who had surgically removed the bottle. When I asked him if it was possible that the beer bottle could have ended up where it did if she had fallen off the bed onto the bottle, he said that it was a possibility. On the stand, however, he claimed that while anything is possible, falling on the bottle was not a reasonable possibility. 'Of course it is possible,' he testified: 'Practically anything is possible.' My client was convicted and received two years less a day. 'You didn't do a nice thing,' said Magistrate Prentice to my client at sentencing. I have sometimes thought of that case when discussing the concept of reasonable doubt with my students, but I have never had the nerve to discuss the facts of that particular case in class.

In September 1959 I entered the bar admission course – the bar ads – then in its first year. The Law Society no longer had a monopoly on legal education in Ontario. The University of Toronto, Queen's, and Ottawa had established – and Western and Windsor would later establish – schools that would offer programs comparable to the Law Society's three-year program at Osgoode Hall Law School. In exchange, the Law Society developed the bar admission course. Every law graduate, from either a university law school or Osgoode, would have to take the six-month course to help ensure they had the required practical skills and knowledge to practise law.

John Arnup, the chair of the Law Society's legal-education committee, worked hard to develop a credible program. J.J. Robinette was nominally in charge of the course. He and Arnup persuaded the leaders of the profession to head up the various sections. Walter Williston headed the civil procedure portion; G. Arthur Martin, criminal procedure; future court of appeal justice Lloyd Houlden, bankruptcy; Donald Lamont, real estate; and John Mullin, corporations. Materials were prepared and distributed to the class.

The first year of the new course was composed almost entirely of University of Toronto graduates. There were as yet no three-year graduates from Osgoode Hall Law School, Queen's, or Ottawa in the course. They would not enter the program until later years. Mixed in with our U of T class were a number of lawyers from other jurisdictions in and outside of Canada who were required to take the course before they could practise law in Ontario. One of these was Immanuel Goldsmith, who had been a barrister in England and was much older than any of his classmates. We were all fond of Manny, who later became senior counsel at McCarthy Tétrault, with his cultured English accent and three-piece suits. He sometimes wrote his notes in Greek and took snuff during seminars. It was during the bar ads that many of us learned how to place snuff in the hollow between the thumb and index finger.

There were only about forty students in that first class, and we were divided into two sections for the seminars. The seminar instructors for each component of the course were outstanding. We had criminal lawyer Austin Cooper for criminal procedure, future justice Bill Anderson for civil procedure, and future court of appeal justice Sam Grange for real estate. They did not come any better and most of us attended all the seminars. We also attended the main lectures. With so few students, any absence would have been noted.

Sometimes substitute lecturers were brought in who would read word for word what had been prepared and distributed to us. One lecture stands out in my memory. Walter Williston of Faskens could not make one of the lectures, and Bill Swackhamer from his firm came to deliver the lecture which had been distributed to us just before the class. There was a typo halfway through the paper. Instead of saying 'It is hard to be definite' about some point of law, it read 'It is hard to be deginite.' One of us spotted the typo and word quickly spread to watch how Swackhamer would handle it. Sure enough, when he came to the passage, which he was clearly reading for the first time, he hesitated, and then read: 'It is hard to be deginite.' Naturally, the class erupted in laughter. This was unfair to Swackhamer, but it reinforced a point that we made at the end of the year when John Arnup asked us for our reaction to the course. Many of us told him it could be much shorter and that there was no need for students to sit through lectures that an instructor would simply read. Forty-five years later, after many changes in the course, that advice has finally been heeded. Students no longer have to attend lectures and the course is now significantly shorter, with more emphasis on lawyering skills and professional responsibility and far less on substantive law.

I did well in the course, winning the Treasurer's Medal and other prizes. Harry Arthurs had chosen to go to Harvard that year, and so this time we were not in direct competition. My name is on the wall at Osgoode Hall as the first winner of the Treasurer's Medal. What a viewer of the wall does not know is that there were fewer than forty students in the course, not the thousand or so who now take the course each year. One prize that I won was a specially bound copy of the rules of practice for the year 1960. That book had a shelf life of about half a year, as each year the rules of practice are amended and, as with telephone books, a new book is produced each year.

Luck had played a role in my doing well. While in the bar ads I taught the law course to those trying to become certified general accountants – my first experience as a law teacher. I had inherited the course from a federal department of justice lawyer, Norm Chalmers, who was a few years ahead of me at law school. Each week I would deliver a lecture in a classroom in the old Chiropractic building (on the site where OISE is now located) on a different legal topic: one week on bankruptcy, another on the *Companies Act*, another on bulk sales and related statutes, and so on. These lectures, by chance, seemed to precede by about a week the bar admission course sections dealing with the same subject areas, and so certainly helped my understanding of the bar ad materials.

Because of my strong third-year marks at law school, graduate study became a realistic possibility. I had not applied during my year of articling, but waited until I was in the bar admission course. Judy would be completing her U of T course in physical and occupational therapy that year and would be ready to work as an occupational therapist, so the timing was good. We were both interested in living abroad.

This was not my first application to study abroad. After my first year at law school I had applied for a Rhodes Scholarship. My chances, I thought, were reasonably good. Athletics were very important for selection as a Rhodes Scholar in those years and, as mentioned in an earlier chapter, I had been on two intercollegiate teams. Hart House warden Joe McCulley, Bora Laskin, and others supported my application. But before the interviews took place I got a letter stating that I was ten days too old. The eligibility rules clearly stated that the scholar had to be under the age of twenty-five on 1 October 1957 when he or she went up to Oxford. I was twenty-four when I started the application process, but would turn twenty-five on 21 September 1957, a problem no one had spotted until then, including me. In retrospect, it was probably far better to finish my law degree at the U of T and go on to graduate work than to have spent two years in an undergraduate program at Oxford.

In the fall of 1959 I applied to a number of American law schools and was admitted with scholarships to the master's programs at Harvard, Yale, and several other schools. In those days almost all U of T graduates who went off to do graduate work in law went to the United States. Few considered going to England, in part because there were very few scholarships for graduate work outside the United States. The Commonwealth Scholarships, established in 1959, were designed to remedy the situation and encourage graduate students to study in other Commonwealth countries. I had not applied to attend an English university and so had not sought a Commonwealth scholarship.

In January 1960 the English law publisher Sweet and Maxwell and the Canadian publisher Carswell set up a scholarship, the Carswell-Sweet and Maxwell Scholarship, for Canadians to study law at Cambridge University, where Percy Maxwell, who had been closely associated with both companies, had studied. With the consent of the committee, the candidate could study at another university in the United Kingdom. Caesar Wright urged me to apply. I think he was on the selection committee. Having his graduates sprinkled around the globe would help promote Caesar's imperial ambitions. Judy and I decided that a year in England would be more interesting than one in the United States, where it would be more of the same. I applied for and was awarded the scholarship, worth $2000 plus return travel to England. I thanked the American law schools that had offered me funds – Harvard and Yale had each generously offered $3000 – and made plans to go to England for the 1960–1 academic year.

At about that time, Dean Allan Leal of Osgoode Hall Law School approached me to see if I was interested in teaching full time at Osgoode when I returned. If I promised to teach for only one year and to work with Desmond Morton, a law professor at Osgoode, who was establishing a program in criminal law, the Law Society would give me $2000 in addition to the scholarship I had already been awarded. That was a lot of money, and was tax-free in those days. Tuition in England was very low, perhaps £100 a year, the equivalent of about $300 at the time. When I returned to teach at Osgoode my full salary would be about the same as the two scholarships combined and the salary would be taxable. I agreed to Osgoode's offer.

After my call to the bar in April 1960, I returned as an associate to Kimber and Dubin, until I left for England in the early summer. As a young lawyer, I was given considerable responsibility. Three cases in particular stand out in my mind. One was a motion before Justice Fred Barlow to strike out a jury notice in a civil case. My recollection is that I won the case, although I cannot remember whether I was trying to keep or strike out the jury notice. I was also involved in a motion before Justice James King to compel a municipality to grant our client a building permit for a large apartment on the edge of a ravine. Doug Laidlaw from

McCarthys – whose office I had searched as an articling student – was on the other side. My client got the building permit. The third case dealt with whether leave to appeal would be given in a summary conviction case argued before the Ontario Court of Appeal, presided over by Chief Justice Dana Porter. My client opposed the granting of leave. I clearly remember that I was in court by myself, with three counsel from Fasken and Calvin on the other side: Walter Williston, John Sopinka, and Bruce Noble. The Court of Appeal sympathized with David over Goliath and I returned to the office proudly announcing my victory. That was the last case I ever argued in court.

Judy and I decided that rather than going to Cambridge, we would spend the year in London. I was accepted at University College, University of London, where the law department was headed by Dennis Lloyd, later Baron Lloyd of Hampstead. We purchased a red Sunbeam Alpine convertible from Rootes Motors – the just-introduced ultra-sleek sports car that tapered up from the front to the rear lights. James Bond later drove a blue Alpine in 1962 in the first Bond film, *Dr. No*. Our Sunbeam, which would be ready for us when we arrived in England, cost about the same as the Carswell-Sweet and Maxwell scholarship. We planned to spend the first summer as well as the following one touring the continent.

We gave up our apartment on the tenth floor of the new Brentwood Towers – it was a relatively fancy building in those days, with swans in the pool in front of the apartment – and stored our few possessions with various relatives. In early July we flew from Toronto's Malton Airport to Heathrow London on a new four-engine Viscount jet.

3

Cambridge and Double Jeopardy

Judy and I arrived at Heathrow in early July 1960 and stayed with our friend Earl Berger, who was pursuing a doctorate in international relations at the London School of Economics. He lived in a basement flat in fashionable Chelsea. The Sunbeam Alpine was ready to be picked up at Rootes Motors on Piccadilly. Our plan was to get the car and leave almost immediately for the Continent.

It seemed to me that it would be courteous to tell Dennis Lloyd, the head of the law program at University College, that I had arrived in England. Manny Goldsmith, my fellow student in the bar admission course, knew him well and had given me his home phone number. I called Professor Lloyd on Saturday morning, expecting him to be pleased to hear from me. 'My dear Friedland,' he said, 'you do not telephone a professor – you send a note. In particular, you do not telephone him at home, and even more particularly on a Saturday.'

This brash colonial had much to learn. Moreover, the incident taught me that in those years in England the telephone was to be used only for emergencies. The experience was somewhat mortifying, and with the added knowledge that the donors of the scholarship preferred that I attend Cambridge University, I decided I would switch from the University of London to Cambridge. I called the director of legal studies in Cambridge, R.W.M. Dias, better known as Mickey Dias, the Ceylonese-born jurisprudence scholar, to tell him that I had now decided to go to Cambridge. Long-distance calls, it seems, were considered emergencies and were therefore excluded from the 'no telephone' rule. We arranged to meet in Cambridge on Wednesday afternoon. He would be waiting for us in the Squire Law Library.

Judy and I drove to Cambridge and met Dias and several other members of the faculty, who were genuinely pleased that the first Carswell-Sweet and Maxwell Scholar had, indeed, chosen Cambridge. We were, of course, late for the appointment. It takes longer than one would think to drive the sixty miles from London to Cambridge, particularly when you are breaking in a new car and have to drive slowly. The discussion took place in the Faculty Combination Room in the so-called 'Old Schools' beside the law library. I had not applied either to the University or to a college. 'What college would you like to attend,' I was asked, as if my family had a long association with one of the colleges. My answer was in the form of a question: 'What college is the closest to the law library?' 'Trinity Hall,' they replied, and so I became a student at Trinity Hall. In fact, I later discovered, Gonville and Caius (pronounced 'keys') was a bit nearer the front door of the law library than Trinity Hall, but Dias and others knew, and I did not, that Trinity Hall had had a strong connection with the law since its establishment in 1350.

I would not have to choose my supervisor or subject area until I returned from the Continent. Since there were no married-student quarters available in those years through the college, we would have to find a flat in or around Cambridge when we returned, provided that it was, under the university's regulations, within six miles – it is now ten miles – of Great St Mary's Church, which is in the centre of the city.

A few days later we set off for the ferry to France. I do not want to turn this book into a travelogue, so I will not go into much detail. We slowly worked our way through France, our ultra-modern-looking red Sunbeam Alpine attracting attention wherever we travelled. In the flea market in Paris we bought a beautiful, authentic African Bambara sculpture, which we left with the Canadian embassy until our return to Paris later that summer. Since we had not made any advance reservations for accommodation, or indeed a firm decision on which countries to visit, we were going to play our itinerary by ear. A postcard home to my folks notes, 'We have a very nice room [in Paris] for about $3 a night for both of us.'

We took a ferry from Brindisi, Italy, to Corfu and then to the mainland of Greece. Travelling through Greece, we visited Byron's grave in

Messolonghi and managed to get last-minute tickets to hear Maria Callas sing *Norma* in the ancient Greek amphitheatre of Epidaurus, an experience which has been hard to equal. It would have been even more memorable had we not fallen asleep towards the end of the opera lying on the grass at the very top of the stone steps. We flew to Israel, our first of many trips there. For both of us, the trip stemmed more from a sense of duty than from a close identification with the country. That would come in later trips, particularly after we lived there for four months in the fall of 1979. One memorable experience was in seeing – accidentally – a forest of over a thousand trees in the Upper Galilee overlooking the Hula Valley, dedicated to the memory of my grandfather, Samuel Rogul, who, as stated earlier, had a strong interest in Zionism. We drove back to France to pick up our African sculpture, travelling through Greece and Yugoslavia. President Tito had finished a new road without a speed limit through the middle of the country. Wherever we went in Yugoslavia there were always crowds around the Sunbeam Alpine. We felt like royalty. We did not, however, feel like royalty in Sarajevo when we could not find a hotel room. We eventually managed to find a place to sleep in a remarkably large bathroom in a former grand hotel. In Greece, the most interesting accommodation was at Meteora/Kalambaka, a functioning monastery in the middle of Greece, perched on the top of a flat mountain. Visitors, sitting in large wooden baskets, were hauled up the steep cliff to the top with ropes and pulleys.

We arrived back in England in early September and stayed in Cambridge for about a week with fellow Torontonians Bob and Ruth Ehrlich and their little boy, Tom. Bob was finishing his second year doing research on diabetes. He was later the pediatrician of our three children and our families continue to be close. Finding accommodation was not easy, but we settled on a modern flat with hot-water heating – then relatively rare – in the small village of Fen Ditton, about two or three miles down the Cam River from Cambridge and therefore easily within the 'six mile from St Mary's' rule. Judy had a job as an occupational therapist at Fulbourn mental hospital, not far from Fen Ditton. We had our car, so getting back and forth to Fulbourn or Cambridge was not a problem. What we had not counted on was that nobody would visit us in Fen Ditton. Few fellow students had cars.

Moreover, my idea that I would become part of the Fen Ditton community – having a beer with the locals in the pub – never came to pass. We lasted in Fen Ditton until January, when we moved to a cold and damp set of rooms on Chesterton High Street in the city. Fortunately, some time before we moved, the heavy clothing that we had shipped from Canada finally arrived in Cambridge. It had come across the Atlantic by ship over the summer, but there had been a tallymens' strike and the goods were kept under lock and key at the Southampton docks. For most of the fall, I wore a lightweight seersucker jacket. A number of faculty members commented on my attire and expressed concern that I would catch a cold.

My attachment to Trinity Hall was tenuous. In those years there were no graduate colleges and for the most part the colleges, devoted almost all their attention to their undergraduate students. There was, for example, no special room in the college for graduate students. Indeed, there was no place in the university specifically devoted to graduate students. The Graduate Centre beside the Cam River was not built until several years later. I used the college as a mailing address and for the occasional lunch. Most of my lunches were at the cafeteria-style restaurant above the Arts Theatre or at the Eagle, a pub in an alley close to the law library.

On several occasions I was invited to the high table at Trinity Hall for a special dinner. At my first such dinner, honouring some patron from perhaps five hundred years earlier, I did not know what to expect. The English, like most refined people, always ask the guest, who does not know what to do, to go first. Perhaps this was to put the guest at a disadvantage. One incident sticks in my mind. After dessert (or was it after the savoury, a strange spicy delicacy, such as sardines, that comes after the main meal), a waiter came around asking if I would like a dessert wine. There were three empty glasses in front of me and I was offered Port, Madeira, and something else. My host invited me to choose. Unfortunately I had not watched what others at the table had done – they had, of course, selected one of the three choices. I said 'a little of all three,' which confirmed in everyone's eyes that colonials did not know how to behave.

When visitors came to Cambridge, we always showed them the college and, in particular, the magnificent garden beside the old library. We have a picture of that garden in our home in Toronto, taken by David Thomas, a law fellow of the college who has written highly regarded books on sentencing. The garden has always been a model for us to strive to duplicate. I got to know some of the fellows, particularly the law fellows, such as Tony Bradley, a constitutional lawyer, who went on to be the dean of the faculty of law at Edinburgh. We became friends and have kept up with each other's careers over the years. Another law fellow was T.E. Lewis, whose specialty was torts. I often chatted with a retired law fellow who had a room at the college, J.W. Cecil Turner, who was the editor of Kenny's *Outlines of Criminal Law*. The bursar, Charles Crawley, an accomplished classicist – who later published a fine book on the history of Trinity Hall, which I would later carefully examine when I wrote my history of the U of T – was always helpful and invited Judy and me for tea from time to time. Nevertheless, I did not feel particularly close to the college, and when I was asked at year's end for two pounds for a life membership in the Trinity Hall Alumni Association, I said that I would think about it. The reaction was so pronounced – I may have been the first person in six hundred years to 'think about it' – that I quickly handed over the two pounds.

I knew who I wanted as my supervisor – Sir Ivor Jennings, the master of my college, Trinity Hall. He was, I believed, the great international and constitutional law scholar, and I wanted to study and write in the international law area. I sent him a note asking for an appointment to see him – you can be sure I did not phone him. 'I am here to study international law,' I told him when we met, 'and I would like you to be my supervisor.' 'My dear Friedland,' he said, 'you have the wrong Jennings. I am the constitutional Jennings. The international lawyer is R.Y. Jennings.' I retreated sheepishly and looked up the publications of R.Y. Jennings. Since he had not published a great amount, I concluded that he would never amount to much, and so I decided to approach another great name in Cambridge, Glanville Williams. I should add that R.Y. Jennings became an important and distinguished international lawyer, eventually becoming the president of the World Court. He was former Supreme Court of Canada justice Frank Iacobucci's supervisor, when he was a student at Cambridge.

I went to see Glanville, who agreed to supervise my work. He was a remarkable scholar in many fields, including torts, jurisprudence, contracts, and criminal law. I had agreed to teach at Osgoode Hall Law School for the coming year and to work with Desmond Morton in the criminal-law area, and so criminal law seemed to be the appropriate subject on which I should concentrate – indeed, more appropriate than my first choice, international law. Moreover, it was at the time Glanville's principal area of interest. He was then working on the second edition of his monumental work on the general part of the criminal law. We eventually developed a research topic that I would work on for my year in Cambridge: bars to prosecution. At that point, I had not planned to go on for a PhD or to have a long-term teaching career. Cambridge did not then offer an LLM degree, and I was content with a diploma in comparative legal studies. The decision to turn my work into a doctorate did not come until after I returned to Canada.

Glanville Williams, who died in 1997 at the age of eighty-six, was one of the common-law world's greatest scholars. His scholarship was superb. A memorial tribute in the *Medical Law Journal* stated that 'few, if any, can claim the breadth or brilliance that he displayed over a very long and distinguished career ... His breadth of learning is unlikely to be seen again.' He was also the author of a book, *Learning the Law*, which had its first edition in 1945 and its thirteenth edition in 2006. It is widely used by persons studying, or contemplating the study of, law. No doubt it was the royalties from that book in particular that allowed him to drive a Jaguar.

He was a shy and gentle person. The entry in the *Dictionary of National Biography* accurately states: 'In appearance Williams was short, trim, and bespectacled, with sharp features and a fine head of yellow curly hair, which in later life turned white. In manner he was calm, reasonable, and quietly spoken, although tenacious in argument.' Glanville held strong beliefs on a great number of subjects. An active advocate for the right to abortion and euthanasia, he was also a pacifist who had refused to serve in the military in the Second World War. It was rumoured that his pacifism cost him the high honours he deserved. I always wondered whether he had been offered a knighthood and refused it. When I was the dean of law in the 1970s I proposed Glanville for an honorary degree at the University of Toronto. The honorary-degree committee approved and President John Evans offered the degree to Glanville, who graciously declined the honour. He said that he did not want to make such a long trip without his wife, Lorna, who was not up to it. After his death, it was revealed in the *DNB* that he had been offered a knighthood, but had declined it, 'partly from modesty, and partly because he thought it incongruous that a man who had refused to wield a bayonet should be the theoretical bearer of a sword.'

We became friends over the years. Although Judy and I were never invited to his home, Glanville would entertain students in his rooms at Jesus College. On one such occasion he invited me and other graduate students for banana-split sundaes, a delicacy he had enjoyed while a visiting professor at New York University Law School several years earlier. He did not have great social skills. During one visit to Cambridge a number of years later, Judy and I and the children paid a visit to Glanville at his college. Glanville and I walked slowly around the fellows' garden talking law, with Judy and the children walking about ten paces behind us. It was an awkward experience which Judy has never let me forget.

Glanville's brilliance was such that I often found it hard to have a sustained conversation with him. His comments were incisive and left little scope for further comment. He did not engage in the normal small talk or banter that helps keep conversations going. It was not his fault, for few were his equal intellectually, and I was certainly not one of them. Many years later, I interacted with Northrop Frye on a series of lectures I was organizing at the law school on crime in literature. We met on a number of occasions and I found the interchanges exactly the same as I had experienced with Glanville. Their intellects and personalities were very similar.

I was to write my one-year diploma thesis on bars to prosecution, which would encompass all the numerous bars to prosecution that fell outside the normal defences involving the act and the mental element. We envisioned chapters on time limitations, diplomatic immunity, territorial limitations on jurisdiction, double jeopardy, and several other subjects. I would start with double jeopardy. I never got beyond double jeopardy. Not only did it occupy that year in Cambridge, but also another nine-month period in 1963 when I returned to Cambridge to complete the residence requirements for the doctorate, plus another four years back in Canada, teaching and desperately trying to complete the manuscript. How Glanville and I could possibly have thought that I could complete bars to prosecution in one year remains a mystery to me.

Glanville wanted me to submit the thesis more quickly than I wanted to do – 'I cannot help feeling ... you are being a perfectionist,' he wrote to me in 1965 when I applied for another extension – but I wanted the manuscript to be in sufficiently good shape that I could submit it to a publisher without much further work. I had seen and continue to see cases of doctorates that are never reworked into a book. The person moves on to other endeavours, or the subject matter becomes out of date, or in the meantime another book is published in the field. As a result, the researcher abandons five or more years of intense work. This may be a blessing in the eyes of some who think that too much obscure work is being published, but it hurts the career of the scholar.

It was easy for me not to have to worry about publication. I had the luxury of not requiring either a doctorate or another book. Tenure was not an issue at the time at Osgoode Hall Law School or at the University of Toronto law school, where I moved in 1965. It was not until 1967 that tenure was officially recognized at the University of Toronto. Moreover, research and publication were not then considered as important at the U of T law school as they later became, and I was not under any outside pressure to finish my doctorate or publish the manuscript. In 1965 – to be discussed in a later chapter – I had published my study of the bail system, *Detention before Trial*, the research and writing of which materially contributed to the delay in completing my work on double jeopardy. Today, deans would want to see more articles earlier in a young academic's career. I had published only one significant article before the bail study. The present tenure process tends to discourage putting all your eggs into one future major publication.

It turned out that double jeopardy was a marvellous topic to research. There had not been a book in English on the topic, yet the concept was one of the most important foundations of criminal justice. In my introductory chapter I state:

> The history of the rule against double jeopardy is the history of criminal procedure. No other procedural doctrine is more fundamental or all-pervasive ... Double jeopardy plays a major role in such areas as recharging an accused with the same or another offence, new trials, Crown appeals, discharging the jury, framing an indictment, sentencing on multiple counts, withdrawing a plea, the relationship between courts, and the recognition of foreign criminal judgments.

I certainly had not realized the potential scope of the subject when I started my thesis and neither had Glanville, who thought, as I have already noted, that I could include double jeopardy as just one of a number of subjects to be covered for the one-year diploma. Double jeopardy is the other side of the criminal-procedure coin. A study of criminal procedure looks at what the various actors in a trial can do. Double jeopardy looks at what happens after a procedural step has been taken in the proceedings. The topic was hard to contain. There was no end of material that had to be studied. In my view, however, it is far better to have a thesis topic that is capable of expansion than to take a topic where there is relatively little material, which the writer has to beat to death.

Double jeopardy prevents the prosecutor from having multiple opportunities to convict an accused. As stated by Justice Hugo Black in the 1957 U.S. Supreme Court case of *Green v. United States:* 'The underlying idea, one that is deeply ingrained in at least the Anglo-American system of jurisprudence, is that the State with all its resources and power should not be allowed to make repeated attempts to convict an individual for an alleged offense, thereby subjecting him to embarrassment, expense and ordeal and compelling him to live in a continuing state of anxiety and insecurity, as well as enhancing the possibility that even though innocent he may be found guilty.' Giving the prosecutor a second crack at the accused allows the prosecution to close gaps in its case, knowing the strategy of the defence.

The term double jeopardy, as noted above, identifies a range of issues in which the legality of subsequent or concurrent proceedings is questioned. Can the prosecutor commence a new proceeding if the charge is dismissed for technical reasons, or if a charge is withdrawn, or if a jury cannot agree on a verdict? Can an appeal court order a new trial following a conviction if there has been an error at the first trial? Can the prosecutor appeal because of an error of law if the accused has been acquitted? Will a court in one country respect a finding by a court in another country or can new proceedings be commenced? Can an accused be convicted on multiple charges arising from a single event? Will the finding or lack of finding of a specific fact in one trial affect the finding of fact in a subsequent trial? The answers to these questions have varied from country to country and from time to time. Thus, I was forced to engage in both a comparative and a historical analysis of the concept.

I traced the doctrine in English law back to the famous dispute between Henry II and Thomas à Becket in 1164, and in other countries to earlier periods. Demosthenes, for example, stated in 355 BC that 'the laws forbid the same man to be tried twice on the same issue.' I spent several months exploring the Henry II/Becket controversy. Becket, the Archbishop of Canterbury, did not want to give the king any authority over his priests. The king, however, wanted his judges, who were starting to exert jurisdiction over much of the kingdom from their base in Westminster, to have the right to punish 'criminous clerks.' The Church in Rome, of course, supported its archbishop, citing early Christian doctrines.

The rule against double jeopardy was well known in ecclesiastical law. It stems from St Jerome's commentary in AD 391 on the prophet Nahum: 'For God judges not twice for the same offence.' The passage in

Nahum 1:9 states that God would not punish the wicked city of Nineveh a second time. In one of my favourite footnotes – perhaps my very favourite – I suggest that God was not, as the Church was arguing, a 'due process' God, but rather a very retributive God. The reason that Nineveh would not be punished twice, as some of the translations of the Nineveh story that I set out in the footnote make clear, is that the initial destruction would be so devastating that there would be no need for a second punishment. The King James version, for example, reads: 'But with an overrunning flood he will make an utter end of the place thereof, and darkness shall pursue his enemies. What do you imagine against the Lord? He will make an utter end: affliction shall not rise up the second time.' The Knox translation – to give a further example – states: 'Believe me, he will take full toll, there shall be no second visitation.' I was helped with this footnote by my fellow graduate student and friend, Peter Richardson, the ecclesiastical scholar and later principal of University of Toronto's University College. I took Henry's side in the controversy because Henry only wanted to punish clerks after they had been found guilty following a hearing in the church courts, and, moreover, the punishments provided in the church courts were nowhere close in severity to those given in the king's courts. But the archbishop was probably right in concluding that Henry would soon have gone further and demanded to try allegedly criminous clerks who had been acquitted in the ecclesiastical courts.

We know the outcome of the controversy from Jean Anouilh's play *Becket* and from T.S. Eliot's *Murder in the Cathedral*, as well as from the 1964 movie *Becket*, in which Peter O'Toole starred as the archbishop and Richard Burton as the king. Becket was murdered by Henry's forces in Canterbury Cathedral. Neither Anouilh nor Eliot nor the movie mentions the double-jeopardy issue, which, in fact, was central to the debate. The reaction to Thomas's murder was such that the king backed off and did not try to exert jurisdiction over clerics, even when they had first been convicted in the ecclesiastical courts. This, I argued, established the foundation for double jeopardy in England. A historical side effect was what was later called 'benefit of clergy,' which helped limit the use of capital punishment in England. Clergy and, later, literate non-clergy accused of a capital crime could plead 'benefit of clergy' and be subject to no penalty or a lesser penalty if they could show that they could read, or at least memorize, a passage. Benefit of clergy was employed as a device to soften the criminal law for hundreds of years, and was not formally abolished until 1827.

By the end of my first year in Cambridge I had made considerable progress on the thesis, writing perhaps a hundred single-spaced typed pages. I would finish a section and submit it to Glanville, who would mark it up, making points about my grammar. He rarely commented on the ideas I was presenting. 'I always find,' he would say, 'that it is best to make the jury plural,' or 'try using a colon here.' It was exasperating. Other graduate students were getting help on the substance of their theses. Some time in the late fall I raised the issue with Glanville. His answer was that I was a lawyer with a good academic record who was much more familiar with the material than he was. He could help me with my writing more than with the law itself.

In retrospect, Glanville was right. I had done very little writing as an undergraduate or at law school, but I had done a significant amount of legal analysis. Glanville had a wonderful writing style – clear and direct. He confessed – to my surprise – that he had had the same problem I was having with my writing when he was doing his Cambridge PhD on 'Liability for Animals,' and had carefully studied the style of the fine historian E.H. Carr, whose writing he had admired. I had read Carr's *The Twenty Years' Crisis* in my undergraduate course on international relations and had found his work very readable, but instead of turning to Carr's work as a model I studied Glanville's writing style. I learned when to use a colon and when a semi-colon (which the reader will see I rarely use) and other grammatical and stylistic techniques, which I should have learned in high school. I have not gone back to E.H. Carr's writing to see how closely my style approximates his, but I expect that there are similarities, via Glanville.

I found that those graduate students who got a lot of help on the substance of their theses often had difficulty finishing them. They relied too heavily on their supervisors' suggestions and followed up too diligently on the supervisors' sometimes off-the-cuff ideas, rather than developing their own. Of course, some students need more help than others. And Glanville was right in judging that I particularly needed assistance in my writing. The techniques that I developed that year are the same ones that I continue to use, even though in those days there were no computers, photocopiers, or sticky notes. (I should add that there was at least one computer in Cambridge – at the Cavendish Laboratory. I was taken there one evening by a Canadian geophysicist, Bosko Loncarevic, whom I had known at the U of T and who was also doing graduate work in Cambridge. It was the size of a tractor trailer and would have had far less capacity or memory than the laptop I am now using.) Fortunately, I had taken a course in typing in high school and had a small portable typewriter. A small storage room on the second floor of the law library was made available to me. I made my notes in spiral binders as I still do. The material could be cut up later and distributed to appropriate files. Because of the photocopier, I can now do the same and keep the original binders. I never understood why most graduate students used file cards, which can easily get mixed up, whereas spiral binders cannot and their pages can be cut up and sorted in the same way cards can. Unlike Glanville, who used glue, I arranged the material using staples and later switched to tape only after the introduction of invisible tape, which can be written on. The file boxes are of the same sort today as I used then. Indeed I still have some of the original dog-eared boxes that I used over forty-five years ago.

Keeping track of material was – and is – the key. One cannot do a major project if one is constantly searching for material that is 'someplace' in one's files. The headings of the file folders and the contents of the boxes were constantly changing in order to reflect my changing ideas about the organization of the material. Flexibility – that is, changing course as the evidence and the quantity of material changes – is crucial to any research project. One should not be a slave to the structure that one happened to start with. The techniques for organizing the constantly changing research material were essentially the same for the writing of the history of the University of Toronto as they were for double jeopardy. I suspect that for most scholars the techniques used for one's thesis continue to be used throughout one's career.

There were no required courses for the diploma or even for the doctorate, should I choose to go on for a PhD. All one had to do – and it was a lot – was to produce the required written work. I wonder whether we do not go too far in North America in requiring course work and comprehensive examinations, as well as a thesis. I did sit in on some courses that particularly interested me, and enjoyed Kurt Lipstein's course in private international law and C.J. Hamson's in comparative law. I also attended the seminar in administrative law given by H.W.R. Wade, but I stopped going to these classes around Christmas time so that I could concentrate on my research. The one class that I continued to take was by F.H. McClintock in criminology, which was both interesting and also allowed us to visit penal institutions. I recall a trip to Wormwood Scrubs in London, where we chatted freely with persons convicted of murder. I often took my students on similar trips, and they were normally as amazed as I had been at how easy it is to talk to murderers.

The majority of prisoners convicted of murder are like the person next door.

We returned to Canada after a second major trip to the Continent, this time visiting the Low Countries and other parts of Europe, including Munich, Vienna, Zurich, and Venice, and then back through Paris to England. Having stayed out of Canada for over a year, we were entitled to bring the car back to Canada duty free. We sailed from Southampton on the *Empress of Canada* in mid-July along with the car and a copy of the famous eleventh edition of the *Encyclopaedia Britannica* of 1911, which we had purchased for £50 from a second-hand bookseller near the Cambridge market (and which we sold thirty years later for about the same price to a scholar of Victorian literature at the University of Toronto). We still have and often use, however, the porcelain cake-cutter which we received for winning the ship-board mixed doubles ping-pong tournament.

I did not submit my thesis for the diploma before I left. I would either finish it when I returned to Canada, limiting it to some aspects of double jeopardy, or perhaps turn it into a doctoral thesis, which would require that I return to Cambridge to complete the residence requirement. At that stage, I was leaning towards the former and planning on joining Kimber and Dubin after my required year at Osgoode.

4

The Enforcement of Morality

We arrived back in Toronto in late July 1961. Judy returned to her work as an occupational therapist at the psychiatric day-care centre (part of the Toronto Psychiatric Hospital) in the former church across from Women's College Hospital.

We went back to the Brentwood Towers, where we had found a one-bedroom apartment on the so-called penthouse floor. We now had an even better panoramic view of the growing, dynamic city to our south and the lake. Viljo Revell's new city hall had started its iconic rise, although Mies van der Rohe's Toronto-Dominion Centre was still in the planning stage. The thirty-four-storey Bank of Commerce Building, completed in 1931, was still the tallest building in Toronto, followed by the Royal York Hotel. The view from the penthouse was spectacular. We have always said that when we eventually move into a condominium from our home on Belsize Drive, we would try to have a comparable view of the present dramatic Toronto skyline.

My office at Osgoode Hall Law School was next to Desmond Morton's – on the second floor of the law-school wing, looking north towards the University Avenue Armouries, the largest in North America when they opened in 1894. We had our own secretary in a small adjoining office and a small research budget. During my time at Osgoode, I watched the Armouries being torn down and the new court house constructed on its site.

Desmond and I constituted Osgoode's Criminal Law Program, although neither of us taught criminal law. That was taught by a practitioner, the great criminal lawyer G. Arthur Martin, who was one of the school's most popular teachers. It was not until I switched to the University of Toronto that I was able to teach the first-year criminal law course. Arthur Martin had an encyclopedic knowledge of the criminal law and a captivating style of delivery. He brilliantly delivered the D.B. Goodman lectures at the University of Toronto when I was dean, yet when we had the lectures transcribed and edited and sent the manuscript to the U of T Press to consider its publication, the Press declined to publish it. Martin's quiet but dramatic emphasis on certain words and phrases and his effective pauses did not translate well to the written form.

Desmond was a provocative and delightful Irishman. I picture him with his dark sunken eyes and somewhat unkempt hair, with a pipe in his mouth, tobacco on his jacket, and often with a glass in his hand. He had graduated in law from Trinity College Dublin in 1951, having served as an intelligence officer in India during the Second World War. Osgoode Hall Law School's Dean Smalley-Baker, who had been appointed after Caesar Wright moved to the University of Toronto in 1949, brought Desmond to Osgoode in 1952. He seemed very much older than me, but in fact was only thirty-four when I joined Osgoode at the age of twenty-nine. His main area of expertise was the law of evidence, and he produced an evidence casebook, first published in 1960. Two years later he delivered a series of CBC Radio lectures, entitled *The Function of the Criminal Law in 1962*, which was published by the CBC. In 1964 he was appointed Regius Professor and dean of law at his alma mater, Trinity College Dublin. He was, however, unhappy there. In part, this was because he was not provided with the secretarial and other support he had become used to at Osgoode.

Desmond returned to Osgoode Hall Law School in 1968, and at the same time became research associate of the influential Canadian Committee on Correction, the Ouimet Committee, which reported in 1969. He moved to the University of Toronto in 1971. A few years later he went on sick leave because of kidney failure, which required dialysis at St Michael's Hospital several times a week. He died in 1989. I was quoted in the obituary in the *Toronto Star* as calling him 'a provocative teacher, an imaginative scholar, and an inspiring colleague ... He knew how to make students think about issues.' I used to visit him regularly at his home and felt very close to him. After I stepped down as dean in 1979, I moved into his old office in Flavelle House.

Apart from the international law and conflicts scholar Jean Castel, the Osgoode faculty was not particularly well known for its scholarship in the years after Wright, Laskin, and Willis left. Allan Leal, who had been appointed dean in 1958 after Smalley-Baker stepped down, had been trying to build up a more scholarly community. Harry Arthurs and Allen Linden, both of whom later developed strong reputations for scholarship, joined the faculty the same year as I did. Turning out lawyers, however, was the main preoccupation of the faculty in those days. On the first day of class each year we were asked to put on our barrister's robes and appear behind Dean Leal in front of the first-year class. The robes were meant to show that we were real lawyers.

I did very little work on double jeopardy in my first year of teaching at Osgoode, in part because I had to prepare for the full-year course I taught on evidence and for a half-year course on personal property. I also taught a seminar on criminology. I do not think I was a particularly good evidence teacher, being inclined to want to let in most relevant material, such as hearsay evidence, in much the same way as the Supreme Court of Canada has been ruling in recent years. The rules, I thought, excluded too much relevant evidence, particularly hearsay, and the hearsay rules took up a large proportion of the course. Most students at Osgoode at the time wanted to learn the rules, and were less interested in learning what the law ought to be. Personal property was a subject that I was not at all interested in, but in those days it seems everybody had to teach a subject or subjects that did not interest them. I liked the criminology course, however. I organized the seminars according to my interests, took the class to various prisons and penitentiaries in Ontario, and enjoyed working with the students on their papers.

Other activities drew me away from double jeopardy. I became involved in a Canadian Bar Association committee on administrative procedures of statutory professional tribunals. A practising lawyer, Gerald Hollyer, and I produced a respectable report on the subject. It went nowhere, and was a lesson to me that it would probably be better to devote my time to scholarship, which might have a greater payoff in influencing government policy. The project that took the most time was my investigation of the bail system in Canada, which will be described in detail in a later chapter. Moreover, in the fall of 1961 I spent considerable time working with Des Morton on a report on gambling.

While I was in England, Desmond had been asked by the attorney general of Ontario, Kelso Roberts, to chair a committee that would investi-

gate the enforcement of the law relating to gambling, usually referred
to as the Morton Committee on Gambling. Its terms of reference were
'To consider the problem in enforcement of the law relating to gambling with reference to the problems in certain other jurisdictions.' It
was a two-person committee, with government economist Rolph Eng
as the other member. I was appointed counsel to the committee, a fancy
designation which allowed me to participate fully in their research and
deliberations. Desmond graciously stated in the acknowledgments to
the report that I 'had participated fully in every phase of the preparation of the Report and the Committee has found his assistance of inesti-
mable value.' This was my first direct involvement in the development
of public policy and I found it both rewarding and interesting. Maybe,
I thought, I should stay in the academic world.

The enforcement of the law relating to gambling was considered a
serious problem at the time. The only major form of gambling that was
then permitted in Canada was pari-mutuel gambling at racetracks.
There were no casinos. Gambling could also take place at bona fide
'social clubs,' but not at other establishments where there was a rake-
off or a charge for playing of more than 50 cents a day. Minor charitable
raffles and similar activities were also permitted, but not large lotteries.
Nor did the law allow sports pools involving more than ten people.
Suppressing illegal gambling was a principal occupation of the Toronto
morality squad.

Gambling laws were being ignored by many citizens. Buying tickets
for the Irish Sweepstakes and other lotteries was illegal, but they were
widely sold throughout Canada. Bookmakers operated illegally in
most major centres. Sports pools were also widely available. Small
gambling operations often exceeded the statutory limits. As with the
prohibition of alcohol, illegal conduct tended to attract undesirable persons, with the inevitable corruption of the police. The Morton Committee took the matter very seriously, stating – a bit too dramatically – that
'if the present illegal gambling operation is permitted to continue ...
either domestic or foreign criminal elements will prosper to such an
extent as to undermine the very nature of our society.' The committee
was concerned about the 'concentration in the hands of criminals of the
vast sums of money expended in unlawful gambling.'

The report to the attorney general was completed in several months.
We studied the legislation in other jurisdictions, examined the secondary literature, and talked to members of Toronto's morality squad and
those in charge of pari-mutuel betting. We went to the Woodbine Race-

track, then near Lake Ontario, and gambled with government money. I do not think we abused our expense account, but I also clearly remember one working dinner where we ate baked stuffed shrimp at the later demolished Prince George Hotel at the corner of King and York Streets.

I was not very impressed with the morality squad. I recall one meeting with several of its senior officers in Desmond's office. They were telling us about arresting a prostitute in a hotel near Jarvis Street. I cannot remember the details, but I will always remember one of the officers saying, without apparent concern about our reaction, that they 'banged her in the doorway,' clearly meaning to my – and Desmond's – ears that they had had intercourse with her. It was a sobering experience.

We had to understand how bookmakers operated. It was not as simple as one would have thought. Illegal bookmaking involving horse racing and sports betting required sophisticated systems of reducing the financial risk by being able to 'lay off' some of the bets. Bookmakers try to balance their books, looking to get a profit no matter who wins the event. In the case of horse racing, the excess risk was sometimes laid off by arranging for someone to place some of the money in bets on the same race at the track. Sports betting required being able to lay off some of the money with large illegal syndicates in the United States. Perhaps it is now different with the large international Internet betting organizations that can withstand the risk.

Sports bookmakers, we discovered, would try to set their odds and point spreads in such a way as to keep the money that they would have to pay if one team won balanced against the money that was at risk if the other team won. If the public favoured, say, the New York Yankees in a World Series game, the person setting the odds might adjust them to make the other team seem like a more attractive bet than it really was in order to induce persons to bet against the Yankees and thus help keep the risk balanced. The bookmakers' profit would come from the slight advantage they would have if the odds, for example, were 6–5 either way. (I believe it was Damon Runyon who said that life is '6 to 5 against.') As stated above, if the so-called 'book' was not balanced, they would try to balance it by laying off some of the money with an underworld organization with deep pockets.

The gambling laws also caught respectable citizens who liked playing cards or other games of chance, such as a close relative of mine who was charged in the mid-1950s as a found-in playing pinochle on Saturday afternoons for small stakes in a nondescript building on Bathurst Street. The club owner would receive a small sum per player per hour –

perhaps 50 cents, which was above the statutory limit of 50 cents a day. I assume that the charges against the found-ins were withdrawn and the owner pleaded guilty. If the participants had been playing pinochle at the private Jewish clubs – the Primrose Club or the Oakdale Golf Club, where there was an annual fee – there would not have been any charges. There were also many prosecutions in those years involving small-time Chinese gaming operations.

The committee concluded that 'most serious consideration be given to the extension of the present exemption relating to pari-mutuel betting so as to permit government-operated off-track pari-mutuel betting on Ontario races.' In no other jurisdiction, the committee noted, 'has it proved possible to effectively prohibit off-track bookmaking or any other illegal gambling enterprise for which there was widespread support.' 'To be enforceable,' the committee stated, 'criminal law must be realistic.' The operation should be in government hands, like the sale and distribution of intoxicating liquor. 'Gambling under government control,' the committee stated, 'may more easily be controlled at a tolerable level.' The proposal was widely applauded by the press, but federal legislation that would permit it was not enacted.

It was a very modest proposal. The committee did not favour extending off-track betting to cover races outside Ontario, nor did it recommend permitting large sports pools, but noted that if they were to be permitted the government should run them. Similarly, the committee made 'no recommendation for or against the creation of any government-operated outlet in the field of lotteries,' stating: 'For the Government to set up a lottery *might* well create a demand rather than satisfy an existing demand.' Further, the committee concluded that the government should not be involved in short-odds betting on sporting events because to do so would involve it in laying off bets and thus being part of the American underworld.

In the short run, the report did not, therefore, directly affect the law relating to gambling. It did, however, help change attitudes with respect to gambling. Over the next forty years there has been a steady increase in the amount of gambling permitted by the Criminal Code and by provincial governments. In 1969 the federal government amended the Code to permit provinces to license charitable organizations to conduct lotteries as long as the proceeds were used for charitable purposes, and also permitted government-run lotteries. Casinos and slot machines at racetracks followed. In 1985 the federal government left the lottery field to the provinces. At the time this is being written, the Alcohol and Gaming Commission of Ontario operates fourteen different lottery games. It owns and has responsibility for, but does not operate, four large casinos: Casino Windsor, Casino Rama, and two in Niagara Falls. There are over 10,000 slot machines in these four casinos. The commission operates five charity casinos in other locations, and seventeen slot-machine facilities, with about 10,000 slot machines, at various racetracks throughout Ontario. Further, the commission has recently taken over the regulation of lotteries from the Ontario Lottery and Gaming Corporation. The Ontario budget for 2006 shows revenue from gambling to the province of Ontario of over two billion dollars. It is clearly big business for the provincial government and the provincial economy.

How the Internet gambling business will be regulated in the future remains to be seen. Internet gambling worldwide is a growing business – with perhaps $10 billion a year or more in transactions. It would appear to be illegal in Canada and the United States, but legal in England. The American federal government has recently started proceedings against foreign owners of Internet sites who were physically apprehended on U.S. territory. The situation is complicated in Canada because many of the sites are run from the aboriginal reserve of Kahnawake. In the long run, it is likely that governments will find some way of controlling the operations and profiting from the large sums involved in Internet gambling, just as they do for horseracing and other forms of gambling.

One of the most significant developments in Canadian criminal justice since the early 1960s has been the legalization of areas of conduct that had been prohibited by the Criminal Code. Obvious examples, in addition to gambling, are abortion and homosexual conduct. Perhaps the key date for legalization of all three was 1969, when the federal government permitted government-run and licensed lotteries, when abortion was permitted if approved by a hospital therapeutic abortion committee, and when homosexual conduct in private was no longer subject to the criminal process. No doubt, Pierre Trudeau played a significant role in promoting these amendments to the Criminal Code as minister of justice in 1967 and as prime minister in 1968. It should be noted, however, that English legislation preceded Canada's in the case of abortion and homosexual conduct and was at the time generally more liberal than Canada's gambling legislation.

The issue of the enforcement of morality was much debated in the early 1960s. The English Wolfenden Committee report of 1957, named after Sir John Wolfenden, the vice-chancellor of Reading University, had recommended that 'homosexual behaviour between consenting adults in private should no longer be a criminal offence.' The committee took the same approach that John Stuart Mill had put forward a century earlier – that 'the only purpose for which power can be rightfully exercised over any member of a civilized community, against his will, is to prevent harm to others.'

The liberal position was contested by the then High Court judge Sir Patrick Devlin, in a 1959 speech, just as Mill's position had been attacked in the nineteenth century by the father of Canada's Criminal Code, James Fitzjames Stephen. Devlin argued that the law 'does not discharge its function by protecting the individual from injury, annoyance, corruption, and exploitation; the law must protect also the institutions and the community of ideas, political and moral, without which people cannot live together.' The Oxford philosopher H.L.A. Hart adopted Mill's liberal position. In the 1960s, the debate was usually referred to as the Hart-Devlin debate. In his speech, Devlin had conceded that 'the limits of tolerance shift' and, further, that one should take into account 'the pros and cons of legal enforcement.' In Canada, the 'limits of tolerance' slowly shifted in all three areas – gambling, homosexual conduct, and abortion – and arguments about the 'pros and cons' of legal enforcement made some measure of legalization more attractive.

I included in my criminal-law casebook the debates on law and morality with an investigation of specific subject areas. These classes normally produced the liveliest and most interesting debates in the course.

An even more revolutionary change than occurred with respect to gambling took place regarding homosexual conduct. In the 1960s homosexuals in Canada could be and were compulsorily committed to mental institutions and some were prosecuted for their conduct. Between 1960 and 1962, 40 per cent of 'sexual deviation' cases at the Forensic Clinic of the Toronto Psychiatric Hospital – the largest single group – were homosexual men. One case that acted as a spur to the amending legislation in Canada was a 1967 Supreme Court of Canada case, *Klippert*, that held that a homosexual could be indefinitely detained in prison as a 'dangerous criminal offender.' Within a generation the treatment of homosexuals changed dramatically from prosecution to equality with heterosexuals. Starting with a landmark Ontario court of appeal decision in 2003, which changed the definition of marriage in federal legislation to permit same-sex marriages, almost all Canadian courts of appeal held that gay and lesbian couples have a constitutional right to marry. Federal legislation was introduced and passed in 2005 permitting such marriages after the Supreme Court of Canada held that federal legislation allowing gay and lesbian marriages would be constitutional.

The history of this change has been told by others. The limited 1969 exemption of private homosexual conduct from prosecution made it less risky for gay and lesbian persons to make their sexual orientation known. Interest groups then formed that promoted further changes. In my U of T history I point out that the first such group in Toronto was created on the U of T campus in the fall of 1969. Human-rights legislation was subsequently changed – or forced by the courts to be changed – to prohibit discrimination because of sexual orientation, and pension and other benefits were adjusted accordingly. The attitudes of a large section of the general public towards homosexual conduct slowly changed over these years from allowing an exemption from criminal conduct to tolerance and then to acceptance of the conduct.

Will other changes relating to other sexual conduct follow? In the late 1970s, the Law Reform Commission of Canada recommended that incest be removed from the Criminal Code. It had not been an offence in Canada until 1892, or in England until 1908. The commission stated in its report, adopting the views of the Wolfenden Committee, that 'It is not the function of the law to intervene in the private lives of citizens and to attempt to cover all sexual behaviour ... Accordingly, in the absence of any exploitation of authority or dependency, it is felt that incestuous behaviour ought not be treated and punished as a criminal act.' The public, however, was strongly opposed to such a change, and Marc Lalonde, the minister of justice, told the House of Commons that he would not accept the recommendation. In the early 1990s, the recommendation concerning the removal of incest from the code was reinserted in a report by the Law Reform Commission that was about to be presented to parliament, but the commission was eliminated by the government before the report was delivered. One wonders whether there may have been a connection between the two events.

Will we see the elimination of the law of incest? Probably not – at least not in the foreseeable future. There are not the interest groups to promote the change in the Criminal Code or to argue for its inclusion in human-rights codes. Indeed, incest survivor groups would strongly oppose it. As we will see in a subsequent chapter, pressure groups are a powerful force in the development of the law. Nor are the courts likely to read incest into the human-rights codes. What will probably continue to happen is that the police will be unlikely to prosecute consenting adults for such conduct. Bestiality is also unlikely to be removed from the Criminal Code because the interest groups involving animal rights would oppose such a change. There is less certainty about changes in the bigamy laws, where there are religious groups in favour of polygamous marriages.

The law concerning abortion was also liberalized in 1969. Until then, there was even doubt whether an abortion performed to protect the life or health of the mother was legal in Canada. The basis for permitting any abortion in Canada followed from the well-known 1939 English case of *Rex v. Bourne*, which had read into the English anti-abortion legislation a defence of necessity for a doctor performing an abortion to save the life of the mother. It did this because of the word 'unlawfully' in the U.K. legislation ('with intent to procure the miscarriage of any woman ... unlawfully uses on her any instrument or other means ...'). Saving the life of the mother, the judge in the *Bourne* case stated, could be expanded to protect the mother's health. In Canada the doubt about the application of the Bourne principle was created when the Criminal Code, which had a section similar to that in the United Kingdom, was tidied up in 1955 and the word 'unlawfully' was dropped. Some then argued that this change removed the defence. It certainly was not meant to have that effect, but enough doubt was cast that it remained difficult to have an abortion in hospitals in Canada. Abortions were still performed secretly by back-street abortionists, similar to those performed in the recent English movie *Vera Drake*, and by doctors willing to risk imprisonment. I personally knew reasonably well one respected doctor in Toronto who was sentenced to two years' imprisonment in the early 1960s because he performed abortions in his office.

After the 1969 legislation, abortion committees were set up in a number of hospitals in Canada. Most readers are familiar with the ensuing story – the role that Henry Morgentaler played, the importance of the various interest groups in promoting change, the Supreme Court of Canada's role in striking down the 1969 legislation in 1988 as a violation of fundamental justice because of the way the law was being applied, and the inability of the government to pass new legislation.

Proposed legislation along the lines of the American Supreme Court case of *Roe v. Wade* was considered too liberal by some and not liberal enough by others. I gave a series of opinions to the federal government in the late 1980s, predicting that the Supreme Court of Canada would uphold *Roe v. Wade*-like legislation. The first opinion was requested by my former colleague Frank Iacobucci, the then deputy minister of justice in Ottawa. A similar request was made concurrently to J.J. Robinette, who, I understand, offered the same opinion as I did (I never saw his written opinion). Subsequent opinions based on further drafts of proposed legislation were given by both Robinette and me to John Tait, who succeeded Frank as deputy minister.

As a result of the inability of the government to reach a consensus, there is no criminal legislation in Canada today dealing with abortion. Understandably, because abortion was not readily available to women across the country before the legislation was struck down, the number of abortions has risen since then. The increase has been mainly in clinics, not hospitals. Over the last few years, however, the number of abortions per live births in Canada has levelled off and remains relatively constant at a little over thirty per one hundred live births – that is, slightly more than 100,000 abortions a year. In spite of the absence of a legislative prohibition in Canada, the rate is still significantly below that in the United States – about fifteen per thousand women in Canada per year, compared with over twenty in the United States. Moreover, the abortions that do take place in Canada are done at an earlier stage than was the case before the legislation was struck down, and as a result complications immediately following the abortion have been cut in half.

It is likely that marijuana (also known as cannabis) will go the way of alcohol and gambling. It will eventually be legalized and controlled by the state. Marijuana was not added to the list of prohibited drugs until 1923. The decision to criminalize the substance, according to the Le Dain Commission that reported in the early 1970s, was made 'without any apparent scientific basis nor even any real sense of social urgency.' Before 1962, according to an RCMP report, there were only isolated cases of marijuana smoking across Canada.

The senate committee on marijuana that reported in 2002 recommended the legalization of the possession and growth for personal use of small amounts of marijuana, as had the Le Dain Commission in the early 1970s. In 2005 the Liberal government proposed to take the intermediate step of decriminalizing the possession of small amounts of the substance – that is, making it a minor offence that can be proceeded against by a ticket under the federal *Contraventions Act*. It would, therefore, still be illegal. If the legislation had been passed, it is likely that it would not have been long before smoking marijuana would have moved from decriminalization to legalization, as happened with homosexual conduct. The legislation died on the order paper when an election was called, and Stephen Harper's Conservative government has said that it has no plans to introduce similar legislation.

As with homosexual conduct, there are strong pressure groups advocating legalization of marijuana, and, as happened with alcohol and abortion, a recognized medical exception for marijuana will play a role in changing perceptions and making enforcement more difficult. There will also be groups, such as Mothers Against Drunk Driving, opposed to change who would be worried about the effect of a change of the law on traffic safety.

It will be interesting to see whether marijuana consumption will increase if federal decriminalization legislation is eventually enacted. Perhaps not. While consumption has not gone up disproportionately in the dozen or so American states that have decriminalized marijuana for personal use, its use has increased in the Netherlands proportionately more than in other European countries.

The Supreme Court of Canada held in 2003 (*R. v. Malmo-Levine; R. v. Caine*) that the existing marijuana laws do not violate section 7 of the Charter. The court stated in a 6–3 judgment (delivered by Justices Charles Gonthier and Ian Binnie) that 'the harm principle' – which states that conduct should only be subject to the criminal law if it is shown to cause harm to others – 'is not the constitutional standard for what conduct may or may not be the subject of the criminal law for the purposes of section 7.' In any event, the court held that the prohibition would have met a harm standard. This tossed the ball back to Parliament.

This brief foray into law and morality shows a clear trend towards decriminalization and then legalization, with the state controlling distribution. In my opinion, this trend will continue into other areas such as prostitution, although the pace of change through legislation in all these areas will, of course, depend on the political composition of the federal government.

The Supreme Court of Canada, as currently constituted, would tend to take the John Stuart Mill / H.L.A. Hart approach to questions of morality in the interpretation of legislation. In the relatively recent decision of *Kouri* (2005) the Supreme Court held that the accused, who ran a 'swingers' club' in Montreal, were not guilty of keeping a common bawdy house for the practice of acts of indecency. Chief Justice Beverley McLachlin stated for the majority of the court that a criminal sanction 'should only attach to render obscene or indecent materials or acts that create a significant risk of harm, incompatible with the proper functioning of society.' Further, the court held, it is up to the Crown to establish 'significant risk of harm' beyond a reasonable doubt.

5

More Double Jeopardy

Some time over the summer of 1962 I decided that I wanted to stay in the academic world – at least for the short term. My classmates in practice were busy winning or losing procedural motions, which as time went on did not interest me as much as it had in my brief period in practice. I had enjoyed working on the gambling study with Des Morton and was excited by the bail project, described in the next chapter. I wanted to return to Cambridge to complete the residence requirements for the doctorate.

I applied for a number of scholarships and received a Canada Council grant for further postgraduate studies. I was told it was the first scholarship given for a doctorate in law by the council, which had been established in 1957. It was sufficient to enable me to return to Cambridge. I had again applied for the Canadian Bar Association's Viscount Bennett scholarship, perhaps the most prestigious of the limited number of scholarships available in Canada. Once more, I was not selected. As is normal, the bar association returned all of the transcripts and the other material I had submitted. By error, however, the CBA also sent me the letters of recommendation that had been submitted on my behalf. The letters were all very positive, but one letter from one of my former teachers at the law school stood out. It was meant to help me and I have never held it against the person who sent it. The fact that the letter was sent to a committee of senior members of the Canadian legal establishment shows that they likely shared similar views about Jews at the time.

The letter stated: 'He is of Jewish religion and while confident in his approach to life, he shows no excessive aggressiveness or resentment that might detract from his charm of manner and tolerance toward others.' I guess I was tolerant of others. I tended, then as now, not to see prejudice in the actions of others. Indeed, I cannot recall ever personally experiencing overt anti-Semitism. Perhaps I was, and am, naive. No doubt, growing up in Forest Hill and centring my life in the academic community cut down on the opportunities to experience such conduct. When I graduated from commerce and finance, a large Canadian steel company, Harris Steel, offered me a position. I did not accept the offer because I had decided to go to law school, but an offer from a large industrial company fortified my view that people exaggerated the extent of anti-Semitism. In the spring of 2005 the *Globe* had a full-page obituary on the owner of Harris Steel, Milton Harris, who – to my surprise – was Jewish.

Dean Allan Leal supported giving me leave, but needed me to teach in the fall of 1962. Jean Castel, who taught international law, was going on leave and someone had to fill in. Leal knew that I was interested in the subject and asked me to teach it. Fortunately, a new edition of Bishop's casebook on international law was published that summer, so I had material that was up-to-date. We followed the casebook, chapter by chapter. Coincidentally, the Cuban missile crisis occurred just as we got to the section on blockades. It was thrilling to be teaching material that was so relevant and important for the future of mankind. (If one did not remember where one was during the Cuban Missile Crisis, people certainly knew where they were the following year when Kennedy was shot in Dallas. I was with my criminology class in Kingston Penitentiary. Nobody knew what was going to happen. There was talk of a possible nuclear attack against the United States. Inmates we talked with were upset about Kennedy's death, but also about their feeling of suffocation at being trapped inside the penitentiary during the crisis.)

Judy and I left for Europe, spending New Year's Eve 1962 watching the fireworks in Funchal, the capital of the Portuguese island of Madeira, and arriving in England in early January. Closing up in Toronto was relatively easy. Allan Leal agreed to look after our Sunbeam Alpine while we were away, and we were able to rent out our apartment in the Brentwood Towers.

I brought with me to Cambridge all my double-jeopardy and all my bail files, hoping to be able to persuade Glanville Williams to allow me to change my thesis topic from double jeopardy to bail. He said that to do so would be a mistake. I had made good progress on double jeopardy and would in the end have two books. He was right, but the next half-dozen years were difficult. It is hard enough trying to complete one book, but finishing two books put great pressure on me. At various times I was sure that I would not complete either. At one point I explored the possibility of returning to the practice of law with Charles Dubin as a way out, but nothing came of it.

I spent the next nine months in Cambridge working exceptionally hard on double jeopardy. We had a small flat in a house on Hartington Grove. Judy did not work. She read and in the early spring became pregnant. Our social life was mainly confined to other graduate students. Judy met Nancy Richardson in a laundromat and Judy and I became good friends with Nancy and Peter, who in the 1970s became the principal of University of Toronto's University College. I had met future Supreme Court of Canada justice Frank Iacobucci in Toronto during the summer of 1962 on his way to Cambridge from University of British Columbia Law School and naturally met him again in Cambridge. He and a fellow graduate student, Nancy Eastham, had been dating each other, and Judy and I established a close friendship with both Frank and Nancy. We attended their wedding in Andover, Massachusetts, two years later with our ten-month-old baby, Tom. Many of our friends were from the Third World. We had two good Ceylonese friends, one a Hindu Tamil, Sam Sanmuganathan, and the other a Buddhist Sinhalese, Sena Wijewardene, who was married to Janaki. We visited both families in Ceylon – later named Sri Lanka – in 1969, and saw them at other times. We visited them in Vienna in 1995, where they were both working for United Nations agencies. Because of the troubles in Sri Lanka, their friendship was on hold and we had to see them separately. Maybe things will change in the future.

On a number of occasions during that year I would go down to London (or is it 'up to London'?) to watch an important trial or appeal. One appeal involved some points of evidence which interested me as an evidence teacher. It would be, I thought, a break from double jeopardy. Four persons had been convicted of murder, but footprint and other evidence had been wrongly admitted and their convictions were subsequently quashed by the Court of Criminal Appeal. At that time, appeal courts in criminal cases in England did not have the power to order a new trial, but had to enter an acquittal. The Crown was understandably unhappy with that result and decided to charge the accused with robbery. Double jeopardy clearly prevented recharges for murder. The accused, Connelly along with others, were convicted of robbery and the case went to England's highest court, the House of Lords, on the question of whether trying the accused for robbery in these circumstances violated the rule against double jeopardy.

In 1964 the House of Lords upheld the robbery conviction, but ruled in *Connelly et al. v. DPP* that in the future all charges relating to a single transaction would have to be tried at the first trial. Not to do so would be considered an abuse of process of the courts and subsequent charges would be barred. The prosecutor would therefore be prevented from unreasonably splitting the case. It was not unreasonable in the *Connelly* case to have done so because, until the *Connelly* decision, the courts had said that murder charges should stand alone and not include other offences.

This was the most important double-jeopardy case since the time of Henry II. The *Connelly* case followed the American Law Institute's Model Penal Code of 1960, which had recommended that all counts related to a single transaction be tried at the same time. It differed from the Canadian law at the time. In the 1963 Supreme Court of Canada case of *Feeley, McDermott and Wright*, for example, the court upheld an Ontario Court of Appeal decision which had stated that the Crown could hold back a charge – in that case it was one of several counts of conspiracy involving the same incident – and that the Crown's decision to do so could not be questioned. The *Feeley* case has not been specifically overruled by the Supreme Court of Canada, but the court has subsequently accepted the doctrine of abuse of process and, indeed, has converted it into a constitutional principle under section 7 of the Charter. This then is the heart of the double-jeopardy issue. It conserves judicial and other resources, tends to prevent inconsistent verdicts, and prevents unfairness to the accused.

I had already finished a respectable draft of my chapter on unreasonably splitting a case before the House of Lords' *Connelly* judgment appeared, and it required extensive rewriting, although not as much as it might have because I had advocated a *Connelly*-like approach. The final touches were put on the chapter on the plane returning from England to Canada, via Boston. We had stopped there to see Judy's brother, Barry, who was working at a Harvard-affiliated hospital and to see Glanville Williams, who was spending some time at Harvard. Glanville read the chapter and liked it. The chapter was later published in the *University of Toronto Law Journal*, as well as in my book.

Some years later I assisted the Law Reform Commission of Canada in developing a legislative enunciation of the principles of double jeopardy. In a paper I submitted to the commission in 1986, 'Double Jeopardy: Draft Provisions,' I made sure that the rule against unreasonably splitting a case became the cornerstone of the concept. In the commission's *Double Jeopardy, Pleas and Verdicts*, published in 1991 (but, unfortunately, never incorporated into legislation), the following rule is set out: 'Unless otherwise ordered by the court in the interests of justice – such as preventing prejudice – or unless the accused acquiesces in a separate trial, an accused should not be subject to separate trials for multiple crimes charged or for crimes not charged but known at the time of the commencement of the first trial' if they 'arise from the same transaction,' as well as in other stated circumstances. The English Law Commission has produced several publications on double jeopardy and has endorsed a restricted version of the *Connelly* principle.

I published a number of chapters from the thesis as articles along the way. The main advantage of doing so is that it requires getting the chapters up to a publishable standard and makes the completion of the whole manuscript easier to achieve. Oxford University Press did not object to my doing so. From a marketing perspective it gives some advance publicity to the book, although not all publishers would see this as an advantage; others might think that it would diminish the potential market. Four of the ten chapters in the book were published as separate articles. Anything more might have caused Oxford to object. One chapter on issue estoppel in the criminal law was published in 1966 in the *Criminal Law Quarterly* and two were published in 1967 in the *University of Toronto Law Journal* – one was the section on unreasonably splitting a case and another was on double jeopardy and the division of legislative authority in Canada. Finally, a two-part article was published in the prestigious English *Law Quarterly Review* on new trials in England following an overturned conviction. The editor of the *LQR*, Professor Arthur Goodhart of Oxford, had been publicly advocating the argument that I was making – that is, that on an appeal from a conviction the Court of Criminal Appeal should have the right to send the case back for a new trial, as in other common-law jurisdictions. Not to do so was taking double jeopardy too far. Up until then, the appeal court could only enter an *acquittal* if there had been an error at the trial. So Goodhart was prepared to give me as much space as I needed to make the argument. In 1989 English legislation eventually allowed the possibility of a new trial after a conviction is quashed.

Another controversial issue was the right of the prosecutor to appeal an acquittal of the accused. English law did not permit it and it is unconstitutional in the United States under their constitutional Fifth Amendment double-jeopardy provision. Canada, however, has permitted such appeals on questions of law since 1930. The double-jeopardy provision in the *Canadian Charter of Rights and Freedoms* has been held not to prevent such appeals. Section 11(h) of the Charter states that any person charged with an offence has the right 'if finally acquitted of the offence, not to be tried for it again and, if finally found guilty and punished for the offence, not to be tried or punished for it again.' The word 'finally' was relied on by the court to justify ordering a new trial after an acquittal in certain cases.

I advocated in my book a modified version of the Canadian law: allowing new trials following a Crown appeal only if the error committed by the prosecutor or the judge could be said with some degree of certainty to be the reason for the verdict. This is the law in Australia. The Canadian law – in my view, improperly – still allows a new trial after an acquittal if the error *may* have been responsible for the verdict. Some day the Supreme Court will recognize that their test is too favourable to the prosecutor and hold that the present Canadian practice goes beyond what the Charter should permit. In a recent case, *Graveline*, the Supreme Court took a step in that direction by holding that there is an onus on the Crown in such cases to satisfy the court that the error of the trial judge 'might reasonably be thought ... to have had a material bearing on the acquittal.' I believe that they should make the hurdle even tougher for the Crown to get over.

Canada rightly still does not permit an appeal from an acquittal – and consequently the possibility of a new trial – on a question of fact. The Crown can appeal only on a question of law. England, however, has recently permitted a new trial based on new evidence in certain cases following an acquittal. One of the examples given in the background papers justifying reopening acquittals was an acquittal of an accused charged with rape because the DNA evidence with respect to semen found in the victim could not be linked to the accused, some time after which new technology becomes available to show that it was the accused's semen. After consultation, the law commission's final report to parliament would have limited new trials in such circumstances to cases of murder.

The government liked the idea of reopening acquittals. It would show that it was being tough on crime. A 2002 white paper had stated that the government should 'rebalance the system in favour of victims, witnesses and communities.' The new *Criminal Justice Act*, which was passed in late 2003, is not, however, limited to murder cases, but contains a list of serious offences, including rape, manslaughter, and armed robbery. Moreover, the legislation would be retroactive and not be limited to reopening cases tried in the future. There are, however, a number of hurdles that the prosecutor has to get over. Only the Court of Appeal can order a retrial, and the court and the Director of Public Prosecutions have to be satisfied that there is 'new and compelling evidence' and that it is 'in the interests of justice' for the appeal court to order a retrial, having regard to a number of factors, including whether the police and prosecutors acted 'with due diligence or expedition' at the original trial.

The English legislation is unfortunate, although it is found in several European legal systems. It is likely that there will be very few cases – perhaps a handful over the years – in which new trials will be ordered. The first case in which a retrial was held under the new law was that of Billy Dunlop, who had been acquitted in 1989 of murdering his girlfriend. He later confessed to a prison officer and was convicted of perjury committed at the murder trial, but could not again be charged with murder because of double jeopardy. When the new law came into operation in 2005 Dunlop was charged with murder, convicted, and sentenced to life imprisonment. The victim's mother had understandably campaigned tirelessly for a change in the law to permit new trials in such cases. The next of kin of victims in Canada, such as Priscilla de Villiers, whose daughter was abducted and murdered in 1991 while jogging, and former member of parliament Chuck Cadman, whose son was stabbed to death in 1992 in a random street attack, have played similar significant roles in changing the criminal-justice system. A single incident or a single person can often have a major effect on changing the law.

The English legislation will, however, have the undesirable effect of creating continuing anxiety for all persons acquitted of serious offences. They will always be vulnerable to a future application for a retrial based on new evidence such as an alleged confession, a possible new eyewitness, or planted or fabricated real evidence. Persons acquitted in England will, as stated by Justice Hugo Black, quoted in a previous chapter, have to 'live in a continuing state of anxiety and insecurity.' Canada should not follow England's lead. Indeed, it is doubtful that the Charter would permit legislation similar to that in England.

Canada does not need legislation to handle one potentially troubling situation, but neither did England: the acquitted accused who had entered the witness box and denied guilt, but later admits that he lied under oath, a topic that I discussed in some depth in my book. The Supreme Court of Canada held in *Gushue* in 1980 that such an accused could later be convicted of perjury if new evidence subsequently appears that was not available at the time of the first trial. A later Supreme Court case, *Grdic*, held that a perjury charge could not be brought if the new evidence had been available at the first trial and could have been discovered if the Crown had exercised due diligence. Noted criminal lawyer Eddie Greenspan once told my class that when a client who has entered the witness box and denies guilt is acquitted, he sometimes gives his client a copy of the *Gushue* case – in effect telling the client to keep his or her mouth shut.

Canadian legislation would, however, be desirable to deal with cases of 'tainted' acquittals, such as the notorious British Columbia case of Peter Gill, in which Gill had a sexual affair with one of the jurors during the trial and was acquitted of murder. A subsequent charge of murder was brought against Gill and two other accused who had not been involved in the matter, but was later dropped, although Gill was properly tried and convicted of obstruction of justice. In such cases of tainted acquittals English legislation enacted in 1996 could serve as a model for Canada.

Double-jeopardy issues are both complex and fascinating. I once ran into a professor of law at New York University who based a whole seminar course on double-jeopardy issues. Over the years I never tired of discussing the issues in my criminal-law class. I particularly liked the discussion of issue estoppel: When will an issue decided in one case bar an inconsistent finding against the accused in another case? Sometimes Canadian courts take the concept too far, holding that inconsistent verdicts in one case will cause a conviction to be overturned. The United States Supreme Court, in contrast, has decided that a jury can bring in inconsistent verdicts, but a judge cannot. The Ontario Court of Appeal has even held that a later acquittal can overturn an earlier conviction if evidence of the conduct alleged in the later acquittal had been admitted in the earlier case as similar fact evidence. (At this point, I know that some readers will be rolling their eyes at why I find this so fascinating.)

Students would usually raise one fact situation that has been the subject of at least one movie and several television dramas: that is, the person who has been convicted of murder when the alleged victim's body has not been found, gets out of prison, finds the victim is, indeed, alive, and shoots him. I predict a conviction for murder in such an unlikely case.

I was probably the only law teacher in the country that spent much time on double-jeopardy issues in the basic criminal-law course. The eighth edition of the casebook which Kent Roach and I produced in 1997 continued to contain a lengthy chapter on the subject. I gave over the casebook to Kent, Patrick Healy, and Gary Trotter, with full rights to do what they wanted with it. The ninth edition appeared in 2004, and the double-jeopardy chapter had disappeared. While the subject is very complex and there are many other criminal law topics – especially concerning the Charter – that instructors wish to include in the basic course, it always held a special place in my course.

The thesis was submitted in 1967 and was accepted by Cambridge for the PhD degree. I was given special exemption from having to attend the oral examination and so I missed that experience, which is an essential part of the process in North America. I do not know how often orals are waived in England. I know that Sir Rupert Cross, the distinguished blind legal scholar from Oxford, was the external examiner and that R.N. Gooderson, a reader in English Law at Cambridge, who taught criminal procedure and evidence, was the internal examiner.

I did not attend the graduation ceremony in Cambridge, although I eventually ordered the elegant Cambridge silk gown – all black with a striking red band down the front and on the inside of the hood. I particularly like the pancake-style Cambridge hat, which always draws compliments from students at convocations. I wanted to wear a Cambridge gown for the 1967 University of Toronto convocation, but the only Cambridge PhD I knew at the U of T was Marshall McLuhan. I often saw him having lunch at the Royal Ontario Museum – on the outdoor terrace of the restaurant overlooking the Chinese tombs – and boldly asked him if I could borrow his gown for the coming June convocation. He was taken aback by the question, but said yes. My colleagues were impressed when they learned whose gown I was wearing. That was the closest I ever got to McLuhan, although I later devoted a number of paragraphs to him in my history of the University.

My manuscript was published by Oxford University Press – technically, the Clarendon Press, Oxford – in 1969. My fear of a competing book occupying the field was almost realized by the simultaneous publication of another book with the same title, *Double Jeopardy*, by an

American scholar, Jay Sigler, that same year. I did not know that Sigler was working on the book, which had also been his doctoral dissertation. Having two competing books published at the same time, one from an American and another from primarily a UK perspective, brought forth reviews comparing the treatment of the subject in each country and of the books themselves. Rupert Cross, who had recommended my manuscript to Oxford, gave it a fine review, comparing the two books in the *Law Quarterly Review*. Cross wrote that I had 'succeeded in producing a work of outstanding importance for academics and practitioners alike' out of my PhD thesis. There were many other very favourable reviews.

Although most scholars consider it my best book, I am reluctant to choose a favourite. It is certainly the one with the strongest evidence of scholarship, but it is very traditional scholarship, unlike the archival scholarship in my true-crime murder books or the University of Toronto history. It does, however, use a historical and comparative approach. Of all my books, it is the one most frequently cited by the courts, including the supreme courts of all of the major commonwealth countries.

I had submitted the final version of the manuscript to my editor at Oxford, Peter Sutcliffe, in November 1967, impressed with the fact that I did not have a contract with Oxford. Everything, I assumed, was being done on trust. When I pointed this out to Sutcliffe in a complimentary manner, he said that this was an oversight and immediately sent me a contract. We had not previously discussed royalties and I was happy with his suggestion that I receive 10 per cent of the published price on books sold in the United Kingdom and 7.5 per cent for books sold elsewhere. I did the index myself, which took more than a solid week. Only an author knows what users are likely to want in an index, and if one has the time it is something an author should do. In early 1969 I saw the first copy of *Double Jeopardy* at the offices of Oxford University Press in Melbourne, Australia, while travelling on my first sabbatical.

Oxford's Clarendon Press was in this case the perfect publisher for me. The quality of production was high and, fortunately, they did not require major changes. The book found its way into most major law libraries throughout the common-law world. Feeling an obligation to give them the right to publish the book, I had first submitted the manuscript, with Glanville William's approval, to Sweet and Maxwell, whose scholarship had sent me to Cambridge. They turned it down, thinking that it would not have sufficient appeal for legal practitioners in its present form to warrant publication by them. I was fortunate to end up with Oxford. Over my career, I would become used to having my first – and often my second and third choice of publisher reject my manuscript. One has to have a thick skin to be an author. The rejection is often based on the understandable ground that the manuscript does not fit the publisher's list, and one usually ends up with a more appropriate firm.

6

Detention before Trial

Judy and I returned to Toronto in the late summer of 1963, and I again took up my duties at Osgoode Hall Law School. In the early fall we purchased a small home for $12,000 at 169 Hillsdale Avenue East, south of Eglinton and east of Yonge. That sum was about double my salary, which had been $5500 when I started teaching at Osgoode in 1961–2 and had risen to about $8000 in 1963. We engaged my former camp counsellor, Jerry Markson, an award-winning architect, to gut the home and design the renovations that added another $10,000 to the cost. We moved into the house in the late fall. This was the first of four major renovations on our two houses and our cottage that Jerry did for us. We are still good friends, which tells me – judging by discussions with others who have undertaken such renovations – that we are both easy to get along with. The Hillsdale home had a striking wooden screen separating the front hallway from the living room which contained the Bambara headdress we had purchased in Paris and other African pieces. The masks were on the far wall of the room, dramatically lit by a pair of spotlights. When I last walked by and peeked into the window of the Hillsdale home, I discovered that the wooden screen was no longer there. Pity.

Our first child, Tom, was born on 4 January 1964. We wanted to pick a name starting with the letter T, after Judy's late mother Tillie, who had died when Judy was ten. I had admired Thomas à Becket, who had played a key role in my double-jeopardy story, and we both liked the young Tom Ehrlich, whom we knew from our first year in Cambridge, when he was about two years old. At the baby naming at Beth Tzedec synagogue, I did not divulge that an archbishop of Canterbury had influenced the choice of name. Judy became a full-time mother, taking courses part-time that would lead to her BA, then to her MA, and eventually to her PhD, in 1988. The BA was done through Woodsworth College, a wonderful addition to the life of the University of Toronto that made it possible for persons like Judy to pursue further education on a part-time basis. The Ontario Institute for Studies in Education, where she did her MA and PhD, provided an equally hospitable environment. She did not go back to work until the mid-1970s, working part-time for Community Occupational Therapy Associates (COTA), a community-based rehabilitation and mental health service provider in the Greater Toronto Area.

I put aside my work on double jeopardy to try to finish my manuscript on bail. As stated in the previous chapter, I had tried unsuccessfully to change my PhD topic from double jeopardy to bail. The bail material had to be given priority now because it was much more time-sensitive than double jeopardy. Moreover, it was important to the Criminal Law Program at Osgoode as well as to the Law Society of Upper Canada, which had financially supported the project, to see the study published.

I had started work on the bail project about two years earlier, in the fall of 1961, between my periods of residence in Cambridge. I was collecting material for my criminology course in the spring of 1961 and came across a recently published article, 'The Bail System and Equal Justice,' by a University of Pennsylvania law professor, Caleb Foote, in the American journal *Federal Probation*. Caleb had worked closely with teams of law students and published a report in 1954 on the bail system in Philadelphia, and a further report in 1958 on the bail system in New York City. Both were published in the *University of Pennsylvania Law Review*. They both showed the unfairness to those kept in custody before their trials.

What would an empirical study of bail practices in Toronto show? Hans Mohr, a bearded, soft-spoken researcher and later professor at Osgoode Hall Law School at York University, wanted to attend my criminology course in the spring of 1962. He had a doctorate in sociology from Graz University in Austria and was interested in quantitative methodology, then rarely used in law schools. At the time, he was doing research at the Clarke Institute of Psychiatry on sexual deviance, and several years later would be one of the authors of the inaptly titled book *Pedophilia and Exhibitionism: A Handbook*. We would talk about the criminal-justice system before and after my seminars. He was very critical of lawyers writing about the legal system without knowing what was taking place in practice. He encouraged me to undertake an empirical study of bail practices and later assisted me with the quantitative analysis.

I invited Caleb Foote to visit Osgoode to discuss his research. Caleb, who later moved to the law school at the University of California, Berkeley, had an interest in the subject of incarceration because, as a Quaker, he had spent several years in a federal penitentiary as a conscientious objector, and was later pardoned by President Truman. He died at the age of eighty-eight in 2006. The dean of the Berkeley Law School described Foote as 'one of the nation's preeminent scholars and teachers in both family law and criminal law.' After I became dean, Foote came to the U of T law school and delivered a brilliant lecture on prisons, making the point that 'if you build them, they will fill them.' The lecture was, unfortunately, never published. If I had to pick two persons who have most influenced my future scholarship I would choose Caleb Foote and Glanville Williams, both of whom happened to be conscientious objectors in the Second World War.

The Law Society of Upper Canada put up $5000 to cover research expenses for the study, and during the summer of 1962 three law students who had been in my criminology seminar were hired as my research assistants: Barry Brown, Charles Gardiner, and Mel Morassutti. As has been the case with many of my projects, I initially bit off too much. The study was to cover bail in all courts in Toronto. In the end, we only collected data on the magistrates' courts, which covered over 95 per cent of the indictable offences in Toronto and all of the summary-conviction Criminal Code offences. The remaining 5 per cent of the indictable offences were tried by a higher court.

The design of the study had been developed in the spring of 1962. A prospective study, that is, one looking at cases that were taking place at the time and future cases, had a number of disadvantages. One is that the cases might take some time before they were completed. Moreover, the very act of sitting in court and observing the process might affect the actions of those being observed. In a pretentious footnote in the introduction to the study I state: 'The writer is informed that those familiar with the physical sciences will recognize the similarity between this and the Heisenberg Uncertainty Principle.' Prospective studies are often used in medical research in order to create a control group, but it is extremely difficult to arrange a control group for legal research because judges would be unwilling to randomly treat people differently as an experiment.

So we chose to study past cases. How large should the sample be? I had taken a course in statistics in commerce and finance and came out of it convinced that the larger the sample the greater the degree of confidence one could have in the results. Some statisticians say that I am wrong, but I cannot get it into my head that a smaller sample is as good as a larger one, assuming both are carefully selected. So we chose to take all of the criminal cases in the Toronto magistrates' courts over a six-month period between the beginning of September 1961 and the end of February 1962, about 6000 cases in all. There was no sampling within that body of cases. We then decided on what variables we would study. Some are obvious, such as the type of offence, the accused's previous convictions, and whether the accused was represented by counsel. In the end, we had about twenty-five variables. Even with 6000 cases, the resulting numbers tended to be very small when sorted by three or four variables. So I was lucky to have initially selected a relatively large sample to study.

The basic source of information was the daily court lists, annotated by hand by the clerk of the court. This was supplemented by data from about fifteen other sources. In mid-June I wrote to Professor Foote that 'the records are better than I thought they would be.' They included the formal informations setting out the charges, microfilmed cash bail records, police records of the previous convictions of persons charged, records on prosecutions for skipping bail, bench-warrant records, Don Jail records, and police-station night bail books. I recall spending an evening looking through the night bail book at Number 1 Division police station in the Stewart Building on the south side of College Street, just west of University Avenue. I chatted with a young man who had been brought into the station and lodged in a cell. Bail had been set by a justice of the peace at $50 and he was unable to raise it. I sympathized with his plight and personally loaned him the money. The police officers were greatly amused. I never saw the accused or the money again. Nor did I put up bail for anyone else during the course of the study.

We received very little assistance from the statistics then being collected by the Dominion Bureau of Statistics. They were seriously out of date and some provinces did not report criminal statistics, as they were required to do. Moreover, the categories were not helpful. The bureau did not, for example, keep records of withdrawals, which consequently raised the conviction rate. I was so upset with the quality of Canadian criminal-justice statistics that I reviewed the bureau's 1960 statistics – found in the bureau's 1962 volume of court statistics – in the *Canadian Bar Review*, one of the few reviews I have ever written, by stating: 'All will agree that the availability of accurate data concerning the administration of criminal justice is an indispensable tool to an intelligent appraisal of the effectiveness of our criminal law, procedure and treatment of offenders ... Even assuming for present purposes that [the reports submitted to the bureau] are honest and accurate, there are none the less aspects of the volume that are very disturbing.' I then set out five specific problems and ended by stating: 'Undoubtedly tremendous strides have been taken by the Dominion Bureau of Statistics in the past number of years to give us a better collection of statistics ... But until the present methods of collection and computation are given a complete re-analysis and revision, those working with the figures would be wise to be cautious.'

Hans Mohr and I also organized a conference in April 1964 at Osgoode Hall Law School on criminal statistics. About seventy persons attended. John Edwards, the director of the U of T's Centre of Criminology, Jim Giffen from the department of sociology, and John Spencer from the school of social work took an active part in the work leading up to the conference. A leading expert on court statistics from the United States, Ronald Beattie, who had had thirty years of practical experience in developing and improving criminal statistics with the California Department of Justice, the United States census, and the United States courts, gave one of the key talks. Hans and I prepared a report on the proceedings, which was later published in the *Criminal Law Quarterly*. The delegates passed a resolution, without dissent, calling for the federal government to set up a national advisory committee to 'conduct a thorough and comprehensive investigation of ... criminal statistics.' The resolution was sent to Justice Minister Guy Favreau, whose parliamentary secretary, Donald Macdonald, had taken part in the conference. I cannot say that the conference had a direct and immediate bearing on improving the collection and analysis of criminal data, but it surely helped to encourage change. Today, the justice-statistics division of Statistics Canada produces well regarded statistics, combined with periodic reports on specific topics.

I wanted to use a computer to sort and analyse the data we had collected, and consulted with persons in the UNIVAC division of Reming-
ton Rand. UNIVAC had built the first commercially sold computer in
the world, used for the U.S. Bureau of Census in 1951. Their offices
were on Bay Street, just north of Wellesley. They agreed to assist without charge. Over the summer my research assistants and I collected
material on each case, and in the fall a larger group of about thirty law
students coded the information, which UNIVAC key-punched and
processed electronically. I thought we were using computers and,
indeed, thanked UNIVAC in the book's preface for advice on the 'possibilities and limitations of computers,' but this was really just mechan-
ical card-sorting. Still, it was just by chance that the punched cards
were sorted mechanically and not put on the large tape drums in the
adjoining room to be sorted by the UNIVAC computer. I cannot therefore claim to have been the first in Canada to use a computer in legal
research, but I think I can claim to be the first lawyer in Canada to do
this form of empirical research in a serious way. The punched cards
used in the process are now with my papers in the U of T Archives.

It was this material and my research notes on the bail project that I
took to Cambridge with me in January 1963, but I was unable to persuade Glanville Williams to allow me to switch topics. I brought the
material back from Cambridge, untouched, and worked on it throughout the academic year 1963–4. That summer a very able research assistant, Philip Alter (who, sadly, died in 2006) helped me organize the
material into a presentable form. The final manuscript had thirty-one
tables and nineteen bar charts or figures.

The study was more or less completed in late 1964. My concluding
chapter stated that 'the release practices before trial which exist for
cases tried in the Toronto Magistrates' Courts operate in an ineffective,
inequitable, and inconsistent manner.' Although I concentrated on
the Toronto courts, the conclusions appeared to be valid throughout
Canada.

In the early 1960s, over 90 per cent of persons charged with criminal
offences in Toronto were arrested. Of those arrested, about 85 per cent
were kept in police custody until their first court appearance. At that
hearing, the magistrate would hold the accused without bail or set an
amount for bail that had to be deposited before the accused was
released. As in the United States, bail in Canada in those days meant
money, rather than, as in England, the person or persons who would

supervise the accused if released. In England, a person putting up bail promised that if the accused did not appear, the person would give the court a certain sum of money. It was not deposited in advance.

'The tragedy of this preoccupation with money,' I wrote, 'is that a large percentage of persons are unable to raise the bail that is set ... 62 per cent of all persons for whom bail was set at their first court appearance were unable to raise it ... Thus, the ability of the accused to marshall funds or property in advance determines whether he will be released.' Although some bail bondsmen operated in the Toronto courts, they did so illegally. In contrast to the United States, the bail-bonding practice was prohibited by the Criminal Code. We had the American system of security in advance and the English system prohibiting bondsmen. It is no wonder that a high percentage of accused were kept in custody pending their trials. The elimination of the routine practice of requiring security in advance was one of my principal recommendations.

The study also showed that being held in custody pending trial can have serious consequences, apart from psychological strain and the possibility of physical abuse while in jail. There was a relationship between being kept in custody and the sentence that an accused would receive, even when the variables were controlled. This is understandable because, for one thing, the accused in custody cannot as easily show that he or she is currently employed – a strong mitigating factor in sentencing. Moreover, those who were not in custody for their trial were more likely to be acquitted than those who were held in custody. In part, this is because those in custody are hampered in the preparation of their defence and tend to appear guilty in the eyes of the trier of fact. Moreover, they look guilty when they come into court from a jail cell.

There are other serious consequences of being held in custody. Recent studies have shown that custody unfairly induces guilty pleas: one such study showed that persons in custody are two and a half times more likely to plead guilty than those not in custody. The same study showed that persons not in custody have more than double the chance of having all their charges withdrawn of those in custody. One third of persons released before trial eventually had all their charges withdrawn, whereas this occurred in only about one tenth of the cases of those in custody. One of the reasons for this is that persons not in custody can work out a diversion arrangement with the Crown in which the charges are eventually withdrawn.

The deleterious consequences of being detained in custody before trial have recently been recognized by the Supreme Court of Canada. Justice Frank Iacobucci referred to my study – he graciously called it 'groundbreaking work' – and the consequences of being kept in custody pending trial in his dissent in the 2002 case of *R. v. Hall*. In the following year, Justice John Major for a unanimous Supreme Court in *Ell v. Alberta* made the same point on the effects of pre-trial custody, again citing my study. The relationship between custody and the result of the case reinforces the view of defence counsel that 'the bail hearing is often the single most important step for an accused person in the criminal process.'

There were other recommendations, such as giving the police greater power to release arrested accused. Summonses were at the time rarely used. I advocated that various steps be taken to put pressure on the police to release persons in appropriate cases. One reason that the police wanted to arrest rather than summon persons was to get fingerprints, as permitted under the *Identification of Criminals Act* if the person was in custody. A possible solution was to permit the police to get fingerprints at a later time if they summoned persons or released them after arrest, a technique which was later adopted in the bail-reform legislation.

In December 1964 I submitted a draft of the manuscript to the University of Toronto Press. It was accepted by the Press and one of the Press's senior editors, Jean Houston, was assigned the task of editing it.

One of the conditions that I insisted upon was that the book be published before the end of June 1965. I was moving from Osgoode Hall Law School to the University of Toronto at the end of that month and felt that it would be unfair to give the credit for the book to the U of T when all of the support and encouragement – and it had been considerable – had come from Osgoode. My recollection is that I had let Albert Abel know that I would be prepared to move to the U of T. Abel probably told Bora Laskin, who likely convinced Caesar that I would be a good addition to the faculty. I was making the change because it seemed reasonably clear in the fall of 1964 that Osgoode was going to move to York University, a move that did not appeal to me.

The ten-minute subway ride from my home in the Yonge and Eglinton area to Osgoode Hall was just right for finishing reading the *Globe and Mail*, and Osgoode's downtown location was ideal from my perspective – close to the courts and the legal profession. The U of T offered those same advantages – indeed, the extra couple of subway stops made it easier to finish the *Globe* and I generally found that I could start and complete my reading of the entire *Toronto Star* on the trip home. The move also offered the possibility of interdisciplinary work with other faculties in a very good university. I remember walking through the campus at dusk on the day that Caesar and I concluded our negotiations. I knew I was joining a great university. Moreover, it was a homecoming for me. Many of my professors were still there and were happy to see me back as a colleague.

It had been a decided advantage to spend the first few years of my teaching career away from the law school where I had been a student. I had not been pushed around by having new courses sprung on me at the last moment, as I might have been if I had started teaching at Caesar's law school. I was able to build up a track record of soon-to-be published scholarship, which may not have been as easy to produce if I had joined the U of T at the start of my career. But that is beside the point, for I had not been asked to join the U of T faculty before then and had not applied for a position. I went into law teaching, it will be recalled, for the Sunbeam Alpine and had not intended to stay very long.

I was appointed as an associate professor, the rank I had at Osgoode. Nobody discussed pensions or tenure when I came to the U of T. At the age of thirty-two, pensions were far in the future for me and I did not have the foresight to ask for credit for my four years of teaching at Osgoode. Tenure was not discussed because the University of Toronto did not formally award tenure in those years. In 1967, after the Haist report on appointment policy, tenure became a crucial part of one's progress through the ranks. In 1968, without any hearing, I was awarded tenure and became a full professor. Today, as mentioned in an earlier chapter, young professors have to produce publications, usually journal articles, every year or they face problems on their three-year reviews and on their tenure hearings. They would not have the luxury – if that is an apt word – of holding back publication until a book appeared, as I did for *Detention before Trial*. Before its appearance in 1965, I had only a couple of publications to my name.

Jean Houston was an excellent editor. She was both the editor and copy-editor. The manuscript was in terrible shape, both in style and in the way I had put the pages together. I had cut and pasted the manuscript, using staples rather than glue or tape. Jean told me that editors do not want to cut their fingers on staples and I had to redo the manuscript using glue. Magic Tape, which can be written on, had not yet been invented. More importantly, Jean forced me to rewrite the concluding chapter in order to draw out the points I had made.

The manuscript was typeset in April. The Press's printing plant was then located at the south end of the main campus in a nondescript building still standing between the Galbraith and Wallberg buildings. To Jean's surprise, I asked if I could spend a few minutes watching the typesetter work on the book and was told that nobody had made such a request before. I watched the linotype operator typing laboriously, with the hot molten lead forming magically into my own words. I have always taken an interest in the physical production of my books, although I never went quite that far again. I should point out, however, that I did not make a similar request to watch my children being born. It was not generally done in those years.

The book was published in June 1965 – less than six months from a very rough manuscript to a finished book. It is hard to overestimate the pride and excitement one feels in the publication of one's first book. As it turned out, there was a surprising amount of attention given to it. Richard Doyle, the editor of the *Globe and Mail*, was interested in the subject and published three lengthy excerpts – the last being a full-page one – over three successive weeks in June on the page opposite the editorial page, then called page seven. Each excerpt included my picture with a caption, the last of which stated that 'Professor Martin L. Friedland, 32, teaches law at Osgoode Hall Law School' and then went on to state that the book would be published on 28 June. Accompanying this last excerpt was an editorial devoted entirely to the book that went from the top to the bottom of the page – a rare occurrence. A CBC television program called *Toronto File* devoted two half-hour programs to the book, consisting almost exclusively of apparently spontaneous, but in fact well-scripted, interviews with the self-effacing author.

There were posters for the book in the book section of Eaton's and in our local W.H. Smith at Yonge and St Clair. Reviews appeared in *Saturday Night*, in *Maclean's*, and in many legal journals in Canada and other countries. No one, especially Martin L. Friedland, 32, would have predicted such a strong reception. No one, that is, except perhaps my parents. I have in front of me the copy of the book that I gave them dated 25 June 1965, which they kept, stuffed with many clippings. I formally dedicated the book 'To my Family' and in the personal dedication I simply said: 'Thanks for everything.' I did not know whether I would ever publish another book, and so I made the dedication a wide one.

Perhaps the interest in the book came from the fact we were just catching up with some of the growing concern in the United States about civil rights. A 1963 U.S. body, The Attorney General's Committee on Poverty and the Administration of Federal Criminal Justice, also known as the Allen Committee after its chairman, law professor Francis Allen, had criticized the bail system and other aspects of the U.S. criminal-justice system, arguing that 'one of the prime objectives of the civilized administration of justice is to render the poverty of the litigant an irrelevancy.' Attorney General Robert Kennedy had convened a conference in Washington in 1964, which I attended along with the Crown attorney for Toronto, Henry Bull. (We all shook hands with Kennedy, but I cannot recall talking to him.) My study was simply part of a much wider international movement to protect the rights of the accused.

In Canada the study attracted the attention of parliamentarians, although it was not the book that was referred to in the House of Commons. That was a small pamphlet, 'Reforming the Bail System,' put out by the John Howard Society of Kingston and printed in Kingston Penitentiary, based on a talk on bail that I had given to the society. One should never underestimate the importance of such vehicles for disseminating one's ideas. The Department of Justice in Ottawa asked me to present my ideas before a group of civil servants in Ottawa. It was an important opportunity. I made careful notes in the front of the book, and as I reviewed them on the plane to Ottawa, while drinking a cup of coffee, the plane lurched and coffee spilled all over the book and over my pants. Needless to say, the experience resulted in my asking airline stewards in the future for only half a cup of coffee. Moreover, appearing before the Department of Justice officials with stained pants may have delayed the implementation of bail reform in Canada. The coffee-stained book is now in the University of Toronto Archives.

An NDP member of Parliament, Barry Mather, who had also read the John Howard pamphlet, contacted me to say that he had been influenced by the document and was introducing a private member's bill, and added that he had 'the undertaking from Mr. Diefenbaker [the leader of the opposition] that he will support it being sent to the Justice Committee for study, an unusual step if it materializes.' It did materialize and a few days later, the chair of the Standing Committee on Justice and Legal Affairs, A.J.P. Cameron, invited me to appear before the committee to comment on Mather's bill, 'An Act Concerning Reform of the Bail System.' I supported the thrust of the bill, which was designed to eliminate security in advance, but the bill did not go further. One problem that I had in my presentation was that about a week before my appearance I had several wisdom teeth extracted. That would not normally have been a problem, except that my dentist had used my lip as a lever to extract one of the teeth, and as a result I had a large scab on my face. So, just as the spilled of the coffee on my pants may have held back law reform, my disfigured face may have played a similar role.

The subject was taken up by Ontario's McRuer Commission on Civil Rights, which reported in 1968, and by the federal Canadian Committee on Corrections, the Ouimet Committee, which reported in 1969. The Ouimet Committee, named after Quebec Justice Roger Ouimet, was very influential in promoting change. The report's chapter on bail, primarily the work of the great criminal lawyer and later judge, G. Arthur Martin, and assisted by the research director, Desmond Morton, relied heavily on *Detention before Trial*. John Turner, the minister of justice, perhaps prompted by his former executive assistant, my friend Jerry Grafstein, wanted legislation on the subject. In 1971 the *Bail Reform Act* was passed.

I had been part of the team drafting the legislation under the direction of John Scollin of the Department of Justice. Irwin Cotler, the minister's executive assistant and many years later the minister of justice, also played a key role in the drafting. Cotler was as bright and full of ideas then as he still is now, although as far as I can recall he had not yet developed his clipped staccato-style of speech. Various sections of the new act encouraged the police to release accused persons before their first court appearance and discouraged the use of cash bail. Today, as noted University of Toronto criminologist Tony Doob has shown in the 1994 study he did for the committee on systemic racism in Ontario, cash bail is infrequently used. Further, release before the accused's first court appearance is used in almost 25 per cent of indictable offences, although I believe it should be used in even more cases. In part, the increase in release before first court appearance is due to the ability of the police to issue appearance notices and obtain fingerprints without arresting the accused, but also has occurred because the Criminal Code allows a civil action in certain cases if the arrest was not reasonable.

The new act wisely set out a series of steps that the justice of the peace should take in deciding whether or on what terms a person should be released. Before the justice makes an order under one of the act's provisions, the prosecutor must convince the court that each less onerous preceding step is inappropriate under the circumstances. The steps build up from the least onerous, that is, an undertaking without conditions, to a recognizance by the accused without sureties, then to a recognizance with sureties, and so on until one gets to the most serious step – the outright denial of bail. The scheme is a good one, and is an example of a sound legislative solution to a complex issue.

The most important question in drafting the *Bail Reform Act* and in subsequent court cases is, When may an accused be ordered to remain in custody? No one disputes the primary ground, that is, to ensure that the accused shows up for his or her trial. The second ground is more controversial: keeping a person in custody because the person may commit further offences. The problem with this ground is that it assumes that the accused is guilty of the offence with which he or she is charged. In a 1947 English case, for example, the court stated that 'housebreaking particularly is a crime which will very probably be repeated if a prisoner is released on bail.' Nevertheless, keeping a person in custody on such grounds had been the practice in England and Canada for many years.

An early draft of the section that permits the court to deny release favoured the prosecution to too great an extent. A person could be kept in custody to prevent the 'repetition of the offence or the commission of another offence.' Later drafts raised the hurdle the Crown had to get over by referring to the 'danger' of committing an offence, which was then changed to 'likelihood' and, finally, to 'substantial likelihood.' The word 'offence' was also narrowed from committing 'another offence' to committing 'a serious offence,' then to committing 'a serious crime,' and still later to committing 'a crime involving serious harm.' The 1971 act adopted the following language: 'substantial likelihood that the accused will, if he is released from custody, commit a criminal offence involving serious harm.'

The legislation was subsequently interpreted by the courts in a very liberal manner – in keeping with the intention of the *Bail Reform Act*. G. Arthur Martin, who had been appointed a judge of the Ontario Court of Appeal, described the act as 'a liberal and enlightened system of pre-trial release.' The Crown claimed, however, that prosecutors found it difficult to keep dangerous people in custody. As a result, there was a reaction against the section of the act that encouraged courts to release persons. Police officers and their wives attacked the legislation. Twelve hundred wives attended a meeting in Toronto and formed an organization to seek tougher bail laws.

Reverse onuses were unfortunately enacted in the mid-1970s, placing the onus on the accused in a number of situations to prove that he or she should be released, rather than on the Crown to prove that the accused should be kept in custody. The reverse onus, for example, was placed on accused persons in cases involving trafficking in narcotics, which has had the effect of disproportionately targeting certain minorities pending their trials. It was also to apply when the accused was alleged to have committed the offence while released on another charge. Moreover, the words 'criminal offence involving serious harm' were broadened to refer to any 'criminal offence.' Perhaps if the initial legislation had not been quite as favourable to the accused, the reaction would not have been so strong and the present legislation would have been better for accused persons. Sometimes one ends up gaining more by claiming less.

These reverse-onus provisions were upheld under the Charter by the courts. Ontario Court of Appeal Justice G. Arthur Martin stated for the court in 1983:

> In general, under the Code, the onus is on the prosecution to justify the detention of the accused ... However, after some four years of experience with the new legislation, Parliament, in response to concern by some segments of the public ... modified the original legislation by placing the onus on the accused in a limited number of offences ... The reverse onus provision ... is a reasonable limitation [under section 1 of the Charter], even if, *prima facie*, it conflicts with s. 11(e) ['not to be denied reasonable bail without just cause']; and we think that it does not.

The Law Reform Commission of Canada stated in a 1988 working paper that the reverse-onus clauses should be repealed, stating: 'The Commission, in the pursuit of fairness and consistency with *Charter* values, believes that the reversal of the ordinary burdens of proof is unjustified whether at the trial or pre-trial stages of the process.' Nevertheless, additional offences have been added to the reverse-onus list.

The Conservative minority government introduced a bill (Bill C-35) in December 2006 that would extend the reverse-onus provision to certain alleged offences committed with a firearm as well as offences alleged to involve a firearm or ammunition while the accused was prohibited from possessing firearms or ammunition. There had been an unusually high number of gun-related homicides in Toronto in 2005, including the tragic killing of an innocent young woman, Jane Creba, shopping on Yonge Street on Boxing Day. Of course, committing an offence with a firearm is a serious matter, and if there were a danger under the existing law that the accused would flee or would engage in other criminal conduct, the justice of the peace could order the accused to remain in custody. But why reverse the onus? It would again affect certain minority groups. Aboriginals in northern communities, in particular, who need and use firearms, would be caught up in this reverse-onus provision, which would further accentuate their high rates of incarceration. What has to be kept in mind is that being held in custody can affect the finding of guilt or innocence, as well as the sentence received. If there is a reverse onus for guns, then why not a reverse onus for all serious offences? And why not even a reverse burden of proof at the trial itself whenever a person is charged with a serious offence – to carry the logic to an extreme? Nevertheless, it is likely that the opposition parties will support the measure and we may have further extensions of the reverse-onus system whenever another 'crime wave' catches the eye of the public.

In spite of the elimination of the dominance of security in advance, the present system is not working well in Ontario. The pendulum has swung too far in the direction of requiring sureties, rather than using release on one's own undertaking or recognizance. In England, sureties are required in only a small fraction of cases. About two-thirds of those who appear for a bail hearing in Toronto today are required to find sureties, and only about half of this number of persons are actually released. The other half, it appears, could not find acceptable sureties. Fewer than 10 per cent of those held for a bail hearing are released on their own undertaking or recognizance.

What appears to be happening is that the requirement to find sureties has taken the place of cash bail as a method of holding accused persons in custody. Although using sureties is far better than using cash bail, it can create problems. The majority of persons who are caught up in the criminal-justice system, many of whom are not from the community where they are arrested, have difficulty finding sureties. Those deciding whether to release a person on bail impose high hurdles, perhaps thinking that there will be less criticism from the public and the media if they keep people in custody than if they release them, with the consequent risk that the accused will engage in criminal conduct.

A recent Statistics Canada special study on custodial remands in Canada from 1986/7 to 2000/1 confirms that remands in custody for those awaiting trial have almost doubled in Canada in those years from about 68,000 to about 118,500. In Ontario, the daily remand count (that is, the average numbers in custody on remand on any day) increased by 63 per cent from 1991/2 to 2000/1, this at a time when crime rates have generally been dropping. Ontario remands for those awaiting trial constitute well over 40 per cent of all such remands in Canada and are significantly higher than the number of persons eventually convicted and sentenced to custody in Ontario prisons. Comparative provincial figures make one wonder why the custody remands have been going up in Ontario, but down in Quebec. Tony Doob suggests that there may be an increasing number of bail hearings in Ontario because in recent years fewer persons are being released by the police before such a hearing.

Because those awaiting trial have not been convicted and are presumed to be innocent, we must find ways of treating with dignity those held in custody. The suggestion that I made in *Detention before Trial* still makes sense to me: 'If persons must remain in custody pending trial, there is no reason why steps cannot be taken to minimize the punitive aspects of detention by providing special remand centres and not imposing any needless restrictions on activities.' We must be careful not to fall into the state of affairs described by one American writer: 'We first administer the major part of the punishment and then enquire whether [the accused] is guilty.'

There is no question that detention before trial is more punitive than time spent in prison after sentencing. The conditions for those held in pre-trial custody are sufficiently undesirable that judges routinely take off two days from the accused's sentence for every day spent in custody. In some cases the ratio is even three to one – and there are cases where it has been four to one. The 'new' wing of the Don Jail – soon to be torn down – was built in 1958 to hold 240 inmates in individual cells. In recent years there have been over 600 in the jail, with many cells holding three inmates.

Other detention centres that I have visited do not treat accused persons with much greater dignity. I must admit that I played a role in the establishment of the new regional detention centres that were designed to replace the century-old county jails. In 1966 I became a member of the Ontario Minister of Reform Institutions Committee on Regional Detention Centres, headed by Joseph McCulley, the former warden of Hart House who had earlier been the deputy commissioner of penitentiaries. The committee included A.M. Kirkpatrick of the John Howard Society, G. Arthur Martin, and architect Harry B. Kohl. Our 1967 report recommended replacing the existing old county jails with something

more humane, but I do not think any members of the committee contemplated the large overcrowded detention centres and 'superjails' –
some remote from centres of population – that have been built in
Ontario over the years.

A particularly impressive program for trying to keep people from
being held in custody is the Ontario Bail Verification and Supervision
Program, operating in the province since 1979 and now financed by the
Ministry of the Attorney General. It had grown out of a project undertaken by the Toronto Rotary Club shortly after the publication of my
book. In 2001–2 the program verified information on such matters as
the accused's roots in the community on about one-third of the persons
who appeared for bail hearings in the courts in the six Ontario cities
where the program operated. About half of the persons verified were
released under the supervision of the bail program. Unfortunately, the
money usually ran out part-way through each year. The program
deserved greater government support, which has since been forthcoming. Its budget has grown from about $2 million a year to over $6 million and the number of cities involved from six to ten, and will soon
reach about fifteen. Recent statistics show that 80 per cent of those in
the program attend all of their court appearances. One particularly
important statistic is that about 40 per cent of persons in the program
are found not guilty or have their charges withdrawn.

Other techniques that should be considered by the courts include
greater use of electronic monitoring and expediting the trials of persons
released who pose a risk of re-offending.

In early June 2003, I spent a day at the Toronto Old City Hall courts to
try to get an impression of the current working of the bail system. I certainly had a sense of déjà vu. The main bail court for Criminal Code
offences was still in the basement of the building – the same small
cramped room that I remembered from forty years ago. Persons came
directly into the glassed-in prisoners' dock directly from the holding
cells. I did not spot a computer in the room. Everything was still done
with written forms being passed back and forth as if in a story by Kafka.
As in the past, persons sitting in the body of the court could not hear
what was taking place and I was forced to move as close as possible to
the front. The CBC series *This Is Wonderland*, set in the Old City Hall,
accurately captured the atmosphere of the present system. Whether
things have changed since I last visited these courts I leave to others to
discover.

The person heading the drama was – to my surprise – not a provincial court judge, but rather a justice of the peace, the overwhelming majority of whom are not legally trained and who do not in practice seem to enjoy the same degree of independence as provincial court judges. Although the Criminal Code permits justices of the peace to handle bail matters, it does not give them the exclusive jurisdiction to do so. When I did my study over forty years ago, it was the magistrate who set bail and the justices of the peace who handled the details involving the acceptance of cash or sureties. If it is true that a bail hearing is the 'single most important step for an accused person in the criminal process,' then it is strange that a provincial court judge is not dealing with these hearings. In other courtrooms I saw provincial court judges holding preliminary hearings, in general a relatively undemanding and far less crucial step in the criminal process. Surely, it should be justices of the peace who handle preliminary hearings, with provincial court judges handling bail hearings.

In spite of the advances made by the *Bail Reform Act*, the system of detention before trial requires more careful examination than it has been given in recent years.

7

Legal Aid

My work on the bail system led to my involvement with the Ontario committee that had been set up in 1963 to explore what the province should do about legal aid. As with the bail system, there was continuing concern about the effect of poverty on accused persons. It was in 1963 that the Supreme Court of the United States delivered its unanimous landmark decision in *Gideon v. Wainwright* requiring legal representation for indigent accused charged with felonies in state courts – before then, the right only applied in federal courts. That was also the year that the previously mentioned American Attorney General's Committee on Poverty and the Administration of Federal Criminal Justice had stated that 'one of the prime objectives of the civilized administration of justice is to render the poverty of the litigant an irrelevancy.'

The committee was set up by the then Ontario attorney general, Fred Cass, and consisted of three members appointed by the attorney general and three by the Law Society of Upper Canada – hence its name, the Joint Committee on Legal Aid. It was chaired by William B. Common, the deputy attorney general of Ontario, who was also a bencher of the Law Society. At about the same time I was also involved with Bill Common on another committee, the Attorney General's Committee on Securities Legislation, usually called the Kimber Committee, which will be discussed in a later chapter. Bill Common was then close to the retirement age of sixty-five. As with Caesar Wright, he seemed much older to me, and, like Caesar, was a heavy smoker. Whenever I think of

Bill Common I picture him bent over coughing uncontrollably for an awkward period, perhaps fifteen or twenty seconds.

My task was described as follows in the preface to the committee's report: 'We retained Professor Martin L. Friedland of Osgoode Hall Law School to survey the extensive literature on legal aid in England and the United States and also to ascertain if any meaningful statistics existed with respect to legal aid and the need for legal aid in Ontario.' I hired two excellent research assistants, Jim Sharples, who had just graduated from Osgoode Hall Law School, and Maurice Coombs, then attending the school. Our study was submitted in late September 1964.

As I look back, I wonder how I survived that summer. I had two research assistants working on legal aid and at least one working on bail. At the same time, I was doing research for the Kimber committee and worrying about whether I would ever complete my work on double jeopardy. To add to this, Tom, our first born, was about six months old. This was about the time that I had tentative but inconclusive discussions with Charles Dubin about moving back to the practice of law with his firm. It could not be as stressful, I thought, as what I was trying to do as an academic. Fortunately, the various projects were eventually completed. My then colleague at Osgoode Hall Law School, the much-beloved R.J. Gray, used to label my activities 'Friedland Enterprises' and to this day, when I bump into him, asks how 'Friedland Enterprises' is doing.

The inadequacy of legal aid at the time can be illustrated by a discussion of the *Fisher* case, which had occurred several years earlier. I got my call to the bar in April 1960. About a month later, I bumped into one of my former classmates, Joe Pomerant, who said that he had just been assigned a capital murder case. A number of us had been taking unpaid legal-aid cases while we were articling – I had a few such cases, including a relatively serious wounding case – but a capital murder was an entirely different matter. Joe would be the only defence counsel. There was no senior or other counsel assigned to the case. The accused, Louis Fisher, was charged with stabbing to death a woman he had met outside a bar and driven to a deserted parking lot.

Joe was a very effective counsel. He had articled with G. Arthur Martin and then went into practice on his own. He modelled his practice after G. Arthur's. Like Martin, he had an oak-panelled office, with a large wooden desk without drawers. Like Martin, he was usually overweight, and again, like Martin, would take steam baths at the Royal

York Hotel. Joe had been a good student, standing second in first-year law and winning the prizes in property and contracts, but then seemed to lose interest in any course unrelated to the criminal law. I would later occasionally ask him to come to one of my criminal-law classes to discuss one of his current cases. He was always able to evoke sympathy from the students for his client no matter how serious the offence. With passion – and sweating profusely – he would move his intense eyes from student to student. One of the cases he discussed in class was the case of 'K,' who had hugged his wife to death and was acquitted by a jury on a defence of automatism. I noted that some students had tears in their eyes during that class.

The defence in the Fisher case was that the charge should be reduced to manslaughter on the basis of drunkenness. Although Joe provided a vigorous defence, Fisher was convicted after an eight-day trial. Today, of course, with rare exceptions, the trial would be substantially longer. His conviction was upheld by the Ontario Court of Appeal by a 3–2 majority, and then by a unanimous Supreme Court of Canada. Joe was the only counsel for the defence on the appeals. On 27 June 1961 Fisher was hanged in the Don Jail – one of the last executions in Canada. Capital punishment was in practice abolished the following year, although it was not formally abolished by parliament until 1976.

Joe received no fee for the preliminary hearing, for the defence at trial, or for the appeal to the Ontario Court of Appeal. He wrote to the Ontario government before Fisher's appeal to the Supreme Court of Canada, outlining hardship and seeking 'some recompense in the vicinity of $1,200 in order that I may be able to maintain my office, and a minimal income to maintain my family.' The request was refused. The deputy attorney general, W.B. Common – the same Bill Common who would later chair the Joint Committee – wrote in an internal memo: 'To do otherwise, would be a complete departure from the underlying principles of legal aid in this Province and if exceptions are made in individual cases in the County of York, it is hardly fair to the contributors to legal aid in the other Counties and Districts in Ontario who offer their services free of charge.' The Ontario government did, however, agree to cover Joe's living expenses while in Ottawa and continued to pay for the transcripts.

Fisher was hanged in spite of the fact that there is no question that if the conviction took place today and an appeal were brought before the Supreme Court of Canada on the basis of the judge's charge to the jury, the court would order a new trial. The key issue in the Fisher case was drunkenness and drunkenness could then, and can today, reduce murder to manslaughter. Fisher gave evidence claiming that he had drunk twenty to twenty-five glasses of beer in the hours before the killing. Today, a judge would ask the jury whether there was a reasonable doubt about the accused's 'intent' to kill or cause bodily harm.

Unfortunately, all those who took part in the case – the judge, counsel, and the expert witnesses – used the concept of 'capacity to form the intent' to kill, rather than simply 'intent to kill' as the test for whether the charge of murder should be reduced to manslaughter. This was accepted law at the time, derived from the 1920 House of Lords case of *DPP v. Beard* and later accepted by the 1931 Supreme Court of Canada case of *MacAskill v. The King*. The Crown's expert testified in cross-examination that 'a person could drink up to 25 bottles of beer over the course of an evening' and still have 'the capacity to form the intent.' The judge and defence counsel did not seem to realize that there was a difference between 'capacity' and 'intent' – that a person could have the capacity to form the intent, but not actually have the intent.

Like others, I also did not at that time grasp the significance of the difference between intent and capacity. I asked a psychiatrist friend, Diz Disenhouse – one of the medical students whom I accompanied on their search for internships in California – how a psychiatrist could possibly have testified that a person had the capacity to form the intent after drinking twenty-five bottles of beer. He pointed out the obvious, that one could have the capacity to form the intent and yet not have the intent. I wonder whether the Crown counsel, Arthur Klein, or the psychiatrist, N.L. Easton, also had recognized the distinction.

Today, it is clear law that the concept of capacity should not be used as the test for drunkenness. Indeed, the Supreme Court of Canada unanimously held in a 1996 case that the 'common law rule which limits the defence of intoxication to the capacity of an accused to form the specific intent is contrary to sections 7 [fundamental justice] and 11(d) [fair trial] of the *Charter*.' The Ontario Court of Appeal had changed the common-law rule even before the enactment of the Charter. Justice John Morden, who was a year behind us at law school, was a member of the court that decided one of those earlier cases. His father, Kenneth Morden, coincidentally, had been part of the majority on the court that decided against Fisher almost twenty years earlier.

A new trial would also be ordered today because the trial judge in the Fisher case would not allow the accused to combine evidence of drunkenness with evidence of provocation or mental disorder to decide whether the offence should be reduced from murder to manslaughter. There was some evidence for both defences. Today, the Ontario Court of Appeal has made it clear that all these defences can be used together to determine whether the accused had the requisite intent.

In the mid-1970s, Joe Pomerant's personal life and his practice started falling apart. Signs of this became evident during the famous Demeter murder case in which he and Eddie Greenspan unsuccessfully defended Peter Demeter against a charge that he had murdered his wife, Christine. Joe was later disbarred and convicted of misappropriating more than half a million dollars from an international drug dealer he had been defending. He was sentenced to five years in prison. A number of us visited him in the medium-security Warkworth Institution, not far from Peterborough, Ontario. Joe had unrealistic expectations of his future. He was sure that the novel he was writing in prison would make him rich. When Joe got out of prison he tried to be reinstated without success. He would visit his classmates from time to time and showed up at several reunions. I had not heard from him for several years when he called in the fall of 2005 to arrange a lunch with Harry and me to celebrate the fiftieth anniversary of our entering law school. We met in the Coffee Mill in Yorkville. Joe had not changed. He still had unrealistic dreams of striking it rich. Who knows, he may succeed. I have always wondered what role the Fisher case played in Joe's career. Having one's first major client hang must have taken its toll.

One of the most dramatic changes in the criminal-justice system since the early 1960s has been in the growth of legal aid. In 1963 the Ontario government contributed only $20,000 to assist the Law Society to administer the scheme for criminal matters. Today, in contrast, Legal Aid Ontario has a budget of about $300 million, with perhaps about half of the money going to fund criminal matters through certificate programs, clinics, staff lawyers, and duty counsel. Legal aid now covers the legal expenses of close to 30 per cent of persons charged with criminal offences, and a much higher percentage of persons charged with indictable offences. In 1963, by contrast, as our research showed, only about 10 per cent of persons charged in Ontario – about 1500 persons in total – received any form of legal aid in criminal matters. Only one person out of six in Ontario who required legal aid or advice in criminal matters was receiving it. Further, over 95 per cent of all persons who appeared in custody for their first court appearance and pleaded guilty did not have a lawyer.

The Joint Committee reported to the attorney general in 1965 and recommended that a new legal-aid plan be brought in to replace the voluntary plan that had been in operation since 1951. It should, the committee stated, be administered by the Law Society of Upper Canada and be paid for by the provincial government. The report rejected an American-style public-defender system and opted for the English-style judicare model, whereby indigent accused persons could choose private counsel paid for by the legal-aid scheme.

The committee did not think much of the public-defender model, stating: 'It has never been seriously considered in England. It has been rejected in Scotland. There is moreover almost no support for the idea in Ontario.' 'The chief advantage of the public defender system,' the committee stated, 'is that it is cheap.' 'On the other hand,' the committee went on to say, 'the system appears to be wrong in principle in that both prosecutor and defender are employed by the same master. Observation of the system in action tends to support the fear that defences will become perfunctory, that little attention can be given to the run-of-the-mill case, that the entire scheme operates on an impersonal production-line basis, and that its overall effectiveness is not impressive.'

I had been less critical of the public-defender system in the study I prepared for the committee, although I recognized the potential dangers. The greater the independence of the agency running the plan, I argued, the less the concern about the independence of counsel. The final sentence of my study suggested a combination of the public-defender and the judicare systems. It was my preferred model, but I had to put it forward in a somewhat gentle fashion, because it was not my job to make such recommendations. I stated: 'One possible plan which should be carefully considered is to utilize the remunerated assigned counsel system throughout the Province, but to use full-time employees of the Law Society in all medium and large-sized urban centres to administer the plan, to offer advice to accused persons, and to handle the defence of relatively uncomplicated cases in the magistrates' courts.'

Perhaps because my view of the public-defender system was far less critical than that of the committee, they objected to the distribution of my study. Although they were generous in their acknowledgment of my work in their report and filed my study with their report to the attorney general, they did not want it otherwise distributed. I objected. I was an academic and one's academic work, I argued, should be made available. The issue of my study's distribution had not been discussed when I took on the task. In the end, a compromise was reached. The study could be sent to law libraries, but not otherwise distributed. From that time on, whenever I undertook similar assignments I would normally negotiate the right to publish, often after a reasonable time delay. In a number of cases, such as my study for the Somalia inquiry and my study for the McDonald Commission on national security, the commission decided, for their own purposes, to publish the study in advance of the publication of their report. Academics, I believe, have a duty to try to ensure that their work is available to other scholars.

This is not the place to give a detailed history of legal aid in Canada. That task remains to be done. The plan kept expanding. The office of duty counsel, for example, was established to offer advice, handle routine pretrial motions, and conduct guilty pleas for indigent persons. Various legal clinics were established throughout Ontario. The clinic system was strongly supported in reports by Justice John Osler in 1974 and Justice Sam Grange in 1978. There are now about eighty such clinics, including those run by students at law schools throughout Ontario.

In 1971 Osgoode Hall Law School established a major clinic in the Parkdale area of Toronto, where students could get credit for a term for working in the clinic. The University of Toronto chose not to follow that route, although in those years Parkdale normally kept a few places open for U of T students. When I became dean at the U of T law school in 1972 I strongly supported the growth of the student legal-aid program. At first the student work was strictly on a voluntary basis, without academic credit. I recall that Steve Grant, John B. Laskin, Barb Jackman, and Rob Prichard – among many others – invested a great amount of their energy in the organization without academic credit. The Law School hired Dick Gathercole to run the program and to teach a course in poverty law. (He later left for British Columbia and became the executive director of the BC Public Interest Advocacy Centre.) It was not until the 1980s that academic credit was given for students taking part in the work of the clinic.

The students had been operating out of cramped quarters in Flavelle House before 1972. We arranged for space on the main floor in the adjoining Falconer Hall, which we had just acquired, but with the growth of the student legal-aid program the space became less and less adequate for the clinic. Clients had no place to wait before meeting with members of the clinic. I wanted to find a proper home for the clinic and arranged with the student directors for it to be housed in a stone coach house and another similar building next to the former meteorological building at the corner of Bloor Street and Devonshire Place that the University made available to us. Some of the clinic's student directors were, however, suspicious of my motives, thinking that I was trying to isolate the clinic, and so they refused the University's offer. The students, who were products of the turbulent 1960s, were some of the more radical students at the law school. I recall, for example, one motion at faculty council proposed by one of the legal-aid directors, who later became the managing partner of one of Toronto's most prestigious law firms, that all lawyers and secretaries at the clinic should be paid the same amount. He no doubt later abandoned that view. The clinic ended up in the Students' Administrative Council building on the west side of St George Street, now part of the Bahen Centre. The clinic eventually acquired its own house on Spadina Avenue – the Fasken Legal Services Building. I still think that the site we had chosen near St George and Bloor was a good one. It was close to the law school and at the intersection of two major subway lines.

The cost to the province of the legal-aid plan kept expanding. In its first year of operation, the plan cost $4 million, and by the end of the next year the cost was $7 million. By 1973 the provincial government's contribution alone was close to $14 million. And it kept growing. Not only were costs rising, but in the early 1990s the federal government started capping its contribution to legal aid. There were no limits on the provincial government's fiscal responsibility, however. It was an open-ended system. The province would simply cover the amount exceeding the annual budget. Between 1980 and 1990 costs increased by 500 per cent and between 1990 and 1995 they increased again by almost 100 per cent. Costs had risen over the previous ten years, 1985 to 1995, from about $75 million to about $350 million.

A crisis developed when the Ontario government announced at the end of the fiscal year 1993–4 that it would no longer cover the almost $40 million deficit that the plan had accumulated that year. A debate took place within the Law Society on whether it should keep the plan. It voted that it should, but continued to struggle to contain costs.

In December 1996 a review committee was established by Attorney General Charles Harnick, with Osgoode Hall Law School professor John McCamus as its chair. My colleague Michael Trebilcock was selected as the director of research. I was asked to prepare a study on the governance of legal-aid schemes. Those preparing papers for the review received drafts of the other papers and met on several occasions to discuss the papers. It was one of the most effective committees with which I have ever been associated. I had two excellent research assistants over the summer of 1996, both of whom had been in my first-year criminal-law class that year: Graham Rawlinson, now a lawyer with Torys, and Katrina Wyman, who is teaching at New York University School of Law. They were joined for part of the summer by a former student, Rob Brush, now with Groia & Company.

The study we prepared for the McCamus committee examined governance structures for legal aid in other jurisdictions as well as the governance of other institutions that receive government money, such as universities and hospitals. A series of criteria, such as independence, accountability, and efficiency, were set out in the study to judge various models of governance. One of the more important criteria was 'innovation and experimentation.' We asked a series of questions. Would the Law Society, which 'seems to be wedded to the judicare system [be open to innovation and experimentation]? ... Will the Law Society innovate and experiment with different models which may be necessary to find the best mix of delivery systems? ... Encourage competition between the various systems? ... Welcome the use of bulk contracts? ... Welcome an increased use of paralegals?' We doubted the commitment of the Law Society to engage in extensive innovation and experimentation. The governance of the legal-aid plan, our study concluded, 'should no longer reside with the Law Society,' even though it may have been an appropriate model in earlier times.

The McCamus review came to similar conclusions and the government brought in legislation, the *Legal Aid Services Act*, in 1998 setting up a semi-independent body named Legal Aid Ontario. The first chair was Justice Sidney Linden, who in the past has led the way in many areas involving the administration of justice. The McCamus report recommended greater use of staff lawyers for both trial and appellate advocacy, bulk contracts, and greater case management.

Thus far, the Ontario plan has increased its use of case management, but has not used bulk contracts, and has used staff lawyers very sparingly. Only four small staff lawyer offices have been set up. This is a step in the right direction, but the bar has been very concerned about this development and Legal Aid Ontario has been moving cautiously. Some provinces, such as Nova Scotia and Saskatchewan, use almost pure staff models. Others, such as British Columbia, Manitoba, and Quebec, use a mixed system of judicare and staff lawyers. I still think that more use should be made of staff lawyers. Duty counsel are now used successfully in Ontario for bail and plea courts, and there is no reason why they could not be as effective for trial courts. If reasonable pay levels were provided – perhaps similar to those of crown attorneys – talented criminal lawyers would be prepared to work for Legal Aid Ontario for part of their careers.

Most lawyers, including this one, believe that more money should be provided for legal aid. Whether this will occur along with the other legitimate demands for public funding, such as health care and education, is another matter. In a capped system, the money has to come from within the budget. One hopeful development was that the federal government under the Liberals started to take a renewed interest in legal aid. The provincial-territorial justice ministers met with the then federal minister of justice, Irwin Cotler, in early 2005 and the government indicated that there would be money specifically dedicated to civil legal aid, which would have the effect of freeing up more provincial money for criminal legal aid. The provinces would, of course, also like the federal government to share criminal legal aid equally with them, but it is unlikely that this will come about because the federal government will not want to go back to the system of open-ended shared costs. The Harper government, up to this point, has not shown a similar interest in legal aid.

The plan, unfortunately, will not likely be able to handle all the demands it faces. Today, legal aid is not given to those who are unlikely to be incarcerated. This is unfortunate. For most offences, first offenders are unlikely to receive a prison sentence and so do not receive legal-aid certificates. Yet this is a group that deserves special attention to ensure that innocent persons are not convicted and receive their first criminal record. Before 1995, Ontario would grant a certificate if a conviction would result in a loss of livelihood, even if it did not result in incarceration. This gave greater flexibility to the legal-aid system because it is usually not difficult to say that a conviction may result in a loss of livelihood. The McCamus report recommended that risk of incarceration be replaced by a more flexible system, as did the Criminal Justice Review – a provincial task force with which I was closely associated – in its 1999 report.

If further funding is not given to the plan, some hard choices will have to be made. Should there be, for example, separate representation on *all* issues for *all* persons charged in a conspiracy to import drugs? Ideally, yes, but this takes away funds needed for others. Should legal aid pay for all Charter arguments for accused persons who have been granted a legal-aid certificate or should there be some peer review through legal aid of the merits of the arguments? Should persons with lengthy criminal records, to take another example, be able to use public funds to contest *every* aspect of a charge? The Joint Committee on Legal Aid felt that the legal-aid system should have the discretion to refuse legal aid for the 'professional criminal' where the application for legal aid is 'without merit.' Representation should, however, not automatically be denied, because as I stated in the study done for the Joint Committee, 'it is often those who have previous convictions who are victims of suspicious circumstances and who are therefore most in need of counsel.' At some point in their criminal careers, however, Chevrolet rather than Cadillac treatment should be provided in order to increase the coverage for others. As in the health-care system, finding the most effective allocation of scarce resources will have to be carefully explored by the legal-aid system – and ultimately by the courts.

Legal Aid Ontario has again been running out of funds. In the fall of 2006 Attorney General Michael Bryant asked John McCamus, who had headed the earlier committee, to investigate the issue once again. Some of the questions raised above may be explored by McCamus.

8

Criminal Courts

Another by-product of my work on bail was that I was invited to do a study on magistrates' courts for the Ouimet Committee, which had been established in June 1965 by Guy Favreau, the federal minister of justice, to study corrections in Canada. Justice Roger Ouimet of the Quebec Superior Court was selected as the chair of the committee, with respected criminal defence lawyer G. Arthur Martin as the vice-chair. Desmond Morton, who had been my colleague at Osgoode Hall Law School and who had recently returned to Osgoode from his disappointing stint as Regius Professor of Law at his *alma mater*, Trinity College Dublin, was named as the committee's 'research associate.'

The committee's terms of reference were very broad. They were 'to study the broad field of corrections, in its widest sense, from the initial investigation of an offence through to the final discharge of a prisoner from imprisonment or parole, including such steps and measures as arrest, summonsing, bail, representation in Court, conviction, probation, sentencing, training, medical and psychiatric attention, release, parole, pardon, post-release supervision and guidance and rehabilitation.' As if that were not wide enough, the committee was subsequently asked to make recommendations on the design of maximum-security prisons.

Its final report, entitled *Toward Unity: Criminal Justice and Corrections*, was published in March 1969. Although the committee had been established by the minister of justice, the report was delivered to the solicitor general because in 1966 the Department of Justice had been split in two and the responsibility for policing and corrections had been transferred to the new Department of the Solicitor General.

The Ouimet report did not deal with the substantive criminal law. Rather, it recommended that the federal government establish another body 'to examine the substantive criminal law.' A few years later – as will be discussed in a later chapter – the Law Reform Commission of Canada was established to take on that task.

No previous study of the criminal process in Canada had been as comprehensive, effective, and influential as the Ouimet report. A great number of the committee's recommendations subsequently were adopted by the federal and provincial governments. Studies completed earlier in the century had been much narrower in focus. The 1938 Archambault report on the penal system of Canada was restricted to federal penal institutions and the 1956 Fauteux report dealt primarily with what is now called the parole system. A 1952 report that had led to the important 1953 revision of the Criminal Code was more in the nature of a housekeeping operation.

My involvement with the committee began with a call from its vice-chair, G. Arthur Martin – probably in December 1966 – asking if I would be interested in doing a study on magistrates' courts. I expressed an interest in the project and followed up an invitation in January 1967 from Justice Ouimet to do a project 'examining the adverse effects of overcrowded dockets and inadequate court room facilities in the administration of justice' by saying that the 'subject is one of great importance and one that particularly interests me.' I agreed to do the study for $50 a day, a third of the amount I was being paid for work I was doing at the same time for the federal government on securities legislation. That is what they offered and because I wanted to do the study I did not seek a higher rate. I have found that in general the more one wants to do a study, the lower the rate of pay. Fair enough.

The draft contract finally arrived in April, a delay due to problems they were having in bringing the provinces on side. The administration of criminal justice is a provincial matter under the *British North America Act* and most provinces jealously protect their turf. Ouimet told me not to start the study 'until such time as our Committee is in a position to advise you of the cooperation of the Deputy Attorneys General of the different Provinces in view of the fact that no finger should be pointed at any particular province and that our Committee's comments would be general and refer to Canada as a whole.'

I made one change in the terms of the proposed contract, which said that the committee had the 'full right to publish in whole or in part, with or without additions, deletions or changes, any interim or final report emanating from you ... with or without acknowledging the author or authors.' Not wanting to be in the same position as I had found myself in when I did the legal-aid study, I wanted the right to publish an article in my own name based on my work at some time in the future. Arthur Martin, with whom I negotiated the amendment, agreed. So the contract was changed to allow me to publish my study 'after the publication of the committee's report or Sept. 1, 1968 whichever is the first.' At the time, September 1968 was about a year and a half away and the date did not seem unreasonable. More on this below.

I hired Dan Webster, now a senior litigator with Bull, Housser & Tupper in Vancouver, who was then just completing second-year law school. We collected as much secondary literature as we could find, as well as annual reports and other documents from police forces and courts across the country. Statistics Canada was improving its output of data, but it was still not as useful as one would have liked, particularly compared to today.

In the late summer I visited the major cities in Western Canada, and also made a side trip to San Francisco, where I looked at a number of new court houses, especially a circular courtroom designed by Frank Lloyd Wright in Marin County. In the fall, I travelled to the Maritimes. I recall the Halifax courthouse overlooking a cemetery, which must have had a sobering effect on accused persons, and a courtroom in St John's, Newfoundland, where Joey Smallwood, I was told, had carved his barely recognizable name on a desk. In each place I met with government officials, judges, and lawyers and spent time observing the functioning of the magistrates' courts. I also sampled the varied cuisine across the country. I have a vivid memory of eating, for the first time, steak tartare – raw ground beef – in a bistro near the Montreal courthouse with a leading defence lawyer, later a superior court judge, René Letarte.

My family accompanied me on the western trip, which did not assist my research, but did result in a picture of me sitting on a horse holding three-year-old Tommy and one-year-old Jenny, with Lake Louise in the background. A picture taken two years later in Sri Lanka (then Ceylon) while I was on sabbatical leave was similar, except an elephant was substituted for the horse. Both Tom and Jenny are lawyers, so perhaps this early exposure to legal research played a role in their careers.

I submitted the study to the Ouimet Committee in early April 1968, having met with the committee in Ottawa in late February to discuss my proposed report. I had given a preview of my ideas at a Canadian Bar Association meeting earlier in February. 'Abolish magistrates' courts, revise system, U of T law professor urges,' was the *Globe and Mail*'s headline for the story. I had suggested that magistrates should have legal training and that the magistrates' courts be merged with the county and supreme courts to form a unified criminal court. The proposal appeared to be well received, although the *Globe* reported that the 'sole burst of applause' at the meeting occurred when the president of the Ontario Magistrates Association, Magistrate Walter Tuchtie, said that 'legally untrained magistrates could sentence a man to life, while supreme courts dealing mainly with divorce and automobile negligence – "dollars" – had to have legal training.'

Justice Ouimet thanked me for the study, stating: 'I wish to thank you wholeheartedly for your very interesting workpaper on Magistrates' Courts – Functioning and Facilities. It will be extremely useful to our Committee and is presently being circulated among the Members. I may add that I was glad to see that you did not hesitate to include a touch of humour which, I am sure, will be fully appreciated.'

I made arrangements for the study to be published in the December 1968 issue of the *Criminal Law Quarterly*. I sent a note to Ouimet in early November telling him about the plan to publish the article in the *Quarterly* – permissible under the contract. I explained that I had decided to publish at this time 'because I will be out of the country on Sabbatical leave from December until the end of next summer and because I wanted the material to be useful in the current discussions on the construction of magistrates' courts across Canada.' I added that 'it appears likely that the *Globe and Mail* will reprint part of the study on page 7.'

I had sent an advance copy of the draft article to Richard Doyle, the editor of the *Globe*, who had been instrumental in arranging the publication of excerpts from my bail study several years earlier. As it turned out, he wanted to publish the whole article, in three separate op-ed pieces. Alan Mewett, the distinguished editor of the *Criminal Law Quarterly*, had no objection to its prior publication, provided the *Quarterly* was mentioned in an appropriate way. Mewett moved from Osgoode Hall to the University of Toronto in 1969 and was a wonderful colleague and a favourite of the students. At his retirement a former student stated that he 'could always be counted on to make the mundane interesting and difficult understandable.' He died in 2001 at the age of seventy, leaving a lasting legacy in the field of criminal law and evidence and through the editorship of the *Quarterly*, which he edited for thirty years until Kent Roach took over in 1998.

The *Globe* followed the three excerpts with a lead editorial under the heading 'Recipe for justice: a proper shaking up,' stating: 'In three articles in The Globe and Mail this week University of Toronto Law School Professor M.L. Friedland gave an exciting foretaste of the quality of analysis we may hope will come from the almost forgotten Canadian Committee on Corrections.' The editorial looked favourably on the concept of a unified criminal court, stating: 'Perhaps none of Prof. Friedland's proposals cuts more deeply into judicial reform than the idea he offers, with reservations, to "abolish the present court structure and the distinction between the jurisdiction of the magistrate and supreme and county courts" ... Professor Friedland's willingness to turn the whole court system on end should be of immense value to the committee which must be concerned with far more than a patchwork transformation of our correctional system.'

Unfortunately, Ouimet did not receive my letter until about ten days after it was sent – the very day that the first excerpt appeared. The letter had been sent in error to the committee's earlier address, then forwarded on to its new address. Ouimet and the committee were understandably upset to have been taken by surprise. The committee, Ouimet informed me on 20 November – the day before the *Globe* editorial appeared – 'were none too pleased with this unexpected publication, and although, strictly speaking, you adhered to the letter of your contract, the general reaction was that they would have appreciated the courtesy of a friendly discussion before you decided to make public your report to our Committee.' 'The reasons expressed in your letter of November 7,' Ouimet went on to say, 'explain the haste with which you proceeded, but the Minister and Governmental authorities may eventually choose to follow our recommendations rather than yours, if we happen to differ!' As it turned out, the committee dealt with my central recommendation on a unified criminal court by ignoring it. One wonders if the committee might have been more inclined to support the recommendation had my letter to Ouimet arrived before the first excerpt appeared.

In my report to the committee, I painted a depressing picture of the magistrates' courts across the country, stating that the court was 'the forgotten child of our system of criminal justice.' 'For the most part,' I wrote, 'the lower courts in the larger urban centres in Canada operate with neither dignity nor efficiency, yet both these qualities are essential to any well-conceived system of justice. A certain degree of dignity is necessary to promote respect for the law and the administration of justice and to create an atmosphere which will help ensure that the rights of the individual are not forgotten. Efficiency helps to conserve much-needed resources and tends to prevent the congestion which in turn militates against the maintenance of a dignified system.'

I identified a number of key problems. One was the often close relationship between the courts and the police. The court was generally referred to as a 'police court.' In most of the principal cities in the West and the Maritimes the police and the magistrates' courts occupied the same building, sometimes euphemistically described as a 'public safety building.' The police liked it that way. One chief of police in a large Canadian city stated in his annual report: 'When apprehension, detention and Magistrate's level of prosecution are conjoined, efficiency of operation in these fields is at its peak.'

Another problem was that because the magistrates' courts had been for the most part a municipal responsibility, a coordinated provincial policy, with adequate funding, was difficult to develop. At about the time I was conducting my study, the provinces across the country were moving to centralize the administration of the criminal courts. In Ontario, for example, the McRuer Commission on Civil Rights played an important role in bringing this about. I might add that the centralization that subsequently took place in Ontario was partially reversed in the 1990s when the Harris government returned the administration of the courts presided over by justices of the peace to municipalities. Toronto was the last municipality to accept this devolution.

The physical facilities of magistrates' courts were for the most part deplorable. In one court in Vancouver, for example, one had to walk through the morgue to get to the courtroom. 'In many courts,' I wrote, 'the only way of providing any ventilation ... is to open the windows, bringing in outside noise and making it difficult to hear what is going on inside the courtroom. This is a choice faced by many courts: whether to hear or to breathe.' This was probably an example of the 'touch of humour' that caught Ouimet's eye. It was used without change in the Ouimet report itself, as were most of the factual findings in my study.

I commented on the design of criminal court buildings, stating: 'Perhaps the first obvious deficiency in design is the too common difficulty of finding the specific courtroom one is looking for – assuming that one has found the proper court building. In many cases there are no visible directions when one enters the building and one is forced to ask a somewhat unobliging clerk where the court is. When there is more than one courtroom in which a case might be tried, it is usually difficult to decipher the posted court list, particularly when there are a great many other persons crowded around the area where the list is posted.' There was – and still is – also the problem of requiring everyone to show up at the same time in the morning, even though cases could not all be dealt with at that time. Dentists, I pointed out, did not require all their patients for that day to show up at nine in the morning.

The study contained ideas on possible shapes of courtrooms – oval, round, and angular – in addition to noting the traditional designs. There was a discussion of the height of the bench and that of the ceiling. A high bench is intimidating and a high ceiling costly. The bench, I thought, should be high enough to permit the judge to be seen and heard and to control the proceedings, but not so high as to be unnecessarily intimidating. I suggested that it be a couple of steps above the body of the court. With respect to height of the ceiling, which can affect the dignity of the court, I drew attention to the then new courthouses in Burnaby, BC, and St Boniface, Manitoba, where skylights were effectively used to provide height and light for the important working area.

As stated earlier, in order to get provincial cooperation for the study, the Ouimet Committee had an understanding with the provinces that I would not criticize individual jurisdictions. My files on the Ouimet Committee contain a letter from the deputy attorney general of Saskatchewan to the committee, stating, 'Mr. Justice Ouimet advised that any report made would not refer in any way to specific cities and provinces, nor any fact given which would enable a reader to know what is referred to.' 'I assume,' he went on to say, 'that this also means that there are not going to be any general statements made that there is such overcrowding and inadequate courtroom facilities in all provinces which would amount to saying that there was overcrowding in Saskatchewan. I do not consider that there is any overcrowding or inadequate courtroom facilities for our magistrates' courts in the cities of Saskatchewan.'

I guess I did not agree with that assumption (although I was careful not to single out individual provinces) because I stated that 'I found a pattern of consistent (though not shocking) delay in almost all of the

Magistrates' Courts in the larger centres in Canada.' Viewed from today's perspective, however, the delay then does not appear very serious. 'In the cases in which both the Crown and defence wished the case to proceed,' I noted, 'there were periods of delay ranging from approximately two weeks to two months.' By today's standards this was speedy justice.

In the 1990s, as will be discussed in a later chapter, I had an opportunity to revisit the criminal courts across the country in connection with my study on judicial independence and accountability for the Canadian Judicial Council. The physical facilities had clearly improved. In my report, *A Place Apart: Judicial Independence and Accountability in Canada*, I noted that the 'present funding system, whatever its defects, has over the past few decades been reasonably good to the judiciary.' I referred to my visits many years earlier for the Ouimet Committee, noting that I had found at that earlier time 'a grim picture.' 'On my visits to courts across the country in connection with the [judicial independence] project,' I stated in *A Place Apart*, 'I was impressed with the facilities for the courts in almost every major city I visited.' There are indications, however, that since my last tour of the courts, physical facilities across the country have been deteriorating. Moreover, the decrease in funding for legal aid, described in an earlier chapter, and the proposed closing of courts in some provinces will cause an increase in the problems in the provincial courts.

The last part of my study for the Ouimet Committee looked at the problem of the status of the magistracy, which, I concluded, 'is at a low level in Canada today.' 'This is a matter of great concern,' I went on, 'because a judicial officer who does not engender respect cannot hope to have the law which he is applying respected. The provision of adequate court facilities and the elimination of the congestion described in the previous sections would no doubt help in raising the status.' I then turned to the status of the judicial officer, stating: 'Ensuring reasonable pay, requiring that all magistrates be lawyers, and designating them as "judges" – steps which have now been taken by a number of provinces – will significantly improve the image of the magistrate. Increasing magistrates' salaries will help attract better men. Requiring that they be lawyers will help to ensure that proper justice will be administered.' The reader will note that the quotes from 1968 are not gender-neutral. This was the standard way of writing at the time, and there were, in fact, very few female judges in Ontario in those days.

Then came the controversial part: 'These changes are very important,' I wrote: 'But they are not enough. A fundamental change in the
position of the magistrate in the judicial hierarchy is necessary. He now
suffers from an inferiority complex because the Criminal Code puts
him in an inferior position by treating him as a third class judge – below
the Supreme and County Court judge.' An example of the inferior status of the magistrate, I noted, was the *trial de novo* procedure set out in
the code and later repealed, which permitted either the accused or the
Crown to appeal from a magistrate's decision in a summary conviction
case and have a complete rehearing of the case by a county court judge.

'The most desirable solution,' I wrote, 'would be to abolish the
present court structure and the distinction between the jurisdiction of
the magistrate and Supreme and County Courts, and to give all those
trying criminal cases concurrent jurisdiction, equal status and equal
pay ... Whatever may have been the justification for the grades of trial
courts in the past (when the magistrate was, in fact, dealing with minor
cases, as in England where to a great extent he still does), it has long
since disappeared in Canada where the magistrate deals with many
serious offences for which an accused can be sentenced by the magistrate to life imprisonment.' It will be recalled that the audience broke
out in applause when Magistrate Walter Tuchtie made this point at the
bar association meeting in February 1968.

The proposed scheme set out in my study was very simple. The
exclusive jurisdiction of the superior courts and the absolute jurisdiction of the magistrates' court should be eliminated and all judicial officers should have concurrent jurisdiction to try all offences, with or
without a jury, in a court perhaps simply called the Criminal Court for
the particular province.

I would have excluded from the new criminal court, partly for political reasons, capital offences, which would continue to be tried by a
supreme court judge and jury. I would also have excluded the very
minor offences that should be tried by another tribunal not necessarily
presided over by a legally trained person. The key question was where
to draw the line for these minor offences. The division between summary and indictable offences obviously draws it at too high a level
because of the potential seriousness of summary-conviction offences.
Perhaps the soundest solution, I suggested, would be simply that for
certain offences (perhaps the present indictable offences) the accused
would have to be tried in the criminal court, and for other offences
could not be sent to jail or fined over a certain low amount unless tried

in the criminal court. Thus the seriousness of the offence, judged by the prosecutor, would determine the court in which the accused would be tried. I added a caveat, however, giving the accused the right to have his or her case tried in the criminal court.

An accused, according to my scheme, would be tried, according to his or her election, either with or without a jury by the first judicial officer who was available, whether it was a superior court judge, a county court judge, or a provincially appointed judge of the criminal court. There was no practical reason why the provincially appointed judge could not also take jury cases, although it is arguable that there were constitutional difficulties. 'After all,' I stated, 'if he is not competent to charge a jury he should not be considered competent to charge himself.'

The proposal was in line with American ideas with respect to the judiciary. The American Bar Association's Model State Judicial Article of 1962, for example, provided for a unified trial court of limited jurisdiction. The American Bar Association Committee commented: 'It is contemplated to set up ... a single, unified judicial system with a single court of original jurisdiction. This follows the recommendation of advocates of judicial reform from Pound to Vanderbilt.' Similarly, the influential report of the President's Commission on Law Enforcement and Administration of Justice concluded in 1967 that 'all criminal cases should be tried by judges of equal status under generally comparable procedures.'

I did not anticipate serious constitutional problems, except perhaps with respect to jury trials. Such a scheme, I speculated, would simply require complementary federal and provincial legislation. The federal government would have to alter radically the court structure set out in the Criminal Code. The provinces would have to enact legislation to make their magistrates as much like federally appointed judges as possible; for example, by designating them as judges, increasing their pay, providing against their removal without just cause, and assuring adequate pensions that did not depend upon the length of service. Quebec, I noted, had gone part-way towards unification. There, the position of the magistrate and the criminal jurisdiction of the county court judge trying cases without a jury were consolidated into the position of district court judge, with all jury trials conducted by a superior court judge.

The study was well received, as the quotes set out earlier in this chapter from the *Globe* editorial indicate. It did not get as good a response in some quarters. *Justice Weekly*, for example, a sensational tabloid that followed court proceedings and thus, as noted earlier, escaped prosecution for obscenity, introduced its analysis with the comment: 'A LEMON BY ANY OTHER NAME.' It did not think much of the idea of requiring that magistrates be lawyers, stating: 'Naturally the professor WANTS ONLY LAWYERS AS PROVINCIAL judges ... seeing that he is a professor in a law school. BUT OUR EXPERIENCE HAS BEEN – and it is a longer one than the professor's ... – that LAYMEN-MAGISTRATES on the whole were as good and OFTEN MUCH BETTER than lawyer-magistrates.' (All capitalization in the original.) It concluded its observations by stating: 'As for jurists having "AN INFERIORITY COMPLEX," as the professor suggests, he must be referring to other [than] the numerous magistrates we have known down through the years – and still know.'

As stated above, the Ouimet Committee's report, published in 1969, accepted most of the suggestions in my study for improving the functioning and facilities of the magistrates' courts, but carefully avoided mentioning unification of the courts. I learned then, if I had not known it before, that superior court judges – and Ouimet was a superior court judge – are generally not enthusiastic about what they consider a dilution of the status of the superior court by expanding its numbers. The same concern was evident a number of years later when recommendations were made by various committees and commissions, such as the Zuber Commission in Ontario in 1987, that the county court be merged with the supreme court. That merger has now been accomplished throughout Canada and is now so well established that I doubt if very many persons would want to re-establish the county court system. Persons such as chief justice of Canada Beverley McLachlin and former chief justice of the Ontario Superior Court Patrick LeSage started their judicial careers as county court judges.

The Law Reform Commission of Canada was established in 1971. The unification of the criminal courts was a natural subject of interest for the commission, of which I was one of the initial commissioners. One of its senior staff members, Darrell Roberts – now a leading counsel in British Columbia – prepared a study paper on the classification of offences and the structure of the criminal courts. Roberts concluded that a unified criminal court was desirable. The commission, however, never went further at that time to prepare a working paper or a report on the subject. Both the chair and the vice-chair of the Law Reform Commission were superior court judges, which may have influenced the decision not to proceed further with the topic.

New Brunswick had a strong interest in a unified criminal court, although it is not clear why such a court was attractive in that province. Perhaps it was because New Brunswick superior court judges heard relatively few criminal cases and missed that interesting aspect of judging. With a unified criminal court they would be able to hear more such cases. Why accused persons were not electing trial by a higher court is also not clear. My guess is that the fee structure of the legal-aid system would help explain it. If legal aid limits the amount that can be claimed for a preliminary hearing, there is less incentive for a lawyer to seek a trial in a higher court. It may also be because of a difference in sentencing practices in the two courts, with heavier penalties imposed in the higher court for comparable cases.

When I did my study on judicial independence for the Canadian Judicial Council in the mid-1990s, I saw first-hand why a unified criminal court was desirable in New Brunswick. Whenever I had a spare moment I would drop into one of its courts to try to get a flavour of what was happening. In Fredericton and Moncton I found the provincial court judges busy with interesting criminal cases, while the superior court judges seemed to be spending their time on small-claims civil cases. Perhaps the couple of days I was in the province were not representative of the true picture, but I note that Carl Baar in his 1991 study for the Canadian Judicial Council confirmed that this division of cases tended to be the pattern in New Brunswick.

In the early 1980s, the attorney general of New Brunswick wanted to create a provincially appointed, unified criminal court. There were, however, questions raised about the constitutionality of the concept and a reference was made by the New Brunswick cabinet to the New Brunswick Court of Appeal. No specific legislation was put forward and it was not known whether the federal government would support a unified criminal court. In a unanimous judgment, the New Brunswick Court of Appeal upheld the establishment of such a court set up by the province with complementary federal legislation. The court would be constitutional whether the unified criminal court had exclusive or concurrent jurisdiction. The Supreme Court of Canada, however, rejected the scheme in the 1983 case of *McEvoy v. New Brunswick*, holding that it breached section 96 of the Constitution, even if the federal government passed the enabling legislation and even if the superior courts retained concurrent jurisdiction to try criminal cases. 'Parliament can no more give away federal constitutional powers than a province can usurp them,' the court stated in a judgment 'By the Court,' adding: 'The effect of this proposal would be to deprive the Governor General of his power under s. 96 to appoint the judges who try indictable offences in New Brunswick.'

This came as a surprise to many persons in an age of co-operative federalism. Peter Russell called the decision 'remarkable.' One can understand why a province should not be allowed to usurp the federal appointing power unilaterally, but why not permit such a transfer if the federal government wants to give it to the provinces, particularly if the superior courts still have concurrent jurisdiction? The Supreme Court decision unnecessarily elevates the importance of the federal appointing power, which on my reading of the history of the *British North America Act* came about almost by chance. The administration of justice was given in the BNA Act to the provinces. It would have been natural also to have given them the power to make judicial appointments. In my study *A Place Apart* I ask why the appointing power was not given to the provinces. My answer: 'Perhaps the main reason is that the key players in Confederation who were moving on to the federal stage wanted to keep patronage over appointments in their own hands.' At an early stage of the deliberations leading to Confederation, one delegate, Sir Samuel Tilley, had urged the delegates to consider 'the adoption of some measure which should entirely remove these appointments from the influence of party politics,' but another participant privately observed in a letter to the Colonial Secretary that the recommendation met with little enthusiasm. 'Considerable reluctance,' he wrote, 'was exhibited by several of the legal members of the conference to forego prizes now apparently within their grasp.' Other delegates argued, however, that the quality of appointments would be better if they were made by the federal government.

One lingering problem following the Supreme Court judgment is the validity of the transfers of criminal jurisdiction to the provincial court that have been made over the years and continue to be made. The Supreme Court in *McEvoy* stated: 'What is being contemplated here is not one or a few transfers of criminal law power, such as has already been accomplished under the *Criminal Code*, but a complete obliteration of Superior Court criminal law jurisdiction.' In fact, the transfers already accomplished were not limited to 'a few,' but included a great number of indictable offences. No one on the seven-member court had a strong background in criminal law. Neither Justices William McIntyre nor Antonio Lamer, both knowledgeable about the criminal law, sat on the case. They would have pointed out that more than 'a few' transfers had already taken place.

A number of persons have argued that their convictions should be overturned because transfers of indictable offences to the provincial courts are unconstitutional, but their arguments have been rejected. In *Trimarchi*, for example, the Ontario Court of Appeal stated in 1987 that it is implicit in the *McEvoy* decision 'that the Criminal Code's present scheme of conferral of jurisdiction on s. 96 courts ... and on the Provincial Courts did not run afoul of the requirements of s. 96. If the Supreme Court was of the view that by reason of s. 96 the Parliament of Canada was disabled from conferring jurisdiction on a provincially-appointed judge to try *any* indictable offence it would have said so, because this would have been a more direct basis for its opinion.' Still, the question remains slightly open whether there might be a point where the transfer of jurisdiction would be considered too much in a constitutional sense. I doubt if that point will ever be reached, assuming that murder and treason remain in the superior courts.

Because of *McEvoy*, the new route to unification would be to have the federal government appoint provincial court judges as section 96 judges. Of course, this is more attractive to provincial court judges, but politically more difficult to achieve. A special committee of Ontario provincial criminal court judges, chaired by Judge David Vanek, brought forward a proposal in 1987 that all trial courts in Ontario be divided into three divisions, the civil, family, and criminal divisions. The committee did not go into detail about how the court should be established, but simply said: 'Initially members of the above courts might be chosen from among Supreme, District or Provincial Court Judges as suitability and preference might dictate.' That meant, in the light of *McEvoy*, that the federal government would make the appointments. Judge Vanek invited me to write a foreword to the report, but I did not want to get caught up in a lobbying exercise, and so declined – even though I supported the concept.

The attorney general of Ontario, Ian Scott, was interested in a unified criminal court and no doubt hoped that the recently established Ontario Courts Inquiry, headed by Court of Appeal Justice Thomas Zuber, would look with favour on the concept. Justice Zuber accepted the idea of a merger of the county court with the superior court, but not a merger with the provincial court. 'It is not apparent,' Zuber wrote, 'that this plan [as suggested by the Vanek committee] contains any substantial benefit to the public in terms of accessibility or efficiency. The unified criminal court would result in a substantial improvement in the lot of those who preside in the present Provincial Court (Criminal Division) but this factor cannot be a sufficient reason to reorganize the court system.' Scott brought about the county court merger and renamed the courts. The former Supreme Court of Ontario, when combined with the county court, would be called the Ontario Court of Justice (General Division), a name that was disliked by the federally appointed judges, and the provincial court was called the Ontario Court of Justice (Provincial Division). The former was subsequently renamed the Superior Court of Justice, which pleased the judges of that court, but stung the provincial court judges, who were now once again implicitly labelled as presiding over an 'inferior court.' And so the battle continues. In Ian Scott's memoirs he refers to what he called 'the odium' with which unification was regarded by many of the federally appointed judges.

Interest in a unified criminal court continued. Peter Russell, in his influential 1987 book *The Judiciary in Canada*, supported the concept, as implicitly did Carl Baar in his 1991 report on the topic for the Canadian Judicial Council, although he was not permitted to make recommendations on the concept. The Law Reform Commission of Canada, headed by Justice Allen Linden, now with the Federal Court of Appeal, also promoted the concept. Linden knew the provincial courts well because his brother, Sidney Linden, was a member of the Ontario provincial court, later becoming its chief judge. In 1989 the commission produced a working paper, *Toward a Unified Criminal Court*, supporting the concept. By contrast, a Canadian Bar Association task force on court reform, chaired by federally appointed justice Peter Seaton of British Columbia, and which included professor of law Thomas Cromwell (now a member of the Nova Scotia Court of Appeal) as research director, was opposed to the concept. The task force stated: 'We are not persuaded that there is a public perception of lower quality justice being administered in the provincial courts. Even if we were, we would not think the unified criminal court would be a necessary or appropriate reform strategy to address this problem. Under a new court structure, inadequate facilities will remain just as inadequate.' The committee suggested that if governments do 'decide that the unified criminal court is a reform worth pursuing, very serious consideration should be given to establishing one or more pilot projects whose operation could be professionally and systematically assessed.' This approach was the one taken before the earlier widespread adoption of the unified family court system.

New Brunswick did not give up. It took the hint given by the Canadian Bar Association and proposed that 'New Brunswick become a pilot site for a Unified Criminal Court.' A detailed consultation document was issued by the New Brunswick Department of Justice in May 1994. According to Carl Baar, 'those efforts were derailed after federal Justice Minister Allan Rock's unprecedented undertaking that federal authorization (by amending the *Judges Act*) would require superior court and provincial bar endorsement of the proposal.'

So far, the new territory of Nunavut is the only jurisdiction in Canada to have a unified criminal court. No doubt other jurisdictions continue to explore the issue. The province of Alberta, for example, has recently expressed interest in the idea.

The provincial court judges have a strong interest in the concept of a unified court and continue to pursue it. A conference, 'Trial Courts of the Future,' was organized by the provincial court judges, to be held in Saskatoon commencing 13 September 2001. I was putting the finishing touches on my paper for the conference early Tuesday morning, 11 September, and preparing to leave for the conference the next day. I was listening to classical music on CBC Radio Two, as I often do, when the news broke that a plane had hit one of the twin towers of the World Trade Center in New York City. I watched the resulting drama on television. The conference was cancelled and was later rescheduled for May 2002, again in Saskatoon. A book of essays delivered at the conference, edited by Peter Russell, has recently been published by the University of Toronto Press, *Canada's Trial Courts: Two Tiers or One?*

A number of provinces, including Ontario and Manitoba, are interested in integrating the courts administratively, if not fully. In *A Place Apart*, I argued that the courts would function more efficiently and with greater independence if their administration were handled by an independent Court Services Agency in which all courts played a role, along with the provincial government. This will be explored more fully in a later chapter on the judiciary. As far as I am aware, no jurisdiction in Canada has yet taken up this suggestion.

Arguments have been put forward that the *Judges' Compensation Case*, decided by the Supreme Court of Canada in 1998, raised the possibility that the Supreme Court will strike down the existing two-tier structure. Judge Gerald Seniuk and Professor Noel Lyon have written in the *Canadian Bar Review* about the 'ambiguous status of the Provincial Court' in the light of the *Judges' Compensation Case*, in which the Supreme Court of Canada used the preamble to the Constitution to require the same procedures for dealing with financial security for provincially appointed judges as apply to federally appointed judges.

A subsequent 2001 Supreme Court of Canada case involving the status of the provincial court, *Therrien v. Quebec*, suggests, however, that the court is not going to upset the judicial apple cart. In that case, then Judge Richard Therrien, who had been dismissed as a Quebec provincial court judge because he had not disclosed when appointed to the bench his criminal conviction in the early 1970s for activities relating to the FLQ, argued that provincial court judges could not be dismissed without a resolution of the legislative assembly. Under the constitution, a federally appointed judge cannot be removed without a joint address by the House and the Senate. In the case of the dismissal of provincially appointed judges in Quebec, it is the Quebec Court of Appeal that makes the determination. The Supreme Court of Canada upheld the flexible approach that had been set out in the 1985 *Valente* case. Justice Gonthier stated for a unanimous seven-judge court that 'the preamble cannot afford greater protection than what is guaranteed by s. 11(d) of the *Canadian Charter*.' *Valente* is therefore still the key decision.

As in other areas of law reform, therefore, the judicial route is not the most promising avenue to bring about a unified criminal court. The *Judges' Compensation Case* will, however, have an impact on the debate. It has brought and will continue to bring about improvements in the salary and benefits of provincial court judges. The gap between superior court and provincial court judges will continue to narrow. The quality of appointments to the provincial court will continue to improve. There is already in each province – for the most part – a good appointment process for provincial court judges. An increasing number of first-rate criminal lawyers will prefer an appointment to the provincial court or treat the two benches with equal interest. There is a growing degree of prestige in the provincial court. The criminal work of the superior courts will continue to decrease, as more and more crimes are tried in the provincial courts. The recent creation of more hybrid offences – offences that can be prosecuted as either summary or indictable offences – is part of that trend. The decrease in legal-aid funding will also be a contributing factor. The work of the superior courts will, however, continue to be significant in the use of judicial resources because of the increased – and in my view, unwarranted – length of murder cases that must be tried in the superior courts. In a recent report on a number of miscarriages of justice in Newfoundland, former chief justice Tony Lamer suggested that there is a lack of expertise in criminal-law matters in some criminal courts in Canada and suggested that appointments from the provincial court could help solve that problem. Another solution, of course, is a unified criminal court.

The interesting criminal cases and Charter issues will increasingly be dealt with by the provincial courts. The public and the politicians will develop a greater appreciation of the important work done by provincial court judges. In time, the idea of a unified criminal court will seem more attractive to many superior court judges. A couple of pilot projects will be tried in a few judicial districts, just as happened in the family-law area. They will prove to be successful. In time, it is likely that there will be a unified criminal court in Canada.

9

Securities Regulation

In January 1964 I received a call from Jack Kimber, the chair of the Ontario Securities Commission, asking me if I would be interested in doing research for a committee he was heading on legislation relating to corporate securities. The previous October, the attorney general of Ontario, Fred Cass, had established a committee – formally known as the Attorney General's Committee on Securities Legislation in Ontario, but usually referred to as the Kimber Committee – with wide terms of reference:

> To review and report upon, in the light of modern business conditions and practices, the provisions and working of securities legislation in Ontario and in particular to consider the problems of take-over bids and of 'insider' trading, the degree of disclosure of information to shareholders, the requirements as to proxy solicitation, procedures as to primary distribution of securities to the public and like matters, and generally to recommend what, if any, changes in the law are desirable.

Improving the regulation of securities was a hot topic in Canada and other countries in the early 1960s. An important study of the subject, the Jenkins Report, had been published in England in 1962 and a thorough six-volume analysis of the area had recently been completed in the United States by Milton Cohen for the Securities and Exchange Commission.

In Canada, the federally appointed Porter Commission on Banking and Finance, chaired by Dana Porter, the chief justice of Ontario, had among other studies been collecting evidence concerning problems related to the distribution of speculative securities. An important background study was done by economist Kendall Cork, who had been a year ahead of me in commerce and finance and who many years later was a fellow board member of the University of Toronto Press. The Porter Commission had reported in February 1964 that there were serious problems. The commission showed that out of over $750 million raised from the public by junior mining companies between 1953 and 1960 only $150 million was spent on exploration. Out of over six thousand public mining companies incorporated in Ontario between 1907 and 1953 only fifty-four had ever paid dividends. It was, the commission concluded, not a very efficient way of raising capital.

The immediate cause for the creation of the Kimber Committee was concern over a controversial takeover bid by Shell Canada for the shares of Canadian Oil. There were at the time no legislative rules for dealing with takeovers, although there had been a voluntary code since 1963, and many thought that insiders in such cases had a distinct advantage over other shareholders because of their special knowledge of the bid.

The original members of the committee had included Kimber, as chair, along with two highly respected securities lawyers, Hal Mockridge of Osler, Hoskin & Harcourt, who acted for such major companies as Inco, and Bob Davies, who, at the age of thirty-eight, was the senior partner of what would become Davies, Ward & Beck, now the high-powered firm of Davies Ward Phillips & Vineberg. Kimber was a gentle, thoughtful, pipe-smoking lawyer, who had left the firm of Kimber and Dubin in 1957 for the less hectic life of a master of the Supreme Court of Ontario. It was not unusual for a master to head the OSC. His predecessor, O.E. Lennox, who had also been a master, was the chair of the OSC for a fifteen-year term, and the first head of the OSC, George Drew, who would later become the premier of the province, was a master when he was appointed the first chair of the commission in 1933. Kimber continued as a part-time master, but became a full-time chair of the commission after the committee that he chaired recommended that the position be a full-time one.

Mockridge, then over sixty, was a shy, circumspect, and reserved lawyer who shunned the spotlight. He gave the appearance of a well-bred senior partner in a large New York or Boston law firm. Davies, by contrast, was aggressive and direct. He expressed his opinions forcefully and held firm views on most subjects. He had recently converted to Roman Catholicism, and I remember him on the airplane during the committee's trip to England devotedly reading the Bible while the rest of us engaged in light-hearted banter. He was as intense a person as I have ever met and, perhaps not surprisingly, he died of a heart attack in 1975 at the very early age of fifty-one. Also on the original committee was Bill Common, the deputy attorney general of Ontario, who at the time also headed the Joint Committee on Legal Aid, discussed in a previous chapter. Finally, there was Lieutenant-General H.D. Graham, the president of the Toronto Stock Exchange, who had asked to be on the committee, but who resigned 'because of other commitments.' The real reason for his resignation was probably because he did not want to be seen as participating in a committee that would likely suggest curtailing the sale of speculative mining shares through the TSE.

The original committee, composed entirely of lawyers, was enlarged in January 1964 to add a number of non-lawyers, including Ian Macdonald, a professor of political economy at the U of T, who was at the time on leave as a government economist and would later become president of York University; Warren Goldring, a financial analyst who had established AGF mutual funds in 1957; and Tom Hutchison, the head of the Canadian branch of the international firm of accountants, Peat, Marwick, now KPMG. Another lawyer, Jack Yoerger, the deputy provincial secretary, was also added to the committee at the time.

I discussed the offer of joining the committee with Dean Allan Leal, who supported my participation, even though I had my hands more than full with a number of other projects. There would be two other staff members: Purdy Crawford, a young lawyer at Oslers, who would go on to become a corporate CEO and still later one of the most, if not the most influential commentator on securities legislation in Canada, and Howard Beck, of Davies, Ward and Beck, who would also become a respected securities lawyer. Crawford had grown up in Nova Scotia – his father was a coal miner – and was a graduate of Dalhousie Law School, while Beck grew up on the opposite coast, in British Columbia, and was a UBC law graduate.

Jack Kimber and I worked out a satisfactory rate of remuneration, $100 a day and a vague title – Legal Associate. I did not want to be called a 'research assistant,' even though that is what I would be. I am not sure why I was asked to do work for the committee. Perhaps Kimber had heard of me when I was an articling student with his old firm.

My background in commerce and finance would have seemed a plus to the committee, although I had not taught company law or securities regulation and did not know very much about capital markets.

I did, however, have expertise in criminal law and up until that time securities regulation was treated primarily as anti-fraud legislation. Indeed, the first major act relating to corporate securities in Ontario, passed in 1928, was entitled the *Security Frauds Prevention Act*. As Chris Armstrong, the historian of the development of Ontario's securities laws, states in his prize-winning book *Moose Pastures and Mergers* – a title that accurately describes the 1960s in Ontario – 'until the mid-1960s the major objective [of securities regulation] was to protect share buyers against fraud resulting from false and misleading claims and the manipulation of prices by brokers and promoters.'

In the nineteen twenties and thirties there were a large number of prosecutions under the Criminal Code for improper activities involving stock brokers and salesmen, including prosecutions for fraud and wash trading (the same person buying and selling the stock to create an artificial market). These prosecutions are described in detail by Armstrong in his again aptly titled earlier book, *Blue Skies and Boiler Rooms*. 'Boiler rooms' were illegal operations in which banks of unlicensed telephone salesmen in basement boiler rooms or similar locations sold shares throughout North America. There was also a section of the Criminal Code relating to what were called 'bucket shops,' wherein there was no intention by the buyer or seller to complete the transaction, and so the activity was considered mere gambling. Another criminal provision, which had been suggested by the federal royal commission on price spreads in the mid-1930s, made it a criminal offence to engage in insider trading, but it seems that no one was ever prosecuted under that particular provision.

The 1928 Ontario *Security Frauds Prevention Act* required that persons selling securities be licensed by the province. In the 1930s Ontario went further and enacted legislation outlawing certain activities, such as cold-calling (without a prior request to call) by a securities salesman at a residence by telephone or door-to-door. Further, in 1945, legislation was enacted in Ontario requiring 'full, true and plain disclosure' in documents called prospectuses, when shares were being sold from the treasury of the company. Enforcement of these provincial provisions was, however, increasingly lax. When Lennox, the chair of the OSC, died in 1962, the number of lawyers with the commission was only two, having fallen from five in the 1950s.

Moreover, there was nothing in Ontario like the so-called 'Blue Sky Laws' that were common in the American states, which gave commissions the power to prohibit the sale of specific securities that were thought to be without intrinsic value. The name 'blue sky law' was the imaginative term used to prevent the selling of 'building lots in the blue sky in fee simple.' Ontario had passed such legislation in the 1920s, but it was never brought into force.

I did not own any shares or spend much time on the business section of the paper and so there was a steep learning curve for me. I first started to dabble in the stock market after the commission reported and turned to Warren Goldring for advice. I had two criteria: the companies had to be socially responsible – this was the 1960s – and had to be at the beginning of the alphabet so that I would not have to turn very many pages of the *Globe* to read the stock-market quotes each morning riding to work on the subway. This was a reaction to my annoyance in my commerce and finance days when Wilfred Posluns, later of Dylex fame, and other classmates would noisily turn the stock-market pages in class. For many years my modest portfolio followed the same rules – only invest in companies from about A to C. It was, however, hard for me to personally block mergers or spin-offs. So, for example, a recent spin-off from Alcan of an aluminum rolling division thrust a company in the Ns (Novelis) into my portfolio. If I were a securities salesman who advised clients to use the 'A to C' strategy for wealth accumulation, I would be kicked out of the business. In any event, with one's portfolio now accessible on line, I rarely look at the stock-market pages. One of my recent picks started with an 'I,' Ivanhoe Mines, a company with interests in Mongolia controlled by Robert Friedland – no relation, but I liked the name.

The meetings of the Kimber Committee were held in the boardroom of Osler, Hoskin & Harcourt, then in a building at the north-west corner of Yonge and King Streets. I prepared memoranda on various aspects of the topics with which the committee had been asked to deal. They covered a wide range of subjects. There were, for example, memos on the duty of a director to shareholders, on tracing transactions on the stock exchange, on aspects of the federal companies act, on Milton Cohen's report for the SEC, on Harvard law professor Louis Loss's views on various issues, on English scholar L.C.B. Gower's writings, and more. These memos have been filed with my papers in the U of T Archives. In looking through them, I must say that I am impressed with the quantity of material I produced – fifteen memos between January and July 1964. Similarly impressive was the number of hours I put in and the bills I submitted.

One difficulty that I encountered was that some members of the committee – in particular Bob Davies – did not want the staff, and particularly me, to participate fully in the deliberations of the committee. I felt strongly that if I was to be a useful member of the team I had to be fully involved in the discussions. Kimber smoothed things over in his calm, fair-minded way. Purdy, Howard, and I were actively involved in all aspects of the policy discussions, but we recognized, of course, that the final decisions were for the committee to make.

In collaboration with Purdy and Howard, I started producing preliminary drafts of the report for the subjects included in the committee's terms of reference. The first such memo, in February 1964, was on insider trading. Later drafts included one in May on take-over bids, and in June on primary distribution on the exchange. By the end of the summer there were drafts on all of the sections of the report.

Public hearings took place in October 1964. I was permitted to participate fully in the questioning. The *Globe and Mail* reported an exchange I had with B. Dale-Harris, the chair of the chartered accountants' committee on securities regulation, in which I asked him what he thought about disclosing the combined salaries of the three most highly paid officers of the company. His answer: 'Putting in the top three is very close to catering to vulgar curiosity.' The Kimber Committee took a similar view and recommended that disclosure be made, without a specific breakdown, of the aggregate salaries of the board and a number of top executives, which would have to include the five highest-paid employees performing similar functions.

It was difficult for the committee members to find the time for sustained collective discussions. Mockridge and Davies, in particular, were constantly being asked to take urgent calls. A decision was taken by the committee to find a retreat where there would be a minimum of distractions. In late November, all members of the committee and the three staff persons went to England, where we would thrash out the report at a small hotel, now called Bailiffscourt Hotel, on the south coast of England near Climping. The hotel was built by Lord Moyne as a private residence in the twentieth century, but was modelled after an ancient castle. This did not stop the telephone calls. Both Mockridge and Davies were involved in issues concerning the recently discovered and controversial Texas Gulf Sulphur mine and were periodically called to the telephone.

The committee flew first class on BOAC to England and we spent the first two nights at the Savoy Hotel. The committee and the other staff members were not receiving any compensation for their work, and so it seemed more than proper to provide good travel and hotel arrangements. They could not, however, travel first class and at the same time put me – the only person receiving compensation – in economy on the plane and in a cheap hotel in London. So, at an early point in my career, I had the luxury of first-class air travel and a large room in the Savoy, with the bed on a raised dais. I did not have to worry about tipping because a memo distributed before the trip instructed us not to tip the porters at the Savoy. The only other time I can recall having first-class travel at the government's expense was when the Law Reform Commission of Canada flew to British Columbia for meetings in late 1971.

We spent the first two days in London meeting with persons from the stock exchange and the board of trade. When we went off for lunch after meeting with the exchange people, the committee members dined with the exchange's board members, and the three staff members joined the president and other officials of the exchange at a separate location, a more valuable experience. The president of the exchange was considered staff. We reciprocated the hospitality by inviting the persons we met with to dinner at a fancy restaurant, the Café Royale in Piccadilly Circle. The evening was memorable because after dinner we went around the table telling off-colour jokes. It was not something that I had experienced in my time at Cambridge, and I do not know whether it was an English or a Canadian tradition. I seem to recall that it was Bill Common who started the joke-telling. Perhaps I told the one, noted in the prologue, that probably got me elected as president of the UC Lit – it was the only joke I knew – but I cannot remember whether I did or not.

The report was more or less drafted in England. It went through a number of further drafts after we returned and was made public on Friday, 26 March 1965. The editorial writers generally liked the report. On the other hand, there was considerable opposition to our recommendations with respect to primary distribution of securities directly from the company or its promoters through the stock exchange. The *Northern Miner* dramatically headlined: 'Eggheads' Report Sheds No Light on Primary Distribution.' That topic drew the most attention.

Canadian securities – and particularly mining stocks – had been receiving a bad name throughout North America. The American comedian George Jessel had a routine involving Canadian securities, which I heard on Johnny Carson's *Tonight Show* at least once during the deliberations of the Kimber Committee. Jessel told about the calls he was getting to buy shares in a hot new mining property in moose pasture country in Ontario. Each call passed on the news that the price of the shares was rising. Jessel kept buying. Again and again, the call came that the price was going up and Jessel kept buying more stock. Finally, he said to the broker, 'Sell!' The punchline was the broker's ungrammatical reply – 'To who?' It drew a terrific laugh from Johnny and the audience. I recall Kimber saying the next morning how destructive such stories were to the Canadian securities industry. Perhaps more than anything else, Jessel's joke bolstered Kimber's conviction that something had to be done.

While the Kimber Committee was collecting evidence, the Windfall affair took centre stage. The question of what to do about the distribution of treasury stock through the exchange had been one of the issues that the Kimber Committee had been asked to investigate. Its terms of reference required the committee to consider 'procedures as to primary distribution of securities to the public.' The Windfall affair showed dramatically how markets could be manipulated and the public duped. The company, an empty shell that had been listed on the exchange and had not been delisted, had acquired some land close to the recently discovered Texas Gulf Sulphur bonanza near Timmins, Ontario. After test drilling and rumours of a successful result, Windfall started selling shares through the exchange. I happened to be at the exchange on Monday, 6 July 1964, the day in which a million and a half Windfall shares were sold, almost one-tenth of the total TSE volume that day. Many of the shares sold belonged to its promoters, George and Viola MacMillan. There was bedlam on the floor of the exchange that day. The price doubled from $1.01 to $2.02, and on later days went higher. When the bubble eventually burst, the investors lost their money. It was like the Bre-X mine affair in Indonesia in the late 1990s. In the Windfall case, the MacMillans delayed announcing that the core they had extracted was worthless. A royal commission to investigate Windfall and the activities of its promoters was set up by the Ontario government, with Justice Arthur Kelly of the Ontario Court of Appeal as the sole commissioner.

The Kimber Committee recommended in its report that primary distribution through the exchange be banned in Ontario, just as it was prohibited in the United States and England. The committee stated:

The Committee is opposed to the system of distributing securities through the facilities of the Exchange, as it is practised in Ontario at the present time. Inherent in the existing system are the dangers, among others, of market manipulation, false rumours, artificial excitement and inside advantages by promoters, brokers and floor traders. Coupled with this is a virtually complete lack of knowledge by the public of the fact that primary distribution is taking place; most people regard a stock exchange as a place where the trading is confined to shares already issued and distributed and where transactions are effected among bona fide sellers and buyers. There is no real disclosure of material facts made to the buyer of speculative securities in this type of primary distribution. For these reasons, primary distribution on the Exchange is inconsistent with a free market.

Perhaps thinking of George Jessel, the committee observed that 'the existing procedure of primary distribution harms the Exchange and indeed the entire securities industry in Canada.' Because the implementation of its recommendation to shift distribution from the exchange to the over-the-counter market would 'have significant consequences,' the committee recommended a two-year transition period.

The Kelly Commission, which reported several months after the publication of the Kimber report, disagreed with Kimber's recommendation for the removal of primary distribution from the exchange. Kelly's solution was to create a separate exchange for speculative mining and similar stocks. Kimber was not enamoured with that idea. After all, there had been such an exchange in the past, the Standard Stock and Mining Exchange, but it had merged with the TSE in the 1930s, with the hope that the senior exchange would be able to control the excesses of mining ventures.

The government did not accept either the Kimber or the Kelly recommendations. The subsequent legislation – the *Ontario Securities Act 1966* – did not bar such primary distribution, but the OSC was given greater control over the exchange. It now had to approve all TSE by-laws and could order the exchange to adopt practices that were in the public interest. In effect, the OSC became an Ontario version of the U.S. Securities and Exchange Commission. Moreover, before primary distribution through the exchange could start, the act required the filing of a new prospectus by a company, which had to be given to purchasers, who would then have forty-eight hours to rescind their purchases. Over the next several years, the OSC introduced rules making such distributions more difficult. More delisting of shell companies took place. Further, companies could not raise more money than they required for immediate exploration needs and promoters' shares were locked in and could not be sold for some period of time. As Chris Armstrong has shown, the use of primary distribution through the exchange as well as the Broker Dealers Association, whose members engaged in such activities, was on a decidedly downward slope, 'well on its way to oblivion.'

In all other areas, however, the Kimber Committee's recommendations were adopted without significant changes and now form the foundation of today's securities legislation across the country. Adherence to the recommendations of the Kimber report was more or less guaranteed by the fact that committee chair Jack Kimber and members Hal Mockridge, Bob Davies, and Tom Hutchinson, along with Howard Beck and Purdy Crawford, played key roles in drafting the legislation, which was enacted in 1966. The primary authors were, not surprisingly, Beck and Crawford. I was not involved in that phase of the work. There have, of course, been many subsequent changes in the legislation giving the investor greater protection. The development of securities regulation laws through legislation is certainly preferable to leaving it to the judiciary to inch their way along in developing the law through a case-by-case method.

Under the 1966 legislation, takeover bids would be subject to statutory rules. Previously, they were governed by a voluntary code developed by bodies such as the Investment Dealers Association and various stock exchanges, but this code was brought in only after the Shell/Canadian Oil takeover. The new legislation closely followed the Kimber report. The object of the legislation was to attempt to level the playing field for all shareholders of the company being taken over. An offer to acquire what would give the offeror 20 per cent of the voting stock had to be kept open for at least twenty-one days to give shareholders an opportunity to consider whether they should sell their shares and to give the offeree company time to inform its own shareholders whether the offer was a good one. The bid had to be accompanied by a circular, giving information about the company making the bid as well as about the offeree company. When there was an all-cash bid, disclosure of the identity of the bidder was not required, but this was changed in legislation in 1978–9 to prohibit anonymous bids. Further, if there was an increase in the price of the bid, all shareholders, including those who had already accepted the bid, would receive the higher amount, and if there was a bid for less than all the shares and it was oversubscribed, the shares had to be taken up on a pro-rata basis.

The committee did not want to discourage bids. In its view, 'take-over bids can, in many cases, have positive advantages to the companies involved, to their shareholders and to the economy generally.' There was, in the committee's opinion, no need to disclose the identity of the bidder if it was an all-cash bid or to inform the offeree company that a bid was going to be made. The object of the proposed legislation was to eliminate the advantages that insiders formerly had and 'to achieve full disclosure on an equitable basis.'

The troubling question of insider trading in a takeover bid, which had been the issue that triggered the creation of the committee, was handled by the insider-trading legislation and would apply to the trading of shares by insiders in the shares of their own company. It did not, however, extend to insiders of one of the companies using their inside knowledge to trade in shares of the other company. So the very concern in the Shell takeover that caused the creation of the Kimber committee was sidestepped. This was subsequently changed by legislation to require reporting by insiders of the bidding company of trades for the six months prior to a successful takeover. Moreover, the equally difficult question of whether a premium could be given for the purchase of a control block without a general offer to all the shareholders was not covered in the legislation, but was 'left to development by the judicial process.' Again, this was subsequently changed by legislation prohibiting the payment of a premium for the purchase of a control block unless the purchase is limited to purchases from not more than five persons (the so-called private-agreement exemption) and not more than a 15 per cent premium over the market price is paid, a reasonable compromise between having no rules on the purchase of control and complete equality for all shareholders.

Insider trading was dealt with in a number of modest ways. The main legislative enactment was to require all insiders to report each month all trades in their company's securities. Insiders included shareholders having 10 per cent or more of a company's voting stock, all directors, and senior officers, including the five highest-paid employees. The committee did not recommend that there be penal liability for improper conduct, but did recommend that legislation permit a person who traded with an insider to bring a civil action for damages if the insider had material knowledge that had not been disclosed. Moreover, the company itself could bring such an action, and the OSC could do so in the name of the company if the company did not act. These recommendations were included in the legislation.

The reporting provisions in the legislation were important and probably have had a significant impact on insider trading. But there was no requirement that tippees, that is, such persons as friends or family members of an insider, were subject to the new insider trading rules. (A Martha Stewart could not have been prosecuted in Canada under the 1966 legislation, even if there were penal sanctions for insider trading.) Moreover, the liability provisions were weak. It would be difficult for a shareholder to know that a trade was made with an insider, particularly if the trade was through a stock exchange. Further, a company would likely be reluctant to sue one of its own insiders. And even if lawsuits were brought, there would not be double liability, as had been recommended in the Kimber report. The possibility of bringing a civil action against an insider for improper trading would therefore not be a strong deterrent. The committee rejected the sensible U.S. rule 16(b) of the *Securities Exchange Act* of 1934, which provided that insiders could only buy or sell shares that they had held for at least six months. This so-called 'short swing' law encouraged actions for damages for breaches of the provision by awarding generous costs to lawyers who brought the actions. It was, however, thought by the Kimber committee to be 'an unseemly procedure.'

The Ontario legislation was a start, and over the years the legislative scheme has been bolstered by including tippees, by creating double civil liability, and by creating penal sanctions. The penalties in the Ontario *Securities Act* for improper insider trading have recently increased significantly. Moreover, the federal government has passed legislation to make such conduct a criminal offence, thus bringing back a prohibition that had first been introduced in the 1930s and subsequently repealed. Section 382.1 of the Criminal Code now provides for a maximum ten-year penalty. It is interesting to note how the code piggybacks on provincial legislation by providing that conduct not prohibited by the applicable provincial legislation is not covered by the section. The Ontario Securities Commission has also been taking the issue more seriously and is bringing more prosecutions, with mixed success. The topic of insider trading alone could be the subject of another book, so I cannot do more than skim the surface here.

The committee's recommendations in other areas were also incorporated in the new legislation. There would be greater disclosure by companies, although the committee did not, as we saw above, cater to 'vulgar curiosity' by insisting on the disclosure of individual salaries, as is now required. The Kimber committee had simply wanted disclosure of the 'aggregate direct remuneration paid by the company and its subsidiaries to all directors and executive officers of the company for services in all capacities.' Changes were made to require greater disclosure in prospectuses and when proxies were solicited by management. The proxy provisions now require disclosure of various financial matters when proxies are solicited, which matches the U.S. federal disclosure requirements. It has always seemed odd to me to use this technique in Canada, where the disclosure could have been done directly as part of normal disclosure by companies rather than by tying it to proxies, which may have been necessary in the United States for constitutional reasons.

The experience of working on the Kimber report was a rewarding one and played an important role in keeping me in the academic world, where similar activities involving the development of public policy were more likely to come along than if I were in practice. Persons involved with the Kimber committee continue to meet informally from time to time. Every five years or so someone arranges a lunch. The last lunch was organized by Purdy Crawford at the Toronto Club in May 2005, and the one before that by Warren Goldring at the National Club. Only five of us are still alive: Warren Goldring and Ian Macdonald and the three former staff members. At the last meeting, Ian had a perfect recall of Bill Commons's joke at the Café Royale.

My involvement with the Kimber committee led to my participation in a federal task force on the *Canada Corporations Act*. The federal cabinet passed a resolution in December 1966 that the act be amended to adopt some of the changes that had recently been enacted in Ontario, specifically those relating to insider trading, takeover bids, and proxy solicitation. The objective, in the words of the cabinet document, was 'to make investment in Canadian corporations as attractive as possible to Canadian investors and to provide to the public the information required, not only for informed investment in specific Canadian corporations, but also for the most efficient investment of capital resources in Canada generally.'

John Turner was primarily responsible for the resolution. He was the registrar general of Canada at the time and his department was responsible for the *Canada Corporations Act*. He established a task force, chaired by Robert Dickerson, a lawyer and an accountant who was on leave to the federal government from the University of British Columbia law school. Task forces were the rage at the time, following John F. Kennedy's many task forces. I agreed to participate in the group, made up almost entirely of academics. My job was to draft the sections relating to insider trading, takeover bids, and proxy solicitation. In addition, Doug Sherbaniuk, my colleague at the U of T law school, and I were to produce a report on the available statistics relating to companies incorporated under federal legislation.

The first meeting of the task force was in early May 1967. We each gave our preliminary thoughts on the areas that had been assigned to us. John Turner came to the meeting, told us how important our task was, and, looking us in the eye, earnestly shook hands with each of us in turn. One felt that he had a good chance of being the next prime minister. The task force met again in early June 1967. June 5th was the start of the 'Six Day War,' when Israel fought its Arab neighbours and in a pre-emptive strike destroyed Egypt's Soviet-built air force. It was a tense period. The task force was meeting in Ottawa that day. Perhaps it was a coincidence, but it turned out that all the Jewish members of the task force chose to sit together at one table at dinner, an unlikely event in other circumstances.

I did not have a particularly difficult assignment. I more or less followed the Ontario legislation, carefully noting any deviations from it. Ron Basford, who had succeeded Turner as registrar general, introduced legislation in the summer of 1969. I made several trips to Ottawa in November of that year, but my active involvement in the project then ceased, because in December I left with my family for a sabbatical abroad. Legislation to amend the *Canada Corporations Act* was eventually passed by parliament in 1972.

When I joined the faculty at the University of Toronto in 1965, Caesar Wright asked me to teach a new optional course on securities regulation. The course consisted of an exploration of the various topics covered in the Kimber report, plus a few others, such as mutual funds. I stopped teaching it in 1969. As stated above, in the early years securities regulation was basically anti-fraud legislation. Over the years it became much more sophisticated, requiring a thorough knowledge of corporate law. David Johnston, later the principal of McGill University and now the president of the University of Waterloo, had expertise in the corporate-law area and a strong interest in securities regulation. He took over the field at the law school. Frank Iacobucci, who taught corporate law, also had an interest in securities regulation and succeeded John Willis as a member of the Ontario Securities Commission. I more or less dropped out of the field for twenty years.

In March 1989, however, I became a member of the Ontario Securities Commission. I had been interested in understanding techniques for controlling conduct. In later chapters I will describe in detail the various projects I was engaged in at the time for the Canadian Institute for Advanced Research. One of these was a study on traffic safety which Michael Trebilcock, Kent Roach, and I had just completed. I thought that a good follow-up study would be to try to understand what techniques worked in the area of securities regulation. Stan Beck, the former dean of Osgoode Hall Law School, was the chair of the commission. We had worked together on the *Canada Corporations Act* task force, and he invited me to join the commission. I certainly did not become a commissioner for the money, because at that time the rate of pay was exactly $200 a meeting, including preparation, with no annual retainer. There was a two- or three-hour meeting of the commission every Thursday morning, as well as various disciplinary and other hearings in which members of the commission were expected to take part.

After two and a half years as a commissioner under Stan Beck and his successor, Bob Wright, I resigned. I felt that I was not pulling my weight as a commissioner on the OSC because I was not able to take part in my fair share of the hearings, which were increasing in number, length, and complexity. Moreover, the area had become so complex that I was spending all my time trying to understand the rules and regulations and was having difficulty putting a decent research project together, which was the reason I was interested in learning more about securities regulation. I had several meetings with two junior colleagues at the law school, Ron Daniels and Bruce Chapman, about collaborating on a project on insider trading, but nothing came of those discussions. I talked with Bob Wright about the possibility of doing a study for the commission on enforcement techniques, but again nothing was concluded.

With the assistance of my summer research assistant, Doug Harris, later the director of policy, research, and strategy at Market Regulation Services Inc., the body charged with controlling equity trading in Ontario, which recently merged with the Investment Dealers Association, I collected a large amount of secondary material on enforcement in the securities industry. I never used the material and eventually gave all the files to a doctoral student, Patrick Osode, who was doing research on insider trading. He received his doctorate and later became the dean of law at South Africa's Nelson R. Mandela School of Law at the University of Fort Hare, the university that Nelson Mandela had attended. My wife and I visited Patrick there in 1996. So my research ambitions may not have been fulfilled, but the material I collected helped an African scholar to get ahead.

That did not end my involvement in the field, because in 2001 Ron Daniels, who was a public director of the Mutual Fund Dealers Association of Canada, suggested that I become a member of the new investor-protection body that the association was establishing. I accepted the offer and served for about a year and a half on that committee. When Daniels resigned from the MFDA in June 2002 – in part because he was overextended and in part because he was going on sabbatical – I was invited to join the MFDA board as a public director. I agreed and also took over Ron's former position as chair of the corporate governance committee.

Bob Wright, whom I served under on the OSC, is now the chair of the MFDA board. The president is Larry Waite, who had been the head of enforcement at the OSC when I was there. The MFDA is a well-run organization which deals with an important segment of the securities industry. The association has a staff of over one hundred persons and an annual budget of over $20 million, while its member firms have collectively about $300 billion in assets under administration. It has been interesting to watch the organization grow and to see the various techniques it uses – licensing, reporting, inspection, requiring internal review and complaints procedures, disciplinary action, criminal charges, etc. – to encourage compliance with good practices by its approximately 150 active members and their 70,000 or so salespersons. I strongly doubt that at this stage of my life I will be able to use this experience to develop a research project on techniques of compliance. In the meantime, it provides an interesting and manageable glimpse into one important part of the securities industry, mutual funds.

Securities regulation is obviously far different today than it was in the 1960s before the Kimber Committee reported. The Ontario Securities Commission is now a much stronger body. I mentioned above that in 1962 there were only two lawyers on the staff of the OSC. Today, there are about one hundred lawyers and a staff of about five hundred. The commission is also more independent than it was, can now control its own budget, and can pay salaries sufficient to attract talented staff and commissioners. Thus far, it has shied away from the aggressive use of criminal prosecutions that have become relatively common in the United States. But with the recent coordination of RCMP and local policing activities into what are called Integrated Market Enforcement Teams (IMET), and an increase in potential penalties in the Criminal Code and the *Securities Act*, coupled with a greater public acceptance of the use of the Criminal Code for the enforcement of securities laws, we are likely to see somewhat greater use of criminal prosecutions in this area in Canada. But judging by the pace of prosecutions in the past few years, one should not expect too much.

One of the central issues that remains to be solved is that of creating a single securities administrator. The Porter Commission had recommended creating a federal regulator, and there have been a great number of committees, task forces, and commissions that have repeated that view. Purdy Crawford has been active for the Ontario government in pursuing that objective. It remains to be seen whether such a federal body will be created or whether there will, instead, be a single administrator responsible to the provinces and the federal government or a model which keeps all the existing provincial regulators and uses a so-called passport system. Ontario and the federal government want a single regulator, whether it be a federal or jointly administered body. The other provinces favour the passport system, whereby approval by one regulator is deemed to be approval by the rest. So we are at an impasse. Ontario would accept the passport system if it were a stepping stone to a single regulator, but at this stage Alberta and Quebec in particular are opposed to moving beyond a passport system. My guess is that the passport model will be adopted, with some uncertainty as to whether it will lead to a single regulator.

10

Machinery of Law Reform

My involvement with various bodies that dealt with issues of public policy led to my interest in the machinery of law reform. In England the newly elected Labour government created a law commission in June 1965, with Leslie Scarman, then a member of the family division of the High Court, as its chair and Professor L.C.B. ('Jim') Gower of the University of London as vice-chair. The force behind its establishment was Gerald Gardiner, the British Lord Chancellor.

Before the English legislation was introduced into Parliament – but with the knowledge that it was in the works – the Ontario government established the Ontario Law Reform Commission, and so Ontario had the honour of creating the first such commission in the Commonwealth. Former chief justice James McRuer of the Ontario Supreme Court, then in the midst of his monumental study on civil rights in Ontario, was named its first chair and Allan Leal its vice-chair. Leal would later resign as dean of Osgoode Hall Law School and succeed McRuer as the chair of the commission. The English Law Commission is still going strong, but the equally successful Ontario Law Reform Commission was terminated by Mike Harris's Conservative government in 1996. In early 2006, Dalton McGuinty's Liberal government announced that it intended to bring back a law reform commission 'to improve the administration of Ontario's justice system and enhance access to justice.' The new commission is located at Osgoode Hall Law

School, in partnership with the deans of the province's seven law schools, the Law Society of Upper Canada, the Law Foundation of Ontario, and the attorney general's department. A research advisory committee has now been established, and University of Toronto law professor Lorne Sossin has been asked by the commission's board of governors to prepare a report on possible research projects that the commission might undertake as its initial priorities.

I hoped to be given a sabbatical in the academic year 1968–9 and wanted to do a comparative study of the process of law reform in the English-speaking world. I had discussed the possibility of such a project with Professor R.M. Jackson of Cambridge University in the summer of 1967 when he had visited Toronto and assisted me with my project on magistrates' courts. Jackson was a justice of the peace in England and the author of an influential text, *The Machinery of Justice in England*. He encouraged me to undertake the project and promised to speak to members of the English Law Commission to sound them out. He also learned while in Toronto that our son Tom, then about three and a half, was a Babar fan. 'I have been making enquiries of a bibliographical nature as to the Adventures of Babar,' he wrote: 'Will you tell me whether Tommy has illustrated copies and if not whether he has any special favourites among the stories?' I replied that he liked all the stories that we had borrowed from the library.

Within a few weeks, Jim Gower, whom I had met through the Laskins when he had visited Toronto, wrote to tell me that Sir Leslie Scarman would be in Toronto in late September and suggested that I meet with him. Allan Leal, who supported the study, arranged for me to take Scarman to the airport, the only spare time that Scarman had during his visit. Leal probably thought I still had the sleek Sunbeam Alpine, which he had borrowed when Judy and I had returned to England in 1963, but we had traded it in after our second child, Jenny, was born in 1966 for a small, practical, boxy Hillman Husky station wagon – the very opposite in terms of style from the Sunbeam. More importantly, I had not had time to have the car washed or cleaned out before picking up Scarman. It was filled with our dog Tippy's hairs and the kids' toys and scuff marks. Leal and McRuer were visibly shocked when they saw that they were sending Scarman off in this manner, although Scarman did not seem to mind.

The discussion went well, and Scarman later wrote me, stating: 'I am most interested in your undertaking a study of the process of law reform.' Ronald St. J. Macdonald, who had succeeded Caesar as dean, was not keen on me taking a full year's sabbatical, but would gladly support a half-year leave. That was acceptable because in those years one received only 80 per cent of one's salary for a full-year sabbatical, but 100 per cent for a half-year. It was agreed that I would be on leave from January 1969 until the end of June.

I applied unsuccessfully for funding from some of the major American foundations. I was diplomatically told by the Ford Foundation, who had been supporting the Centre of Criminology, that they had other priorities. The Russell Sage Foundation and other bodies were also not interested. As with submitting works for publication, one has to have a fairly thick skin to try to get funding for projects. I then turned to Canadian funding bodies and was more successful, receiving funding from the Canada Council, the Laidlaw Foundation, and the Canadian Bar Association's Foundation for Legal Research. It required a fair degree of creativity on my part as well as by the university's office of research administration to permit me to keep most of all three grants. The Laidlaw Foundation covered research activity before I left on sabbatical; the Canada Council gave a three-year grant for standard research expenses, including travel costs; and the Bar Foundation covered some of my living expenses while abroad.

My Canada Council application stated that 'I intend to study and eventually to write a book on the mechanics of law reform in Canada, England, and the United States.' 'Although there has been an increasing amount of activity in reforming specific areas of law,' I wrote, 'there has been no comprehensive analysis of the various pressures brought to bear on the governments involved and the numerous techniques employed for reforming the law. These techniques include: court decisions, Law Reform Commissions, Royal Commissions, Legislative Committees, task forces, etc.'

The subject, I argued, was of both theoretical and practical importance. It is of theoretical importance, I stated, 'because of the analysis of the interrelationship between the legislative and judicial processes.' It was of practical importance 'because it will assist governments, institutions, and individuals interested in law reform in assessing the effectiveness of the various techniques available for introducing changes in the law.' The federal government, I pointed out, had not yet set up a law reform commission and I included in the application the comment by the deputy minister of justice, Donald Maxwell, made in a letter to me that 'we would benefit from the type of study that you have in

mind. I wish to assure you that you may count on our continuing interest in this undertaking.'

I told the Canada Council that I would work on the manuscript for
the two years following my return from sabbatical. 'Hopefully,' I
wrote, the final manuscript can be handed to the publisher at the end of
1971.' Needless to say, it was not. It was not until 1984 that I put
together a collection of articles based on the research.

Our sabbatical plan was to go to New Zealand and Australia, where I
would study law reform in those jurisdictions, and to arrive in England
in March 1969 to be greeted by the daffodils in Cambridge. We would
then spend four months in England. Glanville Williams had helped
arrange for a university flat at 8£ a week at Fen Causeway, which
backed on to the fens, where the cows grazed. Tom would attend the
nearby Newnham Croft primary school. We would find a nursery
school for Jenny when we arrived. In late December, while I was recovering from the flu, we flew via Los Angeles and Tahiti to New Zealand.
It was just before New Year's Eve when we crossed the International
Date Line, thus actually missing the midnight celebrations. The roses
were out in Auckland when we arrived.

New Zealand took law reform very seriously, as it continues to do
today. I met with government officials and with members of the bench,
bar, and academia in Auckland, Wellington, and Christchurch. In Australia I met with persons interested in law reform in Sydney, Melbourne, Canberra, and Perth. I was collecting a great amount of
documentation – material that would soon start to overwhelm me.

My letter to Frank Milligan (of the humanities and social sciences
division of the Canada Council) in mid-April 1969 set out the various
law-reform bodies with whom I had met. I had investigated 'the workings of the New Zealand and New South Wales Law Reform Commissions, the Western Australia Law Reform Committee, the Chief
Justice's Law Reform Committee of Victoria, and the Standing Committee of the Attorneys General of the States and the Commonwealth.'
'There is,' I went on, 'a surprising amount of good material on law
reform.'

We also saw much of New Zealand and Australia. We have pictures
of Tom celebrating his fifth birthday in Auckland, with sparklers on his
cake, and of Jenny learning to swim at an outdoor pool in Melbourne.
Sydney is a spectacular city. We swam in shark-proof pools, surfed on
Bondi Beach, were taken to a koala park outside the city by the chair of

the New South Wales Law Reform Commission, and saw the Sydney Opera House, which was nearing completion. Sydney is also memorable for me because it was there that I first saw a copy of my book on double jeopardy. Oxford had shipped an advance copy to its office there for me to see. Authors will know the thrill of actually holding a new book of theirs in their hands. Sydney was much like Montreal in the immediate post-Expo years. Melbourne was more staid and conservative, and reminded me of Toronto with its Victorian buildings, a growing multicultural community, and a strong university in the middle of the city. Canberra was like Ottawa, a compromise location between the country's two principal cities. Nobody who has visited Canberra at that time of year will forget the ever-present flies. I do not know whether they have solved that problem.

We flew on to England, stopping at Singapore, Colombo, and Teheran. A former student of mine at Osgoode, Gaylord Watkins, now an adviser to a law firm in Indonesia, was teaching in Singapore and showed us some of the sights. Our friends from Cambridge, Sena and Janaki Wijewardane and Sam Sanmuganathan, were in Ceylon while we were there. We stayed with the Wijewardanes for part of the week we spent in Colombo and travelled with them to Kandy to visit the famous Buddhist Temple of the Tooth.

The flight from Colombo to Teheran ran into trouble. One of the jet engines had stopped functioning and the pilot had to unload most of its fuel in flight – not an experience I will ever forget – and stop in Karachi for repairs. There were riots in Karachi and a massive nationwide general strike at the time, and we were not able to leave the airport while the plane was being worked on. There were also signs of instability in Teheran. Electricity and telephone service was periodically interrupted and one felt – without knowing what was actually happening – that the Shah was starting to lose his grip on the country.

We arrived in England in mid-March 1969, and once again I became a fixture in Cambridge's Squire Law Library, which I knew well from my double-jeopardy days. I read widely, made extensive notes, and tried to get a workable structure for the study. No other study that I have ever worked on has produced as many draft tables of contents over the years. Every few weeks over the next dozen years I would try out another draft plan, never finding quite the right one. The content was either too general or too detailed. This continued until, I eventually published a collection of essays in 1984, *A Century of Criminal Justice:*

Essays on the Development of Canadian Law – to be discussed in a later chapter.

I made frequent trips to London to study the work of the English Law Commission. I met with Scarman, Gower, and other commission members. The secretary of the commission, Michael Cartwright Sharp, gave me access to whatever material I wanted. The commissioners also permitted me to attend their formal meetings. One of them, for example, dealt with financial provisions in the divorce bill, another with pecuniary losses in tort actions. I could not have received better cooperation.

I also met with the Criminal Law Revision Committee – a government committee not directly connected with the commission which had been in existence since 1959. It was chaired by Sir Edmund Davies, then a member of the court of appeal. Glanville Williams was a member of that committee, as was Rupert Cross from Oxford. One of the subjects the committee was then dealing with was the use at trial of the accused's criminal record, which was very limited in England at the time. The record could not be put to an accused if he or she took the stand, although there were limited exceptions, such as when the defence attacked the character of a crown witness.

The committee was interested in learning what the practice was in Canada and invited me to one of their meetings. I described how section 12 of the *Canada Evidence Act* permitted the use of previous convictions whenever the accused went into the witness box. Canadian courts had held that a judge had no discretion whether or not to admit the evidence. I urged the committee not to adopt the Canadian position, arguing that it was unfair to the accused because a jury hearing that an accused had previous convictions would likely be less stringent in applying the standard of proof beyond a reasonable doubt. I liked the current English system, which controlled the use of previous convictions, but at the same time, as a trade-off allowed the judge, but not the prosecutor, to comment on the fact that the accused had not entered the witness box. (Under legislation enacted in 1994, the prosecutor in England – in addition to the judge – can now, with some exceptions, comment on the failure of the accused to testify.) When I returned to Canada I wrote an article on the topic for the *Canadian Bar Review*, an article subsequently cited in the well-known 1988 *Corbett* decision, where the Supreme Court of Canada limited the previously absolute right of the Crown to introduce evidence of previous convictions when the accused entered the witness box and gave the judge considerable discretion to exclude the evidence.

Most of my time on my visits to London was spent at the Law Commission. I collected a large amount of material on its first report, *Imputed Criminal Intent*, wherein the commission considered changes in the law relating to the mental element required for murder that had been established in *DPP v. Smith*, a 1960 decision of the judicial committee of the House of Lords. My case study would be a way of understanding the process of law reform in England. It had taken almost two years and twenty meetings to produce the commission's report. One of my many tentative titles was 'The Complexity of Law Reform: Overruling *DPP v. Smith*.' Unfortunately, I never published an article using this material, although it is not inconceivable that I might still do so.

DPP v. Smith, I would argue in my yet-to-be-written paper, may be the most important case decided by an English court in recent centuries because of its subsequent impact on the development of the law. That would be the dramatic introduction to the article. The decision of the House of Lords was that a person could be convicted of murder – at the time, all murder cases in England and Canada were capital cases – even if the person did not have a specific intent to kill or cause grievous bodily harm. An objective standard would suffice. The decision was widely criticized by legal academics and others, many of whom were probably surprised to learn that an objective standard for murder cases had been in the Canadian Criminal Code for many years. The importance of the case was not so much in the decision itself, but in its consequences.

I would show in my article that the case played a major role in the decision to set up a law commission in England in 1965 and contributed in a significant way to the abolition of capital punishment in the United Kingdom in that year. Moreover, the case helped to bring about the breakup of the judicial hierarchy in the Commonwealth, because Australia, for the first time ever, refused to follow a decision of the House of Lords. Even though Canada had abolished appeals to the Privy Council in 1949, Canadian courts had not yet refused to follow a decision of the Privy Council or the House of Lords. My analysis would link Australia's unilateral act of judicial independence to the fact that the United Kingdom was abandoning Australia through its growing involvement with Europe and the Common Market.

The *Smith* case also changed some important judicial practices. The House of Lords issued a practice statement in 1966 that it would no longer consider itself bound by its own previous decisions. The law commission had held back recommending legislation to this effect because the House of Lords wanted to achieve this on its own. Further, in the future the House of Lords would be less inclined than previously to issue unanimous judgments when there were differing opinions held by its judges and would be aware of the danger of moot opinions. The *Smith* case was moot because the attorney general had announced before the appeal was heard that the decision would not result in Smith being hanged. When there is less at stake in a decision, there may be less attention paid to what is being decided.

Thus, the case would tell us something about judicial practices, about the setting up of the English Law Commission, about the relationship between the courts and the legislature, and between those two institutions and the new Law Commission, about the role of pressure groups in the development of the law, and about the techniques of consultation developed by the commission. It would also tell us about how wide or narrow amending legislation should be. Should the amending legislation just overrule the *Smith* case or should it deal generally with the mental element in the law of murder? The Law Commission files are replete with interesting material on all these topics. If I do not, in fact, get back to this subject, as I suspect I will not, I urge someone looking for a good doctoral thesis to explore the case and its implications.

We returned to Canada in early August 1969. I had bundles of documents, many of which had been mailed from Australia and New Zealand. In London I had had the luxury of a research assistant. Eric Salsberg, now a senior corporate executive in Canada, was about to graduate from the U of T law school and article with Torys, but wanted to spend some time in England before starting his articles. He spent several months helping me collect material at the Law Commission and at the Institute of Advanced Legal Studies at the University of London, which he brought back to Canada for me. The material started to overwhelm me. How could I do a comprehensive analysis of the entire field? Further, as I worked on the material I would become interested in a particular aspect of the field and it would turn into a separate study, just as the article on previous convictions did and as the article on *DPP v. Smith* was threatening to do.

My available research time kept shrinking. As we will see in a later chapter, I became heavily involved in university politics shortly after I returned to Canada. Moreover, my appointment to the Law Reform Commission of Canada in the spring of 1971 curtailed most of my research plans, and my appointment in early 1972 as dean of the U of T law school also significantly limited the time I could spend on the project. I would, however, continue to hire research assistants while asking for extensions of my various grants.

I continued to plug away on articles on specific topics. One of the more interesting issues in judicial lawmaking is prospective lawmaking. I was assisted in this research by Peter Jewett, currently at Torys and one of the country's leading securities lawyers. My article on the topic, 'Prospective and Retrospective Judicial Lawmaking,' was published a few years later in the *University of Toronto Law Journal*. The subject is interesting because traditionally judges have said that they are not making law, but are only declaring it. In this light, judgments would necessarily be both prospective and retrospective. But, in fact, judges do make law, and so giving a new law retrospective effect can be unfair to those who relied on the earlier law.

The UK House of Lords recently held that prospective lawmaking should only be used in very exceptional circumstances. In contrast the U.S. Supreme Court has made widespread use of the technique, particularly in constitutional decisions in the criminal-law area. Whenever it changes the law, the court makes a decision in a subsequent case as to whether the change should be fully retroactive (as it was, for example, in *Gideon v. Wainwright*, which required counsel for indigent persons in serious criminal cases) or applicable only to future cases and, if so, at what stage in the process the new decision would kick in. So, for example, cases changing the rules on police line-ups would only affect line-ups held after the Supreme Court decision. In all cases, however – as an incentive to bring appeals – the person who caused a change in the law could take advantage of the new law.

As far as I know, mine is still one of the few articles in Canada on the topic of prospective judicial lawmaking. The Supreme Court of Canada has never formally recognized the practice, although it has, in effect, used it from time to time when it has struck down a law or required a new procedure, but has delayed the application of the decision for a period of time to allow the police or other agencies to adjust to the change or to allow parliament or a legislature to bring in legislation dealing with the issue. So, for example, in *Brydges*, which required the police to tell an accused about the availability of a particular legal-aid service, the police were given thirty days to prepare new caution cards. This is, in effect, prospective lawmaking. As in the American cases on prospective lawmaking, Brydges was permitted to take advantage of the new law. The subject also came up recently when the Supreme

Court of Canada limited the full retrospective application of rights under the Charter to Canada Pension Plan payments for survivors of gay and lesbian partners.

Another specific article was prepared in the mid-1970s on pressure groups and the development of the criminal law. Peter Glazebook, a criminal-law teacher at Cambridge, was organizing a volume of essays honouring Glanville Williams, who was about to retire. Peter asked me to contribute an 8000-word essay on the theme 'Reshaping the Criminal Law,' which I was honoured to do. I had recently completed a project on gun control in Canada – to be discussed in a later chapter – and was struck by the importance of pressure groups (or, as they are sometimes called, interest groups) on the development of the criminal law in that area. With the assistance of John Unger, now a tax lawyer at Torys – many of my research assistants have ended up at Torys – I produced a paper that analysed the importance of pressure groups in the development of the law.

I opened the paper with the statement 'There is nothing new about pressure groups influencing the development of the law. Thomas à Becket and the Church in the twelfth century dispute with Henry II, and the Barons who forced King John to grant Magna Carta in 1215, are early, if extreme, examples.' 'In spite of their importance in the legal system and the growing number of studies of pressure groups,' I stated, 'the subject continues to be one that is "wrapped in a haze of common knowledge," and lawyers have, for the most part, left it to political scientists, sociologists and economists to attempt to penetrate the haze.' I pointed out in the article that 'Glanville Williams, the leading criminal law reformer of the twentieth century, had been closely identified with a number of [pressure groups]: for example, the Abortion Law Reform Association, the Euthanasia Society, and the Haldane Society.' I looked at the range of pressure groups and their tactics. I also examined in some detail the use of the courts by pressure groups.

Because I wanted the article to meet Glanville's exacting standards, I worked very hard on it. I was, however, worried about the word limit. My paper was turning out to be much longer than 8000 words. Glazebrook had warned me that he would be 'fairly stringent' about the limit. As a result, I divided the paper in two and send him the part of the article relating to pressure groups and the judiciary. I had left out the material on pressure groups and parliament, where the gun-control material was analysed. Not surprisingly, Glazebrook was disappointed in what I had sent him. I did not know what to do and sent him the whole article, asking him to choose which half he wanted to publish, the part on the judiciary or the part on legislatures. He decided to publish both halves – about double the length he had initially wanted.

I was very pleased with the solution, as later were the reviewers. One review in the *Journal of the Society of Public Teachers of Law* wanted even more material, stating: 'He uses the example of the Canadian controversy on gun control to illustrate the variety of types of pressure group and the range of tactics they employ. There is also illuminating discussion of the increasing role of pressure groups in seeking to influence the way the criminal law develops by court decisions, especially through the device of claiming standing in civil proceedings. One wishes that Friedland had the room here to expand this analysis by linking it up with the general discussion which he alludes to about political interests and law reform.'

The key question for me was whether Glanville was happy with the article. In the fall of 1978, Judy and I went to England to attend the dinner in his honour at Jesus College. Glanville knew that a book of essays was being prepared, but he had not yet seen it. Sir Edmund Davies presented it to him at the end of the dinner. Glanville was then to deliver his remarks. Instead of standing up to speak, Glanville leafed through the book page by page. It was a long dramatic period of time – perhaps only five or ten minutes, but it seemed much longer. We all watched and waited. He then gave his thoughtful reply. I wrote to Glazebrook after I returned home to Canada, stating, 'It's one of those events that none of us will ever forget.' Glanville liked the article.

Throughout the 1970s I wrote drafts of a number of sections of a manuscript on law reform. There was a lengthy paper – almost 100 typed pages – on 'Parliament and Law Reform,' which was not restricted to criminal law. Nor was another draft paper, entitled 'Some Less Obvious Lawmaking Techniques,' in which I looked at ways courts hide lawmaking by, for example, construing legislative intent, or by the construction of documents, or by deeming what a 'reasonable' person would do, or through judicial discretion or the doctrine of abuse of process.

Should I restrict the book to the criminal law or should I have a broader focus? This was one of the basic issues with which I continued to grapple. As stated above, a plethora of draft tables of contents continued to be produced. I have one draft done on a paper restaurant placemat, dated the 15 March 1976, with the title 'Changing the Law: A Study of the Process of Law Reform.' The outline is not restricted to the criminal law. I must have been having lunch with Frank Iacobucci to discuss my plan because at the bottom of the outline Frank has written 'OK by me! F.I.'

I continued to teach a seminar on law reform for a number of years while I was dean. I enjoyed the seminars, which fit in well with my research for the book, although I did not know what shape it would assume. The seminar covered such topics as law commissions, committees and commissions, judicial lawmaking, bills of rights, and pressure groups. I would try to bring in experts for some of the sessions. Alan Borovoy, the general counsel of the Canadian Civil Liberties Association, was always interesting and provocative on the subject of pressure groups, and federal cabinet ministers John Roberts and Bob Kaplan were knowledgeable about legislative lawmaking. The students would prepare short papers on an aspect of their choosing in three of the subject areas. Rosie Abella, who later became chair of the Ontario Law Reform Commission and, of course, is now a justice of the Supreme Court of Canada, has often generously commented on the influence of the course on her career. Among the other students who were in the seminar that year and who no doubt profited by the discussions on the machinery of reform were Frank Marrocco, later the treasurer of the Law Society of Upper Canada and now a judge, who did a paper on pressure groups, and Neil Gold, the academic vice-president of the University of Windsor.

Before I left on sabbatical I had been invited to a small dinner given in mid-October 1968 by John Turner, the new minister of justice, following Pierre Trudeau's elevation to prime minister. The dinner was in the new wing of the Park Plaza Hotel, as it was known at the time, and was on the day before Turner was to address a special convocation of the Law Society of Upper Canada, where he was planning to announce that he was going to create a Law Reform Commission. He had called the dinner meeting to get advice on the shape of such a commission, and to discuss what its program should be. My invitation probably came through my friend Jerry Grafstein, who knew of my planned project on law reform. It was a distinguished group. My notes at the time indicate that, apart from Turner and Grafstein, it included Gerry Le Dain, the dean at Osgoode Hall Law School, along with two of his colleagues at Osgoode, Alan Mewett and Bill Neilson, Willard ('Bud') Estey, later a member of the Supreme Court of Canada, and Dick Gosse, a member of the British Columbia Law Reform Commission.

Turner asked the group what the priorities of the new Law Reform Commission should be. My notes show that I argued that the commission should get involved in studying the administration of criminal justice. It should try to find out – as I had in my bail study – what was really going on in the process of criminal justice. Turner resisted, saying that the administration of justice is a provincial responsibility. After the meeting, Grafstein said, 'I moved [Turner] a bit,' but he 'didn't want it in the statute for political reasons.' This was the same sensitivity to provincial jurisdiction that had been shown by the Ouimet Committee. The discussion concluded with Turner saying that the creation of the commission was still a year and a half away. Turner announced his plan the next day and the front-page headline in Saturday's *Globe and Mail* was: 'Ottawa plans to set up a law reform commission.'

Everyone at the meeting agreed that there had to be a separate body for law reform. The department of justice, Le Dain said, was simply a '200-man law firm which couldn't think about law reform.' That had been my experience. There was little activity involving law reform in the department. Two years earlier, my fellow Cantabridgian Donald Macdonald, the parliamentary secretary to the minister of justice, proposed that my students prepare bills to be introduced by private members on federal topics, such as expropriation and administrative-law procedures, topics that were crying out for reform. It was an interesting idea, which did not work out, but it shows how little law reform activity was being initiated in the department.

Shortly after I returned from sabbatical in the summer of 1969, I was invited to attend a departmental meeting in Ottawa to discuss the possible shape of a new law reform commission. I gave my thoughts on the effectiveness of the English Law Commission and discussed some of the major decisions that would have to be faced in setting up a commission. Don Maxwell, the deputy minister, then invited me to set my thoughts down on paper. A consulting contract was worked out, and on 20 October 1969 I submitted a nine-page single-spaced memorandum to the department.

In the memo I repeated the pitch that I had made to Turner the year before that 'the Commission will necessarily become involved in studying the administration of criminal justice in Canada, primarily a provincial matter, because the administration of justice (for example police practices, legal aid and court congestion) is directly related to the federal interest in criminal law and procedure.' 'No other body, governmental or non-governmental,' I wrote, 'now takes an overall view of the functioning of the legal system in Canada.' At the top of the list of priorities for a new commission should be criminal justice. 'There is,' I argued, 'a clear need for reassessment and constant review [of] Criminal Law, Criminal Procedure, and Evidence' and pointed out that the Ouimet Committee had barely touched on substantive criminal law, but instead recommended that 'the Government of Canada establish in the near future a Committee or Royal commission to examine the substantive criminal law.' A new federal law reform commission could undertake these tasks.

I argued for sufficient funding to permit the commission to engage in interdisciplinary and empirical research, stating:

> The quality and acceptability of the work produced by the Commission will be greatly enhanced by engaging in empirical studies of the operation of the laws being examined. There is a danger that unless this is built into the planning and budgeting of the Commission, the Commissioners will not have the inclination, the time or the funds to engage in these studies and as a result it is likely that very little work of this type will be done by the Commission. We presently have only a few such studies being undertaken in Canada, and unless the Commission plays a role in promoting them the formulation of our Federal law will be based on guesswork.

There is a section in my memo to the department recommending that the commission engage in widespread consultation, as was then being done by the English Law Commission. Another section discussed the advantages in preparing draft legislation to accompany a report. I suggested a combination of full-time and part-time commissioners with salary and status 'perhaps comparable to a High Court Judge.' I favoured calling the new body a 'law commission' rather than a 'law reform commission.' As in England, the name 'law commission' seems to indicate a wider scope of activity than 'law reform commission.' The suggested name was not accepted at the time, but when the present commission was set up in 1997 after the Law Reform Commission had been closed down in 1992, the name was adopted by Allan Rock, the minister of justice at the time.

My memo was apparently well received by the department. Turner wrote to me, referring to my 'very thorough and perceptive memorandum.' 'I found your comments most useful,' he stated, and added that he hoped 'that before we complete our thinking you might be free to come once again to Ottawa after the turn of the year.'

The memo formed the basis of a public lecture I gave through the University of Toronto's Centre of Criminology. An excerpt from the lecture was published in the *Globe and Mail* ('Advocating a Federal Law Commission to Revamp the Justice System') and the full paper was later published in 1969 in the *Criminal Law Quarterly*. The *Globe* excerpt, to my surprise, was accompanied by a leading editorial entitled 'A faulty reform vehicle.' The *Globe* was particularly concerned about the lack of laypersons on the commission, stating: 'With the legal profession firmly in control of the commission, with no laymen or professionals from other disciplines as commissioners and with enduring ties to the Justice Department limiting its independence, the commission would be so far removed from the public as to be untouchable and, alas, probably unresponsive as well.' A fair criticism.

On 16 February 1970 Turner introduced a bill in the House of Commons to establish the Law Reform commission of Canada. The objects of the commission, the press release stated, were 'to study and keep under review on a continuing and systematic basis the statutes and other laws comprising the laws of Canada with a view to making recommendations for their improvement, modernization and reform.' The commission would have six members, four of whom would be full-time, including the chair and vice-chair, and two would be part-time. The press release noted that the act 'did not require all members of the Commission to be lawyers or judges.'

The bill was given second reading a week later and Turner told the Commons that the first task of the commission would be a complete rewriting of the Criminal Code. 'We will select people,' Turner went on to say, 'who reflect the Government's priorities for the next five or seven years.' He wanted 'young tigers' – 'young enough to have some juice, old enough to have made their mark.' Would I, I wondered, be one of those tigers?

11

The Law Reform Commission of Canada

I thought I might be passed over as a commissioner because in October 1970 I had published an op-ed piece in the *Globe and Mail* – mentioned later in the chapter on national security – criticizing one significant aspect of the federal government's invocation of the *War Measures Act* – its retroactive application. As it turned out, however, I was invited to be one of the 'young tigers' on the Law Reform Commission of Canada. Jerry Grafstein, who worked very closely with the minister of justice, John Turner, had sounded me out in late January 1971. I told him I was 'definitely interested' provided adequate arrangements could be made for a leave from the University. The appointment was to be for five years, although in my own mind I thought it would probably only be for three years. My wife was not particularly keen to be uprooted from Toronto. Not only did our parents live here, but we had just finished completing major renovations to our house on Belsize Drive and our third child, Nancy, had been born in February of that year. Moreover, we had recently returned from nine months abroad in connection with my own career. Judy had been taking courses to complete her BA – she already had an occupational-therapy diploma – and this would interrupt her coursework.

The University was willing to grant me leave, allowing me to continue on the university pension plan and stipulating that I could return to the University 'in as good a position (salary and otherwise) as if [I] had continued on as a full-time member of the Faculty.' Dean Ronald Macdonald had strongly supported the arrangement, telling Simcoe

Hall that 'every effort should be made to work out a satisfactory leave of absence.' Donald Forster, the vice-provost and assistant to the president, was agreeable, taking the position that this was in part 'a tribute to the University.' This was a very generous arrangement, as it tied up a position for a potentially lengthy period of time. The federal cabinet passed an order in council in April, appointing me as a commissioner for a five-year period with a salary of $32,000, substantially higher than the $21,000 that I was receiving from the University that year. I would, however, be giving up consultation income.

We rented a diplomat's home in Rockliffe – at 393 Maple Lane, near Acacia Road. The lease had a so-called 'diplomatic clause' which allowed it to be terminated on three months' notice if the diplomat returned to Canada. Fortunately, we put in a similar clause when we rented our house in Toronto, a clause that we were able to use when we returned to Toronto the following year after I was appointed dean of the law school. The government paid for all moving costs to Ottawa, unlike the University, which wisely said it would pay for only 90 per cent of the costs of moving back to Toronto. The result was that the movers took some of our firewood from our basement in Toronto to Ottawa, but we did not ask them to take any firewood back to Toronto. Universities, I discovered, were generally better at controlling costs than governments.

Ottawa was a wonderful city for a young family. In the one year that we were there, we bought cross-country skis and often skied in the Gatineau Hills, just across the Ottawa River. We also hiked in the Gatineaus, skated on the Rideau Canal, and canoed down the Rideau River. The kids joined their friends in calling at the Governor General's residence down the street on Halloween and climbed the ruins at Mackenzie King's estate, Kingsmere. They attended Rockliffe Public School. Tom did a project on pollution, which included filling a bottle with polluted water from in front of the Eddy Match plant on the Ottawa River, across from the Parliament Buildings. Judy and I had an active social life. We had dinner with the Laskins on several occasions, were invited to a number of parties given by various embassies, and easily made friends with neighbours. It was very much like Cambridge, where many of the residents were outsiders and happy to interact with others living there on a temporary basis. We also had many friends and family members visit us from Toronto. We were very busy.

I felt less satisfied with the pace at work. As we will see, we accomplished a lot in the first year of the commission. Still, I never felt the same intense pressure as I did and as I continue to experience in the academic world, where there is always unfinished work to complete. Activity at the commission increased just before meetings and before other events, but there was not the constant adrenalin flow that one gets in teaching and research in the university. No doubt, the atmosphere is different if one is working in Ottawa in the political arena.

Justice Patrick Hartt was the first chair of the commission, having been appointed before me, and took up his appointment in early April 1971. Pat had been a partner of G. Arthur Martin, was made a QC only nine years after his call to the bar, and had been appointed to the Supreme Court of Ontario in 1966, at the age of forty. He was highly regarded as a criminal lawyer and had progressive ideas about the criminal law. Everyone liked Pat. He had movie-star looks – the *Globe* referred to 'the broad-shouldered, trim-looking Mr. Justice Hartt' – and a winning smile. He left the commission in 1977 to head the Ontario Royal Commission on the Northern Environment, producing an important report in 1978 that recommended that there be an Indian Commissioner for Ontario who would work to settle land claims by negotiation rather than litigation, thereby improving the lot of aboriginals. Pat subsequently became the first such commissioner and held that office until 1983. He retired from the bench in 2000 at the age of seventy-five and became a part-time chair of the review board for mentally ill offenders. I bump into him from time to time and he still looks the same – too young to have retired, just as he formerly looked too young to be a judge.

The vice-chair was Antonio Lamer, who, like Hartt, was appointed a superior court judge at a very early age, in Lamer's case at thirty-six. He also had a stellar reputation as a criminal lawyer, and as a judge had handled some of the FLQ cases. His appointment was delayed until December 1971, although he came to some of the earlier meetings in an unofficial capacity. He would succeed Hartt as chair of the commission in 1976 and would go on to the Quebec Court of Appeal in 1978, and then in 1980 to the Supreme Court of Canada, eventually becoming chief justice. Like Hartt, he had a lively mind and an engaging personality.

The other full-time member was Bill Ryan, a serious-minded academic who sometimes had a twinkle in his eye. He had been the dean of the University of the New Brunswick Law School, and in 1974 would be appointed to the appeal division of the federal court. His sound judgment was a benefit to the commission, just as it was on the bench.

He was the one full-time member without a background in criminal law. There were two part-time members, Claire Barrette-Joncas, a practitioner from Montreal, who would later be appointed to the Quebec superior court, and John McAlpine from British Columbia, a graduate of the Harvard Law School and a highly respected litigator, who is still handling important civil-rights cases today. The three branches of the legal profession – judges, academics, and practitioners – were equally represented as commissioners. Jean Côté, a career civil servant, was appointed the secretary of the commission.

The first formal meeting of the commission was on 27 July 1971, at the commission's temporary offices in nondescript quarters in the West Memorial Building, opposite the National Library and Archives. We would not move to our permanent quarters in the Varette Building on Albert Street until several months later. One of the first decisions made at the initial meeting was to establish a visible presence in Montreal. 'It was agreed,' the commission's minutes state, 'that the Commission needed to establish its presence in the Province of Québec in order to be "visible" in that province and ensure the maximum participation of its citizens in the work of the Commission.' This was just after the FLQ crisis and there was a growing awareness of the threat of separation. Moreover, it allowed the vice-chair to avoid moving to Ottawa. Justice Lamer attended that initial meeting, as did Jacques Bellemare of the University of Montreal and John Edwards of the University of Toronto, who expressed their views on the program of work and the methodology that the commission should adopt.

Our first task was to develop a program of work, which had to be submitted to the minister of justice for his approval. It was clear that tackling criminal law and procedure was to be our main task. The persons appointed reflected the understanding that criminal law would be our main area of concentration. By the third meeting in mid-October we had more or less decided on our subjects of inquiry. There would be six major projects: evidence, general principles of criminal law, substantive offences, criminal procedure, sentencing and other dispositions, and administrative law. Two other subjects were also under consideration: divorce and expropriation.

We had to decide whether to follow the work pattern of the English Law Commission and do most of the work through our own full-time employees or follow the approach taken by the Ontario Law Reform Commission, whereby most of the work was done by outside consultants, usually academics. We chose a middle path. We would hire a number of researchers, both senior and junior, but would also use outside consultants. Because of my background in research and publication I played a very active role in organizing the research teams and hiring many of the full-time researchers and consultants.

When I left Ottawa the following June to take up my position as dean of law, there was a small party at the commission offices. I recall Bill Ryan saying to all the researchers who attended the event that for the most part they were there thanks to my efforts. I did not disagree. We hired a number of excellent persons who were willing to spend a few years in Ottawa. Darrell Roberts, for example, was brought in as the first director of the criminal-procedure project. He had been teaching at the UBC faculty of law, having previously been a litigator for about six years before going to Harvard to do his LLM. He is now a senior litigator for complex civil cases at Miller Thomson in Vancouver. One of the bright junior staff persons was Louise Arbour, who had just completed a year clerking with Justice Louis-Philippe Pigeon at the Supreme Court of Canada. After a number of years of teaching, she was appointed to the trial division of the Supreme Court of Ontario, and rose through the ranks of the judiciary to become a member of the Supreme Court of Canada. She is now the United Nations' High Commissioner for Human Rights.

Among other topics, projects were started on the classification of offences and the concept of a unified criminal court, which was the subject of an earlier chapter in this book. Another major area was the general principles of criminal law. Jacques Fortin, a first-rate criminal-law scholar from the University of Montreal, came to Ottawa to head that project. Tragically, Fortin died of cancer in 1985 at the age of forty-seven, without seeing his excellent work translated into legislation. He had teamed up with Patrick Fitzgerald from Carleton University on many aspects of the work. Fitzgerald, a fine scholar who had a background in jurisprudence as well as criminal law, did an empirically-based project, with the cooperation of the department of consumer and corporate affairs, on strict liability. This work built on a similar project that he had done in the United Kingdom for the English Law Commission before emigrating to Canada. Fitzgerald's study formed the basis of a working paper and a subsequent report by the commission, which was later relied on by Justice Brian Dickson of the Supreme Court of Canada in holding in the well-known – at least to lawyers – *Sault Ste. Marie* case that there should be a 'half-way house' between absolute liability and full *mens rea*. For some offences, Dickson wisely held, an accused should have a defence of due diligence, but the onus should be on the accused to prove this defence on a balance of probabilities. Many of the commission's recommendations became law, not through federal legislation, but rather through interpretation by the courts, particularly after the coming into force of the Charter in 1982.

The commission tackled the entire issue of the mental element in crime, or as it is often called, *mens rea*. (The 'half-way house' study was only a small part of this area of law.) Many, if not most, of the sections of the Criminal Code do not fully set out the *mens rea* requirements that have to be satisfied by the prosecutor. This causes a needless waste of court resources, time, and energy. Many of the cases interpreting individual sections of the code end up in the Supreme Court of Canada. The obvious solution is to set out in the code some definitions of specific words referring to the mental element and to use those words in the sections dealing with substantive offences. This had been the technique used by the American Law Institute's excellent Model Penal Code, which used four basic types of mental state: purpose, knowledge, recklessness, and strict liability. Why the Canadian commission had to spend years trying to improve on this classification was something I always had difficulty understanding.

Keith Jobson, an expert on sentencing, who was then at Dalhousie Law School, was hired to come to Ottawa to head the sentencing and dispositions project. The commission's work on sentencing has in part been reflected in the general principles of sentencing enacted in the Criminal Code in 1996.

Several specific imaginative projects were commissioned. Their subjects came within the mandate of the commission, which called for 'the development of new approaches to and new concepts of the law in keeping with and responsive to the changing needs of modern Canadian society and of individual members of that society.' John Hogarth of Osgoode Hall Law School, another expert on sentencing, undertook an empirical study of alternative dispute resolution in criminal matters in a neighborhood in East York in Toronto. Another far-reaching project – like Hogarth's it was ahead of other work then being done in Canada – was a study by Douglas Schmeiser of the University of Saskatchewan of native persons and the criminal law, though a working paper on the topic was not published until 1991.

Evidence was a subject that I had taught and in which I had a particular interest. It was one of the first projects undertaken by the Law

Reform Commission, and I was part of the team. In early October 1971, a number of outside experts, including Fred Kaufman, a criminal lawyer from Montreal, Horace Krever, then teaching at the University of Western Ontario, and Jean-Louis Beaudoin of the University of Montreal – all three of whom ended up on various courts of appeal – were brought in to offer their advice. An Ontario provincial court judge, René Marin, was subsequently given leave from the bench to head up this project. Ed Tollefson, who had moved from the University of Saskatchewan to the federal Department of Justice, and was an expert on the law of evidence, joined the team on a part-time basis. Neil Brooks, now a professor of tax law at Osgoode, who had clerked with Justice Emmett Hall at the Supreme Court of Canada, did much of the project's groundwork. We also brought in psychologist Tony Doob from the University of Toronto as a consultant. When I returned to Toronto, Tony sat in on my criminal-law course. He has subsequently devoted himself to issues in criminal justice, becoming one of Canada's pre-eminent social scientists in the field.

The law of evidence was a very broad topic. Not only did it encompass evidence in criminal matters, it also dealt with evidence in civil cases in the Federal Court of Canada and evidence before military tribunals. The minister of national defence, Donald Macdonald, wanted us to study the topic, and Marin was happy to do so because of his background in the military. The topic could also cover evidence before federal administrative tribunals.

Unlike most of the other projects, the provinces had been doing work on the civil side of the law of evidence. The Law Reform Commission wanted to assist in coordinating these various evidence projects. The problem was that Ontario had already made considerable progress through its own law reform commission, as had the Quebec group revising the civil code of Quebec. We held a meeting in Toronto in October 1971 with representatives of the Ontario Law Reform Commission, who included the chair of the Ontario commission, Allan Leal, the vice-chair, J.C. McRuer, who was the commissioner in charge of the evidence project, and Alan Mewett, the project's director, who had recently moved from Osgoode to the University of Toronto. I subsequently reported in a memo to the commission that the Ontario commissioners 'were interested, but seemed to be reluctant to delay their work to conduct some form of joint study. They are now at the stage of taking decisions and drafting legislation.' Alan Mewett wrote to Pat Hartt: 'I gather that you hope to rush into your evidence project with all haste.' Mewett suggested that 'substantive criminal law reform should proceed in tandem with evidentiary reform, if not precede it. If this is not done, there may be the danger that the evidentiary tail will wag the substantive dog.' Hartt assured Mewett that the commission had 'every intention of working contemporaneously on substantive, procedural and sentencing matters.'

Administrative law was another subject on the plate of the federal commission, although in the early years the budget would not permit a major study of the area. Bill Ryan was in charge of the project. Phil Anisman, who had just completed his master's of law at Berkeley and would go on to do his doctorate there in securities law, spent two years with the commission working on administrative law. I sent a draft of the proposed project to John Willis, my colleague at the U of T, asking him for his comments. 'The Commission,' he wrote back, 'should in my opinion be practical and specific and not, as McRuer is, ideological and global. You should, in other words, seek specific remedies for specific and actually existing problems and not use (as McRuer did) a global scattergun to scotch horrors that '*might* happen.'' He urged us to 'find out what federal boards or departments are *in fact* exercising what powers to 'interfere' with the liberty, property, livelihood etc. of the citizen and how they *in fact* go about it.' The advice was in line with Willis's view that one should find out how things actually worked before trying to fix them, a point of view with which I agreed. Over the next decade, the commission did much valuable empirical work on specific regulatory agencies.

In January 1972 we sent out a questionnaire seeking input from the legal community and the public on what should be in our official program, which we were planning to send to the minister for approval. We set out the areas that we were considering, which consisted of four in the field of criminal justice, that is, general principles, substantive offences, criminal procedure, and sentencing and disposition, along with a project on family law. The commission was considering three other projects as well because of an interest by the department of justice: one on negotiable paper, another on certain aspects of expropriation, and a third on the *Interest Act*. We asked the public to let us know 'whether the areas we are now considering are desirable ones for study, whether there are matters within these areas to which we should give immediate priority, and whether there are other legal areas of federal concern deserving our attention.' In a talk I gave to the Lawyers' Club of Toronto in March 1972 on the commission's work I acknowledged that the response was 'somewhat disappointing,' and noted that anyone who has sought comments from the legal profession or the public will 'know that perhaps the only thing that will get a strong response is the failure to ask for a response.'

The *Globe and Mail* did not think much of the exercise. In a lead editorial the paper referred to the so-called young tigers and outlined the process, concluding: 'Finally, when all the debate is over, all the submissions heard, all the amendments and changes made, Mr. Justice Hartt will have a list of subjects that he can start to study. And that's how Mr. Turner has his young tigers work. Meow?'

This was somewhat unfair. As I stated in my talk at the Lawyers' Club: 'Like good tigers in the legal jungle, we have been stalking our prey very carefully before attacking it.' In early March we met with all the provincial law reform commissions to discuss ideas for cooperation, and in December we met again with the British Columbia Law Reform Commission, as well as with the BC legal community. That was my first trip on the new Boeing 747, with its upstairs lounge for those in first class – the commission tended to travel first class. There was only one other person in the upstairs lounge on the plane – a former student, David Peterson, the future premier of Ontario, who had graduated from the law school several years earlier.

In July 1971 Ronnie Macdonald wrote to members of the faculty that he was stepping down as dean of law at the University of Toronto and joining the faculty at his alma mater, the Dalhousie Law School. This came as a complete surprise to me. He had been appointed in 1967 before fixed terms were instituted at the University of Toronto. Under the new rules, decanal appointments at Toronto were normally for seven years, and Ronnie still had two more years to go before he would have completed seven years. His roots, however, were in Nova Scotia and he and his sister, with whom he lived, wanted to return there. Moreover, as we will see in a later chapter, the U of T Law School was not being treated generously by the University with respect to budget and space. In September, Ronnie accepted the appointment as dean of Dalhousie Law School.

I expected that I would be on the short list for dean, particularly after the search committee was announced. Acting provost Donald Forster was the committee chair, and I knew that he respected my scholarship and the work I had done on the governance of the University, a matter to be discussed in a later chapter. His views on the importance of scholarship were strongly shared by the other senior administrators on the committee, economist and dean of the graduate school Edward Safarian and James Ham, the dean of applied science and engineering.

Other members of the committee included alumnus John Morden, who had been a year behind me at law school and who would be appointed a superior court judge in 1973; a student, Craig Perkins, who had been in my criminal-law class and who would later be appointed a superior court judge; and four faculty members, Ted Alexander, Frank Iacobucci, Associate Dean Ralph Scane, and Arnie Weinrib. I was friendly with them all, particularly with Frank. He and I were good friends from our days at Cambridge. Moreover, I had played a major role in bringing Frank to the University of Toronto. When Peter Williamson, a corporate and securities scholar, announced that he was leaving for the Dartmouth business school, I told Caesar Wright about a bright potential academic practising law at Dewey Ballantine in New York City. Frank joined the faculty in 1967 and had his office next to mine until I left for Ottawa.

In early December 1971 I was formally invited to meet with the search committee in the New Year, somehow knowing that Bruce Dunlop and Dick Risk, both of whom were respected members of the faculty, were also on the short list. I had to decide whether to let my name stand. I wanted to be dean and would certainly have thrown my hat in the ring if the invitation had come two years later. My wife, I knew, wanted to return to Toronto. I recall seeking Bora Laskin's advice. He thought the deanship was right for me at this stage of my career, but was it right to leave the Law Reform Commission so soon? In the end, I let my name stand and agreed to meet with the selection committee. One of the factors in making up my mind was the pace of the work of the commission, which I mentioned earlier. Where would the commission be in two or three years' time? Would I be able to look back with pride on what we had accomplished? In contrast, I was confident that I could make a significant difference at the law school.

I met with the committee in a small meeting room on the third floor of Hart House on the morning of Monday, 17 January 1972. I think I was the last of the three to be interviewed. About a week later, Brian Levitt, then a law student and today the co-chair of Osler, Hoskin, & Harcourt, who had continued to work part-time for the provost, called on an unofficial basis to say that I had been selected as dean. The appointment had to be approved by the academic board before it would become official. That approval was given on Thursday, 27 January, and on Saturday there was a brief announcement in the *Globe and Mail*, with a longer story in the *Toronto Star* which included a picture – unfortunately, a picture of an economics professor at York University, Seymour Friedland. Two days later a correct picture was shown with a note stating, 'The Star regrets this error.'

The following week I attended a major National Conference on the Law at the Château Laurier, arranged by John Turner but presided over by the new minister of justice, Otto Lang. The conference featured distinguished international speakers such as the radical educator Ivan Illich and the Australian jurisprudence scholar Julius Stone. There was a reception the evening preceding the conference where I met Pierre Trudeau for the first time. He was certainly not a glad-hander.

On Thursday morning, 3 February – the second day of the conference – a hyperbolic *Globe* editorial appeared under the heading 'New vitality at U of T.' The editorial discussed my appointment as dean along with that of John Crispo as dean of the business school. 'The temptation to fill the Dean's vacancy with an established 'safe' legal figure must have been present,' the editorial stated. 'That it was suppressed in favour of promoting what one may perhaps call a swinging young member of the faculty is a tribute to an imaginative administration.' Needless to say, the word 'swinging' was a subject of much comment that day by those at the conference. The editorial went on to state: 'Professor Friedland is a brilliant legal thinker and innovator, and a teacher of formidable reputation. He is a member of the Law Reform Commission and a consultant to government. But he is also a figure of dissent and perhaps even a gadfly to the legal Establishment.' It would be hard to live up to that advance billing as a swinging gadfly.

The sociologist Hans Mohr, who had assisted me with my bail study, filled my position on the Law Reform Commission, and after Bill Ryan was appointed to the Federal Court of Appeal in 1974, Gerry La Forest, who was then an assistant deputy minister in the Department of Justice and who would later serve on the Supreme Court of Canada, was appointed to take Bill's place. These were strong appointments. As a result, I felt less guilty about leaving the position so soon after arriving.

This is not the place to give a history of the Law Reform Commission of Canada. I leave that task to others. The commission produced excellent work over the years – Justice Allen Linden was a particularly effective president for most of the 1980s – but in the February 1992 budget,

Brian Mulroney's Conservatives announced that the commission was to be shut down as a cost-cutting measure. I found that hard to believe, but I knew they were serious when about a month after the announcement a courier delivered a parcel to my office which contained my picture that had been hanging on a wall at the commission's offices in Ottawa. Again, I will leave it to others to analyse the work of the new commission, established by Allan Rock in 1997 and simply called the Law Commission, which was gutted by Stephen Harper's Conservatives in 2006. The legislation establishing the Law Commission was not repealed, but instead its budget was reduced to zero. With a minority government, repealing the legislation would not likely have been passed by Parliament.

After I left the Law Reform Commission in 1972, I continued to have significant involvement over the next twenty years on a variety of projects. My work on codification of the criminal law will be discussed in a later chapter. I was also a consultant to a commission working paper on national security, *Crimes against the State*, published in 1986, as well as to a working paper on double jeopardy, *Double Jeopardy, Pleas, and Verdicts*, published in 1991. Further, I participated in a commission conference on incentives in the legal system in 1990. But my main further involvement was my work on access to the law, a subject of great importance to citizens, which will be discussed in the next chapter.

The Law Reform Commission of Canada did excellent work in its twenty or so years of existence. It was, in my opinion, short-sighted to shut it down. Some such body is clearly needed in Canada, particularly one with a strong emphasis on criminal law and procedure.

12

Access to the Law

One area that had particularly interested me while I was a member of the Law Reform Commission was legal language and the form of the law. Pat Hartt had a strong commitment to the concept and the commission took the issue seriously. How can one make the law more comprehensible to the average intelligent citizen? This came within the mandate of the commission to develop 'new approaches to and new concepts of the law in keeping with and responsive to the changing needs of modern Canadian society and of individual members of that society.'

An intriguing idea put forward to the commission by law professor Clarence Smith of the University of Ottawa was that if one drafts legislation initially in French in the civilian style and then translates into English one can achieve more clarity than if one starts drafting in English in the traditional common-law style. The possible reason for this will become clearer in the discussion below. Smith had successfully drafted a penal code in that manner for the West African country of Cameroon. Bill Ryan and I discussed the subject of drafting at a meeting on the subject with Gerry La Forest, at the time with the Department of Justice, and with Jean Beetz of the University of Montreal, both of whom were later appointed to the Supreme Court of Canada. 'The whole area is a fascinating one,' I wrote to Beetz after the meeting, 'but is not an easy one to solve.'

The commission asked me to continue to work on the issue after my return to the University of Toronto in 1972. Legislative drafting was part of the problem, but the real stumbling block, I realized, was that laypersons would never be able to use the existing legal materials. They would not know whether the subject matter was federal or provincial or, as was often the case, both. Even if they knew where to look, they would not know how to access the statutes or the relevant case law. For the next year and a half I worked on the project of trying to make the law more accessible. I made a number of trips to Ottawa to discuss the issues with the commission. The law school supported the project, as did the University of Toronto, and eventually a fifty-thousand-dollar contract for research expenses, including a small honorarium for me, was concluded between the University and the Law Commission to enable me to do research on the project.

In February 1974 I presented a paper on the project at a meeting of the Institute of Public Administration of Canada, excerpts of which were reprinted in the *Globe and Mail*, with the whole article later published in *Canadian Welfare*. The talk opened with the following general comments:

> The State has an obligation to ensure that its laws are available in an understandable fashion to laymen. This proposition may appear self-evident; yet very little attention has been given toward accomplishing this objective in Canada – or indeed, as far as I am aware, in any common-law country.
>
> In fact, very little attention has been given towards making our laws comprehensible even to lawyers. Governments have left the task of explaining the law largely to private enterprise, and in Canada the commercial publishers and the legal profession have done relatively little to assist the lawyer or the layman.

I proposed a possible solution. 'Let me put forward one scheme,' I wrote, 'that in my opinion warrants careful consideration. That is, to prepare and provide specially prepared sets of legal materials in public libraries and other places such as county law libraries and school libraries so citizens can determine their rights and obligations without necessarily first going to lawyers.'

The materials could be used by citizens, I went on to say, but, more importantly, could be used by intermediaries who regularly provide legal information, such as accountants, civil servants, police officers, librarians, paralegals, and teachers. They would also be useful to lawyers offering legal advice.

The preparation of such materials, I acknowledged, would be a vast undertaking and could not be done without heavy government subsidization. It would require taking all the law and identifying those categories most useful to non-lawyers. There might, I speculated, be perhaps a hundred separate categories in the final product. The basic statutory material would be reproduced along with the regulations and, where directly relevant, some of the case law. The texts would combine federal and provincial law because citizens do not divide their problems into federal and provincial areas. The librarians serving the collection would require some training in order properly to understand the materials with which they would be dealing.

An accompanying *Globe* editorial called it 'an intriguing proposal.' Librarians, a number of whom had helped me develop the ideas, liked the concept. One professor of library science wrote to the editor of the *Canadian Library Journal* stating, in part: 'Dean Friedland has given us a far-reaching challenge. Can we, through the Canadian Library Association and other library association forums, take the initiative in implementing his ideas?' Lawyers were divided. Law Society bencher Peter Cory wrote that it was 'an excellent idea and one that should be ardently supported.' Earl Cherniak, however, a distinguished bencher and an old friend, wrote: 'Dumbest thing I ever read!' Most lawyers were somewhere between the two opinions. Chief Justice Bora Laskin was 'apprehensive about leading people to believe that they can work out their own legal salvation by consulting public library holdings.' Nevertheless, he said he was sending a copy of the speech to the National Librarian, Guy Sylvestre, who later wrote to me that 'the suggested ways of making the law accessible to laymen coincides with the philosophy of the public library movement ... We agree that to create new legal materials will be helpful to the general public.'

The speech to the institute coincided with the start of my detailed work on the project, which eventually resulted in a book, *Access to the Law: A Study Conducted for the Law Reform Commission of Canada*, published in 1975 by Carswell/Methuen. I was greatly assisted by Peter Jewett, a gold-medallist graduate of the faculty of law who had been my research assistant for two summers while at law school and who took a leave of absence from Torys for a year to work on the project as its associate director. His then wife, Linda, who was trained as a librarian and later became a lawyer, was the assistant director. They conducted most of the studies that we undertook.

I had the guidance of an excellent advisory committee, consisting of

Lyle Fairbairn, who had been the assistant provincial director of legal aid, Francess Halpenny, dean of the faculty of library science, Ian Montagnes, general editor of the University of Toronto Press, political scientist Peter Russell, and John Swan from the faculty of law. I met with them frequently and they assisted me in formulating the conceptual framework for the study and in analysing its results. Ian Montagnes had the support of the director of the Press, Marsh Jeanneret, who had graduated from W.P.M. Kennedy's law school, liked the concept, and wanted the U of T Press to play a role in producing the materials as a public service.

We collected data on where people turn to for information about the law and legal advice and on the accuracy of the answers they receive. Visits were made by the Jewetts to centres across Canada to study the various organizations from which citizens then obtained legal information and advice. Interviews were conducted with and questionnaires completed by persons from legal-aid and assistance centres, government information offices, community information centres, libraries, and police departments.

People, we discovered, get legal information from a wide variety of sources, including, to a surprising extent, from the police. We tested information given from a number of sources and found that it was often inaccurate. With the help of psychologist Tony Doob from the U of T's Centre of Criminology, we set up experiments at the Science Centre of Ontario, where persons tried, but failed miserably, to use the statute books to find information.

We looked at existing statutory language and asked a linguist, Professor Harold Gleason, and a psychologist, Professor Paul Kolers, to assist us in examining legal language. Both looked at Canadian statutes and concluded that legal language is structured differently from ordinary language. Legal language, they noted, could be vastly improved if the order of clauses within sentences simply followed more closely other forms of English writing.

Professor Kolers pointed out that English is a 'right-branching' language, in which the qualifications and exceptions normally come after the verb. By contrast, legal language usually starts out with the qualifications and exceptions. Professor Gleason made a similar point, stating: 'There is a principle of English style that can be stated somewhat as follows: If, in any two-part construction, there is an appreciable difference in length between the two, then it is usually preferable for the shorter one to precede ... A convenient designation for a construction which runs counter to this preference is "front-heavy."' Legal language is normally front-heavy.

One can trace this awkward style of legal drafting to the most influential book ever published on legal drafting, George Coode's 'On Legislative Expression,' published in 1843. His work is still – mistakenly – regarded by most experts as a guide to good drafting. Coode broke down drafting into four components in which logical order took precedence over grammar. He stated:

> The rule to be observed is of such simplicity as to make its utterance appear almost an absurdity; but simple as it is, it is the most frequently neglected of any rule of composition. It is, that wherever the law is intended to operate only in certain circumstances, those circumstances should be invariably described BEFORE any other part of the enactment is expressed.

This rule, unfortunately, produces a 'left-branching,' 'front-heavy' construction, which non-lawyers have trouble understanding. Non-lawyers will normally read a section from the beginning and will therefore be forced to keep in their mind all the qualifications that may not apply in their case. Lawyers go straight for the verb, knowing that that is where the action is. I have always wanted to do a study tracing the eye movements of non-lawyers and lawyers reading a statute. That is yet another study waiting for someone to take on.

I earlier referred to the fact that drafting first in French and then translating into English might make the English more readable. The reason may well be that this would avoid the awkwardness of the Coode style of drafting.

The access project had evolved over the years. In the early stages, the plan was to actually start and finish the project by producing perhaps two hundred loose-leaf volumes on selected subjects. But the Law Reform Commission started getting cold feet. Pat Hartt wrote to me in December 1972 that 'there is a great interest in the Commission in the enterprise of attempting to make the law more accessible to the general public, but I think it is fair to say that there is apprehension about becoming engaged in what seems to be developing into a major publishing enterprise.' I then shifted ground to advocate a pilot project with sample drafts only. The budget was reduced accordingly to $50,000, which covered the costs of the work of the Jewetts and other expenses, including my $5000 honorarium.

Models were prepared and extracts from seven of them were included as an appendix to the *Access to the Law* book. Lawyer and author Jack Batten prepared a model on the *Mechanics' Lien Act*, Alan Mewett did one on eavesdropping, and my former research assistant, Eric Salsberg, did another on the Ontario Land Speculation Tax, to give only three examples.

The book received good reviews, particularly, to my surprise, in South Africa. Any country with a large population and relatively few lawyers needs to find solutions other than reliance on the advice of lawyers. The *Globe* followed up its earlier editorial with a detailed analysis under the heading 'To bring the law to the people.' They supported the idea of better training for those offering advice and then stated: 'It's his other suggestion that introduces the giddiness of a good idea – and like any good dramatist, he saves it for the last in his book. Why not write a whole new encyclopedia of the law for laymen? ... In times of constraint, priorities have to be firmly set. Surely a suggestion such as this belongs [on] the list.'

There was much activity in Canada on improving access to the law during the second half of the 1970s. Various organizations were active in producing brochures on legal subjects for citizens, new legal-aid clinics were established, and governments paid lip service to improving the drafting of legislation. No action was taken, however, to provide the type of encyclopedia that I had advocated.

Butterworths of Canada did, however, go part way in that direction. In the mid-1970s they started exploring the possibility of producing something like *Halsbury's Laws of England*, a multi-volume set of books on various legal subjects. While this was really meant for the legal community, it was a worthwhile project. The legal community needed help as much as laypersons did. In 1977 I joined the project's board and was honoured to join J.J. Robinette, Willard ('Bud') Estey, and others in that capacity. The series was formally announced two years later. After several years of experimentation with the project, Butterworths abandoned it in 1982. There was not, they concluded, enough of a market in Canada to make it profitable. Lexis Nexis, which recently took over Butterworths, announced, however, that it would be producing a series of about fifty volumes covering about one hundred areas, called *Halsbury's Laws of Canada*. A number of volumes – primarily designed for lawyers – have already been published.

In September 1980 Ellen Roseman, a regular columnist for the *Globe*, gave her support to the ideas I had been advocating, ending her column by adopting the final line in my book: 'Surely it's time for the law to be available to those it is meant to govern.' I got a call later the same day from Jean Lengellé, the former warden of Hart House, who was the director of the negotiated-grants division of the Social Sciences and Humanities Research Council. He had read the Roseman article and wanted me to apply for a negotiated grant to do the project. He followed up the next day with a written request. I replied: 'It seems to me that I shouldn't think about undertaking any new venture for at least a few years. I have a project on the Process of Law Reform that I have to complete and I don't think that it would be wise to get involved in anything else at this time.' Perhaps I should have tried to work something out. I was likely to get the funding and the timing would have coincided with the introduction of personal computers, although the Internet was still more than ten years in the future.

Just after the turn of the millennium, I returned to thinking about access to the law. My work on the history of the University of Toronto was almost finished and would be published in early 2002. The U of T history had been a mammoth undertaking, which many said could not be done, yet I was about to complete it successfully. I felt confident that I could handle the access-to-the-law project that I had promoted about thirty years earlier. The unfinished project still haunted me. I was convinced that it could be done and that it would make a significant contribution to society, particularly to jurisdictions that had relatively few lawyers. I had discussed the concept with government officials on a trip to South Africa in 1995 to visit our son Tom and his future wife Jacque, who were spending six months there while Tom worked in a legal-aid clinic in Cape Town. I also thought about the project when I was in China in 2000 talking with judges about judicial independence. There was a clear need for better access to the law throughout the world.

The Internet was now a reality. By the early 2000s, 75 per cent of Canadians had access to it. Almost all students were skilled in its use and so the number of users would continue to rise. Moreover, the cost of computers and high-speed Internet connection was going down. High-speed access in Canada had doubled in the previous two years and was at almost 50 per cent for those using the Internet.

I carefully searched the Internet to see how much had actually been done on the Web to advance access to the law. I discovered that a great amount had been accomplished to access *primary* sources of law, but that very little had been done to make those sources comprehensible to the average intelligent citizen. There were a vast array of websites devoted to the law, but most were composed of simple answers to 'frequently asked questions.' Many law firms had websites that gave insights into the law, but they were primarily designed to attract business for the firms and not as a substitute for a lawyer's skills. The commercial publishers had more sophisticated sites, but they were only available at a substantial cost, which made them inaccessible to the average person. Moreover, they were meant for professionals.

We buy our cars and books on the Web now. We seek medical information there. Indeed, as this was being written, three major American health organizations – for cancer, diabetes, and heart disease – announced that they had set up a website (www.patientinform.org) 'to help consumers navigate the bewildering world of health research.' The law is one of the last institutions to take significant advantage of the Internet to provide reliable information for the layperson. One free website devoted to the law stood out, the University of Montreal's CanLII (www.canlii.ca), which makes all the Canadian case law and statutes easily available for free. The site, which has been supported by the Federation of Law Societies and the federal government, is extremely valuable, but there is no analysis of subject areas. It just gives the bare bones of the law.

Legal-aid lawyers and clinics desperately need a Web-based tool similar to the one we had proposed. In my study on the governance of legal-aid systems, which I had done in 1997 for the McCamus committee on legal aid, I had urged the committee to recommend something like the access-to-the-law project, but this suggestion did not find its way into the McCamus report. I had also discussed the concept in the past with Judge Sidney Linden, who had become the chair of the newly created Legal Aid Ontario. He was enthusiastic. Legal Aid had a large budget – approaching $300 million a year – and such a project could in the long run save the organization money, apart from making the law more generally accessible. It would be widely used by the seventy or so (now about eighty) legal clinics in Ontario and by lawyers and others called on to give legal advice. The president of Legal Aid Ontario, Angela Longo, a tough-minded career civil servant, was, however, worried that it would divert money from the organization's primary mission, that is, delivering legal services, particularly at a time when the legal-aid tariff was still very low.

Judge Linden suggested that the Law Foundation of Ontario be brought into the picture, and so I attended a meeting with Linden,

Longo, and Ron Manes, the chair of the foundation, who was sold on the project. A strong proponent of access to justice, Manes headed the Access to Justice Committee of benchers of the Law Society. I later met with the committee, which included former attorneys general Marion Boyd and Charles Harnick. The committee liked the project and the former AGs indicated that they would pass their views on to the current attorney general.

In April 2002, a month after my U of T history was published, the Law Foundation provided me with a research grant of $60,000 for the project. I would be able to go seamlessly from one project to another. I would get $20,000 for expenses to get the project under way and the other $40,000 if I could get a matching $60,000 from the provincial and federal governments. Thinking that would not be difficult, I approached the Ontario attorney general's department and the federal Law Commission for a partnership arrangement. Their involvement was essential. If the demonstration project could not get this relatively small amount of government support, I feared it would limp along and not be able to demonstrate its usefulness. In the meantime I could start work.

I put an ad in the law school's weekly bulletin, *Headnotes*, seeking a summer research assistant. One of the applications came from Eliott Behar, who was about to graduate from British Columbia's University of Victoria law school. Apart from his legal skills, he had designed websites and knew much more than when to right-click a mouse, a skill that still eludes me. He spent six months working with me on the project.

We created a number of models to show how a website could be designed, picking areas that were mainly dependent on statute law, with some federal areas, such as pardons in criminal matters and getting a divorce, and some provincial areas, such as landlord-tenant law and legal aid. Case law was selectively included in the materials, with links to actual cases. There were also links to other useful websites. The models only covered parts of the subjects, and were not to be relied on for accuracy, but they were meant to demonstrate that the project would work. The reader can still find these models at www.law-lib2.utoronto.ca/accessmodels/index.htm, using the name 'access' and the password 'attl.'

As it turned out, the Ontario government was not willing to support the work 'at this time.' Mark Freiman, the deputy minister, was sympathetic to the project but was worried about costs. 'What is unknown,' he rightly pointed out, 'is the long-term potential cost of sustaining and

updating the services. My concern is that such costs would be very considerable.' 'More significantly,' he went on, 'there is a pressing demand
within the ministry to apply the limited funds that are available for
technology to modernizing our own systems, something that the min-
istries in the government's justice sector have been striving to achieve
through the Integrated Justice Project.' He therefore concluded that he
was 'not in a position at this time to recommend to the Attorney General that the ministry commit to your project. I say this despite the
understandable enthusiasm that many who have reviewed the proposal have offered.'

One can understand Freiman's reluctance to get involved, considering, as we now know, that the Integrated Justice Project, in which the
government had invested hundreds of millions of dollars, has been a
failure and has been abandoned. I had estimated in my proposal that
the cost of the access-to-the-law project might be somewhere between
one and two million dollars a year, but that was just an educated guess.

Nathalie Des Rosiers, the president of the Law Commission and now
the dean of the civil-law section of the University of Ottawa law school,
had expressed an interest in the project and was willing to put aside
some money for it, but was not sure how much she could deliver. Her
fellow commissioners may have been worried that the work had
started with the old Law Reform Commission. 'The link of the project
with the previous LRC is not the most attractive feature for us,' she
wrote, 'because we were marketed as "different."'

The success of the project therefore depended on convincing the
Ontario attorney general's department with a more elaborate demonstration project. I was exploring this approach with the Law Foundation when I learned that both the Ontario and the federal governments
were cutting back on the funds they were using for Internet projects.
Ontario, for example, was putting a hold on its own important project
on Ontario statutes. The federal government had started its own limited access-to-the-law website, devoted almost entirely to links to other
websites, which was having problems and was subsequently abandoned. Much of this I learned at a stimulating international conference
on Law Via the Internet in Montreal in early October 2002.

I decided that the time was not right to proceed with the larger demonstration project, and so I reluctantly withdrew my application for
further funding from the Law Foundation. I used the initial $20,000 to
pay Eliott Behar's salary, to write a final report on what was then available on the Web in Canada and other countries, and to describe what

our project had accomplished. The report included the production of a limited number of models on the website described above and examined what further steps could be taken. What we had done, I stated in my report to the Law Foundation, was 'designed to demonstrate that the concept is sound and that a larger long-term project should be undertaken.'

I continue to believe that the access project should come under the wing of provincial legal-aid operations. Legal Aid Ontario has a large administrative structure, with an arm's-length relationship with the government, and needs this type of information for its eighty or so clinics and its research facility for lawyers handling legal-aid matters. I ended my brief report by repeating the concluding sentence from my earlier study: 'Surely it is time for the law to be available to those it is meant to govern.'

It is highly unlikely that I will be the one to undertake that task, but I urge governments and my colleagues in the academic world to continue to explore the concept. I strongly believe that it would make a significant contribution to the administration of justice in this country and internationally.

13

Deaning and the University

My seven-year term as dean started officially on 1 July 1972, although Judy and I would not regain possession of our house until 1 August. In June we travelled from Ottawa through the Maritimes on a holiday, renting a cottage on the recommendation of Gerry La Forest for a couple of weeks on the north shore of Prince Edward Island. Early one morning, Tom and I went out on a lobster boat to take part in the morning haul from the lobster traps. That experience proved to be useful because I would later bring it up during class discussion of the Supreme Court's 1970 *Pierce Fisheries* case, which involved the *mens rea* requirement for the regulatory offence of possessing undersized lobsters. I have a picture of myself on the boat, carefully holding a large lobster, which I at one time contemplated putting in my casebook.

My involvement with the faculty had been fairly intense for the five-month period after my official appointment in late January. I made a number of trips to Toronto to meet with the faculty and later with the student body. My former research assistant, Bert Bruser, who had become the president of the Students' Law Society, had arranged a 'champagne breakfast' with his fellow students. A colleague, Brad Crawford, and his wife Diane, who had wanted to have a good-bye party for Judy and me before we left for Ottawa, held a welcome-home party instead. Bob Kaplan, at the time an MP in Ottawa, had a lunch in my honour with fellow U of T law alumni in the parliamentary lunch room, with baked Alaska for dessert.

Coincidentally, Harry Arthurs was appointed the dean of Osgoode Hall Law School at about the same time. The *Toronto Star* did an article on the two classmates and friends who were appointed deans of the two Toronto law schools. Harry and I quickly developed a number of cooperative ideas, such as the sharing of library resources and permitting students from each law school to take part in the other school's upper-year seminars. This sharing better utilized scarce library resources and broadened the curriculum at both schools, but it was also good public relations to show our respective administrations that we were trying to be as efficient as possible. The rivalry between the two schools continued throughout the decade – for the benefit of both institutions.

I felt that the faculty and students genuinely thought I could make a difference at the law school and looked forward to my tenure. I had good relations with all members of the faculty and seemed to be liked and respected by the students. The alumni, most of whom I knew personally, were pleased that for the first time a graduate of the faculty had become dean. Ronnie Macdonald, who would become the dean of Dalhousie Law School, sent me a gracious note on 1 July, the date that my appointment took effect, stating that there was, 'a universal feeling of contentment as well as enthusiasm over your appointment.'

The previous seven years – since I had left Osgoode Hall Law School and joined the faculty in 1965 – had not been good ones for the faculty of law. More space and greater library and other resources were desperately needed, the students were complaining about the quality of teaching, and many individuals, including my predecessor Ronnie Macdonald, felt that there had to be a greater commitment to scholarship in the faculty.

In the summer of 1968, Ronnie appointed me to chair a committee on research in the faculty. His note to me said, 'Personally as well as professionally I regard this as one of the most important of all our Faculty Committees.' The committee also included Ian Baxter, Jim Milner, and Stephen Waddams, all of whom supported more scholarly publication. An earlier 1966 report from a committee on teaching and research, chaired by Milner, which I had joined shortly after I arrived back at the faculty, had been very cautious about expecting faculty members to publish books or articles. One draft of that report stated that 'promotion of faculty members should follow successful teaching and research,' but defined research broadly to include 'reading and thinking, the results of which show only in classroom activity,' without requiring publication. The final report sent to Caesar Wright in 1966 had gone somewhat further, stating that 'the Faculty should recognize that all members from time to time in their research will be led to inquire into matters that they should publish elsewhere than in the classroom' and that 'research leading to publication' should be 'encouraged and facilitated.' Younger colleagues today may, no doubt, be surprised at the relatively lax attitude towards publication in the 1960s. Times have certainly changed in the faculty of law at the University of Toronto and at most other law schools, where lack of publication has a major negative impact on tenure, promotion, and merit pay.

As chair of the 1968 committee on research, I sent a memo to each member of the faculty, asking them to describe what research they were doing. This information was not then being collected by the dean, as it is today. Without identifying the authors, here are some of the responses in a relatively small faculty: 'I am working (very slowly and painfully) on a ... casebook'; 'the only research I am doing is for the Ontario Law Reform Commission on ...'; and 'the honest answer to your question is a devastating *NONE*.' Caesar Wright had not encouraged faculty members to apply for grants or to publish articles or books. Indeed, there was resentment by some of the faculty over Ted McWhinney's ability to get research funding and his record of publication. I recall one faculty meeting during Caesar's deanship when someone stood up to get something and another person quipped to almost universal laughter: 'While you're up, get me a grant.' The committee tried to change the faculty's attitude towards research, bringing as visitors to the faculty Professor Myres McDougal of Yale to talk about legal research and Professor Robert Alford of Wisconsin to talk about interdisciplinary empirical research. It was at about that point that I left for a sabbatical, described in the chapter on the machinery of law reform.

The faculty's physical resources were clearly inadequate. At the time we were confined to Flavelle House, with all the student facilities in the basement. The law library had only about 50,000 volumes. A report was prepared by the faculty in 1968 at the request of President Claude Bissell. It called for an enlargement of the facilities currently available to the faculty and a doubling of the faculty to result in a faculty-to-student ratio of one to twelve. This was needed for the 450 students then at the law school. Even greater resources would be needed if the size of the faculty increased to 675 students, as the faculty was willing to accept. There were only about half a dozen graduate students in those years, and the faculty wanted to increase their number to between fifteen and twenty-five.

There was a crisis atmosphere in the law school. In the summer of 1969, President Bissell sent a dramatic memorandum to the teaching faculty and the legal members of the board of governors, stating:

> I have been greatly concerned about the Faculty of Law in the University of Toronto. In 1968 the Faculty prepared a report, which was subsequently discussed in the President's Council with no conclusive results. It was apparent, however, that the Faculty was falling behind in all of the basic areas that determine academic quality ... The question now before us is whether we want to retain a first class Faculty of Law, or whether we want to abandon the enterprise entirely, for it is inconceivable that the University of Toronto would accept mediocrity in a major field.

A meeting that included recipients of Bissell's memo was held in the board room of Simcoe Hall in late September 1969, but no remedial action was taken at the time.

In February 1970 Faculty Council sent a 'Statement' to the president and the board of governors requesting that the board 'take immediate, extraordinary steps to deter the full development of the crisis which threatens the very continued existence of the Faculty in this University.' 'Toronto,' the statement asserted, indirectly pointing to Osgoode Hall Law School in its new quarters at York University, 'now lags behind other Ontario law schools in physical and administrative facilities, library collection and staff, faculty salaries, and financial support for graduate studies and faculty research. Not only have other law schools matured, in the sense of overcoming Toronto's initial lead, but it is beyond doubt that they are pulling rapidly ahead of Toronto in all major respects.' The decline would continue if nothing was done, so that 'it may then become a question of whether the Faculty of Law can or should continue to exist at the University of Toronto.'

No action was taken by the board of governors because they were more or less paralysed into inaction in those years. A Commission on University Government – inelegantly called CUG – which had been set up by the University in 1968, reported in October 1969. The commission unanimously recommended that the board of governors and the senate be scrapped and replaced by a unicameral governing body. The senate was primarily responsible for academic issues and the board for physical planning and financial matters. The commission's further recommendation that there be parity between faculty and students became the central issue in the subsequent debates.

I played a significant role in those debates as a member of the President's Council, a body that Bissell had set up in 1965 to advise him, as he had lost confidence in the ability of the board to do so. The council consisted of a number of elected faculty members, the senior university administrators, several members of the board of governors, and, later, a number of students. It acted as a bridge between the senate and the board, but also could give guidance and direction to the president, guidance that would increasingly be needed over the next half-dozen tumultuous years.

Jim Milner, one of the faculty members on the President's Council, died suddenly in the spring of 1969 while I was abroad on sabbatical. When I returned to Canada that summer, I decided that I would run for the vacant position. I was elected and was thereupon thrust into the middle of the debate on university governance. A programing committee was set up in October 1969 by the president, with the concurrence of the major organizations on campus, to try to determine the University's views on the CUG report.

Perhaps because I had not taken any public position on the issues, I was chosen to chair the programing committee, which included the chairman of the faculty association, Fred Winter; the president of the Students' Administrative Council, law student Gus Abols; another member of SAC, Ken McEvoy; the Graduate Students Union president, Michael Vaughan; and another member of the President's Council, historian Robert Spencer.

The activities of the programing committee are described in detail in a chapter of my history of the University. Suffice it to say here that during the course of the academic year the committee organized and encouraged discussion within the University of the many difficult issues raised in the CUG report. The committee struggled to find a way of reaching some form of consensus within the University on the issues. How could this be done in such a complex institution? Bissell later wrote in his memoirs that the answer that the programing committee proposed was 'both simple and bold ... to form a constitutional assembly, a broad and generous representation of the whole university, which would debate and vote on a series of specific resolutions that had emerged from the discussions of the preceding few months.' The constituent assembly, which would become known as the University-wide Committee (UWC), had widespread support throughout the University and was endorsed by the President's Council.

Over a three-day period in early June 1970, the UWC met in a large room in the Ontario government's Macdonald Block, on the east side of Queen's Park Crescent. Vice-president Robin Ross, whose office helped organize the assembly, later wrote that the UWC was 'the largest, boldest and most ambitious Presidential Advisory Committee ever struck or likely to be struck in the University of Toronto.' The committee was made up of 160 persons: 40 faculty members; 40 students; 40 academic and non-academic administrators; and 40 others, including 20 alumni representatives and 10 members of the board of governors. Understandably, the board did not endorse the exercise and refused to take part, though several board members attended as observers.

By a narrow margin (60–54) the UWC rejected the concept of parity between faculty and students. Eleven models were in contention at the meeting for the composition of a unicameral governing body. The final vote resulted in a recommendation for a 72-member body, with students having two-thirds the number of faculty members. The board did not agree with the result, later reporting to the government that 'a majority of the members of the Board have strong convictions' that a bicameral model is preferable to the unicameral system, and that if a unicameral system were to be adopted it should be a much smaller body with a majority of government appointees.

The year that I spent as chair of the programing committee was probably the most stressful in my academic career. There were strongly held views on all sides of the issues. I attended all the sessions of the University-wide Committee and worked behind the scenes with many of the key participants to try to ensure that it would not fail. If it had, I felt, it would have been my fault, because I had strongly promoted the concept of a large constituent assembly. Perhaps the tensest moment was at the very end of the proceedings. In order to induce the faculty and student organizations to take part in the whole endeavour, one of the ground rules was that either the faculty or the students by a majority vote could force a further meeting in the fall at which the decisions concerning the top governing structure could be revisited. If one of the parties had voted against the UWC results, it is unlikely that such a meeting would have been held.

The faculty was reasonably content with the compromise outcome of the UWC meeting, but a number of students were not. After discussion in their caucus, however, the students decided not to require a fall meeting, but stated that they unanimously 'deplore the outcome of these deliberations' and would come forward with a strong minority report. No such report was ever prepared. In general, wrote Bissell in his memoirs, there was 'a sense of immense relief, even a note of jubilation at the outcome.' I certainly felt both the relief and the jubilation. The following day I received a note from Bissell stating: 'I am writing to thank you for your great work during the last few months. You were the one largely responsible for the effectiveness of the all-University Committee, and the University is grateful.'

Any changes to the University of Toronto's governing structure required provincial legislation. In the spring of 1971, Bill Davis's Conservative government decided to go ahead with a new act along the lines proposed by the University-wide Committee. I appeared before the legislative committee that dealt with the bill and urged the government to follow the will of the University as expressed in the UWC. I outlined the procedure that had been followed and stated: 'This was the voice of the University.' A unicameral system was introduced with a greater number of faculty than student places, but the government wisely accepted the board's view that it should be a smaller body – fifty members – and that government appointees and alumni representatives should together form a majority of the council. The *University of Toronto Act, 1971* was passed in July 1971.

I personally liked the decision to have an equal number of internal and external members forming the governing council. It gave the governing body a measure of independence. My one regret was that the faculty did not have sufficient clout in the new structure. As dean, I spent two years as one of the presidential appointees on the new body and could observe its workings. The problem was that academic administrators – the persons most knowledgeable about the issues being discussed – were not members of the governing body, unless they happened to be elected to one of the faculty positions. In contrast, the faculty had controlled the senate in the earlier bicameral structure.

My view with respect to the composition of the governing council can be seen in the structure of the University-wide Committee, which I had promoted. The academic administrators, along with non-academic administrators, formed a separate large category equal in number to the faculty. I considered academic administrators to be the same as faculty members and so the faculty would have a strong voice on the governing body. In my view, most bodies tend to reproduce themselves.

The Commission on University Government, for example, recommended a structure very much like the commission itself. I thought the same would likely happen with the University-wide Committee, but I was wrong. The faculty did not accept academic administrators as pure faculty. Perhaps this was because those on the UWC had spent most of their years at the University under a system whereby deans and chairs tended to be life appointments, rather than appointments for a term of years, as had recently been instituted at the University.

Over the years, as I have shown in my history, changes have been made in the governing structure of the University to increase the participation of academic administrators in the work of the governing council. The most significant change occurred in 1988 during George Connell's presidency, whereby the academic-affairs committee and the planning and resources committee of the governing council were combined into a large academic board that would have a majority of academics and academic administrators. My impression is that the governing structure is now working reasonably well. I have not heard much agitation in recent years for the University of Toronto to return to a bicameral system. Still, it is worth pondering why no other major academic institution in North America that I am aware of has followed Toronto's lead.

With all the turmoil within the University during the 1960s, it is not surprising that the law school's problems were placed on the back burner.

The one thing that I bargained for on behalf of the faculty before accepting the offer of the deanship was more space. The provost, Don Forster, was willing to give us the ground floor of Falconer Hall, then occupied by the School of Continuing Studies, at the time called the Extension Department. The University planned eventually to tear down the building so that there would be a view of the music building from Queen's Park Crescent. With the growing concern about protecting Toronto's historic buildings, I believed that Falconer Hall would never be demolished, and I was reasonably confident that with our foot in the door we would eventually be able to take over the whole building, which we did.

I did not really bargain for my salary, saying that I was content to receive what I was receiving at the Law Reform Commission, which was $35,000 a year. My adjusted notional salary from the law school that year would have been $24,500, so this was a substantial increase.

Today, the University would have ensured that part of that sum would be a stipend for being the dean, which would have disappeared when I ceased being dean and returned to the faculty. In 1972, the concept of a limited term for a dean was still relatively new, so I simply got a salary of $35,000. The subsequent yearly increases were always generous. At the end of my term as dean my salary was over $50,000, and seven years later it was over $100,000. I recall Rob Prichard saying when he was dean that he wanted my salary to be high enough that I would not try to become a judge for financial reasons. I never did apply to become a judge. Perhaps I might have applied if I had grown tired of developing new projects and had wanted the issues to come to me for decision, rather than generating them myself. That day never came.

I was given a great amount of advice before I took office. Jerry Grafstein advised me to do what John Turner had done as minister of justice: make a list of my long-term objectives and keep them in a handy drawer. I did that, but I did not publicize the list because, as I recall telling President John Evans, if I did so I would likely not achieve them. I also remember the advice that Gerry La Forest, who had been the dean of law at the University of Alberta, gave. Take the long view, he advised. I would, he correctly noted, have my ups and downs, but my tenure would be successful if the faculty was a stronger institution at the end of my term of office than it was at the beginning. Judged by that standard, I believe that my deanship was a success.

I achieved three of the objectives I had written down on the list before I formally took office. One was to improve the first-year program by giving each student a small group experience. Up until then, all the first-year classes were in two seventy-five-person sections. Professor Caleb Foote of Berkeley, who had helped me with my bail project, discussed in an earlier chapter, had told me how successful the small-group program was in first year at his law school, so I decided to try to implement it for the fall term. This required rearranging at short notice the teaching loads of a number of faculty members, not an easy thing to do at any time, and not something I could have done without strong faculty support. I instituted what I called the 'course assignments committee,' made up of some of the most respected persons in the faculty. This became, in effect, the executive committee that I would call on to give me advice on all the difficult issues the faculty would face. This body was a more effective sounding board than a group formed of the heads of the permanent faculty committees, which my predecessor had sometimes used. All subsequent deans have used such a group, which still goes by the same rather innocuous name – the course assignments committee. With Associate Dean Ralph Scane's help and with the backing of the course assignments committee, the small-group program was instituted that fall.

Like the course assignments committee itself, the small-group program has stood the test of time and is still an important part of the faculty's teaching program. The first-year class is broken down into small groups of about fifteen students who take one of their courses in the small-group context. This approach enables students to engage in oral discussions, which many students are not inclined to do in the larger sections. It also allows them to get to know one professor and a relatively small group of students reasonably well. It therefore breaks down the anonymity of a large institution. The arts and science faculty has been experimenting with such an approach in recent years. The small-group program also solved the problem of how to deal with legal writing, which had been taught – unsuccessfully – as a large course outside the regular ones. Instead, it became integrated into one of the basic courses, with the assignments worth a large percentage (today, 70 per cent) of the final mark in that course, which itself would have a higher weighting than other courses. Legal writing, therefore, now tends to be taken seriously by the students.

The course assignments committee also assisted me in remedying another issue on my list: too much outside work by faculty members, which can be one of the most destructive conditions in any law faculty. I later saw this occurring in two other Canadian law schools, which I had been asked by the administration of those universities to examine. Faculty members who properly devote their time to teaching and research become discouraged and disheartened if they see other colleagues doubling or tripling their salaries by doing an excessive number of outside arbitrations and other activities. Even before I took office, I had worked out, with the approval of the provost, an arrangement with one faculty member who had, in effect, two full-time jobs – one at the faculty of law and another at another institution. Frank Iacobucci and I had our offices across the hall from this individual, and we knew that he spent relatively little time at the faculty. Over the years, the course assignments committee helped control these situations, which were among the most difficult problems I faced as dean. An individual would say that his workload was none of my business as long as he was meeting his classes and doing a reasonable amount of research. The Crispo rules, named after business school dean John Crispo, that were introduced in 1972 helped because they required one to report outside activities to the dean. One of the reasons that the U of T law school is a strong institution today is because major outside activities have to be cleared with the dean and are carefully controlled. Such activities can be beneficial for the faculty member and the institution, and so should not be unreasonably curtailed, but it should not be up to the faculty member, who has a clear conflict of interest on the issue, to determine whether the activity should be undertaken. Since my retirement I have sat on the faculty committee giving advice to the dean on merit increases, and can see that there is relatively little paid moonlighting going on – perhaps too little now.

In 1991 I prepared a report on conflicts of interest at the University, which in a modified form was adopted by the University of Toronto in 1994 and, I am told, by York University and other institutions. President Rob Prichard had asked me to do the report, knowing how seriously I had taken the issue as dean. My report adopted many of the principles that we used in the faculty of law, the main one being that major outside activities required the consent of the administrator to whom the person reported. The administrator could, for example, help ensure that there was an academic payoff to the work, such as a resulting publication.

Another objective on my list was to try to bring the law school closer to the University. I arranged a series of talks to be delivered at the law school during my first year as dean, which were scheduled for a time slot when we had arranged that there be no classes. I was able to put together an outstanding list of speakers on the topic 'Courts and Trials: A Multidisciplinary Approach,' which was published in 1975 as a book by the University of Toronto Press. The series was well received in the faculty and in the University. The poster setting out the series of speakers remained up on bulletin boards throughout the University for the whole academic year. It was making the point that the law school was open for business with other disciplines. I recall John Crispo, the dean of the business school, asking me: 'Who does your PR work?'

Philosopher Reginald Allen talked about the trial of Socrates; mathematician Anatol Rapoport about theories of conflict resolution and the law; psychologist Tony Doob about psychology and the law of evidence; philosopher Charles Hanly on the Truscott case from a psychoanalytic perspective; political scientists Peter Russell on judicial power and Donald Smiley on courts and human rights; sociologist Jim Giffen on the control of addictions; economist Don Dewees on courts and economic regulation; and historian Ken McNaught on political trials. Many of the faculty at the law school embraced the interdisciplinary approach to studying legal issues. Shortly before Dean Ron Daniels left for the University of Pennsylvania in 2005 he wrote an editorial in the alumni magazine which stated that Caesar Wright had brought the law school *to* the University and I had brought it *into* the University. I was pleased to be remembered for this.

Two outstanding academics, Michael Trebilcock and Ernie Weinrib, had joined the faculty the same year that I became dean. They both strongly supported an interdisciplinary approach to the study of law. Ernie was cross-appointed to the classics department and Michael developed, with the assistance of a young faculty member, Rob Prichard, a strong international reputation in the relatively new area of law and economics. In the mid-1970s we had applied for a Connaught grant to start a program in law and economics with Michael as the director. The application was successful and the program, which is still going strong, has received support from other sources for over thirty years.

The Connaught Fund, which resulted from the sale of the university's Connaught Laboratories in the early 1970s, has been very important to the University. In the mid-1970s, this endowed fund was yielding about $2 million a year. The fund was – and still is – the largest pool of capital available for research that the University has ever achieved. I recall being on a small committee in those early years with George Connell and John Polanyi that set out the ground rules for the distribution of the funds. We wanted it to have as wide an impact as possible. Many of the innovative and often interdisciplinary programs in the University owe their existence to the Connaught Fund. Some, of course, did not flourish. For example, the law school received a start-up grant in the 1970s for a program in law and social welfare, which did not continue after the initial period of funding. I also had my eye on increasing the interdisciplinary work of the school by trying to bring the Centre of Criminology and the Centre for Industrial Relations within the orbit of the law school. Both centres resisted these overtures. They wanted to keep their independence, and were probably right to do so.

Improving teaching and scholarship were crucial issues on my list of priorities. Throughout my deanship I encouraged faculty to take both teaching and scholarship seriously. We made a fuss whenever a book was published, holding book launches and passing new books around meetings of faculty council. Scholarship also played a significant part in merit increases, and we assisted faculty members in applying for grants. It did not take long for the message to sink in.

We tried to enhance the quality of teaching in the faculty. Teaching evaluation procedures were improved. Further, an excellent resource person, Richard Tiberius, who had been working on improving teaching in the faculty of medicine, was made available for any faculty member who wanted help. In order to encourage a good response I was, I recall, the first person to volunteer and gained a lot of insight on how my teaching was perceived by students. Tiberius would sit in on my classes and later talk to the students on their perceptions. I continued to work on my teaching materials, producing two new editions of my criminal-law casebook while dean, one in 1974 and another in 1978. Throughout my deanship I taught a full load, reduced only by one-half course. It sent a good message to others, and if it meant fewer and shorter meetings, so much the better.

We also introduced a small clinical component into some of the courses. Students would have the chance to draft a statement of claim with a practitioner for their civil-procedure course, would work with a practitioner in incorporating a small corporation for the company-law course, and would help a practitioner draft a simple will for their wills and trusts course. Individuals within and outside the university community who wanted a free will drafted volunteered for the program. These clinical additions seemed to be successful, but have since disappeared from the law school. The scheme made good sense because few students had ever seen a real statement of claim, or the document incorporating a corporation, or even a will.

Students were encouraged to take part in the legal-aid program, which was starting to flourish at the law school. We built a course around the program and hired Dick Gathercole, now doing legal advocacy work in British Columbia, to handle the course and be an adviser to the program. In addition, the directed research program was started, which was designed to enable an upper-year student to work on a project under the supervision of a faculty member for a number of hours' credit. We also developed what were called 'cluster programs' for students who thought they knew what they wanted to do after graduation. Frank Iacobucci offered the first cluster program in the faculty – on business planning. We also explored various methods of teaching. John Evans came to talk to us about the problem-solving case method he had so successfully developed at the McMaster medical school. Most thought that the McMaster method not appropriate for a law school, although a number of courses, such as ones in business planning, used aspects of the technique.

All in all, it was a period of change, experimentation, and development. Much of the credit goes to the students, who generally were the most activist of any period in the history of the faculty. These were the same students who had changed the way universities operated in the late 1960s. I was usually able to find an acceptable middle ground between the radical ideas of some of the students and the more conservative views of some members of the faculty.

From the beginning, I took a very positive attitude towards the future of the faculty. I would make the point that we had excellent students and a fine faculty and could be even better than we were. My earlier experience on the university's budget committee when I had been on the President's Council showed me that struggling divisions were not as likely to be supported as generously as the more dynamic ones.

The faculty of law received strong support from President Evans, who started his term as president at the same time as I became dean. He was an outstanding president during a period of financial stringency in universities. I was certain that he would eventually become the prime minister of Canada, but he could not get by the hurdle of winning the election in the Rosedale riding over the popular former mayor of Toronto David Crombie. Evans recognized that the law school was a strong institution and could be made much stronger with modest financial support. He was used to large budgets in medical schools. Compared to any major or even medium-sized department in a medical school, the law school's budget was miniscule. My recollection is that our budget kept expanding at a time when most budgets in the university were contracting. Unlike today, fundraising was not a major part of a dean's activities. Even the University had not done much fundraising. By the end of Evans's tenure in 1978 the University's fundraising campaign had pledges of only $21 million, a very small amount compared to the billion dollars raised during Robert Prichard's tenure.

I also was greatly assisted by a succession of dedicated associate deans, who supported the changes we were making – Ralph Scane, Frank Iacobucci, whom Evans snatched to become the University's vice-president of internal affairs, Bruce Dunlop, and Ted Alexander. In my first year, we hired an assistant dean, Marie Huxter, who had graduated from the law school several years earlier. I had an excellent secretary, Patricia Dawson, who was with me for the full seven years I was dean. She had been secretary to the chair of chemistry at McGill and so was used to the academic world.

The dean's office was, and still is, on the second floor of Falconer Hall. Because the faculty was now in two buildings, we tried to find ways to bring the faculty together. One technique was the 'Friday lunch.' Every Friday the faculty would meet in the small dining room attached to the upper dining room in Hart House. We paid for our own lunches. Between ten and fifteen persons would show up and there would be a ten-minute introduction to some topic, followed by a discussion until about two o'clock. I recall Alan Mewett leading one lively talk on whether the state should punish a refusal to use seat belts.

To further encourage the faculty to meet, the former office of the dean on the second floor of Flavelle House became a faculty room. As an incentive to drop in, all current periodicals, law reports, and recently acquired books were displayed there for a week after cataloguing and before being returned to the library. We instituted a system of placing the periodicals on a separate shelf for each day of the work week, where they would remain for a week, until the new batch for that day arrived. One could therefore easily tell which periodicals were new. I would visit the faculty room at least once a day to look at the new material. A great deal of faculty business was conducted on those visits to the faculty room or by my dropping into a colleague's office. I rarely summoned faculty members to my office, because I remembered the anxiety I had experienced when asked to come to Caesar's office without knowing why he wanted to see me. I should add that the snooker table purchased in those years also helped bring faculty members over to the faculty room, but has since disappeared. So has the practice of displaying new periodicals in the faculty room, perhaps because they are now reasonably accessible on the Web.

Perhaps because of my experience in standing helplessly in front of Caesar's desk, I did not choose to keep the desk. Bruce Dunlop got it and I ordered the same style of desk I had had at the Law Reform Commission. The office came with a washroom. Visiting the dean's washroom became an important part of the first-year students' orientation tour. Meeting the dean, it seems, was incidental.

I supported various student activities. As a former editor, I encouraged the activities of the *Faculty of Law Review*. We were able to obtain funds from the Tory law firm to enable students to spend part of a summer working on a law review project. Mooting became more important than it had been in my days as a student. The most important moot in the 1970s was the annual Jessup international moot. I think we won the Canadian Jessup moot five years in a row, with the world championship being won in 1976 by Patricia Jackson and Richard van Banning, both of whom went on to practice with Torys.

I had a good relationship with the student body and would often have lunch in the student cafeteria in the basement of Flavelle House. The student newspaper always treated me fairly. In one of the fall issues in my first year, Michael Leshner, later famous for his advocacy of the recognition of gay marriages, did a humorous interview, which started like this:

Q. I think we should begin by finding out something about the young Marty Friedland, where you went to school and the like.
A. Well, I don't know how to answer that. I had a relatively conventional upbringing. I had a mother and a father and brother and a dog and I grew up in the north end of Toronto.
Q. Can you give us a few particulars on your family?
A. A wife, three kids and a dog. My son, Tommy, who is now eight, used to want to be a law teacher and write books with his Daddy; he's now more concerned with being a hockey player. Nancy is almost two, but still hasn't given much thought to the future. Jenny, who is six, would probably like to be a law student and spend every day colouring fancy books, like the students do here.
Q. And the dog?
A. Our dog has caused me great embarrassment. As a law professor I should obey the law and not allow him out of the house without a leash. Nevertheless, he refuses to understand the law and barks if not let out. The only possible solution is to let him out unattended with a leash on him. Whether I can beat a charge if prosecuted, I don't know.

The interview ended with:

Q. I understand that you have never forgiven Harry Arthurs for winning the Dean's Key instead of yourself. Would you care to comment?
A. You forget, Michael, that I am now in a position to award one to myself.

On my retirement as dean, the University gave me – at my wife's suggestion – a boxed set of the complete symphonies of Mozart performed by the Berlin Philharmonic with Karl Böhm conducting. Unfortunately they were long-playing records and I switched to CDs shortly after they were introduced in 1982. My colleague Stephen Waddams gladly took them and has given them a good home. The faculty gave me a magnificent engraved gold pocket watch, but I no longer wear a vest and the watch remains in my safety deposit box.

The student body set up a prize in my name for the best article published in the law review each year by a U of T student. I still turn out to present that award, the amount of which was embarrassingly low by today's standards and has been bumped up to a respectable sum by several donations from me. The students also instituted a cup, called 'The Marty,' for the person who won the annual squash tournament at the school. I do not know where the cup is, and have not seen any mention of it in the student paper for many years.

After my deanship I returned to be a regular member of the faculty – the only former dean who has done so. I continued to be active within the University outside the faculty of law, as a senior fellow of Massey College, a cross-appointed member of the Centre of Criminology, a participant in a number of search committees, and for several years a member of the honorary degrees committee and the University's research board. I also took part in a faculty association committee in 1981 at the request of my friend and former squash partner, UTFA president Michael Finlayson, on alternatives to the memorandum of agreement that had been negotiated in the late 1970s. Moreover, I continued to be asked to help resolve various difficult issues within the University. I will only touch on them briefly because of the relatively sensitive nature of the assignments.

In the early 1980s I chaired the first hearing in the University held to decide whether a tenured professor should be removed because of allegedly improper conduct – in this case plagiarism in an article in a student newspaper on one of the suburban campuses. At the time there were only two choices – dismissal of the faculty member or doing nothing. The panel, which included chemist John Polanyi, was persuaded by the defendant's counsel Ian Scott that although the faculty member should have acknowledged the source of the material in his article, removal would be too harsh under the circumstances. Intermediate penalties would today be possible in such a case.

I was also asked by St Michael's College in the mid-1980s to chair a committee to examine the bizarre conduct of a faculty member who had been dismissed from his position as head of the Celtic Studies program. We agreed with the decision by the College that he be removed from his position as head of the program. There were clearly psychiatric problems, and some years later the faculty member resigned from the University for health reasons.

In the late 1990s I chaired a tribunal set up by the faculty of medicine to handle one aspect of the Nancy Olivieri affair – whether a junior faculty member should be disciplined for his conduct in using research data which Dr Olivieri claimed belonged exclusively to her. The tribunal held that it would be unfair to discipline him in the special circumstances of the case, but we advised the faculty that better rules and procedures were needed in the hospitals to handle situations such as the one that Olivieri found herself in. In my history of the University of Toronto I acknowledged in a footnote my involvement in the matter and simply state in the text:

> The regulation of research and ethical procedures and their enforcement in the hospitals did not keep up with the growth of research, as became evident in the controversy in the 1990s involving the Hospital for Sick Children and the development of a drug to treat the iron overload associated with the disease thalassaemia. The controversy, brought to public attention by the haematologist Nancy Olivieri, had the long-term consequence of convincing everyone that harmonization of the differing hospital rules on research procedures was necessary, particularly in the area of drug trials.

The University also asked me to examine problems in two professional faculties: architecture and management studies. In the mid-1980s Provost Frank Iacobucci invited me to chair – political scientist Peter Russell was also a member – a committee looking at turmoil in the faculty of architecture. Architects, we discovered, have strong personalities and strong opinions. In particular, one provocative faculty member had been a lightning rod for various complaints. We recommended various changes in the faculty and were critical of the acting dean. Our report did not, however, solve the issues, and several years later Simcoe Hall tried – unsuccessfully – to shut down the faculty. It is today solely a graduate faculty and seems to be doing well.

Management Studies was having problems in the late 1990s, and Provost Adel Sedra asked me to look into the situation as a one-person committee. Many faculty members were upset because one member – a highly regarded teacher and scholar – was doing little teaching in the regular programs but was receiving more than two thousand dollars a day, in addition to his regular salary, to teach in the executive programs. It was a messy situation because of his personal relationship with the person running the executive programs. I found fault with the faculty member, who was doubling his salary through these faculty-run executive programs, with the person running the program, and with the dean, who resigned a year later. I recommended a number of changes to control excessive moonlighting, particularly with respect to executive programs, and made recommendations on how a more collegial atmosphere could be developed in the faculty. I also recommended that the faculty establish a form of executive committee, such as the so-called course assignments committee in the faculty of law. The report was never made public, but President Prichard and Provost Sedra took steps to implement some of the changes that I recommended. As far as I can tell, the faculty, now called the Rotman School of Management, is today, under Roger Martin's deanship, a strong, confident faculty.

After my deanship ended, I continued – indeed, I increased – my involvement with the University of Toronto Press. My first two books, *Detention before Trial* and my criminal-law casebook, had been published by the Press in the 1960s and I had been a member of the Press's scholarly publishing committee in the early 1970s. Provost Jack Sword chaired that large, unwieldy committee, which met infrequently in the circular chamber in Simcoe Hall. In 1973 President John Evans set up a small committee, chaired by former President Bissell, to examine scholarly publishing at the University. It concluded that a much smaller committee – a manuscript review committee (MRC) – be established. Such a committee was established, with Jack Robson, the distinguished editor of the *Collected Works of John Stuart Mill*, as its chair and with about ten other members, one of whom was Derek Mendes da Costa of the faculty of law. In order to protect the scholarly reputation of the Press, the manuscript review committee has to give its stamp of approval to manuscripts put forward by the various editors of the Press for approval.

When Mendes da Costa was appointed as the chair of the Ontario Law Reform Commission in 1977 and could no longer serve on the committee, Robson called me for my advice on a possible replacement. He may have been calling to sound me out on my own participation, but before he had a chance to do so, I volunteered to join the committee – and have been a member ever since. When my term as dean ended in

1979, I took a leave of absence from the committee for a year when I went on sabbatical, then rejoined it again in the fall of 1980. In the spring of 1983 Jack recommended to President Jim Ham that I be appointed vice-chair of the committee, a recommendation that was approved by Ham on 30 June 1983, his last day in office.

Jack died of a heart condition at the age of sixty-eight in 1995, and I was appointed by Rob Prichard to serve as the chair of the committee. My first meeting as chair was in the fall of 1995 – meeting number 145. I have continued to chair the committee. The 250th meeting was held in March 2006. At some point, I will have to retire from the committee, although I will do so reluctantly. As I say to potential new members of the committee, it is the one committee in the University that persons do not want to leave.

Most manuscripts come with two or more readers' reports. The author responds to the reports, not knowing who wrote them, although the members of the MRC do. There are usually more than a dozen manuscripts to be considered at each monthly meeting from September to June. At some meetings, every member of the seventeen-member committee has one manuscript to read. With the assistance of the secretary of the committee, I assign the manuscripts to individual members, trying to match their interests and expertise with the manuscripts to be discussed. The meetings start at 9:30 in the morning – on Fridays for the past dozen or more years – and continue without a break until about 12 noon.

The meetings are intellectually exciting. There is a wide range of disciplines represented. Members will give a one- or two-page report on a manuscript and then there will be a general discussion. We go behind the readers' reports to make our own assessment of the manuscript in the light of the reports. The process may be unique among scholarly presses, which tend to rely almost exclusively on readers' reports. There is more wit and laughter on the MRC than on any other committee in the University with which I have been associated. Each month we eagerly await medievalist Andy Orchard's always clever report.

Not only have I been involved with the academic health of the Press, but I have also been intimately involved with its financial health. I served on a committee in the early 1980s, chaired by John Lyerle, the dean of the graduate school, to try to obtain better funding for the Press, which was $2 million in debt. I also served as a member of the search committee to select a replacement for Harald Bohne, who was retiring as director of the Press. We were unsuccessful in landing the right candidate and a member of the search committee, George Meadows, with a background in publishing, was asked in 1990 to become the Press's director for one year. He had comfortably retired from business at age fifty-two and wanted to devote himself to sailing and other leisurely activities. The one-year term turned into a fourteen-year term. The sailing was, as it turned out, a plus for the Press. The much anticipated June meeting of the MRC was held during George's tenure at the Royal Canadian Yacht Club on the Toronto Island.

In 1990 President Prichard asked me to join the board of the Press. Jack Robson did not wish to continue as a board member along with his position as chair of the MRC. I have been a member of the board since then. Meadows proved to be a strong and dynamic director and his term was extended until his retirement in 2004. During that period, from 1990 to 2004, the financial health of the Press improved, such that almost every year the Press turned a profit. The number of books published increased from about 80 to about 150 a year. The number of bookstores run by the Press on the three campuses expanded.

I also served on the search committee that chose John Yates to replace George as president. John had extensive experience in publishing, most recently as the president of legal publisher Butterworths Canada. Under his leadership the Press continues to be in reasonably good shape. The financially risky printing division was sold in 2006. Scholarly publishing is continuing to produce important and prize-winning books, and the various bookstores and other components of the Press continue to support scholarly publishing. As this is being written I am serving on the search committee for a new vice-president for scholarly publishing.

Moreover, I have continued to publish most of my books with the Press. Over the course of the past forty-plus years I have worked closely with ten editors at the Press. I doubt if any non-employee in the history of the Press has worked with more editors or has been more involved. My first editor was Jean Houston, who, as discussed in an earlier chapter, helped turn my very sloppy manuscript, *Detention before Trial*, into a book. A few years later, Francess Halpenny, the managing editor, skilfully edited the first edition of my criminal-law casebook in the course of one weekend. In 2001 – with equal skill – she became the textual editor of my history of the University of Toronto. Prudence Tracy, who covered the classics and law, edited several of my books in the 1970s and 1980s, but tragically died of cancer in the early 1990s at the age of fifty-one. Gerry Hallowell, who specialized in history, was the editor of *The Case of Valentine Shortis* in the mid-1980s. Virgil Duff, who covers the social sciences and who has been a fixture at learned-society meetings over several decades, took on the volumes that came out of the sanctions-and-rewards project and also was the editor of *The Death of Old Man Rice*. Ron Schoeffel, now retired, but still actively involved in the Erasmus and Northrop Frye series, was responsible for the U of T history. The present manuscript is being edited by Len Husband. As a member and later the chair of the MRC, I also worked closely with Ian Montagnes, the editor-in-chief in the 1970s and 1980s, with his successor, Bill Harnum, the vice-president of scholarly publishing, and with Suzanne Rancourt, who took over from Ron Schoeffel as the secretary of the MRC. The legendary R.I.K. Davidson, now deceased, is just about the only past editor with whom I was not directly involved.

The Press has been a major force in Canada's cultural life and has brought a significant amount of credit to the reputation of the University of Toronto. To flourish, however, it requires financial support. The sales of the vast majority of scholarly books do not cover the costs of publication. What is needed is an endowment. Maybe some benefactor reading this chapter who has an affinity for scholarship and books will come forward and set up an endowment for the Press that will allow it to enhance its list of publications, as happened with the Mellon-financed Bollingen Foundation at the Princeton University Press.

Another important institution to which I have had a close personal attachment is the Osgoode Society for Canadian Legal History. The vast majority of its books are published by the U of T Press. The Society was started at the initiative of Chief Justice Roy McMurtry in the late 1970s when he was the attorney general of Ontario. At the time of its founding, I had done little work in legal history, but after the publication of my Lipski book in 1984, I was invited to join the society's board. I have been an active member since then.

Roy McMurtry succeeded Brendan O'Brien as the chair of the board. Peter Oliver, a professor of history at York and a fine scholar, was the editor-in-chief from the society's inception until his untimely death from esophageal cancer at the age of sixty-six in the spring of 2006. Peter was primarily responsible for the society's successful publication record, which now stands at close to seventy books. I am pleased that one of my books, *The Case of Valentine Shortis*, published in 1986, is included in that list, as is this volume. The society also has an active program of oral histories. There have been about four hundred interviews, primarily of lawyers, judges, and academics, consisting of about 75,000 pages, a valuable resource for present and future scholars. No other legal-history society that I am aware of has been so successful. My colleague Jim Phillips has replaced Peter as editor-in-chief.

Like the U of T Press, the Osgoode Society is an organization with which I am proud to be associated. The law and the legal profession have been important factors in the development of Canadian society. Without the creation of the Osgoode Society, much of the history of that development might have been lost.

I will end this chapter with a biased quote from my history of the University of Toronto with respect to my contribution to the development of the law school and its future:

> Under Friedland's deanship, the faculty deliberately moved more directly into the University, by increasing the amount of interdisciplinary work and placing a greater emphasis on scholarship. A succession of strong future deans – Frank Iacobucci, Rob Prichard, Bob Sharpe, and Ron Daniels – would appear to have brought the school to the position dreamed of by Sidney Smith: 'a Law School that would rank first in Canada and be among the leading schools of the North American continent.'

The only thing I would add to that quote is that Dean Mayo Moran has maintained the momentum.

14

Gun Control

Like many of the issues that I have worked on over the years, gun control has remained a controversial topic. Indeed, it has become even more contentious in Canadian public policy over the past fifteen years. The election in 2006 of the federal Conservative government under Stephen Harper turned in part on the issue of gun control, particularly the issue of the registration of long guns.

The story of gun control illustrates the danger of a good idea being carried too far. The decision to have all long guns registered, including existing guns, was not wise. It has proved to be virtually unworkable and hugely expensive, and, most important, has diverted attention away from the major problem, handguns. If a more gradual approach to the control of long guns, as recommended by a task force that I had been associated with in the mid-1970s, had been adopted, the licensing of almost all existing long guns would by now have been accomplished through the passage of time.

In June 1975 I was asked by Roberto Gualtieri, the coordinator of a federal Working Group on Gun Control, to undertake a 'jurisprudential analysis of possible gun control proposals.' Roberto, a former Rhodes Scholar, was at the time with the Treasury Board, and had frequently been given the task of handling difficult policy issues. The gun-control initiative was housed in the solicitor general's department, with input from the Department of Justice and the RCMP. There was some urgency to complete the work because of the government's agenda and because Gualtieri had made arrangements to go trekking in the Himalayas late that summer. He was, however, having trouble with his back, and for several of the meetings I attended in Ottawa he conducted the proceedings lying flat on his back. Nevertheless, he did go trekking.

I had never owned a gun and knew very little about them. My first recollection of firing a gun was in high school, when students – I assume only male students – would from time to time go to the Forest Hill police station on Eglinton Avenue to shoot rifles in the basement firing range. I cannot recall whether this was mandatory. There were several other occasions when I fired a gun. The summer I spent in the air force after grade 12 gave me the opportunity to go skeet shooting, and I recall shooting rats on a farm outside Toronto on one occasion and hunting wild boars in northern Nigeria – we did not encounter any boars – when I went on a World University Service study tour to West Africa the summer before entering law school.

A contract was worked out which required me to hand in a preliminary draft of my report by the end of July 1975 and to submit the final report on or before the end of August. The contract outlined the purpose of the project: 'To identify and describe possible policy instruments that could be used to control the availability and misuse of firearms, and to evaluate them from a legal, procedural and constitutional point of view.' I would have the right to publish my study a year after it had been completed, or earlier with the consent of the solicitor general's department.

I was able to hire a law student, Arnie Herschorn, now a lawyer with Minden Gross, who had just finished first year. He had a PhD in philosophy from Princeton and knew about as much about guns as I did. We collected whatever statistics we could and combed the secondary literature for information about the use of guns and their control in Canada and other countries. We also gained some first-hand experience with guns by going skeet shooting at a club somewhere west of Toronto and by shooting handguns at the Hart House firing range. I still have on my office wall the target – signed by the then president of the Hart House gun club and professor of Hispanic studies, Alan Gordon – which demonstrated that I could without difficulty hit the chest-level target with a handgun, even though I had never before fired one. There are clean holes in the target made by a powerful .45 calibre handgun, jagged holes from a .38, and much smaller holes from a .22. Guns, I discovered, are classified according to the diameter of the inside of the barrel.

I submitted a first draft of the study at the end of July 1975, with a note to Gualtieri stating: 'I must say that I don't think I have ever enjoyed working on a project as much as I have enjoyed this one. It's a fascinating area.'

The final draft of the sixty-page study was submitted towards the end of August. It started with a discussion of the pressure for change in gun regulation in Canada. Interest in reform developed even though there had been significant legislation in the late 1960s which had attempted to find a proper balance between protecting the interests of society in controlling the illegitimate use of guns and, at the same time, not unduly hampering legitimate users. I took the position that even if one personally dislikes the use of guns, 'it is difficult to argue that target shooting – an Olympic sport – is not a legitimate activity.' Similarly, I went on to say, 'hunting is part of the Canadian tradition,' quoting a current official publication of the Ontario government which stated that 'the sport of hunting ranks historically as one of our province's first recreational pursuits.'

As is often the case, the immediate cause of pressure for change was a series of tragic incidents involving the deaths of a number of innocent people. Thirteen persons had died of gunfire and arson at a Montreal club in January 1975, and three persons died in a high school in Brampton, Ontario, in May of that year. These incidents provided the public with concrete examples of the potential consequences of the availability of guns. Tragic events had also spurred action for change in the United States. The 1968 U.S. *Gun Control Act* had been quickly passed under the shadow of the shootings that year of Robert Kennedy and Martin Luther King. Moreover, stricter gun laws were being advocated by the police in Canada following the deaths of a number of police officers from firearms in the previous two years, particularly the killing of two officers in Toronto and another two outside Moncton, New Brunswick.

A further impetus for reform was the Canadian government's desire to abolish capital punishment. As a trade-off, the police and the public were to be given some assurance that crime would be effectively dealt with. The proposed legislation introduced in 1976 that followed from our report, Bill C-83 (*An Act for the better protection of Canadian society against perpetrators of violent and other crime*), dealt with wiretapping, dangerous offenders, and parole, as well as gun control. The police, who were strongly opposed to the abolition of capital punishment, were to be protected by greater control over firearms, since guns prove the one real threat to a police officer's life. Shooting a police officer had previously been a capital offence. A similar sequence of events occurred in England in 1965 when capital punishment was abolished: the government introduced strong gun-control legislation before the vote on capital punishment.

Much of my study concentrated on the issue of handguns. They were not yet a problem in Canada because of the stringent control over handguns since the nineteenth century. The number of murders committed in Canada with handguns in the 1970s was still relatively low compared to the United States, although it was rising. In 1970 there were only thirty-three murders in Canada committed with handguns (fewer than 8% of all murders), but this had risen to seventy-one in 1974 (about 13% of all murders). In comparison, Detroit alone had 280 handgun homicides in 1968. In the same year, about 18,000 new registrations for handguns were issued in Detroit, as opposed to only about 14,000 new registrations in all of Canada. It would be important, I argued, to maintain stringent controls so that handguns would not become prevalent in Canada.

Canada's low handgun ownership rate probably accounted for the relatively low rate of homicide by handguns. If handguns are not readily available they will not be readily used, stolen, accidentally discharged, or mistakenly employed. Moreover, if the level of handgun ownership is kept low, then citizens will not be as likely to feel that they have to acquire handguns in order to feel secure.

For the most part, the nineteenth-century Canadian laws simply attached criminal penalties to certain undesirable conduct. So, for example, Canada handled the conduct portrayed in many Western movies of armed villains coming to town by making it an offence 'if two or more persons openly carry offensive weapons in a public place in such a manner and under such circumstances as are calculated to create terror and alarm.' Another section of the Criminal Code made it an offence to point a firearm at another person. In 1892 the first permit system was enacted relating to handguns. A certificate by a justice of the peace was required, unless the person feared an assault. This was tightened up in 1913 by requiring a permit even if there was 'reasonable cause to fear an assault.' Penalties for breaching these provisions were increased in 1933, including a sentence of two years in addition to any other sentence if the offender carried a handgun while committing a criminal offence. The following year, 1934, the government brought in new legislation providing for the registration of all handguns, wherever kept. This, in brief, is the history of some of the major steps taken by various governments over the years to control handguns in Canada.

As a result of the 1968–9 legislation, there were three categories of firearms in Canada – prohibited weapons, restricted weapons, and long guns, which were left unregulated. I recommended in my study that fully automatic weapons and sawed-off shotguns be added to the list of prohibited weapons. The provisions with respect to restricted weapons, primarily handguns, appeared to be working reasonably well. Permits were required and each handgun had to be registered. Careful background checks were made. Still, I recommended further tightening of the controls. Protection of life or property, I argued, should not be a reason for having a handgun, except in extreme cases. Further, I would have severely limited the collector category by not permitting persons to start or add to a collection of handguns, except for firearms over one hundred years old. I noted that most people who were obtaining handguns probably belonged to the collector category. Collections of guns pose a danger because they can be stolen.

I next turned to long guns, which up to that point were subject to virtually no controls, even though many more murders in Canada were committed using rifles and shotguns than with handguns. In addition, there were a large number of accidents and suicides that took place with long guns. One-third of all suicides were accomplished with firearms, predominantly long guns. A person could simply go into a hunting-goods or hardware store and purchase a long gun. It was also possible to purchase a long gun by mail order. There were no background checks or waiting periods. I therefore advocated creating a new category in addition to prohibited and restricted weapons: controlled weapons. This would include all rifles, shotguns, and air guns. The main control would be a licensing system in which the applicant would initially have to pass a competency test as well as undergoing a background check. I did not propose that the legislation would be retroactive, stating:

> One of the key questions is whether a licence should be required for all persons who now possess long-guns. The problem is that there may now be close to 10 million long-guns in Canada. Many persons will not apply for a licence. One does not want to establish a system which automatically makes a large number of persons guilty of offences, or that requires considerable invasions of privacy in order to license the owners of all long-

guns. The best solution is to provide that no one can *purchase* or *use* a controlled firearm or any ammunition without a licence. This will slowly sweep into the licensing system most of those who now have guns.

The licensing system would prevent an individual from buying a gun on the spur of the moment for an illegal purpose. It would not be necessary to have a cooling-off period; the system itself would supply one. As with handguns, the legislation would impose conditions, including one that the gun and ammunition be stored separately and securely. Another consequence of the licensing system would be that dealers in long arms would have to be licensed and would have to keep records of their sales of guns and ammunition so that the authorities could ensure that sales were not made to persons without licences.

I did not advocate the *registration* of long guns, even though I fully supported the continued registration of handguns. The difference between licensing and registration in terms of the gun-control debates is that persons are licensed and guns are registered. Although the registration of long guns may theoretically be desirable, such registration, I observed in my report, 'would be administratively very difficult and would be costly in terms of the benefits which might accrue.' Only infrequently could a gun left at the scene of a crime be traced to the perpetrator. Relatively few registered guns are used in criminal activity. The vast majority are obtained illegally.

There were other control techniques discussed in the study, such as the imposition by legislation of civil liability for all firearms as a technique of control. Courts had been ruling that a gun was not an inherently dangerous object, even though it obviously is one. Further I advocated that gun owners, just as car drivers, should be required to obtain insurance before obtaining a licence to use a gun.

I struggled with the question of mandatory minimum criminal penalties. The advantage of having a minimum penalty as a deterrent is obvious. The disadvantage is that it takes out of a judge's hands the power to shape the sentence to fit the circumstances of the case and the background of the offender. In general, I was opposed to minimum penalties, although I conceded that much could be said in favour of raising some of the maximum potential penalties in order to show parliamentary concern over the issue of gun control. There was, however, some justification for imposing a minimum sentence for certain *second* firearms offences, as the Criminal Code does with impaired driving. Much could also be said for a minimum sentence when a firearm is used to facilitate the commission of certain offences, if one could be sure that the circumstances warranted severe treatment. If some form of minimum sentence were thought to be desirable, then the code might provide, for example, a minimum sentence to be added to any other sentence if the accused was otherwise sentenced to, say, a penitentiary term (that is, two years or more) for that other offence.

In early September 1975, the solicitor general's department prepared a memorandum to cabinet based on the studies done by the working group. Bob Moncur from the solicitor general's research division, who was responsible for drafting the memo, sent me a draft of it, asking for my comments, and stating: 'As you will see, it does not differ greatly from your own paper so you can appreciate how valuable your report was.' The document contained many of the ideas that I had advocated, including imposing civil liability for firearms, prohibiting certain weapons, requiring a demonstration of real need for a handgun or other restricted weapon, and requiring a licence for the future purchase of long guns and ammunition. The document stated: 'In order to impact on the potential firearm *user*, an important option to consider is that of licensing all prospective purchasers of firearms or ammunition. This would have the benefit of discouraging the casual buyer, would introduce a cooling off period into initial firearms or ammunition purchases and would heighten appreciation of firearm ownership.' This was specifically included in the final 'recommendations' section. I was pleased.

Roger Tassé, the deputy solicitor general, gave me permission to publish my study in the December 1975 issue of the *Criminal Law Quarterly*, even before legislation had been finalized, perhaps because my paper supported the thrust that the government was taking. My article was picked up by various newspapers. The *Globe* gave it a very positive editorial, which started by agreeing with my suggestion that there should be civil liability for damage caused by guns, including liability when someone loans a gun, just as there is liability for damage when one loans a car. The editorial complimented my 'ingenuity' in making this suggestion and went on to state: 'He makes a number of other suggestions and, like vicarious responsibility, most of them are good. For instance, he says that gun owners, like car owners, should be required to carry insurance. That owners of all guns, regardless whether they own handguns or long guns, should be licensed.' On this latter point, the writer did not realize that I had limited my recommendation to future purchases or use of guns or ammunition. The *Toronto Star*, which had given the study a headline on the first page, made a similar misinterpretation in its editorial, stating: 'Friedland recommended that all shotguns and rifles be licensed.' I have not checked what the editorial reaction was outside Toronto.

I received a fair number of letters from the public about my suggestions, almost all negative. One stated: 'You sound like a stupid two year old school kid with your narrow minded gun control. Any one with a brain in his head will leave good enough alone.' Another presented the slogan that 'GUNS DO NOT KILL PEOPLE, PEOPLE KILL PEOPLE!' and stated, 'A firearm is just like any other piece of sporting equipment – tackle, golf club, pair of skiis, skates, baseball bat or what have you.' By contrast, Professor Alan Gordon of the Hart House gun club wrote that he was 'prepared to support' most of my suggestions.

The legislation, Bill C-83, was given first reading in February 1976. In one very significant respect, it went further than the cabinet document that I had seen, which had limited the licensing of long guns to future purchases of guns or ammunition. Section 88 of the bill provided that 'every one who, not being the holder of a licence under which he may lawfully have in his possession firearms or ammunition, knowingly has in his possession any firearm or ammunition' is guilty of an offence.

I have not been able to discover who was responsible for the change. Was it the solicitor general, Warren Allmand, or the minister of justice, Ron Basford, who had taken over the justice portfolio from Otto Lang in September 1975? It is likely that both Allmand and Basford, from large urban centres, agreed to the change. But maybe, like the *Globe* and the *Star*, they did not realize that they were departing from the cabinet document that had limited licensing to future activities. Another possibility is that a member of the Department of Justice or the parliamentary draftsman had made the change. It could have been instigated by Prime Minister Trudeau, although there is nothing in the various books on his life that I have examined that show his attitude towards firearms.

Basford stated on second reading, in March 1976:

For citizens who wish to own or use common firearms for legitimate purposes, a number of control systems were considered closely by the Government – total prohibition, firearms depositories, gun registration and possessor licensing. They were the subject of a full study carried out by

Dean Martin Friedland for the Government during 1975. Of these, the one that is the only balanced and reasonable approach to the problem of controlling misuse of firearms is a system of licencing persons who possess guns.

The cabinet document and my study had not, as stated above, said that licensing should be required for persons who 'possess' guns. I had said that licensing should be required for persons who 'purchase' a long gun or ammunition or 'use' an existing gun. The cabinet document had also restricted licensing to future purchasers. The difference may not be great and may not be easily understood by most persons, but it may have made the difference between the passage and non-passage of Bill C-83. If it had not been retroactive, the opposition would likely not have been as great. Many of the ten million or so long guns in Canada are in attics, and their owners have little intention of ever using them. They could have been swept into the licensing system if persons purchased ammunition. Moreover, the legislation could have been limited to the use of a firearm off the person's property. So a farmer shooting rodents on his own property would not require a licence, just as a farmer does not require a licence for a vehicle used on his property.

Because of strong opposition to the bill, it was withdrawn by the government. In April 1977, Bill C-51 was introduced, with the licensing provision limited to the future acquisition of long guns – hence the name 'firearms acquisition certificate' in the legislation. There was no mention of the purchase of ammunition or of the *use* of existing long guns. Bill C-51 was enacted. I must admit that I did not make as much at the time of the difference between the 1976 legislation and what my study had proposed. I thanked Gualtieri for sending me the bill, which I said looked very good on a quick reading.

The passage of the 1977 legislation was assisted by publicity given to gun-related events. One such event was a coroner's inquest in Toronto for Ernest Lamourandire, who in September 1976 had been discharged from the Clarke Institute of Psychiatry, purchased a high-powered rifle, went to the top of a building and wounded five persons in the streets below before killing himself. I testified at the inquest that a licensing system for the purchase of long guns would likely have prevented this tragedy. Again, the *Globe* and the *Star* weighed in with strong editorials supporting my testimony. The *Star* stated: 'Hunters and wildlife associations – as well as gun manufacturers themselves – who are waging such a bitter campaign against a tougher gun control law in Canada might do well to ponder the testimony of Martin Friedland ... at Toronto's "sniper" inquest this week.' The editorial set out the number of murders and suicides with rifles and shotguns and agreed that this toll could be significantly reduced with a licensing system for all firearms. They quoted from my earlier study to counter the objection by hunters to the red tape involved in getting a licence: 'But as Friedland pointed out, "the few seconds it takes to fill out a document are nothing compared with the hours people are prepared to spend waiting for a duck to come by."' The coroner's jury urged that the Ontario government introduce gun-control legislation if the federal government did not.

My work on gun control led to two further academic papers. One was an article published in 1978 on pressure groups and the development of the criminal law, briefly described in an earlier chapter on the machinery of law reform, which I prepared for a book in honour of my PhD supervisor, Glanville Williams. The gun-control issue beautifully illustrated the influence of pressure groups. The justice and legal-affairs committee that heard evidence on Bill C-83 had received submissions from a great number of individuals and groups, thirty-eight of which it published. The subsequent Bill C-51 was strongly opposed by a number of groups, but those supporting it were not well organized. The minister of justice, Ron Basford, publicly urged Canadians who wanted tougher rules to voice their opinions. The legislation, he warned, would founder without support. One new group, the National Firearms Safety Association – one of the first in Canada representing victims and their families – appeared. The association was formed as the result of initiatives by a Vancouver widow whose son had been killed by a firearm. Today, as is well known, victims and their families are major players in the criminal-justice system.

I looked in my article at the ad hoc, issue-oriented groups formed to lobby against the firearms legislation. One powerful organization opposing Bill C-51 was CASAL, the Canadian Association for Sensible Arms Legislation. It was an alliance of organizations, being composed of over twenty-five clubs representing, according to their spokesman, half a million people. Coalitions among groups are well known in the lobbying business. The more persons making the same point, the more the legislators will take note. If their alliance collapses, however, the result may well be worse for the lobbyists than if there had been no coalition in the first place. This appears to have happened with respect to

CASAL. Its head was a highly respected former RCMP commissioner, Colonel L.H. Nicholson, who had been associated with wildlife groups in the fight over Bill C-83. When the time came for presenting briefs to the justice and legal-affairs committee on Bill C-51, the coalition split apart. Colonel Nicholson appeared on behalf of the Canadian Wildlife Federation and refused to endorse the CASAL position that there should be a right to collect automatic weapons. After the CASAL presentation the wildlife association sent a telegram to the justice and legal-affairs committee 'dissociat[ing] our organization from any statements or briefs presented in the name of CASAL.' This may have been the turning point in the debate.

Since the mid-1960s, police groups had become active lobbyists on criminal-justice issues. In 1971, for example, the Canadian Police Association appeared before the justice and legal-affairs committee on the bail issue. After the passage of the *Bail Reform Act* – as stated in an earlier chapter – groups of police and wives of policemen (1200 wives attended a meeting in Toronto and formed an organization) pressed for a 'tightening up' of the legislation. There was not a unanimous front, however, on gun control. The policeman wearing his police cap wants gun control, whereas the policeman wearing his sportsman's cap does not. So the Canadian Association of Chiefs of Police supported Bill C-83, while some of the police associations (the equivalent of unions) took a more ambivalent position.

In my article I quoted Alan Borovoy, counsel to the Canadian Civil Liberties Association, saying that 'pressure without reason may be irresponsible, but reason without pressure is ineffectual.' For a number of years, Alan would come to my seminar on law reform to discuss pressure groups. Such groups used a wide variety of tactics in the gun-control debate, including mass meetings, delegations, advertisements, petitions, and letter writing. The lobbying was intense. One Manitoba MP stated that he received a petition signed by five hundred persons from a village with a population of only one thousand. Another said that he had received over five thousand letters. Gun clubs stressed their power to influence votes. The aforementioned Colonel Nicholson stated with respect to Bill C-83 that the MPs 'are going to be left with the clear impression that if they support the bill they are going to suffer.'

Some American writers have taken the position that such groups are all–important in society. A.F. Bentley, whose influential work on pressure groups, *The Process of Government*, was published in the United

States in 1908, stated that 'society itself is nothing other than the complex of the groups that compose it ... When the groups are adequately stated, everything is stated. When I say everything I mean everything.' My study of gun control and other issues showed that if groups are not 'everything,' they are nonetheless more a part of our political and legal system than is usually acknowledged. In the paper I showed how Canada and other countries have fostered and encouraged pressure groups and have brought them more openly into the decision-making process.

The second paper arose out of an invitation in 1980 to participate in a seminar at Harvard University comparing Canadian and American gun-control laws. The seminar was sponsored by the University Consortium for Research on North America at the Harvard Center for International Affairs. As it happened, the Canadian solicitor general's department had wanted me to do further work on gun control, which it supported, financially and otherwise. I was to talk about the Canadian experience and Father Robert Drinan, then a congressman with an interest in gun control, was to discuss the American experience. Drinan, who died in early 2007, was a Catholic priest and a professor at Georgetown University Law Center who had been the dean of law at Boston College before entering politics. He resigned from Congress at the end of 1980 because Pope John Paul II had demanded that all priests withdraw from electoral politics. (Many think that Drinan was the target of this order because of his pro-choice position in the abortion debates.) In his last official day in office, 31 December 1980, Drinan wrote to me about what he planned to say, stating: 'I would expect that I would be talking about the history of proposed gun legislation in the United States. I would stress the fact that it is a very intractable topic and that the prognosis for reform legislation is poor.'

The seminar took place at the Center for International Affairs in early March 1981. Drinan pointed out that there were over two hundred million firearms in the United States, and that although only fifty million of these were handguns, handguns accounted for 90 per cent of criminal and accidental firearms misuse. He emphasized that the real problem was handguns, pointing out that in all but one of the ten assassinations or attempted assassinations of presidents or presidential candidates, the assassin had used a handgun. Handguns were used in every third robbery and in every fourth aggravated assault. He concluded his talk by stating: 'The splendid example of the ways by which Canada has curbed virtually all violence by handguns should serve as an example and an incentive for the United States to move forward with a national comprehensive law that would seek to eliminate a hideous situation in a nation which proudly proclaims that it has a profound respect for the sanctity and inviolability of all human life.'

In my own paper I stressed the dramatic difference in handgun use between the two countries. My opening paragraph stated: 'In 1979 there were fewer than 60 homicides committed with handguns in all of Canada. Metropolitan Toronto, with more than 2,000,000 persons, had only four handgun homicides that year. In contrast, in 1979, handguns were used in almost 900 killings in New York City, about 300 in Metropolitan Detroit, and 75 in Metropolitan Boston ... There were over 10,000 handgun homicides in the US in 1979, almost 20 times the Canadian *per capita* rate.' I added that statistics for more recent years were, in general, not dissimilar to the 1979 figures.

I went through the history of gun control in Canada, showing that, in general, legislation in Canada closely parallels movements for reform in the United States. The difference is that Canada has been able to pass strong legislation, whereas the United States has not. I examined why this was, and continues to be, so. Near the top of the list, I suggested, is the fact that the criminal-law power was given in the 1867 *British North America Act* to the federal government. The American model was deliberately rejected. As a result, in Canada legislation need be passed by only one government, not fifty, as in the United States. Canada therefore does not have to face the difficult problem of widely varying standards from one jurisdiction to another and the consequent easy migration of handguns from loose-control to tight-control jurisdictions. Not only can the federal government in Canada set a uniform standard, but through the Royal Canadian Mounted Police it plays a greater role in administering the legislation than is usual in the criminal law.

The Mounties have been important for another reason. They were the vehicle used by the federal government to help ensure the peaceful development of the Canadian West. Canada did not have a 'wild west' because the law preceded development. The role of Mounties in the West is one of those myths that turns out to be true. The development of the American frontier found no counterpart in Canada. Moreover, many of the Mounties settled in the West when their tour of duty was completed, thus giving stability to a potentially volatile region. According to an 1887 report by an RCMP official, the handgun was sufficiently foreign to Canadian society that the Mounties – unlike current movie-goers who have been brought up on Westerns – were unsure where to wear their pistols. The report noted that 'the men of the western plains of the United States, who are acknowledged to be the most expert pistol shots in the world, invariably wear it on the right side, with the butt at the rear.'

The different attitudes towards law and order on each side of the border are reflected in the literature of each jurisdiction. The hero of American fiction is often the stranger who takes the law into his own hands, whereas the hero in early Canadian fiction is the Mountie. In one novel by the popular author Ralph Connor, published in 1912, the Mountie walks into a gambling den where a 'bad-man' is flourishing his gun:

'Put it down there, my man. Do you hear?' The voice was still smooth, but through the silky tones there ran a fibre of steel. Still the desperado stood gazing at him. 'Quick, do you hear?' There was a sudden sharp ring of imperious, of overwhelming authority, and, to the amazement of the crowd of men who stood breathless and silent about ... the gambler slowly laid upon the table his gun ... The man, still silent, slunk out from the room. Irresistible authority seemed to go with the word that sent him forth, and rightly so, for behind that word lay the full weight of Great Britain's mighty empire.

Both countries came into existence as a result of the American Revolution, but whereas the United States was founded as a result of defiance of authority, Canada was the result of obedience to the Crown. Moreover, the revolution resulted in a large number of law-abiding United Empire Loyalists coming to Canada, where there was and is no right to revolution, no declaration of independence, no 'right to bear arms,' no tradition of civil disobedience, and no violent civil war. What we have, instead, in the simple phrase of our constitution, is 'Peace, Order and Good Government.'

I concluded my talk by observing that if Canada had not carefully controlled the possession of handguns for the past century it is likely that the Canadian crime rate for serious offences would be substantially higher than it is today, although for historical and cultural reasons it would, no doubt, still be far below the American rate. The Canadian system combines limitations on the reasons for possession of handguns, careful screening of applicants, vigorous judicial sentencing, and strong federal action. It may be – I suggested – that the United States has something to learn from Canada on this issue.

The article was to be included in a book by the organizers of the series on lessons across the border, but nothing came of that project. I published it in a book of essays, edited by Tony Doob and Eddie Greenspan, honouring my colleague and friend John Edwards, the founder of the Centre of Criminology at the University of Toronto. It was also included in my collection of essays *A Century of Criminal Justice*. A shortened version of the article was published as a full-page feature in the *Globe* in April 1981, under the headline 'The Gun in Canada.' Its publication was prompted by the attempted assassination of Ronald Reagan several weeks earlier.

On 6 December 1989 Marc Lépine tragically massacred fourteen women at the École Polytechnique, an engineering school in Montreal, and then committed suicide. December 6 has been officially designated the National Day of Remembrance and Action on Violence against Women. The event provided the impetus for significantly changing gun-control legislation in Canada.

The Progressive Conservative government introduced hard-hitting legislation in 1991. Third reading was given on 5 December, the day before the second anniversary of the massacre. New pressure groups, such as the still-effective Canadian Coalition for Gun Control, had been formed and were advocating strong action. The act provided for better screening of applicants for long guns and a minimum twenty-eight-day waiting period before a licence would be issued. The penalties for firearm-related offences were substantially increased, more weapons were placed in the prohibited and restricted weapons categories, and the gun collector category was further narrowed. It was a good package.

The Liberals, who attained office in 1993, were committed to even more ambitious measures. The promise of a gun registry had been in the Liberal Red Book of pre-election promises. Moreover, the following year, at the Party's biannual convention, a resolution unanimously adopted asked for tighter gun-control legislation. In his address to the convention, Prime Minister Jean Chrétien stated with respect to gun control: 'I believe that the time has come to put even stricter measures in place ... I will be asking my Minister of Justice to examine your resolution very closely and to draft tough gun control legislation.'

The resulting legislation, Bill C-68, was indeed tough. A large number of mandatory minimum sentences were introduced and new search-and-seizure sections were enacted. The heart of the legislation, and its most controversial provision, was the establishment of a new gun registry for all existing and future long guns. The 1995 act received royal assent on 5 December, the day before the sixth anniversary of the Lépine massacre.

I have followed the debates on the gun-registry issue, although not in as much depth as I had studied the earlier legislation. We know that the auditor general of Canada found in 2002 that the registry's cost would be $1 billion higher than the original estimate. It is hard to say what effect the legislation has had on crime because the long-gun registry came along shortly after the strong 1991 legislation. We are told that about seven million long guns are currently registered, but if the solicitor general's estimate in the 1970s that there were over ten million guns in Canada was correct, there are, perhaps, well over three million unregistered guns. Thus, the registry is not very reliable.

We have recently learned from the 2005 murder statistics in Toronto – as I had been arguing in my writings – that the real problem is handguns. Fifty-two of the seventy-eight murders in Toronto in 2005 were committed with firearms, and in all cases but one the gun used was a handgun. Across Canada, the handgun was used in 60 per cent of homicides committed with firearms in 2005. These are far different from the 1979 statistics set out earlier, which noted there were only four homicides with handguns in Toronto and sixty in Canada. If the funds used for the long-gun registry had been devoted to countering the smuggling, possession, and use of handguns, we would be a lot safer today than we are. The Toronto figures for 2006 show a significant decrease in the use of handguns in murder cases, which tends to show that if the police concentrate on handguns – which they have recently done – public safety will be substantially increased.

I did not enter the public debate when the 1995 legislation was being discussed. Among other projects, I was in the middle of my study on the judiciary, and had not kept up on the gun-control topic for about ten years, with the exception of an appearance on Peter Gzowski's radio program *Morningside* in the late 1980s following a specific gun-related incident. Moreover, persons who spoke against the registry were considered by many city folk to be 'right-wing nuts,' a label I did not wish to acquire. I did, however, send my articles and a letter to the deputy minister of justice, George Thompson, in early 1995, stating:

> As you know, I have my hands full with other matters and I wasn't going to enter the gun-control debate, but I thought I should go on record (by sending this letter to you) to the effect that concentrating on the use rather

than the possession of long-guns would be, in my view, a better policy option. Of course we should continue to require registration of handguns. Indeed, I would go even further and eliminate entirely the collector category. You can share these letters with the Minister, if you wish. Indeed, you can make whatever use you want of this letter and the articles.

Thompson later told me privately that he agreed with my arguments, but that politics had trumped my analysis.

In June 2006 Stephen Harper's minority Conservative government introduced a bill (C-21) to eliminate the long-gun registry. It is unlikely, however, to be enacted by the minority government because the opposition parties would probably defeat the government on this issue. What we are seeing instead is the registry being dismantled administratively by regulation and through the budget, rather than through legislation. If the Conservatives form a majority in the next election, the long-gun registry legislation will likely be repealed.

Harper's government had introduced a bill (C-10) in the spring of 2006 increasing the penalties for crimes involving guns, but the legislation was less draconian than many had anticipated. The Department of Justice had, it seems, convinced the politicians that the courts might not uphold minimum penalties that were too tough. If the bill is made law, the result will be an increase in minimum penalties for certain offences in which restricted or prohibited weapons are used – an increase from four to five years for some offences and a ten-year minimum for some repeat gun-crime offenders. I still think that it would be better to limit the application of any minimum penalties to repeat offenders and to cases where the convicted person is otherwise sentenced to a penitentiary term. Minimum penalties have unexpected consequences and can significantly increase the penitentiary population, particularly for some minority groups, including aboriginal offenders.

In the earlier chapter on detention before trial I discussed and criticized the proposed federal legislation (C-35) reversing the onus of proof on the question whether an accused should be released on bail in a case involving firearms. That bill can be traced to the large number of homicides in Toronto in 2005, ending with the random killing downtown of Jane Creba on Boxing Day.

The history of gun control is replete with policy being influenced by specific events. A tragic shooting at Dawson College in Montreal in September 2006 will also have an impact on the future debates. It will encourage the present government to be even more draconian than they otherwise would be in terms of minimum penalties and will also provide a further stimulus to pass the reverse-onus bail provisions when firearms are alleged to have been used. With respect to the gun registry it will cut both ways, viewed by some as another indication that guns are dangerous and that a registry for all guns is required and by others as proof that the registry will not help because the guns used at Dawson College were, in fact, registered. The deadliest mass shooting in modern U.S. history took place at Virginia Tech in Blacksburg, Virginia, in April 2007. Thirty-two persons were killed by a lone gunman with handguns. Perhaps this tragedy will be the catalyst for greater control of handguns in the United States.

When new legislation on the long-gun registry is introduced, assuming that it is, I hope that the position that had been advocated in the cabinet document in 1975 is carefully examined. Be tough on handguns and devote resources to their control. Scrap the registry, which tries to keep track of over ten million long guns, and bring in a scheme requiring licences for persons who acquire long guns or ammunition or use long guns off their own property.

15

National Security

In the summer of 1977 a royal commission was established by the Trudeau government to examine issues relating to national security. The commission, officially designated the 'Commission of Inquiry concerning certain activities of the Royal Canadian Mounted Police,' was popularly known as the McDonald Commission, after its chairman, Alberta Queen's Bench Justice David McDonald. McDonald was hardworking and scholarly, important qualities in producing the commission's well-thought-out three-volume report in 1981. I had dealings with him when I did my study on judicial independence in the mid-1990s because of his strong views on that topic. He was a natural for the Alberta Court of Appeal, but was not appointed to that court until 1996. His links with the Liberal Party did not help his chances of elevation during the Mulroney years. I wrote a note congratulating him on his appointment and received a gracious note of thanks saying how much he was looking forward to his work on the court of appeal. The note arrived three days after he had died suddenly of a heart attack.

The McDonald Commission was set up following a number of revelations concerning the activities of the RCMP, which showed that the Mounties had not been spending all their time singing love songs in the Rockies. It was revealed, for example, that in Quebec in the early 1970s the Mounties had, without a warrant, entered and removed documents from the premises of a press agency; had similarly removed from private premises computer tapes containing membership lists of the Parti

Québécois; had issued a fake communiqué urging FLQ extremists to continue on a course of revolutionary action; had burned down a barn to prevent a meeting taking place; and had engaged in many other questionable activities.

As a result of these disclosures, the commission – whose other members were Guy Gilbert, a prominent Montreal lawyer, and Donald Rickerd, the then head of the Donner Canadian Foundation – was set up, with a mandate to inquire into RCMP activities 'not authorized or provided for by law,' as well as to advise on policies for the future. The policy aspects of its mandate, with which I became involved, were as follows:

> To advise and make such report as the Commissioners deem necessary and desirable in the interest of Canada, regarding the policies and procedures governing the activities of the RCMP in the discharge of its responsibility to protect the security of Canada, the means to implement such policies and procedures, as well as the adequacy of the laws of Canada as they apply to such policies and procedures, having regard to the needs of the security of Canada.

My friend political science professor Peter Russell was appointed the research director of the commission. Like McDonald, he was a Rhodes Scholar. No political scientist in Canada has made a greater contribution – perhaps on a par with another friend, political scientist Alan Cairns – to the analysis of legal issues from a political-science perspective, with studies ranging from aboriginal justice to the role of the judiciary and from constitutional politics to national security.

The commission, through Peter, invited me to prepare a paper on the legal aspects of national security. This would include, I stated in my letter to the commission in early February 1978, 'the Official Secrets Act; state privilege; criminal offences involving security; potential defences such as necessity, entrapment, mistake of law, and superior orders; aspects of the War Measures Act; special powers of search and seizure; and generally, the legal contours of the concept of national security.' 'All in all,' I went on to say, 'a large task, but one which I believe should be handled as one coherent study.' The finished manuscript, I thought, would be about one hundred typed pages in length and would be available in the fall of 1978, with a 'reasonable draft' ready by the end of August 1978. The contract provided for sixty days' work. I was going abroad on a one-year sabbatical in the summer of 1979 and wanted to complete the work before I left. I asked for the right to publish the study after the commissioners' report was made public, and suggested that since there had been very little written in Canada on the issues I would be dealing with, it might improve the level of debate if the study were to be published even earlier.

As it turned out, the commission published the study, along with one by John Edwards on ministerial responsibility and another by Ned Franks on parliament and national security, in early 1980 before the publication of the commission's report. The commissioners stated in a brief note at the beginning of the studies that they hoped that each paper would 'provoke and stimulate the reader to express his or her own considered views to the Commission.' For some reason, the prime minister, who was then Joe Clark, had to personally approve the publication in advance of the commission report, and so on the back of the title page one finds the statement: 'The Prime Minister has approved the publication of this study in advance of the final report of the Commission.' Clark had a very short mandate before he lost the next election to Trudeau in early 1980, but fortunately he had time to approve the publication of these three studies.

I did not have much of a background on issues relating to national security, except for working with Ken McNaught on an essay he did on political trials in Canada for the collection I edited in 1975, *Courts and Trials: A Multidisciplinary Approach*, and for an op-ed piece I did for the *Globe and Mail* shortly after the *War Measures Act* had been proclaimed on 16 October 1970. In the *Globe* article I complained about the retroactive nature of the regulations that had been passed by the government immediately after the *War Measures Act* had been declared at 4 a.m. on the morning of 16 October. The regulations made it an offence to be a member of the Front de Libération du Québec (FLQ) from the time that the regulations were passed.

It was, I argued, unjust to prosecute persons for membership in an organization which was not illegal before the regulations were passed and from which they had not had the opportunity to withdraw. When the Nazi party and other similar organizations had been declared to be illegal in 1940 by regulations passed under the *War Measures Act*, the Canadian government gave Nazi party members and others advance warning so they could resign from their organizations. As the reader will note from my discussion of gun control and my advocacy of prospective judicial lawmaking, I dislike retroactive laws.

Over four hundred FLQ members were arrested without prior notice in the early morning of 16 October but, as it turned out, no one was convicted of being a member of the FLQ. It seems that at four in the morning the government either forgot, or could not arrange, to have the regulations published in the *Canada Gazette*, which was not done until 11 a.m. later that day. The *Regulations Act* clearly states that 'no person shall be convicted for an offence consisting of a contravention of any regulation that at the time of the alleged contravention was not published in the *Canada Gazette*... unless ... reasonable steps had been taken for the purpose of bringing the purport of the regulation to the notice of the public, or the persons likely to be affected by it, or of the person charged.' This, of course, had not been done. Nor did the government declare the *Regulations Act* not to be operative, as it could have done. As a result, persons arrested could later argue that in the seven-hour period between 4 a.m. and 11 a.m. they had decided to dissociate themselves from the FLQ. Maybe the drafters of the regulations knew this and never intended to prosecute persons for being members of the FLQ. The *Regulations Act* states that although persons cannot be convicted if regulations are unpublished, they are still valid for other purposes. Perhaps the government only wanted the power of search and arrest to help them find the persons who were holding Quebec cabinet minister Pierre Laporte. As it turned out, the invocation of the *War Measures Act* likely precipitated the murder of Laporte.

About a month later, John Turner, the minister of justice, arranged a small meeting at Montebello Lodge in Quebec to discuss aspects of the declaration of the *War Measures Act*. I attended, as did a number of others, including Alan Borovoy and Alan Dershowitz, a good friend of Turner's executive assistant, Irwin Cotler. For some reason, I do not have a clear memory of the exchanges that took place over what I recall was a two-day meeting and do not have any notes of the meeting.

I have a clearer memory of a talk I gave a few months later at the University of Buffalo Law School on 'Civil Liberties and the FLQ Crisis.' The law school was then in downtown Buffalo and a large rally against the war in Vietnam was taking place that very day close to the school. During my talk, police sirens periodically blared in the streets and the small number of people who had shown up to hear my address slowly left – I hope to watch what was happening outside. By the end of the talk there were few remaining.

I would obviously need a lot of help for the McDonald commission study. Once again, I was able to hire two first-rate research assistants:

Chris Grauer, who had just completed second year, and Ian Kyer, who had completed first year. Both are now leading lawyers, the former in Vancouver and the latter in Toronto. Chris also worked for me during the following summer, which enabled me to put some finishing touches on the manuscript. All three of us went through security clearance, in my case up to 'top secret.' I had not realized at the time that there was a still higher classification for persons doing work with the now publicly acknowledged Communications Security Establishment, which engages in electronic surveillance of foreign signals. I went through another 'top secret' check in 1996 when I did a background study for the Somalia inquiry and again in 2003 when I did work for the Arar Commission. I guess they like to keep their security checks up to date.

My published study began with the following statement: 'I start this study on the legal dimensions of national security with a confession: I do not know what national security means. But then, neither does the government.' In retrospect, that was a bit too cheeky. Most view the concept – I went on to say – as one that they cannot define, but, 'like obscenity, they know it when they see it.'

My paper was not directly concerned with the structure of the Canadian Security Service, nor with the government's responsibility for its operation. The service was at the time under the control and direction of the commissioner of the RCMP, who was responsible to the solicitor general of Canada in all matters, including those of security. A 1969 royal commission, the Mackenzie Commission, had recommended that a civilian organization replace the security function of the RCMP, but this had not been accepted by the government, and instead a civilian director was appointed to head the service. Prime Minister Trudeau stated in the House in June 1969: 'We have come to the conclusion that current and foreseeable security problems in Canada can be better dealt with within the RCMP through appropriate modifications in their existing structure than by attempting to create a wholly new and separate service.' The McDonald Commission, however, agreed with the Mackenzie Commission, and this time the advice was followed. A separate security service, the Canadian Security Intelligence Service (CSIS), was set up in 1984. Following the events of 11 September 2001, the RCMP has become more directly involved in security matters, a subject that will be investigated in the next chapter.

My two-hundred-page paper – it was twice as long as I had predicted – was broken down into six parts, including an introduction and conclusion. Part two analysed the various criminal offences in the code relating to national security, such as treason, sedition, sabotage, riot, and mutiny. This part also included a discussion of the espionage provisions of the *Official Secrets Act*. Section 3 of the act covered espionage and section 4 the leakage of government information.

The more controversial aspect of the act was section 4, the leakage provision, which was dealt with in part three of my study. The comparable provision in England had been given a very wide interpretation – all government information, whether 'classified' or not, was subject to the section. A former attorney general of England described the breadth of the British section by stating that it 'makes it a crime, without any possibility of a defence, to report the number of cups of tea consumed per week in a government department.' If one substituted 'coffee' for 'tea,' I noted, 'the comment could have been equally applicable in Canada.' The press had been concerned about this section. Are members of the press subject to prosecution or search for publishing information that came to them under the door or, less likely, over the transom (one rarely sees a transom anymore) in a brown envelope from a government employee? Canadian courts had given the section a more restricted meaning than was assumed to be the law in the United Kingdom. The matter was not clear and I urged clarification of the Canadian law.

Part four covered police powers and national security. I examined such controversial subjects as wiretapping for national-security purposes, surreptitious entry to place a bug, opening mail, informants and entrapment, and possible defences to such activities, such as necessity and following superior orders. Many of these issues were far from clear and I recommended that they be clarified by legislation.

This part of the study also looked at emergency powers. When could the state call in the military or declare martial law? When could the *War Measures Act* be used? Should intermediate legislation be enacted that would be politically less difficult for the government to invoke? I thought intermediate legislation was probably not a good idea. If special legislation was needed to deal with a particular emergency, it could, as in England with respect to IRA terrorism, be passed by Parliament. Such legislation should, however, be ready for passage by Parliament at some future time. Because Canada was bound by the International Covenant on Civil and Political Rights, which spelled out certain rights that could not be overridden in an emergency, these rights would have to be protected. The McDonald Commission also recommended that 'draft regulations be debated in public *before* a crisis develops, to ensure that proper attention will be paid to civil liberties.'

The debate that the McDonald Commission had recommended took place in 1988 when the government replaced the *War Measures Act* with the *Emergencies Act*, which sets out in greater detail what can be done by the executive in various types of emergencies. It is a substantial improvement over the previous law. Separate parts of the act deal sensibly with public-welfare emergencies (part 1), public-order emergencies (part 2), international emergencies (part 3), and war emergencies (part 4). The legislation also provides for compensation to any person 'who suffers loss, injury or damage as a result of any thing done' under the act. Unlike the *War Measures Act*, which specifically stated that the Canadian Bill of Rights did not apply to its measures, the *Emergencies Act* is subject to the Charter, as well as the Bill of Rights. The act's preamble also says that any temporary measures 'must have regard to the United Nations International Covenant on Civil and Political Rights, particularly with respect to those fundamental rights that are not to be limited or abridged even in a national emergency.' These provisions made it unnecessary to spell out such safeguards in the legislation. The only safeguard specifically mentioned – meant to prevent a recurrence of the internment of persons, such as of Japanese Canadians in the Second World War – was a section saying that the government could not make orders or regulations providing for the 'detention, imprisonment or internment of Canadian citizens or permanent residents ... on the basis of race, national or ethnic origin, colour, religion, sex, age or mental or physical disability.'

Parliament is to be recalled, the act states, 'at the earliest opportunity after the declaration [of an emergency] is issued.' The cabinet decision is valid for varying lengths of time depending on the category of emergency. A public-order emergency is valid for thirty days unless revoked or continued in accordance with the act, an international emergency for sixty days, a public-welfare emergency for ninety days, and a war emergency for one hundred and twenty days. Each of the emergencies has a specific definition. A public-order emergency, for example, is defined as 'an emergency that arises from threats to the security of Canada and that is so serious as to be a national emergency,' with 'threats to the security of Canada' given the same meaning as under the CSIS act. Further, 'national emergency' is defined as 'an urgent and critical situation of a temporary nature that (a) seriously endangers the lives, health or safety of Canadians and is of such proportions or nature as to exceed the capacity or authority of a province to deal with it, or (b) seriously threatens the ability of the Government of Canada to preserve the sovereignty, security and territorial integrity of Canada – and that cannot be effectively dealt with under any other law of Canada.' This confines this type of emergency to really serious matters.

Part five of my study investigated the role the judiciary should play in national-security matters. I suggested that the judiciary should be involved in granting warrants for all electronic and other intrusive surveillance, except possibly in the narrow case of the surveillance of embassies and foreign agents. As in the U.S. federal courts, a special panel of judges could hear such cases. The judiciary should also be involved in granting the power to open mail in security cases. When I did my study it was the solicitor general of Canada who authorized interceptions on the grounds of national security. I wanted judicial warrants to be required, again with the possible exception of the surveillance of embassies and foreign agents. As I stated: 'This use of the judiciary will act as a barrier to a government using electronic surveillance for internal political purposes,' and quoted the U.S. Church Committee of 1976, which had stated that its 'examination of forty years of investigations into "subversion" had found the term to be so vague as to constitute a license to investigate almost any activity of practically any group that actively opposes the policies of the administration in power.'

The study was well received by those who were asked by the commission to comment on it before publication, with the exception of John Starnes, who had been the first civilian director of the security service of the RCMP. He was opposed to the judiciary being involved in security matters. 'Before any decisions were to be taken to involve the judiciary so directly in such vital areas of Security Service operations,' he wrote, 'I would like to see undertaken an exhaustive examination of exactly how such a system would work in practice, using specific cases to illustrate the range of complex problems involved.' He also did not like my opening paragraph, where I acknowledged that I did not know what national security meant, stating: 'Clearly, if one is to write a paper on the legal dimensions of national security it is necessary first to know what "national security" means.' As I admitted above, maybe my comment was a bit too cheeky.

When the report was published, the *Globe* editorial, in contrast, rather liked my opening statement that I did not know what national security meant. 'Nor we suspect, does anybody,' they commented.

'Prof. Friedland argues,' the editorial went on to say, 'that the law regarding national security, like all other law, ought to be specific ... That in a nutshell, is [his] point – and it is an excellent point, though he wanders from it.' Of course the editorial liked the suggested reform of the *Official Secrets Act*, but felt that I wandered when I suggested that the police should be given the right to open mail with a judicial warrant. It seemed to me to be equivalent to wiretapping. The academic reviews were good, in general agreeing with a British reviewer in *Public Law* that I had produced a 'thorough and scholarly account of the law of "national security."'

After completing my study, I continued doing work on contract for the commission. I read drafts of sections of their reports and was invited to Ottawa to discuss particular aspects of the commission's mandate. This relationship continued after I started my sabbatical in Israel in the summer of 1979. It proved difficult, however, to get material to me on a timely basis. The easiest way was for the commission to send it to the Canadian embassy in Tel Aviv through the so-called diplomatic bag. But getting it to me in Netanya, a seaside town north of Tel Aviv, posed a problem because we did not have a telephone to enable me to make arrangements for delivery. As it turned out, my son Tom and Canadian ambassador Joe Stanford's son attended the American International School in Hertzliya, midway between the embassy in Tel Aviv and our apartment in Netanya. The ambassador simply gave the documents, normally labelled 'top secret,' to his son, who in turn gave them to Tom, who brought them home to me after school. So much for 'top secret.'

Shortly after we arrived in Israel I participated in a conference on 'Peace vs. Violence' held at the Jerusalem Hilton. Prime Minister Menachem Begin, whom Judy and I met and who six months earlier had concluded a peace agreement with Anwar Sadat of Egypt, was a keynote speaker. It was a time of considerable, though guarded, optimism. My talk was entitled 'Adhering to Rules of Criminal Procedure in Cases of Terrorism.' I asked whether the rules of procedure and evidence should be different in cases of terrorism from those of other serious offences, such as murder or treason. I did not think so. Until the court has pronounced the accused guilty, we do not know if the accused is guilty. I went on:

> The rules of procedure that most countries have developed are in almost all cases designed to sort out the guilty from the innocent. There are other

functions, but that is the primary function. Tampering with the criminal trial rules will necessarily make it more likely that an innocent person is convicted; take almost any rule of criminal procedure and evidence and you will see that it will affect the outcome of the trial.

I noted that the subject of the panel on which I was participating was 'Respect for the rights of the accused,' not 'Respect for the rights of the terrorist.' This was an obvious, yet often forgotten, distinction. I then illustrated the consequence of changing some of the rules of procedure by discussing the harmful effect on an accused person of denying bail or disregarding the rule against double jeopardy. An emergency situation may, however, change the balance. Israel was clearly in an emergency situation within the meaning of the UN Covenant allowing for a derogation of rights in an emergency. A year earlier Israel had brought in an emergency-powers law which allowed the minister of defence to hold persons for up to a year, subject to judicial supervision. Seventeen persons were being held under that law: sixteen in the administered territories and one in Israel. 'It seems to me,' I observed, 'that this new law is a great credit to Israel's search for the proper protection of human rights even in an emergency situation.' I concluded the paper by saying that 'there are situations involving terrorism which call for drastic emergency action, but until that stage is reached the ordinary law and procedural safeguards should not be diluted.' This was easy for an outsider to say. When Canada was faced with a serious threat of terrorism following 9/11, as we will see in the next chapter, I felt that some of the modest incursions on civil liberties introduced to thwart terrorism were justified.

Several months later, I gave a talk on national security at a faculty seminar at the Tel Aviv faculty of law, in which I went through some of the major conclusions of my study for the McDonald Commission. The talk was published in the *Israel Yearbook on Human Rights*, with an addendum by a bright young member of the Tel Aviv faculty, Baruch Bracha, who showed how the points that I dealt with were being handled in Israel. Included in his addendum was a discussion of emergency powers in Israel. His conclusion was similar to mine at the earlier conference in Jerusalem. 'It appears,' he wrote, 'that, confronted as the State is with extraordinary security factors, Israeli law maintains a proper balance between the demands of the emergency situation on the one hand, and the freedom of the individual on the other.'

After coming to England for the second half of my sabbatical, I gave a number of talks at various universities in the United Kingdom on the subject 'National Security: Some Canadian Legal Perspectives.' One of the talks was a Special University Lecture, arranged by my friend Graham Zellick, later the vice-chancellor of the University of London, delivered at Queen Mary College in the University of London in February 1980. I knew that there was going to be a large crowd at that lecture, in part because it was well publicized, but mainly because an advertisement in *New Society* and perhaps other journals had billed the speaker as 'Milton Friedland' rather than 'Martin Friedland.' Many persons were interested in what the famous University of Chicago economist Milton Friedman had to say. The hall was packed. After thanking Graham for his introduction, I stated: 'Last weekend's *New Society* had a notice concerning this lecture. They got the title right, but they called me Milton Friedland. Some of you might be here under the mistaken impression that I am the world famous economist who will be talking about national security and the free enterprise system.' As with my talk at the University of Buffalo, people started leaving, although there was still a respectable number who courteously remained.

I also completed a study for the McDonald Commission during my sabbatical on entrapment, a subject of considerable interest to the commission. The study, 'Controlling Entrapment,' was subsequently published in the *University of Toronto Law Journal*. 'Undercover agents,' I wrote, 'come in many different shapes and guises, but there are two basic categories: undercover police officers, and informers who co-operate with the police for pay or other consideration.' In both cases, their conduct ranges from being passive observers to being active participants. But as one sociologist, Gary Marx, has warned, 'there are pressures inherent in the role that push the informant toward provocation.' Indeed, I went on to say, there is a risk that the agent may go even further. 'The spy,' stated Leon Chafee, 'often passes over an almost imperceptible boundary into the *agent provocateur*, who instigates the utterances he reports, and then into the fabricator, who invents them.'

The recent and ongoing prosecutions against a large number of alleged terrorists in Toronto that are now unfolding will vividly bring out the danger of informers, because one of the key actors in the conspiracy to use explosives for terrorist purposes was also an informer for the RCMP. The issue of entrapment will undoubtedly be raised by the defence. How it will play out remains to be seen.

A number of techniques were explored in the paper. Judicial approval in advance was, I concluded, not a sound option because it would require an undesirably close interaction between the police and the judiciary. Nor would judicial discretion to exclude evidence be desirable because the technique would not cover many cases of improper entrapment. Guidelines, however, were desirable, with disciplinary action to be taken if they are breached. Further, there should be approval of the conduct at a senior police level. I also advocated that a limited defence of entrapment be set out in the Criminal Code. I preferred a simple factual test for the trier of fact, whether it be a judge or jury. The accused should be acquitted, I suggested, if the trier of fact is 'satisfied that the police or their agent's conduct in instigating the crime has gone substantially beyond what is reasonable, having regard to all the circumstances, including, in particular, the accused's pre-existing intent.' The test, therefore, combined an objective test with a subjective element, rather than choosing one or the other, as is normally required in the literature on the topic.

The McDonald Commission agreed that an entrapment test should be enacted in the Criminal Code. Their suggested defence was similar to the one that I had advocated: 'The accused should be acquitted if it is established that the conduct of a member or agent of a police force in instigating the crime has gone substantially beyond what is justifiable having regard to all the circumstances, including the nature of the crime, whether the accused had a pre-existing intent, and the nature and extent of the involvement of the police.' The government did not, however, deal with this question in its follow-up legislation. A defence was, however, later developed by the Supreme Court of Canada, which treats entrapment as a question of law in determining whether the police have induced the commission of the offence. The issue of entrapment is therefore determined by the judge, not the jury. This necessarily results in long legal arguments and references to earlier cases, a point that I will stress in a later chapter on the advantages of legislation over judge-made law. Justice Lamer gave a non-exhaustive list of ten factors that might be taken into account by the judge. A factual test would be preferable.

When I returned to Canada in the summer of 1980 after my sabbatical, I continued as a consultant to the commission. The commission wrapped up its work just before the summer of 1981.

In 1983 the government prepared a bill in response to the McDonald report, which adopted the main conclusion of the commission that the security service be removed from the RCMP and given to a new body, the Canadian Security Intelligence Service (CSIS). I gave evidence on the bill before a special committee of the senate, chaired by Michael Pitfield, formerly the chief clerk of the privy counsel. My submission, which was published in mid-September 1983 as an op-ed piece in the *Globe*, dealt with a number of matters that I had covered in my national security study for the McDonald Commission.

The two-hour session with the senate committee, from 7:30 until about 9:30 in the evening, covered a range of topics that I raised in my written submission, such as wiretapping safeguards, possible immunity for undercover agents, a more limited definition of 'threats to the security of Canada,' and a stronger review body (SIRC) than the one proposed in the legislation. The members of the senate committee were very knowledgeable – indeed surprisingly knowledgeable – about the issues we discussed. I felt that I was participating in a good law-school seminar discussion.

'Implicit in my analysis for the McDonald Commission and my remarks here,' I stated at the outset of the discussion, 'is the assumption that there have been, and will continue to be, serious threats to the security of Canada.' I then went on to observe:

> Inherent in the subject matter, however, is the danger that attempts to meet these threats may involve conduct which unnecessarily threatens civil liberties. The task of finding the proper route through this maze, one which protects the security of the nation and yet does not unnecessarily encroach on civil liberties, is not an easy one.
>
> In my opinion, the present bill takes a route that in many respects favours the interests of the state to too great an extent. The bill has been drafted by reasonable people on the assumption that it will be administered by reasonable people. I would prefer, however, that the bill be drafted on the assumption that at some future time it may be administered by unreasonable, mean-spirited persons.

With respect to wiretapping for national-security purposes, to give only one example of matters covered in the discussion, I said that I preferred the proposed use of judicial approval in advance as set out in the bill to the ministerial approval formerly required, but suggested a number of changes, such as ones to prevent 'judge-shopping,' to provide that the standard of proof for a warrant was 'reasonable belief' rather than the lower standard of 'reasonable suspicion,' to deal with the question of the legality of 'surreptitious entry' through legislation, and to require the yearly reporting of national-security wiretaps.

I had said very little about the central issue in the debate, the establishment of CSIS, simply stating in my introductory remarks that 'on balance I agree with the arguments favouring the separation of the Security Service from the RCMP.' The committee wanted me to elaborate. The factor that influenced me the most, I said, was the ability and the inclination of the separate security service to hire university graduates in such fields as international relations and foreign languages more readily than would the RCMP.

My *Globe* article ended with the following succinct conclusion: 'To sum up, the bill should be re-drafted to strengthen the review process, to clarify and confine the scope of 'threats to the security of Canada,' to re-think the protection to be provided to employees of the security service, to deal with informers, and to increase the safeguards on the use of intrusive investigative techniques.' The bill was redrafted and many of the safeguards that had been suggested by me and others were enacted. I had worked hard on my submission and was pleased with Pitfield's comments at the end of the session: 'We are grateful for the thoroughness and incisiveness of your advice, and the effort you have put into this matter for us. Your brief will be a most useful one, I can promise you that.' I chose not to check whether he said the same to others who appeared.

The CSIS act was proclaimed in the summer of 1984. The following October I attended a seminar for about twenty-five persons organized by the Security Intelligence Review Committee at Meech Lake in the Gatineau Hills. I was impressed with the operations of SIRC under its first chair, former cabinet minister Ron Atkey. I was later invited to give evidence in the five-year review of the CSIS act by a special House of Commons committee, but declined. I had moved on to other projects and felt that without a lot of work I could not make a significant contribution to the review.

Because of my work for the McDonald Commission, I became heavily involved during the 1980s with the Law Reform Commission of Canada in helping prepare a draft working paper for the commission on 'Offences against the State.' The work started in 1981 when Frank Muldoon was the president of the commission, and was eventually published in 1986 when Justice Allen Linden was president. No final report, however, was published by the Law Reform Commission.

There was some delay in starting the study for the Law Reform Commission. As we will see in a later chapter on codification, the federal government decided in October 1979, during Joe Clark's tenure as prime minister, that 'a thorough review of the Criminal Code should be undertaken as a matter of priority.' The review would be a three-way cooperative effort between the Department of Justice, the solicitor general's department, and the Law Reform Commission of Canada. It was not clear who should have responsibility for offences involving national security. Offences against the state appeared to be within the mandate of the Law Reform Commission, yet they were also of great interest to the solicitor-general's department, which had responsibility for the security service, and to the Department of Justice, which had the responsibility for prosecuting offences under the *Official Secrets Act*. Both the solicitor-general's department and the Department of Justice had been doing work on redrafting this act. In 1980 Stephen Skelly of the Department of Justice had produced a detailed confidential paper on the act for the department, drawing heavily, with appropriate acknowledgment, on my recently published study on national security.

It took some time to sort out whether the matter could be handled by the Law Reform Commission. In late 1981 I had discussions with Jacques Fortin and Patrick Fitzgerald, who were in charge of the commission's substantive criminal-law project. After I produced a discussion paper for the commission on national-security offences, I was authorized by Muldoon to talk to the various government officials interested in the area. I had discussions with the deputy solicitor general Fred Gibson; the assistant deputy solicitor general Mike Shoemaker, who had been a year behind me at law school; the deputy minister of justice, Roger Tassé, with whom I had worked on securities regulation when he was the deputy registrar general; and Stephen Skelly, an assistant deputy minister in justice.

One of the main concerns of the departments was whether the federal government would lose control of the right to prosecute if offences under the *Official Secrets Act* were placed in the Criminal Code. Although Chief Justice Laskin in one case had taken the position that the federal government could give itself the right to prosecute offences in the Criminal Code, Justice Dickson in dissent was firmly convinced that if an offence was in the code it would be a provincial responsibility to prosecute it. Even today, the matter is not entirely clear, although it seemed to me then – and still seems so now – that an offence's inclusion in the Criminal Code should not be decisive, even though the prosecution of most criminal offences will come under section 92(14) of the

Constitution Act, whereby the provinces have authority over 'the administration of justice in the province.' Criminal offences in the code that relate to national security could come under the federal 'peace, order and good government' clause as well us under the criminal-law power. When the CSIS act was passed in 1984, the companion *Security Offences Act* was also enacted. It allows the federal government to issue a fiat to establish exclusive federal power to prosecute when an 'alleged offence arises out of conduct constituting a threat to the security of Canada.' The federal government is prosecuting the current terrorism-related cases in Ontario. I cannot conceive of the possibility of the Supreme Court of Canada saying that that statute is unconstitutional.

There were probably other issues relating to a potential turf war between the justice department, headed by Mark McGuigan, and the solicitor general's department, headed by Bob Kaplan, both of whom I knew well.

The matter appears to have sorted itself out, because I got the following cryptic handwritten note, dated 23 December 1982, from Frank Muldoon, who appeared to me to have been reading too many spy novels:

Marty

On the matter of our mutual interest and concern, I am informed that messages have been transmitted between Dr. McGuigan and Mr. Kaplan.
Ergo, I am also informed, I shall learn what's what from Dr. McGuigan relatively soon in 1983. I am given some reason to hope that it will be as we proposed.

All the best.

Sincerely

Frank Muldoon

This appeared to mean that we could go ahead with a working paper on offences against the state. Meetings were therefore set up with the two departments involved. In April 1983 I attended a meeting in Ottawa with Muldoon and another commissioner, Alan Reid, which was attended by Solicitor General Kaplan and the senior people from his department, Fred Gibson, Mike Shoemaker, and Ed Finn, who would become the first director of CSIS. Similar cooperation was given by the Department of Justice, and in early June 1983 I finally received a copy of Stephen Skelly's 1980 paper on the *Official Secrets Act*.

I continued my work for the commission, producing, with the help of my summer research assistant, Paul Schabas, now a senior litigator at Blakes, a sixty-five-page draft working paper, which I sent to the commission during the summer of 1984. Justice Allen Linden of the Ontario Supreme Court had become the commission's president, having been appointed in the summer of 1983 after Frank Muldoon was appointed to the trial division of the Federal Court. There were consultations on the document in Montreal in December 1984 with a group of academics selected by the Canadian Association of Law Teachers, and another meeting with an advisory panel of senior judges, which included G. Arthur Martin, Fred Kaufman, and Gerry La Forest. There had been an earlier consultation in Hull with government officials. Linden asked me after the three consultations ended to send him some notes of my impressions. I acknowledged that there were a number of good points that would have to be taken into account, particularly with respect to achieving consistency between the working paper and other reports that the commission was producing, such as the one on *mens rea* concepts in the commission's general part of the code and another study on extraterritorial jurisdiction.

'On the principal points in the paper,' I wrote, 'I didn't hear anything that caused me to change my mind. Some points worried me, but on balance I'll stick to the main conclusions,' which I then succinctly outlined:

> There was no substantial dissent on ... for example: the abolition of the distinction between treason and high treason; keeping the offence of harming her majesty as part of the law of treason; keeping revolutionary conduct, if violent or illegal ... as part of the law of treason; keeping the concept of allegiance for extra territorial offences; eliminating the limitation periods; getting rid of the offence of sedition; integrating into the Code the espionage part of treason with the espionage provisions of the Official Secrets Act; catching espionage of information that is not 'secret and official' if used for a prejudicial purpose, but not information that is already in the public domain; etc.

I urged Justice Linden to ensure that consultation with other government departments take place before the working paper was released. I pointed out that 'consultation with the Department of External Affairs, the Department of National Defence, the Solicitor General's Department, the Security Service, and the Department of Justice had not been done' and stated that 'it would be a mistake to proceed with even a Working Paper without careful discussions with each of those divisions.'

It was now up to the commission to finalize the working paper. The redrafting of the paper was done by Patrick Fitzgerald and his niece, Oonagh Fitzgerald, now a senior lawyer in the Department of Justice. They took a very philosophical approach to many of the issues, which is not surprising because Patrick was a noted jurisprudence scholar. Jacques Fortin had died of cancer the month after the December consultations. Moreover, a new co-coordinator of the substantive criminal-law projects, François Handfield, had recently been appointed. When I saw the document again in the fall of 1985, it had been completely restructured. I have not examined the commission records – assuming they have been preserved – to see how the overhaul came about.

The new document started with a historical discussion of national-security offences, including a learned, but in my view unnecessary, discussion of early Germanic and Roman laws. Justice Linden asked me to comment on the new draft. I was hesitant to be too critical of what · appeared to be a *fait accompli*. 'I thought there was a bit too much on the early Germanic and Roman law,' I gently wrote, adding: 'Maybe you should start with the 1351 statute.' I found this very early history particularly odd because the commission had reduced the size of the document. They had, for example, reduced my 248 footnotes to 147. I also thought that it was better to discuss the history of various provisions when discussing specific offences. 'Personally,' I wrote to Linden, 'I like dealing separately with the historical discussion of each major section, but I may be wrong...'

Further, I had taken the position in my draft of the working paper that an illegal unilateral declaration of independence by a province would come within the treason section. The new working paper said it would not and did not recommend that it be added. In my letter to Linden, I stated: 'You say that a Unilateral Act of Independence is not treason,' and I then asked: 'Would it be treason if the secessionist province resisted a Federal move to reestablish its authority?'

I had similar concerns with many of the other parts of the document. I complained about limiting espionage to 'classified national security information,' stating, 'I don't agree. I would make it wider than that.'

Further, 'I would impose a duty on persons to warn the authorities when they know of a planned violent overthrow of the government.' The new draft stated that the threat in these cases 'is not so immediate as to justify imposing a duty on the citizen.' I also had concerns with the handling of the 'leakage' provision, stating, 'I'm not sure that the leakage provision, as drafted, belongs in this part of the Code.' And so on. In retrospect, I wonder why I did not make the language of my response stronger. Perhaps I thought that a gentle approach would get better results. Nevertheless, when I was asked how I wanted my contribution noted in the published document, I said to Linden: 'Put me at the bottom of the list.'

Linden replied, thanking me for my memo and stating: 'We will certainly incorporate most of your suggestions before publication.' Some changes were made, but the very philosophical approach taken in the paper remained. I was not privy to the comments received on the document and have not looked at the archival records. I note, as stated above, that the commission never brought in a report on the subject. A report by the commission, *Recodifying Criminal Law*, did, however, incorporate the proposed draft section on 'Crimes against State Security,' along with other substantive provisions, but there was little commentary on these sections in the report. The commission was closed down by the government in 1992. The offences of treason and sedition therefore still remain in the Criminal Code in much the same form as they were before the McDonald Commission studied the subject.

The *Official Secrets Act* has, however, recently been abolished as part of the government's reaction to the terrorist attacks in the United States on 11 September 2001. The government used that occasion to introduce a new *Security of Information Act*, which tidied up and replaced the *Official Secrets Act*. When I had given evidence to the senate committee on the CSIS act in 1983 and had said that the OSA should be revised, the chair of the committee, Michael Pitfield, who had been the clerk of the Privy Council and knew the politics of the issue, stated: 'It seems to me that we will be waiting until hell freezes over before anyone tries to do it.' It took the events of 9/11 to get it changed.

Unfortunately, the key sections of the new *Security of Information Act* continued to use the ambiguous language of the *Official Secrets Act*. We still do not know, for example, what the words 'secret official' in the wrongful communication of information part (section 4) refer to where an offence is created for a person to have 'in his possession or control any secret official code word, password, sketch, plan, model, article, note, document or information ...' Did it refer only to 'code word' and possibly 'password,' or does it apply to all information? Some lower courts in Canada had held the former, contrary to the interpretation that had been given to similar words in England. Surely it would have been sensible to clarify this in the legislation.

The issue has recently been brought to a head, because in October 2006 Justice Lynn Ratushny struck down section 4 in a case testing a search warrant against an Ottawa journalist, Juliet O'Neill, who was investigating an aspect of the Maher Arar affair. Ratushny held that the section was unnecessarily broad and vague and therefore violated the accused's right to fundamental justice under section 7 of the Charter. Moreover it violated section 2(b) – freedom of expression – of the Charter when applied to a journalist. The government decided not to appeal and perhaps we will soon see new and more carefully defined proposed legislation to handle the problem of leaked information – or, perhaps not.

It seemed a shame that the Law Reform Commission did not bring in a report on offences against the state. They might have if they had followed my earlier draft working paper, which had gone through a process of careful consultation with judges, academics, and government officials. As I will argue in the later chapter on codification, 'law reform is affected by a great number of factors apart from the merits of the proposals. Then, as now, a combination of politics, personalities, and pressure groups affected the outcome.' I will leave to later researchers the task of determining precisely how this might apply to offences against the state.

16

More National Security – Terrorism

My involvement with national-security issues was minimal during the 1990s. I had moved on to other projects. By September 2001, I had more or less completed the University of Toronto history. The only significant work still to be done was the index, which I planned to undertake myself. I never was able to do so. I got caught up again in national-security issues, and was fortunate to be able to obtain a skilled indexer to do the history's index.

On the morning of 11 September 2001, as mentioned in an earlier chapter, I was at my home computer working on a paper that I had to deliver the next day in Saskatoon on criminal-court unification. I normally listen to classical or jazz music while working – either my own discs or CBC 2. Shortly before 9 a.m., the CBC broke in to say that a plane had hit one of the twin towers of the World Trade Center in New York City. Judy and I then watched the drama unfold on television.

The following week, the law school asked political scientist Janice Stein to give a talk to the faculty on the international implications of September 11th. During the discussion – to my surprise – she turned to me and asked me what I thought about the terrorist attacks. Drawing on my work for the McDonald Commission, I gave an off-the-cuff analysis of the problems that Canada and the United States faced in collecting intelligence on potential terrorist threats. The reaction in both countries to the excesses of the RCMP and the FBI in the 1970s had caused both countries to limit wiretapping and to tie the hands of undercover agents. Moreover, the budgets of the security services in both countries had been cut over the years, thus further limiting their activities.

I further developed those ideas in a short paper I presented several weeks later to a law school constitutional roundtable on 'Terror's Challenge to Law.' I worked hard on that short paper, using the Internet to gather factual information quickly. I was surprised at how much was now available on national-security issues through government and other websites. The websites of CSIS and SIRC, the review agency, clearly showed that the Canadian government was well aware of the threat of terrorism. I noted:

> Report after report details the concern over terrorist attacks. There is, for example, a public report in May 2000 on 'International Terrorism: The Threat to Canada,' and another in December 1999 on 'Chemical, Biological, Radiological and Nuclear Terrorism,' as well as one the same month on 'Trends in Terrorism.' Osama bin Laden is mentioned in a number of papers and the word Afghanistan starts appearing more frequently in more recent years. Ahmed Ressam, the so-called millennium bomber, appears in several studies after he was apprehended crossing the border. These are the unclassified papers. There is also a long list of secret and top secret papers that are listed.

I sent my paper to Janice Stein for her comments, stating: 'I am indebted to you. If you hadn't turned to me for a comment when you came to the faculty I wouldn't have started thinking about the issues.' She urged me to send it to the *Globe*. I did send it, but withdrew it when I learned that new security legislation was about to be tabled in Parliament. It would be better to comment publicly after I had seen the bill.

I'm not sure how it came about, but the Department of Justice asked me if I would examine the legislation on terrorism that they were about to introduce. It is likely that Dean Ron Daniels told Morris Rosenberg, the deputy minister of justice, about some of the expertise in the faculty of law. Rick Mosley, the assistant deputy minister in charge of policy in the department, called me on 16 October – the day after the legislation, Bill C-36, was given first reading in the House of Commons – and asked me to act as a consultant to review and comment on the bill. I was to pay particular attention to some of its more controversial aspects, such as preventive arrest, evidence gathering, and the extension of the power of the Communications Security Establishment (CSE) to gather electronic information without a warrant. He wanted my comments in ten days' time.

The legislation – the *Anti-Terrorism Act*, but still known today as Bill C-36 – was very complex and required an investigation of many areas with which I was unfamiliar. It also required some familiarity with the proposed American and UK legislation. I had permission to discuss the subject matter with persons in the government who were more knowledgeable than I was about the issues, and in the process I had helpful talks with a number of department of justice lawyers – in particular, Michael Duffy, a justice lawyer assigned to CSIS, George Dolhai, a lawyer involved in special federal prosecutions, and Stan Cohen, senior counsel in the human-rights section of the department. All three commented on my draft before I submitted it to the department. In my letter of thanks to Stan Cohen, I stated that 'it was one of the toughest tasks I have ever done.'

Two weeks after handing in my memorandum I participated in a conference – 'The Security of Freedom' – organized by the faculty of law and attended by over 350 individuals. My talk was entitled 'Police Powers in Bill C-36' and in a footnote I acknowledged that it was in part drawn from my memo prepared for the Department of Justice. The papers for the conference were published as a book, *The Security of Freedom: Essays on Canada's Anti-Terrorism Bill*, by the University of Toronto Press less than two weeks after the conference ended – a remarkable achievement.

I will quote from my published paper rather than my memo to the Department of Justice in order to avoid the unlikely possibility of charges under the *Security of Information Act*. Again, as in my earlier talk, I noted that the threat from terrorism was well documented. In my talk I quoted one expert, Paul Wilkinson, who had prepared an unclassified CSIS paper, in which he stated: 'In view of the fact that attacks by terrorist groups have become increasingly lethal over recent years, it is wise to plan for a continuing trend towards massive car and truck bombings in crowded city areas, and "spectacular" terrorist attacks ... designed to capture maximum attention from the mass media, to cause maximum shock and outrage.' This clearly applied to September 11, except that planes were used rather than cars and trucks. My belief that the threats should be taken seriously coloured my view that the modest changes proposed by the government were reasonable under the circumstances. Later events in Madrid, London, and elsewhere show that society cannot be too complacent. What Canada was proposing was nowhere near the response in the United States and Great Britain to terrorist threats.

My principal concern with Bill C-36 was that it transferred responsibility for many aspects of national security back to the RCMP. The McDonald Commission had recommended that national-security matters be taken over by a civilian agency, a recommendation that had been adopted by the government after a thorough examination of the bill by the Senate's Pitfield Committee. Terrorism was and is part of the CSIS mandate. Bill C-36, I argued, 'gives too much emphasis to prosecution and punishment. We are not going to feel or be much safer if half a dozen terrorists are prosecuted and punished after terrorist attacks. Our emphasis should be on discovering and thwarting terrorist activities before they occur. It is obviously far better to prevent destructive action before it occurs than it is to prosecute and punish persons afterwards.' The Pitfield report had put it well: 'Law enforcement is essentially reactive. While there is an element of information-gathering and prevention in law enforcement, on the whole it takes place after the commission of a distinct criminal offence. The protection of security relies less on reaction to events; it seeks advance warning of security threats, and is not necessarily concerned with breaches of the law.' 'The proposed bill,' I argued, 'reverses much of what was accomplished in the 1980s, that is, controlling excess zeal by the police in the area of national security.'

It would be interesting to know how this shift came about. It might, in part, have been engineered by the RCMP, who always regretted the loss of the security service. It might also stem from the Department of Justice being in charge of drafting the legislation: lawyers tend to think of law enforcement and prosecution to solve problems. Perhaps a different bill – with the creation of fewer new offences – would have emerged if the solicitor general's department – which was responsible for national security and CSIS – had been in charge. Still, some new offences were inevitable because a United Nations resolution called for controlling the financing of terrorism. When the cabinet documents are made public many years hence we may have a clearer picture of how the assignment to the justice department came about. It may have happened because a strong minister, Anne McLellan, was in charge of justice and a relatively weak minister, Lawrence MacAulay, in charge of the solicitor general's department. Or it may have been, as Eddie Goldenberg – Chrétien's chief policy adviser – suggests in his memoirs, that the deputy minister in the department of justice, Morris Rosenberg, was liked and respected by Goldenberg. Moreover, CSIS had been weakened financially throughout the 1990s. Its report for the previous year showed a decrease in employees from about 2700 persons in the early 1990s to about 2000.

The security service was forgotten in the bill. 'Surely, the exercise of special powers relating to terrorism,' I argued, 'should require the consent of CSIS.' Of particular importance, I observed, was the fact that 'the powers given to the police under Bill C-36 are not subject to the review of SIRC.' This was an obvious defect, which five years later was examined in Justice Dennis O'Connor's study of the subject in his Arar report and will probably also be discussed in former Supreme Court of Canada justice John Major's study of the Air India affair.

I then examined each of the controversial provisions in the bill relating to police powers. The definition of 'terrorist activity,' which was the foundation of some of the police powers, was, I believed, too broad. I had no difficulty with the sections dealing with wiretapping with a warrant. The bill made it easier for the police to engage in wiretapping by permitting wiretaps in national-security matters to last for a longer period than in other cases, to permit a judge to extend the period before notice of the tap has to be given to the person subject to the tap, and to allow wiretaps without having to show that 'other investigative procedures have been tried and have failed' or are 'unlikely to succeed.' 'One would have thought,' I observed, 'that where there is a serious threat to national security, wiretapping with a judicial authorization should be at or near the top of the list of techniques that could be used.' Indeed, I suggested that the legislation go further and, as in the UK legislation, provide procedures for obtaining keys for encrypted communications.

One significant change brought about by the proposed legislation was the recognition in the bill of the formerly secret Communications Security Establishment (CSE), an organization of about one thousand persons, which provides the government with foreign signals intelligence, obtained by gathering and analysing foreign radio, radar, and other electronic emissions. The mandate of the organization would be expanded. Formerly, it could only intercept communications that did not originate or terminate in Canada. The legislation now provides that the minister of national defence will be able to authorize interceptions involving individuals in Canada 'if the interception will be directed at foreign entities located outside Canada.' In my talk I state that this extension 'is a troubling aspect of the bill.' 'Why is the Federal Court of Canada not approving electronic surveillance involving persons in Canada?' I asked, and went on to state:

> I do not, of course, know the technicalities of how the CSE presently iden-
> tifies the place that a telephone, radio, or internet signal originates or ends
> up. I presume that they may discover this while they are recording some-
> thing. They should be permitted to preserve the material, with the Minis-
> ter of National Defence's approval, until an application can be made to the
> Federal Court.

Perhaps the test in such cases should be 'reasonable cause to suspect,' rather than the normal 'reasonable cause to believe.' Further, why are the activities of the CSE not being reviewed by the five-person Security Intelligence Review Committee, which examines the work of CSIS after the fact? The review is now done by a single retired or supernumerary judge. It is generally easier, I believe, to co-opt a single retired judge than it is to co-opt a group, such as SIRC.

In 2006 the issue of President George W. Bush's personal authoriza-tion of similar surveillance had become a matter of controversy. Bush claimed that he has executive power to authorize such activity under the war power, in spite of congressional legislation spelling out what wiretapping can legally be done. In January 2007, with a Democratic Congress, Bush agreed that in the future judicial authorization would have to be sought in all national-security cases.

There is no doubt that the procedure before the federal court can be improved. As I understand the practice, when CSIS obtains a court authorization which results in evidence relevant to a criminal charge, all of the wiretaps have to be turned over to the defendant, whether the wiretap is introduced into evidence or not. I do not believe that this should be necessary if the evidence is not used for prosecution pur-poses. Further, it should be possible to use the independent federal courts, without making the process of obtaining national-security wire-taps too difficult.

Investigative hearings were permitted by Bill C-36. A person could be ordered to appear before a judge to give evidence – and arrested with a warrant if he or she fails to appear. The judge had to be satisfied that there were 'reasonable grounds to believe' that a terrorism offence had been committed or would be committed and that the person summoned had 'information that may reveal the whereabouts' of the perpetrator or of a person who 'may commit a terrorism offence.' Failure to comply would result in committal to jail for contempt of court. This process was new, but, as I stated in my talk, not particularly troubling. It was not troubling because there are many cases where persons are compelled to give evidence under oath, such as inquiries before fire marshals, royal commissions, and securities commissions. Similarly, persons who have knowledge of a criminal offence can be called at a preliminary hearing, although in such a case the compulsion occurs after a charge is laid. In the United States witnesses can be forced to testify before a grand jury as 'material witnesses' before charges are laid (as was the case in Canada for many years) and in the United Kingdom the *Terrorism Act* makes it an offence in certain circumstances for a person to fail to disclose information if the person 'believes or suspects that another person has committed' certain offences, a far more coercive process than an investigative hearing. Further, it was likely that the investigative-hearing process could not be used against a prime suspect because of the right against self-incrimination under sections 11(c) and 7 of the Charter. Moreover, a witness, under the legislation, had the right to counsel at any stage of the proceedings. Thus, the procedure was a relatively mild one.

Although I did not find the investigative-hearing section troubling, I did wonder 'what the provision will actually accomplish' and whether it was 'worth including in the bill.' If the person has relevant information, I speculated, he or she will have an incentive to cooperate with the police to avoid the possibility of being charged with a substantive offence – and the range of offences under the legislation is very wide. The investigative-hearing procedure was only tried in one case, to investigate someone during the Air India proceedings, twenty years after the event. The technique was challenged by counsel for the witness, but was upheld by the Supreme Court of Canada (citing my chapter in the terrorism book). There is much to be said for the dissenting view, however, that the section was not designed for such a situation. As it turned out, the prosecutors did not pursue holding an investigative hearing in the Air India case, perhaps because the Supreme Court also had held that there was a presumption that the investigative hearing had to be public.

The legislation was subject to a sunset clause. In February 2007 a majority of the House of Commons voted not to renew the provision relating to investigative hearings.

The section of Bill C-36 on requiring a recognizance with conditions, I stated, was also not unreasonable. It allowed the police to arrest a person without a warrant on the basis of 'reasonable suspicion' that he or she will commit a terrorist offence and for the court to impose conditions. This would have been like the current peace bonds found in the Criminal Code, whereby a person who has grounds to fear for his or her safety can seek to have a judge impose conditions on the person posing the potential threat. There are, however, several differences. The arrest for terrorism could be made on the lower standard of 'reasonable suspicion' and not the test normally used in the Criminal Code, 'reasonable belief.' But the lesser standard of suspicion was the test that had been used in the *Official Secrets* Act since it was first enacted in 1911. This section of Bill C-36 also allowed the judge to hold the person for a total of seventy-two hours – three times greater than the twenty-four-hour maximum period normally used in the code. The Supreme Court of Canada, in *Hunter v. Southam*, its first Charter case involving search and seizure, had recognized that a lower standard of proof may be acceptable under the Charter in matters involving national security. Whether it is justified depends on the threat posed. 'My own view,' I stated, was that a lower standard was 'clearly acceptable for terrorist offences under a restricted definition of terrorism.' As far as I am aware, the section was never used. Like the provision for investigative hearings, it was not renewed by the House of Commons.

Another area that I dealt with in my talk was undercover agents, which Bill C-36 did not cover. As stated above, the existing law created a problem for undercover operations. Canadian courts had held that without legislation peace officers could not breach *any* laws in pursuit of their lawful activities. The Ontario Court of Appeal, for example, held in a 1989 case that a police officer could not go through a stop sign without specific legislative authorization, and in 1999 the Supreme Court of Canada held that an undercover police officer could not offer to sell drugs to a dealer in a so-called reverse sting operation, although they could buy drugs because specific legislation allowed such purchases. I noted that a bill was about to be passed dealing with organized crime and law enforcement, which permitted some law-breaking with various controls. Although this would cover police handling national-security matters, it would not cover members of CSIS because they are not peace officers. In my view, it should cover them.

I concluded my paper by stating:

> This review of special police powers has argued that some additional police powers should be added, such as the power to deal with encryption and to make undercover operatives more effective by permitting some illegality. Other powers, such as investigative hearings, are probably unnecessary. Still others, such as wiretapping and arrest on suspicion, are justified to deal with the very serious problem of terrorism. In all these cases, however, the definition of terrorism should be more limited, the consent of CSIS or the Solicitor General of Canada should be required, and the Security Intelligence Review Committee should play a greater role in reviewing any actions taken.

The five-year review of the anti-terrorism act has not finished its report as this is being written, although we know that the sections relating to investigative hearings and recognizances with conditions have not been renewed. In mid-May 2007, however, the public safety minister, Stockwell Day, announced that he planned to revive both sections in new legislation. We will see whether these sections are introduced and, if introduced, passed. We will also see what the parliamentary committees dealing with the review of the act will say with respect to other provisions. I expect that they will leave the legislation more or less as it is, but will impose another sunset clause.

My concern about the lack of review of the RCMP's national-security activities was not dealt with in the legislation. It became an issue, however, after the publicity given to the Maher Arar case in 2004. In the fall of 2002, Arar (a Canadian citizen) was taken by U.S. officials from New York and flown to the Middle East, where he was held for ten months in a Syrian jail, tortured, and allegedly 'confessed' to having been trained as a terrorist in Afghanistan.

There were calls for a commission of inquiry, but the government resisted. The matter was being looked into by the RCMP oversight body, the Commission for Public Complaints against the RCMP, which had been established in 1988, but the RCMP was not cooperating with the commission. Shirley Heafey, the commission's chair, wanted greater powers, noting in a statement in late January 2004 the wide powers given to the Security Intelligence Review Committee (SIRC) when

CSIS was set up and the limited powers that her commission possessed. Several months earlier, Reid Morden, a former director of CSIS, had made the point that CSIS was subject to careful scrutiny, but 'in contrast the RCMP has little or no oversight or review, with the exception of a responsive official, the RCMP Complaints Commissioner.'

On 28 January 2004 the cabinet set up a royal commission to investigate the facts in the Arar case and also to determine what review body should supervise the RCMP's increasing role in the area of national security. The auditor general of Canada, Sheila Fraser, had prepared a report several months earlier recommending that 'the government ensure that agencies that collect security intelligence be subject to appropriate levels of external review and disclosure.' The day that Paul Martin's Liberal government took office in mid-December 2003, the prime minister undertook to establish an arm's-length review mechanism for the RCMP's activities with respect to national security. The government was obviously not willing simply to expand the powers of the complaints commission.

Associate Chief Justice Dennis O'Connor of the Ontario Court of Appeal was appointed the sole commissioner. He has a sterling reputation as a judge and was highly regarded as the sole commissioner several years earlier investigating the tainted-water tragedy that occurred in Walkerton, Ontario. That earlier inquiry also had a factual and policy component.

Although public attention has focused on the factual inquiry, in the long run the policy issue may prove to be more important. 'Under the policy mechanism for the RCMP national security activities,' the government press release stated, 'Mr. Justice O'Connor will examine domestic and international review models. He will make such recommendations as he considers advisable on the creation of a new mechanism and in doing this, he will consider how the recommended mechanism would interact with other Canadian review bodies.'

The Arar Commission asked Patrick Macklem of the University of Toronto law school to help organize a one-day session to give advice to the commission on its mandate. The private session was held at the law school in mid-April 2004, with Justice O'Connor and the counsel assisting the commission in attendance. My task was to comment on 'independent review mechanisms: domestic and comparative models.'

'There are many issues for the Arar Inquiry to consider,' I observed, stating the obvious: 'A decision cannot be made by the Inquiry until there is a thorough examination by the Inquiry of all the intelligence gathering and anti-terrorism activities in Canada and the forms of accountability to which they are subject. Other countries use other techniques and these will have to be examined as well.' 'The key question for the Inquiry,' I went on to say, 'is whether the oversight should be given to the RCMP's Commission for Public Complaints, as suggested by its chair, or to the Security Intelligence Review Committee (SIRC), or to an entirely new body?'

I liked the SIRC structure, whose five-member board, with the assistance of staff, ably reviews the activities of the over 2000-person CSIS after the fact and produces special studies. Past members have included Bob Rae, Roy Romanow, Jean-Jacques Blais, Gary Filmon, and Ron Atkey, knowledgeable and sophisticated individuals appointed to hold office 'during good behaviour' for up to five years with the option of re-appointment.

I was less optimistic about the ability of the Commission for Public Complaints against the RCMP as a review body, stating:

> In contrast, the RCMP has well over ten times that number of employees – about 30,000. Only a very small part of its activity relates to national security. The Commission for Public Complaints against the RCMP is, as its name states, a complaints body. It is not a general review body. It has its hands full dealing with complaints about drug enforcement, corruption, and a vast array of other matters. The Commission publicly complains about its backlog. In its March 2003 report it stated that 'the caseload at the end of March 2003 was comprised of over 400 cases awaiting evaluation.' Should it add national security? Does it – and can it – have the knowledge and sophistication necessary to deal with national security issues? Would adding a national security review function change the focus of the review body more than is desirable? Would the tribunal's review apply to matters other than national security?

I also recommended that the commission examine the role of the Inspector General for CSIS in the solicitor general's office. The inspector general, appointed by cabinet, concentrates on CSIS and reports to the minister on its activities, including giving the minister a certificate on the extent to which he or she is satisfied with the various CSIS reports to the minister. I particularly wanted the commission to study the use of inspectors general in the United States, who are widely used by the federal government to control waste, corruption, and improper conduct. I had earlier examined the role of the American inspectors general when I did my study *Controlling Misconduct in the Military* for the Somalia inquiry in the mid-1990s. I was impressed with the use of the office in the United States, particularly in the military.

In my presentation at the Arar symposium I discussed what might be the dividing line between the RCMP complaints body and SIRC or any new body, assuming that the review was not given to a beefed-up RCMP review body. This difficult question would be the commission's greatest challenge. I asked:

> When is a matter one of national security? There is an overlap between preventive intelligence gathering activity and regular policing. The Air India case is an obvious example. Perhaps one could say that matters investigated under certain Acts, such as the Terrorism Act, should be under the review powers of the other agency. This would require spelling out which sections of the Criminal Code or other Acts should be included. The legislation could also include for outside review any warrant where the application is based in whole or in part on national security grounds. This will be a challenging exercise.

A few weeks later, the Arar Commission, which had chosen a formal advisory committee several months earlier, asked me to be a consultant to do further work as a 'special adviser' to assist them in preparing a background paper on the inquiry's policy issues. I was asked to look at national-security review mechanisms in the United States and review procedures for police forces in Canada. Fortunately, I had already hired two first-rate recent graduates from the faculty of law, Bill Thompson and Shaun Laubman, who were to help me with the present book, but who were more than happy to switch to national-security issues. By chance, both had taken courses on national security at law school. Bill had a strong interest in criminal law and Shaun had considerable knowledge of American constitutional law from his undergraduate studies.

The division of responsibility was therefore clear. Shaun would help with the examination of the review mechanisms in the United States and Bill would assist me with the review of police activities in Canada. The final documents were delivered to the Arar Commission at the end of the summer, were published on their website, and were drawn upon for their consultation paper. Readers can view the commission's consultation paper, dated October 2004, on its website (www.ararcommission.ca).

Along with other members of the commission I met with Shirley Heafey and members of her staff in Ottawa, and in Toronto with the Ontario Provincial Police and the Toronto Police. One of the officers who took part in the meeting with the Toronto Police was a staff superintendent in charge of detective operations, Bill Blair. Blair was particularly impressive, and a number of us attending the session predicted that he would be the next chief of police for the City of Toronto, a prediction that proved correct.

I did not take part in any further work for the commission after helping with the consultation draft. The commission published its report dealing with factual events relating to the Arar case in September 2006, finding that Arar had not been involved in any terrorist organization and was innocent of any improper conduct. In December 2006 Justice O'Connor's 630-page second report on review mechanisms was released: *A New Review Mechanism for the RCMP's National Security Activities*. The commission recommended that the RCMP Complaints Commission be given an expanded and revitalized role with respect to complaints relating to the RCMP in the national-security area and at the same time that the Security Intelligence Review Committee (SIRC) be given the responsibility for reviewing a number of other agencies, such as transportation, immigration, and foreign affairs. The Communications Security Establishment (CSE) would continue to be reviewed by a single retired judge. There would be a four-person body called the Integrated National Security Review Coordinating Committee, made up of the heads of the three bodies and an outside chair that would coordinate the work of all three review agencies.

Justice O'Connor's scheme may work, but I would have given SIRC the right to take over any cases involving national security that it wanted from the RCMP Complaints Commission and the Communications Security Establishment reviewing judge. There are examples of such pre-emption in the U.S. security agencies. How can SIRC do its job of controlling CSIS effectively if it does not know what is happening in the other two bodies? There are some investigations that require the prestige and expertise of a body like SIRC, qualities that are not likely to be found in the RCMP review body. This approach would require, of course, that SIRC be kept fully informed of what the other two review agencies were doing. I believe there should be one strong independent body with the capacity to review all national-security matters. As stated above, I did not take part in the deliberations leading to the second Arar report and was not privy to the arguments that convinced O'Connor to recommend what he did.

Two further investigations are ongoing, the commission on the Air India disaster, conducted by former Supreme Court justice John Major, and an investigation of three more Arar-like cases involving alleged incarceration and torture in foreign jails, being conducted by former Supreme Court Justice Frank Iacobucci. Whether they will look into the question of review mechanisms and, if they do, whether they will agree with Justice O'Connor's solution, remains to be seen.

17

Codification of the Criminal Law

At the University of Toronto, deans receive a one-year paid administrative leave at the end of their deanship. I intended to use that year, 1979–80, to complete my project on the machinery of law reform, which I had been working on since 1967. The Donner Canadian Foundation agreed to provide me with research funds, which would help pay for some of my research expenses. I was determined to finish the project, which was continuing to be an albatross around my neck.

Judy and I had decided that the family would spend about four months in Israel and the rest of the leave in Cambridge. I brought some of the albatross – in the form of a large number of files – with me to Israel, and the rest of the documents were sent to Cambridge to await my arrival there in late December.

We had rented a large apartment on the seafront in Netanya – a few buildings south of the Park Hotel, where a terrorist suicide bomber would later kill a large number of persons at a Passover dinner. We loved Netanya, a relatively compact city about thirty kilometres north of Tel Aviv, which caters to holidaymakers. Judy had distant relatives living in Netanya and other relatives living on a moshav – a cooperative agricultural community – close to the city. Another of Judy's relatives lived on a kibbutz on the border with Lebanon. As far as I know, I do not have any relatives in Israel, although several uncles had lived there in the 1930s. Our three children attended the American International School outside Hertzliya, midway between Netanya and Tel Aviv.

We had purchased a new Renault 12, which we had picked up in Paris and drove through France and Italy. We took a ferry from Brindisi to Corfu, drove through Greece, and sailed from Piraeus to Haifa. During our time in Israel we covered the country from the Golan Heights in the far north to Eilat in the south. The Sinai was then part of Israel, and we climbed Mount Sinai at dawn and toured the ancient monastery of Saint Catherine's. We spent the Jewish New Year in the ancient city of Safed, staying in the apartment of Wolfe Goodman (of the recently disbanded law firm Goodman and Carr) and attending a Reform service held outdoors. I still keep in my tallis (prayer shawl) container some pressed olive leaves and passion flowers that I picked up walking to the service.

I had been given visitor-professor status at both the Tel Aviv University Law School and the Hebrew University Law School in Jerusalem. Once a week I would take the awe-inspiring drive to Jerusalem for a seminar I gave on law reform. Judy and I never tired of the drive up to the hills of Jerusalem. My seminar was fun. I had about thirty very talented students in the class, many of whom had finished their army service and therefore tended to be somewhat older than law students in Toronto. The seminar worked well. I covered many of the same topics I covered in my course in Toronto – legislative lawmaking, judicial lawmaking, administrative lawmaking, committees and commissions, etc. – blending Israeli and Canadian examples. The seminar I remember best was one on pressure groups. Every person in the class was an active member of some pressure group – left and right political parties, religious and non-religious organizations, the army, a kibbutz, and many more. They clearly recognized the power of pressure groups in shaping the development of the law.

I had brought material with me on codification of the law, hoping to complete a chapter on the topic and perhaps others while in Israel. Judy and I were also hoping to start a novel and we made some progress, but soon abandoned the project because each of us was feeling guilty not doing our academic work. Judy was working on her MA and was doing part of her practicum in Israel. I still have the drafts of the novel and maybe this will be a post-post-retirement project. It was to be a Middle East spy thriller – I had just finished work on national security – concerning the possibility of a seismic fault which would make Israel self-sufficient in energy. I did the library research and Judy developed the characters. The plot is no less realistic today than it was in 1979.

Sitting on the balcony in our apartment in Netanya overlooking the

Mediterranean, I wrote about the history of codification in English law, starting with Jeremy Bentham and his promotion of codification. I touched on the efforts to codify the criminal law in the United States by followers of Bentham, and described the Indian criminal code that was drafted by the great historian Thomas Macaulay and brought into force shortly after the Indian Mutiny of 1857.

Codification of the law, including the criminal law, has not been as prevalent in the common-law systems as in the Continental civil-law systems. One of the main reasons for the common law's resistance to codification may be related to the close identification of legal and scientific thought in England in the seventeenth century. The most famous scientist of the time, Sir Francis Bacon, was also one of the most famous jurists, and lawyers were actively involved in the founding of the scientific Royal Society of London and in its work. Lawyers were part of the general intellectual community and were influenced by and, in turn, influenced scientific ideas. The chief justice of England, Sir Matthew Hale, the first major writer on the criminal law in England, was, for example, both a scientist and a lawyer. I see a close relationship, therefore, between the Baconian method of scientific empiricism and the common law's case-by-case method of building general principles from specific instances. Both use the inductive approach. Similarly, one can see a close relationship between the Continental Cartesian method of deductive analysis and the concept of codification, which goes from general principles to specific applications.

In writing the chapter on codification, I left one footnote blank. It dealt with a criminal code prepared for the island of Jamaica in the 1870s by a future English judge, R.S. Wright. I could not find out very much about Wright's code from the sources that were available to me in Israel. I decided to wait until I got to England to fill in the footnote. A professor at the Hebrew University, Yoram Shachar, told me about his experiences at the Public Records Office in London doing research on the history of the Israeli criminal code and urged me to visit the archives when I got to England. He told me how thrilling it was to work in the archives. I had never done any archival work.

We left Israel's sunshine around Christmas 1979 and arrived at Heathrow to the usual 4 p.m. winter darkness. I would be a visiting scholar at the Cambridge Institute of Criminology, then on West Road. Professors Glanville Williams and Kurt Lipstein had arranged for a large flat for the family in Clare Hall, a relatively new graduate college founded in

1966. The flat was large enough to hold a Canada party on 18 February 1980, the day that the Liberals under Pierre Trudeau won the election over the Conservatives under Prime Minister Joe Clark.

I loved Clare Hall, particularly the way it attempted to make our children feel part of the community and to integrate visiting scholars with graduate students and fellows. I also liked the cafeteria-style system that was used for seating at lunch time. One had to take a seat in the dining room in the order in which one emerged after getting one's food. As a result, one was usually mixed with students and fellows, and the ensuing conversations had an interdisciplinary flavour.

We had sold the car before we left Israel and all had bicycles. Tony Doob, who had been in Cambridge the year before, had donated two bright red bicycles to us, which we in turn bequeathed to Richard Ericson, who was arriving the following year. I don't know who has the red bicycles today.

Shortly after arriving in Cambridge, I went down to the relatively modern Public Records Office at Kew, outside London. One could leave Clare Hall at about 7:30 in the morning, take a fast train to London, change to a train to Kew, and arrive at the archives at about the time they opened. And one could visit the nearby Kew Gardens when they closed. One look at the Colonial Office records relating to the R.S. Wright code for Jamaica showed that the story was worth more than one footnote. It was not just a code for Jamaica that was being developed by Wright, but a code to be considered for adoption by all the colonies. Moreover, James Fitzjames Stephen, the noted jurist, had been involved in reviewing Wright's code, and it was during that review that Stephen decided to draft his own code. There were therefore two competing codes in the latter part of the nineteenth century, Wright's code and Stephen's. It was Stephen's code that was adopted in 1892 in Canada and most other Commonwealth countries.

Digging through the archival records was a wonderful experience. Every file tells a story. The Colonial Office adopted the practice of having the most junior person comment first on an issue, with the next most junior person commenting next, and so on, in much the same way, I understand, that the Supreme Court of Canada discusses how a case will be decided. There were also records in the files of the Lord Chancellor's office and in various libraries, particularly the Cambridge University Library. The footnote grew into a paragraph, and then into a short article, which I thought might be suitable for the *Criminal Law*

Review, and then into an article with 324 footnotes, which was quickly accepted by Professor Patrick Atiyah for publication in 1981 in the first volume of the new *Oxford Journal of Legal Studies*.

'R.S. Wright's Model Criminal Code: A Forgotten Chapter in the History of the Criminal Law' is my favourite article and had a profound effect on my subsequent work. As we will see in a later chapter, my interest in Justice Stephen led to my interest in the Lipski case, which in turn led me to the Shortis and Patrick cases. The R.S. Wright article was the first time I used a narrative approach for academic purposes, as I also did later for my three true-crime books. It was primarily the true-crime books, I believe, which influenced the committee choosing the person to write the history of the University of Toronto to select me. The history followed the style of the murder books. So the article had a major effect on my subsequent career.

The article opened my eyes to the obvious, that is, that a code reflects the philosophy and views of its drafter. Here we had two very different codes representing the differing philosophical and jurisprudential positions of the two drafters. I had been studying and teaching criminal law for twenty years and had accepted our criminal code – which was essentially Stephen's code – as more or less inevitable. But now I had two different models and came to appreciate why many scholars in various fields like taking two or more models to analyse a problem.

An understanding of Wright's left-wing liberal code placed Stephen's more authoritarian code in its proper perspective. Wright was in many respects a radical, supporting land nationalization and the abolition of the House of Lords. He promoted women's rights and played an active role in the growing labour movement, the latter causing him to wish to curtail the power of a conservative judiciary to develop the law. When Wright was appointed to the superior court, he at first declined the knighthood that went with the office, but at the urging of other judges eventually accepted it. Stephen, by contrast, was very conservative, was opposed to the universal franchise, wanted the law to enforce morality, and trusted the judges to develop the law. Disraeli once said that Stephen would have made an excellent leader of the Conservative Party. I have Spy prints from *Vanity Fair* on my office wall of the two judges, hanging uncomfortably beside each other. The caption under Stephen's picture is 'The Criminal Code,' and under Wright's, 'He declined a Knighthood, but thought better of it.'

Here are several examples from the two competing codes of how their different philosophies played out in the drafting of specific sections. Take the political offence of sedition, where the differences are clear. Wright allowed the citizen wide scope to criticize government policy, limiting a seditious purpose to 'a purpose to excite any of Her Majesty's subjects to the obtaining by force or other unlawful means of an alteration in the laws or in the form of government.' Stephen's code, however, allowed far less scope for free speech. In his code sedition included an intention to bring the government of the United Kingdom or any part of it into 'hatred or contempt,' or 'to raise discontent or dis-affection amongst Her Majesty's subjects.' Stephen wanted to control the proletariat. Wright wanted to encourage them to complain.

Stephen – who had written a book opposing John Stuart Mill's liberal approach to the enforcement of morality – would punish buggery or bestiality with a possible penalty of penal servitude for life, and with a *minimum* penalty of ten years' imprisonment. Wright's code treated those offences as 'public nuisances.' Further, Wright's abortion section was much more liberal than the section drafted by Stephen, who would permit an abortion only 'for the preservation of the life of the mother.'

Wright's support of the labour movement influenced his view of the offence of common-law conspiracy, which he would have restricted to a conspiracy to commit a 'crime,' that is, an offence punishable on indictment. Stephen would have punished conspiracies to commit offences punishable on summary conviction and most probably conspiracies to engage in some conduct which was not itself subject to a criminal penalty. The one thing that I knew about Wright before learning about his role in drafting a criminal code was that he had written a book that is still used today, *The Law of Conspiracies and Agreements*, but I had not known that it had been written to try to discourage the judges from continuing to use the law of conspiracy to curtail strikes and picketing by unions.

Wright's code also differed from Stephen's in the way it dealt with the mental element in crime. Like the American Law Institute's first-rate Model Penal Code, which has been adopted by most American states, Wright's code set out for each offence the mental state required for each element of the offence and defined that mental state in an introductory section. Stephen opposed this view, taking the position that one could leave it to the judges to develop the requisite mental state for each element through judicial decisions. 'A code without general definitions of general elements,' Wright rightly stated in answer to Stephen's view, 'would miss the greatest advantage of codification.' As a result, the present Canadian Criminal Code generally leaves it to the judiciary to work out what the accused's mental state should be. Most criminal-law courses in Canada today spend perhaps half the year figuring out what the judges have been saying about the mental state for various offences. This is a waste of time for law students and a waste of time for judges. It often requires numerous appeals to the Supreme Court of Canada to work out the mental state for an element of a crime, when it could have been done more directly and effectively through legislation.

Stephen's draft code – which was revised by a royal commission on which Stephen was a member – became the dominant code in the colonies, being adopted in Canada, New Zealand, and Australia. Wright's code of criminal law and another code on procedure were both rejected in Jamaica, although adopted in several other colonies in the Caribbean. The criminal code, although not the code of procedure, was then enacted in the Gold Coast and was supposed to be the code for other UK colonies in Africa, but the chief justice of Northern Nigeria favoured a code based on the Stephen model that had been enacted in Queensland, Australia. The Northern Nigerian code was then adopted by Southern Nigeria, swept up the east coast of British Africa, and then continued over to Cyprus and Palestine.

To make matters worse for Wright's code, in 1900 one of Stephen's sons, H.L. Stephen, asked the Colonial Office if he could revise and bring Wright's code up to date. The permanent officials thought that it would be a mistake, but the colonial secretary selected Stephen to do it. He emasculated Wright's code, eliminating, for example, the mental-element provisions. That was the death knell for Wright's code.

Stephen's code was not, however, enacted in England. There were a number of reasons often advanced, such as the extensive changes it made to the law, the lack of parliamentary time to deal with the subject, and the change of government in 1880. My study added several more reasons. One was organized labour's reservations about the code and another was concern about the quality of Stephen's work shared by a number of influential people. Parliamentary draftsmen were not impressed with Stephen's code, and were of the opinion that Wright's code was the better one. Further, the draftsmen agreed with Wright that a more gradual approach to codification in England was desirable.

Stephen's code is in some respects clumsily constructed. Here are two examples of confusing provisions in Stephen's code that Canadian lawyers take for granted, but are not as good as Wright's comparable provisions. Stephen broke offences down into indictable and non-indictable – that is, according to the procedure for trying the offence. This has caused confusion because – without getting too technical – many indictable offences today (minor theft, for example) cannot be tried by indictment. It would have been better to classify offences according to the seriousness of the crime. Wright kept the distinction, as the Americans have, between felonies and misdemeanours, stating with respect to felonies: 'It seems inexpedient to throw away a term which already carries associations of grave reprobation.' Stephen's introduction of the term 'homicide' into murder and manslaughter also adds a confusing element – read any charge to the jury in a murder case and you will understand how difficult it is for the jury to grasp what the judge is saying. Wright, by contrast, defined murder directly without reference to homicide.

The whole story – one more sad tale in the politics of legislation – will have a familiar ring to those who have been or are now engaged in producing a new criminal code. In my conclusion I ask, 'What conclusions can be drawn from the story of Wright's Jamaica Code?' My answer: 'Perhaps it is simply the obvious one that law reform is affected by a great number of factors apart from the merits of the proposals. Then, as now, a combination of politics, personalities and pressure groups affected the outcome.'

I ended the article by commenting on the fact that a biography of Stephen written by his brother Leslie does not mention Wright. Moreover, the less than enthusiastic entry for Wright in the *Dictionary of National Biography*, of which Leslie Stephen was the founding editor, was written by one of James Fitzjames's sons, Herbert, and does not mention Wright's work on codification. I end the paper by stating: 'It almost seems as if the Stephen family tried to eliminate Wright from the history of the codification of the criminal law.'

My article helped right the balance, but I had the chance to go further. I was asked if I would do a piece on R.S. Wright for the new *Dictionary of National Biography*. I was in the middle of the U of T history, however, and did not want to be diverted. I felt that I would have to do a lot more work on Wright's involvement in the labour movement, which I considered probably as important to society as his work on codification. Therefore, I sent the DNB a copy of my article, which they obviously knew about already, and asked them to pass it on to the person whom they selected to do the entry. Fortunately, they chose Peter Glazebrook, who already knew my article well, having been one of the three people I thanked in a footnote for reading the paper and making helpful comments. (The other two were Glanville Williams and Rupert Cross.) The new entry is now out. Peter has given Wright the credit he justly deserves.

The time and effort spent on the R.S. Wright article meant that I did not come home from my sabbatical with a draft of the book on the process of law reform I had hoped to complete. I thought that perhaps a collection of essays on law reform would be a good substitute. The problem was that I could not decide what papers to use. I must have had dozens of possible titles for the collection, but nothing seemed right. One title that came close was 'The Mulberry Bush: Studies on the Reform of the Criminal Law.' In the meantime, I had just completed or was working on other papers – such as those on entrapment, the Charter, national security, and gun control – which did not fit comfortably into a book on law reform. In the end, Carswell agreed in late 1982 to publish a book of essays then titled *Essays on Criminal Justice: Politics, Personalities and Pressure Groups*, the subtitle drawn from the R.S. Wright article. The book came out in 1984 under a new title, *A Century of Criminal Justice: Perspectives on the Development of Canadian Law*. This title came from the last essay in the book, an analysis of three murder cases from 1882 which I had done for the centenary of the Royal Society of Canada. The lead essay was still the R.S. Wright article. The book also included the essay on pressure groups that I had done for the book honouring Glanville, as well as new articles on the division of powers, the Charter, and gun control. It received some very favourable reviews, such as one by Justice Allen Linden, then president of the Law Reform Commission of Canada, who wrote in the *Canadian Bar Review* that the book contained 'a smorgasbord of intellectual delights served up by one of Canada's master chefs.'

Once again, I had gotten out of the academic quicksand alive. I sent a copy of the book to Don Rickerd of the Donner Canadian Foundation, which had been supporting my research, thanking him for his support and for the flexibility that the foundation gave me in pursuing my research. Most projects that I have worked on and for which I have received funding end up deviating substantially from what I had said that I would do. This is inevitable in research. One idea leads to another. It would be a mistake to limit where the evidence takes you. I have spoken to scientists about this and they tell me it happens all the time in scientific research.

My interest in codification continued over the following years. During the 1980s there was an attempt by the federal government to expedite the development of a new criminal code. The Law Reform Commission of Canada had been publishing many excellent studies, but a new code still seemed far off. In October 1979, when the Clark government was in office, federal and provincial ministers responsible for the various aspects of the criminal justice system in Canada met in Ottawa and unanimously agreed that 'a thorough review of the Criminal Code should be undertaken as a matter of priority' and that 'the review should encompass both substantive criminal law and criminal procedures.'

This 'comprehensive and accelerated review' was centred in the Department of Justice, which worked closely with the solicitor general's department and the Law Reform Commission. I was involved in the review. During the 1980s I did work for all three bodies, as well as preparing a paper on the structure of sentencing from a historical perspective for the Canadian Sentencing Commission, which had been set up in 1985 and issued a fine report in 1987. The process of codification was gaining momentum.

I also produced papers for the solicitor general on the Charter and the division of criminal powers under the constitution while continuing to work with the Law Reform Commission on various projects, such as double jeopardy and national security, which would eventually fit into a new code. Moreover, I had a contract with the Department of Justice to give advice on various aspects of the code. I attended a number of consultation sessions, including one near the Gatineau Hills in Quebec, another at the Inn on the Park in Toronto, and still another at Toronto's King Edward Hotel – a two-day meeting held shortly after Mark McGuigan became the minister of justice. They were busy years for law reformers.

An excellent document emerged from the Department of Justice in 1982, *The Criminal Law in Canadian Society*. This was primarily the work of Jack Macdonald, a non-legal member of the department (who later moved to British Columbia). There was a lot of activity in the Department of Justice and other departments, as well as the Law Reform Commission, and the government announced that a code would be ready for the one hundredth anniversary of the enactment of the first code in 1892. When I delivered the Viscount Bennett Memorial Lecture at the University of New Brunswick in 1992, devoted to the centenary of the 1892 code, I pointed out the obvious: the deadline had passed without the appearance of a new code.

Moreover, in late February 1992, the federal minister of finance, Don Mazankowski, announced in his budget speech that the Law Reform

Commission of Canada, along with a number of other federal agencies, would be eliminated for financial reasons. The chances of a new code therefore decreased even more. The Law Reform Commission was resurrected in 1997 with a new name, the Law Commission, and with a new mandate that did not include the production of a new criminal code. In any event, as stated in an earlier chapter, the commission was effectively closed down in 2006 by the Conservative government withdrawing its funding.

In the spring of 1992 a subcommittee of the Standing Committee on Justice and the Solicitor General conducted hearings on the general part of the code. That year I gave a seminar at the law school on the reform of the criminal law. Its objective was to generate a brief to be presented to the committee. Each student prepared a paper on one of the topics contained in the general part, which formed the basis of the brief. The seminar was similar to the law-review seminars I had given in the early 1980s, which were designed to produce a special issue of the law review on a given topic. I did one in 1983 on the general part of the Criminal Code which was very successful. Two of the papers published in the law review (an article by Ed Morgan on necessity and one by Paul Schabas on drunkenness) have been cited by the Supreme Court of Canada. The following year Bob Sharpe and I conducted a seminar on the Charter, which again produced a good issue of the law review.

I appeared before the subcommittee in June 1992 with two students from the seminar, Sharon Nicklas and Orlando da Silva. Our work was well received, the chair of the committee referring to our 'excellent' document. I made the suggestion to the subcommittee that it would be desirable to enact the Criminal Code in stages. The problem with putting a whole code before Parliament as a package is that it is not likely to be enacted. There are many controversial issues in any criminal code: police powers, abortion, gun control, and hate literature, to name only a few. Special-interest groups will mount campaigns against the provisions that they dislike and it will be difficult to gain acceptance of the package as a whole.

This happened in the United States when the federal government tried to bring in a new federal criminal code. In 1966 the Johnson administration established through Congress a powerful National Commission on Reform of Federal Criminal Laws. The commission, under the chairmanship of the governor of California, Edmund G. Brown, produced a *Final Report on a Proposed New Federal Criminal Code* in 1971. It could not make it through Congress – it was not right wing enough for President Richard Nixon – although various subsequent attempts have been made over the years to have a new federal code enacted. In 1990 the Society for the Reform of the Criminal Law asked me to participate as one of the opening keynote speakers at an international conference in Washington designed to put pressure on governments, including the American government, to develop new criminal codes. I was paired with Herbert Wechsler, who had been the principal architect of the American Model Penal Code. I discussed codification in the Commonwealth, drawing of course on my R.S. Wright paper.

The Law Commission in England started working on a new criminal code in 1968, but a code has still not been produced. The project was turned over to a group of legal academics in the 1980s, without great success. In the early 1990s England decided that a more gradual approach was needed, and since then the Law Commission and the government have been chipping away at the task by bringing in separate parts of a new code. Much has been accomplished. The process may now be speeding up because in July 2002 the government produced a white paper, *Justice for All*, in which it stated its intention to codify the criminal law.

In my view, a gradual process is the best approach for the Canadian government to follow. In the mid-1990s the government brought in some good sections on sentencing, based in part on the report of the sentencing commission. The next important step is to enact a new general part, followed by a code of procedure, and then a new code of evidence. It is important to have a new code, as will be discussed in the next chapter, for the sake of the effectiveness of the criminal-justice system. Well-thought-out provisions in all of these areas will cut down on the complexity and therefore the length of trials and will play a significant role in improving the administration of criminal justice in Canada.

18

The Charter

There is little question that the most dramatic change in criminal justice in Canada since the enactment of the Criminal Code in 1892 has come through the *Canadian Charter of Rights and Freedoms*, enacted in 1982. Indeed, the Charter may be the most important development in criminal law since English criminal law was introduced into Canada following the defeat of the French in 1763. The Charter, as a constitutional document, has had the effect of transferring to the judiciary the major role in reforming criminal law and procedure.

The Charter has certainly played a far more important role in criminal justice than the Diefenbaker *Bill of Rights* – a federal statute enacted in 1960 – which applied only to federal legislation. After the enactment of the Charter, accused persons, supported by various pressure or interest groups, with the assistance of government and other funding, started challenging many laws and practices in the courts. In the first year and a half after its enactment there were more than 125 Charter cases reported in the *Canadian Criminal Cases*. In contrast, within a year and a half after the *Bill of Rights* was enacted there were only about a dozen cases involving the *Bill of Rights* in the same series of law reports. The Charter has continued to play a significant role in the development of the criminal law.

The enactment of a constitutional charter of rights had been part of Pierre Trudeau's agenda since he entered politics. The repatriation of the constitution coupled with a charter of rights was a special priority after he succeeded Joe Clark in 1980 to begin his fourth term as prime minister. Canada had signed the United Nations International Covenant on Civil and Political Rights in 1976, and at the same time had signed the optional protocol which gives individuals within Canada the right to complain to the Human Rights Committee of the United Nations about alleged violation of rights set out in the Covenant. Canada therefore had an international obligation to bring in a document that covered the provinces as well as the federal government – and provincial legislation was not covered by the *Bill of Rights*.

The public appeared to support the enactment of the Charter. Parliament was not highly regarded at the time. Joe Clark, the leader of the Opposition, still looked and sounded like a campus politician. In contrast, Chief Justice Bora Laskin and other members of the Supreme Court were well respected. Laskin therefore indirectly influenced the enactment of the *Charter of Rights and Freedoms*, looking and acting like a wise Solomon-like figure, whom the public could trust to deliver sound judgments under a new charter of rights. As it turned out, however, Laskin did not participate in deciding any cases under the Charter.

The Charter has been widely acclaimed by Canadian citizens. For some – including, I think, the majority of law professors – the Charter has taken the place that Holy Scripture once occupied. Others are more sceptical. I fall somewhere in between. There have been some very positive results of the Charter in the area of criminal justice. In other respects, however, it has held back the development of the criminal law, for at the very time that the Department of Justice, the solicitor general's department, and the Law Reform Commission of Canada were attempting to expedite the development of a new code of criminal law and procedure, the Supreme Court of Canada seized the initiative to reform the criminal law, forcing the government to react to what the Supreme Court was actively doing. As I will argue below, lawmaking through the legislative route is generally far superior to lawmaking by the judiciary. If the Supreme Court had not been as aggressive as it had been, it is likely that Canada would now have a well-thought-out, balanced code like the 1962 American Law Institute's Model Penal Code, which, with various changes, has been adopted by the majority of states in the United States.

My comments here are restricted to the role of the Canadian courts in the area of criminal law and procedure. I have few complaints about the Supreme Court's decisions on sometimes more contentious issues such as aboriginal rights, equality rights, and electoral rights. Indeed, I welcome the court's involvement in those difficult subjects. These are areas where, in the words of Chief Justice Beverley McLachlin, the courts can provide 'protection against the tyranny of the majority.' Further, I have few complaints about the actual results reached by the Supreme Court in the field of criminal justice. My complaint is that its overly ambitious approach to reforming the criminal law has in fact held back rational development of the law through the legislative route. In this regard, it would, in my view, have been preferable for the Supreme Court to have been more deferential to Parliament and to have encouraged Parliament to take the lead. This is not a question of legitimacy, but, as I will argue below, of institutional competency. ·

The activism of the United States Supreme Court in the 1960s and 1970s no doubt became a role model for Canada's Supreme Court. One of the court's first Charter decisions, *Hunter v. Southam*, delivered in 1984, adopted an American-style approach to search and seizure. The U.S. Supreme Court, as is well known, had been active in those decades in developing the criminal law, although as Robert Harvie and Hamar Foster have shown, it was less aggressive than the Supreme Court of Canada became. The U.S. Supreme Court had, of course, been forced to play an active role because in the United States the criminal law is, for the most part, a state responsibility, and only the Supreme Court could impose minimum standards on a system that cried out for standards. But in Canada the constitution gives the federal government exclusive legislative authority over criminal law and procedure. The legislative route was open in Canada and the structure was in place for developing a new comprehensive code.

The fault has to be equally shared by Parliament, which allowed – and perhaps even encouraged – the initiative to be seized by the Supreme Court by not continuing to pursue the legislative agenda aggressively. There are few votes to be gained in changing the criminal law, unless the legislation promotes a law-and-order agenda. Every contentious provision, particularly those involving law and morality, such as abortion and homosexual conduct, will alienate a significant number of voters, whatever the government decides to do. Better to have that anger directed at the courts, the government of the day might think.

Like most persons who had been involved in thinking about criminal justice, I did not expect that the Charter would have such a dramatic effect on the development of the criminal law. In the year and a half after the Charter was enacted, I gave a number of talks on it to various groups of judges and lawyers across the country, which resulted in a 1983 article in the *Manitoba Law Journal*. I took the view that 'the Charter will help protect us from tyranny, but will not replace Parliament as the body to develop the criminal law.' I then added: 'It is suggested that this is the proper use of the Charter.'

In the article I applauded the approach that had been taken up until then by the provincial courts of appeal, noting that 'changes that have been made by the courts have been of a marginal nature,' and then adding that 'the changes have been important, taking some of the harshness out of some laws and further individualizing the criminal justice system.' I concluded the article by stating: 'A broad, but careful, approach has been given by the appeal courts so far, and undoubtedly a similar approach will be taken by the Supreme Court to the Canadian Charter of Rights and Freedoms.' At that point, the Supreme Court had not decided any Charter cases. My prediction of the approach that the court would take was, of course, wrong.

My initial involvement with the Charter was through a select committee established by the Canadian Jewish Congress in the summer of 1980. When I returned to Canada from my sabbatical in July 1980, a letter was waiting for me from the noted McGill public law scholar Maxwell Cohen, inviting me to participate in a Congress committee on the Constitution of Canada. The first meeting of the members of the committee, who were drawn from across Canada, was at the end of July in the boardroom of Holy Blossom Temple. At that meeting I was asked to serve on the drafting committee, along with Max Cohen, David Lewis, the former head of the New Democratic Party, and Professor Irwin Cotler, at the time the president of the Canadian Jewish Congress. Joe Magnet, a constitutional law scholar at the University of Ottawa, was later appointed as the research adviser.

I was assigned the task of preparing an initial document on legal rights under the Charter, sections 7 to 14, those rights most directly related to the criminal process. 'The arguments for entrenching legal rights in the Constitution,' I wrote, 'are less persuasive than in the areas of political, language and mobility rights. Entrenchment of rights necessarily transfers some law-making power from Parliament and the legislatures to the courts, from elected to appointed persons.' Nevertheless, on balance, I wrote, legal rights should be entrenched.

I was, however, concerned about two key sections of the Charter relating to the criminal law, sections 1 and 7. The proposed section 7 was precisely the same as the present section, which provides: 'Everyone has the right to life, liberty and security of the person and the right not to be deprived thereof except in accordance with the principles of fundamental justice.' Section 7, I observed, might turn out to be one of the Charter's most important provisions. I liked the words 'fundamental justice,' used in the section, better than the words used in the *Bill of Rights*, 'due process of law,' a phrase given a very narrow interpretation by the Supreme Court of Canada under the *Bill of Rights*. It had, however, been given a broad interpretation under the American *Bill of Rights*. The U.S. Supreme Court had expanded the phrase in the well-known *Lochner* decision in 1905 to include what is called 'substantive due process,' and had used the concept to strike down over the years much progressive legislation, including important components of the New Deal legislation in the 1930s.

There was, however, a danger, I suggested, that Canadian courts would use 'principles of fundamental justice' to go further than society would wish them to go. (Nobody contemplated – certainly not David Lewis – that the Supreme Court of Canada would dismantle significant aspects of Quebec's health-care system in the 2005 *Chaoulli* decision as a violation of fundamental justice.) It would be wise, I suggested, specifically to limit the section to 'procedure' by amending the section to read: 'in accordance with procedures consistent with the principles of fundamental justice.' The select committee's report did not, however, adopt this suggestion and made no comment on section 7, except to state that it 'assumes that ... the word 'everyone' in section 7 embraces persons in Canada illegally.' The interpretation of section 7 will be dealt with more fully below.

I was also concerned about how the language of section 1 would be interpreted in an emergency, or indeed in any situation. I preferred to have a specific clause dealing with emergencies, as the UN Covenant did, that limited the extent to which rights can be denied in such cases. It is during emergencies that rights tend to be abused. The select committee took a similar view and recommended that the Charter not contain the present section 1, but that an emergency clause be added to the Charter. I would have left the balancing of rights in other situations to be handled through the interpretation of individual rights. As we know, an emergency clause was not added, but section 1 was strengthened by substituting the words 'demonstrably justified' for the weaker words 'generally accepted.'

It was the combination of the later interpretations of sections 7 and 1 that caused the later major shift in the development of criminal justice from Parliament to the courts. The interpretation of section 7 broadened the scope of rights that would be protected, while section 1 put a burden on the government to justify any limitation of rights.

I prefer that change come through legislation, if that route is possible. Perhaps my earlier active involvement with legislative solutions in areas such as bail, legal aid, securities regulation, and gun control influenced my view. There are clear advantages in using the legislative route. I am not going to give much weight to the often-heard argument that judges are not elected and so it is undemocratic to have judges take over the role that legislatures are intended to fulfil, except to note that the Charter was also designed to protect democratic rights and that taking over the traditional role of Parliament as a lawmaker interferes with those rights. Here, I am going to deal with more practical arguments, stressing the institutional competence of each body.

Through the parliamentary committee system, for example, the legislature will have available a better system of consultation than the judiciary has and, unlike the judiciary, such committees can produce interim reports and draft legislation for comment. In the well-known 1990 *Askov* case on unreasonable delay, for example, which resulted in about 50,000 pending cases later being dismissed, no interveners appeared before the Supreme Court to assist in the development of the law. No interveners apart from two provincial attorneys general appeared in *Duarte*, decided in the same year, where the court said that a listening device required judicial approval in advance, even if one of the parties consented. Further, Parliament has better access to statistical and social-science research than has the Supreme Court. Again, using the *Askov* case as an example, the Supreme Court gathered some of its own statistical data, but that data turned out to have been used incorrectly.

With a comprehensive legislative bill, one section can be placed in the context of other provisions, and trade-offs can be made to keep a proper balance in the system. Courts understandably concentrate on the particular issue with which they are dealing. Let me give an example of such a trade-off that I think would have been an improvement over the current system. I believe that the former English system of not in general allowing the accused's criminal record to be introduced into evidence and at the same time allowing the trial judge to comment negatively on the failure of the accused to testify is preferable to the Canadian system. In Canada, the prosecutor can, with some restrictions, introduce the accused's record if the accused takes the stand, but the trial judge cannot comment on the accused's failure to testify. The Canadian system tends to keep the accused out of the witness box. The former English system – modified in 2003 to permit more use of previous convictions – tended to encourage it. With the current interpretations of the Charter on self-incrimination, however, the former English approach would not be possible.

Moreover, legislation is normally prospective and not retrospective, applying only to future cases, whereas court decisions – again, the *Askov* case is an example – are normally both prospective and retrospective, thus creating problems for the administration of justice, and in many cases, unwarranted windfalls for cases tried under the former law that are still subject to appeal. I have been told that some counsel appeal convictions simply hoping that a new decision may give them a ground of appeal while the case is in the system. The American approach of determining which constitutional decisions are prospective only would be better than the present Canadian system. The Supreme Court of Canada engages in a modified form of prospective lawmaking when it states that a decision will not take effect for a period of time. In the 1990 *Brydges* decision, for example, in which the Supreme Court decided that the police not only have to tell an accused that he or she has the right to counsel, but also have to say that legal aid and duty counsel are available, the court gave the police thirty days from the date of the judgment to react to the change. This has been done in a number of other cases, such as the *Chaoulli* decision relating to health care. The court should do this in more cases, and should, for example, have done it in the new decisions defining reasonable doubt.

However difficult it may be to interpret a legislative provision, at least the legislature speaks with one voice. Supreme Court decisions, in contrast, are often lengthy, with multiple opinions, some concurring and some dissenting, and are often difficult for non-lawyers – and indeed for lawyers – to comprehend. They usually require very close analysis and complex arguments. To give just two examples: The insanity decision of *Swain*, decided in 1991, covers over seventy-five pages in four separate reasons for judgment in the *Canadian Criminal Cases*, plus eleven pages for the headnotes; and the delay case of *Mills*, decided in 1986, covers eighty-one pages in four reasons for judgment, plus nine pages for the headnotes. Recent judgments do not appear to be getting much shorter or less complex, although it seems the court is trying to do better.

Moreover, Supreme Court judgments often necessitate further clarifying judgments by the court because of matters overlooked in the earlier judgment. The recent series of cases on the reasonable doubt rule is a good illustration. It would have been better to have developed this area of law outside traditional judicial decision-making. In England, the courts sometimes use extra-judicial 'practice directions' to guide future practice, while the United States federal courts adopt evidentiary rules through regulations. The Supreme Court of Canada could probably adopt a similar approach through its rule-making powers, which would cover all criminal cases and would, no doubt, soon become the law for provincial matters.

I am particularly concerned about the fact that courts, unlike legislatures, do not like drawing fixed lines, but normally try to determine on which side of an imaginary line a case falls. A court-developed imaginary line normally requires trial judges to examine a large number of factors to determine the outcome of the cases before them, often resulting in long legal arguments and lengthy proceedings at the trial level. Look at most Supreme Court of Canada decisions – both Charter and non-Charter cases – and you will see that a decision at trial requires that a host of factors be taken into account by the trial judge in deciding an issue. Rather than a simple factual determination for the law of entrapment, for example, as suggested by the McDonald Commission on national security in the early 1980s, the Supreme Court has imposed a legal test that requires the examination of a large number of factors. In the *Mack* case on entrapment, the court lists nine factors that should be considered and then adds that 'this list is not exhaustive.' Similarly, in order for a judge to decide whether hearsay evidence should be admitted or an expert should be heard, he or she has to take a list of factors into account.

Sometimes a simpler rule is better. An example, familiar to all law students, is the development of the law of civil negligence. Before the British House of Lords decided *Donoghue v. Stevenson* in 1932, each case of civil negligence in England and Canada required a careful analysis of earlier cases dealing with the law of causation. In *Donoghue v. Stevenson*, however, the House of Lords produced a simpler rule involving a finding of a reasonable person's standard of care, which is much easier for a judge or jury to understand. Such simplification tends to turn a legal issue into a factual issue. This approach does not eliminate all the problems, but I believe that it helps to decrease them.

In a recent speech, Chief Justice Beverley McLachlin warned the Canadian Bar Association that 'proceedings in criminal cases are crumbling under the weight of pre-trial motions.' Ontario Court of Appeal Justice Michael Moldaver, in an even stronger speech to the Criminal Lawyers' Association annual conference in 2005, stated that 'long criminal trials are a cancer on our criminal justice system and they pose a threat to its very existence.' To a considerable extent, the judiciary has created the problem.

The judicial process can be costly in terms of appellate decisions, which often involve a large number of state-financed lawyers as interveners, but more importantly in the time taken in the later application and interpretation of those decisions by trial judges. How many adjournments are sought with an eye to arguing 'delay' and how many subsequent lengthy arguments are the direct result of the *Askov* decision? How much of the available legal-aid budget is now used to develop the law through the judicial process and then apply it in individual cases? One expert on legal aid in Canada, Albert Currie of the federal Department of Justice, stated: 'The Charter has had a dramatic impact on criminal legal aid. Charter litigation has had the effect of driving up costs, by making the law more complex, and by introducing constitutional bases for arguments.' Funds spent on these long trials are no longer available for other deserving legal-aid cases.

Having comprehensive legislative, rather than judicial, solutions to search and seizure, entrapment, double jeopardy, disclosure, hearsay, and speedy trial procedures – to mention only a few areas that could have been, and in most cases were being, developed through the legislative route – would have created fewer problems in the administration of criminal justice than having the rules developed by the courts. The *Askov* case, for example, might not have been necessary if Parliament had enacted speedy trial laws, as was attempted, without success, in 1984. Most American jurisdictions have time limits that, with good cause, can be departed from. Moreover, Parliament would likely not have said that a stay was the *only* remedy available for unreasonable delay. To have a complete stay gives the accused too great an advantage. The British House of Lords recently refused to adopt the remedy used in the *Askov* case. There are other options. The judge could, for example, ensure that the accused is not kept in custody and could order that the trial be expedited. The delay could even be reflected in the penalty imposed. A comprehensive legislative scheme could help ensure compliance by a whole series of intermediary orders, preventing delay long before the time is reached for the draconian retrospective stay of proceedings after the unreasonable delay has already occurred.

It is also important to note that legislation can be changed by Parliament. In contrast, court decisions which rely on the Charter become part of the Constitution and limit what Parliament can do. There has, of course, been what is called a 'dialogue' between the courts and Parliament, but Parliament enters the debate with one hand loosely tied behind its back. Parliament cannot change a constitutional decision unless it exercises its power of override, which for political reasons it is reluctant to do, or gets a constitutional amendment, which is an unrealistic prospect, or eventually wears down the will of the Supreme Court, as it did in the 2002 *Hall* case relating to the grounds for denying bail.

Constitutionalizing decisions tends to hinder change and experimentation, which might improve the system of criminal justice. In my various talks in the early years of the Charter I urged the courts not to rush to constitutionalize the criminal law, unless it was absolutely necessary. Why not reach the same result, if one can, I asked, by developing ordinary criminal-law concepts, such as the doctrine of 'abuse of process'? I recall Chief Justice Dickson sitting in the front row listening to a talk I was giving to the Canadian Bar Association in 1983. We chatted afterwards, and it was apparent to me that my arguments had not persuaded him.

The Supreme Court of Canada did not *have* to take such an activist stance in the criminal law area. Let me give two examples, the *Oakes* and the *BC Motor Vehicle Act* cases, probably the two most important criminal-law judgments delivered under the Charter.

In the 1986 *Oakes* case, the Supreme Court, without the benefit of a full discussion of the issue by counsel in the case, placed a heavy onus on the government to uphold a law under section 1 that was found to have breached a substantive section of the Charter. (The issue in *Oakes* was whether a section in the *Narcotic Control Act*, placing the onus on the accused found in possession of a narcotic to prove that he or she was not in possession of it for the purpose of trafficking, was a violation of the presumption of innocence section of the Charter. The court held that it was and then turned to examine whether it could be upheld under section 1.) Canadian courts have tended to give a very literal meaning to the substantive section and then turn quickly to section 1. It would have been preferable, in my view, for the courts to first do the balancing under the substantive section, as the American courts do, and as Canadian courts now tend to do under section 7, where there is therefore no onus on the government. Chief Justice Brian Dickson's judgment in the *Oakes* case provides a series of tests which require, among other things, that the government action be shown to 'impair "as little as possible" the right or freedom in question.' Moreover, Dickson stated, the onus on the government 'must be applied vigorously.' The passages in the judgment relating to section 1 are rightly identified by Robert Sharpe and Kent Roach in their recent fine biography of Dickson as 'five of the most important pages ever written in Canadian constitutional law.'

The vast majority of cases decided against the government have turned on the 'minimal impairment' aspect of the *Oakes* test. Section 1, however, had been designed to help the government, not to impede its legislative abilities. As Roy Romanow, one of the principal architects of the Charter, and his co-authors have written: 'The clause was designed to encourage judicial deference to legislative choices even though they affected civil liberties.' In a talk at a Canada-Israel conference on the Charter in 1992 at the Hebrew University, I urged the Israelis, who were considering introducing a charter, to spell out carefully what they actually want when drafting a limitation clause, such as Canada's section 1, and not to leave it to later judicial interpretation.

Chief Justice Dickson was determined to use the Charter to develop the law through the judicial process. In *Hunter v. Southam*, the year before the *Oakes* decision, Dickson had shown, according to Sharpe and Roach, that he was 'determined to play a leading role in defining the scope and impact of the Charter generally.' Indeed, shortly after the Charter was enacted, Dickson had signalled that he would take a bold approach, stating in a talk at Dalhousie's faculty of law: 'When the occasion cries out for new law, let us dare to make it.'

In the *BC Motor Vehicle Act* case, decided in 1985, the Supreme Court gave a very broad meaning to section 7 of the Charter, which provides that 'Everyone has the right to life, liberty and security of the person and the right not to be deprived thereof except in accordance with the principles of fundamental justice.' (The issue in the case was whether a legislative provision in British Columbia that provided for 'absolute liability' for driving without a valid licence was contrary to the principles of fundamental justice.) The section in the *BC Motor Vehicle Act* case did not have to be so broadly interpreted and – according to most of those involved in the creation of the Charter – was not intended to be so interpreted. Not only did the court expand the words 'fundamental justice' to include what the Americans call 'substantive due process,' but it gave a very expansive and vague meaning to the phrase. 'The principles of fundamental justice,' Justice Lamer wrote, 'are to be found in the basic tenets and principles, not only of our judicial process, but also of the other components of our legal system ... Whether any given principle may be said to be a principle of fundamental justice within the meaning of s. 7 will rest upon an analysis of the nature, sources, rationale and essential role of that principle within the judicial process and in our legal system, as it evolves.'

It is hard to think of a standard that would give the courts greater scope to develop the law in almost any way they think it should be developed. Shortly after he retired from the court, Chief Justice Lamer told the *Lawyers Weekly* that the *BC Motor Vehicle Act* case was his 'most satisfying moment' on the court. The case, he said, 'announced that a majority of the court, at least, would take a post-modernist approach – a contextual approach – to interpreting the Charter and applying it,' whatever that means. Lamer wanted to use the Charter to make changes in the criminal law. He had been the vice-president and then the president of the Law Reform Commission of Canada throughout the 1970s and had been frustrated by the lack of progress in bringing forward and implementing the commission's recommendations.

The Supreme Court has used section 7 in a surprisingly large variety of cases. In a recent edition of his book *Charter Justice* Don Stuart devotes over 170 pages – almost one-third of the book – to section 7. Decisions using section 7 include the *Stinchcombe* decision involving disclosure by the Crown, *Morgentaler* on the right to an abortion, *Hebert* on self-incrimination, *Swain* on the consequences of being found not guilty by reason of mental disorder, *Ruzic* on the defence of duress, and the many cases requiring the accused to have a certain mental state before being convicted. And there are many more.

After I completed my book on the history of the University of Toronto in 2002 and went back to the field of criminal justice, I systematically went through all the cases in the *Canadian Criminal Cases* over the previous five years. I was struck by the increasing number of decisions that rely on section 7 of the Charter, which has certainly become the workhorse for the development of criminal-law policy. In the *O'Connor* decision in 1995, the Supreme Court even held that section 7 encompassed abuse-of-process cases. Thus, areas that were traditionally part of ordinary criminal law, such as entrapment and aspects of double jeopardy, would now seem to have been constitutionalized under fundamental justice.

The Supreme Court has also been constitutionalizing the law of evidence under section 7. Of course I knew about the cases involving self-incrimination, but until I did a report in 2005 on a judicial-conduct case for the Canadian Judicial Council – requiring me to relearn the law of evidence, which I had not taught for forty years – I had not realized how many evidence matters are now covered by section 7. One can see its operation, for example, in the solicitor-client privilege rules. It was first used in 1991 in the *Seaboyer* case, in which the court said that a law which interferes with the accused's 'right to present full answer and defence' violates section 7. In that case, the court struck down a provision in the Criminal Code limiting the use of the prior sexual conduct of the complainant. 'In short,' Justice McLachlin stated, 'the denial of the right to call and challenge evidence is tantamount to the denial of the right to rely on a defence to which the law says one is entitled.' Moreover, it is an infringement of section 7, she went on, to 'exclude evidence the probative value of which is not substantially outweighed by its potential prejudice.' Both statements in the *Seaboyer* case give great scope to permit counsel to introduce Charter arguments with respect to evidentiary issues.

The result of the movement to make the rules of evidence responsive to the needs of the particular case, David Paciocco and Lee Stuesser argue in their book on evidence, has not come without a cost: 'Flexibility is being achieved at the expense of certainty. The rules of evidence have never been easy to apply. Yet many of those rules of evidence now require more detailed evaluation and produce less predictable results than ever before.'

Will the use of section 7 keep expanding? The recent marijuana cases of *R. v. Malmo-Levine* and *R. v. Caine*, decided by the Supreme Court of Canada in 2003, show a more restrained application of section 7 and appear to have slowed down the expansion of the section. The majority of the court refused to accept the argument that the so-called 'harm principle' was a principle of fundamental justice, stating: 'In short, for a rule or principle to constitute a principle of fundamental justice for the purposes of s. 7, it must be a legal principle about which there is significant societal consensus that it is fundamental to the way in which the legal system ought fairly to operate, and it must be identified with sufficient precision to yield a manageable standard against which to measure deprivations of life, liberty or security of the person.'

In contrast with *Malmo-Levine*, however, the majority of the court (4–3) in the 2005 health-care case of *Chaoulli* used section 7 and an equivalent provision in the *Québec Charter of Human Rights and Freedoms* to strike down the existing single-tier health-care system in Quebec because' of an unreasonable wait-time endured by a person who needed a hip replacement. Although not involving a criminal case, the decision shows that section 7 may continue to expand. Chief Justice McLachlin and Justice Major, relying on the *Morgentaler* case, stated that 'prohibiting health insurance that would permit ordinary Canadians to access health care, in circumstances where the government is failing to deliver health care in a reasonable manner, thereby increasing the risk of complications and death, interferes with life and security of the person as protected by s. 7 of the *Charter*.' The prohibition, they stated, was done 'in an arbitrary manner, and is therefore not in accordance with the principles of fundamental justice.' A majority of the court restricted the decision to Quebec, although it is hard to say why it should not apply throughout Canada. Thus, the growth in the use of section 7 may not be over.

In the spring of 1991 both Judy and I had half-year sabbaticals. She had started teaching at the University of Toronto in 1982, becoming the chair of occupational therapy in 1991. We first spent six weeks in Asia, where I gave a number of talks on the Charter. The trip had originally been planned to take place several months earlier, but the first Gulf War intervened, making travel uncertain and possibly dangerous. Tension was still high in India, where we started the trip. For security reasons, we did not go to the Punjab, where I had planned to visit Punjab University law school in Chandigarh, headed by Virendra Kumar, who had received his PhD at Toronto when I was dean. The main centres we visited were Bombay, Bangalore, Madras, Calcutta, and New Delhi. Although I had travelled widely, I had never before experienced the extreme poverty and shanty-town quarters of millions of people that we saw on the way from the Bombay airport to our hotel. Our luxurious hotels made the poverty seem even more extreme. The Oberoi hotels, where we stayed in most of the Indian cities we visited, were the finest we had ever experienced.

I gave a formal talk on the Charter at the National Law School of India University in Bangalore. The evening before the talk, as I recall,

Judy and I each received bouquets of roses, and just before the talk I was given a coconut to drink. I had done some work on the Indian constitution for the purpose of the talk, and in the discussion afterwards there was considerable interest in comparing how the Indian Supreme Court had used their section 21, which is comparable to the Canadian section 7, to expand judicial power. The main interest, however, was in the Canadian section 15, the equality section, even though it was hardly mentioned in my talk and was not an area with which I had great familiarity. Affirmative action relating to specified castes and tribes was a contentious issue in India. I did the best I could. The Bangalore law faculty wanted to explore the possibility of establishing a link with the Toronto faculty. When I returned home, Dean Robert Sharpe pursued the initiative, but in the end nothing concrete developed, although a number of members of the faculty have maintained personal links with the school, which appears to continue to be the strongest in India.

Judy, in turn, gave a formal talk, which I attended, at a hospital with a strong Canadian connection – the Christian Medical College in Vellore, about fifty kilometres west of Madras. It was a sweltering day, with temperatures well over 100 degrees Fahrenheit. After the talk, we were taken on an unforgettable tour of the compound for lepers, whose staff included a number of occupational therapists. One could not avoid the signs of impending death wherever one went in India. In Calcutta we visited one of Mother Teresa's hostels. Once the pride of the British Empire, Calcutta was probably the most impoverished city we visited, but since we had been in India for several weeks the Calcutta visit did not have the same impact as our first experience in Bombay.

The Indian election was to take place later that month. In Madras there were ten-foot-high cut-outs of the candidates placed along the streets, including the Congress candidate Rajiv Gandhi, who was assassinated by a Tamil Tiger in Madras in May, several weeks after our visit there and shortly after we had left India. Security had been very high wherever we went in India. When I was searched before being allowed to enter a courtroom in the Indian Supreme Court in New Delhi, I had to leave outside the courtroom the small package of wooden Stim-U-Dents I had in my pocket.

The courthouses in the major cities were enormous. The one in Calcutta, built in the 1870s, was said to be more elaborate and larger than the law courts on the Strand in London. The scenes were straight out of Dickens, with bundles of papers tied with pink ribbons piled in every courtroom and with a large number of litigants and their lawyers waiting for their cases to be called. The court libraries had very few Canadian books or series of reports. I recall meeting with a senior barrister in the library in the Calcutta courthouse. He had seen me looking through an old catalogue and asked me what I was looking for. I told him honestly that I was checking to see if the library had any of my books. His reply: 'If you presented us with one, yes; if not, no.' Fortunately, the Indian Law Institute in New Delhi has a fairly good selection of Canadian materials – including seven of my books – but not the *Dominion Law Reports*. The position in Canada is even worse with respect to Indian material. The Supreme Court of Canada stopped subscribing to the *All India Reporter* in 1984.

In Hong Kong, I gave a talk on the Charter to the law faculty at the University of Hong Kong and to lawyers at the attorney general's department. There was intense interest in the Canadian Charter because the territory was to be taken over by China in 1997 and they were naturally worried about the almost inevitable loss of rights. Moreover, Hong Kong was about to introduce a bill of rights. Indeed, a bill of rights was enacted as an ordinance the following month, June 1991. It closely followed the International Covenant on Civil and Political Rights because the Hong Kong government did not want to be seen as trying to put one over on its soon-to-be masters. A number of questions in a discussion with lawyers from the attorney general's department revolved around the 1985 *Singh* decision, in which the Supreme Court of Canada had held that any person in Canada, even those who had entered illegally, could challenge their detention or deportation order all the way up to the Supreme Court. They were concerned that this would encourage illegal immigration and also tie up the courts. They were using me as a sounding board as they were fine-tuning the document, which I knew was being developed but had not realized was so imminent.

Throughout the Asian trip – which also included visits to universities in Shanghai, Tokyo, and Kyoto – I expressed pride in our judiciary and in the Charter. I would mention my concern about how activist the Supreme Court had been, which I believe has held back the development of criminal codification, but on the whole I spoke favourably of what had been accomplished. Perhaps this was simply the tourist not wanting to criticize his country while abroad. 'This review of the Canadian Charter,' I said in the conclusion to my paper in Bangalore, 'shows that the Charter has had a profound and for the most part a beneficial effect on criminal law and procedure. It has taken some of the harsh-

ness out of the criminal law and introduced a number of new procedural rules.'

In the previous two chapters I repeated a statement that I had written in
the early 1980s that law reform is 'affected by a great number of factors
apart from the merits of the proposals. Then, as now, a combination of
politics, personalities and pressure groups affected the outcome.' I will
leave to future historians the task of analysing in greater detail the personalities that brought about the decisions discussed here. The influence of pressure groups should also be carefully analysed. In an article
on pressure groups that I published before the introduction of the
Charter I had stated that they are 'more a part of our political and legal
system than is usually acknowledged.' They have become even more
important because of the Charter. The rights revolution in Canada, as
in the United States, has been, as one writer, Charles Epp, observes, the
result of 'deliberate, strategic organizing by rights advocates.' Epp goes
on to argue that 'strategic rights advocacy became possible because of
the development of ... the support structures for legal mobilization,
consisting of rights-advocacy organizations, rights-advocacy lawyers,
and sources of financing, particularly government-supported financing.' The Women's Legal Education Action Fund (LEAF) is an example
of one such group. In the fall of 2006 the Conservative government gutted the funding for such organizations.

I have to acknowledge, however, that it is possible to argue that, even
without judicial activism, a new criminal code may not have been produced. As we saw in the previous chapter on codification, the contentious nature of many of the issues would have made the introduction of
a comprehensive new code politically difficult. In the last chapter I
pointed out that the U.S. federal government started the quest for a
new federal criminal code in the 1960s, but the political nature of the
various provisions has thus far prevented its passage. Similarly,
England started to produce a new code in the 1960s and is still at it. Yet
now that the foundation has been laid by the Supreme Court of Canada
it may be easier to produce and enact a new code in this country.

Moreover, the activism of the Supreme Court of Canada has had the
very positive effect of helping prevent Parliament from going down the
American route of harsh penalties and the overuse of incarceration. In
1987 the Supreme Court held, for example, in the *Smith* case that the
minimum penalty of seven years' imprisonment set out in the *Narcotic
Control Act* for trafficking in narcotics was 'cruel and unusual' punish-

ment under section 12 of the Charter. The test, the court stated, is whether 'the sentence is so unfit having regard to the offence and the offender as to be grossly disproportionate.' Seven years would now be just a routine sentence in the United States. The law-and-order sentencing schemes there – at both the state and federal levels – have resulted in many mandatory penitentiary sentences. As a result, as Tony Doob and Cheryl Webster have recently shown, the U.S. incarceration rate has risen from roughly 100 persons per 100,000 in 1963 to over 650 per 100,000 today, by far the highest rate in the world. In contrast, the Canadian incarceration rate, which had been the same as the American rate was in 1963 – around 100 per 100,000 – is still almost exactly that rate today. The crime rate in the two countries is about the same. It is unlikely that the Canadian parliament would have taken the American path, but the Supreme Court has made it constitutionally difficult to do so.

The Harper government introduced a Canadian version of the American 'three strikes' law in October 2006 (Bill C-27). It requires a judge to *presume* that a person is a dangerous offender unless the contrary is proved by a convicted person on a balance of probability in certain cases. The prosecutor, who would have to apply to have the person so designated, could do so if the person was convicted of one of a list of so-called primary offences (such as assault causing bodily harm, sexual assault, or incest) for which a sentence of two years or more would be appropriate in the circumstances of the case and when the convicted person had previously been convicted of two designated offences (which include assault and breaking and entering) and had been sent to the penitentiary for each of them. Persons found to be dangerous offenders are sentenced to an *indefinite* term in the penitentiary. Passage of the new bill could possibly dramatically increase the penitentiary population in Canada, an outcome that is both undesirable and unnecessary. As Tony Doob from the University of Toronto's Centre of Criminology stated after the legislation was introduced: 'A large amount of research in the U.S. has been overwhelmingly consistent in showing that these changes in sentencing have no effect. In terms of deterrence, it's just nonsense.'

I doubt if the legislation will pass under a minority government, and if it did, I doubt that the Supreme Court of Canada would uphold it when it is challenged. The result of the law would in many cases be 'cruel and unusual punishment.'

Let me stress the point. The U.S. and Canadian incarceration rates were about the same in 1963, but the U.S. rate is now about six times higher than the Canadian rate. In my opinion, the fact that Canada did not follow the American lead – which I applaud – is one of the most important non-developments in criminal justice in Canada in the past fifty years.

The federal government should again take the initiative and take up the task of producing a new code of criminal law and procedure. Furthermore, the Supreme Court should encourage the government to do so. A well-developed code, sensitive to the decisions of the Court, would likely survive Charter challenges. The Court would probably respect the choices made by Parliament as part of a comprehensive criminal code.

19

The Trials of Israel Lipski

In the spring of 1981 I started looking for a project that would build on my interest in Mr Justice James Fitzjames Stephen, one of the most important figures in the history of the criminal law and one of the two principal players in the saga that I had just published on R.S. Wright's model criminal code. I knew that Stephen had been involved in a number of interesting murder cases, such as the well-known Maybrick poisoning case. I started to play around with a plot – part-fictional – that would involve Stephen, the Maybrick case, Stephen's youngest son J.K. Stephen, and perhaps Stephen's niece Virginia Woolf. In spite of Stephen's strong moral views, he was an opium smoker and I would speculate on whether Stephen had been smoking opium when he presided over the much-criticized Maybrick case. I would also examine whether J.K. Stephen was, in fact, Jack the Ripper, as some writers have claimed. I never went much further because in the course of this investigation I came across the Lipski case.

I had seen brief references to this case, which Stephen had tried in 1887, but did not know much about it except for the fact that Lipski was a Polish Jew who had been hanged for murder in London. I was curious about the case and went over to the University of Toronto's Robarts Library to see what I could find out by consulting the London *Times* on microfilm. This was in April 1981. I had already set my criminal-law exam and would not receive the exam papers and seminar essays for a couple of weeks. An interesting study could be done on what professors do during this wonderful, relatively free period in the spring of the year. My guess is that much of the best imaginative work in universities takes place in this two-to-three week time, after the intense pressure of teaching and setting exams and before one's summer research assistants come on board.

Slowly turning the handle of the microfilm reader – I don't think any of them were electric in those days – I became fascinated with the Lipski case. The alleged murder and the eventual hanging of Lipski took place over a two-month period during the summer of 1887 – while Queen Victoria's Golden Jubilee celebrations were taking place. The fact that the Jewish community was involved in the case made it particularly interesting for me. 'Terrific!' I wrote in my notebook on 6 May, and prepared a three-page outline, which turned out to be close to the outline I eventually used for the book. *The Trials of Israel Lipski: A True Story of a Victorian Murder in the East End of London* was published in early 1984.

I did not, however, know at the time whether there were good records of the case in England. I wrote to the National Archives in Kew, where I had spent considerable time on the R.S. Wright article the previous year. My contact at the archives advised me that the records were held by the Home Secretary and were closed for one hundred years. I would have to seek permission to see the documents six years before they would be officially open. Permission was quickly granted.

I was scheduled to organize a panel and give a talk that summer at the annual Cambridge conference for Canadian lawyers that was run by an organization presumptuously titled the Canadian Institute of Advanced Legal Studies, as if it were the Canadian equivalent of the Institute for Advanced Study in Princeton. I would be able to see the papers at the Home Office while in England. As an aside, I should say that this conference run by the institute was excellent. The institute had been formed in the 1970s through the initiative of the Canadian High Commissioner in London, Paul Martin Sr. As the University of Toronto dean of law, I had been consulted about the concept, and thought it would prove to be for the most part a boondoggle for lawyers to write off the cost of a visit to England. In fact, it has proved to be a valuable vehicle for serious debate and continuing education. One memorable panel that year was chaired by Paul Martin on the patriation of the constitution. The participants included three of the principal architects of the deal struck by the so-called Kitchen Cabinet later that year: the federal minister of justice, Jean Chrétien; the attorney general of Ontario, Roy McMurtry; and the attorney general of Saskatchewan, Roy Romanow.

My visit to the Home Office convinced me that the Lipski case, which I had started to work on once I knew that some records of the case were available, deserved a book-length treatment. I arranged to have the documents copied and sent to me in Canada. The records, which were more extensive and more interesting than I had expected, included many documents on the fight for a reprieve and a full transcript of the two-day trial. As I stated in the preface to the book: 'I realized that this case, which has never been the subject of a major study, could serve as a good vehicle for analyzing the criminal process. It also would enable me to study material on Jewish immigration from Eastern Europe, the role of the Press and the impact of a *cause célèbre* on the process of law reform.' This was followed in the preface by a paragraph that I would use, with appropriate modifications, in my two later true-crime murder books:

> The story will place one trial in the context of the social, political and eco-
> nomic conditions of the time. A trial may in theory be an objective pursuit
> of truth, but in practice there are many subjective factors which influence
> the course of events. Justice may in theory be blind, but in practice she has
> altogether too human a perspective. The Lipski story is, no doubt, more
> dramatic, and the wealth of material richer, than in most cases; yet, by
> looking at this extreme example one can better understand some of the
> factors that may influence any criminal trial: the personality of the judge;
> the adequacy of counsel; the reaction of the press; the cry of popular opin-
> ion; the vulnerability of the Government; and many more.

In the final chapter of the book I added: 'The case shows the inherent fallibility of the trial process and the constant danger of error. Society should think twice before shifting the balance too far in favour of the prosecution. Further, the case strengthens the arguments against capital punishment.'

The book reflected my long-held view of the dangers of capital punishment. Although capital punishment had been abolished in the United Kingdom and Canada in the late 1960s, there was still considerable controversy about its abolition and there were moves in England at the time to reintroduce it. Some reviewers used the Lipski book as ammunition against the death penalty. In the early 1960s I had prepared notes for an interview on television – I think it was for *Canada AM* – in which I urged the government to put its weight behind a private member's bill to abolish the death penalty in Canada. My recollection is that at the last minute the producers found a better-known commentator to put the case against capital punishment. I still have my notes, which state that 'any examination of our legal system reveals that there may be the possibility of a miscarriage of justice.' I repeated the often-used argument that 'a penalty which is irrevocable should only be imposed by a tribunal which is infallible' and pointed out that 'most lawyers don't have as much confidence in the infallibility of our legal institutions as most laymen.'

My earlier work on double jeopardy, bail, and legal aid all contributed to my belief in the fallibility of the judicial process. Further, I had read a large number of transcripts and had handled several legal-aid cases while articling and realized how hit and miss the system was. In the 1960s I had helped a number of criminal lawyers, including Roy McMurtry and Arthur Maloney, with their appeals. I had also worked on one *cause célèbre*, the Steven Truscott case. In 1959 Truscott had been convicted of the murder of Lynne Harper and was sentenced to be hanged. While attending the Bar Admission Course in early 1960, I sat in – as an interested observer – on part of Truscott's unsuccessful appeal to the Ontario Court of Appeal. Thereafter, his sentence was commuted to life imprisonment. The Supreme Court of Canada subsequently refused leave to appeal. There was agitation for a new trial for Truscott after Isabel LeBourdais published her 1966 book, *The Trial of Steven Truscott*. That same year, the minister of justice ordered a new hearing before the Supreme Court of Canada which provided for the possibility of hearing new evidence. G. Arthur Martin was asked to represent Truscott. Martin asked me to assist him in preparing legal arguments on a number of points of evidence that he was going to argue. I was honoured to do so, particularly because he offered to pay me the same hourly rate that he was receiving from the government, $30 an hour.

I became familiar with the Truscott case and could see, once more, the inherent frailty of the judicial process. All the usual problems were there – the problems with identification evidence, with expert evidence (particularly evidence relating to lesions on Truscott's penis and the deceased's stomach contents), with statements made by the accused, with the use of similar-fact evidence, and other issues. In the end, the Supreme Court of Canada, after hearing evidence from Truscott, who had not testified at the trial, and from various experts, dismissed the appeal. Only Justice Emmett Hall would have ordered a new trial.

I decided to use the Truscott case in the first printed edition of my casebook on criminal law and procedure, which was to appear for use in September 1968. 'The Truscott case has been chosen for intensive examination,' I stated in the introduction of the casebook chapter 'The Trial Process,' 'because of the great number of problems which it covers and because many persons feel that the case raises serious questions about the adequacy of our system of justice.' I continued to use the case in subsequent editions, but for the 1989 edition Kent Roach, who had become my co-editor, persuaded me to substitute the Donald Marshall Jr case, which was not only more current, but also raised issues of racism. Kent has recently published a scholarly article on the use of such materials, arguing that 'it is both possible and desirable to include a case study of a wrongful conviction in the curriculum of a standard criminal procedure course.'

The Truscott case continued to be debated in legal circles, and even though Truscott had been released on parole from prison in 1969, a number of lawyers working with the Association in Defence of the Wrongfully Convicted took up the case. In 2001 the association presented a massive application to the minister of justice, asking that the case be reopened and that Truscott's conviction be overturned. A few years ago, I received a call from an official in the Department of Justice asking if I would allow my name to go forward as a possible commissioner to investigate the case. I informed the official that I had two serious conflicts of interest. One was that I had worked on the case over thirty-five years earlier, and the second was that my daughter Jenny, who had articled and worked for two of the lawyers involved in the application, James Lockyer and Phil Campbell, had worked on the brief to the minister of justice. Former Quebec Court of Appeal Justice Fred Kaufman was named commissioner and reported to Minister of Justice Irwin Cotler that there was 'a reasonable basis to conclude that a miscarriage of justice likely occurred.' The minister referred the case to the Ontario Court of Appeal, which has recently reserved judgment after a lengthy hearing. My daughter Jenny was once again involved in the case. I will return to the Truscott case in a later chapter.

The book on the Lipski case was more or less completed in about a year, a relatively short period in comparison with most other manuscripts I have worked on. It seemed to write itself. As always, I was assisted in my research by some excellent research assistants. John Atkinson, a law student who had grown up in Ireland, worked on the case for much of the summer of 1981 and the following summer spent a month in England tracking down leads, including trying to link the case to the Jack the Ripper murders. Shortly after the book was published, tragically, John died of cancer. At the family's request, I gave the eulogy at his cremation at Mount Pleasant Cemetery. I was also assisted by Stephen Perry, now a distinguished professor of jurisprudence at the University of Pennsylvania, who did research for me in various English archives in the fall of 1981 while completing graduate work at Oxford. Paul Schabas, now a leading litigation lawyer at Blakes, also worked on the project.

Lipski was my first book in which a word processor was used, though I did not personally use it. I still wrote the drafts in longhand and a secretary typed them on the word processor, which I remember as a rather large boxy machine, built by a Canadian company whose name I have forgotten. It was not until I wrote the history of the University of Toronto in the late 1990s that I personally typed a long manuscript on a computer.

As stated above, my initial outline proved to be close to the one I used for the manuscript, with one important exception. In an early draft I had started the book by giving away the ending, writing: 'On Monday morning August 22, 1887, Israel Lipski, a Polish immigrant Jew, was hanged for the murder of Miriam Angel.' Shortly after that, I was telling a young colleague, Barry Reiter, now with Bennett Jones, about the case while we were walking over to the athletic centre to play squash. He asked me why I told the reader at the beginning of the book that Lipski had been hanged. It was a good question. Readers would not know the case and certainly would not know the outcome. I made the decision to give away at the outset the fact that Lipski was convicted, but not that he was hanged. In my preface to the published book I refer to Justice James Fitzjames Stephen's charge to the jury, in which he stated that he had 'never known a case which presented so many remarkable and singular features' and then I add: 'This book is the story of that trial, the conviction, and the fight for a reprieve.' Many readers were shocked to find at the end of the book that Lipski had been hanged.

In my other historical crime books, I did not even give away the fact that the accused had been convicted. This meant, of course, that I had to be careful about the titles to chapters and, more important, the pictures in the books. The penultimate chapter in the Lipski book, for example, was entitled 'Approaching the end;' rather than simply 'The end.' In my second book, *The Case of Valentine Shortis*, I had some marvellous pictures of Shortis in the penitentiary, which I could not use because it would give the story away for the many persons who first leaf through a book to look at the pictures. Similarly, in the third book, *The Death of Old Man Rice*, I could not use a wonderful picture of the aged Patrick, who was sentenced to be executed, returning to New York City from Sing Sing Penitentiary many years after his trial.

In researching the Lipski book, I was intrigued by the contrast between the wealthy Jews in the West End of London and the recent immigrants in the East End. Rabbi Simeon Singer, who attended to Lipski's spiritual needs in prison, had said in a sermon at the time that 'in no spot on the globe and probably at no period in the world's history has there existed so glaring a contrast between riches and poverty as in this city and in this age of ours.' The statement has a contemporary ring to it and could be delivered in most places of worship today. Similarly, the anti-immigrant sentiment in the nation in those years – there was then unrestricted immigration to England – particularly at a time of unemployment and difficult economic conditions, also has a contemporary relevance. At the time, the population of the East End of London had a large percentage of Jews and there were strong anti-Semitic feelings in the country. Today, that area of London has a large proportion of Muslims who suffer from comparable anti-Muslim attitudes. One of the most startling facts in the book was the role of the Jewish Board of Guardians – a relief organization – in sending Jewish immigrants back to Eastern Europe. Fifty thousand persons were returned between 1880 and 1914 in a scheme that was inaptly called 'The Exodus.' It is no surprise, I point out in the book, that when Theodor Herzl came to England advocating a homeland for the Jews, he was welcomed by the established Jewish community, who were looking for an alternative to immigration by impoverished Jews from Eastern Europe to the United Kingdom.

Many of the characters in the case were larger than life. These included Stephen, the judge, whose revealing letters to his wife during and shortly after the trial I found in the Cambridge library. He was the brother of the literary figure Leslie Stephen and, as noted earlier, the uncle of Virginia Woolf. There was also Henry Matthews, the Home Secretary, who was the first Catholic in the cabinet since the seventeenth century. It was believed that if Matthews made the wrong decision about whether Lipski should hang and had to leave the cabinet, Ireland would be more likely to achieve independence from the rest of the United Kingdom. Lipski was supported in Parliament by a radical Scottish socialist MP, R.B. Cunninghame Graham, who was described by recent biographers as a 'mixture of Hamlet and Don Quixote' and who became the model for some of George Bernard Shaw's more outlandish characters. Perhaps the most enigmatic figure was W.T. Stead, the editor of the *Pall Mall Gazette* and the founder of what was called 'the new journalism,' who championed Lipski's case in his paper.

The book's first paragraph gives the basic outline of the story: 'On Tuesday morning, 28 June 1887, in the East End of London, Miriam Angel was found dead. Nitric acid had been poured down her throat. Israel Lipski, a twenty-two-year-old Polish immigrant Jew, was charged with her murder.' The case against Lipski seemed very strong. His attic room, where he was starting a business making sticks for umbrellas, was one floor above Mrs Angel's room and Lipski was found in her room under the bed, apparently unconscious, with nitric acid in his mouth, suggesting that he had tried to commit suicide after murdering Mrs Angel. There was evidence that the door had been locked from the inside. Lipski claimed that two of his workmen had committed the crime while he was out getting supplies. They had, he said, then tried to murder him. Lipski's fiancée and his solicitor believed in his innocence.

The public and the press took a great interest in the case. Murder charges in England were then surprisingly rare. Lipski was the only person to be accused of murder at the Old Bailey that summer, and there were only thirty-five murder convictions throughout 1887 in all of England and Wales. The interest in the case was partly because the issue of unrestricted immigration – particularly Jewish immigration from Eastern Europe – was controversial at the time. There was also fascination in the fact that this was what later became known as a 'locked-door' mystery, an important genre of murder mysteries, but unknown to me when I started writing the book. How could Lipski be innocent if the door was locked from the inside?

Lipski was represented by a lawyer with little experience in the criminal law. His inept cross-examination of the two workmen that Lipski claimed were the guilty parties was summarily cut off by Justice Stephen. The judge's charge to the jury made it clear to the jury that he, Stephen, believed that Lipski was guilty. According to the *Times* reporter, Justice Stephen stated:

There were only two motives which could be put forward for the commission of the crime – passion and avarice. There was nothing taken from the deceased's room, because there was nothing to take, and the circumstances did not seem to support the motive of avarice. It was more probable that passion was the motive for the crime, and that if that were so it would rather be the act of one man than two.

After a two-day trial, it took the jury only eight minutes to bring in a verdict of guilty.

Over the next four weeks, the Home Secretary, assisted by Justice Stephen and others, had to decide whether Lipski would hang. It became publicly known that Stephen was troubled about the unfairness of his address to the jury, which clearly encouraged the jury to convict. The judge admitted to his wife in one letter: 'The man was not quite properly defended and I myself did not exactly hit the right point in summing up.'

There was, moreover, real doubt about Lipski's guilt. Even Queen Victoria followed the case closely and was concerned about whether Lipski would hang. The execution was postponed for a week. On the evening before Lipski was to hang, while the Home Secretary and Justice Stephen were continuing their deliberations on whether there should be a reprieve, Lipski 'confessed' to Rabbi Simeon Singer. Singer then authorized the public release of the confession, and the following morning – 22 August 1887 – Lipski was hanged. When the black flag was raised, confirming that Lipski was dead, the crowd of over five thousand persons that had gathered outside of Newgate Prison let out three loud cheers.

This sensational trial had a number of consequences. It temporarily stopped the growing trend of trial by newspaper, because of Stead's humiliation in having supported Lipski. It also slowed down the movement for a court of criminal appeal (eventually established in 1907) because many persons, including the influential Justice Stephen, thought that a review by the Home Secretary was the better system. Further, the discussion of the case in Parliament led to the rule that a case still under review by the Home Secretary should not be discussed in Parliament.

The Lipski case fanned the flames of growing anti-Semitism in England, leading eventually to restrictions on immigration. The case can also be linked to the Jack the Ripper cases in 1888, the year after

Lipski was hanged. One of the Ripper murders took place on a street one block away from where Lipski had lived, and the person responsible was heard to shout 'Lipski' when the prostitute was stabbed to death. It is possible that someone was trying to place the responsibility for the murders on the Jews, perhaps to curtail further immigration to England.

The case shows the inherent frailty of the criminal process. Lipski may have confessed to a murder he did not commit rather than face a lifetime in prison. When told of the possibility of a reprieve, he said: 'Oh, I would rather die.' Moreover, a confession would permit him to place on record a view of the facts – a killing in the course of robbery – far less serious in his view, likely, than a murder committed out of lust. A confession by Lipski, Rabbi Singer may have thought, would end the controversy surrounding the trial and might help calm the troubled waters and prevent even greater problems for the Jewish community. In his sermons at the time, Singer spoke generally of martyrdom.

Not everyone believed that Lipski's confession was genuine. The radical editors Belfort Bax and William Morris (the famous designer) wrote: 'There is nothing to be surprised at in Lipski's confession. Indeed, it was just what was to be expected ... Under the circumstances the world should be given to understand that he has confessed, and "admitted the justice of his sentence," [and this] was absolutely essential to the stability of the government, of the system of capital punishment, and to the credit of our judicial machinery generally.'

As to whether Lipski was, in fact, guilty, those who have studied the case, I stated in the book's final paragraph, are likely to agree with a letter written in the *Pall Mall Gazette* shortly after the hanging: 'The Whitechapel mystery will remain a mystery.'

I sent the manuscript to a number of publishers in England – contrary to the publishers' preferred rule against multiple submissions at the same time. In early December 1982 I heard from Macmillan London that they would like to publish the book. Not only was I pleased to have a major house accept the manuscript, but I was particularly happy to have the company that had published Justice Stephen's books a century earlier. Lord Hardinge of Penshurst, my principal editor, wrote that he had read the book and had also sought the advice of experts. 'We are all agreed,' he stated, 'that this is a formidable piece of research, most elegantly presented ... Let me add finally how much I personally enjoyed and was intrigued by this fascinating story, so meticulously presented.'

He included a report from an anonymous reader, who I later found out was the writer and critic Julian Symonds, who wrote that it was 'an excellent piece of work: finely organized, agreeably written, and making good use of the trial transcript ... a good account of the social background, and some brilliant sketches of the well-known people who became involved in the case.'

I could not have been happier. Macmillan offered a significant advance of £2000 and generous royalties, something that academic authors are unaccustomed to receiving. The publisher required few changes. Lord Hardinge wanted me to cut down a bit on the use of the transcript, which I readily agreed to do. He also wanted the title changed, from *The Whitechapel Mystery: The Trials of Israel Lipski* to *The Trial of Israel Lipski*. In the end, we settled on *The Trials of Israel Lipski* because I liked the ambiguity of the word 'Trials.' The publisher even managed to arrange that Macmillan of Canada bring the book out in Canada for a relatively low price – well under $20. Most English books in those years priced themselves out of the Canadian market, unless they were also published, rather than just distributed, in Canada.

The book came out in mid-February 1984. Judy and I had been planning to spend a week in London – Judy's brother Barry and his wife Ann were living there for the year – so we arranged the trip to coincide with the book's publication date. There were a number of radio interviews and Judy and I had lunch with Lord Hardinge at a restaurant called the Vecchia Parma on the Strand. The first reviews came out in that week's Sunday papers, just before we got on the plane to return to Canada. 'This fascinating and disturbing case,' wrote the reviewer in the *Observer*, 'is meticulously analyzed by Professor Friedland.' The *Guardian's* reviewer concluded: 'He tells an excellent tale, all the more moving for its cool, dispassionate revelation of the State's injustice perpetrated against one of the many strangers within the gates.' I was particularly pleased by the lead review in the *Sunday Times* by John Mortimer, a barrister and the well-known author of *Rumpole of the Bailey* and many other books. He wrote: 'The story he tells is a fascinating one, which includes an apparently motiveless crime, a locked room and the distinguished Mr. Justice Stephen who, although he may not have been Jack the Ripper's father was certainly Virginia Woolf's uncle and was most anxious to discover that sex was at the bottom of it all.' There was also a glowing full-page review by a Jewish judge in the *Jewish Chronicle*, who stated that it is 'as intriguing as any Conan Doyle or Agatha Christie novel.' Equally favourable reviews followed in the academic journals, the *British Journal of Criminology* referring to the book as 'masterly and fascinating' and the *Law Quarterly Review* as 'a book of absorbing interest.' To my surprise and dismay, most English reviewers gave away the ending.

The English reviews caught the eyes of reviewers in Canada, who first learned about the book from the English papers. Robert Fulford devoted a column to the book in the *Toronto Star* before its Canadian release date, noting the 'exceptionally favourable' English reviews. It was widely reviewed in all the major Canadian papers. Many of the leading lawyers in Canada, including J.J. Robinette, Eddie Greenspan, and Clayton Ruby, wrote reviews, a cross-country tour took place, and interviews were arranged by the publisher with a number of well-known radio personalities, such as Peter Gzowski, Vicki Gabereau, and Valerie Pringle. Macmillan Canada ordered more books from England, although in the end they did not sell all they ordered.

The book was short-listed for an English Crime Writers' Dagger Award and won the 1984 Crime Writers of Canada Arthur Ellis award for non-fiction. The prize, consisting of a politically incorrect wooden figure being hanged, is now prominently displayed in my office. When you pull the cord, the arms and legs splay apart. The book was not, however, quickly snapped up by an American publisher, although eventually it was published by a small house, Beauford Books, which changed the cover from the tasteful English design to one showing a gruesome murder. Again, the American newspaper and academic reviews were flattering.

A number of companies have over the years acquired options to produce a movie, but so far none has been made. The closest it came to happening was through an Australian company. A movie producer there, Valerie Angel-Newstead, wrote to me asking who had the rights to the movie. Under the contract, I shared the rights with Macmillan. Ms Newstead explained her personal interest in the case. She was the eldest granddaughter of the husband of Miriam Angel, the woman that Lipski had been convicted of murdering. After the murder Mr Angel had brought from Poland and subsequently married Miriam Angel's sister, a not uncommon practice at the time. Ms Newstead arranged for me to meet in New York with an Australian writer, Sam Lipski – no relation to Israel Lipski, but another striking coincidence – who had written a scene-by-scene 'treatment.' Ms Newstead wanted to make the movie partly in Australia, which had many old Victorian buildings, and partly in England. Some of the best English character actors, such as John Mills, Donald Pleasance, and Nigel Hawthorne, had expressed an interest in playing roles in the movie. Unfortunately, she could not get financing. Those financing movies at the time did not like the ambiguity in the story. Lipski should either have been guilty or innocent. With two sons-in-law in the movie and television business, I have not given up hope that a movie will eventually be made.

The Lipski story recently gained a new life. A few years ago I was asked to prepare an article on Lipski for the new Oxford *Dictionary of National Biography*, which I was happy to do. Lipski fitted into a series of articles the DNB was producing on immigrants to England who have had an important impact on English society, a description that Lipski, of course, fits. No doubt, Justice James Fitzjames Stephen and his brother Leslie Stephen, the founding editor of the DNB, would be surprised to learn that Lipski now shares space with them in that august publication.

20

The Case of Valentine Shortis

I got such a kick out of researching and writing the Lipski case that I wanted to see if I could replicate the experience with a Canadian case. Was the critical success of the Lipski case an accident? Was a case study a good method of analysing the criminal process? In my search, I limited myself to the period from about 1880 to the First World War, a time when communications over long distances were by letter rather than by telephone. As a result, there would likely be better documentation than after that date. I examined a number of Canadian cases that were mentioned in various true-crime anthologies or had been prominent in the newspapers in those years. I wanted a case that had interesting characters and, if possible, political ramifications. And, of course, I wanted a case that was not well known, so that an element of suspense could be created.

One case that was prominent in the Toronto papers in the early years of the century was that of the Hyams twins, who were charged with the murder of the younger brother of one of the twins' fiancée in an elevator 'accident' allegedly arranged to collect the insurance that had been placed on his life. One of the leading American defence lawyers, Francis Wellman – still known for his book on cross-examination – took part in the defence, although he was not permitted to gown because he was not a member of the Law Society of Upper Canada. There was a full transcript, but as the case ended in an acquittal, there were no records of the case in Ottawa. In the end, I rejected the case because there was not enough background documentation and also because the Hyams twins were Jewish and I did not want to be known as the person who gave prominence to alleged Jewish murderers.

In the spring of 1983 I went to Ottawa to examine the Capital Case Files in the National Archives. All convictions for murder in Canada – and in that period all murder cases were capital cases – are preserved there. The relevant documents were sent to Ottawa to determine whether the cabinet would exercise its power of commutation. Files would normally contain a transcript of the trial proceedings, any decisions of the courts of appeal, the views of the trial judge, further inquiries made by officials in the Department of Justice, and information sent by the convicted person, his lawyer, his family, and others relating to the case. I systematically went through all the files in the relevant years hoping to find a good case.

I had been to the National Archives on several previous occasions, once to examine Canadian materials relating to the codification of the criminal law for my R.S. Wright article and once to collect material for a talk I had been asked to give in Ottawa in June 1982 on the occasion of the one hundredth anniversary of the founding of the Royal Society of Canada. I was to be part of a panel, chaired by Queen's law professor William Lederman, which included Walter Tarnopolsky talking about race relations and Rosie Abella about the rights of women and children. I was to examine changes in Canadian criminal law and procedure over the previous century and consider how similar trials would be conducted today.

Murder and treason were the only capital offences in Canada at the time. In 1882 there had been only eight murder convictions in all of Canada, including the West, which certainly confirmed the view of historians that Canada was a more peaceable and law-abiding country than our neighbour to the south. Out of the eight Canadian cases from 1882, five occurred in Ontario, and I selected three of those for discussion. (In one of the other cases the file was missing and the fifth case was similar to one of the three I had chosen.) I compared the three cases, which had taken place in Napanee, Milton, and Toronto, with trials in 1982. 'I am struck,' I wrote, 'by the fact that the trial of serious criminal cases has not changed as much in the past 100 years as almost all other areas of the law, and, indeed, of society ... The present-day lawyer would feel very much at home in a courtroom 100 years ago, and lawyers of that time would be surprised at how little change has occurred over the course of the century.'

The locale of murders has, of course, changed, reflecting changes in society. One of the three murders took place on a farm, another in a stable. And the weapons have changed: two of the three murders were committed with an axe, a weapon which is rarely used today. The motives, however, have not changed over the years – jealousy, anger, and revenge will be with us for some time.

The issues in the three cases could have been argued in the same manner one hundred years later. The same key arguments, I observed, regarding the accused's mental state in the Toronto case, the admissibility of the confession in the Milton case, and the insanity of the accused in the Napanee case could all have taken place in a courtroom in 1982. I went on to note a number of changes that had taken place outside the formal structure of the trial, such as new techniques of police and scientific investigation, the use of legal aid, and the introduction of parole. There were also some significant changes within the trial, particularly the placing of the onus of proof on the prosecution and giving the accused the right to give evidence on his or her own behalf.

There were, however, major changes outside the trial itself. The time taken before a case is heard and the length of the trial have grown enormously since 1882 and are even more of a problem in Canada today than when I gave the talk in 1982. Two of the three trials in 1882 took place within three months of the murder and the third within six months. It will be recalled that in the Lipski case the trial took place a month after the murder. Perhaps even more striking is the length of the trials. The Toronto case took one day to try, the Milton case two days, and the Napanee case three days. Today, in many cases it is hard to pick a jury in that time, let alone try the case. (I will deal with the issue of the lengthy trial in a later chapter.)

In spite of these differences, I concluded that 'the criminal process has not been subject to radical change, nor is it likely to undergo such change in the future, as many of the procedures have now been included in the Charter of Rights and thus entrenched in the Constitution. So a present-day lawyer would also likely feel at home in a major criminal case a century from now.'

The presentation was well received. As it turned out, I was invited to become a fellow of the Royal Society the following year, 1983. I was the first member of the society from the University of Toronto Law School since Bora Laskin had been a law teacher. I believe I was sponsored by Harry Arthurs, who had become a member the previous year, and Walter Tarnopolsky, who had been one for several years. I cannot say that I have been a very active member, however. Until recently, there has not been much to do, except proudly add FRSC after one's name. I went to my induction in Vancouver that year and gave a five-minute talk at a lunch where the new fellows talked about themselves. I recall saying that my first experience with research was as one of the subjects of John Seeley's study of Forest Hill Village in his book *Crestwood Heights*. I also attended a meeting in Ottawa in late 2003, when I formally received the Sir William John Dawson Medal for 'important contributions to knowledge in multiple domains,' but was not asked to say anything except 'thank you.'

For a number of years, the various deans of the U of T Law School looked to me to help organize the nominations for new fellows. We have a strong faculty and the number of members of the Royal Society has increased significantly. Michael Trebilcock, Stephen Waddams, and Ernest Weinrib were early, easy choices. At present, there are over ten members who are or were associated with the faculty of law. As with all nominations for prizes and awards, one has to prepare the nomination carefully and try not to put more than one person forward in the same year. For three years in the late 1990s I was a member of council of the society's humanities and social sciences division, and so I know the difficulty of choosing new fellows from the pool of excellent candidates.

I was also a member of a Royal Society committee on Tobacco, Nicotine, and Addiction that reported in 1989. The committee had been set up at the request of the federal Department of Health and Welfare to determine whether nicotine was addictive. The tobacco industry was denying that it was and did not want a warning to that effect put on cigarette packages. It was a scientific committee, but a lawyer was added to cover any potential legal issues. The tobacco lobby, of course, claimed that there was no scientific evidence that nicotine was addictive, but that smoking was a social habit instead. The Centre for Addiction had, however, done interesting studies which convinced me – if as an ex-smoker I needed convincing – that cigarettes were addictive. In one experiment they had conducted, mice in a cage had the option of choosing to take liquid from a feeder which also contained nicotine or from another feeder without nicotine. Over time, the mice would favour the one with the nicotine by a wide margin – and this was not because it was a social habit. I think of that expert committee whenever I see the words 'cigarettes are highly addictive' on a package of cigarettes. I also think that a picture of mice heading towards the nicotine feeder would make an excellent TV ad against smoking. The Royal Society has recently been restructured, and one of its new missions – with generous financial support from the Canadian government – is to be part of expert panels to be set up by a new body, the Canadian Institute of Academic Medicine, which was founded by the Royal Society, the Canadian Academy of Engineering, and the Academy of Health Sciences. We will probably be seeing more expert panels making recommendations on policy issues of national importance.

There was no clear-cut winner in my search for a case to follow Lipski in the many files that I went through in the National Archives in Ottawa. With some reservation, I selected the case of Valentine Shortis, who was charged with murder in Valleyfield, Quebec, in 1895. My reservation was because this was not a 'who done it' but rather a 'why done it.' It was clear that Shortis had shot and killed two men in the office of the Montreal Cotton Company as they were counting the money for the payrolls that were to be disbursed to the workers the next morning. The only possible defence was insanity.

It turned out to be as interesting as the Lipski case. It was a cause célèbre in Quebec, the *Montreal Gazette* describing the trial as 'the most remarkable that has ever taken place in Canada.' As with Lipski, I attempted to place the case in its social, cultural, and political context. The political context was surprisingly fascinating. The case unfolded during some of the most dramatic events in Canadian political history: the Manitoba schools question; the cabinet revolt by the so-called 'nest of traitors'; and the 1896 election in which Sir Wilfrid Laurier swept Quebec and became the prime minister of Canada. The Shortis case played a role in that crucial election.

The records in the National Archives were extensive and there were good records in other places – in the provincial archives in Quebec City and Toronto, as well as in Kingston Penitentiary and other places. I had received a small research grant from the University's Connaught fund. As dean of law I had been involved in setting up the fund, and was now a beneficiary. I was able to hire a number of excellent research assistants over the next few years, including – to mention only those connected with the law school – Kent Roach, who was just completing first year, and Richard Owens, who recently spent a number of years as the executive director of the law school's Centre for Innovation Law and Policy. Other persons collected material for me in England. Gordon Cameron, now with Blakes, went down from Oxford to search for material in the Colindale newspaper library in London and Steven Rosenhek, now with Fasken Martineau, visited the Aberdeen family estate in Scotland to look at documents and had the pleasure of having tea with the present Lady Aberdeen.

I like to think that the summers that Kent spent working with me while he was at law school helped influence him to pursue an academic career. I knew about him before he entered law school because Peter Russell had sent me a copy of a first-class paper he had written for Peter on national security. Like Peter, Kent is prematurely bald. There is a clear resemblance to the Seinfeld character George Costanza, played by Jason Alexander. Kent has turned out to be among Canada's leading scholars – enormously productive and innovative, with enthusiasm for whatever he is working on.

I more or less followed the same format as I did for the Lipski case, trying to build up as much suspense as possible. At one point I contemplated telling the story through Shortis's mother, but soon abandoned that approach. The book's title did not emerge until close to the end of the process. Among the various possibilities were 'Valentine's Day,' 'The Shortis Files,' 'The Valleyfield Killer,' and even 'A Royal Bastard.' One problem that I faced in the course of my research was the new *Privacy Act*. One cannot now just go to the National Archives and demand to see documents. Some official first has to make sure that the requested documents do not harm the privacy of any living person. There were many documents in the Shortis files that were initially denied to me, even including letters from Wilfrid Laurier. Rather than fight the matter head on, I successfully argued that I came under one of the exceptions in the act.

The Shortis trial had lasted twenty-nine days, the longest trial in Canada up to that point. Part of the reason for its length was the fact that half the jury spoke French and the other half English, and so evidence in one language had to be translated into the other. Moreover, there had to be jury addresses in both French and English. The case attracted interest because, as in the Lipski case, there were relatively few murders at the time. In 1894, no one from Quebec had been convicted of murder, and there had not been a hanging in the province since 1890.

The bare facts of the case can be briefly stated. Francis Valentine Cuthbert Shortis was born in Waterford, Ireland, on St Valentine's Day,

1875. Valentine, as he was called by his family, was the only child of exceptionally wealthy parents. He had difficulty at school and later in learning his father's business. His father decided that his son would have to learn to stand on his own two feet. In September 1893, at the age of eighteen, Valentine sailed alone to Montreal. He eventually obtained a job as a private secretary to the general manager of the Montreal Cotton Company in Valleyfield, Quebec. It was not long before he was let go from his job, but he remained in Valleyfield, spending considerable time with his girlfriend, Millie Anderson.

On Friday evening, 1 March 1895, Shortis went to the main office of the Montreal Cotton Company. The men counting out the pay packets knew him and let him in. When the men were about to place the pay packets in the safe, Shortis took a loaded gun they kept in a drawer and shot one of the men. A second man was shot dead as he went to phone for the doctor. The first person managed to crawl into the darkened factory, and Shortis followed the trail of blood by lighting matches. When Shortis found him, he shot him in the head. Miraculously, this person did not die but was able to summon help. In the meantime, Shortis shot and killed the night watchman on his rounds.

The prosecutor was convinced that Shortis was sane, as were the townspeople, who were certain that the motive was robbery and that Shortis wanted the money to go west with his girlfriend. The lawyer for the defence took the position that Shortis was insane and received judicial permission to take evidence in Ireland about Shortis's erratic and violent conduct while growing up there.

The trial took place in Beauharnois, in the Valleyfield area. A change of venue to Montreal had been resisted by the government for political reasons – it did not want to alienate the local voters – despite the fact that the local citizens had tried to lynch Shortis and were clearly biased against him. Four thousand persons had attended the Catholic funeral of the French-speaking person who had been shot and one of the largest number on record attended that of the Protestant English-speaking victim. In spite of the conflicts between French and English in other parts of the country, the citizens of Valleyfield were united in their grief and in their hatred of Shortis.

The case enabled me to explore a number of aspects of the history of psychiatry, the insanity defence, and the treatment of the criminally insane in Canada. The law of insanity in the 1892 Criminal Code was similar to the section in the code today – both are based on the old M'Naghten rule, but there was one crucial difference between the

M'Naghten rule and the 1892 code. The M'Naghten rule states that an accused can show that he or she is not guilty by reason of insanity if the accused has a 'defect of the mind' and either does not appreciate the nature and quality of the act or does not know that the act was wrong. Note that the rule is disjunctive. One only had to come under one of its two heads to establish a verdict of not guilty by reason of insanity.

The 1892 code, however, placed an 'and' between the two heads, rather than an 'or.' This made it very difficult for an accused to succeed with an insanity defence. Counsel in the Shortis case tried to expand the definition to include irresistible impulse, but did not challenge the conjunctive nature of the section. Similarly, the judge accepted it without question and refused to go beyond the section. Shortis's insanity plea failed and he was convicted of murder.

The conjunctive 'and' was consistently used in criminal trials in Canada until 1931, when this restrictive interpretation was questioned by the Ontario Court of Appeal in the *Cracknell* case, although the point had not been argued by counsel. The chief justice of Ontario, Sir William Mulock, stated for the court: 'That this change was a mistake on the part of the draughtsman appears to me obvious ... Thus, in order to establish his defence it was not necessary to prove both incapacity to appreciate the nature and quality of his act and also absence of guilty intent. In my opinion ... the word "and" should not be construed literally.' So, as I state in the book, for almost forty years – between 1892 and 1931 – accused persons in Canada who raised the defence of insanity had to satisfy both heads of the insanity test. I examined a number of cases of seriously insane persons who were hanged between those years and found a number who would clearly be found not guilty today. I concluded that the number of people in Canada who have been unjustly hanged because of, to use Chief Justice Mulock's words, 'a mistake on the part of the draughtsman' will never be known.

I learned a great amount about the four psychiatrists who gave evidence – unsuccessfully – for the defence. They were the leading psychiatrists in Canada. The most junior of the four was James Anglin from the recently opened Verdun Protestant Asylum in Montreal. The second witness, Dr C.K. Clarke, after whom the Clarke Institute of Psychiatry at the University of Toronto is named, was a remarkable man. A Canadian doubles tennis champion and later an original member of the violin section of the Toronto Symphony Orchestra despite the loss of two fingers, he was at the time the medical superintendent of the 600-bed Rockwood Asylum in Kingston. The third psychiatrist to give evidence was also somewhat larger than life. Dr Daniel Clark was the medical superintendent of the 700-bed Toronto Lunatic Asylum. He had made a considerable amount of money on placer mining during the California Gold Rush and had later edited a book of poetry and written a novel.

The most remarkable of all the defence psychiatrists was undoubtedly R.M. Bucke, the superintendent of the 900-bed London Lunatic Asylum, the largest in Ontario. The number and size of mental hospitals in those years is striking. Bucke's appearance revealed much about his fascinating background. Obvious to all was a decided limp, the result of the amputation of one foot and part of the other when, many years earlier, he and a prospecting companion had been lost in a blizzard in the American West. Bucke had left home at the age of sixteen, spending five years in the United States plying the Mississippi, working in the Louisiana swamps, and searching for gold and silver in the West. Also apparent to everyone was the remarkable physical resemblance and similarity in dress between Bucke and the recently deceased American poet Walt Whitman. Bucke, who became Whitman's literary executor, identified Whitman with the Messiah and *Leaves of Grass* as the Bible of the future for the next thousand years. All four psychiatrists stated that Shortis was insane and would never recover.

In 1989 I gave a talk on the Shortis case as the Kenneth Gray Memorial Lecturer at the Canadian Psychiatric Association annual meeting in St John's, Newfoundland. There is no doubt that my portraits of the larger-than-life psychiatrists made many in the audience ponder over their rather humdrum lives in comparison to those of their counterparts one hundred years earlier.

Would the verdict be the same today? Most psychiatrists would disagree with the diagnosis by the defence psychiatrists that Shortis was suffering from 'moral insanity' (later termed schizophrenia). Rather, as Dr Vivian Rakoff, the former head of the Clarke Institute, and others informed me, his condition would now be considered within the *Diagnostic and Statistical Manual*'s category of 'antisocial personality disorder.' The mental disorder would be enough to get the issue to the jury, but a jury would not likely be convinced that Shortis did not appreciate the nature and quality of his act or know that it was wrong, even with today's disjunctive insanity rule and the expanded legal interpretation of the words 'appreciate' and 'wrong.'

For me, the most interesting part of the case was the fight for a reprieve and the political repercussions of the case. Shortis was to hang on 3 January 1896, and his family went to extraordinary lengths to try to have the sentence commuted to life imprisonment. Shortis's parents went to see officials in Ottawa and spoke to influential politicians. Mrs Shortis visited Lady Aberdeen, the wife of the governor general, whom the Shortises had known when Lord Aberdeen was the representative of the queen in Ireland. Lady Aberdeen was naturally very sympathetic to Mrs Shortis's plea to save the life of her only child.

The decision was to be made by the cabinet, which devoted four meetings to the question in December 1895. An election was looming and members of Mackenzie Bowell's Conservative government were certain that if they commuted the sentence the opposition Liberals under Wilfrid Laurier would be able to say that the Conservatives hanged a Frenchman, Louis Riel, who had also pleaded insanity ten years earlier and, moreover, had a recommendation of mercy from the jury, but reprieved an English-speaking person. Under the Liberals, Laurier would argue, there would be equal justice for all.

In one meeting the cabinet voted 7–5 for hanging. Lord Aberdeen then talked individually to nearly all the members of the cabinet, as he apparently had the right to do. Lady Aberdeen wrote an intriguing note to the minister of justice, Charles Hibbert Tupper, saying 'there is an aspect of the matter which I want to lay before you in a few words and so as friends, I ask you to come and hear this.' What Lady Aberdeen told the minister of justice was never revealed, but at the last cabinet meeting dealing with the issue the vote was 6–6, which allowed the governor general to commute the sentence.

There was a very strong reaction against the commutation. Shortis was burned in effigy, persons tried to break into the prison to lynch him, and seven cabinet ministers – the so-called 'nest of traitors' – left the federal cabinet. Most important, the decision to allow the governor general to commute the sentence had a major effect on the 1896 election, as the Conservatives had feared.

The election of Laurier was an important event in the history of Canada, as many historians have argued. The Shortis affair, however, has not been recognized as contributing to the result, yet it is crystal clear to me that it influenced the election. The very last words spoken before Parliament was prorogued involved the Shortis case. Laurier opened the campaign in Valleyfield and made much of the Shortis case, arguing, as the Conservatives knew he would, that the Conservatives hanged Louis Riel but reprieved Valentine Shortis. The newspapers throughout this period carried many stories about the case. Laurier's chief lieutenant, Israel Tarte, ran in Valleyfield. In the end, Quebec voted overwhelmingly for Laurier (49 seats to 16 for the Conservatives), although the rest of the country was more or less evenly divided. One can never be sure what is responsible for election results, but it is clear to me, at least, that the Shortis case was a major factor in that crucial election.

The final third of the book deals with the institutions where Shortis was confined. It enabled me to trace the history of corrections over a lengthy period and to show the changes in penal philosophy over the years. Shortis spent ten years at St Vincent de Paul Penitentiary in Montreal, then fourteen years in the new wing for the criminally insane in Kingston Penitentiary. Shortis's parents, with the assistance of Lady Aberdeen, continued to press for better conditions for Valentine. Starting in 1914, he was moved to Guelph, then to Burwash (near Sudbury), back to Guelph, up to the new facility for the criminally insane at Penetanguishene on Georgian Bay, and then finally back to Kingston. Thus, I was able to cover the construction and operation of most of the major penal institutions in Canada at the time. One of my principal conclusions to the study was as follows:

> The story touches in a selective manner on the history of corrections in Canada, from the punitive origins of Kingston Penitentiary through the period of rehabilitation to the present period of uncertainty. Our mammoth penal system, it can be seen, was not the outcome of sustained, logical growth. To a great extent it has been the result of accidents, economic factors, the desire to use existing structures, and the shifting demands of public opinion. What we have today was not inevitable.

Lady Aberdeen was able to play a role in Shortis's fate through her friend William Lyon Mackenzie King, whom she had met when she and her husband were visiting the University of Toronto and Mackenzie King (then called Willy) was a student. King was, in part, responsible for Shortis's transfer to Guelph Reformatory and then, as prime minister, for Shortis's release from Kingston Penitentiary on a ticket of leave. Shortly before noon on Saturday, 3 April 1937, after serving 15,071 days – over forty-two years – in continuous confinement, Valentine Shortis, now sixty-two, was a free man. He was – and the record may possibly still hold – the longest-serving prisoner in Canadian history.

Shortis moved to Toronto under an assumed name, Francis Cuthbert, and died in 1942. The papers then disclosed his true identity, the *Telegram* remarking on 'his goatee, monocle and cane, known to hundreds' and the *Star* reporting, wrongly, that he had been 'educated at Oxford ... the scion of an aristocratic Irish family.'

In the conclusion of the book I talk about the inherent danger of predicting future conduct: 'Shortis was declared 'incurably insane' in 1895 by the very best psychiatrists in Canada; he later became, in the eyes of many, a distinguished, Oxford-educated, cultured gentleman.'

I have revealed too much of the story already, and so will not go into some of the speculative twists and turns at the end of the book, particularly as to what Lady Aberdeen may have told the minister of justice. I will reveal, however, that some of Shortis's supporters believed that his father was the illegitimate son of Queen Victoria's husband, Albert.

As in the Lipski book, I talk about the frailty of the criminal process, saying: 'Justice may in theory be blind, but in practice she has altogether too human a perspective ... The result of the trial, the commutation, the question of Shortis' release may in part have been influenced by the slip of a draughtsman's pen in preparing a criminal code, the improper failure to grant a change of venue, the extreme rivalry of counsel, the reaction of the press, the cry of popular opinion, the vulnerability of the government, a mother's tears, a father's wealth, the strong feelings of the family and friends of the victims, the continuing interest of Lady Aberdeen and her friendship with prominent politicians, and much more.'

The book, *The Case of Valentine Shortis: A True Story of Crime and Politics in Canada*, was published by the University of Toronto Press and by the Osgoode Society. There was a launch – along with other Osgoode Society books – in Convocation Hall at Osgoode Hall during a blizzard in late November 1986. A paperback edition of *Shortis* was brought out a few years later and has been reprinted several times because it is being used in some university courses to show the development of criminal justice in Canada. For a number of years it was used as a text by Desmond Glynn of Ryerson University for a CJRT Open College radio series on the history of crime in Canada.

As with *Lipski*, the book got excellent reviews. My favourite was by Donald Akenson, a Queen's University professor and author, in the *Canadian Historical Review*, who wrote that it is 'a book full of wonders ... done with high craft and with a sense of pace and story line that usually is found only in writers of fiction.' I also liked the review by Margaret Cannon, a reviewer of crime books for the *Globe*, who wrote that it 'is a superior nonfiction book ... carefully researched and documented and can be savored by scholars as well as ordinary readers.' Again, there was a cross-Canada book tour and interviews, including one on *Morningside* with Peter Gzowski. Over the course of my career I had more than half a dozen interviews with Gzowski, who always knew the material well and asked perceptive questions. Peter had been the editor of the *Varsity* at the University of Toronto when I was a student and I had known him over the years. He was, however, always careful not to talk to me before the interview, even though when it took place at the CBC studio on Jarvis Street he had to pass the waiting room where I was sitting. He wanted the interview to be completely spontaneous.

Before the manuscript for the book was completed, I had used the Shortis case as the basis for the inaugural E.M. Culliton lecture at the University of Saskatchewan – named after a recently retired chief justice of Saskatchewan. After its publication, there were many lectures – from the previously mentioned talk at the Canadian Psychiatric Association annual meeting in Newfoundland to one at the University of Victoria law school in BC. I vividly recall my talk at the Manitoba law school. The slide projector would not work and I gave the talk pretending that the slides were actually being shown. It was a success. Many years later, my wife and I had prepared a slide show about our son Tom for a dinner the night before his wedding in Atlanta. When it was our turn to give our talk, we discovered that one of us (probably me) had left the slide tray in the hotel, where we had been practising our prepared patter. My previous experience in Manitoba was put to use and we pretended that the slides were up on the screen – for example, 'There's one of Tom building sand castles in PEI.' It was also a success, many persons thinking that it was planned that way and that there never were any slides.

I also gave a slide presentation in Dublin and was supposed to give one to a historical society in Waterford, Ireland. It had been carefully arranged by Tom Power, a professor of history at St Thomas University in New Brunswick, who was a native of Waterford, but when I got to Waterford, the lecture at the Granville Hotel had been cancelled, for reasons that were never clear to me. The organizers claimed that they never received confirmation that I was coming. I was sure that it was a conspiracy to suppress any discussion of the case that might reveal details about Shortis's background. I thought that perhaps the solicitor who had records about the case, but had refused to reveal them to me, was behind it.

The solicitor, Fergus Power, who had witnessed the will of Shortis's father and handled his estate, had refused to examine any of the records of the Shortis family because of what he described as 'the sensitive nature of the matter.' The visit was not a total disaster, however. I met in the lobby of the Granville Hotel the next evening with Tom Power's parents and several others and told them the story of Valentine Shortis. My notes, written on the train from Waterford back to Dublin state: 'It was more fun than if I had given a lecture. Glasses of beer kept appearing; I think I had three pints. (I usually stop at one.) They were convinced that there is more to the story ... The session ended about midnight.' If there is more to the story, I still have not discovered it. I met the next morning with the solicitor, Fergus Power, who claimed not to have any information that would assist me further. My note states that if he 'knows more about the case than he let on, then he is a very good actor!' Over the years, I received letters from a number of relatives of the characters in the book – from relatives of Valentine Shortis, of his girlfriend Millie Anderson, of the manager of the Montreal Cotton Company, and of one of the persons killed – but they contained no new revelations.

No relatives of Shortis were in the film business, unlike in the Lipski case, but the book came closer to becoming a movie than the Lipski book did. There were discussions with a number of producers, including Telescene Film Group in Montreal. The company, run by Robin Spry, wanted 'the story to be shot as a docu-drama to be produced in collaboration with the National Film Board.' Serious discussions were under way with Donald Brittain, the brilliant NFB director who had been nominated for several Oscars, when Brittain suddenly died at the age of sixty-one in July 1989. Telescene wrote to me a few weeks later, saying that 'in spite of this unfortunate turn of events ... the Film Board still maintains their interest in collaborating with us, and we are now attempting to find another talented director to work on this project.' Nothing further developed, however.

21

The Death of Old Man Rice

The Shortis book was published in the spring of 1986. That summer I explored the possibility of doing an American historical crime book to form a trilogy with my Lipski and Shortis books. With the help of a summer research assistant, Tim Endicott, now teaching law at Oxford University, I looked at murder cases in New York City from the late 1890s to the First World War. I was particularly interested in New York City because my father had grown up there before moving to Toronto in the 1920s, I still have relatives there, and, of course, my wife and I always welcome an excuse to visit the city.

Tim went through the index to the *New York Times*, noting any murder case with a large number of entries that looked interesting, and came up with seven such cases. Most had already been the subject of a book, such as the Chester Gillette case, on which Theodore Dreiser had based his novel *An American Tragedy*, and the case of Harry Thaw, who had killed the famous architect Stanford White. Also included on the list was the case of Albert T. Patrick, a lawyer who had been convicted in 1902 of the murder in New York City of William Marsh Rice, the founder of Rice University in Houston, Texas. No book had apparently been written about the case. My notation beside the case on 24 June 1986 says simply, 'looks good.'

The case had almost been forgotten, in spite of the fact that at the time it was given front-page coverage by the New York newspapers and had been described by one paper as 'America's most remarkable murder case' and by another as 'one of the most remarkable trials in all history.' Because readers today would not know what happened to Patrick I could maintain some drama in telling the story, as I had tried to do in the two earlier books.

I then contacted Rice University. The Woodson Research Centre at Rice's Fondren Library had, of course, a strong interest in the case. They confirmed that no book had been written about it, although there were a number of articles, which they sent me along with a bibliography. They told me that they had a number of scrapbooks containing newspaper clippings about the case, as well as some boxes of material that were open to the public.

I thanked them for the articles and sent them my Lipski and Shortis books so they would know the type of book I was considering writing. I was not at the time certain that the Rice murder was the case for me because the available archival material seemed somewhat skimpy. The Rice archivists were, however, obviously impressed with the scholarly nature of my earlier murder books and revealed that, in fact, they had a roomful of material on the case – about seventy-five linear feet of documents – which archivists will tell you is a lot of material. These documents were not open to the public and required the permission of the Rice President's Office, which was quickly granted.

The material had been given to Rice University by a prominent character in the story, James A. Baker, Jr, the grandfather of the former secretary of state. There was a full transcript of the case, as well as the New York lawyers' and district attorneys' files and various court records. Particularly valuable were the letters and telegrams sent between the New York and Houston lawyers – the long-distance telephone was still not in use in those years. The five scrapbooks prepared by the prosecution contained extensive newspaper clippings, with detailed and sensational accounts of the case. One of the headlines in Hearst's *Evening Journal* was eight inches high. Another newspaper stated that more had been written about Patrick than about any other individual, with the possible exception of the president of the United States. There was also a large quantity of material in the archives in Albany, New York, deposited by a former governor of New York, David B. Hill, who had acted for Patrick on his appeal to the New York Court of Appeals. I could therefore examine the case from both the prosecution and the defence perspectives.

Because of the extensive archival records, I decided that I would take on the case. The book, *The Death of Old Man Rice: A True Story of Criminal*

Justice in America, published jointly by the University of Toronto Press and the New York University Press, did not, however, appear until 1994. The complexity of the case and the location of the records, scattered across the United States, were, in part, responsible for the delay. This also probably explained why no one else had written a book on the case. I made several trips to Houston and to New York, as well as to Albany and Washington. A more important reason for the delay was that other academic pursuits, discussed in later chapters, had a higher priority. I was assisted in my research by a number of first-rate research assistants, including Paul Michell, now a litigator in Toronto, who has taught international commercial arbitration at the U of T law school.

My three murder books in fact form a good trilogy. As it turned out, each book appears to capture the essence of the society in which the case occurred. As I stated in the preface to the third book, 'the Lipski story is one of class and prejudice in England; Shortis is about race and religion in Canada; and the Patrick/Rice case is about wealth and ambition in the United States.'

The Rice case certainly involved great wealth. Rice was probably the richest Texan in the United States. Would his wealth go to the Rice Institute, later renamed Rice University, in Houston, as Rice had designated in a will executed by him in 1896, or would it go to Albert T. Patrick, who had drafted a later will for Rice in the year 1900, which Rice had apparently signed? James A. Baker and his Houston law firm, Baker and Botts, were certain that the later will was a forgery and spent hundreds of thousands of dollars supporting the prosecution of the murder charge and defending the validity of the earlier will. There was also great wealth supporting Patrick. His sister was married to one of the richest men in Philadelphia, John Milliken – when he died in 1919 his estate was worth over $25 million – who helped finance the defence to protect the family name and also because Patrick had promised him a share in Rice's estate if the later will was upheld.

Ambition can be seen in the determination of the prosecutors – assistant district attorney James W. Osborne and district attorney Williams Travers Jerome – to get a conviction to help further their political ambitions. Everyone in the case was on the make, including Patrick and his associates, whom I concluded were guilty of forgery, but probably not murder. James A. Baker wanted to establish a major university in Houston and to have a large pool of capital which would help the development of Houston and the fortunes of his law firm, all of which was accomplished. The cornerstone of Rice University was laid in 1911 and the pool of capital was then about $10 million. Today, Rice University, one of the most highly regarded smaller academic institutions in the United States, has an endowment of well over $3 billion.

The book reiterated the theme, developed in my earlier two books, of the inherent frailty of the criminal process. 'All three cases,' I wrote, 'show ... the many nonlegal factors that may influence any criminal trial, then and now' and 'the danger of shifting the balance too far in favor of the prosecution and strengthen the arguments against capital punishment ... Recognizing the inherent fallibility of the process ... helps keep us on our guard against miscarriages of justice.'

One reason I like researching murder books is because I learn a great amount about a wide range of interesting subjects that I might not otherwise have known. Here are a few examples from the Rice case.

The effect of embalming became the crucial issue in the murder charge against Albert T. Patrick. The book starts with an undertaker coming to 'Old Man Rice's' apartment on Madison Avenue:

> At about ten o'clock on a balmy Sunday evening in late September 1900, Charles Plowright, a Manhattan undertaker, arrived with his assistant at 500 Madison Avenue. He had been telephoned by the superintendent of the apartment building about an hour earlier and asked to make the necessary funeral arrangements for the remains of William Marsh Rice, a wealthy, aged Texan living in New York.

Patrick was in charge of the arrangements. He wanted the body cremated immediately, but the undertaker explained that it would take some time to get the furnace at the crematorium to the required temperature. Because of the warm weather the undertaker recommended embalming, which was immediately done. Before the cremation could take place, however, the police intervened and an autopsy was conducted.

At the trial the prosecution argued that the murder was committed at Patrick's direction by Rice's valet, Charlie Jones, by administering chloroform to Rice. The valet so testified at the trial, although he had given several conflicting stories before the trial began. The defence contested Jones's evidence and said that Rice died a natural death from eating too many bananas. (A full-page review of my book in the *London Review of Books* was simply headed: 'Bananas.') The prosecution experts testified that the autopsy showed congestion of the lungs caused by chloroform.

The defence tried to argue at trial and on appeal – unsuccessfully – that the congestion was caused by the embalming.

I had to learn a great amount about embalming – my research was done before the television series *Six Feet Under*. In Rice's case, the embalming fluid was pumped into his body through the right brachial artery on the underside of the right arm above the elbow. I was interested in seeing an actual embalming and spoke to a number of embalmers in Toronto, but they felt that families would not want some stranger in the room observing the procedure. I discovered that there is a funeral-service program at Humber College in Toronto, and its director was willing to let me observe an embalming. The person I dealt with had an interest in the history of embalming and arranged to have the embalming done by the same method as in the Rice case, that is, using the right brachial artery rather than the carotid artery in the neck, the one that is commonly used today.

There were about ten students embalming two cadavers, bodies that had not been claimed by anyone for burial. The students, I observed, were serious-minded and somewhat older than one would expect. A number of those I spoke to had already been working in funeral parlors and wanted to upgrade their skills and pay. After about two hours of embalming and cosmetic work, the bodies looked surprisingly presentable. The experience helped me understand the voluminous evidence at and after the trial relating to embalming.

I must say that this was one of the more interesting – if not the most interesting – fact-finding forays I have ever done in the name of research. In earlier chapters I described pari-mutuel betting at Woodbine for the study on gambling and target and skeet shooting for the study on gun control. In a later chapter I will describe a study of traffic safety in which I and other participants drank wine and then took a breathalyzer test to determine what it feels like to be over the legal limit.

Patrick was convicted and sentenced to death in March 1902. The jury obviously believed the evidence of Jones, the valet. The conviction was upheld by a majority on appeal to the New York Court of Appeals. Further applications for a new trial and appeals in the federal courts, including to the Supreme Court, were also unsuccessful. Jones, it should be noted, was never prosecuted for any offence, and he returned to Texas, eventually committing suicide much later in life with a .38 revolver.

The New York Medico-Legal Society, with the financial support of

Patrick's wealthy brother-in-law, John Milliken, had conducted experiments supporting Patrick's defence that the congestion in the lungs was caused by the embalming fluid and not by chloroform. The society organized meetings of embalmers who showed that embalming fluid would indeed reach the lungs. Nearly thirty-five hundred New York physicians signed a petition demanding an independent commission of inquiry into the medical aspects of the case. Each successive New York governor would be invited to attend these demonstrations. Even Sir Arthur Conan Doyle and Dr Joseph Bell, who was the model for Sherlock Holmes, got involved and supported the defence. This was possibly the only American case in which Conan Doyle became directly involved.

Because of this new expert evidence, Patrick's sentence was commuted in 1906 to life imprisonment, and in 1912 he was given a pardon and released from Sing Sing Penitentiary. I sent a draft of the manuscript to a number of leading experts – Dr Fred Jaffe of the Ontario Centre of Forensic Sciences, Dr Alan Van Poznak, a professor of anesthesiology at the New York Hospital–Cornell Medical Center, and to Dr Charles Hirsch, the chief medical examiner of New York City – who all agreed with Patrick's experts that chloroform would not cause recognizable changes in the lungs.

I also sent the manuscript to a husband and wife team of embalmers in Chicago, Edward and Gail Johnson, who are acknowledged experts on the history of embalming. They had absolutely no doubt that the embalming fluid would reach the lungs and that Patrick was therefore innocent of murder. They later wrote a lengthy review of the book in their profession's leading journal, *American Funeral Director*, under the heading 'The Patrick Case: How the Nation's Embalmers Saved an Innocent Man from the Electric Chair.' My editor at New York University Press, Niko Pfund, told me that for some time he kept a copy of the review on his wall. Few academic books get reviewed in undertakers' journals.

I also became knowledgeable about forgery. If Patrick was not guilty of murder, he was almost certainly guilty of forgery. My advice to would-be forgers is to make sure two or more forged signatures are not exactly the same. When the head of New York's detective bureau, 'Gentleman George' McCluskey, saw two of the cheques purportedly signed by Rice, his first remark was 'There is a wonderful similarity in the two signatures,' and then, placing them under his magnifying glass, he added, 'Yes, a wonderful similarity.' All the handwriting experts engaged by the prosecution, including the author of the still widely used text *Osborn on Questioned Documents*, made the same point. Rice's signatures, which occurred on all the pages of the will, were almost exactly the same. Yet when they examined signatures by Rice on various documents he signed the day he died, the signature varied considerably. One expert stated categorically that 'where two signatures have been shown to be exactly alike in every particular ... one must be a forgery.'

I found a respected handwriting expert in Houston, Janet Masson, who wrote that 'the evidence validating the conclusions reached by [the handwriting experts] is just as powerful and persuasive today as it was when presented at the beginning of the century.' She produced transparencies of Rice's 'signatures' on the pages of the 1900 will for the purpose of superimposing one on the other. They line up almost perfectly. It is difficult to disagree with her conclusion that 'the four signatures were traced using the same presumably genuine signature as a model.'

In addition, I learned a considerable amount about death by the electric chair, just as in the Lipski case I had found out much about the techniques of hanging. Patrick was on death row in Sing Sing Penitentiary for a number of years until his sentence was commuted to life imprisonment. The death house in Sing Sing had been constructed in 1888. Formerly, executions in New York were conducted, as in England and Canada, in the county where the trial had been held. During Patrick's time on death row, however, New York executions took place at Auburn, Sing Sing, and Dannemora penitentiaries. The world's first electrocution took place at Auburn in 1890, and thereafter all the executions in New York would take place in one of the three state prisons.

The story of how New York seized on electrocution as the preferred technique is fascinating. Electrocution replaced hanging in New York as the result of a state legislative commission on techniques of execution that was established in the 1880s. By chance, there was at the time great rivalry between two systems of supplying electricity for general use in the country, Edison's direct current system and Westinghouse's alternating current. Edison's strategy for gaining the upper hand was to show how dangerous Westinghouse's alternating current was. It could kill. The legislative commission looking at techniques for execution then seized upon this fact, watched some demonstrations of its lethal quality on animals, and recommended that hanging be replaced by electrocution in the state prisons. Hanging was officially replaced by electrocutions in New York State in 1888.

I also learned much about the growth of Houston and of law firms in North America. Houston, which is now the fourth largest metropolis in the United States, was then a city of under fifty thousand. In the nineteenth century, the leading city in the area was the coastal city of Galveston, Texas. Houston was inland, connected by a waterway to Galveston, forty miles to the southeast. Houston surpassed Galveston in population for the first time in 1900, and would double its population in the next ten years, while Galveston's declined. The major reason for that decline was the devastating hurricane there on 8 September 1900, two weeks before Rice died, which the defence alleged caused him anxiety and contributed to his death. Over six thousand people perished in what was – and still is – the greatest natural disaster in U.S. history. Houston, being away from the coast, was much less seriously affected. As this is being written, the southern United States is still recovering from the devastation caused by Hurricane Katrina. I am surprised that I did not see any mention in the papers I read about the Galveston hurricane of 1900.

I was interested in the growth of Baker and Botts over the years. In 1900 it was a four-man firm, not unlike other important corporate/commercial law firms at the time in New York, Chicago, and Toronto. The firm was not a collection of sole practitioners, as many firms were, but an example of the new breed of law firm then emerging – a true partnership in which all the members of the firm shared responsibility for the work. At the time I wrote the book, the firm had offices on ten floors of the fifty-one-storey One Shell Plaza dominating the Houston skyline, and over four hundred lawyers in offices in Washington, New York, and other major cities, also not unlike other corporate/commercial law firms in New York, Chicago, and Toronto. It now has over seven hundred lawyers and no doubt will continue to grow.

As in my other murder books, one sees the influence of external factors playing a role in the case's outcome, factors such as overly aggressive prosecutors with political ambitions, the influence of the press in moulding public and professional attitudes, and the ability of the participants, in turn, to manipulate the press. We also see the power of money – vast fortunes were available to each side – to bring about results. In the early stages, the wealth of those who favoured upholding the earlier will played a role in helping bring about the conviction by offering enormous financial, fact-finding, and research support to the prosecution. In the later stages, Milliken's wealth financed the various steps leading towards the pardon. The ability to take these steps and to mobilize professional and other groups – then and now – often depends on the money available.

Another conclusion that I drew from the case is the great danger inherent in the manner in which the legal system uses expert testimony. The practice at the turn of the century was not significantly different from the practice today. Expert witnesses can be bought, cornered, neutralized, and manipulated. A further major concern the case highlights is the risk of relying on an accomplice's testimony. An accomplice such as Jones obviously has much to gain by supporting the prosecution. In the end, we have in the Patrick case the spectacle of Jones confessing – probably falsely – to murder and yet not being prosecuted for any crime.

The book consisted of exactly one hundred chapters divided into seven parts, with four pages of pictures at the beginning of each part. I dedicated the book 'to my late father, Jack Friedland, who grew up in New York City in the early years of the century before moving to Toronto. Whether the family ever discussed the Patrick/Rice murder is not known.' The publisher obtained good endorsements to put on the cover. Eddie Greenspan was given prominence with his comment: 'A fascinating, engrossing, riveting book about a most remarkable murder case.' I had sent a copy of the manuscript to James A. Baker III to see if he would make a comment that could be used. He was willing to say that he 'found the book fascinating,' which was used on the U.S. edition. I am not sure he read enough of the book to know that I was alleging that his grandfather may have framed Patrick on the murder charge.

The book was widely and well reviewed. It came out at about the same time as the trial in the O.J. Simpson case and a number of reviewers referred to that case. A reviewer in the *Journal of the American Medical Association* started his review by quoting from the dust jacket of the book: 'One of the most remarkable trials in all history ... a gripping tale of murder and intrigue ... the influence of the popular press, the purchase of expert witnesses ... the issue of the death penalty, and the advantage of wealth.' The reviewer then went on to write: 'The O.J.

Simpson case, right? Wrong!' A review in the *Harvard Law Review* also referred to the O.J. case, stating:

> Even without Court TV, Patrick's trial for first-degree murder gripped the nation and created a media feeding frenzy quite similar to the current coverage of the O.J. Simpson case. Martin Friedland provides a compelling account of Patrick's legal battles, from the initial trial to the Death Row appeals. The book should prove particularly interesting for law students because the Patrick trial raised many issues that remain controversial today: the proper role of the media in celebrity murder trials, the purchase of expert witnesses, and the risk that the death penalty may sometimes cause innocent people to be executed.

These are exactly the points I hoped would be made about the book.

The book later came out in paperback. So far, no one has taken an option for a movie, although there have been several nibbles. I gave a number of talks on the book, including a talk at legal historian Bill Nelson's seminar at NYU and another to the Medico-Legal Society of Toronto. One interesting follow-up is that I made contact with Patrick's only living grandchild, Mimi West, who now lives with her husband in retirement on Vancouver Island, following their careers in the American military. Patrick's two daughters were raised by one of his sisters. Ms West told me that she never met her grandfather Albert, and did not know about the case until she was in her thirties. I met with her when I was in Victoria, British Columbia, doing my study on judicial independence. She and her husband took me to dinner at the very traditional English-style Union Club, where she took great pleasure in introducing me as the person writing a book about her grandfather, who had been on death row in Sing Sing.

I subsequently spent considerable time and effort in trying to find a good fourth murder case, hoping for one from a Third World country where the records would be in English, but so far I have not found one. After carefully going through the index of the *London Times* and selecting three possible Indian cases, I collected considerable material on a murder committed in the Bengal area in 1907. By chance, a student who had been in my first-year small group, Poonam Puri, now a professor at Osgoode Hall Law School, was going to India that summer and agreed to examine the material in the archives in New Delhi to see what material was available. She wrote an excellent memo, showing why the

Bengal case was the most promising one to explore. A bomb had been thrown by a Hindu nationalist at the carriage of a hated magistrate, but the terrorists had the wrong carriage and killed the wife and daughter of an Anglo-Indian barrister, who, ironically, was sympathetic to the aspirations of the Indian nationalists and had been actively involved in the early years of the Indian National Congress. This was the first bomb thrown for a political purpose in India and provoked a strong reaction from the British authorities.

The trouble with the case, for my purposes, was that I could find little information about the English side of the case, in spite of several trips to the India Office in London. Yet, I knew a great amount – almost too much – about the Indian side. Indeed, a book had been published about the use of violence in Bengal in that period. I put the case aside when I started the U of T history, but I still have all my boxes of material and it is possible that I might tackle it again when this memoir is finished.

Another case which intrigued me was one that I discovered when I was in Victoria, BC, in 2002 to give a talk to University of Toronto alumni on my recently published history of the University. My wife and I visited the cemetery of the very old Victoria synagogue – much older than any synagogue in Toronto. There was a reasonably large Jewish community in Victoria in the nineteenth century who had come up from California because of the gold rush on the Fraser River. The oldest tombstone in the cemetery was inscribed with the words:

In Memory of
Morris Price
Killed at Cayoosh, BC
Buried May 6, 1861
First Interment in this Cemetery

Price had been a merchant on the Fraser River who was robbed and murdered by two aboriginals. Both were tried and convicted by the well-known travelling judge Matthew Begbie and were hanged. There were several brief records of the case in the British Columbia Archives, but not enough to fill in much detail, unless I were to fictionalize most of it, which I may do.

So, I'm still looking for an interesting follow-up case that I can tackle.

Writing the true-crime books not only fortified my concern about the frailty of the criminal process, to be discussed in the next chapter, but also helped spark an interest in crime in literature. In 1985 I started organizing a law-school course on the topic. I was not – I freely admit – very knowledgeable about literature. My undergraduate degree was in commerce and finance, and my program did not, as far as I remember, even offer an elective course on literature. I tended to read – and still do – non-fiction. So my reading of novels – let alone novels dealing with crime – was limited. There was, however, one spurt of reading Dickens in the mid-1960s when I was invited to address the Dickens Fellowship of Toronto on 'Dickens and Crime.' My fellow participant was Harry Girling, a professor of English at York University. We selected four Dickens novels dealing with crime. I was to talk about crime and Girling was to talk about the novels. It turned out that he talked about crime and I talked about the novels. I vividly recall that meeting held in a packed lecture room in Wycliffe College at the University of Toronto. It started with someone singing something like: 'Where are the yeomen of yesteryear?' I thought I was back in the nineteenth century.

My idea for the law-school course was to ask individual members of the English department at the University of Toronto to conduct a seminar on a book involving crime that interested them. A number of members of the department – in particular, Jack Robson and Michael and Jane Millgate – were very helpful in identifying persons and books that might be considered. I would offer the seminar in both 1986 and 1988. The English scholars, with my participation, would lead the discussion. The students would read as many of the books as they were able to and would be graded on the basis of a research paper on one of the legal themes explored in the seminars.

Law attracts a large number of students with a background in literature, and the course was oversubscribed and apparently well received. The student papers were almost uniformly excellent. The course was particularly successful from my perspective because I was able to read a large number of novels and plays that I had never read before – and I did not feel guilty about not sticking to my academic work. This *was* my academic work. It also made me think more deeply about crime and justice. As the entry in the law-school calendar stated, the series was designed to provide 'insights into aspects of crime, the criminal process, and the history of the criminal law by analyzing the way perceptive writers have dealt with matters relating to crime.' Each of the works studied also considered the wider question of the meaning and forms of justice.

I was able to attract a distinguished list of participants. English literature has always been one of the U of T's strongest departments. No one that I approached declined the offer to take part. They all liked the concept. The understanding was that some time after the second run-through they would produce a publishable paper which would be included in a book of essays to be submitted for publication.

The book, *Rough Justice: Essays on Crime in Literature*, was published in 1991 in hardcover and paperback by the U of T Press. The subtitle, it will be noted, was crime *in* literature. The course was not on law *and* literature, a growing, if amorphous, field that involves areas such as law as literature and theories of interpretation. The book received a number of good reviews, although it was not reviewed as widely as I had expected. The critic W.J. Keith wrote that it was 'an excellent idea for an interdisciplinary course and book ... It appears to have been a notably successful enterprise, and offers an inspiriting example for more imaginative efforts to break down the formidable barriers between academic disciplines ... I learned a lot from this book, which is both serious and accessible.'

The first essay was by Northrop Frye on crime and sin in the Bible. It was Frye's last published essay. He died in 1991, just before the book was published, and the collection was dedicated to his memory. The series, which was open to the wider university community, usually attracted a couple of dozen persons not registered in the course to its seminars, held in the solarium in Falconer Hall. The number of persons who showed up for Frye's seminar was so large that at the last minute we had to transfer the seminar to the moot courtroom, which could barely hold the numbers who wanted to listen to Frye. Perhaps people sensed that this might be one of the last occasions to hear the great man. Unlike all the other contributions, Frye's did not contain any footnotes, but he allowed me and my research assistant, Doug Harris, who had a strong background in English literature, to add them. Doug, now an expert on securities regulation, also helped me write the introduction.

The last essay was by Josef Škvorecký, the Czech writer, who had been teaching a course on detective fiction. He analysed that genre from a personal perspective. Frye and Škvorecký were the bookends, and in between were eleven papers by acknowledged experts such as Jack Robson on Charles Dickens's *Our Mutual Friend*, Michael Millgate on William Faulkner's *Sanctuary*, and Ted Chamberlin on the life and writings of Oscar Wilde – to name only participants who were or subsequently became University Professors. There were essays on English,

American, and Canadian authors. The two Canadian papers were Dennis Duffy's on Rudy Wiebe's powerful novel of the Riel case, *The Scorched-Wood People*, and Ann Saddlemyer's analysis of two Canadian plays, George Ryga's *Indian* and Sharon Pollock's *Blood Relations*, which look at the treatment of native people and women, respectively, in a white, patriarchal society.

The title *Rough Justice* was chosen for the collection because many of the essays show that a form of rough justice was accomplished in the end. In Faulkner's *Sanctuary*, for example, a key character was executed for a murder he could not have committed because he was murdering someone else at the time. Similarly, there was doubt about the legal guilt of Clyde Griffiths in *An American Tragedy* and of Bigger Thomas in *Native Son*, but no doubt about their moral guilt. I was particularly interested in those three American books because they tended to display what I was finding in *Old Man Rice*, which I was then working on: politically ambitious district attorneys, inept lawyers, an aggressive press, and hostile public opinion.

The book was launched at the Rooftop Lounge of the Park Plaza Hotel – every author's dream venue. The trade journal *Quill and Quire* noted that I seemed 'in a jubilant mood.'

There has been a recent resurgence of interest in law and literature at the law school, with several courses being offered in 2006–7 and with plans to introduce combined law and literature degrees, as is now done in other areas, such as law and management studies and law and social work. My seminars and the resulting book perhaps contributed in a limited way to this development.

22

The Frailty of the Criminal Process – Some Observations

Over the past several decades there has been a growing acknowledgment by the judiciary and others of the frailty of the criminal process. In Canada the miscarriages of justice in the well-known trio of cases *Marshall*, *Milgaard*, and *Morin*, along with a number of others, have made the public and the judiciary more receptive to recognizing this fact. In the past there was a reluctance to recognize that the system is fallible. In the *Truscott* case, for example, the judge who conducted the trial later urged both the federal and Ontario governments to prosecute Isabel LeBourdais for public mischief because her book on the trial stirred up controversy. The recent report by former chief justice of Canada Antonio Lamer on three miscarriages of justice in Newfoundland – also all murder cases – is a further example of the frailty of the process. 'Any system that depends on human beings is, by virtue of that very feature, fallible,' Lamer wrote, adding: 'This helps to explain why tunnel vision is seldom the result of personal malice ... and why wrongful convictions are not aberrations but are rooted in systemic problems.' A large number of cases are currently under review. A list of some of the major ones can be found on the website of the Association in Defence of the Wrongly Convicted (AIDWYC, www.aidwyc.org).

In the Supreme Court of Canada's extradition decision in 2001, *Burns and Rafay*, the court unanimously refused to extradite the accused to the United States to face the death penalty, stating: 'In recent years, aided by advances in the forensic sciences, including DNA testing, the courts

and governments in this country and elsewhere have come to acknowledge a number of instances of wrongful convictions for murder despite
all of the careful safeguards put in place for the protection of the innocent.' The Supreme Court would not – unless there were 'exceptional
circumstances' – permit extradition to another country unless there was
an assurance by the state requesting extradition that the death penalty
would not be imposed. The court did not say what was meant by
'exceptional circumstances.'

In other common-law jurisdictions there has also been greater recognition in recent years of the possibility of wrongful convictions. The
governor of Illinois, for example, in early 2003 commuted the death
sentences of more than 150 persons on death row. Because of a number
of wrongful convictions in England involving alleged Irish terrorists,
Britain introduced a Criminal Cases Review Commission in 1995. Up to
the end of June 2006 the commission had received well over 8000 applications for review and had referred over 330 cases to the Court of
Appeal as provided for in the legislative scheme, of which almost 200
convictions were quashed by the court. In 2004–5, 45 cases were
referred by the commission to the Court of Appeal out of almost 1000
applications. About one-third of the referrals in recent years have been
for murder cases.

The 1989 report by the royal commission on the Donald Marshall Jr
case was the first Canadian commission to carefully dissect how a person could be wrongly convicted of a crime. It was also, according to
Chief Justice Lamer, 'the first time in Canadian legal history, that a
wrongful criminal conviction was ever formally acknowledged by a
public institution.' The commission recommended that an independent
review process be established by the federal government. In 1993 Canada improved its process of reviewing convictions outside the regular
court system by setting up the Criminal Conviction Review Group – an
internal review system in the Department of Justice. Further improvements were made by amendments to the Criminal Code in 2002,
whereby the review group was given the powers of a commissioner
under the *Inquiries Act* and therefore could compel witnesses to give
evidence under oath. (See sections 696.1–696.6 of the Criminal Code.)
Moreover, the legislation gave the minister the power to delegate to a
lawyer or former judge the investigation of a conviction, along with the
minister's special powers. The process is overseen by a special adviser,
retired Quebec justice Bernard Grenier, whom I had known when he
worked for the Law Reform Commission in the 1970s. In spite of these

changes, it would seem preferable to adopt the more independent British system.

The present Canadian system has far fewer applications for review than the British system. In 2003–4, there were only twenty-nine applications for review in Canada and in 2004–5 only thirty-five. One of the cases from 2001 was the Steven Truscott murder conviction, discussed in an earlier chapter. After a thorough review by former Quebec Court of Appeal justice Fred Kaufman, minister of justice Irwin Cotler concluded that 'there is a reasonable basis to conclude that a miscarriage of justice likely occurred' and referred the case to the Ontario Court of Appeal, which heard fresh evidence in the fall of 2006 and formal arguments in early 2007. My daughter Jenny was gowned and sitting at the counsel table in the fresh-evidence hearing before the five-judge panel chaired by Chief Justice Roy McMurtry. I attended the proceedings one morning to hear important evidence given by an entomologist on the likely time of death, judged by the size of the maggots on the deceased's body, which in turn would indicate how long they had been there. Jenny and I then went for lunch! I also dropped in for part of the formal argument and watched the televised proceedings, the first time that a court of appeal hearing in a criminal case in Ontario has been televised. The decision is expected in the late spring or early summer of 2007.

Part of the reason for the lower number of review applications in Canada is that provincial offences are not covered by the federal legislation. Another reason is that the British legislation has been interpreted by the English Court of Appeal to allow the court to take into account in deciding the appeal developments of the common law after the conviction, although later legislative changes will not affect the conviction. It is not clear how Canadian courts would interpret the comparable Canadian legislation. If, for example, the Fisher murder conviction in the early 1960s – discussed in an earlier chapter on legal aid – were the subject of a review in Canada, would the court of appeal take into account the changes in the common law relating to the defence of drunkenness? Perhaps not, but what will the court of appeal deciding the Truscott case do on issues of disclosure, which have changed dramatically because of the Supreme Court's *Stinchcombe* case? These are difficult questions and would probably have been considered by the reviewing authorities in Canada and England in the decision about whether to send a case back to the courts in the first place. When cases are sent back, what will Canadian courts of appeal do? Would it make any difference if the change with respect to the duty to disclose had been brought about by legislation rather than by the common law? It may be that the courts will devise a qualitative test in the Truscott case which will depend on a large number of factors. There is likely to be a balance between fairness to the accused in the light of liberal developments in the law and the need to have some controls on the number of old cases that can be reopened.

The time that has elapsed since the original conviction is likely to play a role. The closer that event is to the present the more likely that the court will take the change into account, just as they would if the time for appeal had not elapsed or the convicted person was still in the appeal system. The English Court of Appeal has heard cases where the convictions were made and the executions carried out many decades ago, such as those of James Hanratty and Ruth Ellis, both of whose convictions were upheld.

How about reviewing a possible miscarriage of justice in the Lipski case in Britain? It is theoretically possible, but the English Court of Appeal has been very critical of using scarce judicial resources to decide ancient cases referred to the court. In the case of James Hanratty, who was hanged in 1962, the court pointed out that 'a case of this age must be exceptional to justify this level of expenditure,' and in that of Ruth Ellis, hanged in 1955, the court stated: 'We have to question whether this exercise of considering an appeal so long after the event ... is a sensible use of the limited resources of the Court of Appeal ... Parliament may wish to consider whether going back many years into history to re-examine a case of this kind is a use that ought to be made of the limited resources that are available.' So, even though the present chair of the British commission, Graham Zellick, is an old friend – he was a visiting professor at the U of T law school on two occasions while I was dean – I do not think that the commission would be willing to consider taking up the case of Israel Lipski.

In 2006 Michael Bryant, the attorney general of Ontario, introduced the Ontario Criminal Conviction Review Committee (OCCRC) to review criminal convictions in Ontario. The committee was headed by the respected former defence counsel and Quebec Court of Appeal judge Michel Proulx, who died in early 2007. The fact that the matter could also be the subject of a review by the federal minister of justice does not deprive the Ontario committee of jurisdiction. It is also assigned the task of 'providing expert advice and guidance to Crowns across the province in dealing with some of the difficult issues relating to potential miscarriages of justice, developing educational and policy initiatives aimed at the prevention of miscarriages of justice, and developing protocols and best practices for dealing with these cases and preventing future miscarriages of justice.' As originally set up, there would be six senior Crown counsel from across the province on the committee, representing the appellate, policy, and trial perspectives on the issues. This is an expanded version of a special Ontario committee, described below, in which I participated that gave advice to the attorney general on matters arising from the inquiry conducted by Fred Kaufman into the Morin conviction. A number of defence lawyers and others were on that earlier committee. The Ontario Bar Association has already complained that defence lawyers should be included on the OCCRC.

A valuable report on the prevention of miscarriages of justice by a federal/provincial group of prosecutors, chaired by the assistant deputy attorney general of Canada, D.S. Bellemare, and the assistant deputy attorney general of Manitoba, Rob Finlayson, was published in 2004 and an international conference on the subject held in October 2005. The report's analysis drew heavily on the recent Canadian inquiries. The identification of problem areas fits in well with the lessons that can be learned from my three early murder cases.

The prosecutors identify eyewitness identification as an issue, as have many commentators over the years, and recommend that line-ups be conducted in as fair a manner as possible, without, for example, the person conducting the line-up knowing who the suspect is. Readers of *Lipski* will recall that he was identified by a druggist as the person who bought nitric acid from him. The 'show-up' identification was made, however, after the police took the druggist to the hospital ward where Lipski was being guarded by a policeman and simply asked him if this was the man. Further, the report recommends that the witness be told that the actual perpetrator may not be in the line-up, and the witness therefore need not feel that he or she must make an identification, and that all statements made during the line-up be recorded, if possible, by audio- or videotaping.

Members of the public may not be as aware as psychologists and lawyers are of the weakness of eyewitness-identification evidence. The Innocence Project in New York identified 101 of the first 130 wrongful convictions identified by DNA evidence as being at least partly the result of mistaken identification. A similar, although less dramatic, pattern exists in Canada. In earlier periods, eyewitness identification was given greater weight than circumstantial evidence, which required a special warning (called the rule in *Hodge's Case*) that the jury had to be satisfied beyond a reasonable doubt that the circumstantial evidence was consistent with the accused's guilt and inconsistent with any other rational conclusion. That warning with respect to circumstantial evidence is no longer given, but a special warning is required for eyewitness evidence.

The prosecutors' report next identifies false confessions as a serious problem. Over one-quarter of the U.S. post-conviction exonerations based on DNA evidence involved false confessions. There are, of course, many reasons for false confessions, such as torture in the case of Maher Arar case, who confessed to being an al-Qaeda agent while being imprisoned in Syria. In Canada the principal motive would seem to be 'hope of advantage.' In the Lipski case I speculated on reasons why he might have falsely confessed to murder. Assuming that Old Man Rice's valet, Charlie Jones, made a false confession of murder, as seems likely, hope of advantage in pinning the ultimate blame on Patrick would have been the reason for his confession. Jones was never charged with any crime. The report recommends that the entire interview – not just the final statement – of a suspect in custody, be recorded in investigations involving offences of significant personal violence. Lamer also recommended in his Newfoundland report that all police interviews be videotaped or audiotaped in major crime investigations. This is a growing practice in Canada. Most police services in Ontario videotape statements taken from those suspected of committing serious crimes. The Toronto Police Service videotapes virtually every statement provided at police facilities by persons accused of committing criminal offences. The practice is also growing in the United Kingdom and the United States. Illinois was the first state to require by legislation that all custodial interrogations of persons accused of homicide be electronically recorded. Alaska and Minnesota had previously required such recordings if a court so ordered.

The federal/provincial committee also identified as a serious problem in-custody informants, which was an issue in a number of cases. This type of testimony was thoroughly discussed by Fred Kaufman in the Morin inquiry and by former Supreme Court of Canada justice Peter Cory in his report on the Thomas Sophonow case, another case of a wrongful conviction. It was also the subject of comment by Lamer in his recent report. Jail-house informants have much to gain from saying that the person in the next cell admitted his or her guilt. The committee's report contains forty-two recommendations on the topic, more than for any other problem area. One-fifth of the committee's report is devoted to the issue.

The report's central recommendation – that a committee composed of senior prosecutors unconnected with the case carefully review every proposed use of in-custody informers – follows the policy adopted in Ontario as a result of the Morin case. Shortly after Morin's acquittal, which had been conceded by the Crown because of newly discovered DNA evidence, the Ontario attorney general's department realized that it had to change some of its policies. One proposed new policy was to control the use of in-custody informers.

As it happened, I had been peripherally involved in helping to develop that policy. In the summer of 1997 I became a member of an advisory committee that assisted the attorney general's department in developing new policy in this and other areas. The committee, chaired by crown counsel Scott Hutchison, consisted of four senior managers of prosecutions and included former Court of Appeal justice David Griffiths, three top defence counsel, Bruce Durno, Michelle Fuerst, and Earl Levy, the Alberta deputy minister of justice, the director of public prosecutions in Nova Scotia, and me. The advisory committee commented on Crown-produced drafts, which were then presented to the Kaufman committee. The committee met again in 1999 – after Kaufman reported – to form what was called the Attorney General's Kaufman Report Implementation Advisory Committee.

The policy developed for in-custody informants requires that such evidence can only be introduced in legal proceedings where there are sufficient indicia of reliability and a compelling public interest for introducing the evidence. In addition, the evidence cannot be adduced without the approval of an In-Custody Informer Committee, consisting of senior Crown counsel not connected with the prosecution. Further, informers offering false testimony are to be prosecuted.

The Ontario Court of Appeal added more protection in 2002, holding in the *Baltrusaitis* murder case that in cases of in-custody informants a special warning by the trial judge is required, similar to the warning – called a *Vetrovec* warning – that is normally used when an accomplice gives evidence, where there is also a strong incentive to lie. A new trial was ordered. At the first trial, the jail-house informant probably had played an important role in the conviction, being the last witness called in the Crown's case. At the second trial, the witness was not used and the accused was acquitted.

Expert testimony also loomed large in the committee's report. There were serious problems with expert testimony in the Truscott case with respect to the time of death as determined by the contents of the deceased's stomach, and in the Morin case with respect to hair and fibre comparison evidence that was said to come from Morin. No doubt, the Ontario Court of Appeal will have much to say about the Truscott expert evidence. Expert testimony has recently been called into question in both Canada and England concerning testimony by doctors in cases of the alleged murder of children – pediatrician Sir Roy Meadow in England and pediatric pathologist Charles Smith in Canada. In April 2007 the Ontario government appointed Justice Stephen Goudge of the Court of Appeal to lead a public inquiry into the oversight of Ontario's pediatric forensic pathology system in the wake of a review by the chief coroner into the work of Dr Smith. Under the terms of reference, the report is expected within one year.

Expert evidence is being increasingly used. There was very little expert evidence in the Lipski case – evidence that would likely have been available today and would easily have determined if it was Lipski's semen in the deceased's body. By the time of the Patrick trial fifteen years later, scientific evidence was more widely used. But as we saw in the Patrick case, there are dangers with expert testimony. The market for experts can be cornered, as happened in the Patrick case with handwriting experts, and medical expert evidence may be inaccurate, as we saw in the evidence obtained after the Patrick trial that showed the experts at trial were wrong in determining that chloroform caused the irritation in the lungs, which led to the conclusion that Patrick was guilty of murder.

Finding the right solution to the problem of expert evidence is not easy. In Ontario, the police and the Crown rely on the Centre of Forensic Sciences. How can government-paid scientists maintain an arm's-length relationship from the Crown? Would it be better to give the courts a greater say in what experts can be called or would this be inconsistent with the adversary process?

This is not the place to analyse in detail the various issues that contribute to miscarriages of justice. That would require a book, one which my colleague Kent Roach is now writing. Apart from the above points, high up on most lists would be the adequacy of counsel in conducting the defence, which was identified as a problem in the Lipski case, where the trial was conducted by a commercial lawyer when one skilled in the criminal law was called for. The adequacy of disclosure is another important area, although less so today in the post-*Stinchcombe* era than when Marshall, Milgaard, and Morin were tried. *Stinchcombe* imposed a duty on the police and prosecutors to disclose all relevant evidence to the defence. Of course, there was even less disclosure in my three true-crime murder cases. One problem identified by Lamer in his report is the fact that many superior court judges in Canada do not have strong backgrounds in criminal law. He encouraged the federal minister of justice to be vigilant in identifying the need for criminal-law experience when judicial vacancies occur. 'There is a rich source which has largely gone untapped,' he observed, 'in the provincially appointed courts of this country which do exclusively criminal work.' Having a unified criminal court, as I discussed in an earlier chapter, would help solve this problem.

Being held in custody pending trial can also contribute to wrongful convictions because the accused is less able than he or she would have been if out on bail to gather evidence for the defence. Failure to go into the witness box should also be explored. Sometimes there are tactical reasons for an accused not giving evidence, such as fear that the accused will not make a good witness. That is understandable, but it is regrettable if the accused does not give evidence because he or she has a criminal record. The law should better protect the accused from having previous convictions used if the accused gives evidence. My solution (discussed in an earlier chapter) was, except in special circumstances, to prevent previous convictions from being put to an accused who testifies, but in exchange to permit the judge to comment adversely on the fact that the accused did not testify.

One issue that was not on the list of the federal/provincial recommendations is the problem of double jeopardy. It is often forgotten that Morin's conviction arose after he had been acquitted of murder and a new trial had been ordered by the Ontario Court of Appeal. This gave the Crown another crack at the accused. As stated in the earlier discussion of double jeopardy, I think that we have too lenient a test for sending a case back for a retrial after an appeal from an acquittal. The Supreme Court of Canada now permits a new trial if the verdict at the first trial might not have been the same if the error had not been made. In my view, the hurdle should be harder for the prosecution to get over, such as in cases where the error at the first trial was responsible for – and not just may have contributed to – the acquittal. It should also be noted that the conviction in the Sophonow case came after a hung jury and two further trials, where the convictions were overturned.

Over the years, trials have gotten longer and longer. The Lipski case lasted two days, while the three murder trials that I explored from 1882 were each of under one week's duration. The Shortis case of 1895, which lasted twenty-nine hearing days, was the longest criminal trial in Canada up to that time, and the Patrick case of 1902, which lasted two months, was then the longest in New York City. The Shortis and Patrick cases would be considered relatively short by today's standards, as would the Truscott and Fisher trials from the late 1950s and early 1960s, which lasted eight and ten days respectively.

Many murder cases today last for months, if not years. In his 2005 Sopinka lecture to the Criminal Lawyers Association, Ontario Court of Appeal justice Michael Moldaver – who, I should add, stood out in my criminal-law class in the early 1970s – devoted his talk to the long trial. 'I don't like what I am seeing. Criminal trials are spinning out of control.' 'More and more,' he went on to say, 'they seem to go on endlessly, often for months and sometimes years at a time. Sadly, they have taken on a life of their own and if they haven't already done so, they are fast becoming the masters of a system they are meant to serve.' More recently, Chief Justice Beverley McLachlin noted with concern: 'Not too many years ago, it was not uncommon for murder trials to be over in five to seven days. Now, they last five to seven months.'

The arguments against lengthy trials rightly focus on the use of valuable judicial, legal-aid, prosecutorial, police, court, and other resources, which are then not available for other needs. Such trials also have an effect on the public's and, particularly, the jury's view of the administration of justice. There is another important effect: a lengthy trial with many interruptions and adjournments will affect the jury's ability to get at the truth. Sometimes this results in wrongful convictions, but sometimes it results in wrongful acquittals, which should also be of concern. Jurors and, to a lesser extent, judges surely have difficulty in keeping evidence heard a year earlier in their heads. My own experience as a fact-finder when I conducted Ontario Human Rights cases in the 1970s and 1980s brought this fact home to me. I had at least fifteen of these cases over the years. Many for various reasons had to be adjourned for periods of time during the hearing, and I found that I usually had trouble clearly recalling the evidence I had heard weeks earlier and had to rely on my notes. In teaching I also found that last year's lecture notes were almost useless. One had to prepare most parts of the lectures almost from scratch.

In an earlier chapter I analysed the role that the Charter has played in encouraging lengthy proceedings. Something should be done to control these trials. Charter arguments go on for days, even weeks or months. In contrast, the Supreme Court of Canada on matters that have national significance gives each side one hour to make their arguments. Why can a counsel at trial go on for days presenting legal arguments? Should the trial judge have the right to set a limit on how much time may be taken in the examination and cross-examination of witnesses? Should the trial judge be able to impose reasonable time limits on arguments? Are appeal courts too quick to say that rights have been denied when debate has been curtailed? Should there be greater use of written arguments? Should there be techniques developed to discipline counsel through costs and other sanctions that do not threaten the integrity of the trial? Should legal aid only pay for a certain number of hours for presenting legal arguments, without approval of an increase in hours? Legal Aid Ontario takes the position in these major cases that if the judge is willing to hear the argument then legal aid should pay for it, although it places a limit on the time allowed for case preparation.

Some lengthy arguments, as discussed in the chapter on the Charter, are caused by the Supreme Court's decisions, which require the trial judge to take into account a large number of factors in making a decision on such issues as unreasonable delay, disclosure, and the introduction of hearsay evidence. One of the themes that I developed earlier is that it is usually better to use legislation than judge-made law to develop policy in the criminal-law area. Federal legislation or federal rules would normally draw clearer lines than the judges can, and would therefore simplify, and cut down the length of, arguments.

The issue of how to handle mega-trials has plagued the administration of justice throughout Canada. Almost all provinces have experienced them, and there is increasing concern about how to handle the issue. Yet it is not just the Air India and biker-gang type of cases that result in lengthy trials. 'The long criminal trials about which I am speaking,' Moldaver said, 'are your standard, ordinary, every-day murder trials, sexual assault trials, robbery trials, drug trials and the like.'

In 2005 I was asked by the Canadian Judicial Council (a body made up of all the federally appointed chief justices in Canada) to act as special counsel to examine a judge's conduct, which had been was called into question during a very long criminal trial. My task was to act as a fact-finder. I will not identify the judge or even the jurisdiction involved. It was a relatively simple murder case, but it consisted of 40 days of pre-trial hearings and 130 days for the trial, plus other proceedings, spread over a period of more than two years. The transcript that I read consisted of over 30 volumes – approximately 6000 pages – and that covered only about half of the proceedings. I concluded my report with a plea that the Council examine the issue of the mega-trial. I ended my 2005 report to the council by stating:

> In my opinion ... the Canadian Judicial Council should take this on as one of its initiatives. As you know, many of the cases that the CJC's Judicial Conduct Committee has had to deal with have arisen in the context of a mega-trial. How do other countries control the length of trials? What standards are possible? A strong federal body, such as the Canadian Judicial Council, is needed to establish national standards, just as the Council did with *Ethical Principles for Judges*. This is a national problem. I urge the CJC to examine the issue.

Since then, the Ontario Superior Court of Justice, through the Chief Justice's Advisory Committee on Criminal Trials, has studied the issue and made a number of sensible recommendations. Its 2006 report, entitled *New Approaches to Criminal Trials*, was prepared by six members of the Ontario Superior Court and four others representing the attorney general of Ontario, the federal Department of Justice, and the defence bar. The committee, chaired by criminal-law experts Justices David Watt and Bruce Durno, drew on a 1999 report by a committee established by the attorney general of Ontario that had also tried to make the system more efficient and had covered a wider range of matters than the later committee, such as bail, alternative dispositions, and ways of coordinating the various components of the criminal-justice system. I had played a significant role in researching and writing the 1999 report, *Report of the Criminal Justice Review Committee*, but as the 2006 report noted, those recommendations have been ignored by many judges and counsel.

The 2006 report concentrated on ways 'to make criminal trials more efficient, more focused, and shorter.' Detailed recommendations were set out on such matters as the pre-trial conference, trial scheduling and management, limiting legal-aid funding for legal arguments in court, and requiring more written proceedings. The committee concluded by stating:

> Through fundamental changes to the pre-trial system, enhanced require-
> ments regarding pre-trial application notices and supporting material,
> more effective trial management and case management, we are confident
> that the recommendations have the potential to shorten trials, without sac-
> rificing the interests of the accused or the prosecution ... However, [these
> changes] in themselves will not achieve the objectives. What is needed is a
> fundamental change in attitudes and habits on behalf of all participants in
> the criminal justice system, a system whose participants often do not
> readily embrace change.

This report is an important contribution to the problem, but I believe that the Canadian Judicial Council should heed my plea for a national study.

23

Sanctions and Rewards in the Legal System

In the spring of 1984 I was sounded out about the possibility of becoming involved in a program involving law and health that the recently created Canadian Institute for Advanced Research (CIAR) was considering establishing. (The acronym has recently been changed to CIFAR, with its forward-looking allusion.) Rob Prichard, who was then on sabbatical at Harvard and who would start as the dean of law on 1 July, sent me a document developed by the president of the CIAR, Fraser Mustard, a distinguished medical scientist and the former dean of the McMaster University medical school. CIAR, which had been formed as an independent think tank in 1982, links together experts from across Canada and outside the country to investigate various fields. Until 1984, its activities had been restricted to the sciences.

Mustard and his friend John Evans, the former president of the University of Toronto, who is never far from most creative new ideas in Canada, wanted to develop a program that looked at the determinants of poor health outcomes, in the case of medicine, and antisocial behaviour, in the case of law. 'A basic issue in health and law,' Mustard wrote in a background document, 'is the quality of the evidence concerning factors contributing to such things as antisocial behaviour, adverse health effects and the value of interventions to prevent or treat the problems.' The CIAR, he suggested, could 'provide a base for the development of a different intellectual focus in health and law from that which is dominant in many of our institutions today.' Both fields could use existing databases and create new ones. Perhaps the two areas of health and law, they thought, could be combined in one program.

Prichard's covering note said that he wanted to speak to me about the program, adding, 'It is not nearly as crazy as it first seems.' I assume that Mustard and Evans had asked Rob to sound me out. Fraser's view, according to historian Craig Brown's recent history of the CIAR, was that it was desirable to have a social scientist lead the development of the program. Academic lawyers, it is often forgotten, are really social scientists. I was not, however, ready to become involved, as I was trying to finish a number of projects, including my book on Valentine Shortis. I was, nevertheless, interested in the concept and wanted to be kept informed of developments.

As it turned out, the CIAR council did not want the health and law programs to be developed together. Law professor Michael Trebilcock, who was a member of council, argued that although the work proposed needed to be done, especially in law, 'the talent was thin on the ground and care should be taken not to lead [researchers] on a wild goose chase.' Prichard was then asked by Mustard to work with John Hagan, a productive sociologist who had been cross-appointed to the faculty of law, to set up a working group of Canadian professors and law deans to explore the feasibility of creating a program in Law and Society. The timing was opportune within the scholarly legal community because the concept of more empirical interdisciplinary work had been promoted in Harry Arthurs's influential 1983 report Law and Learning, sponsored by the Social Sciences and Humanities Research Council.

I became a member of the law-and-society working group, and over the next nine months I participated fully in its activities, which consisted of a large number of meetings and a symposium at which two Yale Law School professors, George Priest and Stanton Wheeler, among others, presented ideas. In February 1985 Prichard, Hagan, and I presented an interim report to the CIAR's research council, recommending that a research program in sanctions and rewards be established. Rob wanted me to be involved in the program and wanted to make sure that what the task force was proposing had my support. I played a major role in helping to develop the proposal and thought that the area was rich with possibilities. Justice Allen Linden, the president of the Law Reform Commission of Canada, wrote to Prichard: 'The theme of Sanctions and Rewards is a brilliant unifying concept which I agree can tie together many different types of studies in different fields.' The final report was presented to the CIAR council in June 1985.

The arguments in favour of studying sanctions and rewards were well presented:

> After a good deal of discussion, debate and consideration, we concluded that the subject of Sanctions and Rewards could provide the necessary organizing principle around which the work could proceed. A central issue of concern to virtually all areas of law is how to influence behaviour and the role that different legal instruments can play. Whether the instrument is civil liability, criminal liability, bureaucratic, administrative and regulatory justice, tax and subsidy schemes, moral suasion or any other, the constant and common issue is how we can effectively influence behaviour. The topic of Sanctions and Rewards provides unity and focus on the one hand but embraces many contexts and issues since it is relevant to almost all settings in which law is involved with conduct, behavior and social change.

The report was adopted by the council, including its recommendation that an implementation group be struck to proceed further with investigations of possible research into these areas of law. Specific projects within the program were not identified because, as the report stated: 'It is critically important to prefer people over particular projects.'

Mustard then asked me if I would head the project. My notes of the meeting stated simply: 'They want me to do it and I can set my own agenda, I think.' The formal letter asked me 'to join the Canadian Institute for Advanced Research as an Associate with responsibility for developing the Institute's program in "Sanctions and Rewards"' for the coming academic year and then to serve as a senior fellow for a period of three years, during which time I would be responsible for implementation of the first stage of the program.

I immersed myself in the project. In early September 1985, I started the first of twenty-nine spiral binders containing ideas and notes on the literature about the subject. This is the technique I had used twenty-five years earlier when I wrote *Double Jeopardy*, and the one I continued to use for most of my later projects. As previously discussed, the binders could be photocopied, cut up, and distributed to appropriate files. Again, as was often the case, the first entry in the first binder – relating to injunctions and damages – resulted from a conversation over lunch with one of the faculty's greatest repositories of knowledge, Stephen Waddams, who can penetrate through the haze and shed light on almost any legal subject involving either public or private law.

It was a great project. In an early memo to Mustard I wrote: 'As you could, no doubt, tell from our discussion the other day, I am excited by the possibilities that are emerging as I talk to people and study the literature on the topic. I think we can make a substantial contribution to one of the central issues in law – why are laws obeyed and what are the best techniques for gaining compliance with the law.'

The project would proceed in three stages. In the first stage, a symposium would be held at which scholars from a variety of disciplines would prepare papers investigating the subject of sanctions and rewards from the perspectives of their own particular disciplines. In stage two, teams of scholars who would have attended the earlier symposium would tackle individual projects. The third stage would be a major project related to a single area, perhaps road traffic, under a general title such as 'The Automobile in Society.'

Traffic safety was an ideal project, I wrote in my memo to Mustard, because it allowed us to study both civil and criminal liability – the central components of present techniques of enforcement. The field was also good because there was a substantial amount of data on accidents available through insurance companies, departments of highways, special foundations and groups concerned with accidents. The fact that much thought had already been given to this area meant that we could test some tentative hypotheses. We could, for example, examine the interrelationship between the degree of enforcement, the quickness of intervention, and the penalties imposed. I also liked the subject area because comparative studies are easier with a standard product such as an automobile. Finally, I noted, the subject was obviously important in itself because of the enormous personal, social, and economic costs of accidents. Traffic safety was then, and continues to be, a serious issue. Throughout the world, according to a 2004 World Health Organization report, traffic accidents are the second leading cause of death for persons aged five to twenty-nine. In Canada, death by traffic accidents is more than five times the murder rate.

Stage one came close to being what we had hoped. The symposium, which was held in May 1986 at the Millcroft Inn in Alton, Ontario, an hour's drive northwest of Toronto, worked well. We gained insights into strategies and approaches that would assist us in the further stages of the program. We started with a paper by historian John Beattie, who showed that the criminal law has typically worked to control crime and social disorder by means of sanctions rather than rewards. This raised the issue of whether rewards should be more widely used. If sanctions are used, how severe should they be? Is certainty of punishment more effective than fear of a more severe punishment which may not be applied? Sociologist H. Laurence Ross examined the 'deterrence hypothesis' – that is, that the effectiveness of a threat of punishment is a function of its severity, certainty, and swiftness. He concluded that 'a number of studies in widely different contexts seem to coalesce on support for the deterrent effect of measures aimed at increasing the certainty of punishment, though mainly in the short run, and on rejection of the deterrent effect of measures aimed at increasing the severity of punishment.'

Economist Philip Cook had also studied the concept of deterrence. As he stated in his paper, 'belief in the efficacy of the deterrence mechanism comes naturally to economists, whose theoretical perspective presupposes that observed behaviour is the consequence of well-informed, rational choice.' Even if all persons do not act rationally, he went on to say, this does not mean that deterrence does not work for others. Cook agreed with Ross about the importance of certainty. Research, he noted, shows that a stated chance of a $1000 fine is more of a deterrent than half the stated chance of a $2000 fine. Cook also pointed to evidence suggesting that when one crime is successfully deterred, another substitute crime may see a corresponding increase, and discussed the geographic displacement of crime in response to changes in enforcement patterns. Introducing exact-fare collection machines on buses, for example, may increase the robbery risk at convenience stores. He also raised the issue of decreasing opportunities, such as by introducing more stringent regulations requiring identification numbers for auto parts, and rules making it an infraction to leave a parked vehicle unlocked.

Law scholar Robert Rabin, who explored the deterrent effect of civil liability on conduct, had serious concerns about the role of deterrence in the tort system. Insurance blunts the impact of civil liability. Greater attention should therefore be paid, he concluded, to techniques that create and maintain an incentive to take care, such as co-insurance, deductible amounts, and the use of experience ratings in setting premiums.

These are just four of the ten provocative papers presented at the symposium. Criminologist Frank Zimring made a plea for empirical research using what he called 'the field experiment,' wherein one studies changes in specific law enforcement or punishment before and after a particular policy shift occurs. A child psychologist, Joan Grusec, discussed child behaviour, criticizing B.F. Skinner's conclusion that positive reinforcement is better than punishment. Her own research showed that 'moderate levels of punishment, administered by a humane and caring agent' so that the relationship between cause and effect is clear, are just as effective as positive reinforcement. Being too harsh, however, will defeat the objective of having the individual internalize the rule and accept it as his or her own.

Organizational psychologist Hugh Arnold observed, in contrast, that 'there is an emerging consensus that the effects of punishment on performance are not as strong as the influences of reward.' The use of punishment in an organization, he pointed out, 'has a tendency to create resentment, anger, and hard feelings toward the punishing agent and the organization in general.' Anthropologist Pierre Maranda also encouraged the use of rewards. Our own legal system, he observed, is characterized by 'rigid sets of laws that are mostly repressive; that of other, simpler societies, by flexibility and fluid adaptation emphasizing rewards.' The trouble with rewards, he stated, is that it requires a greater effort to achieve compliance through rewards than through sanctions: 'The threshold of fear is relatively low, that of seduction much higher.'

Political scientist Carolyn Tuohy provided language that categorizes three basic compliance mechanisms: the command mechanism, such as the criminal law; the exchange mechanism, such as market exchanges and the negotiating table; and the persuasion mechanism, such as the education system. Similarly, lawyer Christopher Stone gave us language to categorize compliance variables, identifying four different control strategies: harm-based liability rules, penalties, standards, and rewards. Stone also raised a number of important issues concerning the target of the various control strategies. Should it be the agent who actually causes the harm, or the enterprise, or both? Should the law target only part of an enterprise, such as a corporate division or a plant? Should advisers such as auditors and lawyers be liable for their clients' wrongdoing?

The program was off to a good start. We had a list of questions for our further research on sanctions and rewards. As I stated in the preface to the volume, *Sanctions and Rewards in the Legal System: A Multidis-*

ciplinary Approach (published by the University of Toronto Press in 1989):

> A number of themes run through many of the papers: Does deterrence actually work in the criminal and civil areas? Are rewards more effective than sanctions? Is internalization of values the best technique for gaining compliance? Will certainty of penalty have a greater deterrent effect than severity of penalty? Will enforcement displace one type of crime for another? What target or targets should enforcement be aimed at? Is it better to concentrate on 'designing out' undesirable conduct?

The second stage of the project involved empirical studies of specific subjects, covering a range of legal areas. We tried to involve a lawyer and a social scientist in each project, although we were not always successful in doing so. We also met collectively on several occasions so that each project would profit from the experience of the others. Although our original intention was to leave the traffic-safety study until the third stage, we started to tackle it as one of the specific studies. *Regulating Traffic Safety*, authored by Michael Trebilcock, Kent Roach, and myself, was published by the University of Toronto Press in 1990 and was also included as one of the seven case studies published at the same time by the Press in *Securing Compliance: Seven Case Studies*.

The subjects of the studies ranged from securities regulation and prostitution to environmental protection and family violence. Also included were studies of compliance with tax laws and of workplace safety and, as stated above, an extended analysis of techniques for regulating traffic safety.

There is often more than one technique used for controlling the same conduct. The first chapter of *Securing Compliance* by legal historian John McLaren and criminologist John Lowman, which studied prostitution in three major cities in Canada between 1892 and 1920, showed a wide diversity of approaches, sometimes operating at the same time in different jurisdictions. The authors identified four 'discourses': the 'moral' discourse, which was responsible for the introduction of the added punishment of whipping as a possible penalty for a second conviction for procuring; a 'public order' discourse, which served as an all-purpose control device for the police to facilitate general ordering of the streets, and in the process, to control other disreputable groups besides prostitutes; a 'pragmatic tolerance' discourse, whereby prostitutes were unofficially confined to and left undisturbed in 'red light' districts; and a 'public health' discourse to minimize the public-health risks associated with the sex trade. A further approach is a system of official licensing, which today is increasingly being taken more seriously as a policy option because of the deaths of a great number of prostitutes in Vancouver and the disappearance of a large number of prostitutes in Edmonton.

Different compliance techniques can be adopted by different agencies and even by the same agency at different times and in different regions. In their study of the regulation of financial markets in Ontario in the 1980s, Philip Stenning and his colleagues from the Centre of Criminology showed that the Ontario Securities Commission concentrated on the sanctioning model, whereas the Toronto Stock Exchange preferred what the authors call 'behavioural ordering,' which can be achieved through any number of strategies, including sanctions, threats, rewards, incentives, persuasion, and the design of facilities. Although the two approaches have tended to merge in the two institutions in recent years, their analysis still holds true. From my perspective as a director for the past few years of a self-regulatory organization, the Mutual Fund Dealers' Association of Canada, I observe that its enforcement group looks at prosecution – criminal or administrative – as a last resort and uses such techniques as licensing, disclosure, inspection, and education to gain compliance with the law.

Is it better to use criminal or administrative proceedings? In a paper on the activities of two administrative agencies in British Columbia, legal scholars Richard Brown and Murray Rankin concluded that . administrative penalties are more effective than criminal sanctions. In their study, they compare the administrative penalties used by the Workers' Compensation Board of British Columbia with the criminal penalties used by the Waste Management Branch. Administrative penalties, they state, have a number of significant advantages for regulators: . 'The administrative process responds to risk rather than to harm, does not unduly stigmatize offenders who are thought not to warrant moral opprobrium, applies a standard of absolute as opposed to strict liability in at least some cases, entails minimal operating costs, and imposes monetary penalties large enough to have a reasonable prospect of deterring offenders.' Criminal prosecutions scored poorly on all these counts. The authors argued that regulators should be given a choice between using administrative and criminal sanctions on a case-by-case basis.

Some agencies use criminal proceedings very sparingly. Lawyer Neil Brooks and psychologist Anthony Doob looked at tax evasion and showed that the Department of National Revenue – now called the Canada Revenue Agency – for the most part relies on behavioural ordering rather than prosecutions. In the 1980s, there were fewer than three hundred prosecutions a year for tax evasion in each of Canada and England. The prosecuting authorities select clear-cut cases to prosecute and they publicize subsequent convictions. By prosecuting clear cases, the authorities are more or less assured that other taxpayers will not sympathize with the wrong-doers, and thus the 'dramatization of the moral notions of the community,' to use Thurman Arnold's phrase, will be more starkly presented. For the most part, the Canada Revenue Agency relies on behavioural ordering, such as matching income with disclosure, audits, and reassessments. The low number of prosecutions also conceals the fact that extensive cheating on taxes goes on in society, which, if better known, might encourage other taxpayers to cheat because 'everyone is doing it.' The low number of prosecutions can be contrasted with the very high number of prosecutions in the enforcement of road traffic laws, discussed in a later section of this chapter. What does the department of national revenue know that the police do not?

Other authors showed the complexity of the sanctioning process. Economist and lawyer Donald Dewees examined why the government of Ontario was successful in reducing mercury discharge from chloralkali plants, but far less successful in limiting sulphur dioxide discharges (which cause acid rain). In part, this was because mercury pollution could more easily be traced to its source, and so the possibility of significant lawsuits was a serious threat. Moreover, there was technology available at a moderate cost to control mercury pollution, unlike what was then available for sulphur dioxide. Dewees's overall conclusion was that where regulation is apparently successful it 'does not exist in a vacuum,' and 'the factors that make regulation successful also yield other pressures, such as tort liability and public opinion, leading toward the same outcome.' Sociologists John Hagan and William McCarthy and legal scholar Carol Rogerson examined family violence from a perspective that showed the breadth and complexity of the sanctioning process. They show a link between child abuse, homelessness, and juvenile delinquency. The law, they observed, punishes the delinquent and not the child abuser. Their conclusion is that 'an effective, long-term solution to family violence may lie in the social transformation of family structure,' a transformation that the use of criminal penalties cannot bring about.

Michael Trebilcock and I worked on the traffic-safety study. I had always wanted to work with Michael, an expert on law and economics, who has one of the most imaginative minds at the faculty of law. Yale law professor George Priest, who had done work on civil liability for accidents, had agreed to work with us on the project, but as it turned out was not able to participate. Kent Roach was our research assistant during the summer of 1986 after his second year of law school, and also did a directed research project for me on drunk driving during his third year. His involvement during this period and later when he joined the faculty was so helpful that we made him a co-author. The traffic study was to be one of the seven studies, but it was also designed to allow us to do further empirical work on the next stage of the project.

It turned out that there never was a further stage of the sanctions-and-rewards project for reasons I will convey in the next chapter. This is yet another example of a project – like the study of the machinery of law reform – that was never completed in the way that I had intended. But this is par for the course. I recall a conversation I had in Cambridge with my supervisor, Glanville Williams, who was one of the most productive legal scholars that the United Kingdom has ever produced. I could not believe it when he pointed to his filing cabinets and said that most of the space was devoted to projects that had not been completed.

In our study, *Regulating Traffic Safety*, we thoroughly reviewed the literature on the various techniques that have been or could be applied to promote safety. We looked at prosecutions, civil liability and insurance, licensing, rewards, and the control of opportunities. As one knowledgeable reviewer stated: 'This book challenges all the truisms about traffic safety. It presents a no-nonsense scholarly appraisal of all the issues surrounding traffic safety regulation, based on best available evidence.'

Most of the effort to control accidents in the past has concentrated on changing driver behaviour, particularly through the use of surveillance and prosecution. The prevalence of deterrence methods can in part be explained by the introduction of the automobile just as methods of policing were shifting emphasis from inspection and compliance to apprehension and the 'deterrence model of policing.' There are today well over a million convictions a year in Ontario for violations of traffic laws. The reader will recall that there are only about three hundred prosecutions each year for tax avoidance. Our overall impression was that 'we have concentrated and continue to concentrate our resources too heavily on changing driver behaviour' and that 'switching some of the resources now devoted to policing and prosecutions to improving car and road design and to curtailing activity levels of high-risk classes of drivers would ... improve road safety.'

Before the 1960s, almost all traffic safety regulation had been directed at influencing the behaviour of the driver and preventing crashes. Starting in the late 1950s, traffic safety experts and eventually policy-makers began to realize that reducing the frequency of crashes and the damage sustained when they occurred – which is the primary objective of traffic safety laws – could be attained by other forms of environmental regulation, such as through car and highway design. American crusader Ralph Nader played a major role in this shift.

Prosecutions take up a large proportion of court resources. Some estimates suggest that drinking-and-driving related offences take up over one-third of court time. A British study showed that road traffic offences occupied 50 to 70 per cent of magistrates' court time. As with the tax system, we should be somewhat more selective in prosecuting offenders. We are likely to have fewer accidents and save more lives if some of the resources now used in prosecutions were devoted, for example, to more frequently repainting the white lines on highways and adding more warning devices that alert the driver that he or she is about to go off the road. As with the tax system, we should use more administrative penalties. The alcohol ignition-interlock device could, for example, probably be imposed through a provincial administrative hearing – without a criminal prosecution. Why not force drivers who are found with a blood-alcohol reading of .05 to instal an ignition-interlock device? Those are the persons who could easily slip into the group that drives with an alcohol blood content over .08. Although the legal limit in Canada is .08, the police can now prevent a person from continuing to drive if there is a reading of .05. Research shows that risk of a crash starts to rise significantly at about .05, the most common legal limit in many other high-income countries.

What does it feel like to be over the legal limit? In order to find out, we conducted an experiment at the law school one afternoon during the summer of 1988. The faculty and summer research assistants were invited to a wine and cheese reception late in the afternoon – a typical law-school event following a visiting speaker's address. We had cleared the 'experiment' with the office of research administration at the University. Attendees would keep track of the number of drinks they had and when a person thought that they were over the limit he or she would leave the room and take a breathalyzer test from an Ontario Provincial Police officer in the next room. After several glasses of wine,

I started feeling woozy. As I was one of the hosts, I stuck around longer than I should have. When I left, I had never felt so intoxicated in my life. After taking the breathalyzer test, I went directly to the men's washroom, was sick to my stomach, and then took a taxi home. The breathalyzer reading showed that I was just about at the legal limit. Some of my colleagues, I should add, did not show the same drastic effects of a similar consumption of wine. The experiment confirmed my view that we should be tougher on drinking and driving and should lower the legal limit.

Our study also questioned the current enforcement of speed limits. Is it speed that is a problem or the variation of speed? Who creates the problem: the person keeping up with traffic or the person weaving in and out of traffic above the speed of the normal flow? Police now pick off the easy cases of drivers going above the limit on clear stretches of highway because it is easier to clock their speed and signal them to pull over than it is with the person weaving in and out of traffic. Would it be better to frame the law such that it is an offence to drive in an unsafe manner in the light of the traffic and road conditions? California permits a defence if the speed was 'reasonable or prudent, having due regard for weather, visibility, the traffic,' and so on.

We discovered in our traffic-safety study that the law has much to learn from the epidemiologists who widen their investigations to include more than the conduct of the driver. The so-called Haddon matrix, named after William Haddon, a respected epidemiologist in the field of traffic safety, is widely used in traffic studies. The matrix provides grids that distinguish human, vehicle, and environmental factors in accidents and breaks down accidents temporally into pre-crash, crash, and post-crash phases for analysing potential interventions. This new injury-control perspective challenged traditional legal interventions based on concepts of fault, negligence, and individual responsibility. A similar approach to controlling and reducing harm through means other than the criminal process can be used in other areas, from securities regulation to hard drugs and from military misconduct to terrorism. Kent Roach recently applied the analysis in his book on terrorism, *September 11: Consequences for Canada*. Such an approach should be at the forefront in the discussion of policy operations to control undesirable consequences in all fields.

This was probably the most important conclusion to our study, that is, that there are often better techniques for controlling undesirable conduct than the use of the criminal process. The British gas-suicide study is probably the best example of the effective use of other techniques for designing out unwanted conduct. In 1963, suicide by domestic gas accounted for over 40 per cent of suicides in England. My wife and I were in England in 1960–1 and again in 1963 and knew how careful we had to be to make sure that the gas was turned off. The lethal quality of the gas was, however, almost completely eliminated between 1963 and 1975, and the annual number of suicides from all causes in England declined dramatically, at a time when suicides continued to increase in most other European countries.

There would, however, likely be some adjustment, compensation, or displacement effect with any improvement in traffic safety or in other areas. Cars with steering locks that make them difficult to steal may well encourage an increase in the theft of older cars without such locks. The use of specially designed tires for use in winter conditions might dispose persons to drive faster than they otherwise would. The question is whether there is a positive safety benefit or whether, as some psychologists have argued, the benefit is lost by what is called 'risk homeostasis.' We concluded in our study that the compensation did not come close to removing the advantage of the safety feature in question. With safety belts, for example, we concluded that it is unlikely that drivers will significantly increase their driving risks just because they are belted. Drivers do not want to experience an accident, even if it is less severe than it might be without the driver being belted.

The study also examined the use of civil liability, which can be helpful – directly or by increased insurance rates – in controlling accidents, both by reducing exposure levels and by creating incentives to take care. Licensing techniques were also an important aspect of controlling conduct by reducing driving by high-risk drivers. Inexperienced drivers, we advocated, could be subject to greater restrictions on the use of alcohol than other drivers, and speed limits for such drivers, to take another example, could be at the lower range of reasonable driving speeds. Since publishing our study, there has been an increased use of licensing in most countries, with graduated licensing for inexperienced drivers.

We also advocated greater use of rewards than at present. Many institutions, we pointed out, including religious bodies, prisons, universities, and businesses, rely more on rewards than sanctions. This approach could be expanded to other areas. In addition to rewarding good drivers through the insurance system, we could, for example, give free licence renewals, or lottery tickets with the chance of substantial prizes, to drivers who do not have accidents or traffic tickets during the previous year. The use of small incentives has been used in some jurisdictions to encourage the wearing of seat belts.

We were intrigued by a reward system then being used by the Toronto Transit Commission (TTC), which at the time had won the North American transit safety award for eighteen of the past twenty-one years. Its system of rewards for safe driving was likely part of the reason for the remarkable record. The TTC ran a program within each of its then ten divisions called 'Safety Bingo.' Each driver had a regular bingo card and every day a new bingo number was drawn. The drivers started filling up their cards. The first driver within the division to get a line completed got a small token prize. Completing two lines resulted in a better prize, such as a flashlight; completing three lines could get the person something like a toaster, and so on. Now comes the critical point. One accident by a driver that is that driver's fault and causes the driver to be off work for more than one day wipes out not only that person's bingo card but all the other bingo cards in the division. Everyone must start the game again with a clean card. So the person with the accident is letting down perhaps three hundred other drivers, many of whom might have been close to winning a prize.

Such a scheme is used with various modifications by other companies. It gives persons a reason for thinking about safety while they are driving. Moreover, peer pressure adds an incentive to be careful. It may be that the modesty of the actual reward enhances the behavioural effect of the reward program. As Queen's University psychologist Gerry Wilde, who assisted us with our work, stated: 'If drivers can be induced to engage – even temporarily – in new behaviour in order to earn an incentive, their attitudes and subsequent behaviour will change accordingly. The effects of such temporary commitments will be larger as the incentive or external justification offered is smaller.'

There were a large number of important issues that we could explore in the next phase of the sanctions-and-rewards project. The two books that we published received respectable reviews in the scholarly journals, although I was personally disappointed that the traffic study did not have more of an impact in the scholarly literature. I presented a number of papers on sanctions and rewards and the traffic study, including at the U of T's Centre for Health Promotion and at a British Columbia conference on traffic safety.

During this initial period, I was putting together a paper tying

together some of the ideas. The paper – one more that remains in my filing cabinet or has been transferred to the archives – was a thirty-page
analysis entitled 'View from the TeaMasters: An Introduction to Sanctions, Rewards and Other Techniques for Achieving Compliance with
the Law.'

As I discussed in the chapter on my law-student days, I like working
in restaurants to study or develop ideas. I find that background noise
helps one concentrate on one's work. For many years, I would prepare
my two o'clock criminal-law class in the Jamie Kennedy restaurant at
the Royal Ontario Museum, and lately I prepared my Woodsworth
criminal-justice course and my two-week intensive course relating to
the material in this book at the Intercontinental Hotel on Bloor Street.
The back outside room at Grano Restaurant on Yonge Street is also an
excellent location during nice weather.

In the 1980s I would often work in a restaurant at the north-west
corner of Yonge and Davisville, close to where I live. It is now a Tim
Horton's, but was then called 'The TeaMasters.' While sitting in the restaurant I got the idea of analysing sanctions and rewards from what I
could observe outside the window. From that vantage point I could see
the whole world of sanctions and rewards, with a bank across the road
that enabled me to discuss controlling fraud and robberies, a restaurant
that served liquor that brought in the question of drunkenness and
impaired driving and health concerns, and the TTC station across the
road and its handling of workers' compensation, accidents, destruction
of property, and cheating on fares, as well as its rewards program.
There was also a busy intersection with all the problems for drivers of
obeying signals and avoiding pedestrians, and the important matter of
left- and right-hand turns. And on and on. I gave a number of presen-
tations of the paper at the faculty and elsewhere, but, unfortunately
never completed it for publication. It would, I thought, eventually fit
into a later stage of the sanctions-and-rewards project – if we ever
reached that stage.

24

Borderline Justice and Other Studies of Law and Society

Plans for the next stage of the sanctions-and-rewards project, meant to build on stage two, were well under way. One of the projects would be an expanded inter-disciplinary and empirical study of traffic safety that would take us beyond the descriptive study that we had published. I had been meeting individually and collectively with Ezra Hauer, a traffic-safety specialist in the faculty of engineering at the University of Toronto, Herb Simpson, the head of the Traffic Injuries Research Foundation in Ottawa, Gerry Wilde, a psychologist from Queen's University, and my brother-in-law, Barry Pless, a pediatrician and epidemiologist with an interest in accidents, from McGill.

Michael Trebilcock had decided that he wanted to work on a project on medical malpractice in stage three. We also wanted Tony Doob and Neil Brooks to continue their work on the tax system, as well as have John Hagan and Carol Rogerson continue their study of domestic violence. John Hagan was to join me as a fellow of the Canadian Institute for Advanced Research (CIAR). Another planned project would have involved two Quebec scholars from the University of Montreal, Jean-Paul Brodeur and Hélène Dumont, to work on police deviance, but they had to withdraw because each had new administrative responsibilities. And there were other persons and projects that we were considering.

One problem with moving forward, however, was that some members of the CIAR's research council felt that the sanctions-and-rewards project was too narrow, a view that was apparently shared by the new advisory committee of the law program, chaired by Principal David Johnston of McGill. It seemed to me then, and seems to me now, that sanctions and rewards was as broad a topic as any that could be successfully undertaken. According to Craig Brown's history of the CIAR, the advisory committee recommended to the research council that 'the program's perspective and approach be broadened to address in depth how law worked in society and how the law interacted with other social controls.' Moreover, the CIAR wanted to bring in more Quebec scholars interested in law and society. The Quebec thrust would likely have been supported by David Johnston and by other Quebec-based members of the committee, such as sociologist Guy Rocher and law dean François Chevrette of the University of Montreal.

I recall that there was considerable resistance to the appointment of Michael Trebilcock as a fellow until after some Quebec scholars had been appointed. The CIAR was of the view – and it was hard to disagree – that the program was too much Toronto-based, with John Hagan and me as full fellows, and with Trebilcock a natural to join us in the future.

Rod Macdonald, the dean of law at McGill, suggested a comparative project involving commercial law. A Quebec-based node of the law project was then established to accompany the sanctions-and-rewards projects. Macdonald and legal scholar Jean-Guy Belley of Laval organized the Quebec-based network and later became fellows of the law-and-society program.

One way or another, the main thrust of the program gravitated towards Quebec. It was a very frustrating period for me as director. Not only was the sanctions-and-rewards program akin to herding cats (legal academics at the time were not used to cooperative projects), but the growth and coordination of a Quebec-based thrust to the program – one which I had some difficulty understanding – made the law program much like nailing jelly to the wall. To add to the problems, the future funding of the law program was uncertain.

Craig Brown notes in his history of the CIAR that I told Fraser Mustard that the program was becoming too 'diffuse.' All in all, I concluded that it would be better if Rod Macdonald became the director of the program after my three-year term was completed at the end of June 1989. The new program would be called Law and Society, a name that was later changed to Law in Society, and still later to Law and the

Determinants of Social Order. I would, however, remain a fellow of the program and continue my work on sanctions and rewards.

I have to take some blame for letting the program slip out of my grasp. Not only was I feeling frustrated by pressures coming from many sides, but I became deeply involved with another project. Towards the end of 1986, the Ontario Department of Financial Institutions asked me if I would chair a task force on inflation protection for employment pension plans. The topic was an important and difficult one. The government wanted to do something about the large surpluses in pension plans, but could not decide on a policy that would satisfy both labour and management, each of whom claimed that the surplus was rightfully theirs. Hence the creation of a task force. The issue had been in the public arena for some time because inflation was high (in double digits in the early 1980s) and pensioners without inflation protection – that is, most pensioners in the private sector – were being hurt. At the same time, pension funds had large surpluses, which many companies were claiming as their own – Conrad Black's use of the surplus in the Dominion Stores plan comes to mind – or which at least, they claimed, allowed companies to take 'pension holidays,' that is, not contribute anything to the fund. Employers and employees fought court battles over who owned the surpluses, and the Ontario government subsequently placed a moratorium on withdrawals by employers pending the task-force report.

I did not know much about pensions, although I had taken a couple of courses in actuarial science as an undergraduate. I do not believe, however, that the minister of financial institutions, Monte Kwinter, or the cabinet knew that I had ever studied actuarial science. I recall Ian Scott, the attorney general and an old friend, telling me some time later that when the matter came up in cabinet and someone asked, 'What does Friedland know about pensions?' Scott said, 'Nothing, but he'll have a good one at the end of his work on the task force.'

I worked out a satisfactory arrangement with Fraser Mustard. The pension task force could not wait and I wanted to do it, having never previously chaired a major committee. The task force worked hard for over a year. Its other members, Syd Jackson, the chair and former president of Manulife, and Cliff Pilkey, the former head of the Ontario Federation of Labour, had strong opinions on the issues, particularly Cliff. We worked well together, although in the end Cliff followed the official union position that all the money belonged to the workers. The majority report reached what I believed was a reasonable compromise position. The company could only claim the funds as their own if they gave all *future* retired workers inflation protection that amounted to 75 per cent of the cost-of-living increase, based on the consumer price index (CPI), minus 1 per cent, a carefully worked-out formula. We encouraged companies to grant increases to retirees through some special rules, but did not make it mandatory. Cliff, however, would have applied the formula retrospectively. The solution of the majority owed something to the sanctions-and-rewards study. It offered the companies a reward if they offered a reasonable amount of inflation protection.

It was a busy year. In early 1987 the Institute of Policy Analysis at the University of Toronto organized a one-day workshop for the pensions task force in which experts discussed the various issues. With the assistance of our director of research, David Conklin, we commissioned a large number of research projects. The task force met frequently during the year at our offices on Bloor Street. (The rubber plant from my office there is still in my law-school office. Should I have given it back to Kwinter?) We also established, and met on a number of occasions with, a research advisory committee consisting of several pension experts: Shiraz Bharmal, John Ilkiw, Don Lee, Jim Pesando, David Short, and Michael Wolfson, some of whom also did research papers for us. In addition, over the summer of 1987 we had two first-rate law students, Jeff Trossman from the U of T, now at Blakes, and Dave Lametti from McGill, now teaching there.

I gave a number of talks during our deliberations, such as a presentation to a large conference on pensions and, after our report had been released, to the Canadian Institute of Actuaries and to the American Bar Association, which was meeting in Toronto during the summer of 1988. We requested and received submissions from a great number of organizations, firms, and individuals, many of whom presented their views at our public hearings. The progress of our work was closely followed by the press, particularly the financial press. I have one editorial cartoon on the wall of my office showing me trying to steer the boat with Jackson and Pilkey rowing in opposite directions. The task force met for three days in December 1987 at Westover Inn in St Mary's, Ontario, to try to finalize our ideas.

We produced a three-hundred-page report as well as three volumes of research papers, which were published by the government in English and French. I was proud of what we had accomplished – on time and within budget. The government appeared to be impressed with the report and was interested in implementing our recommendations. Murray Elston, the minister of financial institutions, called it a 'very thorough and well-reasoned report.' A government consultation paper proposing changes in the legislation was issued in 1989, but in the end a formal bill was not introduced. Many of the ideas were, however, brought into effect through the collective-bargaining process, and the report probably had some influence on future court cases dealing with surpluses in pension plans.

Part of the reason that the impetus for change was lost was that the economy was starting to lose steam – the market tumbled tumultuously one Friday in October 1987 during our deliberations – and employers said that any increased costs would jeopardize jobs and might cause the abandonment of defined benefit plans. Moreover, inflation was starting to ease, which reduced the need for change. Inflation during the 1990s was very low, typically between 1 and 3 per cent per year. In fact, that would have been a good time to implement the report because employers would not have strongly resisted the change if it was clear that they could have the surplus after providing for inflation. It is now unlikely that anything will be done in the near future. No one is worried about the problem today. If, however, inflation ever reaches high levels again, people will regret that the report was not implemented when inflation was low. In the meantime, the courts continue to struggle to resolve the problem of who owns pension surpluses. This is another case – as with the development of the criminal law – where legislation would have been a better solution, but the issue was controversial and so was largely left to the courts.

In fact, the formula – 75 per cent of the CPI minus 1 per cent – was later used by Bob Rae's NDP government in Ontario in the early 1990s to decrease payment for certain public programs where less than full inflation protection was thought to be desirable. It was referred to as the 'Friedland formula,' not quite the legacy that I had hoped for.

The law-and-society program continued to struggle under Rod Macdonald's direction. Mustard reported to the CIAR's research council in late 1989, according to Craig Brown's history, that Macdonald was still working on 'defining the intellectual framework,' and that the 'program is struggling.' Harry Arthurs took over from David Johnston as chair of the advisory committee in the summer of 1990 and Arthurs and Macdonald developed two foci for the program. One was the 'the concept of normativity as involving both instrumental and symbolic elements' and the second was 'the notion of legal pluralism.' I must say that I was sceptical about whether these foci could make any significant breakthroughs within the CIAR program. Moreover, I had trouble understanding the meaning of the word 'normative.' Does it refer to what 'is' or what 'ought to be'? In some disciplines it means 'is,' and in others 'ought.' On the first page of one document prepared by Rod he used the words 'normativity,' 'normative,' or 'norm' twenty-five times. Whenever I hear these words today – and one hears them constantly – I have to stop and ask myself what they mean or what they add to a statement. But this is obviously my problem, because most legal academics use the word normative at least once in every talk. One clue that I might be on the right track, however, is that my Microsoft spell-check program has just noted that the word 'normativity' is unknown to it. One could, perhaps, equally criticize my use of the word 'sanction' in the sanctions-and-rewards program. Does it mean punishment or does it mean approval? It can mean either.

It is not for me to analyse in detail the subsequent development of the law-and-society program, which Craig Brown has described in his history of the CIAR. New researchers – all bright and accomplished – were added, including Liora Salter, a sociologist from York University. In early 1993 Macdonald and Salter prepared a 'framework' document, the goal of which was – ambitiously – to 'reformulate the theoretical paradigm' of law. The reformulated theoretical framework, again according to Brown, 'would seek to discover where state law fits into the regimes of society's norms, what these norms are and how they are influenced by law. The framework would also examine how the norms related to one another and the relationship between state law and customary law.' A tall order.

This new framework, entitled 'Law and the Determinants of Social Order,' kept expanding. The following year a new dimension was added, called 'The Institutions of the New Economy.' Other researchers were brought in. Then another theme, entitled 'Law in Everyday Life: Imagining Justice,' was introduced, with additional researchers. Liora Salter took over the program in 1995, and Harry Arthurs and Guy Rocher, among others, joined the research team. The growth in numbers sometimes reminded me of a pyramid scheme. Nevertheless, I participated in almost all the many meetings and tried to adjust my work, as best I could, to the themes being explored.

Fraser Mustard stepped down as the president of the CIAR, and on 1

July 1996 political scientist Stefan Dupré became president. Faced with a budgetary crisis, he recommended to the CIAR executive that the Law and Determinants of Social Order program be closed down as of 30 June 1997. Because of the demands it made on the institute's time and resources, Dupré concluded, 'trying to save this program did not make sense.' Harry Arthurs is convinced that the program was doing first-class work and could have made a major contribution to the law. He may be right. I do not know what Rod and Liora now think, though I do know that they felt the same frustration I had experienced in not being sure of what the expectations for the program were, along with the feelings of 'herding cats' and 'trying to nail jelly to the wall.'

When it became clear that the law program was going in a different direction, I decided that I would not do further work on traffic safety. We had, I thought, made a decent contribution in that area. I would, instead, concentrate on applying what we had learned about sanctions and rewards to the control of those administering the criminal-justice system, which was closer to my areas of expertise than traffic safety. In December 1988 I had given the Moran Lecture at Dublin University on 'Controlling the Administrators of Criminal Justice.' The paper, later published in the *Dublin University Law Journal* and the *Criminal Law Quarterly*, examined the many techniques that are used to control the police, prosecutors, judges, and others in order to get them to exercise their powers properly. I covered a wide range of activities in the administration of criminal justice, including wiretapping, search and seizure, entrapment, bail, delay, and sentencing.

My colleague Kent Roach and I then started examining the issues in greater depth. We agreed to collaborate on a major study, which we tentatively called 'Toeing the Line: Controlling the Administrators of Criminal Justice,' and started giving an upper-year seminar on the subject. At that stage, there was not a significant empirical component to the project, although, as with the traffic-safety study, we would collect what data were available. Our study would benefit from the traffic-safety study in that we would apply something like the Haddon matrix – perhaps the most important insight we had gained from the earlier work – to the examination of techniques for controlling the participants in the administration of criminal justice.

We decided to add to our project an empirical comparison of the administration of criminal justice in Niagara County, New York, and Niagara County, Ontario. I had been interested in such a comparison since the 1960s, when Professor R.M. Jackson of Cambridge University and I discussed a possible tripartite study of the administration of justice in three adjacent counties in Ontario, Quebec, and New York. Nothing came of that idea, but it resurfaced when we were discussing a traffic study using three cities in those three contiguous areas. Again, that did not work out.

At about the same time, one of Canada's leading criminal lawyers, Michael Code, who had been in my first-year criminal-law class in 1973 and with whom I had kept in close touch over the years, consulted me about his returning to law school to do a master's degree. I encouraged him to do so. Michael started his LLM in the fall of 1990, with Kent and I jointly supervising his work. He would join us in working on the project.

The three of us examined a number of possible counties in Ontario, Quebec, and New York, and eventually chose the two Niagaras. They each had a population of about 300,000, with the major cities of Niagara Falls in each county being separated from each other by the Niagara River. Each had a county town of comparable size – Welland in Ontario and Lockport in New York. We spent some time in each county, meeting with judges and prosecutors and determining how we would proceed with the project. That fall, the three of us put in a proposal to the SSHRC for funding. It was successful. The referees had high praise for the proposal, not only commending the concept, but pointing out that we had not asked for enough money. We also had a great tentative title for the manuscript, 'Borderline Justice.' A good title is half the battle.

Michael Code completed his master's degree in 1991 on the topic of court delay, comparing how delay was handled in the two counties. He spent considerable time at the court offices in Lockport and Welland, studying their files and meeting with the judges and court officials. Michael's book *Trial within a Reasonable Time*, published in 1992, concluded that the American legislative approach to delay was better than Canada's Charter-driven judicial approach. He had been the winning counsel in *Askov* (1990), the leading delay case in Canada, yet he believed that the judicial approach was not preferable. Michael continued his interest in the project, but did not have time to do any further research because he had been appointed the assistant deputy attorney general for criminal justice for Ontario – a position of enormous influence in the criminal-justice field. He then returned to practice and was one of the lead defence counsel in the Air India case. In 2006 he was appointed to the full-time faculty at the U of T law school.

Kent and I continued our work on the project, enjoying the help of a succession of excellent research assistants each summer. In addition, the student seminar papers helped us with our ideas. Over two successive weekends in the spring of 1992 we spent time riding with the police in each county. On the first weekend, I spent three days with the Ontario police and Kent with the New York police. The following weekend we switched. My lengthy notes, written up immediately after each weekend, show how stimulating the experience was. The differences between the two jurisdictions were significant. On the New York side the police force consisted of a number of local, independent police forces. On the Canadian side one force, the Niagara District force, covered two counties, Niagara North and Niagara South. We were interested in Niagara South.

The larger Canadian force had more sophisticated equipment, such as computers in squad cars and modern communications systems. Surprisingly, with comparable crime rates, there were almost three times the number of squad cars in Niagara Falls, New York, as there were in Niagara Falls, Ontario. Even in Ontario, however, the police presence was highly visible. In both jurisdictions we were constantly passing other squad cars. This supported the research that Richard Ericson had done in the early 1980s (published in his book *Reproducing Order*) showing that that was just what the police were trying to do – keep order by their visible presence. On one notorious drug-dealing corner of Niagara Falls, New York, the officer I was with made his presence strongly felt. My notes state: 'We actually never got out of our car on Highland. It would have been intimidating. Joe felt most had guns. He passed the street 40 times that night, sometimes coming up side-streets with his light off, sometimes sitting at the corner of a main intersection, sometimes in a parking lot where most of the people were hanging around at the corner.'

In fact, there were very few arrests on either side of the border. One of the officers that I rode with on the American side told me that he had not 'Mirandized' (his verb) a person in a month. It was instructive to learn that New York law, unlike Canada's, does not require that a Miranda warning or any mention of the right to counsel be given (unless the accused asks for counsel) before a breathalyzer test is administered. Has Canada gone too far in the other direction with respect to informing the accused of the right to counsel in such cases? On one evening in a station in Niagara Falls, Ontario, it was touch-and-go whether the breathalyzer test could be given, because the lawyer who was supposed to be on duty had not telephoned back. The test has to be administered within two hours, if it is to be admissible into evidence. At ten minutes before the deadline the legal-aid lawyer called and, of course, informed the accused that he had to take the test or would be charged with failing to take it, which is equally as serious an offence. The accused took the test. His recorded alcohol content was .23 – about three times the legal limit. I was surprised, because I was having an intelligent chat with him while we were waiting, which proves, I guess, as discussed in the previous chapter, that the capacity of various persons to hold their liquor differs widely.

There was enormous discretion exercised on each side of the border. Persons who were clearly impaired were sometimes permitted to leave their cars and go home. In one case on the American side, the person was allowed to continue driving and was even given back his large open bottle of beer. In one instance in Ontario, a clear case of assisting a suicide was overlooked. Fights were broken up, but no charges laid. Sometimes, however, one wondered why charges were laid. Persons were frequently being arrested on the American side for urinating in parking lots, but not for fighting.

Our observations also supported the conclusion of another book by Ericson (and Kevin Haggerty), *Policing the Risk Society*, that the police spend much of their time producing reports on incidents for the use of others. Charging a person with impaired driving can take hours of paperwork. The police possess enormous discretion on whether to charge persons, and one of the factors they take into account is the potential avoidance of paperwork. Police find it more interesting to drive around the city, observing persons who seem out of place, stopping cars on various pretexts, driving with sirens blaring to act as a back-up, and chatting with prostitutes.

I was constantly aware of the dangers faced by the police. Whenever we stopped a car and the officer asked for the person's driver's licence, which was often in the glove compartment, I was sure that a gun would emerge. I stood far behind the officer. My notes from the Ontario visit state: 'I was outfitted with a bullet proof vest, worn under my shirt, which I eventually got used to. The Kevlar vest, they say, will not stop a 45, but will slow down a 38 and stop a 22. Some wear them; some don't. The sergeant, who was rather heavy, didn't. He was fatalistic about what might happen.'

When I got to the American side, I met with the chief of police. My notes state: 'I told him that I had a bullet-proof vest in Ontario, hinting that I would like one in N.Y. He did not bite, suggesting that many officers did not wear them – I guess older officers like him don't. On two occasions he warned me to "be careful."' The next night, the officer conducting the briefing before the squad cars went out referred to a report they had received that a police officer would be shot that summer. My notes state: 'I went back and asked the Lieutenant for a vest. They couldn't find one, but he'd call us back if they did. About an hour later we were called back and I put it on. Joe [the officer I was riding with] had also said that my white shirt made me particularly visible at night.'

Guns were clearly more important on the American side. The two officers that I rode with in Ontario had *never* fired their guns and doubted if others in their platoons had either. They had occasionally drawn their guns, but were reluctant to do so because a report has to be filed whenever a gun is drawn, and, as stated above, the police dislike writing reports. In contrast, the police on the American side would often have their gun drawn when responding to a threatening situation. My notes about one of the policemen that I drove with on the American side state: 'He carries a gun when he is not on duty. He feels empty without one. He doesn't like coming to Toronto cause he can't bring his gun. He keeps it on his ankle.'

We were also struck by the power of police organizations to influence policing. The police union in Niagara, Ontario, had insisted on two-person cars, which are not required on the American side, and which might explain why there are fewer patrol cars on the Ontario side. There were also different shift patterns on each side of the border. In Ontario, the police had twelve-hour shifts with two days on and two days off. This meant that they tended to go home after their shift, and with two days off they became more integrated into their local community. In contrast, there were eight-hour shifts on the American side, so the officers tended to go out for a beer with fellow officers after their shifts.

Now, as to the crucial question of whether Ontario police are doughnut lovers. The answer, according to our very limited survey, is 'Yes.' What do they eat on the other side of the border? Again, with some hesitation, we would conclude that they eat pizza. One evening the officer I was riding with got a call to proceed at once to a spot under a certain bridge. We went there, I recall, with our siren on. When we arrived, we found about half a dozen other police cruisers. Someone had obtained – I'm not sure from where – a large number of pizzas, which we happily consumed.

As the work of the law-and-society program shifted, we tried to fit our work into the wider framework. The description of our project was redrafted to fit into the new 'normativity' framework. I left that task to Kent. My heart was not in it. Here is a sample of what he creatively produced in one memo: 'Canadian criminal justice at the level of symbolic discourse and legal doctrine has undergone much normative change. At the same time, there is significant normative dissonance because many criminal justice officials resist the charter and the public is not certain that criminal justice is heading in the right direction.'

We did work on plea bargaining, which fit in well with the broader program because it occurred outside the formal law – 'in the shadow of the law,' as it is sometimes described. At a later stage we reformulated a description of the project to fit into 'Law in Everyday Life.' For that endeavour we would, for example, examine, in addition to plea bargaining, the day-to-day encounters between citizens and the police and how discretion is exercised. We would also look at the effect of technology on policing and compare the regionalized police force in the New York with the more centralized administration of justice in Canada. We kept adjusting our focus to fit into the wider CIAR endeavour.

For a number of reasons, Kent and I wanted to finish our project, as best we could, as quickly as possible. In March 1996 I informed Liora that our work on the two Niagaras project was coming to an end. The material we had collected was becoming somewhat out-of-date. Moreover, we both had become involved in other significant projects while working on 'Borderline Justice.' I had prepared a report on judicial independence and accountability for the Canadian Judicial Council, published in 1995, which will be discussed in the next chapter, as well as publishing *The Death of Old Man Rice* in 1994. In addition, in the spring of 1995, I had started a study on accountability in the military for the Somalia inquiry, to be discussed in a later chapter. Kent had published his prize-winning book *Constitutional Remedies* in 1994, and had other projects on the go. It was clear that we would never publish the book we had intended to write.

We published two more major articles on the project under the title 'Borderline Justice,' Kent took the lead on a one-hundred-page paper published in 1996 in the *American Journal of Criminal Law*, comparing policing in the two Niagaras, while I took the lead on a paper published in 1997 in the *Israel Law Review* on whether accused persons choose jury or non-jury trials in the two jurisdictions.

One of the principal conclusions of the policing article was that although the criminal-procedure rules were similar on each side of the border, the manner in which the rules are implemented and the police organized in the two Niagaras reflect important differences between the two nations. We wrote:

> The traditional Canadian love of government and deference to authority mean that centralized administrative authority plays an important role in most aspects of policing. Police complaints, police governance, affirmative action and even the drawing of firearms are all monitored by centralized authority in Ontario. In contrast, American traditions of localism and suspicion of big government mean that local police forces remain the norm and few state-wide requirements are placed on the police. Police practices are regulated more by the threat of civil liability and damage awards from local juries than by the elaborate, expensive and centralized administrative regulation found in Ontario.

'Most of the differences between policing in the two Niagaras,' we concluded, 'are based on informal and organizational factors, not the law governing police powers.'

In the article on juries, we explored why juries are seldom used in Ontario, even when they could have been, and why juries are almost always used in New York, even when a jury could have been waived and a judge chosen. There are fewer than five hundred jury cases in criminal matters each year in Ontario. Of course, the election of judges in New York, rather than their appointment, as in Canada, is part of the answer. Judges who have to face re-election in partisan elections may want to appear as law-and-order judges. We examined statistics throughout the United States and concluded that states that appoint judges tend to have more trials by judge alone (called bench trials) than states that elect judges. We also speculated that the way cases are assigned affects the decision. In New York the judge who is to hear the case has handled all the pre-trial proceedings, including bail applications, and so may know too much about the accused compared to a jury, which would know very little. And there are other factors, such as knowing before trial in New York whether an accused's criminal record will be admitted. In Ontario this is not known until the trial is under way, and defence counsel may not want to take the chance that a jury will know about the accused's prior record. A judge is not likely to give such evidence as much weight as a jury would. There is, we concluded, a more general reason for the selection of juries in the United States. Their selection 'is consistent with the more populist grass-roots approach in American society which tends to mistrust government, compared with the traditional respect for authority in Canada,' a point made in an earlier chapter discussing gun control.

Like the law-reform project described in earlier chapters, the project's result was not exactly what we had intended – we had wanted to publish a book – but we did manage to get out of it alive, with a credible record of publications and with ideas that would influence the future work of scholars, including Kent and me. My later work on the judiciary and my study for the Somalia inquiry certainly benefited from the earlier work, as did Kent's work on terrorism. A book-length manuscript on 'Borderline Justice,' I believe, would have made a significant contribution to legal scholarship. The concept was terrific and it is likely that if we had not become involved in other activities and had ploughed ahead without concern for the broader law-and-society program we would have completed it. Collaborating with a small group of colleagues can produce excellent work. Collaborating with too many colleagues spread across the country may prove less successful – at least in legal fields.

The law-and-society program continued to evolve. In early 1996 Liora circulated a document with a new direction: 'What Use is Law?' It would have two new themes: 'Law in Turbulent Times' and 'The Turbulence of Law.' Maybe these were good themes, but they were straying far from our 'Two Niagaras' project. I wrote to Liora saying that 'it might be best to let me sit out this round.' A few months later the CIAR closed down the program.

25

A Place Apart:
Judicial Independence and
Accountability

In late 1992 I was approached by Deans Robert Sharpe of the University of Toronto and James MacPherson of Osgoode Hall Law School to see if I would be interested in undertaking a study for the Canadian Judicial Council on judicial independence and accountability. Bob and Jim, now judges on the Ontario Court of Appeal, had each been the executive officer for Chief Justice Brian Dickson and had been asked by the council for their advice on how the council should proceed with such a study.

The Canadian Judicial Council is composed of all the federally appointed chief justices and associate chief justices in Canada – thirty-eight in total, and was chaired at the time by Chief Justice Antonio Lamer. The council, which had been established by legislation in 1971 by the minister of justice, John Turner, grew out of the annual conference of chief justices that John Edwards of the University of Toronto's Centre of Criminology had established in 1964. The council would, as was stated on second reading of the legislation, 'provide a national forum for the judiciary in Canada, and ... strive to bring about greater efficiency and uniformity in judicial services and to improve their quality.' It would also provide a new and better forum to investigate complaints against the federal judiciary, at the time handled by the Department of Justice, which could be followed by an ad hoc commission, such as the much-criticized inquiry several years earlier into the conduct of Justice Leo Landreville.

A wide-ranging study was thought necessary in the early 1990s because many matters involving the independence of the judiciary were then the subject of debate. One important question was what role the judiciary should play in the running of the courts. In 1981 Jules Deschênes, the chief justice of Quebec, had written a report in collaboration with Professor Carl Baar on the issue. The Deschênes report, entitled *Masters in Their Own House* (*Maîtres chez eux*), which had been commissioned by the council, advocated greater administrative and budgetary independence for the judiciary along the lines of federal courts in the United States. Since the report's publication relatively little progress had been made, and some members of the council wanted action. Although the council's Judicial Independence Committee did not feel that creating an updated version of the Deschênes report was 'either necessary or desirable,' the full council rejected that approach and wanted the independence committee to 'consider what steps should be taken to renew council's interest in the subject matter of the Deschênes report.' In early 1992 a twenty-seven-page draft report was prepared by the chief justice of British Columbia, Allan McEachern, a strong advocate of greater independence. Because of the setting up of my study, a final version of McEachern's draft was never prepared.

Another issue then being debated was the disciplining of judges. The then minister of justice in the Mulroney government, Kim Campbell, had met with the full council in March 1992 and had expressed concern about the discipline process. 'Some of my provincial and territorial colleagues,' she told council, 'had serious concerns that judicial independence was being used as a shield from public scrutiny.' Some former judges, her colleagues were suggesting, had avoided disciplinary hearings by claiming a medical disability, and in some of these cases the former judge had returned to gainful employment while continuing to receive a full pension.

The judiciary had other concerns, such as the possibility that some form of judicial evaluation would be brought in and that sensitivity training through judicial education would be imposed. Nova Scotia was considering introducing judicial evaluation, and former Supreme Court of Canada justice Bertha Wilson chaired a committee that was about to bring in a report for the Canadian Bar Association that might recommend compulsory sensitivity training. Members of the judiciary were concerned about what Justice Wilson would recommend. Indeed, her report, *Touchstones for Change*, recommended that 'sensitivity courses for judges on gender and racial bias be made compulsory not only for newly appointed judges but for all judges,' although the committee later agreed to drop the compulsory aspect of the recommendation. In general, in part because of the growing role of the judiciary under the Charter, there was increasing public concern that the judiciary be accountable for its actions in a more public and understandable fashion.

It is not surprising, therefore, that, at its meeting in September 1992, the council agreed with a recommendation from the Judicial Independence Committee 'that the Council should retain the services of a distinguished academic to provide the Committee with the best possible advice on questions of judicial independence and accountability.' The committee consulted with deans Sharpe and MacPherson and with Chief Justice Lamer's current executive officer, Tom Cromwell. It may be that the committee wanted Sharpe, MacPherson, and Cromwell to undertake the research themselves, but it was soon recognized that it would be better to have an independent academic who had more time to devote to the task. I had not taken public positions on any of the topics, and so it was probably thought that I could examine the issues reasonably objectively. Hence, my selection for this interesting project. Tony Lamer, with whom I had worked on the Law Reform Commission of Canada, supported my involvement, writing to me in December 1992 that it was 'wonderful news' that I might get involved, and adding: 'I know you would be of great help to the Council in addressing these important issues and it would give me great personal pleasure to have you take on this project.'

It took some months to work out the details of the contract. The Treasury Board initially took the position that the project was unnecessary, but in the end the money was found, particularly because the Department of Justice wanted the study to be done. The total budget, spread over a two-year period, was to be slightly under $100,000, including my fixed honorarium of less than half of that, which probably worked out to be under $50 an hour. I wanted to do the project and was content with the remuneration, even though I had recently been doing projects for the Ontario and federal governments at more than three times that rate.

The contract was signed in June 1993 and the Canadian Judicial Council issued a press release indicating the study's wide scope:

The study, which will have the active co-operation of the Federal Department of Justice and the Federation of Law Societies, is expected to be completed in early 1995 and will examine a range of issues involving the judiciary from appointment to discipline. Professor Friedland will explore the subject from an historical, comparative and contemporary perspective.

Some of the many topics to be studied are the effect of the Charter of Rights and Freedoms on judicial independence; whether judicial independence should be further constitutionalized; techniques for selecting judges; confirmation hearings; the role of the chief justices; the role of the judiciary in the administration of the courts; the composition and functioning of judicial councils; the relationship between provincial and federal judicial councils; the discipline of judges; performance evaluations; setting remuneration; and retirement policy.

The chair of the Judicial Independence Committee, with whom I would have much involvement, was Richard Scott, the chief justice of Manitoba. Scott was practical, unflappable, respectful of others, and a pleasure to work with. He was also a marathon runner – during the time I was involved in the project he ran and completed the Boston Marathon. I was given two years to complete my own marathon. Throughout, he was supportive of my work.

I met with the Judicial Independence Committee on a number of occasions to report on my progress, as well as with a subcommittee, consisting of Scott and three other members of the independence committee, that was set up to offer advice and to keep an eye on what I was doing. The other members were Chief Justice Roy McMurtry of Ontario, who had grown up around the corner from me in Forest Hill and whom I had known and respected for many years; Chief Justice Allan McEachern of British Columbia, with whom I would have a number of disagreements; and Associate Chief Justice Pierre Michaud of Quebec. McEachern was feisty and down-to-earth, and had strong opinions on most of the subjects I dealt with – often contrary to my own. He was particularly concerned about my proposed recommendation that future judicial appointments should require retirement at age seventy. Even though my recommendation was that only judges appointed in the future would be subject to the new age limit, he thought that under the circumstances it would be difficult for him to stay on past age seventy, which he was approaching. I met with these four high-powered judges for lengthy sessions on several occasions. In the preface to my study I state: 'I enjoyed the lively interchanges with that group and it is probably safe to say that not one of them agrees with all my recommendations.'

Bob Sharpe and Jim MacPherson acted as special consultants and were key participants in the project's earlier stages, but both were appointed to the trial division of the Ontario Supreme Court during my work on the project and moved somewhat into the background because, as judges, they had a potential conflict of interest with some of my recommendations. As it turned out, Bob's appointment was made in the spring of 1995, while I was completing the project. I was asked to be the acting dean at the U of T law school until a new dean was selected, which added to the burden of finishing the project on time. *Frank* magazine – in, I think, my only appearance in its pages – said that I was 'wheeled out' as acting dean.

There were two issues of academic independence that first had to be worked out. One was an assurance that the work would be published. The formal contract did not include such a clause, but correspondence with the council made it clear that there was an understanding that the work would be published, either in my name or with appropriate acknowledgment of my work. I did not care who had copyright on the work, but was concerned that it be published. The arrangement tended to satisfy me, but I continued to be nervous that the council would try to suppress or bury the study. I would be told from time to time that certain members of council did not want it published. Non-publication would have proved difficult under the *Access to Information Act*, and also because I had widely distributed for comment a draft of the report – perhaps even more widely than necessary to protect against its suppression – to judges, government officials, academics, lawyers, and others. Any attempt to bury it would have been unsuccessful and would have created very negative publicity for the council. The comments I received on the draft were extremely helpful in my final revisions. Just about all persons to whom I sent it took their responsibility seriously. Another issue was the clause in the contract that stated that I would 'treat as confidential and not divulge, unless authorized ... any information obtained in the course of the performance of the contract.' I did not seek to change the contract, but got the agreement of council that I could use 'any information obtained for academic purposes.'

As with my other research projects, I had excellent student assistance. At the very early stages I was assisted by Jeffrey Piercy, now practising law in Calgary, and at the very final stages by Gillian Roberts, now with the Crown Law Office in Toronto. In between, Poonam Puri, now a professor at Osgoode Hall Law School, and Caroline Ursulak, now practising in Toronto, did excellent work on the project.

Poonam and Caroline had finished second year and had been in my small group in first year. Both did directed research under my supervision on judicial independence in their third year, Poonam on court administration, and Caroline on judicial selection. I could not have asked for better research assistants. Some of the research material, along with my many handwritten drafts, notes, and extensive correspondence, has been deposited in the U of T Archives for the use of future scholars.

In the spring of 1994, after I had done considerable research and had formed some tentative ideas, I travelled to every province and territory in Canada, meeting with chief justices, other members of the judiciary, government officials, lawyers, and academics. The process of consultation was often tricky. Federally appointed judges have a lobby group, called at the time the Canadian Judges Conference, that does not always agree with the positions taken by the Canadian Judicial Council. In setting up meetings with regular judges, I made sure that members of the conference were well represented. I usually met separately with court of appeal judges. I also met separately with provincially appointed judges, sometimes with and sometimes without their chief judge being present. In selecting members of the legal profession with whom to consult I sought the advice of the Canadian Bar Association, individual law societies, and the Federation of Law Societies of Canada. My meetings with academics were based on my knowledge of what they might be able to contribute to my work.

These meetings were very helpful in sorting out my thoughts. Moreover, I was also able to see parts of the country that I might not otherwise have seen, such as Yellowknife in the Northwest Territories, and Whitehorse in the Yukon. In Whitehorse, the courthouse and the attorney general's department were in the same building, constructed in the mid-1980s, but separated by an atrium with an upper walkway between the two sides. The judges objected to the walkway because it gave the appearance of too close a connection between the courts and the executive. The solution was to place several large potted trees on the walkway, which prevented passage between the two sides. I took a number of pictures of the walkway, which at one point I thought might appear on the cover of my report. I do not know if the trees are still there. The visit to Whitehorse was particularly memorable because I was able to tack on a trip through the Yukon and Alaska with Judy, who had flown up from Toronto for a few days. Judge Barry Stuart, a former academic, had suggested a wonderful weekend trip for Judy and me, with a ferry ride from Haines, Alaska (with its soaring American eagles), to Skagway, the base of the gold rush, and then back to Whitehorse.

As noted above, the study was not limited to federally appointed judges. If I was to make sensible recommendations about the judiciary in Canada I would have to devote time and attention to the provincially appointed judges, who outnumber their federal counterparts. This approach was appreciated by the provincial court judges, although I recall that when I gave a talk at the provincial court judges' annual meeting in Moncton after the report was published, several judges publicly chastised me for not dealing with the sensitive topic of unification of the criminal courts, which I had written about many years earlier. I explained that I already had my hands full dealing with the topics that were clearly on my plate. Nevertheless, some of my proposals recommended closer cooperation between the federally and provincially appointed judges in such matters as the administration of the courts and the development of a code of conduct.

In the preface to the study I gave special thanks to the executive director of the council, Jeannie Thomas, who 'took an active interest in all aspects of the project from the initial stages to the physical production of the Report, including its translation into French.' Similarly, the Department of Justice cooperated fully. I had helpful meetings on a number of occasions with deputy minister John Tait and his successor George Thompson, and with Andrew Watt, then head of the Judicial Affairs Unit, and with other members of his unit. I also had a number of lengthy frank discussions with Chief Justice Lamer. In the preface I thank Peter Russell from the University of Toronto and Carl Baar of Brock University, 'the two foremost Canadian academic experts on the judiciary,' stating that 'from the outset, they helped me shape the study, shared their extensive libraries with me, and read drafts of my chapters.'

There was extensive correspondence with many other knowledgeable individuals. I received, for example, a ten-page single-spaced handwritten letter from Bertha Wilson, pointing out the issues she had faced in producing her *Touchstones* report. If judges, she stated, 'don't show respect for women and visible minorities in the courtroom, how can we have confidence in their impartiality in dispute resolution?' She ended her letter with these simple but powerful words:

Working with the Royal Commission on Aboriginal Peoples has been a great experience for me. It has opened my eyes to another culture and another view of the world. And, in particular coming on top of the Gender Equality Task Force, it has made me realize how important respect for others is and how much pain and misery we can inflict through perpetuating stereotypes and condoning sexism and racism in our human relations.

I also spent a productive week in England, meeting with a number of knowledgeable academics, such as Robert Stevens, who had recently written a book on judicial independence, with some key people in the Lord Chancellor's office, with the chair of the Law Commission, Sir Henry Brooke, and with the Lord Chief Justice of England, Peter Taylor. I met for an hour with the Lord Chief Justice before court in his office at the Law Courts in the Strand. There were pictures of his predecessors on his wall. Seeing a picture of Chief Justice Mansfield, one of the greatest common-law judges of all time and my favourite judge when I was a law student, sent a shiver up my back. I also met with a number of barristers, including David Pannick, who subsequently wrote a favourable article ('Wanted: judges to judge the judges') on my report in the London *Times*. The visit to England was particularly valuable because change was in the air in the United Kingdom, but was not yet publicly documented, such as changes in the appointment process and the administration of the courts.

During the course of my research and writing, I gave a number of talks on various aspects of the subject: for example, to the Canadian Institute for the Administration of Justice in Ottawa, to the midwinter meeting of the Canadian Bar Association in Prince Edward Island, to the annual meeting of chief judges of provincial courts in Winnipeg, to the Ontario Court of Appeal in Niagara-on-the-Lake, and to Department of Justice personnel in Ottawa. I was also invited by the Supreme Court of Canada to address a delegation of Romanian judges organized by Justice Peter Cory and, the following year, a delegation of Hungarian judges organized by Justice John Major. I vividly recall meeting one of the Romanian judges and asking him when he had arrived in Canada. He told me that he was, in fact, Justice Major, whom I had not seen since we were students at law school forty years earlier.

The most important event was a full-day Canadian Judicial Council seminar in Ottawa on 30 March 1995 for all the members of council. A draft of my report, which the council had distributed, would form the basis for the seminar. I would give a ten-minute introduction to each topic, followed by reactions by several persons, and then there would be comments and questions from members of the council. Those who agreed with what I had to say on a topic tended to remain silent. It was an all-day barrage, but I survived. Indeed, I found it exhilarating.

The chair of the independence committee, Richard Scott, provided some positive feedback, along with many thoughtful comments, writing: 'I must say that it was a pleasure once again to leisurely rummage through the Report, particularly with the benefit of the March seminar, and a further month to ruminate on some of the more controversial recommendations. Your Report like good wine seems to become more mellow as it "matures."'

The one aspect of the report that judges particularly seemed to dislike was my calling the promise of a substantial pension to every newly appointed judge a 'signing bonus.' As Ontario Court of Appeal Justice Coulter Osborne wrote: 'Your reference to a "signing bonus" does not bother me all that much. It does, however, introduce a rhetorical element which will inevitably be plucked out of the report by the media from sea to sea at the expense of other more substantive observations. On balance, I would think that the reference is better unsaid than said.' Even the 'unflappable' Scott commented that if I used the phrase, 'unfortunately all of your other careful and specific comments about the necessity of having a good, even a generous pension for the judiciary would be lost in the media frenzy that would undoubtedly follow.' According to my notes made at the time, Chief Justice McEachern telephoned to say that my comments about generous pensions would 'earn me the undying enmity of the judiciary.' I decided to remove the harmless phrase, to the relief of many members of the judiciary. I had not anticipated such a reaction, but I learned that it may be a smart move to introduce in a draft something that would attract the lightning and perhaps thereby somewhat temper the reaction to other parts of a report.

As with most of my projects, I was uncertain what title to give to the manuscript. Sometimes one never finds an appropriate title and settles for a purely descriptive one, such as the not particularly exciting *The University of Toronto: A History*. At some point during my research I came across a comment in the Canadian Senate in 1932 by former prime minister Arthur Meighen that 'a judge is in no sense under the direction of the Government ... The judge is in a place apart.' *A Place Apart: Judicial Independence and Accountability in Canada* became the title of the book. It was a terrific title. Shortly after the book's publication, however, my friend Horace Krever, the erudite Ontario court of appeal justice, sent me a note pointing out that 'eight years before Meighen used the phrase, it was used at an Imperial Congress ... with reference to persons with venereal disease.' I replied: 'Please do me a great favour and don't spread it around about the origins of "a place apart." I'm in enough trouble with your colleagues as it is!'

The four-hundred-page report was published in English and French in June 1995. The French version, as seems to happen in such cases, was over forty pages longer. The press release quoted Chief Justice Lamer as stating:

> Our hope when we commissioned Professor Friedland to examine these issues was that he would provide the basis for an informed debate on what is necessary to secure the strength, independence and, above all, public confidence in our courts and our judges. He has done that ... With this report we can begin a process my colleagues and I consider essential to the continuing health of our courts as a vital institution of Canadian democracy. For this, I offer Professor Friedland my profound thanks.

The report received a good reaction in most of the major daily papers and the legal weeklies. An editorial in the *Ottawa Citizen*, for example, was headed 'Accountability of our judges needs reform,' and that in the *Edmonton Journal* 'How to guarantee a stronger judiciary.' Most articles and editorials focused on my recommendations concerning the appointment of Supreme Court of Canada justices and that concerning judicial evaluation. I appeared on a couple of TV shows, including a CBC program called *Face Off*, and a number of radio programs, such as *As it Happens* and various talk shows, including one hosted by former prime minister Kim Campbell from Vancouver. I also spoke at the annual meeting of the Canadian Bar Association in Winnipeg and at various other meetings, such as one of federal court judges in Montebello, Quebec, and the annual meeting of the provincial court judges in Moncton. Further, I gave a talk entitled 'Reflections on *A Place Apart*' at the University of New Brunswick as the Viscount Bennett Lecturer – the same Viscount Bennett whose scholarship I did not win when applying to do graduate work. I gave another to the Society for the Reform of the Criminal Law at Whistler, British Columbia. These were subsequently published in the *University of New Brunswick Law Journal* and the *Criminal Law Forum*, respectively. The number of talks given in connection with *A Place Apart* was comparable to the number given in connection with my later book on the history of the University of Toronto.

Allan Rock, the minister of justice, met privately with the council – I was not invited to attend – at its meeting in Toronto in September 1995 and commented favourably on the report, congratulating council 'for having asked Professor Friedland to prepare a report which I believe will be helpful as a framework for issues of great concern to the judiciary and to the public.' He noted that the department had 'an outstanding commitment to examine the conduct provisions of the Judges Act' and stated that 'Professor Friedland's discussion of the issues is a very good starting point for a review.' He also wanted changes in judicial education, particularly for newly appointed judges, found the suggestion of fixed terms for chief justices 'very interesting,' and liked what I had to say about 'the value of judicial performance and self-evaluation.' He undertook, however, not to take any action on the report until he had further views of the judicial council.

For reasons of space, I can only briefly touch on some of the issues that I covered in the report. Let me start with security of tenure. At what age should a judge retire? I suggested that future retirements should be at age seventy, which would be in line with a recent change in England. Most European countries have mandatory retirement at age seventy or younger. In fact, seventy had been the age of retirement for judges of the Federal Court of Canada and for county and district court judges in Canada, but shortly after the enactment of the Charter a federal court judge challenged the distinction between those judges and superior court judges as discriminatory under the Charter and won at trial. The government decided not to appeal and instead of lowering the retirement age for all future judges to seventy, as I believe would have been desirable, raised the age for all federally appointed judges to seventy-five. There does not seem to be much interest today in reducing that age limit.

Just as we do not want judges retiring too old, we do not want them retiring too young. One of the reasons that judges in Canada are seen as independent is that they have nothing to gain by the decisions they make. A judge who is permitted to retire at a full pension at too young an age may in many cases start a new career – business? politics? – and the public will then start wondering whether his or her judgments may have been designed to further their later career. Of course judges would like such an opportunity – who would not? – but the important question is whether it is good for society. I thought that an actuarially reduced pension at an earlier age would be acceptable to handle cases of hardship, as in England, such as having to look after a sick spouse, but I thought it would be a mistake to encourage early retirements by offering a full pension. Unfortunately, in 1998 the federal government accepted the judges' argument and brought in amending legislation that provides that in certain cases – when the age of the judge and number of years of service combined is eighty or more years – a full pension may be payable before age sixty-five after fifteen years' service. I think we will come to regret that amendment.

I also discussed the issue of what should be done with a judge who is incapacitated or disabled because of illness or infirmity. At present, such a judge is dealt with through the discipline process, with incapacity through disability being treated as a lack of 'good behaviour.' It would be better, I argued, to treat such a case in the same way it is dealt with in other parts of society, that is, through long-term-disability status. We should not assume today that incapacity due to disability is necessarily permanent. The determination of incapacity should be made by the judiciary, and a further replacement appointment authorized after such a determination. This is now the practice in the U.S. federal system. If the incapacitated judge recovers, he or she would return to the bench.

Financial security was also a subject of considerable interest. One wants salaries to be high enough, when combined with good pensions, to attract a pool of excellent candidates. But even if a very large portion of the bar were willing to accept an appointment at a much lower salary, we would still want to pay judges well to ensure their financial independence – for our sake, not for theirs. As I stated in the report, subsequently quoted with approval by the Supreme Court: 'We do not want judges put in a position of temptation, hoping to get some possible financial advantage if they favour one side or the other. Nor do we want the public to contemplate this as a possibility.' The question of how judicial salaries should be determined was a hot topic when I did my report. Many judges wanted binding arbitration. The present masochistic method of establishing judicial remuneration for federally appointed judges by a commission every three years was questioned in the report. Would it not be better to deal with judicial remuneration as part of the review of other senior salaries paid from government funds, such as those of deputy ministers and army generals, as is now done in England, the United States, and Australia?

I thought that it was desirable to have some form of a commission to offer advice to the government, although I thought it unlikely that the courts would say that such a commission was constitutionally required. As it turned out, in the *Provincial Judges Compensation Case* in 1997 the Supreme Court of Canada not only held that commissions must be established for all judges, federal and provincial, but that the government is required to accept a commission's recommendations unless it can convince a court that there is a 'rational' reason for rejecting them. I certainly had not anticipated that they would go that far, and in a 2001 talk in Vancouver on the occasion of the three-hundred-year anniversary of the *Act of Settlement*, which established judicial independence in England, I criticized the case, stating:

> Thus the judiciary have created a clear potential conflict of interest by judicializing the process. If the government 'chooses not to accept one or more of the recommendations,' Chief Justice Lamer stated, 'it must be prepared to justify this decision, if necessary in a court of law.' The judges are therefore in a real sense determining their own compensation ... In other situations, permitting a person to be a judge in his or her own cause would be a ground for reversing a judgment ... Would it not have been wiser to have simply required the establishment of a compensation tribunal and also required the government to respond within a set period of time and then leave it to public opinion to judge that response?

Three members of the Supreme Court of Canada were in the audience that day and my words may have hit a sensitive nerve. In any event, in subsequent cases the Supreme Court has narrowed the role of the courts in these situations, such that it is now relatively easy for a government to reject a recommendation from a commission. In a 2005 decision (*Provincial Court Judges' Assn. of New Brunswick v. New Brunswick*) a unanimous court rejected challenges to a number of provincial governments' decisions not to follow commission recommendations. The Supreme Court stated that a court's review should be 'a deferential review which acknowledges both the government's unique position and accumulated expertise and its constitutional responsibility for management of the province's financial affairs.'

One chapter of the report that convinced the Canadian Judicial Council that change was necessary was the one in which I strongly recommended the drafting of a code of conduct. I looked closely at the code of conduct for federally appointed judges in the United States and thought it would be a good starting point. The U.S. code is used primarily for guidance and is not as directly tied to discipline as are most of the state codes. Its use of comprehensive advisory opinions is also very helpful, as are its confidential opinions on specific issues. At the Canadian Judicial Council meeting in the spring of 1995 – at the same time that the full-day seminar on my draft report took place – the council decided to go ahead with a new code of conduct. The working group of the independence committee that had been established to work with me, along with Lamer's executive officer, Tom Cromwell, took on the task. In order to make it clear that the document is advisory in nature, it is entitled *Ethical Principles for Judges*. It is a good document. My one real regret is that it was not drafted in conjunction with the provincial court judges. The drafters acknowledge input from the Canadian Association of Provincial Court Judges, but I believe it would have been better to have worked more closely with these judges, perhaps by including a number of them as members of the committee. The principles relating to the conduct of judges should not vary from court to court.

Other issues dealt with in the report included performance evaluation and the role of the chief justices. In both cases I drew on my experience in the academic world. Teaching evaluations are a valuable aspect of the academic world today, although they were virtually unheard of forty years ago. Some form of periodic evaluation of how judges conduct proceedings would, I stated, enhance the effectiveness of the judiciary. They would be most useful if they were designed and administered by the judiciary and were not publicized. I also liked term appointments for chief justices and recommended seven-year terms, reflecting my experience as a dean. Dick Scott thought that ten years would be better. Perhaps he is right, but some limited term would be good for the judiciary. I also recommended that it would be desirable for members of the court to take part in recommending a new chief justice, just as faculty members take part in the selection of senior academic administrators in the universities.

Another area where I thought that the experience of the academic world might be helpful was in the administration of the courts. For the most part, the attorney general departments throughout Canada run the courts, except for matters that are crucial to judicial independence, such as deciding which judge will hear a case. Many judges want greater administrative and financial independence, such as the U.S. courts and the Supreme Court of Canada now have. I noted that in contrast to the judiciary, universities in Canada are wholly responsible for the administration of their institutions. They are given grants from the government, receive tuition and funds from other persons and institutions, and more or less control the way that money is spent. Many judges would like to have the same system. But academic staff do not have the final say in how university monies are spent. In most universities there is a board of governors or governing council, the majority of whose members do not have a direct potential conflict of interest in the decisions made. If the judges want greater institutional independence, they should be willing to work within a system that provides some checks and balances.

It is desirable that such a system be established. There is need for some separation or buffer between the judiciary and the attorney general, the chief litigator before the courts. Moreover, it is desirable to give the judiciary greater control over their working conditions on the theory that people work more effectively if they have control over their work environment. Further, it makes sense to have the three levels of courts working together. There are ways of sharing resources and streamlining court procedures to be found if there is a cooperative effort among the courts.

In *A Place Apart* I explore a number of administrative models. The one I favoured was a board of judicial management encompassing all three levels of the judiciary. The board could consist of judges and various non-judicial appointees in approximately equal numbers. The board would appoint the administrator of the courts, would allocate the budget among the three levels of courts, would attempt to streamline and coordinate the work of the courts, and would prepare the estimates that would be channelled through the attorney general's department. Judges would still have control over the assignment of cases and other matters at the core of judicial independence. The system would not turn judges into administrators. It would, however, give the judiciary a greater stake in running the court system and incentives for running the courts more efficiently.

In the late 1990s the Ontario government – with my involvement – started examining the issue, but in the end the superior court judges did not want to participate. They feared, it seems, that the government would be using a court-services agency to implement budgetary cuts. The Ontario government continues to be interested, however. Ontario Attorney General Michael Bryant, who had read a talk that I gave in late 2003 in which I said that 'it is not desirable for the judges to be under the thumb of the Attorney General, the chief litigator in the courts,' stated at the opening of the courts in early 2004: 'I'd like to think that mine is an affable, collaborative thumb, but 'twas not always so and may not be tomorrow, so now is the time consider the role of the judiciary in administering the courts.'

The Canadian Judicial Council itself has taken a new interest in the subject and commissioned a study by my colleague Lorne Sossin and several others, which resulted in a report published in September 2006 by a subcommittee of the council entitled *Alternative Models of Court Administration*. The report lays out various options. The model favoured by the subcommittee and endorsed by the council combines what was referred to as 'limited judicial autonomy' with an 'independent commission.' The latter would not be composed of either judges or persons from the attorney general's department, but would be similar in function to a provincial auditor or ombudsman. The role of such a commission, which could range from being a full administrative-services commission to having a simpler dispute-resolution mandate, is still to be determined. A process of consultation with stakeholders across the country is now under way.

I had a lengthy chapter in the report on discipline. My impression of the council's procedures was positive: 'The Council gave me full access to all of their complaint files ... My overall opinion is that the Judicial Conduct Committee and the Executive Director have dealt with the matters received carefully and conscientiously. I never sensed that any matter was being "covered up" by the Council after a complaint was made to it.' The council, of course, liked that conclusion. Nevertheless, I had a number of suggestions for improvement. I recommended that thought be given to the procedures to be followed if a joint address of both houses of parliament were to be undertaken – now the only method of removal – against a federally appointed judge. For example, something more than a bare majority should be required. I also wanted to include judges who were not chief justices when consideration is given to having a formal inquiry. Further, I suggested that there be public disclosure – in a sanitized form – of all complaints dealt with, plus a periodic external review of all the decisions made in the complaints process. The American federal judicial practice of giving a judge's chief justice the chance to resolve minor complaints before the matter was dealt with by the judicial council also appealed to me. Moreover, I wanted the council to be given explicitly the right to publicly or privately reprimand a judge. The council had previously taken the position that their job was only to decide whether there was a case for removal. My examination of the council's origins led me to conclude that they already had such a power, which needed to be acknowledged.

A number of changes were subsequently made in the council's procedures to make the system somewhat more open. I had also recommended as a matter of policy that provincial attorneys general not have the power to demand that the council undertake a formal inquiry. Such a power, I believed, should only be in the hands of the federal minister of justice. The power was recently upheld as constitutionally permissible by the Federal Court of Appeal, reversing a trial court which had held otherwise. The judge who is the subject of the complaint has now sought leave to appeal the court of appeal decision to the Supreme Court of Canada.

Finally, there is a chapter on appointments, a matter that has been in the news with the changed composition of the judicial-appointments committees that vet applications for appointments and with the appointment of Marshall Rothstein of the Federal Court of Appeal to fill the Supreme Court of Canada vacancy created by Justice John Major's retirement. On the latter issue, Prime Minister Stephen Harper selected Rothstein in 2006 from a list of three names sent to the minister of justice by a committee made up of parliamentarians, lawyers, and others. The list of three had emerged from a list of six names sent to the committee by the former government. There was then a hearing before a parliamentary committee in which Justice Rothstein was gently questioned. Unlike an American confirmation hearing, the committee did not vote on the issue.

The procedure followed was strange. The committee that put forward the names should have been the one to interview the candidates to determine whether each person's name should have be put forward. Having the parliamentary committee interview the person already selected by the government is simply a rubber-stamping formality. Moreover, the earlier committee should have been able to suggest names not put forward by the government.

All in all, I still like the scheme I suggest in *A Place Apart*. In my model there would be a special nominating committee for each appointment to the Supreme Court. The committee could consist of nominees of the province or provinces traditionally associated with the particular appointment, nominees of legal groups, and nominees of the federal government. I had not contemplated that parliamentarians would be on the committee, but it should be open to have them. The committee would present a short, possibly ranked, list of names to the government. Now comes the important part. If the government went outside the list, a public confirmation hearing would be held, perhaps by a joint committee of the House and Senate. There would obviously be strong pressure for the government not to go outside the short list of recommended candidates. Such a system would be a compromise between the American system requiring a confirmation hearing for all appointments to the Supreme Court and the Canadian system where, at the time I wrote my study, there were none. The special nominating committee would in a sense be a substitute for a confirmation hearing. It would be a proxy for the public. Maybe the scheme will be looked at again when the next appointment comes up. The next person on the court to have to retire is Justice Morris Fish, who will turn seventy-five in 2013, although it is likely that someone will take an early retirement before then.

Of potentially greater significance is the change made by the Harper government in the process for selecting superior court justices. Committees across the country have played a significant role in vetting persons who apply to become a federally appointed judge. Until recently they classified the persons as 'recommended,' 'highly recommended,' or 'not recommended.' The government has in recent years chosen from the 'recommended' and 'highly recommended' categories. The system had been working reasonably well, although in my view it gave the government greater discretion than is desirable to choose whom they wanted as judges. However, the Harper government has now reconstituted the vetting committees in a number of important respects. It has eliminated the category of 'highly recommended,' which, in effect, gives the government wider scope to appoint whom they want. It has also added a police representative to each committee and given the representative from the judiciary on each committee a vote only in the case of a tie. Given that restriction, the government has the power to control the committees with its right to appoint four representatives to an eight-member committee.

This is politicizing the process more than is desirable. University of Ottawa law professor Ed Ratushny, who has been a student of the process for decades, told the Canadian Press: 'It is part of a bigger picture where this government seems to have a strong underlying distrust of the (current) judiciary. I can't imagine what objective they could have in mind, other than to look for lawyers who will be hard-assed, law-and-order judges.' I put it more strongly than is my custom in public statements. As the *Globe and Mail* stated: 'University of Toronto professor Martin Friedland, an expert on judicial independence and the committees, said the expansion of Ottawa's control over committees that are supposed to be a check on federal politicking is "shocking, because it's such a blatant attempt to control the outcome."'

I barely touched on the possibility of the election of judges in *A Place Apart*, stating that 'the existence of elections ... are not models that appear to have much if any support in Canada,' even though they are used for a number of state courts in the United States. A recent Canadian survey indicates, however, that there is, indeed, a surprising amount of support for electing judges. It would be a disaster. Few things would be more destructive to the independence of the judiciary than to have judges campaign for office accepting contributions to pay for their campaigns, let alone having to run on a law-and-order platform.

I was pleased with the reception of *A Place Apart*. Moreover, it continues to play a role in public-policy debates, is occasionally cited in judicial decisions, and is given to every newly appointed federal judge in Canada. I believe that it has also had some impact internationally. The chief justice of the Constitutional Court of South Africa, Arthur Chaskalson, noted in a talk at the faculty of law that the report had been of assistance in South Africa on a number of issues, and I know from discussions with Chief Justice Aharon Barak of Israel that the report has been used there.

In 2000 I had the privilege of joining the chief justice of Saskatchewan, Ed Bayda, and Professor Ratushny on a trip to Beijing, where we spent a week with a group of young Chinese judges discussing issues of judicial independence and accountability. It was a fascinating experience. The introductory chapter of *A Place Apart* had been translated into Chinese, as had the Canadian Judicial Council's document *Ethical Principles for Judges*. Corruption of the judiciary – and there are about 200,000 judges in China – is a serious problem. The Chinese judges found it interesting that bribery and corruption are not specifically mentioned in the Canadian ethical-principles document, although such conduct is covered under one of the articles which says that 'Judges should not engage in conduct incompatible with the diligent discharge of judicial duties or condone such conduct in colleagues.' No doubt, all the Chinese judges noted another article which provides that Canadian judges 'should refrain from ... membership in political parties.' Some of the Chinese judges participating in the seminars were active members of the Communist Party. Perhaps for this reason, other

Chinese judges remained silent in open discussions about this serious gap in the guarantees for judicial independence in their country.

The judges' college where the seminar took place was to translate the entire report into Chinese. Indeed, a draft translation was produced and Chief Justice Beverley McLachlin wrote a preface for the book, but, as far as I know, the translation was never formally published. I am not sure why. Perhaps, on closer examination, there were sections that advocated too much judicial independence.

The study would seem to have been a key factor in my promotion in 2003 from an Officer to a Companion of the Order of Canada. Although a number of subject areas were mentioned in the citation when I became an Officer in 1990, the only one specifically referred to in the citation as a Companion was my study on judicial independence and accountability, which states I had 'authored one of the most definitive studies of the role of the judiciary in our country.' There was no mention of the recently published history of the University of Toronto.

I was, of course, pleased to be bumped up to the rank of Companion, although I am aware that few people know the difference between the various levels of appointment. Companions form a very select group. The Order allows for only 165 living Companions at any one time. No doubt, people who hope to become Companions are eying my health. At the official ceremony only two persons became Companions, the singer and songwriter Joni Mitchell and me. My children, understandably, seemed more interested in Joni than in their father. I do not wear my snowflake pin very often, except on relatively formal occasions, and tend to wear the Companion pin even less, sometimes feeling like an imposter when I do so. I was more comfortable being an Officer. Nevertheless, I normally wear the pin when I meet with judges – and did so throughout my work on *A Place Apart* – to remind them that they are not the only persons that should be treated with respect.

It is a tricky business knowing when to wear one's pin. I do not wear it to the synagogue, for example, and tend not to wear it at weddings and funerals, particularly not at funerals. I usually leave it up to Judy to decide. I also tend not to wear it around the University. On one occasion, however, I was putting it on in the men's washroom at the law school before going to a relatively formal dinner. The pin slipped and went down the drain in the sink. I had a spare one and did not bother trying to recover it. Many years from now, some plumber will discover it and ask his or her spouse: 'Guess what I found today?'

26

Controlling Misconduct in the Military

My work on sanctions and rewards and my study of the judiciary led to a fascinating study for the Somalia Commission of Inquiry on techniques for controlling misconduct in the military. The inquiry had been set up by the federal government in March 1995 to examine various aspects of the operation of Canadian forces in Somalia, including the torture and death by members of the military of a young defenceless Somali, Shidane Arone. His death on 16 March 1993 became a crucial defining moment for the Canadian military, just as the My Lai massacre of defenceless civilians in Vietnam – precisely twenty-five years to the day earlier – had been a defining moment for the military in the United States.

The Commission of Inquiry into the Deployment of Canadian Forces to Somalia was headed by Federal Court of Appeal Justice Gilles Létourneau, a former academic who had been the chair of the Law Reform Commission of Canada. The other commission members were Robert Rutherford, a supernumerary Ontario superior court justice with a military background, and Peter Desbarats, the dean of the graduate school of journalism at the University of Western Ontario. Although I met with the commissioners from time to time, my principal involvement was with Stanley Cohen, the commission secretary, who had been seconded from the Department of Justice. I knew Stan well because he had done graduate work at the U of T law school in the mid-1970s when I was dean, and I had later worked with him on a number of projects in the 1980s when he was the director of research for the Law Reform Commission. He was of great assistance in helping me formulate the scope of my study.

The contract negotiated in the spring of 1995 included a brief description of the work that I would do: 'The work would cover the area of control of deviant behaviour in the Military. The emphasis would be on the chain of command system, leadership, disciplinary actions and decisions, as well as looking at other techniques for controlling undesirable behaviour. The study would look at the subject from a conceptual, comparative and to some extent, historical perspective.' The contract proceeded on the assumption that the study would be published by the commission, but if it was not, then I would have the right to publish it after the publication of the commission's report. The commission wanted a fairly tight time frame. I was to complete the study within a year.

The contract provided about half of the budget for research assistance. I have always found that research assistants are important in my research. For this project, they were crucial. As I wrote to Stan Cohen: 'The project would not be an easy one for a number of reasons. It would, of course, require a general understanding of military organizations. Further, my superficial search into the literature indicates that much of it – and I assume that there will be material out there some place – will be hard to find.' One matter – to give one example – that continues to cause me to scratch my head in wonder, but never seems to bother members of the military, is why a brigadier is higher in rank than a major and a major higher than a lieutenant, but a lieutenant-general is higher in rank than a major-general and a major-general higher than a brigadier-general. Like lawyers, the military have ways of keeping the uninitiated in their place.

I had excellent research assistance for this project. Caroline Ursulak, who had worked with me on the judiciary study, was given a short leave of absence from her law firm to do background work for me on the military justice system. Caroline had some experience in military matters because after completing her master's in international affairs and before coming to law school, she had worked for three years for a Canadian military defence association. I also hired Rob Brush, who had been in my first-year small group, had been the gold medallist in political science at Western, and also had a master's in political science. In his third year of law school, Rob would do an excellent directed research project under my supervision on the difficult topic 'The Place of Rules of

Engagement within the Military Justice System,' which I forwarded to the Somalia inquiry for its use. I also wanted to find someone with military experience, and so wrote to the Royal Military College in Kingston, asking if they knew of a law student or young lawyer who had a military background. It turned out that there was such a student who had just finished first year in our own faculty. Craig Martin had been the gold medallist in the history program at RMC and for the next four years had been a naval lieutenant in Victoria and Halifax. He was able to provide the background that all of us needed, particularly on the military police and on informal methods of discipline. For a time while in the military he had been the officer responsible for the administration, discipline, and direction of thirty men on *HMCS Preserver*. These research assistants are typical of the many I have had over the years. The reader will understand why I have dedicated this book to them.

My personal knowledge of military matters was very limited, being based on three months in the air force in the summer of 1950, as described in the prologue. Having just finished grade 12 and needing a summer job, I became one of a group of about fifty students who joined 400 Fighter Squadron to get a taste of military life. I received an honourable discharge after the summer.

I have always liked planes, and so when I turned sixty I started taking flying lessons at the Toronto Island Airport. For the better part of a year, I would spend Saturday mornings at ground school and in the air. I completed the ground-school training with flying colours, even though I seemed to be asking more naive questions than anyone else. My objective was to fly solo, but I did not achieve that. After I had spent about ten or fifteen hours in the air, always with an instructor, my in-laws were involved in a serious car accident. Under the circumstances, spending half a day a week taking flying lessons seemed a bit frivolous. So I stopped the lessons and never took them up again.

My research assistants and I combed through the military libraries at National Defence headquarters in Ottawa, the Canadian Forces College library in Toronto, and the Judge Advocate General's library in Ottawa. Craig met with military police at National Defence headquarters and Caroline with military-justice personnel. I had lengthy interviews with many knowledgeable members of the military. Lieutenant Colonel Kim Carter, who was part of the liaison group with the Somalia inquiry and later became the chief military judge and a full colonel, was particularly helpful, as were members of the Judge Advocate General's branch. I

had discussions with many other knowledgeable commanders, lieutenant commanders, and lieutenant colonels, although, again, I am still not
certain of the proper hierarchy of those ranks. On one visit to Ottawa to
meet with the JAG people, I was invited to lunch in the officers' mess, a
particular treat that the JAG staff did not want to miss – it was arctic
char day. I was impressed with the officers' mess, but less impressed
with the bare, almost primitive premises where the JAG officers and
persons that I met at National Defence headquarters worked. I hope
that working conditions have improved since I was there.

As with my other research projects, I built up file boxes of material
and was constantly rethinking the organization of the material and
structure of the study. The paper grew in length. In early January 1996
I wrote to Stan Cohen, saying, 'The paper is substantially longer than I
expected. On the other hand it was substantially more interesting to do
than I expected.' The printed version of the paper, *Controlling Misconduct in the Military: A Study Prepared for the Commission of Inquiry into the
Deployment of Canadian Forces in Somalia*, was over 180 pages long. I
received excellent feedback on drafts that I sent out, particularly from
Stan. I also received valuable comments from Kent Roach, with whom
I had worked on the sanctions-and-rewards projects; from Deborah
Harrison, who had been studying women and the military for the commission; and from various persons with military backgrounds, such as
Douglas Bland, Charles Cotton, Jack Vance, and Professor Janet Walker
of the Osgoode Hall Law School, who had written on military justice.

A preliminary draft was handed in on 29 February 1996 – a leap year
– in accordance with the contract, and the final draft was delivered in
June. I noted that the study contained 'a lot of background material that
might prove useful to persons making policy submissions to the Commission' and that the commission 'might consider releasing the final
version at an earlier stage, rather than waiting until after your report is
published.' Other commissions, including the McDonald Commission
on national security, I reminded them, had followed that route. I was
told that the commission was planning on publishing the background
studies along with their final report. I will discuss later in this chapter
the odd circumstances the following year that brought about the publication of my report, along with others, before the publication of the
commission report.

The project was particularly interesting to me because of the light it
shed on ways to control conduct in non-military situations. There are

many valuable aspects of military justice and other techniques used by the military to control undesirable conduct. The military, like the academic world, uses rewards as a way of motivating desirable conduct, a technique that is not used – as discussed in an earlier chapter – to the extent it could be to control undesirable conduct in civilian society. Further, the military, like the tax system, does not come in with its heavy guns – courts martial in the case of the military – whenever wrongdoing is discovered. Administrative sanctions are often used, as are summary proceedings. Summary trials at the time I did my study constituted 98 per cent of all military trials.

In civilian society we give too much prominence to criminal proceedings. We punish and stigmatize. The military, in contrast, generally tries to reintegrate the wayward soldier back into military society. Soldiers that cannot be reintegrated under any conditions, as one sociologist has observed, 'must be punished or expelled from the Army in such a way as to maintain the legitimacy of the Army in other soldiers' (and civilians') eyes.' Reintegrative shaming, such as occurs in summary proceedings before the commanding officer, has been making a resurgence in criminological theory. As criminologist John Braithwaite states in his book *Crime, Shame and Reintegration*, 'Reintegrative shaming is superior to stigmatization because it minimizes risks of pushing those shamed into criminal subcultures, and because social disapproval is more effective when embedded in relationships overwhelmingly characterized by social approval.' In the civilian criminal-justice system – this is particularly so in the United States – we tend to push wrongdoers into criminal subcultures by imposing too harsh penalties.

I canvassed the general literature as well as the specific studies on misconduct in the military. Military personnel are, by the nature of their activity, aggressive. As military historian Anthony Kellett observed, 'If an army is to fulfill its mission on the battlefield, it must be trained in aggression.' The wonder is that there is not more spillover criminal activity by members of the military than there is. It does, however, occur for certain types of crime. Authors have identified, for example, a high level of spousal abuse in the military. This could be a spillover into personal lives of violence used elsewhere for legitimate purposes, reflecting 'a subculture in which physical aggressiveness is positively valued.'

Physical aggressiveness, I noted, is particularly valued for paratroopers – and it was paratroopers who were sent to Somalia. Paratroopers were volunteers from other units who had passed the formal parachute jumping course and had met higher physical-fitness standards than those in other infantry units. In my study I quoted an article by a Canadian major who wrote in 1975: 'Jumping encourages self-confidence, determination, self-reliance, masterful activity, aggression, courage, and other items symptomatic of the Phallic-narcissistic type, all of which are very important in the military setting, especially in paratroop commando units, which rely heavily on individual action and are aggressive in nature.'

My study questioned the use of an airborne unit for peacekeeping missions. Their presence, I suggested, may be counterproductive. The U.S. military, for example, had to remove airborne troops as occupation forces from Yokohama after the Second World War because of alleged rapes, robberies, and murders. Further, it was parachutists who killed thirteen Catholics in Northern Ireland on Bloody Sunday in 1972. (Recent reports have also documented the use of torture by members of an American airborne regiment, known locally as the 'Murderous Maniacs,' against detained Iraqis.) It is not surprising, therefore, that in 1995 the Canadian government closed down the airborne division, although a special counter-terrorism unit (known as JTF2 – Joint Task Force II) was later established and is still in operation.

Another issue that I explored was the disturbing evidence of alcohol abuse. There is a high level of alcoholism in the military, in part because of the easy access to cheap alcohol on most bases. In one survey of the Canadian military in 1989, almost half the respondents reported being sick as a result of alcohol abuse, and about one-third had had blackouts during that year. A 1994 random survey of almost two thousand regular-force members concluded that 'a fifth of members had been drunk four or more times in the last three months and one in twenty-five show evidence of significant problems related to their alcohol use.' Restricting alcohol consumption, I concluded, was an important ingredient in controlling undesirable conduct. Some of the videotapes shot in Somalia and repeatedly shown on television showed soldiers drinking large quantities of beer. In contrast, the U.S. forces did not permit their troops to use alcohol in Somalia.

In subsequent missions abroad, including in Bosnia and Afghanistan, the Canadian military has limited soldiers to two drinks of alcohol per person a day. The 2004 DND annual report notes, however, that for deployed operations, drug and alcohol misconduct constitutes almost one-third of all charges laid, whereas for the military as a whole it represents about 10 per cent. So alcohol and drugs are still a problem. I have seen no TV coverage of problem drinking in Afghanistan, but perhaps because liquor is not widely available in a Muslim country and is not permitted on American bases it is easier to control drinking there than in other jurisdictions.

The selection of military personnel is the starting point in controlling misconduct. With full conscription, the military will roughly reflect the general population, but with an all-voluntary army, as Canada has, this is not necessarily so because economic necessity will be a strong factor for those seeking a military career. After conscription was ended in the United States in the early 1970s, the quality of the recruits dropped, such that the reading level of the average soldier dropped from the twelfth-grade in 1973 to the fifth-grade level in 1980. In the good economic times of the mid-1980s the quality of the applicants in Canada declined, and many of these subsequent recruits ended up in Somalia. The minimum qualification for recruits is still a grade 10 education, even though for civilian police it is normally at least the completion of high school. Moreover, at the time I did my study there were inadequate checks made of the recruit's prior criminal record and no psychological testing. The military has informed me that grade 10 is still the minimum education level, and that psychological tests are still not given, but the recruiters are careful to check criminal records.

The Canadian force in Somalia was virtually an all-male force, whereas 12 per cent of the much larger U.S. force was composed of females. There were few acts of violence by U.S. personnel in Somalia. Thus, I raised the question in my study whether the presence of a large number of women in the U.S. military units might have helped control misconduct, and suggested that more women be selected for peace-keeping operations in the Canadian military. Female children are not normally socialized to be as aggressive as males. Moreover, one U.S. study showed that 'women were less likely than men ... to view the locals negatively.' That study contrasted the approach by women to that of male combat troops, who tend to adopt a 'warrior strategy' and 'construct negative stereotypes of Somalis and perceive them as the enemy.' There was therefore a danger that many of the combat-ready Canadian Airborne forces approached their task as 'warriors' rather than as humanitarians. Having women in the contingent might have had a beneficial effect on the behaviour of the Canadian troops. The Canadian military has, however, changed. At least one in ten of the more than two thousand Canadian troops in Afghanistan are women. This may have assisted in creating a better attitude towards the

Afghans than to the Somalis. From what I have read and seen on TV, the troops appear genuinely to want to help the local citizens. But all it takes is one incident of torture or murder to cause an investigation which may turn up disturbing revelations.

A full study comparing the missions in Somalia and Afghanistan would make an excellent graduate thesis.

One clear change between the Somalia and Afghanistan missions is the greater use of military police. There were clearly too few military police in Somalia. Only two such officers were sent there for a Canadian force of more than one thousand persons – less than one-fifth of 1 per cent of the force. By comparison, military police accounted for about 7 or 8 per cent of the U.S. force in the first Gulf War in 1990–1. One reason for the failure to send more military police was that cabinet, in spite of recommendations by the military for more troops, had set a firm upper limit on the number that could be sent, and personnel were needed for military operations. Further, the operation was originally to be a United Nations operation, and in such cases the UN supplies the police. The military recognized and continues to recognize the importance of having military police. In the early 1990s there were about 1300 authorized security and military-police positions in the Canadian Forces out of a total regular force of somewhat under about 65,000 persons – that is, about 2 per cent. There was one military police position for every fifty members of the military. Outside the military, the figure is one tenth that amount – about one police officer per five hundred persons.

Adequate numbers of military police are particularly necessary when prisoners are taken or other persons detained in order to get the captured combatants away from the front-line troops, whose emotions tend to run high. One senior Canadian officer observed that 'if there had been a military police presence in theatre both of the Somalia incidents [4 and 16 March 1993] which brought such discredit on the Canadian forces in general and the Airborne Regiment in particular may have been avoided.' The lesson from Somalia was quickly learned, and in the subsequent mission to Bosnia in 1995 Canada sent a larger number of military police for the thousand-member force assigned to NATO. The same is true for the force in Afghanistan. Having an adequate number of appropriately trained military police accompany Canadian Forces is now standard procedure.

I made a number of specific recommendations in my chapter on the military police which were designed to achieve greater independence for the police from command influence. One change suggested was to have the career prospects of military police determined outside the regimental chain of command. Another was to permit the military police to bring charges for military offences without the consent of the commanding officer. Still another was to consider adopting something similar to the U.S. Criminal Investigation Division, a military body that investigates all serious offences but whose command structure is independent of the units to which accused persons belong. In general, these changes have subsequently been made.

The longest chapter of my study was on military justice, in which I described the relatively complex system of courts martial and summary proceedings. The 1992 Supreme Court of Canada decision in *Généreux* had settled the question of the constitutional legitimacy of a separate system of military justice. The key constitutional question that remained was the validity of the system of summary proceedings conducted before commanding officers and delegated officers.

The military justice system is the core technique for controlling misconduct in the military. When less-harsh controls – leadership, loyalty to one's unit or comrades, administrative sanctions, and rewards – fail, it is the military justice system that is expected to deter improper conduct on and off the battlefield. There is no question that summary proceedings are very important to the Canadian military, just as they are to all military forces. They provide a relatively quick, easily understood, non-legalistic, and reasonably fair system of imposing minor penalties on military personnel. As stated above, summary proceedings are the most widely used form of proceeding, accounting for perhaps 98 per cent of military trials.

In the two years after the Charter was enacted in 1982 the number of summary proceedings dropped by over one-third. They remained relatively low up to the time of the Somalia inquiry, even though the number of Canadian Forces members had increased slightly in that period. Further, from the years 1986 to 1991 the use of detention went down significantly. This trend was contrary to that found in the civilian criminal-justice system. Moreover, Canadian Forces courts martial in and out of Canada were also low, compared with 1983. I suggested that it may well have been apprehension about the constitutionality of the military justice system after the introduction of the Charter in 1982, together with new and more onerous regulations and statutory changes, that were partly responsible for the decline in the use of the military justice system.

In the chapter on military justice I recommended several important changes, which, I believed, would influence the Supreme Court of Canada to uphold the summary-justice procedure, were it to be challenged. One change was to limit the power of the commanding officer to give a punishment of detention to a maximum of about thirty days, rather than the ninety days then permitted. Another was to ensure that a person charged had the opportunity to consult with a military lawyer (or with a civilian lawyer at his or her own expense) before making the decision to waive the right to elect trial by court martial. A third change that I thought should be considered was to permit a member sentenced to detention by a commanding officer to have a right to a new trial by court martial. If those changes were made, I concluded, the Supreme Court of Canada would very likely uphold the procedures on the basis of waiver of rights, or because summary proceedings did not come within section 11 of the Charter, or if the possibility of a thirty-day detention did violate the Charter, that it was a reasonable limit on rights under section 1. The various changes to the law on military justice will be described in a later section.

A further chapter of the study examined external systems of control. I recommended that Parliament should have a greater role in the scrutiny and development of defence policy. There were at the time no annual reports to Parliament by the military or the Department of Defence. Nor was there an annual report to Parliament by a review group such as the Security Intelligence Review Committee in connection with the security service. Parliament had also given up an important area of review by not examining orders in council and other statutory instruments relating to the military.

I suggested in my study and at a special symposium organized for the inquiry by the Ottawa-based Institute of Governance that two types of review were desirable. One would be a body internal to the military, comparable to the U.S. inspector general of the army. This is an important office, with inspectors general of lesser rank throughout the army who receive complaints, allegations of impropriety, and requests for assistance. The other type of review should be a civilian body outside the military that reports to Parliament. This could be an office like the Security Intelligence Review Committee, an external military ombudsman, or a statutory inspector general such as the position introduced in the United States in 1983. Both the internal and the external body should, as in the United States, receive complaints from civilians as well as the military, provide anonymity to persons reporting, and have toll-free hotlines to make it easier for persons to call. There should be no requirement for military personnel to exhaust internal redress-of-grievance procedures before their concerns were dealt with. The government subsequently chose to introduce an ombudsman.

My study was handed in at the end of June 1996. I then more or less forgot about the subject and went on to other projects, although I followed the press accounts of the problems that the commission was facing. The government was clearly unhappy with the pace and scope of the work of the commission.

In mid-January 1997 I got a call from Stan Cohen informing me that the government was truncating the commission's activities and imposing an early reporting deadline. It wanted the commission to write and hand in its report by the end of June of that year. The commission still had much work left to do. It had not yet heard witnesses relating to what happened in Somalia and would only have time to hear from two in-theatre commanders, Colonel Labbé and Lieutenant Colonel Mathieu. The commissioners were already obligated to hear witnesses identified as necessary by the parties to the proceedings. The final date for hearing evidence would therefore be the end of March.

The government, Stan Cohen informed me, was at the same time setting up a Special Advisory Group on Military Justice and Military Police Investigative Services, to be chaired by Brian Dickson, the former chief justice of Canada, who had a military background, to investigate the military police and military justice, two of the subjects that I had dealt with in my as-yet unpublished study. The advisory group was to report to Defence Minister Doug Young in two months – by 15 March 1997. I reminded Stan – it was more an 'I told you so' – that I had recommended on several occasions that the commission publish some of the background studies in advance. Publication might have prevented an end-run around the commission.

A few days later, I got a call from Brian Dickson, whom I knew reasonably well and whom I greatly respected. We had known each other since the days when his son Brian had been in my law-reform seminar and was graduating from the U of T law school, in 1970. On several occasions when he was a serving judge, Chief Justice Dickson had invited me to have lunch with him in the Supreme Court dining room. He had been told by my friend Bob Sharpe, at the time a superior court judge in Ontario, who was writing Dickson's biography, that I had completed a study on the very subjects Dickson would be exploring.

Dickson told me that he had not known about the study until Bob spoke to him about it. Bob knew all about my study. Indeed, I had started negotiating the contract with the Somalia inquiry when Bob was still dean of the law school, and he therefore had to approve my undertaking the work. I cannot recall whether I suggested to Bob that he tell Dickson about my study or whether Bob did it on his own. I have no note of such a discussion, but it would not surprise me if I had initiated it.

Dickson wanted to obtain a copy of my study. He and his fellow members – retired Lieutenant General Charles Belzile and businessman and former parliamentarian Bud Bird – had a major project to finish in two months and wanted the benefit of my analysis. I told him that it was up to the Somalia inquiry to give him a copy of the report, although my view was clear that it would be 'intolerable' for him not to have it. Justice Létourneau later called to thank me for my position in supporting the commission.

Dickson requested a copy of the study from the office of the Privy Council, who approached the Somalia inquiry, which would not give a copy to the government. There was a contest between the inquiry and the Privy Council Office. On 4 February Stan Cohen called to say that the Privy Council had capitulated, with the approval of a cabinet committee. One of the members of the Somalia inquiry, Peter Desbarats, later published a book about the inquiry, entitled *Somalia Cover-Up*, in which he described what took place day-by-day. The entry for Wednesday, 5 February 1997 states: 'We've resolved a nasty little tussle behind the scenes' and then referred to the 'concerted attempt' by the special advisory group 'to gain access to our research on military justice.' He goes on to state:

It's widely known among the legal and academic community that Prof. Martin Friedland of the University of Toronto had completed a wide-ranging study for us by the end of last year.

Access to this study would provide the panel with an up-to-date theoretical base for its findings, but why would we assist the 'competition' in this way? Shouldn't that just confirm Young's implied assertion that his experts could do, in a few months, what it had taken us more than two years to achieve? This was the unfortunate rivalry that the minister had created.

Our response was to provide the study only if we were given control over the publication of all our studies. Some of us have become so suspicious of the government that we believe the Liberals might not only delay publication of our report after the end of June, on some pretext or other, but prevent us from publishing our research.

Today we received a government order giving us control over our own publishing schedule, and the Friedland study is on its way to the advisory group. We intend to publish it about two weeks before the minister announces his reforms.

My report was published in record time in both official languages, an impressive accomplishment. It seems to have been well received. I will mention only two responses. I liked the one from Barnett Danson, a former minister of national defence, who wrote: 'Like so many reports, I was about to put it in the pile beside my bed until I had an opportunity to scan it. But then I made the mistake of starting to read it and found it intensely interesting. The emphasis on preventing misconduct struck a special chord for me as a former soldier and as MND.' He then went on to make a number of thoughtful observations, including that 'we are belatedly paying a high price for the mystique of the paratrooper, a role which your report properly refers to as an [outdated] requirement for modern defence forces.' Many persons found the report very readable. I blushed when the master of Massey College, John Fraser, who was then investigating an issue involving military discipline, wrote in the *Toronto Star*:

> I was very grateful to pick up a Canadian government study on military justice ... *Controlling Misconduct in the Military* ... The author is the multi-talented Martin L. Friedland, the former dean of the University of Toronto's faculty of law and the author of at least 15 books – all of them distinctive and readable, which makes him a blessed oddity among legal polemicists. This study is written with all the master's familiar touches: succinctness, pithiness and eloquence.

The Dickson special advisory group invited me to meet with them as a paid consultant for several hours on 12 February a week after receiving my study. My appearance was with the consent of the Somalia inquiry. I was to be picked up from the Ottawa airport and, as a memo from the group's executive officer states, 'whisked to our downtown office.' In the academic world we are rarely 'whisked' any place.

The advisory group had gone over my study very carefully and we had an excellent discussion about the issues. I later received a gracious letter of thanks from Dickson. I also received a note from the commission counsel Guy Pratte, after their report was handed in, stating: 'Having your report in our hands was of great help in more ways than I can explain.' The group's report specifically mentioned that they had 'access to an exhaustive study prepared and completed in 1996 by Professor Martin Friedland of the University of Toronto, which touches upon many of the matters falling within our mandate.' I also reviewed an opinion that Pratte provided to the group on the Charter aspects of the military justice system. In the meantime, I had been reviewing drafts of the Somalia report and commenting on some of their background papers. Being paid by the two competing groups was somewhat awkward, but there was full disclosure to each group of my involvement with the other.

The Dickson group produced a fine report. I sent a note to Dickson, stating: 'I read your report over the week-end. It is a very impressive document – on time and probably under budget. I agreed with most of your recommendations and was pleased and honoured to have played a role in assisting the advisory group.'

The document followed many of the suggestions I had made in my study. They rightly recognized that 'in recent years the application of military discipline with the Canadian Forces has been overly cautious and inconsistent because of concerns by commanding officers about uncertainties over the effect of the Canadian Charter of Rights and Freedoms.' 'Consequently,' they went on to say, 'we have recommended certain changes in the summary trial process which we hope will encourage confidence in the use of this important method of discipline and leadership.' 'The main instrument of [the] disciplinary process,' they stated, 'is the traditional summary trial process, which permits the chain of command to administer discipline and justice in a swift, decisive and final manner, both under combat circumstances in times of war and in training circumstances in times of peace.'

They recommended, as I had, that for summary proceedings the maximum period of detention be reduced from ninety to thirty days and that a person charged be given the opportunity to consult with legal counsel before waiving trial by court martial. The commanding officer who was involved in the charge, they stated (as I had), should not be involved in the hearing, and there should be a right to ask for a review of a conviction that was subject to a waiver by the next level of command. They also recommended greater independence for the military police as well as a more independent National Investigative Service. Further, they suggested that a 'responsible and independent office' should be created to provide an avenue for complaints and concerns by individual members of the Canadian Forces with respect to any matter that touches on the military justice system or any other concerns of military personnel, and that this body report directly to the minister of national defence.

Not everyone was happy with the Dickson recommendations. Guy Pratte faxed me an article that had appeared in the *Montreal Gazette* on 1 April 1997 by retired Colonel James Allan, who had commanded the Canadian contingent of the UN peacekeeping forces in the Middle East. He commented on the Dickson report by stating, in part:

> The public relations devoted to getting out Young's 'reforms' has obscured the much more substantive work being done by various experts for the Somalia commissioners. For example, Prof. Martin Friedland's report on the military justice system is better than the one prepared for Young by Justice Brian Dickson. Friedland correctly stressed the role of Parliament as an independent oversight body external to the military.

I was flattered, but was content to have played a role in Dickson's fine work.

The Somalia inquiry's report, *Dishonoured Legacy*, published that summer, took a somewhat different approach than Dickson or I had taken on military justice. It accepted the need for summary proceedings before commanding officers, but limited their use to minor military misconduct. The commission would prohibit the use of summary trials for the most serious service offences, including criminal code offences tried as service offences. In other cases, summary proceedings could not be used if detention was sought, although confinement to barracks would be possible. This would have forced the military to proceed by court martial in many more cases, including, for example, cases of theft and possession of narcotics. Moreover, the Somalia inquiry would have given all military personnel the right to trial by jury before a civilian court whenever the offence carried a possible penalty of five years or more. This would, of course, have brought many more military cases into the civilian courts.

The Somalia inquiry did not try to engage in a debate with the Dickson proposals. The commissioners probably felt that they did not have sufficient time to do so, as they were scrambling to complete their lengthy report by the end of June 1997. The report was too detailed to be easily absorbed by the press and the public, consisting of over 1600 pages in five volumes, covering a wide range of topics. Moreover, I found that it was not particularly well organized. It is difficult to write a report with an axe hovering over one's head. I have only examined its sections on military justice, and do not feel competent to discuss other areas of the commission's report.

A special Senate committee had been formed in early April 1997 to continue to explore the issues that the Somalia inquiry did not have time to examine, but the committee met on only two occasions. At the end of April Parliament was prorogued for a June 1997 election, putting an end to its existence.

The government now had two reports to examine, the Somalia inquiry report and the report by the Dickson special advisory group. The government's response, *A Commitment to Change*, was issued in October 1997 by the new minister of defence, Art Eggleton. It accepted most of the recommendations of the Somalia inquiry, but where the inquiry's recommendations differed from those of the Dickson group, the government proposed to implement the latter. In particular, it did not accept the Somalia inquiry's recommendation that summary proceedings be severely limited to minor disciplinary proceedings. Instead, the government adopted the Dickson group's view that summary proceedings be used for any military offence, although detention would be limited to thirty days. It would, however, limit the ability of a commanding officer to try the accused summarily for criminal offences to just eight such offences.

Nothing was said in the government response about giving the accused access to counsel to ensure a true waiver of trial by court martial, probably because this could be implemented without amending the *National Defence Act*. That change was subsequently made by regulation. The government also did not accept the Somalia inquiry's recommendation that the accused have the right to trial by jury in a civilian court whenever the offence carried a penalty of imprisonment of five years or more. As to an external review body, the government chose a military ombudsman rather than an inspector general. To some extent the difference between the two is more a matter of name than function, but it is likely that if the inspector-general route had been taken, the office would have had stronger powers of investigation than that given to the ombudsman.

In a paper published in 1998 in the *Criminal Law Quarterly* as part of a collection of articles honouring Alan Mewett, I wrote: 'The result of the proposed changes will produce a more limited, but still effective system of summary proceedings. In this writer's opinion, this is a desirable outcome.'

The Senate took up the task of examining the bill on military justice – C-25 – in October 1998. I was asked to appear before the committee, but declined. I had had my full say on all these issues and, moreover, was heavily involved in my research on the history of the University of Toronto.

Bill C-25 came into force the following year and seems to have had the desired effect. The number of summary trials more than doubled in 2000–1 and more than tripled in 2002–3. The annual report of the judge advocate general for 2002–3 noted 'the continued willingness of commanding officers to resort to the disciplinary system when necessary' and an 'increased confidence in the system.' The new act called for an independent review of the legislation every five years. In September 2003 Antonio Lamer presented the first such review. He was very positive, stating: 'While Bill C-25 dealt with a variety of issues, one of the main areas was the reform of the military justice system. I am pleased to report that as a result of the changes made by Bill C-25, Canada has developed a very sound and fair military justice framework in which Canadians can have trust and confidence.'

My work clearly played a role in the redesign of the system of military justice. Whether it had an effect on other decisions, such as closing down the airborne regiment, creating a military ombudsman, the increase in women on foreign missions, and the attempt to control the use of alcohol abroad, is difficult to say. I was not privy to any of the decisions in the department. I would hear rumours that my study was being discussed in military circles, but I do not travel in those circles and so do not know.

Like most of the studies I have worked on, this one took unexpected twists and turns. Reforming military justice fits nicely into the conclusion that I offered in the chapter on codification of the criminal law, where I explored R.S. Wright's model criminal code and asked: 'What conclusions can be drawn from the story of Wright's Jamaica Code?' My answer was: 'Perhaps it is simply the obvious one that law reform is affected by a great number of factors apart from the merits of the proposals. Then, as now, a combination of politics, personalities and pressure groups affected the outcome.'

27

Writing the History of the University of Toronto

Another consequence of writing my historical-crime books is that I was asked to write the history of the University of Toronto. Had I not written those books it is doubtful that I would have been so selected.

In early June 1997 I received a telephone call from Ron Schoeffel, the editor-in-chief at the University of Toronto Press, asking if I would be interested in submitting a proposal to a university committee charged with deciding who would be invited to write a history of the University of Toronto. The committee, chaired by Father James McConica of the Pontifical Institute of Mediaeval Studies, wanted a scholarly yet accessible one-volume history. The last history of the University had been published in 1927. In the 1970s, material had been collected for a history, but the project was later abandoned. The new history would be published in the year 2002 – the 175th anniversary of the granting of a charter to King's College, the predecessor of the University of Toronto.

I had, of course, known about the project, but had not previously indicated any interest in it. I told Ron that I would think about whether I would submit a proposal. I was not sure that I wanted to undertake the task. Was there enough archival material from which to draw? Could the story be told adequately in one volume? How would the information be organized? Would I find the endeavour intellectually rewarding? Over the course of the following six weeks I prepared a detailed proposal, helped by two excellent summer research assistants, Graham Rawlinson and Katrina Wyman, who had just completed first-year law school and who were working with me on various legal projects, including one on legal aid. Graham, who had come into law school with a graduate degree in history and is now a lawyer with Torys, and Katrina, who had a graduate degree in political science and now teaches at the New York University law school, were enthusiastic about the project.

I became very interested in the prospect of writing the history. It quickly became clear that an almost overwhelming amount of primary material was available in the University of Toronto Archives and at other locations. Moreover, there was an abundance of secondary material, such as autobiographical writing by former administrators – President Claude Bissell, Dean Ernest Sirluck of the graduate school, Chief Librarian Robert Blackburn, and many others. An extensive collection of doctoral theses, biographies, taped interviews, and departmental and other histories related to the University of Toronto could be used.

It would not be easy. The University of Toronto is not only a very old institution by Canadian standards. It is also a very complex institution. In part, the complexity is due to the number of constituent colleges, such as St Michael's, which joined the University in 1881, followed by Victoria College in 1890, and Trinity College in 1904. The colleges were responsible for teaching a number of subjects in the humanities and the University for teaching the social sciences and pure sciences. This division, which has subsequently been modified, was worked out in the 1880s and reflected the subjects that Victoria wanted to continue teaching when it joined the University. In addition, there are a large number of professional faculties, dominated by engineering and medicine. The faculty of medicine, with its many teaching hospitals, divisions, and links to other faculties, was particularly complex. There were no histories at the time of the largest divisions in the university: the faculties of arts and science, medicine, engineering, or graduate studies.

A one-volume history, I thought, would pose problems of selection, but that would make the task more interesting. The presentation of the material would also be a challenge. I hoped to make the history one that people would want to read from beginning to end, rather than just concentrate on their own areas of interest. A chronological approach seemed the best way to accomplish this. The faculty of medicine, for example, would be dealt with in a number of places rather than within a single chapter. Similarly, instead of treating broad themes, such as academic freedom or curriculum development, as individual chapters, I would discuss these themes in appropriate places throughout the book.

I planned relatively short chapters, as I had done in *Old Man Rice*, which would look at specific issues and events – often turning points – in the University's history. A chapter would start on a particular date and look backwards at what led up to an issue or event, and then take the story forward in time. After completing the book I learned that starting somewhere in the middle of a story is a well-known literary device – *in medias res*, used by Homer in the *Iliad* and the *Odyssey*. At the time, however, I simply wanted to tell a story in an interesting manner and also make a scholarly contribution to the literature.

One of the key issues was determining the date on which the history would end, which I decided would be the year 2000. I wanted the story to have a happy ending. While I could have ended things at an earlier point, one at which I had neither known the key players nor partici-pated in the events, that would hardly have been the history the Uni-versity wanted, or the one I was interested in undertaking. As earlier chapters of the present book show, I grew up in Toronto and went to the University for both my undergraduate and law degrees. I came to the University in 1951, knew Sidney Smith in the 1950s, and worked closely with Claude Bissell on university governance in the 1960s. I was dean of law in the 1970s when John Evans was president, hired Robert Prichard as a law teacher, and so on. After my post-graduate work at Cambridge University and teaching at Osgoode Hall Law School, I returned to the Faculty of Law in 1965. As I stated in the prologue to the book: 'For better or worse, I am not a detached observer. But then, who would be?'

My proposal was presented to the selection committee in late July 1997, and an interview was arranged. Others, I was told, were inter-viewed as well. Some subsequently identified themselves to me and gave me the benefit of their expertise. It was a strong committee, com-posed primarily of historians – Father McConica, who had been involved in writing the history of Oxford University, Natalie Zemon Davis, who had written the very readable *The Return of Martin Guerre*, my squash partner Vice-president Michael Finlayson, social historian Franca Iacovetta, and graduate school dean Michael Marrus, along with Bill Harnum and Ron Schoeffel of the Press. I understand, but did not know it at the time, that President Prichard was keen to have me do the history.

Most, if not all, members of the committee were familiar with one or more of my historical crime books. I told them that I would try to write the history in the same way, trying to keep the reader interested and linking the history to the cultural, political, and social life of the city, the province, and the country.

In the fall I was informed that I had been selected. The contract with the University of Toronto Press allowed me about 200,000 words of text and the equivalent of 100 pages of pictures. Notes – there are about 400 pages of them – would be published separately by the Press and would also appear on the University of Toronto Press's website (see www .utppublishing.com, then go to 'downloads'). I was provided with a substantial sum for research assistance and a good honorarium. I also negotiated with the University for special treatment in the archives, where I would have a separate room for my research assistants and would be permitted to have my own photocopying machine. We all took special training in photocopying archival material – e.g., do not use the automatic feeder. It would have been very difficult – if not almost impossible – to have done the project in the time available if we had had to wait to receive copies of documents from the archives in the normal way. When the project was over, some of the equipment, including a small refrigerator, which my research assistants had used, was donated by the Press to the archives.

I was about to turn sixty-five, and at the University of Toronto at that time one officially retired at the end of June of the year in which one reached that age. The history turned out to be a perfect post-retirement project. Over the next four years, I spent perhaps 90 per cent of my research time on the endeavour. I cannot think of a more intellectually stimulating project to have undertaken.

The history of the University of Toronto is the history of Toronto, the history of Ontario, and the history of Canada. It is intimately connected with events outside the University. One can trace over the years, for example, both Canada's and the University's transition from dependence on Great Britain and fear of the United States to a lessening of British influence and an acceptance of American culture and ideas. I had experienced part of this transition as a young law student. This change would have upset the founder of the University, John Strachan, who had urged the creation of a university in Upper Canada to counter American values. In the United States, he argued, 'the school books ... are stuffed with praises of their own institutions, and breathe hatred to everything English ... Some may become fascinated with that liberty which has degenerated into licentiousness, and imbibe, perhaps unconsciously, sentiments unfriendly to things of which Englishmen are proud.'

Life at the University clearly was affected by the two world wars, the cold war, and the Vietnam war. The opening up of the University to various groups as students and as faculty members also reflects developments in society generally. What was happening in society can be seen, for example, in the admission of women to University College in the 1880s or in the expansion of the University in the 1960s to accommodate the 'baby boomers' born after the Second World War. And it can be seen in the University's growing ethnic, cultural, and religious diversity in the 1990s, a reflection of Canadian immigration patterns in the 1960s and 1970s. And so on.

The project was also an exploration of the history of ideas. The early periods show both the fierce conflicts in the country and in the University over the role of the Christian religion in public institutions and the tensions among the different Christian denominations. Charles Darwin's ideas permeated much of the intellectual debate in the second half of the nineteenth century. The ideas of many of the major intellectual figures on the world's stage made their way onto Toronto's. Thomas Huxley, a Darwinian, was turned down for a position at the University in the 1850s. James Mavor, a follower of Karl Marx, was hired as the professor of political economy in the 1880s. Ernest Jones, Sigmund Freud's biographer, taught psychoanalysis in the medical school before the First World War, and Leopold Infeld, one of Albert Einstein's collaborators, taught in the mathematics department in the 1940s.

An institutional history of a university, I discovered, can be a wonderful way to look at many political, cultural, and intellectual issues. Because the currency of universities is knowledge and ideas, they are often forced to deal with external forces. During the summer of 2002 I gave a talk to U of T alumni and others at the Canadian Studies Centre in Berlin. A number of persons from Berlin's Humboldt University, formerly known as the University of Berlin, attended and participated in the discussion. Their university, which was founded in 1810, has, of course, been buffeted by external forces to a far greater degree than has the University of Toronto – including by fascism and communism. One could write the history of Europe and of ideas by looking at Humboldt University – twenty-nine Nobel prizes up to 1933 and none after that.

The University of Toronto grew dramatically over the past century. In 1900 there were well under 2000 students, in 1950 there were about 10,000, and by 2000 there were over 50,000 students on its three campuses – the largest number of students at any university in North

America. Since then, the U of T has continued to grow, and now has almost 70,000 students, 60,000 of them being full-time.

The growth has been particularly evident in the number of graduate students. The PhD degree was introduced at the University of Toronto in 1897, with the first PhD being awarded in 1900. The number of PhD students increased very gradually over the years. By the year 1921 only forty persons had received PhDs. By the mid-1980s, however, there were about three thousand doctoral students enrolled. Today, engineering alone has over a thousand graduate students, with about 40 per cent pursuing doctorates. Moreover, most programs in the University now require a first degree before entry. The mission of the University of Toronto has shifted significantly towards post-graduate work.

Coupled with the growth in the number of graduate students has been a dramatic increase in research at the University. During the First World War, the head of the National Research Council estimated, the entire country had 'not many more than 50 pure research men all told.' The total sum spent by the federal government for university research from 1912 to 1915 had been less than $300,000. Today, the research budget of the University of Toronto alone is greater than $350 million, plus a comparable amount for research in the teaching hospitals.

The financing of universities has also changed. I was surprised to learn that at the beginning of the last century the Ontario government contributed very little to universities. The total U of T budget in 1900 was on average under $125,000 a year, and the provincial government contributed annually only $7000 of that amount. Today, the provincial government contributes over half a billion dollars to the U of T for general operations. For the most part, in earlier periods the federal government stayed out of education. The Massey Commission, which reported in 1951, changed that. Universities, the commission stated, which were 'nurseries of a truly Canadian civilization and culture,' were 'facing a financial crisis so great as to threaten their future usefulness.' Direct federal support to universities began almost immediately, rising from $7 million in 1951–2 to some $100 million in 1966–7.

A recurring theme in the history of the University is how to control those financing the University. In the early days it was the church, and later the provincial government, that had direct effective control of the University. Up until the change in the governing structure in 1906 (described below), all appointments were made by the provincial cabinet. The most striking exercise of the power of appointment occurred in 1853, when the government decided to appoint the undistinguished

Reverend William Hincks as the professor of natural science at the University instead of Thomas Huxley, who had submitted references from Charles Darwin and many members of the scientific establishment in Great Britain. William Hincks was, it should be noted, the brother of the premier of the province.

Another issue is that of governance, which influences how the institution functions. The 1906 *University of Toronto Act* changed the way the University was to be governed. A government-appointed board of governors was established to deal with financial issues and a senate to handle academic matters. The University would be removed from direct government control. The report of the provincial royal commission that led to the change was obviously strongly influenced by the businessmen on the commission, such as Joseph Flavelle. The board of governors would be like a corporate board of directors appointed by the government – in effect, the shareholders – and be removable at the pleasure of the government. The workers, that is, the faculty and the administrative staff, were excluded from membership on the board. Only the president would be a member.

This bicameral structure, consisting of a board and a senate, lasted for two-thirds of a century. Moreover, it influenced the structure of the new universities that were founded in the West and elsewhere. It was not until 1972, as described in an earlier chapter of this book, that a new *University of Toronto Act* merged the two bodies – the senate and the board of governors – into one unicameral governing council. The 1972 act, in my view, has helped the University of Toronto to cope with change, bringing all the estates together to make financial and academic decisions, which are difficult to separate. It took some time, however, to work out some of the problems with the new structure, the most important of which was that the role of the faculty – who had played a major role in the old senate – was significantly diminished. In the late 1980s, however, a new academic board was established which gave the faculty a greater say in policy issues. My impression is that the governing structure is now working reasonably well. I have not heard much agitation in recent years for the U of T to return to a bicameral system. Still, as mentioned earlier, it is worth pondering why no other major academic institution in North America of which I am aware has followed Toronto's lead.

One question that I would sometimes get after giving a talk on the U of T history was whether I came across anything that surprised me. One surprise was the fact, mentioned above, that we did not hire Thomas

Huxley. Another was to learn that Frederick Banting's fame as a Nobel Prize winner for the discovery of insulin in 1922 probably held back research in the University because a large part of the resulting research money that flowed its way went to Banting, who was not, in fact, a very good researcher. But perhaps the greatest surprise is that up until the Second World War, the heads of the chemistry department, including Lash Miller, after whom the chemistry building was named, did not believe in atomic theory. 'Don't get involved with those fellows ... in chemistry,' John McLennan, a distinguished professor of physics at the time, after whom the physics laboratories are named, advised graduate students. I also learned about a person I had never heard about, A.B. Macallum, a physiologist who became the head of the National Research Council in Ottawa during the First World War, and was perhaps the U of T's greatest scientist before the Second World War.

I will not speculate on who was the University's greatest scientist during the second half of the twentieth century. One of the contenders has to be John Polanyi, whose 1986 Nobel Prize in chemistry for his work on lasers played a role in changing the fate of the University of Toronto. Not only did it help to improve morale in the University, but it encouraged the federal and provincial governments to start funding excellence and not just provide funds according to the number of students. This has helped the U of T enormously.

I have sometimes been asked my opinion on when might have been the best time to have been a student at the University. I particularly liked the 1920s. The University was a dynamic institution in the years before the Depression under the leadership of President Robert Falconer, one of my favourite presidents. Scholarship, research, and graduate studies were becoming more important. Moreover, the University of Toronto was the dominant force in intercollegiate sports and was particularly successful in men's and women's hockey. Most of the members of the men's hockey team graduated in 1926 and formed themselves into the Varsity Grads, which competed in the 1928 Olympics in St Moritz, Switzerland. The team easily won the gold medal, beating Sweden 11–0, Switzerland 13–0, and Great Britain 14–0.

The other decade I liked was the 1950s, when I attended the U of T. The first paragraph of that chapter of the history, entitled 'Easy Street,' states:

It was good to be a student in the 1950s. By 1950, almost all the veterans had graduated, and overcrowding was no longer a serious problem. It would be more than a dozen years before the first wave of baby boomers would appear on campus. The economy was strong, and there was relatively little unemployment. Employers were desperate for university graduates, particularly if they were men. Anyone could go on to law school, with whatever marks. Moreover, the public expected that the 'good times' would continue. There was neither the seriousness of the post-war veterans, nor the intensity of the students of the 1960s. This was the apolitical, silent generation of students who attended football games, spent hours each day playing bridge, and were not particularly worried about their future.

I could not have asked for better research assistance on this project. In my prologue to the history I thank eleven research assistants, including Graham and Katrina, who had helped me formulate the proposal. In the spring of 1998 I had put a request in the law school's weekly newsletter for one or two summer research assistants. The candidates were so impressive that rather than hiring one or two, I ended up hiring five persons that summer from the law school, all with strong backgrounds in history – Michael McCulloch had a doctorate in nineteenth-century Canadian history and David Bronskill a master's in history – as well as two historians, Charles Levi and Sarah Burke. Charles, who had just submitted his doctorate in history at York University under Paul Axelrod, became my principal research assistant over a three-and-a-half-year period. He was – and is – a fabulous researcher. If there was a document that needed to be found, Charles would find it. Michiel Horn of York University described Charles in the acknowledgments to his book on academic freedom as 'incomparable.' I agree, and note that Horn is using Charles to assist him with his forthcoming history of York. Sara Burke, now teaching at Laurentian University, helped me collect material on women in the University. After the book was published, Colin Grey, now doing a doctorate in law at NYU, assisted me in preparing the notes for the Press's website.

The U of T Archives was also superbly helpful, particularly the senior archivist Harold Averill, who helped guide my researchers, and generously commented on drafts of the manuscript, as did others. A list of the sixty-one persons within the University who read some or all of the manuscript is contained in an appendix to the book. I doubt if any manuscript ever published by an academic at the University of Toronto received as much careful vetting as did the history of the University.

The Press, as usual, was wonderful to work with. Ron Schoeffel was in charge of the project, and was always helpful on the book's structure. One of the persons whom I asked to read a draft of the manuscript was the Press's former managing editor, Francess Halpenny. Her comments were so useful that she was asked to become the principal manuscript editor of the book, a task to which she brought the same skill and care she brought to the editing of my criminal-law casebook thirty-five years earlier. I had intended to do my own index, but became involved in national-security issues following the terrorist attacks on 9/11 and ran out of time. An experienced indexer, Ruth Pincoe, produced an admirable index.

I was also assisted by the research material collected by English professor Robin Harris, who had been appointed University Historian in 1970 and had spent the next thirteen years either full-time or part-time on the task, assisted by numerous talented research assistants. In 1974 professor of history Gerald Craig was added to his team and was assigned the task of writing the history up to the *University of Toronto Act* of 1906. Harris would cover the period from 1906 to 1972. Each volume was to be separately published under the author's own name. Illness clearly played a key role in Craig's inability to complete his part of the project. Professor Harris eventually deposited his papers in the archives in 1983. In a background document accompanying the material he described the main problem he faced in writing the history: 'The problem I could not solve was the presentation of the material in human terms.' He illustrated the issue by discussing Kathleen Russell, the director of the nursing program in the 1920s, to whom he planned on devoting three pages.

'The trouble is,' Harris went on to say, 'that between 1906 and 1972 the University of Toronto had between 100 and 200 Kathleen Russells' – people such as Bernard Fernow, the first dean of the faculty of forestry, and William Pakenham, the first dean of education – and so he concluded: 'I have decided to call a halt.' It was clear to me that I could not possibly write the history of each division of a university as complex as the University of Toronto. That is for each division to carry out, as many continue to do.

An issue that had to be faced was how the sources should be dealt with. We decided to put the notes, numbering about 10,000, on the U of T Press's website. These are also available in hard-copy form through the Press, an arrangement which was insisted upon by the Federation of the Humanities and Social Sciences before they would give a grant.

The Press had applied in the usual way for a grant, forwarding two perceptive, positive reader reviews. As it turned out, the Press never received the grant because everyone had forgotten the rule that no grant is available if more than 5000 copies of a book are produced in the initial printing. The Press had printed 6500 copies.

The use of the Internet for all the notes was a first for the Press, and was subsequently written up in the journal *Scholarly Publishing*. Another Press author, Constance Backhouse, had used the Internet for a number of very lengthy footnotes, but the rest were at the back of her book. To have done so for the U of T history would have made the book unnecessarily unwieldy in size. We were, however, able to include in the book thirteen pages on the sources used for each chapter, with an eighteen-page bibliography limited to those sources. I worked closely with the Press for months trying to get the most user-friendly format for the website. The notes are in Adobe's PDF format. One can click on individual chapters or the entire text. Another advantage of using the Internet is that one can do an electronic search of the notes. Putting the notes on the Internet sounds terrific, but my impression is that the electronic version is not used very often. It is encouraging and perhaps surprising, however, to know that after half a dozen years it is still available on the Web.

Still another advantage is that the notes can be changed, as I did in a few cases to correct errors discovered in the text after the book went to press. One significant addition was the discovery that Charles Levi made just before the book was published – too late to be included in the text. He had found a memo from registrar Robin Ross to Claude Bissell in 1959 making it clear that the faculty of medicine discriminated against Jews as late as 1959. Up until finding that note I felt that I could not go further in the text than stating that 'it appears reasonably clear from both the anecdotal and the statistical evidence available that discriminatory practices prevailed for a period of time' after a discretionary admission policy was introduced in 1942. I have not otherwise added to the notes since they were prepared.

I was not familiar with the literature on writing history when I wrote my book, but I did explore this aspect later when I had to address a learned-society symposium on the University of Toronto and its histories. As I read the literature, I kept wondering how the U of T history fit into the various theories. The manuscript certainly fits into a narrative mode. It also attempts to place the history in the context of the times by looking at relevant social, political, and economic conditions. Is it 'top down' or 'bottom up,' to use the language in the literature? I guess it is both, but mainly top down. It is hard for an institutional history to avoid discussing presidents and other senior administrators. But I did not divide the chapters according to presidents. The mention of a new president was usually dealt with in the middle of a chapter.

Where relevant, I tried to include detailed descriptions of events from the students' perspectives, such as the chapter on the admission of women and the student strike of 1895. It is not, however, a history of students or of women. Others can still write their own books on those subjects without worry that the field has been covered. In some places I go into great detail to describe an event. Some of these – such as the student strike of 1895 or the election of Canon Cody as chancellor in the 1940s – may be the U of T equivalents of the Balinese cockfights described by anthropologist Clifford Geertz. They become symbolic windows into a larger society.

From the time I started the project, my plan was to take the story up to around the year 2000. The final chapter, I thought, might record a personal stroll through the St George campus on the last day of 1999, in which I would reflect on the past and maybe speculate on the future. I was not sure where to start the walk, or, indeed, whether I would actually go on it. As it turned out, on 30 December 1999 the optometrist phoned to say that my new lenses had arrived. I could pick my glasses up at the Eaton Centre the next morning. I did so, and took the walk, describing it in the present tense in the last chapter, which I called an epilogue to match the preface, which I called a prologue. It was a bit of a gamble, but it seems to have worked well, according to almost all of the reviews.

I was pleased with the reviews. My favourite was by P.B. Waite, a distinguished professor of history at Dalhousie, who had written the history of that university. In the first sentence of his review in *Historical Studies in Education*, he stated: 'One did not really believe it could be done. Not in one volume, not by one author, not with any grace or charm.' Five pages later he concluded: 'As one looks at this marvelous work, one can only say how wrong we were ... It is not often in a book review that one can truly say, compliments all round, to publisher, designers, researchers, but especially to the author. One thinks of Tolstoy's remark out of the Russian countryside, "the footsteps of the master cultivate the soil."' I must admit that I do not really understand the last sentence, but I take it as a significant compliment. I should add that the book has won a number of prizes: the City of Toronto's Heritage Award, the Champlain Society's Chalmers Award, and the Ontario Historical Association's Talman Award.

I recently became immersed again in U of T history because I was asked to write an introduction to a book being prepared by former architecture dean Larry Richards on the architecture of the University of Toronto, to be published by the Princeton Architectural Press. Who knows what else may result?

I gave a great many talks on the book, both before and after it was published. I went across the country, talking to alumni groups, and in addition gave talks to specific groups interested in certain aspects of the history: for example, to women's groups, to a conference organized by the physiology department to celebrate the one hundredth anniversary of the first PhD awarded at the University, to members of Hart House, to faculty at University College, to graduate students in history, to major donors to the University, to professional historians, and so on.

The talk I remember best was the one I gave on 15 March 2002, the 175th anniversary of the founding of the University and the official date for the book's launch. The Great Hall was packed. My remarks came after those by Chancellor Hal Jackman, President Robert Birgeneau, and James Bartleman, the lieutenant governor of Ontario. I started my brief talk by stating: 'It is not every day that an academic launches a book in the presence of a lieutenant governor and a former lieutenant governor – as well as a chancellor and a former chancellor.' I then read a few selections, ending with a statement made in 1858 by President John McCaul at a banquet celebrating the completion of the construction of the magnificent University College. The passage reads: 'President McCaul eloquently predicted that long after his bones had turned to dust, there would remain "an institution which freely offers the advantages of an education of the highest order to all who are qualified to avail themselves of its benefits, and enables the [children] of the poorest and humblest man in the land to compete on equal terms with the children of the most affluent and the most influential."' I added that this was 'a statement we should continue to take to heart today.'

I then presented the very first copy of the book that I saw to President Birgeneau, with the following inscription:

March 15, 2002

To President Birgeneau:

This copy is for the president's office in Simcoe Hall so that in moments of leisure you and future presidents can read about some of the great and not-so-great presidents of the past. You and perhaps your successors can take comfort in the fact that your office is not now the subject of a sit-in – see chapter 36 on student activism in the 1960s – and that you do not have to use a fire hose to quell a student riot, as President Loudon felt compelled to do in the 1890s – see page 160.

With best wishes,

M.L. Friedland

Epilogue

As the reader will gather, I have thoroughly enjoyed my career in the academic world. I have been surrounded by first-rate colleagues and talented students. The projects have all been interesting, and my contributions to the law and public policy have been personally rewarding and generously rewarded. My work has led to changes to the law and to other institutions. Whether there will be other challenging projects in the future remains to be seen.

My present plan is to continue teaching for at least another year the so-called 'intensive' course at the law school that I taught this past year, based on the material in this book. As to my future research, I doubt if I will ever undertake another massive project like the history of the University of Toronto or the study of judicial independence and accountability. I may, however, try to write a book on the murder that took place on the Fraser River in British Columbia in 1861, mentioned in an earlier chapter. There is not enough archival material available on this case to replicate the historical murder books that I have written, so I will blend known facts with fiction. I recently gave a talk at Massey College on Julian Barnes's *Arthur & George*, a brilliant merging of fact and fiction relating to a historical criminal case that brought about the establishment of the Court of Criminal Appeal in England. Over the years I have toyed with trying just that sort of book, but in the end always stayed with the known facts.

Judy and I will no doubt continue to travel as we have in the past. As the previous chapters show, an academic career does not hold one back from seeing the world, although much of our travel has not been connected with our work, particularly in recent years. Last year we travelled to Poland and Central Europe and the previous year to South-East Asia, and we have just returned from Peru and Patagonia. While there are not very many places still to cover – the pyramids and parts of India are still on the list – we can always return to some of our favourite countries, including England, Israel, and Italy.

We will see what lies ahead, but if the earlier chapters teach us anything, it is that things never work out quite the way one thinks they will. Chance and seemingly almost arbitrary choices always play a role in one's life. I never dreamed that I might have an academic career until some time during first-year law school. None of my high school or undergraduate teachers or classmates ever suspected that I would be a serious scholar. If they did, no one ever said anything to me about it.

Most readers can tell a similar story of the role that chance has played in their own lives. I was lucky, for example, to have been selected for the World University Service study tour of West Africa in 1955, which whetted my appetite for intellectual adventure. I was also fortunate that Dean Caesar Wright had offered to cover my first year's tuition after I returned from that trip so that I could attend the University of Toronto law school, with its stimulating atmosphere. Students rarely know how well they will do at law school. Who would have guessed that Caesar Wright would read out to the first-year class my term paper as a model answer to his torts test?

It was also accidental, as the reader will recall, that I went to Cambridge University for post-graduate work and that I ended up doing my research in the field of criminal law under Glanville Williams. And if the Law Society of Upper Canada had not offered me a scholarship on condition that I teach for one year at Osgoode Hall Law School I probably would not have become a law teacher but instead would have become a litigator with Charles Dubin, and more than likely would later have sought a position as a judge. Further, if I had not become involved in a number of stimulating public-policy inquiries early in my career, I may not have remained in the academic world. The reader will recall many other examples from earlier chapters, and can, no doubt, give similar examples from his or her own career.

Yet, in retrospect, there is a measure of continuity in one's career – one thing does lead to another. At law school and later as an academic, I would look through the new law journals. In my first year of teaching, while looking through the journals, I happened to come across an article on an empirical study of the bail system in the United States by Caleb Foote of the University of Pennsylvania. This led to my empirical study of detention before trial in the Toronto courts, which led to my work on legal aid, which led to further empirical studies. Similarly, the discovery of R.S. Wright's nineteenth-century model criminal code while on sabbatical in 1979 led to my work in the Public Record Office in England, which led to my three murder books, which, in turn, were partly responsible for my selection to write the history of the University of Toronto.

I am not sure that I am able to say how it was that I was able to succeed in the academic world. I tend not to be introspective, but I will try. To start with, my family expected me to succeed in whatever I did. My grandfather, it will be recalled, wrote in my bar-mitzvah book that I should be 'a credit to [my] family and an honour to the Jewish race,' and my mother wrote that I should 'aim high.' My parents were always caring and positive. And while one cannot choose one's parents, one can choose one's life partner. I chose well.

Judy encouraged me to undertake an academic career and supported my future scholarly activities. After a number of years as a full-time mother she also became an academic, later becoming the chair of the department of occupational therapy at the University of Toronto. As a result, she was as engaged as I was in research and writing and did not resent the time I spent on my academic work. Our three children, Tom, Jenny, and Nancy, have always provided stimulation and amusement. Both Tom and Jenny became lawyers – Tom a litigator and partner with Goodmans, Jenny a criminal lawyer – and Nancy a photo-based artist. They and their equally engaging and engaged partners have so far produced six wonderful grandchildren.

I guess I was personally ambitious to succeed. I wanted to do well as a law student and as a scholar and to influence public policy through my books and studies. The competition with Harry Arthurs at law school and as fellow deans – mentioned several times here – probably played a positive role in both our careers.

Another characteristic of mine that helped is that, like my parents, I am reasonably easy to get along with. I tend not to take uncompromising positions. I have no enemies that I know about. This certainly helped as dean and even in my research, which usually required cooperation with others. I recall that at the Learned Society meeting to discuss the University of Toronto history one scholar made the point that everyone in the University helped me collect material because I seemed to be 'such a nice guy.' I am not so sure I am, but I will leave that to others to decide. I have also been described in print as 'self-effacing,' a description that may be retracted after this book is published.

Concentrated hard work also paid off. I learned that as an undergraduate, not through my courses, but through athletics. Without an overabundance of talent, but with practice and determination, I was able to make two intercollegiate teams. Playing sports also helps one to bounce back from defeat. I recall reading some place that the head of one of London's major teaching hospitals liked choosing former athletes to head departments because they are used to winning and losing. In the academic world, as in competitive sports, one has to develop a thick skin. As a scholar, I routinely had papers and books initially rejected by my publisher of choice. It goes with the territory.

Being somewhat adventurous – my early travel is a good example – and filled with curiosity – think of my stamp and butterfly collections and building crystal radio sets – probably played a role in my later work in breaking away from traditional legal scholarship. I never engaged in research which simply 'chased a judge around a stump,' an unforgettable phrase used by law professor John Willis to describe much legal scholarship when I started teaching. I looked for more imaginative ways to understand the law and where it should be heading.

I loved the process of research – getting an idea for a project, gathering information, not knowing exactly where one is going, and constantly reorganizing the material. The writing was usually started long before the research was completed. One can clarify one's thinking through these early drafts and can adjust the writing as more information is collected. There are, therefore, initial drafts, further reworkings and reorganization, and constant rewriting. As I have stated many times in the previous chapters, the ultimate product is often far different from the one that had been planned and described in the initial grant application. There is little point in dutifully following too closely an original plan that was conceived before much serious research was undertaken.

Writing never became particularly easy for me, but I learned that creating a manuscript, whether an article or a book, requires perseverance and many drafts. I also enjoyed the process of publication, from copyediting and peer review to proofreading and indexing. I thought of it all not as a burden, but as a necessary and interesting part of the process. The reader will recall that I even sought permission to watch my first book being typeset in hot lead. I find the publication process fascinating, so it is no surprise that I have been heavily involved with the University of Toronto Press for over forty years.

Perhaps my real talent is to be able to stick with a topic for years and never get bored with it. In part this is because almost all the topics that I have written about are very broad and multi-dimensional, and I almost always treated them from a historical, comparative, and contemporary perspective. I did that, for example, for double jeopardy, national security, sanctions and rewards, and the present book. Each manuscript required bringing together masses of material on related subjects, so it was difficult to get bored. My most recent project, which involved a new field for me, copyright law and practice, was a report for the collective Access Copyright on the proper distribution to publishers and creators of the relatively large sums collected from users. It was very complex. I did not discuss this report in an earlier chapter because under the contract the collective has a year to try to decide how to deal with my report before it is made public.

My work was usually interdisciplinary, which added a further dimension to most projects because I was forced to learn something about a discipline other than law. My bail study was as much a work in sociology as in law, double jeopardy was in part historical, access to the law required some knowledge of psychology and linguistics, sanctions and rewards and pension reform delved into economics and other disciplines, and most topics involved political science. The writing of the history of the University of Toronto required at least a superficial understanding of many disciplines. If I do the book on the British Columbia murder case I will have to immerse myself in the anthropological literature. I consider my involvement in interdisciplinary work probably my most important contribution to legal scholarship. It also had an impact on teaching and scholarship at the faculty of law at the University of Toronto, which in turn influenced academics in other law schools.

I promoted scholarship, both doctrinal and interdisciplinary, at the law school, through my role on the research committee in the 1960s and as dean in the 1970s, by encouragement and by example. A tenure-stream academic has a dual responsibility to be a good teacher and an effective scholar. My attention to the conflict-of-interest rules as dean and my later work in the 1990s on conflict-of-interest rules for the University are a reflection of my view that academics have to concentrate on advancing knowledge and making those advances public. In almost all cases I was able to publish the work that I did for outside bodies. The conflict-of-interest rules give academic administrators the ability to ensure that colleagues get some academic payoff from their outside work.

In an earlier draft of this final chapter I tried to sum up some of the main themes in my work. One was the frailty of the criminal process; another, the need to find the right balance in the development of the criminal law; and still another, the desirability of having a well-financed independent body like a law commission to develop ideas. I also had a section on the form of the law and another on alternatives to the criminal process. It did not work. Readers to whom I sent the manuscript found the final chapter repetitious and downright boring. I was not sure what to do. I then went off by myself – as the reader knows I often do in such situations – for a long lunch, sat in a quiet corner of the Coffee Mill in Yorkville, ordered a Hungarian cabbage roll, and thought about what I should do.

I concluded that those readers were right: there would be no point in simply repeating what I had stated in earlier chapters. The real conclusion is that change in the law and in institutions is like life itself. It is filled with chance and unforeseen results. The same is true of the legal process. As I stated on a number of occasions, justice may in theory be blind, but in practice she has altogether too human a perspective. There is no inevitability in how things turn out. Individuals and events seemingly unrelated to an issue always seem to play a role in the outcome. The growth and development of the law should always be understood in a wide context, and not be limited to the merits of the proposal under consideration.

This then concludes the story of 'my life in crime and other academic adventures.' It has been a stimulating journey for me. Where the path will take me in the future is, of course, uncertain, but if this book is any guide, there are sure to be some further unexpected twists and turns along the way.

One such turn occurred within the past month. Judy and I purchased a condominium and sold our home on Belsize Drive that we have lived in for almost forty years. Judy, always the occupational therapist, had been making the point for several years that we should move into a condo while it would be fun to do so and not a necessity. At about the time this book appears in print we will be moving from the north end of the city into a condo on the waterfront, south of Queen's Quay, built in the 1980s on top of a historic 1920s warehouse that now contains offices, shops, and a theatre. Our suite has a fine view of sunsets over Lake Ontario to the west, and of Ward's Island to the south and the CN Tower to the north. I only wish that the building was not still referred to as the 'Terminal Warehouse.'

Notes on Sources

Much of the material in this memoir is drawn from memory, from my books, reports, and articles, and from my personal papers in the University of Toronto Archives. There have been three deposits of my personal papers made to the Archives. The first was a large deposit (152 boxes) in 1998 (Accession no. B98-0006) and there were two deposits in 2002 – one of further personal papers (Accession no. B2002-0023) and another of papers relating to the writing of *The University of Toronto: A History* (Accession no. B2002-0022). All of the material relating to the U of T history (94 boxes) is open to the public, but much of the other material is closed for a number of years. There will likely be another deposit of papers in the next year or two. There is a detailed finding aid for each of the accessions, and so I have not identified in these notes the precise location within the accessions where material can be found.

Preface. Page ix, para 1: 'Criminal Justice in Canada Revisited' (2004) 48 *Criminal Law Quarterly* 419.   **Page x, para 2:** M.L. Friedland, 'R.S. Wright's Model Criminal Code: A Forgotten Chapter in the History of the Criminal Law' (1981) 1 *Oxford Journal of Legal Studies* 307 at 345.   **Page x, para 3:** Martin Friedland, *The Trials of Israel Lipski: A True Story of a Victorian Murder in the East End of London* (London: Macmillan, 1984) at 11–12.

Prologue. Material relating to the early history of the law school can be found in Martin L. Friedland, *The University of Toronto: A History* (Toronto: University of Toronto Press, 2002) and Ian Kyer and Jerome Bickenbach, *The Fiercest*

Debate: Cecil A. Wright, the Benchers, and Legal Education in Ontario, 1923–1957 (Toronto: Osgoode Society for Canadian Legal History, 1987).   **Page 5, para 2:** My papers in the Archives.   **Page 5, para 3:** *U of T: A History* at 438.   **Page 6, para 2:** *Ibid.* at 440.   **Page 7, para 1:** *Ibid.* at 676.   **Page 11, para 1:** *Ibid.* at 385.   **Page 14, para 1:** *Brown v. Board of Education* (1954), 347 U.S. 483.   **Page 17, para 3:** My papers in the Archives.   **Page 18, para 1:** *Ibid.*   **Page 18, para 2:** Norman Rogul, *Fursby: The Life and Times of Norman Rogul* (Toronto: published privately, 2004).   **Page 22, para 4:** Forest Hill Collegiate Institute yearbook, *The Forester*, 1950–1.   **Page 23, para 1:** John R. Seeley et al., *Crestwood Heights: A Study of the Culture of Suburban Life* (Toronto: University of Toronto Press, 1956).   **Page 24, para 1:** Alan C. Cairns, 'My Academic Career: The Pleasures and Risks of Intro-spection' in Gerald Kernerman and Philip Resnick, eds., *Insiders and Outsiders: Alan Cairns and the Reshaping of Canadian Citizenship* (Vancouver: UBC Press, 2005) 329 at 332.

Chapter 1, Legal Education. Page 27, para 1: Martin L. Friedland, *The University of Toronto: A History* (Toronto: University of Toronto Press, 2002) at 441.   **Page 29, para 1:** The Schiff quote is from Philip Girard, *Bora Laskin: Bringing Law to Life* (Toronto: Osgoode Society for Canadian Legal History, 2005) at 67.   **Page 29, para 3:** For a discussion of Laskin's legacy, see Girard, *Bora Laskin*, and Martin Friedland, 'Laskin and the University' in Neil Finkelstein and Constance Back-house, eds., *The Laskin Legacy: Essays in Commemoration of Chief Justice Bora Laskin* (Toronto: Irwin Law, 2007).   **Page 31, para 2:** The memorial service for Al Abel can be found at (1978) 28 *University of Toronto Law Journal* 364.   **Page 32, para 2:** *The Queen v. Jennings*, [1966] S.C.R. 532.   **Page 34, para 1:** The quote from Robin-ette is from *U of T: A History* at 306.   **Page 34, para 3:** R.C.B. Risk, 'The Many Minds of W.P.M. Kennedy' (1998) 48 *University of Toronto Law Journal* 353.   **Page 34, para 4:** For the cottage lakeshore trail, see Ian Kyer and Jerome Bicken-bach, *The Fiercest Debate: Cecil A. Wright, the Benchers, and Legal Education in Ontario, 1923–1957* (Toronto: Osgoode Society for Canadian Legal History, 1987) at 165–7 and Girard at 153–4.   **Page 37, para 3:** The review by Abel can be found in (1957) 42 *Iowa Law Review* 471.   **Page 39, para 2:** M.L. Friedland, 'Regu-lation of Economic Activity by Criminal Law: Decline of the Trade and Com-merce Power' (1957) 15 *University of Toronto Faculty of Law Review* 20.

Chapter 2, Articling and the Bar Ads. Much of the material in this chapter is from memory and my archival material.   **Page 43, para 1:** The Sirluck story can be found in Martin L. Friedland, *The University of Toronto: A History* (Toronto: University of Toronto Press, 2002) at 467.   **Page 43, para 2:** Conversations with Murray Chusid.

Chapter 3, Cambridge and Double Jeopardy. See, generally, Martin L. Friedland, *Double Jeopardy* (Oxford: Clarendon Press, 1969). **Page 58, para 1:** Charles Crawley, *Trinity Hall: The History of a Cambridge College 1350–1975* (Cambridge: University Printing House, 1976). **Page 58, para 3:** Glanville Williams, *Criminal Law: The General Part*, 2nd ed. (London: Stevens & Sons, 1961). **Page 59, para 2:** Andrew Grubb, 'Glanville Williams: A Personal Appreciation' (1998) 6 *Medical Law Review* 133 at 133 and 137. **Page 59, para 3:** *Oxford Dictionary of National Biography*, vol. 59, 194 at 195. **Page 61, para 2:** *Double Jeopardy* at 3. **Page 62, para 1:** *Green v. United States* (1957), 355 U.S. 184 at 187–8. **Page 63, para 1:** *Double Jeopardy* at 327, n. 1.

Chapter 4, The Enforcement of Morality. **Page 68, para 3:** *Report of the Canadian Committee on Corrections (Toward Unity: Criminal Justice and Corrections)* (Ottawa, 1969) (Chair: Roger Ouimet); 'J. Desmond Morton Quelled Prison Riot' *Toronto Star*, 30 Nov. 1989. **Page 70, para 1ff.:** Drawn from personal papers in the Archives and *Report of the Attorney General's Committee on Enforcement of the Law Relating to Gambling* (1961) (Chair: J.D. Morton). **Page 72, para 4:** See, generally, Patrick J. Monahan and A. Gerold Goldlist, 'Roll Again: New Developments Concerning Gaming' (1999) 42 *Criminal Law Quarterly* 182. **Page 74, para 1:** 'The Report of the Committee on Homosexual Offences and Prostitution' Cmnd. 247 (1957) (Chair: John Wolfenden). **Page 74, para 4:** See, generally, David Kimmel and Daniel J. Robinson, 'Sex, Crime, Pathology: Homosexuality and Criminal Code Reform in Canada, 1949–1969' (2001) 16 *Canadian Journal of Law and Society* 147 at 157ff.; Tom Warner, *Never Going Back: A History of Queer Activism in Canada* (Toronto: University of Toronto Press, 2002); the 40% statistic is from Kimmel and Robinson at 158; *Klippert v. The Queen*, [1967] S.C.R. 822; *Halpern v. Canada (Attorney General)* (2003), 225 D.L.R. (4th) 529 (Ont. C.A.); *Reference re Same-Sex Marriage*, [2004] 3 S.C.R. 698. **Page 75, para 2:** *U of T: A History* at 526–7; *Haig v. Canada*, [1993] 2 S.C.R. 995; *Vriend v. Alberta*, [1998] 1 S.C.R. 493; Donald Casswell, 'Moving toward Same-Sex Marriage' (2001) 80 *Canadian Bar Review* 810; *M. v. H.*, [1999] 2 S.C.R. 3. **Page 75, para 3:** Law Reform Commission recommendations concerning incest are in Law Reform Commission of Canada, *Sexual Offences* (Working Paper 22) (1978) at 30 and 26; public opposition to decriminalization noted in Law Reform Commission of Canada, *Evaluation of the Comments Received on Working Paper 22 'Sexual Offences'* by Carole Kennedy (1978); recommendation rejected in House of Commons, *Debates*, 2 February 1979 at 2831 (Hon. Marc Lalonde); recommendation repeated in Law Reform Commission of Canada, *Sex Crimes Recodified*, An Addendum to *Report 31: Recodifying Criminal Law (1987)* (unpublished, 1991); timing of the LRC's elimination noted in John Barnes, 'Sex Crimes, Prostitution and Pornography: A Posthumous Report of the Law Reform Commission of Canada' (1994) 73 *Canadian Bar Review* 553.   **Page 76, para 2:** *The King v. Bourne,* [1939] 1 K.B. 687; J.J. Lederman and G.E. Parker, 'Therapeutic Abortion and the Canadian Criminal Code' (1963) 6 *Criminal Law Quarterly* 36; *Vera Drake* (2004).   **Page 77, para 1:** *Roe v. Wade* (1973), 410 U.S. 113; my Department of Justice opinions on the abortion issue are in my personal papers in the Archives.   **Page 77, para 2:** Statistics on abortion can be found in Statistics Canada, 'Therapeutic Abortions, 1995' *The Daily,* 5 Nov. 1997, 28 Mar. 2003, and 11 Feb. 2005; Statistics Canada, 'Induced abortions per 100 live births,' available online; and U.S. Census Bureau, 'Table 96. Abortions – number, rate, and ratio by race: 1975 to 2002' in *Statistical Abstract of the United States: 2007,* available online.   **Page 77, para 4:** Special Senate Committee on Illegal Drugs, *Cannabis: Our Position for a Canadian Public Policy* (Ottawa, 2002) (Chair: Pierre Claude Nolin); *Final Report of the Commission of Inquiry into the Non-Medical Use of Drugs* (Ottawa, 1973) (Chair: Gerald Le Dain).   **Page 78, para 4:** *R. v. Malmo-Levine; R. v. Caine,* [2003] 3 S.C.R. 571 at 633.   **Page 79, para 1:** *R. v. Kouri,* [2005] 3 S.C.R. 789 at 794.

Chapter 5, More Double Jeopardy. See, generally, Martin L. Friedland, *Double Jeopardy* (Oxford: Clarendon Press, 1969).   **Page 82, para 3:** *Connelly et al. v. DPP,* [1963] 3 All E.R. 510.   **Page 83, para 2:** *Connelly et al. v. DPP,* [1964] A.C. 1254; the *Connelly* principle was applied in the recent controversial Bermuda case of *Middleton v. DPP,* [2007] Bda L.R. 28, involving a Canadian victim.   **Page 83, para 3:** *R. v. Feeley, McDermott and Wright,* [1963] S.C.R. 539.   **Page 83, para 4:** M.L. Friedland, 'Double Jeopardy and the Rule against Unreasonably Splitting a Case' (1967) 17 *University of Toronto Law Journal* 249.   **Page 84, para 1:** Law Reform Commission of Canada, *Double Jeopardy, Pleas and Verdicts* (Working Paper 63) (1991); English Law Commission, *Double Jeopardy and Prosecution Appeals* (Report 267) (2001).   **Page 84, para 2:** M.L. Friedland, 'Issue Estoppel in Criminal Cases' (1966–7) 9 *Criminal Law Quarterly* 163; M.L. Friedland, 'Double Jeopardy and the Division of Legislative Authority in Canada' (1967) 17 *University of Toronto Law Journal* 66; M.L. Friedland, 'New Trial after an Appeal from Conviction – Part I' (1968) 84 *Law Quarterly Review* 48, and 'New Trial after an Appeal from Conviction – Part II' (1968) 84 *Law Quarterly Review* 185.   **Page 85, para 1:** *R. v. Morgentaler, Smoling and Scott* (1985), 22 C.C.C. (3d) 353.   **Page 85, para 2:** *Vallance v. The Queen* (1961), 35 A.L.J.R. 182; *R. v. Morin,* [1988] 2 S.C.R. 345; *R. v. Graveline,* [2006] 1 S.C.R. 609.   **Page 85, para 3:** *Criminal Justice Act 2003,* part 10: Retrial for Serious Offences; English Law Commission, Consultation Paper no. 156, *Double Jeopardy* at 36; *Double Jeopardy and Prosecution Appeals.*   **Page 86, para 1:** U.K., H.C., *Justice for All,* Cm. 5563

(2002).   **Page 86, para 2:** See London *Times*, 11 Nov. 2005 and 12 Sept. 2006; see also the BBC 1 'One Life' documentary 'Getting Away with Murder' (2006). **Page 87, para 1:** *R. v. Gushue*, [1980] 1 S.C.R. 798; *R. v. Grdic*, [1985] 1 S.C.R. 810. **Page 87, para 2:** *R. v. Gill* (2003), 180 B.C.A.C. 290.   **Page 87, para 3:** *R. v. Elmosri* (1985), 23 C.C.C. (3d) 503; *Dunn v. United States* (1932), 284 U.S. 390; *R. v. Mahalingan* (2006), 208 C.C.C. (3d) 515, leave to appeal to Supreme Court granted 16 Nov. 2006.   **Page 89, para 1:** Jay A. Sigler, *Double Jeopardy: The Development of a Legal and Social Policy* (Ithaca: Cornell University Press, 1969); Rupert Cross (1971) 87 *Law Quarterly Review* 413 at 413.

Chapter 6, Detention before Trial. See, generally, Martin L. Friedland, *Detention before Trial* (Toronto: University of Toronto Press, 1965).   **Page 92, para 3:** Caleb Foote, 'The Bail System and Equal Justice' (1959) 23 *Federal Probation* 43; Caleb Foote, 'Compelling Appearance in Court: Administration of Bail in Philadelphia' (1954) 102 *University of Pennsylvania Law Review* 1031; Caleb Foote, 'A Study of the Administration of Bail in New York City' (1958) 106 *University of Pennsylvania Law Review* 693.   **Page 93, para 1:** J.W. Mohr et al., *Pedophilia and Exhibitionism: A Handbook* (Toronto: University of Toronto Press, 1964).   **Page 93, para 2:** 'In Memoriam: Caleb Foote, Leading Family and Criminal Law Scholar' in *School of Law, Boalt Hall Enews* (April 2006), available online.   **Page 93, para 4:** *Detention before Trial* at 5, n. 7.   **Page 95, para 1:** (1963) 41 *Canadian Bar Review* 475 at 475 and 478.   **Page 95, para 2:** M.L. Friedland and J.W. Mohr, 'Canadian Criminal Statistics: A Report on the Third Criminal Law Conference, Osgoode Hall Law School, April 3–4, 1964' (1964–5) 7 *Criminal Law Quarterly* 170.   **Page 96, para 3:** *Detention before Trial* at 172.   **Page 97, para 2:** *Ibid.* at 176. **Page 98, para 1:** *R. v. Hall*, [2002] 3 S.C.R. 309; *Ell v. Alberta*, [2003] 1 S.C.R. 857; Sidney Linden in Martin L. Friedland, 'Criminal Justice in Canada Revisited' (2004) 48 *Criminal Law Quarterly* 419 at 435, n. 98.   **Page 100, para 3:** 'Denial of Reasonable Bail' *Globe and Mail*, 21 June 1965.   **Page 101, para 1:** *Report of the Attorney General's Committee on Poverty and the Administration of Federal Criminal Justice* (1963) at 6.   **Page 101, para 3:** Correspondence in personal papers in the Archives; House of Commons, Standing Committee on Justice and Legal Affairs, *Minutes of Proceedings and Evidence*, 16 Nov. 1967.   **Page 102, para 2:** *Report of the Royal Commission Inquiry into Civil Rights* (1968) (McRuer Report), vol. 2, c. 38; *Report of the Canadian Committee on Corrections (Toward Unity: Criminal Justice and Corrections)* (1969) (Chair: Roger Ouimet).   **Page 102, para 3:** Anthony N. Doob, 'Race, Bail, and Imprisonment,' Draft Working Paper for the Commission on Systemic Racism (Toronto, 1994) at 2 and 7.   **Page 103, para 2:** *R. v. Phillips* (1947), 32 Cr. App. R. 47.   **Page 103, para 3:** The various changes are in my papers in the Archives.   **Page 103, para 4:** *R. v. Bray* (1983), 2 C.C.C.

(3d) 325 at 328; re the 1200 wives, see *Globe and Mail*, 12 Feb. 1973.   **Page 104, para 2:** *Bray* at 328–9; *R. v. Pearson*, [1992] 3 S.C.R. 665.   **Page 104, para 3:** Law Reform Commission of Canada, *Compelling Appearance, Interim Release and Pre-Trial Detention* (Working Paper 57) (1988) at 37–8.   **Page 104, para 4:** See 'Fatal Shooting on Yonge St.' *Globe and Mail*, 27 Dec. 2005.   **Page 105, para 2:** 'Race, Bail, and Imprisonment' at 7.   **Page 105, para 4:** Sarah Johnson, 'Custodial Remand in Canada, 1986/87 to 2000/01' *Juristat*, Canadian Centre for Justice Statistics, Statistics Canada – Catalogue no. 85-002-XIE, vol. 23, no. 7, at 6–8 and 11; for a discussion of the Juristat report, see Lou Strezos, 'The Presumption of Innocence behind Bars,' background document presented at the Criminal Lawyers' Association conference, 8 Nov. 2003; correspondence with Tony Doob, 22 Apr. 2007.   **Page 106, para 2:** *Detention before Trial* at 108; Ernst Wilfred Puttkammer, *Administration of Criminal Law* (Chicago: University of Chicago Press, 1953) at 69.   **Page 106, para 4:** Material on regional detention centres is in my papers in the Archives.   **Page 107, para 2:** Ontario, Ministry of the Attorney General, *Bail Verification and Supervision Program* (2002) (unpublished); Ontario, Bail Verification and Supervision Program, *4th Quarter Report 2001/2002* (2002) at 4.

Chapter 7, Legal Aid. See, generally, Martin L. Friedland, *Legal Aid: Working Papers Prepared for the Joint Committee on Legal Aid* (Osgoode Hall Law School, 1964); Ontario, *Report of the Joint Committee on Legal Aid* (1965) (Chair: William B. Common); and Martin L. Friedland, 'Governance of Legal Aid Schemes' in *Report of the Ontario Legal Aid Review: A Blueprint for Publicly Funded Legal Services* (1997) (Chair: John D. McCamus), vol. 3, 1017.   **Page 109, para 1:** *Gideon v. Wainwright* (1963), 372 U.S. 335; *Report of the Attorney General's Committee on Poverty and the Administration of Federal Criminal Justice* (1963) at 6.   **Page 110, para 2:** Joint Committee report at 8.   **Page 111, para 1:** *R. v. K.*, [1971] 2 O.R. 401.   **Page 111, para 2:** *R. v. Fisher* (1961), 34 C.R. 320 (C.A.); *R. v. Fisher*, [1961] S.C.R. 535.   **Page 111, para 3:** Letter from J.B. Pomerant to W.C. Bowman, 13 Feb. 1961, Archives of Ontario, RG 4-32, 1960/1344.   **Page 112, para 2:** *DPP v. Beard*, [1920] A.C. 479; *MacAskill v. The King*, [1931] S.C.R. 330; evidence of Crown expert is set out in M.L. Friedland and Kent Roach, *Criminal Law and Procedure: Cases and Materials*, 8th ed. (Toronto: Emond Montgomery, 1997) at 694.   **Page 112, para 4:** *R. v. Robinson*, [1996] 1 S.C.R. 683 at 710; see Ontario Court of Appeal cases of *R. v. Otis* (1978), 39 C.C.C. (2d) 304; *R. v. Dees* (1978), 40 C.C.C. (2d) 58; and *R. v. Seguin* (1979), 45 C.C.C. (2d) 498.   **Page 113, para 1:** *R. v. Rathwell* (1998), 130 C.C.C. (3d) 302 (Ont. C.A.).   **Page 113, para 2:** For more on the *Demeter* murder case, see George Jonas and Barbara Amiel, *By Persons Unknown: The Strange Death of Christine Demeter* (New York: Grove Press,

1977).   **Page 113, para 3:** 1963 statistics can be found in *Legal Aid: Working Papers*, part III at 5, 7–8, and 24 and Joint Committee report at 19–20; more recent statistics can be found in Legal Aid Ontario, *Legal Aid Ontario Business Plan 2004–2005* at 7 and *Legal Aid Ontario Business Plan 2003–2004* at 19.   **Page 114, para 3:** Joint Committee report at 107–8; *Legal Aid: Working Papers*, part IV at 7.   **Page 115, para 2:** *Report of the Task Force on Legal Aid* (1973) (Chair: John Osler); *Report of the Commission on Clinical Funding* (1978) (Commissioner: S.G.M. Grange).   **Page 116, para 2:** 'Governance of Legal Aid Schemes' at 1027–8.   **Page 117, para 2:** *Ibid.* at 1046–7 and 1049.   **Page 117, para 3:** McCamus report at 255.   **Page 118, para 3:** *Ibid.* at 150 and 160; *Report of the Criminal Justice Review Committee* (1999) (Chairs: Hugh Locke, John D. Evans, and Murray Segal) at 31.   **Page 119, para 1:** Joint Committee report at 61–2; *Legal Aid: Working Papers*, part III at 24.

Chapter 8, Criminal Courts. See, generally, M.L. Friedland, 'Magistrates' Courts: Functioning and Facilities' (1968) 11 *Criminal Law Quarterly* 52, and M.L. Friedland, 'The Provincial Court and the Criminal Law' (2003) 48 *Criminal Law Quarterly* 15.   **Page 120, para 2:** *Report of the Canadian Committee on Corrections (Toward Unity: Criminal Justice and Corrections)* (1969) (Chair: Roger Ouimet) at 1.   **Page 121, para 3:** *Report of the Royal Commission to Investigate the Penal System of Canada* (1938) (Chair: Joseph Archambault); Canada, Department of Justice, *Report of a Committee Appointed to Inquire into the Principles and Procedures Followed in the Remission Service of the Department of Justice of Canada* (1956) (Chair: Gérald Fauteux).   **Page 123, para 2:** *Globe and Mail*, 5 Feb. 1968.   **Page 124, para 2:** *Ibid.*, 21 Nov. 1968.   **Page 125, para 1:** 'Magistrates' Courts' at 52–3.   **Page 127, para 2:** Martin L. Friedland, *A Place Apart: Judicial Independence and Accountability in Canada* (Ottawa: Canadian Judicial Council, 1995) at 220.   **Page 129, para 3:** American Bar Association Committee, *Report of the Task Force on the Administration of Justice* (Washington, 1967) at 92.   **Page 130, para 1:** *Justice Weekly*, 14 Dec. 1968.   **Page 130, para 2:** Ouimet report at c. 9; *Report of the Ontario Courts Inquiry* (1987) (Chair: T.G. Zuber).   **Page 131, para 2:** Carl Baar, *One Trial Court: Possibilities and Limitations* (Ottawa: Canadian Judicial Council, 1991) at 75.   **Page 131, para 3:** *Reference Re Establishment of a Unified Criminal Court of New Brunswick* (1981), 62 C.C.C. (2d) 165 (N.B.C.A.); *McEvoy v. New Brunswick*, [1983] 1 S.C.R. 704 at 720.   **Page 132, para 2:** Peter H. Russell, *The Judiciary in Canada: The Third Branch of Government* (Toronto: McGraw-Hill Ryerson, 1987) at 60; *A Place Apart* at 234; correspondence of Lieut. Gov. Gordon to Edward Cardwell, 26 Sept. 1864, as cited in G.P. Browne, *Documents on the Confederation of British North America* (Toronto: McClelland & Stewart, 1969) at 47.   **Page 132, para 3:** *McEvoy* at 719.   **Page 133, para 1:** *R. v. Trimarchi* (1987),

40 C.C.C. (3d) 433 at 443 (Ont. C.A.). **Page 133, para 2:** *Report of the Provincial Criminal Court Judges Special Committee on Criminal Justice in Ontario* (1987) (Chair: David Vanek), part IV: 'The Criminal Court of the Future' at 78. **Page 133, para 3:** Zuber report at 79. **Page 134, para 1:** Ian Scott with Neil McCormick, *To Make a Difference: A Memoir* (Toronto: Stoddart, 2001) at 181. **Page 134, para 2:** see Russell at c. 3; *One Trial Court* at c. 7; Law Reform Commission of Canada, *Toward a Unified Criminal Court* (Working Paper 59) (1989); *Report of the Canadian Bar Association Task Force on Court Reform in Canada* (1991) (Chair: Peter Seaton) at 113. **Page 134, para 3:** New Brunswick Department of Justice, Consultation Document, *A Proposal for a Unified Criminal Court* (1994) (unpublished). **Page 135, para 1:** Carl Baar, 'Judicial Independence and Judicial Administration: The Case of Provincial Court Judges' (1998) 9 *Constitutional Forum* 114 at 117. **Page 135, para 2:** See Dave Hancock, Alberta Minister of Justice and Attorney General, 'Notes for an Address: Trial Courts of the Future Conference' (2002). **Page 135, para 3:** Peter Russell, ed., *Canada's Trial Courts: Two Tiers or One?* (2007). **Page 135, para 5:** *Re Provincial Court Judges*, [1998] 1 S.C.R. 3; Gerald T.G. Seniuk and Noel Lyon, 'The Supreme Court of Canada and the Provincial Court in Canada' (2000) 79 *Canadian Bar Review* 77 at 79. **Page 136, para 1:** *Therrien v. Quebec*, [2001] 2 S.C.R. 3 at 51; *R. v. Valente*, [1985] 2 S.C.R. 673.

Chapter 9, Securities Regulation. See, generally, *Report of the Attorney General's Committee on Securities Legislation in Ontario* (1965) (Chair: J.R. Kimber). Much of the material, including memoranda, can be found in my papers in the Archives. **Page 138, para 1:** Kimber report at 6. **Page 138, para 2:** English Board of Trade, *Report of the Company Law Committee*, Cmnd. 1749 (1962) (Chair: Lord Jenkins); *Report of Special Study of Securities Markets of the Securities and Exchange Commission* (1963) (Director: Milton H. Cohen). **Page 139, para 1:** Canada, *Report of the Royal Commission on Banking and Finance* (1964) (Chair: Dana Porter); E. Kendall Cork, *Finance in the Mining Industry: A Study Prepared for the Royal Commission on Banking and Finance* (1962). **Page 139, para 3:** See Christopher Armstrong, *Blue Skies and Boiler Rooms: Buying and Selling Securities in Canada, 1870–1940* (Toronto: University of Toronto Press, 1997). **Page 141, para 2:** Christopher Armstrong, *Moose Pastures and Mergers: The Ontario Securities Commission and the Regulation of Share Markets in Canada, 1940–1980* (Toronto: University of Toronto Press, 2001). **Page 143, para 4:** 'Bosses Salaries: Sop to Vulgar Curiosity or an Essential Part of Analysis?' *Globe and Mail*, 9 Oct. 1964. **Page 144, para 4:** *Northern Miner*, 1 Apr. 1965. **Page 145, para 2:** Ontario, *Report of the Royal Commission to Investigate Trading in the Shares of Windfall Oils and Mines Limited* (1965) (Commissioner: Arthur Kelly).

Page 146, para 1: Kimber report at 60.   **Page 147, para 1:** Armstrong, *Moose Pastures* at 265.   **Page 147, para 2:** Bill 66, *The Securities Act, 1966*.   **Page 148, para 2:** Kimber report at 20–1.   **Page 149, para 2:** *Ibid.* at 17.   **Page 154, para 2:** Ontario, *Five Year Review Committee Final Report: Reviewing the Securities Act (Ontario)* (2003) (Chair: Purdy Crawford).

Chapter 10, Machinery of Law Reform. The material in the chapter is mainly drawn from my personal papers and from my collection of essays *A Century of Criminal Justice: Perspectives on the Development of Canadian Criminal Law* (Toronto: Carswell, 1984).   **Page 155, para 2:** Ontario, Ministry of the Attorney General, news release, 4 Jan. 2006.   **Page 160, para 4:** M.L. Friedland, 'Comments: Cross-Examination on Previous Convictions in Canada' (1969) 47 *Canadian Bar Review* 656; *R. v. Corbett*, [1988] 1 S.C.R. 670.   **Page 161, para 1:** *DPP v. Smith*, [1961] A.C. 290.   **Page 161, para 4:** Practice Statement (Judicial Precedent), 26 July 1966, [1966] 3 All E.R. 77.   **Page 163, para 2:** M.L. Friedland, 'Prospective and Retrospective Judicial Lawmaking' (1974) 24 *University of Toronto Law Journal* 170; *National Westminster Bank v. Spectrum Plus*, [2005] 3 W.L.R. 58.   **Page 163, para 3:** *Gideon v. Wainwright* (1963), 372 U.S. 335.   **Page 163, para 4:** See also Sujit Choudhry and Kent Roach, 'Putting the Past behind Us? Prospective Judicial and Legislative Constitutional Remedies' (2003) 21 *Supreme Court Law Review* (2d) 205; *R. v. Brydges*, [1990] 1 S.C.R. 190; *Hislop v. Canada (Attorney General)*, 2007 S.C.C. 10.   **Page 165, para 1:** M.L. Friedland, 'Pressure Groups and the Development of the Criminal Law' in P.R. Glazebrook, ed., *Reshaping the Criminal Law: Essays in Honour of Glanville Williams* (London: Stevens & Sons, 1978) 202.   **Page 165, para 2:** G. Maher (1980) 15 *Journal of the Society of Public Teachers of Law* 84 at 85.   **Page 165, para 4:** These unpublished documents are in my papers in the Archives.   **Page 167, para 2:** *Globe and Mail*, 19 Oct. 1968.   **Page 167, para 4:** This memorandum is in my papers in the Archives.   **Page 169, para 2:** *Globe and Mail*, 15 Dec. 1969; M.L. Friedland, 'The Process of Criminal Law Reform' (1969–70) 12 *Criminal Law Quarterly* 148.   **Page 169, para 4:** John Turner is quoted in 'It's a Big Carcass Waiting' *Globe and Mail*, 23 Feb. 1970.

Chapter 11, The Law Reform Commission of Canada. Material in this chapter is mainly drawn from my papers in the Archives, which contain copies of many of the Law Reform Commission documents from this period.   **Page 170, para 1:** 'Can Crime Be Retroactive? Trial under the War Measures Act' *Globe and Mail*, 28 Oct. 1970.   **Page 172, para 2:** 'New Commission Chairman Wants Public Involved in Task: Law Reform Too Important to Be Left Solely to Judges, Lawyers, Hartt Says' *Globe and Mail*, 1 Apr. 1971.   **Page 174, para 3:** *R. v. Sault Ste. Marie*, [1978] 2 S.C.R. 1299.   **Page 175, para 4:** Law Reform Commission of Canada, *Studies on Diversion: East York Community Law Reform Project* (1975); Douglas A. Schmeiser, *The Native Offender and the Law* (1974); the 1991 Law Reform Commission report was *Report 34: Aboriginal Peoples and Criminal Justice* (1991); *The Law Reform Commission Act*, R.S.C. 1970, c. 23, 1st Supplement.   **Page 177, para 3:** Martin L. Friedland, 'The Work of the Law Reform Commission of Canada' (1972) 6 *Law Society of Upper Canada Gazette* 58 at 59.   **Page 178, para 2:** 'Tiger into Tabby?' *Globe and Mail*, 25 Jan. 1972.   **Page 179, para 2:** See, generally, Martin L. Friedland, 'Frank Iacobucci and the University of Toronto' (2007) 57 *University of Toronto Law Journal* 155.   **Page 180, para 1:** '2 Appointments Are Announced by U of T' *Globe and Mail*, 29 Jan. 1972; *Toronto Star*, 26 Jan. 1972.   **Page 180, para 3:** *Globe and Mail*, 3 Feb. 1972.   **Page 181, para 2:** Law Reform Commission of Canada, *Crimes against the State* (Working Paper 49) (1986); Law Reform Commission of Canada, *Double Jeopardy, Pleas and Verdicts* (Working Paper 63) (1991); M.L. Friedland, 'Rewards in the Legal System: Tenure, Airbags, and Safety Bingo' (1993) 31 *Alberta Law Review* 493.

Chapter 12, Access to the Law. The main source for this chapter is the book I published with Peter and Linda Jewett, *Access to the Law: A Study Prepared for the Law Reform Commission of Canada* (Toronto: Carswell/Methuen, 1975) and my papers in the Archives.   **Page 183, para 2:** 'Making Law Available to the People' *Globe and Mail*, 11 Feb. 1974; Martin L. Friedland, 'Law for the Layman' (1974) 50 *Canadian Welfare* 4.   **Page 184, para 2:** 'Law on the Self-Help System' *Globe and Mail*, 11 Feb. 1974; letter to the editor of *Canadian Library Journal* from J.P. Wilkinson, Professor of Library Science, University of Toronto, 12 Feb. 1974, in my papers in the Archives.   **Page 185, para 5:** *Access to the Law* at 67. **Page 186, para 2:** George Coode, 'On Legislative Expression' (1843), extract cited in Elmer A. Driedger, *The Composition of Legislation* (Ottawa: Queen's Printer, 1957) at 185.   **Page 187, para 2:** *Globe and Mail*, 15 Nov. 1975.   **Page 188, para 1:** 'The Governed Deserve Law Guide: Professor' *Globe and Mail*, 4 Sept. 1980.   **Page 189, para 3:** Martin L. Friedland, 'Governance of Legal Aid Schemes' in *Report of the Ontario Legal Aid Review: A Blueprint for Publicly Funded Legal Services* (1997) (Chair: John D. McCamus), vol. 3, 1017.   **Page 191, para 2:** See, for example, 'Province Cuts Ties with Private Partners: Integrated Justice Project in Tailspin' *Law Times*, 21 Oct. 2002.   **Page 192, para 1:** The report to the Law Foundation (26 Feb. 2003) is in my papers in the Archives.

Chapter 13, Deaning and the University. This material is mainly drawn from my papers in the Archives and from memory. I have not examined official law-school papers that likely have been deposited in the Archives.   **Page 193, para 1:** *The Queen v. Pierce Fisheries*, [1971] S.C.R. 5.   **Page 194, para 1:** 'The Atheist

Reformer Who's Taken over Toronto's Legal Bastion' *Toronto Star*, undated clipping in my papers in the Archives.   **Page 195, para 3:** The report to the University and related documents are in my personal papers in the Archives. **Page 196, para 5:** Martin Friedland, *The University of Toronto: A History* (Toronto: University of Toronto Press, 2002), c. 36.   **Page 198, para 2:** Robin Ross, *The Short Road Down: A University Changes* (Toronto: University of Toronto, 1984) at 52.   **Page 199, para 2:** My remarks to the human resources committee in July 1971 are contained in my papers in the Archives.   **Page 200, para 2:** *U of T: A History* at 619.   **Page 203, para 2:** *U of T Bulletin*, January 1992.   **Page 203, para 3:** Martin L. Friedland, ed., *Courts and Trials: A Multidisciplinary Approach* (Toronto: University of Toronto Press, 1975); 'Message from the Dean' *Nexus*, Spring/Summer 2005, 1 at 1.   **Page 208, para 2:** The 1972 Michael Leshner interview, printed in *Hearsay*, the student newspaper of the time, is in my papers in the Archives.   **Page 210, para 2:** *U of T: A History* at 614–15.   **Page 211, para 2:** The history of the U of T Press is discussed in c. 34 of *U of T: A History*; M.L. Friedland, *Cases and Materials on Criminal Law and Procedure*, 2nd ed., (Toronto: University of Toronto Press, 1968).   **Page 214, para 2:** See Walter Lippincott et al., *A Century in Books: Princeton University Press 1905–2005* (Princeton: Princeton University Press, 2005) at 85–9.   **Page 215, para 3:** *U of T: A History* at 442.

Chapter 14, Gun Control. Much of the material in this chapter can be found in my papers in the Archives and in two of my articles: 'Gun Control: The Options' (1975–6) 18 *Criminal Law Quarterly* 29 and 'Gun Control in Canada: Politics and Impact' in *A Century of Criminal Justice: Perspectives on the Development of Canadian Law* (Toronto: Carswell, 1984) at 113.   **Page 218, para 2:** An edited version of the study is reproduced in 'Gun Control: The Options' at 29. The incidents are set out *ibid.* at 30.   **Page 219, para 2:** The statistics are drawn from 'Gun Control: The Options' at 33–4.   **Page 219, para 4:** This history is set out in greater detail in 'Gun Control: The Options' at 40–6.   **Page 220, para 3:** *Ibid.* at 58.   **Page 221, para 3:** *Ibid.* at 59.   **Page 222, para 3:** 'Liabilities of the Gun' *Globe and Mail*, 18 Dec. 1975; 'Deadly Handguns Should be Banned' *Toronto Star*, 15 Dec. 1975.   **Page 223, para 5:** Canada, Department of Justice, Speaking notes of the Minister of Justice, Ronald Basford, on second reading of Bill C-83 in the House of Commons, 8 Mar. 1976, in my papers at the Archives, at 7.   **Page 224, para 4:** 'Bill Passage Would Have Hindered Sniper's Rifle Purchase, Jury Told' *Globe and Mail*, 18 Nov. 1976; 'Free Sale of Guns Costs Innocent Lives' *Toronto Star*, 19 Nov. 1976.   **Page 225, para 2:** M.L. Friedland, 'Pressure Groups and the Development of the Criminal Law' in P.R. Glazebrook, ed., *Reshaping the Criminal Law: Essays in Honour of Glanville Williams*

(London: Stevens & Sons, 1978) 202.   **Page 226, para 3:** A. Alan Borovoy, 'Civil Liberties in the Imminent Hereafter' (1973) 51 *Canadian Bar Review* 93 at 94. **Page 227, para 1:** A.F. Bentley, *The Process of Government* (Cambridge, Mass., 1908).   **Page 227, para 3:** Robert F. Drinan, 'Handguns and Violence in the United States,' paper prepared for Seminar on Canadian–U.S. Relations, University Consortium for Research on North America, Harvard Center for International Affairs, 3 March 1981, in my papers in the Archives, at 18.   **Page 228, para 2:** 'Gun Control in Canada: Politics and Impact' at 113–14.   **Page 229, para 2:** Ralph Connor, *Corporal Cameron of the North West Mounted Police: A Tale of the Macleod Trail* (1912), as cited in Dick Harrison, *Unnamed Country: The Struggle for a Canadian Prairie Fiction* (Edmonton: University of Alberta Press, 1977) at 77.   **Page 230, para 1:** Anthony N. Doob and Edward L. Greenspan, eds., *Perspectives in Criminal Law: Essays in Honour of John Ll.J. Edwards* (Aurora: Canada Law Book, 1985) 226; 'Gun Control in Canada'; Martin L. Friedland, 'The Gun in Canada' *Globe and Mail*, 11 Apr. 1981.   **Page 230, para 4:** House of Commons, 16 Feb. 1995, at 9719; see, generally, Elaine Davies, 'The 1995 Firearms Act: Canada's Public Relations Response to the Myth of Violence' (2000) 6 *Appeal: Review of Current Law and Law Reform* 44.   **Page 231, para 3:** See 'New Police Strategy Designed to Blanket High-Violence Areas' *Globe and Mail*, 13 Feb. 2006.

Chapter 15, National Security. Most of the material for this chapter can be found in my personal papers, the McDonald Commission report, and my study for the McDonald Commission, *National Security: The Legal Dimensions* (1980). **Page 234, para 1:** The McDonald Commission produced three reports, in four volumes: Commission of Inquiry concerning Certain Activities of the Royal Canadian Mounted Police, 1st report: *Security and Information* (1979), 2nd report, vols. 1 and 2: *Freedom and Security under the Law* (1981), and 3rd report: *Certain R.C.M.P. Activities and the Question of Governmental Knowledge* (1981) (Chair: D.C. McDonald).   **Page 234, para 2:** Martin L. Friedland, 'National Security: Some Canadian Legal Perspectives' in *A Century of Criminal Justice: Perspectives on the Development of Canadian Law* (Toronto: Carswell, 1984) 141 at 141–2.   **Page 235, para 2:** *National Security: The Legal Dimensions* at v.   **Page 236, para 2:** J.Ll.J. Edwards, *Ministerial Responsibility for National Security, as It Relates to the Offices of Prime Minister, Attorney General and Solicitor General of Canada* (1980); C.E.S. Franks, *Parliament and Security Matters: A Study* (1980).   **Page 236, para 3:** Martin L. Friedland, ed., *Courts and Trials: A Multidisciplinary Approach* (Toronto: University of Toronto Press, 1975); 'Can Crime Be Retroactive? Trial under the War Measures Act' *Globe and Mail*, 28 Oct. 1970.   **Page 238, para 2:** *National Security: The Legal Dimensions* at 1.   **Page 238, para 3:** House of Commons, *Debates*, 26 June 1969, at 10636.   **Page 241, para 2:** 'National Security: Some Canadian Legal Perspectives' at 156; U.S. Senate, *Final Report of the Select Committee to Study Governmental Operations with Respect to Intelligence Activities* (1976) at book 2, p. 4.   **Page 241, para 3:** Starnes's comments are in my papers in the Archives.   **Page 241, para 4:** 'An Overdose of Security' *Globe and Mail*, 29 Apr. 1980.   **Page 242, para 1:** [1981] *Public Law* 280 at 281.   **Page 242, para 3:** Martin Friedland, 'Adhering to Rules of Criminal Procedure in Cases of Terrorism' in Judy Davidson, ed., *The Jerusalem Conference on Peace vs. Violence* (conference in September 1979) 152 at 153.   **Page 243, para 3:** 'National Security: Some Canadian Legal Perspectives' was first published in (1980) 10 *Israel Yearbook on Human Rights* 257; Baruch Bracha, 'Addendum: Some Remarks on Israeli Law regarding National Security' *ibid.* 289.   **Page 244, para 1:** 'Listings' 51 *New Society* 378.   **Page 244, para 2:** M.L. Friedland, 'Controlling Entrapment' (1982) 32 *University of Toronto Law Journal* 1 at 1–2.   **Page 245, para 2:** Second McDonald Commission report at 1053; *R. v. Mack*, [1988] 2 S.C.R. 903.   **Page 246, para 1:** 'A Leash for the Watchdogs' *Globe and Mail*, 20 Sept. 1983.   **Page 247, para 3:** Remarks of P.M. Pitfield, Chairman, 6 *Proceedings of the Special Committee of the Senate on the Canadian Security Intelligence Service*, 12 Sept. 1983, at 90.   **Page 247, para 5:** Draft provisions on national security can, however, be found in the Law Reform Commission's 1991 *Report 31: Recodifying Criminal Law* at 125–31.   **Page 248, para 1:** Canada, Department of Justice, *The Criminal Law in Canadian Society* (Ottawa, 1982) at 10.   **Page 248, para 3:** *R. v. Wetmore*, [1983] 2 S.C.R. 284.   **Page 250, para 2:** The draft report can be found in my papers in the Archives.   **Page 252, para 3:** *Proceedings of the Special Committee* at 89.   **Page 253, para 1:** *National Security: The Legal Dimensions* at 41 and 55.   **Page 253, para 2:** *O'Neill v. Canada (Attorney General)* (2006), 213 C.C.C. (3d) 389.

Chapter 16, More National Security – Terrorism. The material in this chapter comes from memory, my papers in the Archives, from my chapter 'Police Powers in Bill C-36' in Ronald J. Daniels, Patrick Macklem, and Kent Roach, eds., *The Security of Freedom: Essays on Canada's Anti-Terrorism Bill* (Toronto: University of Toronto Press, 2001) 269, and from my work for the Arar Commission. **Page 255, para 2:** The talk, 'Terrorism and National Security,' delivered at a constitutional roundtable on 11 Oct. 2001, is in my papers in the Archives.   **Page 256, para 3:** 'Police Powers in Bill C-36' at 281–2, endnote.   **Page 257, para 2:** *Ibid.* at 272–3; Special Committee of the Senate on the Canadian Security Intelligence Service, *Delicate Balance: A Security Intelligence Service in a Democratic Society* (Ottawa, 1983) (Chair: P.M. Pitfield) at 6.   **Page 257, para 3:** Eddie Goldenberg, *The Way It Works: Inside Ottawa* (Toronto: McClelland & Stewart, 2006).   **Page 258, para 2:** 'Police Powers in Bill C-36' at 272; Commission of

Inquiry into the Actions of Canadian Officials in Relation to Maher Arar, *A New Review Mechanism for the RCMP's National Security Activities* (2006) (Chair: Dennis R. O'Connor); see terms of reference for the Air India inquiry, 1 May 2006, P.C. 2006-293; 'Police Powers in Bill C-36' at 276.   **Page 259, para 3:** See *New York Times*, 'In Address, Bush Says He Ordered Domestic Spying,' 18 Dec. 2005 and 'A Spy Program In from the Cold,' 18 Jan. 2007.   **Page 260, para 1:** 'Police Powers in Bill C-36' at 276–8.   **Page 260, para 2:** *Vancouver Sun (Re)*, [2004] 2 S.C.R. 332; *Application under s. 83.28 of the Criminal Code (Re)*, [2004] 2 S.C.R. 248.   **Page 261, para 2:** *Hunter v. Southam*, [1984] 2 S.C.R. 145; 'Police Powers in Bill C-36' at 279.   **Page 261, para 3:** 'Police Powers in Bill C-36' at 280–1; *R. v. Brennan* (1989), 52 C.C.C. (3d) 366 (Ont. C.A.); *R. v. Shirose and Campbell*, [1999] 1 S.C.R. 565.   **Page 262, para 2:** 'Police Powers in Bill C-36' at 281.   **Page 262, para 3:** See 'Those Anti-Terror Clauses' *Globe and Mail*, 18 May 2007.   **Page 263, para 1:** Reid Morden, 'Spies, Not Soothsayers: Canadian Intelligence after 9/11,' Commentary no. 85, Canadian Security Intelligence Service (2003), available online.   **Page 263, para 2:** For Sheila Fraser's remarks, see Office of the Auditor General, press release, 10 Feb. 2004, available online; see also Wesley Wark, 'Martin's New Security Agenda: Feeling Safe Yet?' *Globe and Mail*, 18 Dec. 2003.   **Page 265, para 1:** Martin L. Friedland, *Controlling Misconduct in the Military* (Ottawa, 1996).   **Page 266, para 2:** O'Connor report.   **Page 267, para 2:** See *Globe and Mail*, 'Air-India Inquiry Begins with Victims,' 22 June 2006 and 'Ottawa Will Probe Files of 3 More Detainees,' 13 Dec. 2006.

Chapter 17, Codification of the Criminal Law. The material in this chapter has been drawn from memory, from my papers in the Archives (including letters home), and from three articles: 'R.S. Wright's Model Criminal Code: A Forgotten Chapter in the History of the Criminal Law,' first published in (1981) 1 *Oxford Journal of Legal Studies* 307, then repr. in Martin L. Friedland, *A Century of Criminal Justice: Perspectives on the Development of Canadian Law*, c. 1 (Toronto: Carswell, 1984); 'A Century of Criminal Justice,' first published in (1982) 20 *Transactions of the Royal Society of Canada* 285, later in (1982) 16 *Law Society of Upper Canada Gazette* 336, and finally in *A Century of Criminal Justice*, c. 8; and 'Codification in the Commonwealth: Earlier Efforts' (1990) 2 *Criminal Law Forum* 145.   **Page 270, para 2:** See 'A Century of Criminal Justice' in *A Century of Criminal Justice*.   **Page 273, para 1:** All the examples and most of the facts in this chapter are taken from 'R.S. Wright's Model Criminal Code.'   **Page 273, para 2:** James Fitzjames Stephen, *Liberty, Equality, Fraternity*, 2nd ed., 1874, reproduced with intro. and notes by R.J. White (Cambridge: Cambridge University Press, 1967).   **Page 273, para 3:** R.S. Wright, *The Law of Criminal Conspiracies and Agreements* (Philadelphia: Blackstone, 1887).   **Page 273, para 4:**

American Law Institute, *Model Penal Code: Official Draft and Explanatory Notes* (Philadelphia, 1985); 'R.S. Wright's Model Criminal Code' at 315.   **Page 275, para 1:** 'R.S. Wright's Model Criminal Code' at 325.   **Page 275, para 2:** *Ibid.* at 345.   **Page 275, para 3:** *Ibid.* at 346.   **Page 275, para 4:** *Oxford Dictionary of National Biography*, vol. 60, 487.   **Page 277, para 1:** Canada, Department of Justice, *The Criminal Law in Canadian Society* (Ottawa, 1982) at 10.   **Page 277, para 2:** Report of the Canadian Sentencing Commission, *Sentencing Reform: A Canadian Approach* (1987).   **Page 277, para 3:** 'Criminal Justice and the Constitutional Division of Power in Canada' in *A Century of Criminal Justice*, c. 2; Law Reform Commission of Canada, *Double Jeopardy, Pleas and Verdicts* (Working Paper 63) (1991); Law Reform Commission of Canada, *Crimes against the State* (Working Paper 49) (1986).   **Page 277, para 4:** Canada, Department of Justice, *The Criminal Law in Canadian Society* (1982); Martin L. Friedland, 'Canadian Criminal Justice, 1892–1992' (1993) 42 *University of New Brunswick Law Journal* 175.   **Page 278, para 1:** M.L. Friedland, 'Reforming Police Powers: Who's in Charge?' in R.C. Macleod and David Schneiderman, eds., *Police Powers in Canada: The Evolution and Practice of Authority* (Toronto: University of Toronto Press, 1994) 100 at 101.   **Page 278, para 2:** Edward M. Morgan, 'The Defence of Necessity: Justification or Excuse?' (1984) 42 *University of Toronto Faculty of Law Review* 165; Paul B. Schabas, 'Intoxication and Culpability: Towards an Offence of Criminal Intoxication' (1984) 42 *University of Toronto Faculty of Law Review* 147.   **Page 278, para 3:** Remarks of Blaine Thacker, Chairperson, House of Commons, *Minutes of Proceedings and Evidence of the Sub-Committee on the Recodification of the General Part of the Criminal Code*, 15 June 1992, vol. 2, 4–26 at 26.   **Page 278, para 4:** United States, *Final Report of the National Commission on Reform of Federal Criminal Laws (Proposed New Federal Criminal Code)* (Washington, 1971); for the conference papers see (1990) 2 *Criminal Law Forum* 111–76.   **Page 279, para 1:** 'Codification in the Commonwealth.'   **Page 279, para 2:** see M.L. Friedland, 'Old and New Criminal Codes' (1982) 16 *Law Society of Upper Canada Gazette* 220; U.K., H.C., *Justice for All*, Cm. 5563 (2002).

Chapter 18, The Charter. Material is mainly drawn from the following articles: Martin L. Friedland, 'Criminal Justice and the Charter' (1983) 13 *Manitoba Law Journal* 549, repr. in *A Century of Criminal Justice: Perspectives on the Development of Canadian Criminal Law*, c. 7 (Toronto: Carswell, 1984); and 'Criminal Justice in Canada Revisited' (2004) 48 *Criminal Law Quarterly* 419.   **Page 280, para 2:** 'Criminal Justice and the Charter' in *A Century of Criminal Justice* at 205.   **Page 281, para 2:** See Martin Friedland, 'Laskin and the University' in Neil Finkelstein and Constance Backhouse, eds., *The Laskin Legacy: Essays in Commemoration of Chief Justice Bora Laskin* (Toronto: Irwin Law, 2007).   **Page 282, para 1:**

Beverley McLachlin, 'Judging, Politics, and Why They Must Be Kept Separate,' unpublished luncheon address to Canadian Club of Toronto, 17 June 2003. **Page 282, para 2:** *Hunter v. Southam*, [1984] 2 S.C.R. 145; Robert Harvie and Hamar Foster, 'Ties That Bind? The Supreme Court of Canada, American Jurisprudence, and the Revision of Canadian Criminal Law under the Charter' (1990) 28 *Osgoode Hall Law Journal* 729 and Harvie and Foster, 'Different Drummers, Different Drums: The Supreme Court of Canada, American Jurisprudence and the Continuing Revision of Criminal Law under the *Charter*' (1992) 24 *Ottawa Law Review* 39.   **Page 283, para 1:** 'Criminal Justice and the Charter' at 208.   **Page 283, para 2:** *Ibid.* at 231.   **Page 283, para 3:** Material on the Canadian Jewish Congress is from my papers in the Archives.   **Page 284, para 1:** *Lochner v. New York* (1905), 198 U.S. 45.   **Page 284, para 2:** *Chaoulli v. Quebec (Attorney General)*, [2005] 1 S.C.R. 791. Three judges held that it was a violation of section 7; three that it was not; and the seventh judge was only willing to hold that it violated the Quebec Charter.   **Page 285, para 3:** *R. v. Askov*, [1990] 2 S.C.R. 1199; *R. v. Duarte*, [1990] 1 S.C.R. 30.   **Page 286, para 2:** See also M.L. Friedland, 'Prospective and Retrospective Judicial Lawmaking' (1974) 24 *University of Toronto Law Journal* 170; *R. v. Brydges*, [1990] 1 S.C.R. 190; *Chaoulli*, unreported additional judgment rendered 4 August 2005, Docket 29272.   **Page 286, para 3:** *R. v. Swain*, [1991] 1 S.C.R. 933; *R. v. Mills*, [1986] 1 S.C.R. 863.   **Page 287, para 2:** See *R. v. Lifchus*, [1997] 3 S.C.R. 320; *R. v. Starr*, [2000] 2 S.C.R. 144; and *R. v. Russell*, [2000] 2 S.C.R. 731.   **Page 287, para 3:** *R. v. Mack*, [1988] 2 S.C.R. 903.   **Page 287, para 4:** *M'Alister (or Donoghue) v. Stevenson*, [1932] A.C. 562.   **Page 288, para 2:** Remarks to the Council of the Canadian Bar Association in Montreal, 16 Aug. 2003, at p. 2; 'McLachlin Urges Overhaul of Criminal-Justice System' *Globe and Mail*, 18 Aug. 2003; Michael Moldaver, John Sopinka Lecture on Advocacy, Criminal Lawyers' Association Conference, 21 Oct. 2005.   **Page 288, para 3:** Albert Currie, 'Riding the Third Wave: Rethinking Criminal Legal Aid within an Access to Justice Framework' (Ottawa: Department of Justice, 2000).   **Page 288, para 4:** *Attorney General's Reference No 2 of 2001*, [2003] All E.R. 220 (H.L.).   **Page 289, para 2:** See, for example, Kent Roach, *The Supreme Court on Trial: Judicial Activism or Democratic Dialogue* (Toronto: Irwin Law, 2001) and 'Constitutional and Common Law Dialogues between the Supreme Court and Canadian Legislatures' (2001) 80 *Canadian Bar Review* 481; Peter W. Hogg and Allison A. Bushell, 'The *Charter* Dialogue between Courts and Legislatures' (1997) 35 *Osgoode Hall Law Journal* 75; and *R. v. Hall*, [2002] 3 S.C.R. 309.   **Page 289, para 3:** See 'Criminal Justice and the Charter' at 208–9. **Page 289, para 4:** *R. v. Oakes*, [1986] 1 S.C.R. 103; *Reference re: Section 94(2) of the BC Motor Vehicle Act*, [1985] 2 S.C.R. 486.   **Page 290, para 1:** *Oakes* at 139 and at 137; Robert Sharpe and Kent Roach, *Brian Dickson: A Judge's Journey* (Toronto:

University of Toronto Press, 2003) at 334.   **Page 290, para 2:** Roy Romanow, John Whyte, and Howard Leeson, *Canada ... Notwithstanding: The Making of the Constitution 1976–1982* (Toronto: Carswell/Methuen, 1984) at 243.   **Page 290, para 3:** *A Judge's Journey* at 312; remarks of 29 Oct. 1983, cited *ibid.* at 310.   **Page 291, para 1:** *BC Motor Vehicle Act Reference* at 309–10.   **Page 291, para 2:** *Lawyers Weekly*, 29 Mar. 2002.   **Page 291, para 3:** Don Stuart, *Charter Justice in Canadian Criminal Law*, 4th ed. (Toronto: Thomson Carswell, 2005); *R. v. Stinchcombe*, [1991] 3 S.C.R. 326; *R. v. Morgentaler*, [1988] 1 S.C.R. 30; *R. v. Hebert*, [1990] 2 S.C.R. 151; *R. v. Swain*, [1991] 1 S.C.R. 933; *R. v. Ruzic*, [2001] 1 S.C.R. 687.   **Page 291, para 4:** *R. v. O'Connor*, [1995] 4 S.C.R. 411.   **Page 292, para 2:** See, for example, *Smith v. Jones*, [1999] 1 S.C.R. 455; and *R. v. Seaboyer*, [1991] 2 S.C.R. 577 at 608 and 612.   **Page 292, para 3:** David M. Paciocco and Lee Stuesser, *The Law of Evidence*, 4th ed. (Toronto: Irwin Law, 2005) at 6; *R. v. Malmo-Levine; R. v. Caine*, [2003] 3 S.C.R. 571 at 634.   **Page 293, para 2:** *Chaoulli* at 850 and 859.   **Page 295, para 2:** *Singh et al. v. M.E.I.*, [1985] 1 S.C.R. 177.   **Page 296, para 2:** Charles R. Epp, *The Rights Revolution* (Chicago: University of Chicago Press, 1998) at 2.   **Page 297, para 1:** *R. v. Smith*, [1987] 1 S.C.R. 1045 at 1072; Anthony N. Doob and Cheryl M. Webster, 'Looking at the Model Penal Code Sentencing Provisions through Canadian Lenses' (2004) 7 *Buffalo Criminal Law Review* 139. Tony Doob points out (correspondence of 27 Apr. 2007) that the American data for city jails was not included in the statistics until the 1970s, and when included showed an incarceration rate of 130–50 per 100,000.   **Page 297, para 2:** 'Critics Blast Three-Strikes Laws' *Globe and Mail*, 18 Oct. 2006.

Chapter 19, The Trials of Israel Lipski. See my book *The Trials of Israel Lipski: A True Story of a Victorian Murder in the East End of London* (London: Macmillan, 1984) and my papers in the Archives.   **Page 299, para 1:** See Michael Harrison, *Clarence: The Life of the Duke of Clarence and Avondale* (London: W.H. Allen, 1972).   **Page 300, para 4:** Nancy E. Eastham and Boris Krivy, eds., *The Cambridge Lectures: Selected Papers Based upon Lectures Delivered at the Cambridge Conference of the Canadian Institute for Advanced Legal Studies, 1981* (Toronto: Butterworths, 1982).   **Page 301, para 2:** *Lipski* at 204.   **Page 302, para 2:** *R. v. Truscott* (1960), 126 C.C.C. 109 (Ont. C.A.); *R. v. Truscott*, [1967] S.C.R. 309.   **Page 303, para 2:** M.L. Friedland, *Cases and Materials on Criminal Law and Procedure*, 2nd ed. (Toronto: University of Toronto Press, 1968) at 366; Kent Roach, 'Wrongful Convictions and Criminal Procedure' (2003–4) 42 *Brandeis Law Journal* 349 at 369.   **Page 303, para 3:** See Canada, Department of Justice, news release, 28 Oct. 2004, available online. Fred Kaufman, *Report to Minister of Justice in the Matter of an Application by Steven Murray Truscott* (Ottawa, 2004).   **Page 305, para 2:** *Lipski* at 16.   **Page 306, para 1:** C. Watts and L. Davies, *Cunninghame*

Graham: A Critical Biography (Cambridge: Cambridge University Press, 1979) at xiii, 181ff. **Page 307, para 1:** *Lipski* at 98. **Page 307, para 3:** *Ibid.* at 112. **Page 307, para 5:** For more on miscarriages of justice and the establishment of the English Court of Criminal Appeal, see Martin L. Friedland, *Double Jeopardy* (Oxford: Clarendon Press, 1969) at 233 and Julian Barnes, *Arthur & George* (New York: Knopf, 2006). **Page 308, para 3:** *Lipski* at 184. **Page 308, para 4:** *Ibid.* at 205. **Page 309, para 3:** William J. Fishman, 'Alien Trial' *Guardian*, 16 Feb. 1984; John Mortimer, 'The Murder behind Closed Doors' *Sunday Times*, 19 Feb. 1984; Judge Aron Owen, 'Murder in the Old East End' *Jewish Chronicle*, 17 Feb. 1984. **Page 310, para 1:** Christopher T. Husbands (1985) 25 *British Journal of Criminology* 199; (1984) 100 *Law Quarterly Review* 511. **Page 310, para 2:** Robert Fulford, 'Fascinating Case of British Victorian Prejudice' *Toronto Star*, 31 Mar. 1984; John J. Robinette, 'Trials of Israel Lipski True Victorian Mystery' *Toronto Star*, 13 May 1984; Edward L. Greenspan, 'Harsh New Light on 1887 Murder' *Cornerbrook Western Star* and other papers, 9 May 1984; Clayton Ruby, 'The Sad Tale of the Walking-Stick Maker' *Globe and Mail*, 5 May 1984. **Page 311, para 2:** Martin L. Friedland, 'Lipski, Israel (1865–1887)' *Oxford Dictionary of National Biography*, online ed. (Oxford University Press, 2005), at http://www.oxforddnb.com/view/article/77220.

Chapter 20, The Case of Valentine Shortis. See my papers in the Archives, my book *The Case of Valentine Shortis: A True Story of Crime and Politics in Canada* (Toronto: University of Toronto Press, 1986), and Martin L. Friedland, 'The Case of Valentine Shortis – Yesterday and Today' (1991) 36 *Canadian Journal of Psychiatry* 159. **Page 312, para 2:** The transcript was found in the Ontario Archives. **Page 313, para 3:** Martin L. Friedland, 'A Century of Criminal Justice' was first published in (1982) 20 *Transactions of the Royal Society of Canada*, 285 and in Martin L. Friedland, *A Century of Criminal Justice: Perspectives on the Development of Canadian Criminal Law*, c. 8 (Toronto: Carswell, 1984). **Page 314, para 5:** 'A Century of Criminal Justice' in *A Century of Criminal Justice* at 245. **Page 315, para 3:** Royal Society of Canada, *Tobacco, Nicotine and Addiction: A Committee Report* (Ottawa: The Society, 1989). **Page 316, para 3:** *Shortis* at ix. **Page 319, para 1:** *M'Naghten's Case* (1843), [1843–60] All E.R. Rep. 229. **Page 319, para 2:** For a discussion of this issue, see *Shortis* at 39–41. **Page 319, para 3:** *R. v. Cracknell* (1931), 56 C.C.C. 190 at 193 (Ont. C.A.); *Shortis* at 41. **Page 320, para 3:** 'The Case of Valentine Shortis – Yesterday and Today.' **Page 320, para 4:** *Shortis* at 65 and n. 13. **Page 321, para 3:** *Ibid.* at 159. **Page 322, para 2:** *Ibid.* at 291. **Page 323, para 4:** *Ibid.* at 290–1. **Page 323, para 6:** Donald Harman Akenson (1987) 68 *Canadian Historical Review* 622 at 622. **Page 324, para 1:** Margaret Cannon, 'Two Prize-Winners Take Second Bows' *Globe and Mail*, 15 Nov. 1986.

Page 325, para 3: Material on a possible film can be found in my papers in the Archives.

Chapter 21, The Death of Old Man Rice. Material on this chapter can be found in *The Death of Old Man Rice: A True Story of Criminal Justice in America* (Toronto: University of Toronto Press, 1994) and in my personal papers on the case, most of which were donated to the Fondren Library at Rice University. The rest are in the U of T Archives.   **Page 326, para 1:** In addition to Tim Endicott and Paul Michell, a number of other research assistants helped me gather material, including Fred Pletcher and Craig Godsoe, both of whom are handling complex corporate matters for Borden Ladner Gervais in Vancouver, and Jennifer Webster, who is practising family law in Toronto.   **Page 326, para 2:** *People v. Gillette* (1908), 191 N.Y. 107.   **Page 327, para 1:** *Denver Post*, 28 Nov. 1912; *Houston Chronicle*, 28 Nov. 1912.   **Page 329, para 2:** *Old Man Rice* at ix and 380–1.   **Page 329, para 4:** *Ibid.* at 6.   **Page 329, para 6:** *London Review of Books*, 20 Apr. 1995. **Page 331, para 1:** *Old Man Rice* at 335.   **Page 331, para 3:** *American Funeral Director*, Jan. 1995.   **Page 331, para 4:** *Old Man Rice* at 42.   **Page 332, para 1:** *Ibid.* at 45.   **Page 332, para 2:** *Ibid.* at 379.   **Page 333, para 3:** See Kenneth J. Lipartito and Joseph A. Pratt, *Baker & Botts in the Development of Modern Houston* (Austin: University of Texas Press, 1991).   **Page 334, para 3:** *Old Man Rice* at xii.   **Page 334, para 4:** (1995) 273 *Journal of the American Medical Association* 66 at 66.   **Page 335, para 1:** (1995) 108 *Harvard Law Review* 797 at 797.   **Page 336, para 2:** Peter Heehs, *The Bomb in Bengal: The Rise of Revolutionary Terrorism in India 1900–1910* (Delhi: Oxford University Press, 1993).   **Page 338, para 2:** W.J. Keith (1991) *Canadian Book Review Annual* 283 at 283.   **Page 339, para 3:** 'Bookends' *Quill & Quire*, November 1991, at 30.

Chapter 22, Frailty of the Criminal Process – Some Observations. This chapter draws on earlier chapters and several reports on miscarriages of justice. **Page 340, para 1:** Nova Scotia, Royal Commission on the Donald Marshall, Jr, Prosecution, *Commissioners' Report* (1989); *Reference re: Milgaard (Can.)*, [1992] 1 S.C.R. 866; Ontario, The Commission on Proceedings Involving Guy Paul Morin, *Report* (1998) (Commissioner: Fred Kaufman), available online; see 'Truscott Judge Wanted Author Prosecuted' *Globe and Mail*, 31 Jan. 2007; the Lamer Commission of Inquiry Pertaining to the Cases of Ronald Dalton, Gregory Parsons, and Randy Druken, *Report and Annexes* (2006) (Chair: Antonio Lamer) at 172; see also *Report of the Commission of Inquiry into Certain Aspects of the Trial and Conviction of James Driskell* (2007) (Commissioner: Patrick LeSage), available online.   **Page 340, para 2:** *United States v. Burns*, [2001] 1 S.C.R. 283; *ibid.* at 294 and at 296.   **Page 341, para 2:** See Martin L. Friedland, 'Criminal Justice in Canada Revisited' (2004) 48 *Criminal Law Quarterly* 419 at 425; for the most up-to-date statistics see the CCRC statistics available online; for 2004–5 statistics, see U.K., Criminal Cases Review Commission, *Annual Report 2004–2005* at 11, available online.   **Page 341, para 3:** Marshall Commission report; Lamer report at 167; see, generally, 'Criminal Justice in Canada Revisited' at 426.   **Page 342, para 2:** Fred Kaufman, *Report to Minister of Justice in the Matter of an Application by Steven Murray Truscott* (Ottawa, 2004); see Canada, Department of Justice, news release, 28 Oct. 2004, available online; 'CBC to Televise Truscott Appeal' *Globe and Mail*, 18 Jan. 2007.   **Page 342, para 3:** *R. v. Stinchcombe*, [1991] 3 S.C.R. 326.   **Page 343, para 2:** *R. v. Hanratty*, [2002] 2 Cr. App. R. 30; *R. v. Ellis*, [2003] EWCA Crim. 3556.   **Page 343, para 3:** 'Judgment Summary' of *Hanratty*, reported online; *Ellis* at para 90.   **Page 343, para 4:** See Ontario, Ministry of the Attorney General, news release, 24 May 2006, available online.   **Page 344, para 2:** Federal/Provincial/Territorial Heads of Prosecutions Committee Working Group, *Report on the Prevention of Miscarriages of Justice* (2004) (Chairs: D.A. Bellemare and Rob Finlayson).   **Page 344, para 4:** *Ibid.* at 42–3.   **Page 345, para 1:** *Hodge's Case* (1838), 168 E.R. 1136; the need for a warning re circumstantial evidence was rejected in *R. v. Cooper*, [1978] 1 S.C.R. 860; for the need to warn re the frailty of eyewitness evidence, see *R. v. Sutton*, [1970] 3 C.C.C. 152 (Ont. C.A.), *R. v. Spatola*, [1970] 4 C.C.C. 241 (Ont. C.A.), and *R. v. Howarth* (1970), 1 C.C.C. (2d) 546 (Ont. C.A.).   **Page 345, para 2:** Bellemare and Finlayson at 58.   **Page 346, para 5:** *R. v. Baltrusaitis* (2002), 162 C.C.C. (3d) 539 (Ont. C.A.); *R. v. Vetrovec*, [1982] 1 S.C.R. 811.   **Page 347, para 2:** For the establishment of the Goudge inquiry see Ontario, Ministry of the Attorney General, news release, 25 Apr. 2007, available online.   **Page 347, para 5:** See also the (2007) 52:2 *Criminal Law Quarterly* issue, which is devoted entirely to the subject of wrongful convictions.   **Page 348, para 1:** Lamer report at 164.   **Page 348, para 2:** See also my discussion of this issue in c. 10, above.   **Page 348, para 3:** *R. v. Morin* (1987), 36 C.C.C. (3d) 50.   **Page 349, para 3:** Michael Moldaver, John Sopinka Lecture on Advocacy, Criminal Lawyers' Association Conference, 21 Oct. 2005; Beverley McLachlin, 'The Challenges We Face,' unpublished remarks to Empire Club of Canada, Toronto, 8 March 2007; see also 'Top Judge Sounds Alarm on Trial Delays' *Globe and Mail*, 9 March 2007.   **Page 350, para 4:** Moldaver, Sopinka Lecture.   **Page 351, para 1:** Canadian Judicial Council, *Ethical Principles for Judges* (Ottawa, 1998).   **Page 351, para 2:** The Chief Justice's Advisory Committee on Criminal Trials in the Superior Court of Justice, *New Approaches to Criminal Trials* (2006) (Chairs: David Watt and Bruce Durno), available online; Ontario, *Report of the Criminal Justice Review Committee* (1999) (Chairs: Hugh Locke, John D. Evans, and Murray Segal).   **Page 352, para 1:** *New Approaches to Criminal Trials* at paras 408–9.

Chapter 23, Sanctions and Rewards in the Legal System. Much of the material in this chapter is drawn from my papers in the Archives and from three books resulting from the CIAR project: Martin L. Friedland, ed., *Sanctions and Rewards in the Legal System: A Multidisciplinary Approach* (Toronto: University of Toronto Press, 1989); M.L. Friedland, ed., *Securing Compliance: Seven Case Studies* (Toronto: University of Toronto Press, 1990); and Martin Friedland, Michael Trebilcock, and Kent Roach, *Regulating Traffic Safety* (Toronto: University of Toronto Press, 1990).   **Page 353, para 1:** See Craig Brown, *A Generation of Excellence: A History of the Canadian Institute for Advanced Research* (Toronto: University of Toronto Press, 2007).   **Page 354, para 2:** *Ibid.* at 71.   **Page 354, para 3:** *Ibid.* at 81.   **Page 355, para 2:** *Report of the Task Force on Law,* Submitted to the Canadian Institute for Advanced Research (1985) (Chairs: Gisèle Côté-Harper, John Hagan, and J. Robert S. Prichard) at 16.   **Page 355, para 3:** *Ibid.* at 27.   **Page 356, para 4:** Margie Peden et al., eds., World Health Organization, *World Report on Road Traffic Injury Prevention* (Geneva, 2004) at 4.   **Page 357, para 1:** *Sanctions and Rewards*; H. Laurence Ross, 'Sociology and Legal Sanctions' *ibid.* 36 at 39.   **Page 357, para 2:** Philip J. Cook, 'The Economics of Criminal Sanctions' *ibid.* 50 at 67.   **Page 358, para 1:** Joan E. Grusec, 'Sanctions and Rewards: The Approach of Psychology' *ibid.* 109 at 113.   **Page 358, para 2:** Hugh J. Arnold, 'Sanctions and Rewards: An Organizational Perspective' *ibid.* 137 at 152 and 142; Pierre Maranda, 'An Anthropological View of Sanctions and Rewards' *ibid.* 156 at 157 and 164.   **Page 359, para 1:** *Sanctions and Rewards* at 12.   **Page 360, para 3:** Richard Brown and Murray Rankin, 'Persuasion, Penalties, and Prosecution: Administrative v. Criminal Sanctions' in *Securing Compliance* 325 at 348.   **Page 361, para 1:** Thurman W. Arnold, 'Law Enforcement – An Attempt at Social Dissection' (1932) 42 *Yale Law Journal* 1 at 8; see also Jon Elster, *The Cement of Society: A Study of Social Order* (Cambridge: Cambridge University Press, 1989).   **Page 361, para 2:** Donald N. Dewees, 'The Effect of Environmental Regulation: Mercury and Sulphur Dioxide' in *Securing Compliance* 354 at 387; John Hagan, Carol Rogerson, and Bill McCarthy, 'Family Violence: A Study in Social and Legal Sanctions' *ibid.* 392 at 427.   **Page 362, para 3:** Evelyn Vingilis (1991) 3 *Journal of Motor Vehicle Law* 111 at 111.   **Page 362, para 4:** *Regulating Traffic Safety* at 4.   **Page 363, para 2:** Ralph Nader, *Unsafe at Any Speed: The Designed-In Dangers of the American Automobile* (New York: Grossman, 1965).   **Page 363, para 3:** U.K., Department of Transport, Home Office, *Road Traffic Law Review Report* (1988) (Chair: Peter North) at 25.   **Page 364, para 3:** W. Haddon, 'On the Escape of Tigers: An Ecologic Note' (1970) 60 *American Journal of Public Health* 2229; Kent Roach, *September 11: Consequences for Canada* (Montreal: McGill-Queen's University Press, 2003).   **Page 365, para 1:** R.V. Clarke and P. Mayhew, 'The British Gas Suicide Story and Its Criminological Implications' (1988) 10 *Crime and Jus-*

tice: An Annual Survey 79.   **Page 366, para 3:** G.J.S. Wilde and P.A. Murdoch, 'Incentive Systems for Accident-Free and Violation-Free Driving in the General Population' (1982) 25 *Ergonomics* 879 at 887–8.

Chapter 24, Borderline Justice and Other Studies of Law and Society. Much of the material in this chapter can be found in my papers in the Archives.   **Page 369, para 1:** Craig Brown, *A Generation of Excellence: A History of the Canadian Institute for Advanced Research* (Toronto: University of Toronto Press, 2007).   **Page 369, para 5:** *Ibid.* at 210.   **Page 370, para 2:** Ontario, *Report of the Task Force on Inflation Protection for Employment Pension Plans* (1988) (Chair: Martin Friedland).   **Page 371, para 4:** Task Force on Inflation Protection for Employment Pension Plans, *Research Studies*, vols. 1–3 (1988).   **Page 372, para 1:** Remarks of Murray Elston, Legislative Assembly of Ontario, *Debates*, 2 Mar. 1989.   **Page 372, para 4:** Brown at 211.   **Page 374, para 1:** *Ibid.* at 224.   **Page 374, para 2:** (1989) 11 *Dublin University Law Journal* 10; (1988–9) 31 *Criminal Law Quarterly* 280.   **Page 375, para 4:** Michael A. Code, *Trial within a Reasonable Time: A Short History of Recent Controversies Surrounding Speedy Trial Rights in Canada and the United States* (Toronto: Carswell, 1992); *R. v. Askov*, [1990] 2 S.C.R. 1199.   **Page 376, para 2:** Richard V. Ericson, *Reproducing Order: A Study of Police Patrol Work* (Toronto: University of Toronto Press, 1982).   **Page 377, para 3:** Richard V. Ericson and Kevin D. Haggerty, *Policing the Risk Society* (Toronto: University of Toronto Press, 1997).   **Page 379, para 4:** Kent Roach and M.L. Friedland, 'Borderline Justice: Policing in the Two Niagaras' (1996) 23 *American Journal of Criminal Law* 241; Friedland and Roach, 'Borderline Justice: Choosing Juries in the Two Niagaras' (1997) 31 *Israel Law Review* 120.   **Page 380, para 1:** 'Policing in the Two Niagaras' at 351–2.   **Page 381, para 3:** 'Choosing Juries' at 156.

Chapter 25, A Place Apart: Judicial Independence and Accountability. Material is mainly drawn from my papers in the Archives, my study for the Canadian Judicial Council *A Place Apart: Judicial Independence and Accountability in Canada* (Ottawa, 1995), and Martin L. Friedland, 'Judicial Independence and Accountability in Canada' (2001) 59 *The Advocate* 859.   **Page 382, para 2:** Remarks of Albert Béchard, House of Commons, *Debates*, 14 June 1971, at 6666.   **Page 383, para 1:** Jules Deschênes, *Masters in Their Own House: A Study on the Independent Judicial Administration of the Courts* (Ottawa: Canadian Judicial Council, 1981).   **Page 383, para 3:** Canadian Bar Association Task Force on Gender Equality in the Legal Profession, *Touchstones for Change: Equality, Diversity and Accountability* (Ottawa: CBA, 1993) (Chair: Bertha Wilson) at 285.   **Page 389, para 2:** Robert Stevens, *The Independence of the Judiciary* (Oxford: Clarendon

Press, 1993); London *Times*, 24 Oct. 1995.   **Page 391, para 3:** *Ottawa Citizen*, 19 Aug. 1995; *Edmonton Journal*, 18 Aug. 1995; Martin L. Friedland, 'Reflections on *A Place Apart: Judicial Independence and Accountability in Canada*' (1996) 45 *University of New Brunswick Law Journal* 67; Martin L. Friedland, 'Judicial Independence and Accountability: A Canadian Perspective' (1996) 7 *Criminal Law Forum* 605.   **Page 393, para 3:** *Re Provincial Court Judges*, [1997] 3 S.C.R. 3 at 116.   **Page 394, para 1:** Article in *The Advocate* at 862.   **Page 394, para 2:** *Provincial Court Judges' Assn. (New Brunswick) v. New Brunswick*, [2005] 2 S.C.R. 286.   **Page 395, para 1:** Canadian Judicial Council, *Ethical Principles for Judges* (Ottawa, 1998).   **Page 397, para 1:** An edited version of Michael Bryant's speech was published as 'AG Vows to Re-examine Courts Administration' *Law Times*, 12 Jan. 2004.   **Page 397, para 2:** Canadian Judicial Council, *Alternative Models of Court Administration* (Ottawa, 2006).   **Page 397, para 3:** *A Place Apart* at 94–5.   **Page 398, para 2:** *Cosgrove v. Canadian Judicial Council et al.* (2005), 261 D.L.R. (4th) 447 (federal court trial division); reversed in 2007 FCA 103 (as yet unreported).   **Page 398, para 5:** *A Place Apart* at 256–7.   **Page 399, para 2:** See *Globe and Mail*: 'Toews Accused of Trying to Politicize the Judiciary' and 'A Flagging Relationship Suffers Another Blow,' 11 Nov. 2006, 'Where Are the Judges?' 3 Jan. 2007, and 'Senior Lawyers Criticize Toews,' 16 Nov. 2006.   **Page 399, para 3:** 'Toews Under Fire for Plan to Let Police Play Role in Vetting Judges' *Canadian Press*, 16 Nov. 2006; 'Tories Deny Goal Is to Stack Court System' *Globe and Mail*, 14 Feb. 2007.   **Page 400, para 2:** 'Two-thirds Back Electing Judges' *Globe and Mail*, 9 Apr. 2007.

Chapter 26, Controlling Misconduct in the Military. Material in this chapter has been drawn from my papers in the Archives, my report *Controlling Misconduct in the Military: A Study Prepared for the Commission of Inquiry into the Deployment of Canadian Forces to Somalia* (Ottawa, 1997), and my article 'Military Justice and the Somalia Affair' (1998) 40 *Criminal Law Quarterly* 360.   **Page 406, para 2:** Lawrence B. Radine, *The Taming of the Troops: Social Control in the United States Army* (Westport, Conn.: Greenwood Press, 1977) at 156; John Braithwaite, *Crime, Shame and Reintegration* (Cambridge: Cambridge University Press, 1989) at 68.   **Page 406, para 3:** Anthony Kellett, *Combat Motivation: The Behavior of Soldiers in Battle* (Boston: Kluwer Nijhoff, 1982) at 89; Deborah Harrison and Lucie Laliberté, *No Life Like It: Military Wives in Canada* (Toronto: Lorimer, 1994) at 43–4.   **Page 407, para 1:** Article by Major J.K. McCollum in *Military Review*, Nov. 1976, quoted in Mobile Command Study, *A Report on Disciplinary Infractions and Antisocial Behaviour within FMC with Particular Reference to the Special Service Force and the Canadian Airborne Regiment* (Ottawa: Department of National Defence, 1985) at 159.   **Page 407, para 2:** Human Rights Watch, 'Torture in Iraq' *New York Review of Books*, 3 Nov. 2005.   **Page 407, para 3:** As cited in a study for the Somalia inquiry done by Eugene Oscapella, 'Alcohol and Drug Policies Affecting the Canadian Forces,' February 1996, at 5.   **Page 408, para 2:** Conversations with various military personnel re recruiting standards. **Page 408, para 3:** Conversations with military personnel re military women in Afghanistan.   **Page 409, para 4:** *Controlling Misconduct* at 54.   **Page 410, para 2:** *R. v. Généreux*, [1992] 1 S.C.R. 259.   **Page 413, para 3:** Peter Desbarats, *Somalia Cover-up: A Commissioner's Journal* (Toronto: McClelland & Stewart, 1997) at 248–9.   **Page 414, para 2:** 'Recent Study Peels Away Army Justice' *Toronto Star*, 1 June 1997.   **Page 415, para 2:** *Report of the Special Advisory Group on Military Justice and Military Police Investigation Services* (Ottawa, 1997) (Chair: Brian Dickson) at 18.   **Page 415, para 3:** *Ibid.* at i–ii.   **Page 416, para 2:** 'Young's Measures Won't Reform Military' *Montreal Gazette*, 1 Apr. 1997.   **Page 416, para 4:** Commission of Inquiry into the Deployment of Canadian Forces to Somalia, *Dishonoured Legacy: The Lessons of the Somalia Affair* (Ottawa, 1997).   **Page 417, para 3:** See 'Military Justice and the Somalia Affair.'   **Page 417, para 5:** *Ibid.* at 485. **Page 418, para 3:** Ministry of National Defence, *The First Independent Review by the Right Honourable Antonio Lamer ... of the Provisions and Operation of Bill C-25* (2003), available online, Foreword at 1.

Chapter 27, Writing the History of the University of Toronto. The main sources for this chapter are my book *The University of Toronto: A History* (Toronto: University of Toronto Press, 2002), and my articles 'Writing the History of the University of Toronto' (2002) 14 *Historical Studies in Education* 282 and 'Reflections: A History of the University of Toronto' in Michael Goldberg, ed., *The University Professor Lecture Series 2002–2003* (U of T Faculty of Arts and Science, 2003) 23.   **Page 424, para 3:** A.B. Macallum, quoted in *U of T: A History* at 261.   **Page 426, para 4:** *U of T: A History* at 382.   **Page 429, para 2:** John P.M. Court, 'Bibliographies and Notes as a Separate Online Publication: A Novel Trend in Support of Scholarly Publishing' (2002) 34 *Journal of Scholarly Publishing* 43; Constance Backhouse, *Colour-Coded: A Legal History of Racism in Canada* (Toronto: University of Toronto Press, 1999).   **Page 429, para 3:** *U of T: A History* at 352.   **Page 430, para 2:** Clifford Geertz, *The Interpretation of Cultures: Selected Essays* (New York: Basic Books, 1973).   **Page 430, para 4:** P.B. Waite (2003) 15 *Historical Studies in Education* 186.   **Page 432, para 1:** I do not know whether the volume is still in the president's office. I still have a copy of the book with the same inscription, but inscribed that morning with such a shaky hand – because of the drama of the occasion – that I had to inscribe another copy.

Epilogue. Page 433, para 2: See c. 21; Julian Barnes, *Arthur & George* (New York: Knopf, 2006).   **Page 435, para 2:** See prologue.   **Page 437, para 2:** The study, 'Report to Access Copyright on Distribution of Royalties,' was handed in on 15 Feb. 2007.

Publications
and Government Work
of Martin L. Friedland

Books

*Detention before Trial: A Study of Criminal Cases Tried in the Toronto Magistrates'
Courts*. University of Toronto Press, 1965; paperback, 1969
Double Jeopardy. Oxford: Clarendon Press, 1969
Courts and Trials: A Multidisciplinary Approach. Editor. Toronto: University of
Toronto Press, hardcover and paperback, 1975
Access to the Law: A Study Prepared for the Law Reform Commission of Canada.
Toronto: Carswell/Methuen, 1975
National Security: The Legal Dimensions. Hull: Canadian Government Publishing
Centre, 1980
*The Trials of Israel Lipski: A True Story of a Victorian Murder in the East End of Lon-
don*. London: Macmillan 1984; New York: Beaufort Books, 1985. Winner,
Crime Writers of Canada Award for Non-Fiction, 1984; finalist, British Crime
Writers Award for Non-Fiction, 1984
A Century of Criminal Justice: Perspectives on the Development of Canadian Law.
Toronto: Carswell, 1984
The Case of Valentine Shortis: A True Story of Crime and Politics in Canada. Toronto:
University of Toronto Press, 1986; paperback, 1988. Finalist, Crime Writers of
Canada Award for Non-Fiction, 1986
Sanctions and Rewards in the Legal System: A Multidisciplinary Approach. Editor.
Toronto: University of Toronto Press, hardcover and paperback, 1989
Securing Compliance: Seven Case Studies. Editor. Toronto: University of Toronto
Press, 1990

Regulating Traffic Safety (with Michael Trebilcock and Kent Roach). Toronto: University of Toronto Press, 1990

Rough Justice: Essays on Crime in Literature. Editor. Toronto: University of Toronto Press, 1991; hardcover and paperback

The Death of Old Man Rice: A True Story of Criminal Justice in America. Toronto and New York: University of Toronto Press and New York University Press, 1994; paperback, 1996

A Place Apart: Judicial Independence and Accountability in Canada. Ottawa: Canadian Judicial Council, 1995

Cases and Materials on Criminal Law and Procedure, 8th ed. (with Kent Roach). Toronto: Emond Montgomery, 1997

Controlling Misconduct in the Military: A Study Prepared for the Commission of Inquiry into the Deployment of Canadian Forces to Somalia. Ottawa: Public Works and Government Services, 1997

The University of Toronto: A History. Toronto: University of Toronto Press, 2002. Winner, Toronto Heritage Award, Floyd S. Chalmers Award, and J.J. Talman Award

My Life in Crime and Other Academic Adventures. Toronto: University of Toronto Press, 2007

Articles and Book Chapters

'Regulation of Economic Activity by Criminal Law: Decline of the Trade and Commerce Power' (1957), 15 *University of Toronto Faculty of Law Review* 20

'Reputation of Disorderly Houses' (1962–3), 5 *Criminal Law Quarterly* 328

'Canadian Criminal Statistics: A Report on the Third Criminal Law Conference, Osgoode Hall Law School, April 3–4, 1964' (with J.W. Mohr) (1964–5), 7 *Criminal Law Quarterly* 170

'Reforming the Bail System' (1966), John Howard Society of Kingston publication

'Issue Estoppel in Criminal Cases' (1966–7), 9 *Criminal Law Quarterly* 163

'Double Jeopardy and the Division of Legislative Authority in Canada' (1967), 17 *University of Toronto Law Journal* 66

'Double Jeopardy and the Rule against Unreasonably Splitting a Case' (1967), 17 *University of Toronto Law Journal* 249

'New Trial after an Appeal from Conviction' (1968), 84 *Law Quarterly Review* 48 and 185

'Magistrates' Courts: Functioning and Facilities' (1968–9), 11 *Criminal Law Quarterly* 52

'Cross-Examination on Previous Convictions in Canada' (1969), 47 *Canadian Bar Review* 656

'The Process of Criminal Law Reform' (1969–70), 12 *Criminal Law Quarterly* 148

'Summons, Arrest, and Bail' (1970), 12 *Canadian Journal of Corrections and Criminology* 30

'The Work of the Law Reform Commission of Canada' (1972), 6 *Law Society of Upper Canada Gazette* 58

'Access to the Law' (1974), 8 *Law Society of Upper Canada Gazette* 127

'Law for the Layman' (1974), 50:4 *Canadian Welfare* 4

'Prospective and Retrospective Judicial Lawmaking' (1974), 24 *University of Toronto Law Journal* 170

'Gun Control: The Options' (1975–6), 18 *Criminal Law Quarterly* 29

'Pressure Groups and the Development of the Criminal Law' in P.R. Glazebrook, ed., *Reshaping the Criminal Law: Essays in Honour of Glanville Williams* 202. London: Stevens & Sons, 1978

'Adhering to Rules of Criminal Procedure in Cases of Terrorism' in Judy Davidson, ed., *The Jerusalem Conference on Peace vs. Violence* 152. Conference in September 1979

'National Security: Some Canadian Legal Perspectives' (1980), 10 *Israel Yearbook on Human Rights* 257

'R.S. Wright's Model Criminal Code: A Forgotten Chapter in the History of the Criminal Law' (1981), 1 *Oxford Journal of Legal Studies* 307

'Legal Rights under the Charter' (1981–2), 24 *Criminal Law Quarterly* 430

'Controlling Entrapment' (1982), 32 *University of Toronto Law Journal* 1

'Double Jeopardy: Some Recent Developments' in Nancy E. Eastham and Boris Krivy, eds., *The Cambridge Lectures, 1981* 17. Toronto: Butterworths, 1982

'Old and New Criminal Codes' (1982), 16 *Law Society of Upper Canada Gazette* 220

'A Century of Criminal Justice' (1982), 20 *Transactions of the Royal Society of Canada* 285 and (1982), 16 *Law Society of Upper Canada Gazette* 336

'Criminal Justice and the Charter' (1983), 13 *Manitoba Law Journal* 549

'Gun Control in Canada: Politics and Impact' in Anthony N. Doob and Edward L. Greenspan, eds., *Perspectives in Criminal Law: Essays in Honour of J.Ll.J. Edwards* 226. Aurora: Canada Law Book, 1985

'Controlling the Administrators of Criminal Justice' (1988–9), 31 *Criminal Law Quarterly* 280

'Codification in the Commonwealth: Earlier Efforts' (1990), 2 *Criminal Law Forum* 145, reprinted in (1992), 18 *Commonwealth Law Bulletin* 1172

'The Case of Valentine Shortis – Yesterday and Today' (1991), 36 *Canadian Journal of Psychiatry* 159

'Rewards in the Legal System: Tenure, Airbags, and Safety Bingo' (1993), 31
  Alberta Law Review 493
'Canadian Criminal Justice, 1892–1992' (1993), 42 *University of New Brunswick
  Law Journal* 175
'Reforming Police Powers: Who's in Charge?' in R.C. Macleod and David
  Schneiderman, eds., *Police Powers in Canada: The Evolution and Practice of
  Authority* 100. Toronto: University of Toronto Press, 1994
'Borderline Justice: Policing in the Two Niagaras' (with Kent Roach) (1996), 23
  American Journal of Criminal Law 241
'Reflections on *A Place Apart: Judicial Independence and Accountability in Canada'*
  (1996), 45 *University of New Brunswick Law Journal* 67
'Judicial Independence and Accountability' (1996), 7 *Criminal Law Forum* 605
'The Right to a Fair Trial' (with Kent Roach) in D. Weissbrodt and R. Wolfrum,
  eds., (1997), 129 *Beiträge zum ausländischen öffentlichen Recht und Völkerrecht* 3
'Borderline Justice: Choosing Juries in the Two Niagaras' (with Kent Roach)
  (1997), 31 *Israel Law Review* 120
'Governance of Legal Aid Schemes' in vol. 3 of the *Report of the Ontario Legal Aid
  Review: A Blueprint for Publicly Funded Legal Services* 1017. Toronto: Publica-
  tions Ontario, 1997
'Judicial Independence and Accountability in Canada' (2001), 59 *The Advocate*
  859
'Police Powers in Bill C-36' in Ronald J. Daniels et al., eds., *The Security of Free-
  dom: Essays on Canada's Anti-Terrorism Bill* 269. University of Toronto Press,
  2001
'Writing the History of the University of Toronto' (2002), 14 *Historical Studies in
  Education* 282
'Reflections: A History of the University of Toronto' in Michael Goldberg, ed.,
  The University Professor Lecture Series 2002–2003 23. University of Toronto
  Faculty of Arts and Science, 2003
'The Provincial Court and the Criminal Law' (2003), 48 *Criminal Law Quarterly*
  15
'Criminal Justice in Canada Revisited' (2004), 48 *Criminal Law Quarterly* 419
'Lipski, Israel (1865–1887)' *Oxford Dictionary of National Biography*, online edi-
  tion. Oxford University Press, 2005
'Frank Iacobucci and the University of Toronto' (2007), 57 *University of Toronto
  Law Journal* 155
'Laskin and the University' in Neil Finkelstein and Constance Backhouse, eds.,
  The Laskin Legacy: Essays in Commemoration of Chief Justice Bora Laskin. Tor-
  onto: Irwin Law, 2007
'Codification and the Charter: Who's in Charge of the Reform of Criminal
  Law?' *Criminal Law Forum*, forthcoming

Government Committees and Commissions

Counsel to the Attorney General's Committee on the Enforcement of the Laws Relating to Gambling (Ontario), 1962

Consultant to the Joint Committee on Legal Aid, 1964–5, and author of background study *Working Papers on Legal Aid*, 1964

Legal Associate to the Attorney General's Committee on Securities Legislation in Ontario (Kimber Committee), 1963–5

Member of the Minister of Reform Institutions' Committee on Regional Detention Centres, 1966–7

Member of the Federal Task Force on the Canada Corporations Act, 1967–8

Consultant to the Canadian Committee on Corrections, 1968–9, and author of background study 'Magistrates' Courts: Functioning and Facilities'

Commissioner of the Law Reform Commission of Canada, 1971–2

Consultant to the Solicitor General of Canada's Task Force on Gun Control Legislation, 1974–5, and author of background study 'Gun Control: The Options'

Consultant to the Commission of Inquiry concerning Certain Activities of the RCMP (McDonald Commission), 1978–80, and author of background study *National Security: The Legal Dimensions*, 1980

Consultant to the Canadian Sentencing Commission, 1985–6, and author of background study *Sentencing Structure in Canada: Historical Perspectives*

Consultant to the Law Reform Commission of Canada and the Federal Department of Justice on the review of the Criminal Code, 1981–90

Consultant to the Law Reform Commission of Canada on offences against public order, 1981–92

Chair of a number of boards of inquiry established under the Ontario Human Rights Code, 1981–93

Chair of the Ontario Task Force on Inflation Protection for Employment Pension Plans, 1987–8

Member of the Royal Society of Canada committee that prepared report *Tobacco, Nicotine, and Addiction* for Health and Welfare Canada, 1989

Member (part-time) of the Ontario Securities Commission, 1989–91

Consultant to the Canadian Judicial Council, 1993–5, and author of study *A Place Apart: Judicial Independence and Accountability in Canada*, 1995

Consultant to the Commission of Inquiry into the Deployment of Canadian Forces to Somalia, 1995–7, and author of *Controlling Misconduct in the Military: A Study Prepared for the Commission of Inquiry into the Deployment of Canadian Forces to Somalia*

Consultant to the Attorney General of Ontario on a possible court services agency, 1996–7

Consultant to the Ontario Legal Aid Review, 1997, and author of background study 'Governance of Legal Aid Schemes'

Consultant to the Ontario Criminal Justice Review, 1998

Consultant to the Commission of Inquiry into the Actions of Canadian Officials in Relation to Maher Arar, 2005

Consultant to Access Copyright, 2007, and author of fact-finding study 'Report to Access Copyright on Distribution of Royalties'

Index

Abel, Albert, 30–1, 36–8, 98
Abella, Rosalie, 166, 313
Aberdeen, Lord and Lady, 317, 321–3
Abols, Gesta ('Gus'), 197
abortion, 59, 73–4, 76ff.; defence of necessity, 76; MLF's legal opinions on, 77; Henry Morgentaler, 76; *Rex v. Bourne*, 76; *Roe v. Wade*, 77; U.S. comparison on, 77; *Vera Drake* (film) on, 76
Abortion Law Reform Association, 164
Academy of Health Sciences, 316
Access Copyright, 437
access to the law, 182ff.; advisory committee on, 184–5; and attorney general's department, Ontario, 190–1; CanLII, 189; development of project on, 183; final report on, 191; form of the law, 182; 'front-heavy' construction, 186; and the Internet, 188–90; and Law Commission of

Canada, 191; and Law Foundation of Ontario, 189–90; and Law Society of Upper Canada, Access to Justice Committee, 190; 'left-branching' construction, 186; and Legal Aid Ontario, 189; legal language, 182; legislative drafting, 183; and librarians, 184; and McCamus committee on legal aid, 189; MLF's post-millennium activity on, 188; need for in developing countries, 187; preparation of models for, 187; research assistance for, 184; Science Centre experiments on, 185; sets of legal materials for, 183; special studies on, 185; talk to Institute of Public Administration of Canada on, 183
Access to the Law (study prepared for Law Reform Commission of Canada). *See* access to the law
Addison, Joseph, 47
Afghanistan, 255, 262; military action

2007 Robert J. Sharpe and Patricia I. McMahon, *The Persons Case: The Origins and Legacy of the Fight for Legal Personhood*
Lori Chambers, *Misconceptions: Unmarried Motherhood and the Ontario Children of Unmarried Parents Act, 1921–1969*
Jonathan Swainger, ed., *The Alberta Supreme Court at 100: History and Authority*
Martin L. Friedland, *My Life in Crime and Other Academic Adventures*

2006 Donald Fyson, *Magistrates, Police, and People: Everyday Criminal Justice in Quebec and Lower Canada, 1764–1837*
Dale Brawn, *The Court of Queen's Bench of Manitoba, 1870–1950: A Biographical History*
R.C.B. Risk, *A History of Canadian Legal Thought: Collected Essays*, edited and introduced by G. Blaine Baker and Jim Phillips

2005 Philip Girard, *Bora Laskin: Bringing Law to Life*
Christopher English, ed., *Essays in the History of Canadian Law: Volume IX – Two Islands: Newfoundland and Prince Edward Island*
Fred Kaufman, *Searching for Justice: An Autobiography*

2004 Philip Girard, Jim Phillips, and Barry Cahill, eds., *The Supreme Court of Nova Scotia, 1754–2004: From Imperial Bastion to Provincial Oracle*
Frederick Vaughan, *Aggressive in Pursuit: The Life of Justice Emmett Hall*
John D. Honsberger, *Osgoode Hall: An Illustrated History*
Constance Backhouse and Nancy Backhouse, *The Heiress versus the Establishment: Mrs Campbell's Campaign for Legal Justice*

2003 Robert J. Sharpe and Kent Roach, *Brian Dickson: A Judge's Journey*
Jerry Bannister, *The Rule of the Admirals: Law, Custom, and Naval Government in Newfoundland, 1699–1832*
George Finlayson, *John J. Robinette, Peerless Mentor: An Appreciation*
Peter Oliver, *The Conventional Man: The Diaries of Ontario Chief Justice Robert A. Harrison, 1856–1878*

2002 John T. Saywell, *The Lawmakers: Judicial Power and the Shaping of Canadian Federalism*
Patrick Brode, *Courted and Abandoned: Seduction in Canadian Law*
David Murray, *Colonial Justice: Justice, Morality, and Crime in the Niagara District, 1791–1849*
F. Murray Greenwood and Barry Wright, eds., *Canadian State Trials, Volume Two: Rebellion and Invasion in the Canadas, 1837–8*

2001 Ellen Anderson, *Judging Bertha Wilson: Law as Large as Life*
Judy Fudge and Eric Tucker, *Labour before the Law: The Regulation of Workers' Collective Action in Canada, 1900–1948*
Laurel Sefton MacDowell, *Renegade Lawyer: The Life of J.L. Cohen*

2000 Barry Cahill, 'The Thousandth Man': A Biography of James McGregor Stewart*
A.B. McKillop, *The Spinster and the Prophet: Florence Deeks, H.G. Wells, and the Mystery of the Purloined Past*